Aversive Conditioning
and Learning

Contributors

A. H. BLACK

ROBERT C. BOLLES

F. ROBERT BRUSH

M. RAY DENNY

HARRY FOWLER

DOROTHY E. McALLISTER

WALLACE R. McALLISTER

STEVEN F. MAIER

JAMES S. MYER

MARTIN E. P. SELIGMAN

RICHARD L. SOLOMON

JOHN THEIOS

Aversive Conditioning
and Learning

Edited by F. ROBERT BRUSH

Department of Medical Psychology
University of Oregon Medical School
Portland, Oregon

ACADEMIC PRESS   New York and London   1971

ACADEMIC PRESS, INC.
111 Fifth Avenue, New York, New York 10003

United Kingdom Edition published by
ACADEMIC PRESS, INC. (LONDON) LTD.
Berkeley Square House, London W1X 6BA

LIBRARY OF CONGRESS CATALOG CARD NUMBER: 70- 127680

PRINTED IN THE UNITED STATES OF AMERICA

Contents

AVERSIVE CONDITIONING

1. Autonomic Aversive Conditioning in Infrahuman Subjects

A. H. Black

2. Behavioral Measurement of Conditioned Fear

Wallace R. McAllister and Dorothy E. McAllister

v

AVOIDANCE LEARNING

PROBLEMS OF PUNISHMENT

List of Contributors

Numbers in parentheses indicate the pages on which the authors' contributions begin.

A. H. BLACK (3), Department of Psychology, McMaster University, Hamilton, Ontario, Canada

ROBERT C. BOLLES (183), Department of Psychology, University of Washington, Washington, D. C.

F. ROBERT BRUSH (401), Department of Medical Psychology, University of Oregon Medical School, Portland, Oregon

M. RAY DENNY (235), Department of Psychology, Michigan State University, East, Lansing, Michigan

HARRY FOWLER (537), Department of Psychology, University of Pittsburgh, Pittsburgh, Pennsylvania

DOROTHY E. MCALLISTER (105), Department of Psychology, Northern Illinois University, DeKalb, Illinois

WALLACE R. MCAALLISTER (105), Department of Psychology, Northern Illinois University, DeKalb, Illinois

STEVEN F. MAIER (347), Department of Psychology, University of Illinois, Urbana, Illinois

JAMES S. MYER (469), Department of Psychology, The Johns Hopkins University, Baltimore, Maryland

MARTIN E. P. SELIGMAN (347), Department of Psychology, Cornell University, Ithaca, New York

RICHARD L. SOLOMON (347), Department of Psychology, University of Pennsylvania, Philadelphia, Pennsylvania

JOHN THEIOS (297), Department of Psychology, University of Wisconsin, Madison, Wisconsin

Preface

Interest in aversive conditioning and learning has increased dramatically in the past ten years, and many research papers have been reported which investigate the variety of behaviors that can be elicited, suppressed, learned, or conditioned as a result of aversive stimulation or its removal. A number of new facts and phenomena have been discovered, but they, along with some old established phenomena, like avoidance learning, are not well understood and remain the subject of experimental analysis. The need to review and integrate this growing literature provided the impetus for collecting together the original papers that make up this volume.

However, a comprehensive review of the entire field was not feasible, and a survey based on a large number of individual research reports was not viewed as likely to meet the need for integration and synthesis. The editor, therefore, attempted to work some sort of compromise between those two alternatives by bringing together the ideas of a number of investigators who have been actively following programs of research on various aspects of aversive conditioning or learning. Their challenge was to integrate their research with that of others; their enticement may have been the opportunity to write about their own research and primary interests at some length. Credit for the ideas contained in this volume, of course, goes to the contributors who allowed themselves to be seduced into the demanding work these chapters represent; the editor merely served as goad and reminder of past deadlines.

Within the book the chapters are arranged topically, although it will be apparent to the reader that the groupings are somewhat arbitrary because many of the chapters contribute to more than one topic heading. The first chapters deal with operant and classical conditioning of responses of the autonomic nervous system and with behavioral measurement of conditioned fear. Both have a strong methodological emphasis because of the complexity of the measurement problem in this area, and both deal with aspects of the mediational functions frequently ascribed to conditioned responses based on aversive stimuli. In the next section, the chapters deal primarily with avoidance learning, and a number of problem areas are discussed. Among them are the effects of response selection on the ease of acquisition, the nature and slow time course of the processes that reinforce avoidance learning, the influence on avoidance learning of prior experience with uncontrollable shock and with reliable and unreliable predictors of shock, an analysis of avoidance learning in terms of a Markov model of short- and long-term memory, and finally, the nature of retention of conditioned fear and the possible hormonal mechanisms that control performance motivated by fear. The last section deals with some of the unexpected effects of punishment which usually, but certainly not invariably, produces suppression of behavior. The emphasis here is on the effects of noncontingent aversive stimuli that may account for the suppressive effects of punishment and on the paradoxical facilitation of behavior that sometimes results from response-contingent shock.

I wish to thank the contributors to this volume for their patience, cooperation and willingness to write and rewrite. Their diligence and hard work made this book possible and my job easier. The final editing was further facilitated by the help and continuing encouragement of my wife.

AVERSIVE CONDITIONING

Autonomic Aversive Conditioning
in
Infrahuman Subjects[1]

A. H. BLACK

McMaster University
Hamilton, Ontario, Canada

I. INTRODUCTION

A. The Organization of the Chapter

The topic of this chapter is a restricted one. Two of these restrictions are shared by the authors of all the chapters in this volume: the limitation to experimental situations which employ aversive reinforcers and to research on infrahuman subjects. The further restriction to autonomic responses, however, is unique to this chapter. The justifications for selecting autonomic responses for special study are dealt with briefly in Section II. Two major concerns become apparent when these justifications are considered. The first concern is with the attempt to employ autonomic responding to distinguish between classical and operant conditioning, to compare the two, and to study their relationship. The second is the analysis of the properties of the response in conditioning. What properties are shared by those responses that can be conditioned by a particular procedure? What determines that one particular response will be selected from among the many that could be conditioned in a given experimental situation? How does one account for the interrelations among various autonomic and skeletal responses during conditioning? These questions can be contrasted with those devoted to understanding other aspects of the conditioning process such as the analysis of discriminative stimulus control, or the isolation of the essential properties of reinforcing stimuli.

---

[1]Although a great deal of research on autonomic conditioning has been carried out in Russia, this literature has not been covered because certain methodological problems make it difficult to employ it in dealing with the particular problems considered in this chapter.

These two issues are emphasized, not only because they have provided major foci for previous research on autonomic conditioning, but also because many of our assumptions and beliefs concerning them require reexamination. Our preconceptions about how the properties of the response (or perhaps, more generally, of the organism) interact with a given conditioning procedure, seem to have led to an inadequate conception of the role of autonomic responses in conditioning. Furthermore, although the contrast between operant and classical conditioning has provided much of the theoretical motivation for carrying out research on autonomic conditioning, the data accumulated over the past two decades give rise to questions concerning the operant–classical distinction. This is not to say that research on either the comparison between classical and operant conditioning or on the nature of autonomic conditioning is useless; rather, the point that I would like to emphasize is simply that the assumption that autonomic conditioning provides an especially useful approach to the understanding of the relationship between classical and operant conditioning may have been unfortunate.

The chapter will be organized in the following manner. In Section II, the reasons for treating autonomic conditioning as a unique topic will be discussed first, followed by an introduction to the problems which arise in attempting to deal with the two issues referred to previously. Research on the operant conditioning of autonomic responses will then be described (Section III) since operant conditioning seems to be somewhat easier to deal with than classical conditioning of autonomic responses which will then be presented (Section IV). The problem of the analysis of the response will be emphasized in these two sections. Classical and operant conditioning will then be compared (Section V). Autonomic responses during skeletal operant conditioning will be dealt with in Section VI, accompanied by comments on the relationship between classical and operant conditioning. In the final section (VII), the conclusions of the previous sections will be reviewed, and the value of research on autonomic conditioning will be reconsidered. One final point must be mentioned. Data on cardiovascular conditioning are emphasized in this chapter, simply because the majority of the relevant experiments have been carried out on this system.

B.   Terminology

1.   In descriptions of classical conditioning, the standard terms CS, CR, US, and UR will be employed for conditioned stimulus, condi-

tioned response, unconditioned stimulus and unconditioned response, respectively. Similarly, in operant conditioning, the terms CS, R, and S^R will be employed to describe the discriminative stimulus, the operantly conditioned response, and the reinforcement, respectively.

2.   There is some disagreement over the specification of the conditions that are necessary and sufficient to produce a change in behavior during conditioning. For example, it has been suggested that the pairing of the CS with the US is not a sufficient condition for producing classical conditioning (Rescorla, 1967). Rather, a dependency between the CS and US must be established by making the probability of the US higher in the presence of the CS than it is in the absence of the CS. This problem will be discussed in Section IV. One would like to be able to refer to the essential relationships among stimuli, responses, and reinforcers for producing conditioning without committing oneself to a particular theoretical point of view as to whether conditioning is produced by pairing events or by establishing a dependency between them. Alternatives to "pairing CS and US," such as "connecting CS and US," "associating CS and US" or "relating CS and US" are ambiguous. It is not clear whether one is talking about the relationship between the events that is specified in the description of the experimental procedure, or about the relationship between the events that is made by the subject as a function of having been exposed to the experimental procedure. We want to refer only to the former type of relationship. Since the alternative terms are somewhat unsatisfactory, the terms "pairing CS and US" or "pairing R and S^R" will be used throughout the paper, without implying a commitment to any particular theoretical position.

3.   Since operant conditioning can occur during classical conditioning and vice versa, the procedure that the experimenter establishes need not be the same as the one that affects the organism. For example, the experimenter may pair a CS and a US in order to produce classical conditioning. In reality, however, the behavior of the organism may also be controlled inadvertently by the operant pairing of the response and reinforcer. Because of the possibility that the relationships between events arranged by the experimenter may be different from those that affect the subject, it is important to distinguish between these two types of relationships. The approach suggested by Jenkins (1968) will be followed in this chapter. The term *experimenter's procedures or experimenter's dependencies* will be used to describe the relationships between events (stimuli, responses, and reinforcements) that are established by the experimenter. The term *empirical procedures* or *empirical dependencies* will be used to describe the actual relationships that are influencing behavior. An exper-

imenter classical conditioning procedure, therefore, can involve both empirical classical and empirical operant conditioning procedures. Similarly, an experimenter operant conditioning procedure can involve both empirical classical and empirical operant conditioning procedures.

4. Even though the different relationships among stimuli, responses, and reinforcers can affect an organism simultaneously during a given conditioning procedure, it is obvious that under certain circumstances one will want to study the effects of one relationship while controlling others. This is especially true of those relationships which are considered to be necessary and sufficient for producing a particular type of conditioning (*i.e.*, pairing CS or US, or pairing R and S^R). The term "effective" will be employed to refer to the essential relationship in a particular conditioning procedure, when other relationships which occur during that procedure are controlled. The term *effective classical component* will refer to those situations in which the relationship among stimuli, responses, and reinforcers that is affecting behavior is the pairing of CS and US, while other relationships are controlled. Similarly, *effective operant component* will refer to those situations in which the relationship among stimuli, responses, and reinforcers that is affecting behavior is the pairing of R and S^R, while other relationships are controlled.

5. The concept "central movement processes" is employed continually in this chapter to refer to central neural processes that are part of the complex control system involved in the initiation and maintenance of overt skeletal responses. The need for such a concept arose in research in which curare was employed to block activity at the neuromuscular junction, thus preventing overt responses. When a stimulus necessary and sufficient for the response is applied under curare, central processes involved in the initiation and maintenance of the movement presumably occur, and impulses which would normally lead to movement travel to the neuromuscular junction where they are blocked. The term "central movement processes" refers to those neural processes that are related to skeletal movement in the normal state, and that also occur in the curarized state when movement would be expected if no neuromuscular block existed.

One could find some empirical measure of central movement process in the curarized state by measuring electrical activity in central structures and/or peripheral motoneurons during overt responding to a given stimulus in the normal state and during the presentation of the same stimulus in the curarized state. Those components of the neural response that were common to the two states could be employed as indices of central movement processes in the curarized state. Presumably, those processes which depend on feedback from overt movement would not fall into this category. (Taub and Berman (1968) have shown, however, that such feedback is not essential for the conditioning of movement.) On the other hand, hippocampal theta waves do seem to be indicators of central movement processes. Vanderwolf (1968) demonstrated that hippocampal theta waves are correlated with active voluntary responses. Dalton (1968), in a recent unpublished Ph.D. thesis in our laboratory, provided confirmation of this result by demonstrating that theta waves accompany active lever pressing avoidance responses to one stimulus, and are absent when the subject avoids shock in the presence of another stimulus by refraining from pedal-pressing. These hippocampal theta waves, then, provide a possible empirical measure of what we have termed "central movement processes."

II. BACKGROUND

In this section, the justifications for carrying out research on autonomic responses as opposed to skeletal responses will be discussed first. The two issues which seem to be prominent in such discussions (*i.e.*, the analysis of classical and operant conditioning and of the properties of the conditioned response) will then be considered.

A.   The Special Status of Autonomic Responses

The first question which should be considered is the reason for treating autonomic conditioning separately from skeletal or somatic conditioning. A readily available answer is that autonomic and skeletal responding can be distinguished by differences in the neural systems underlying each (Patton, 1961), and that this distinction can justify the separate analysis of the conditioning of each type of response. It does not seem, however, that the existence of anatomical and physiological differences is sufficient to justify the categorization of experiments on autonomic conditioning separately from those on somatic conditioning. One would certainly be less inclined to single out the conditioning of autonomic responses if this research on autonomic responses led to the same conclusions as research on the conditioning of skeletal responses. Therefore, not all differences between skeletal and autonomic behavior shall be considered, but rather those differences which imply that research on autonomic conditioning can provide data that could not be obtained from research on skeletal conditioning.

Although Pavlov employed an autonomic response, salivation, in the original research on conditioning, he assigned no special status to autonomic responding. He expected that skeletal responses could be classically conditioned in the same way that autonomic responses were conditioned, and chose salivation for practical, rather than theoretical reasons.

It is essential to realize that each of these two reflexes—the alimentary reflex and the mild defence reflex to rejectable substances—consists of two distinct components, a motor and a secretory . . . We confined our experiments almost entirely to the secretory component of the reflex; the allied motor reactions were taken into account only where there were special reasons. The secretory reflex presents many important advantages for our purpose. It allows for an extremely accurate measurement of the intensity of reflex activity, since either the number of drops in a given time may be counted or else the saliva may be caused to displace a coloured fluid in a horizontally placed graduated glass tube. It would be much more difficult to obtain the same accuracy of measurement for any motor reflex, especially for such complex motor reactions as accompany reflexes to food or to rejectable substances. Even by using most delicate instruments we should never be able to reach such precision in measuring the intensity of the motor component of the reflexes as can easily be attained with the secretory component. Again, a very important point in favour of the secretory reflexes is the much smaller tendency to interpret them in an anthropomorphic fashion—i.e., in terms of subjective analogy. Although this seems a trivial consideration from our present standpoint, it was of importance in the earlier stages of our investigation and did undoubtedly influence our choice (Pavlov, 1927; p. 17).

While the position that both skeletal and autonomic responses could be conditioned in the same manner seems to have been accepted at first, this widespread agreement with Pavlov's position was of short duration. Beginning in the 1930's, distinctions were made between operant and classical conditioning procedures, and the autonomic-skeletal difference was employed in attempts to differentiate between the two types of conditioning. Mowrer (1947) stated that the differences between autonomic and skeletal responses were fundamental in discriminating between types of conditioning. Autonomic changes could be conditioned only by classical procedures, and skeletal responses only by operant procedures. Ko-norski and Miller (1937) were equally direct, although less restrictive, about skeletal responses:

> According to the existing state of knowledge—and we dispose of no facts to the contrary—the conditioned reflex of the new type (our type II) is confined exclusively to striped muscles, while the classical type has no restrictions laid on effectors and includes among them, besides striped muscles, smooth muscles and glands (Konorski and Miller, 1937; p. 8).

The position of Solomon and Wynne (1954) is the same as that of Ko-norski and Miller.

Skinner's (1938) approach was somewhat more complicated and also less categorical. He divided behavior into two types—respondents and operants. According to Skinner, respondents could be elicited by apply-ing a specific stimulus. Operants, on the other hand, provided the exper-imenter with no such eliciting stimulus. In addition, Skinner divided conditioning into types. Respondent conditioning, or type S, was identi-cal to classical conditioning, and was contrasted to operant conditioning, or type R. Since all autonomic responses were most likely respondents, Skinner suggested that one might be able to condition them only by classical procedures.

> The distinction between Types R and S arising from their con-finement to operant and respondent behavior, respectively, implies a rough topographic separation. . . . It is quite possible on the ex-isting evidence that a strict topographical separation of types (of conditioning) following the skeletal-autonomic distinction may be made.
>
> Any given skeletal respondent may be duplicated with operants and hence may also be conditioned according to Type R (operant conditioning). Whether this is also true of the autonomic part is questionable . . . There is little reason to expect conditioning of Type R in an autonomic response, since it does not as a rule natu-rally act upon the environment in any way that will produce a reinforcement . . . (Skinner, 1938; p. 112).

Schlosberg (1937) took still another position. According to his theory, the main distinction between responses is that found between diffuse preparatory responses and precise adaptive responses. He argued that the former could be classically conditioned and the latter operantly con-ditioned. To the extent that autonomic changes could be classified as

diffuse and preparatory, they could be conditioned by classical procedures alone.

> . . . The less specific reactions have no convenient generic
> name. They include various changes in the breathing rhythm, pulse
> rhythm, electrical skin resistance, body volume, pitch of voice, and
> tonic change (23,35,37). Such responses may be referred to as
> emotional, attentional, anticipatory, or preparatory. They "condi-
> tion" rather readily (Schlosberg, 1937; p. 385).

The hypothesis that autonomic responses are susceptible only to classical conditioning procedures seems to have been widely accepted. The
following statement is found in a recent text (Kimble, 1961):

> One fact which supports the division of responses into dichoto-
> mous categories is the following. Although autonomically mediated
> reactions such as the GSR and vasoconstriction are readily condi-
> tioned classically, they seem to be impossible to condition by in-
> strumental methods. The Pavlovians simply state (without docu-
> mentation available in English) that glandular responses cannot be
> conditioned instrumentally. Mowrer (1938) was unsuccessful in an
> attempt at instrumental conditioning of GSR, and Skinner (1938)
> reports that he and Delabarre could not condition vasoconstriction
> by making reinforcement contingent upon the response. Thus, for
> autonomically mediated behavior, the evidence points unequivo-
> cally to the conclusion that such responses can be modified by clas-
> sical, but not instrumental, training methods (Kimble, 1961; p, 100).

Since this text was published, evidence has accumulated which seems to
demonstrate that autonomic responses can be modified by operant conditioning procedures. Some ambiguity exists, however, about the interpretation of these results, and this will be discussed in Section III of this
chapter. No matter what the final resolution of this ambiguity may be,
the attempt to distinguish between operant and classical conditioning by
means of the autonomic-skeletal contrast has provided justification for
the view that autonomic responses are the most appropriate for research
on classical conditioning. Those who assumed that classical conditioning
affected only autonomic responses and that operant conditioning affected only skeletal responses would obviously employ only autonomic
behavior in research on classical conditioning. Those who assumed that
classical conditioning affected both autonomic and skeletal responses,
and that operant conditioning affected only skeletal responses, would
also employ autonomic behavior in research on classical conditioning.

They would select autonomic responses, in contrast to skeletal responses, because of their belief that autonomic responses could not be accidentally contaminated by the effects of operant procedures.

A second reason for focusing attention on autonomic conditioning arises from the intimate relationship that has long been assumed to exist between autonomic changes and emotion (Lindsley, 1951; Mandler, 1962). Almost as soon as information on classical conditioning became available in North America (Watson & Morgan, 1917; Watson & Rayner, 1920), the proposition was advanced that classical conditioning is the process by which emotional states are learned. With the development of the learning theories described above, the hypothesis that the classical conditioning of autonomic changes should provide information on the learning of emotions gained new prominence. Furthermore, theories such as Mowrer's (1947) assigned an additional function to these classically conditioned emotions. They treated autonomic emotional responses not simply as expressions of emotion or indicators of physiological equilibrium, but also as motivators of adaptive skeletal behavior. The archetypal example of this approach is the analysis of avoidance conditioning with a warning stimulus. Classically conditioned fear responses to the CS were assumed to motivate the avoidance response, and the termination of fear was assumed to operantly reinforce it (Mowrer, 1947). According to this view, research on the classical conditioning of autonomic responses was assumed to provide information not only on the acquisition of emotional and motivational states, but also on the way in which acquired motivational states affected operant behavior. This orientation led to two types of research. The first type was research on the classical conditioning of autonomic responses. It was designed to investigate the development of learned emotional states. The second type of research was the attempt to measure changes in autonomic responding during operant conditioning. This was done in order to find out how emotional and motivational states influenced operant conditioning. The former research will be discussed in Section IV and the latter in Section VI.

This dynamic analysis, in which classically conditioned emotional responses are supposed to have an effect on the simultaneous or immediately subsequent operant response, is central to many modern approaches to the problem of emotion. In these approaches, there is and has been controversy, however, over the function of the autonomic response. This controversy seems to be only one battle in the war between centralists and peripheralists. The peripheralists argue that psychological processes are heavily dependent upon peripheral responses and their afferent feedback. The centralists, on the other hand, argue that psychological processes such as learning, thinking, and perceiving can go on independently of peripheral responses. Earlier, the question was whether the occurrence of the autonomic response was a necessary condition for the conscious experiences labeled "emotional" (Cannon, 1929; James, 1884). More recently, the question has been whether the occurrence of the autonomic response is a necessary condition for the motivational and reinforcing effects produced by classical conditioning. The hypothesis that the autonomic response is necessary (Mowrer, 1947) can be contrasted with the view that the occurrence of some classically conditioned central emotional state is alone sufficient (Rescorla & Solomon, 1967). In the latter case, the autonomic response might be used as a measure of the emotional state because of the close correlation often assumed to exist between the autonomic response and the emotional state. As we shall see in Section VI, however, this assumption of a close correlation must be questioned.

A final justification of research on operant autonomic conditioning is closely related to the previous one. It is the use of this procedure in the treatment of psychosomatic disorders. Psychosomatic disorders have been loosely defined as physiological malfunctions influenced by psychological variables. The further assumption seems to have been made that the automonic nervous system is especially prone to the crippling effects of psychological malfunctioning. Therefore, it is only natural that those interested in psychosomatic illness should be very interested in any psychological methods for changing autonomic behavior, in particular, the conditioning of autonomic responses (both classical and operant). The notion of operant control of autonomic reactions seems to be particularly exciting to many psychologists, because they often make the assumption that gaining *operant* control of autonomic responses is identical to gaining *voluntary* control of autonomic responses. (This assumption can, of course, be questioned, as indicated in Section IV,E).

In summary, the following seem to have been the major justifications for the belief in the special status of research on the conditioning of autonomic behavior. The first is the belief that autonomic responses were particularly suitable for the analysis of classical conditioning and useful in making a distinction between classical and operant types of conditioning. Second, the conditioning of autonomic responses was expected to provide information on the acquisition of emotional-motivational states. Furthermore, the analysis of the relationship between classically conditioned autonomic responses and skeletal operant responses was assumed to help our understanding of how emotional and motivational states affected operantly conditioned behavior. Finally, autonomic conditioning was of special concern to those interested in psychosomatic disorders.

These justifications are based, to a large extent, on the differences' between the properties of autonomic and skeletal responses as they relate to differences between classical and operant conditioning. Therefore, this topic will be considered before the data on autonomic conditioning.

B. The Distinction between Classical and Operant Conditioning

It is obvious from the previous section that only against the background provided by an understanding of operant and classical conditioning do the direction and purpose of much of the research on autonomic conditioning make sense. Three main problems must be considered in attempting to provide such a background.

If one takes the distinction between operant and classical conditioning seriously, the first problem must be to describe each precisely. There is little point in attempting to distinguish them if one cannot describe them. The second problem is the analysis of the similarities and differences between classical and operant conditioning. The third problem is the study of the relationship between the two, *i.e.*, when changes in one type of conditioned response occur, what changes occur in the other?

Two requirements must be met in order to describe each type of conditioning. First, one must identify the relationship among stimuli, responses, and reinforcers that is considered to be essential for producing a given type of conditioning. Second, one must determine the effects of this essential relationship on behavior when the confounding effects of other relationships and variables are controlled. In short, one must specify the effective component of a conditioning procedure and then determine its effects. Such a description is often treated as a definition of a type of conditioning. Because this definition depends on the establishment of certain empirical relationships, it is often difficult to distinguish between the definition of a type of conditioning and the experimental analysis of that type of conditioning. This in turn implies that the definition can change as our knowledge grows. For example, there is some concern as to whether the reinforcing event, or some response elicited by it (as suggested in somewhat different ways by Lorenz, 1955 and Premack, 1965) is necessary for operant conditioning. Similarly, on the response side, one might ask whether the outflow of impulses to the effector organ is sufficient, or whether some feedback is also necessary. The answers to questions such as these can obviously lead to a modification in the way we define a type of conditioning. Even though we might expect the definition to change, there does seem to be a certain level at which there has been agreement about the basic description or definition of operant conditioning. It can be defined as a change in response probability which is produced by the presentation of a reinforcing event after the response occurs, even though some disagreements may exist as to just what features of the response, the event and their relationship are essential.

When one turns to classical conditioning, the situation is different. There is some disagreement as to whether the essential feature of the experimental procedure is simply the presentation of a conditioned stimulus (CS) followed by an unconditioned stimulus (US) in temporal contiguity (Rescorla, 1967). There is much greater disagreement, however, in describing the change in behavior produced by the effective component of the classical conditioning procedure. The traditional Pavlovian view states that the classical conditioning procedure leads to an increase in the probability of responses to the CS produced by the same neural centers as the unconditioned response to the US. According to this view, any change in the response to the CS not identical to, or a component of, the unconditioned response is not a classically conditioned response. Many alternative specifications have been employed in recent research on classical conditioning. These specifications vary from those which are more exclusive than the Pavlovian view to those that would include any change in behavior during the CS that can be attributed to the effect of the presentation of CS and US. These problems of describing classical conditioning will be discussed further in Section IV.

The second problem that must be considered in dealing with classical and operant conditioning is determining the similarities and differences between them. Do the empirical classical and operant experimental procedures have the same or different effects on behavior? Does the same[2]

---

[2]One question will recur throughout the course of this chapter: What does one mean by the "same" variation in the parameters of conditioning? For example, can one treat the delay of reinforcement both in classical and in operant conditioning as a change in the same parameter of the two conditioning situations? In what sense is the change in the interval between CS and US in classical conditioning the same as the change in the interval between response and reinforcement in operant conditioning?

A similar problem exists when one talks about the "same" response in the two conditioning situations. The term response usually refers to a set of movements which are classified together on the basis of some criterion. Standard examples are the classification together of all movements which lead to the same outcome (lever depression), or of all movements of a given effector or set of effectors (heart rate as one response and leg movement as another). The class may be very broadly defined (as in the examples given above) or very narrowly defined (as in the case of the eyeblink. Very brief latency eyeblinks are sometimes treated as a different response from long latency eyeblinks). In the extreme case, one could treat every difference in measurable dimensions of effector organ activity as a different response. This would lead to response classes which contained only one member per class. It is clear from this discussion that the question of whether two patterns of movement are to be considered as the same or different responses depends on the particular criterion that one is using to define a response. If the criterion is very narrow the two may be considered different; if the criterion is broader the two may be considered the same.

change in a parameter of the classical and operant conditioning operations (such as an increase in magnitude of reinforcement) have the same
or different effects on behavior? Are there responses that are sensitive to
only one of the two procedures? The lack of agreement about the definition of classical conditioning makes it difficult to deal with these questions. How can we compare two processes if we do not have some
agreement about what one of them is?

Even if there were agreement on the definition of classical conditioning, another fundamental problem must be faced in attempting to compare the two types of conditioning. As noted in Section I,B, operant and
classical conditioning procedures are not mutually exclusive. Although
the experimental dependencies between stimulus, response, and reinforcement that the experimenter arranges to produce classical conditioning are different from those that he arranges to produce operant
conditioning, the empirical dependencies that occur need not be different. If one pairs a CS and US, and some change in behavior begins to
occur to the CS, then one has inadvertently established the condition
necessary for operant conditioning, since the presentation of a reinforcement will follow some change in response.[3] Similarly, if one operantly
reinforces a response in a particular stimulus situation, and the response
begins to occur regularly, then one has inadvertently arranged the condition necessary for classical conditioning, since the US will follow immediately after the CS because of the short latency of the response. Since
both types of conditioning procedures occur together (even though one
has planned to produce only one of them), it is difficult to know
whether to attribute a change in behavior to one or to the other. If
methods could be devised to study each type of conditioning separately,
classical and operant conditioning could be precisely compared. Unfortunately, much early research failed to handle this problem adequately.
A number of control procedures have been proposed recently which are
designed to rule out the effects of classical conditioning during operant
conditioning and vice versa, but many problems still remain (Rescorla &
Solomon, 1967).

Finally, there is the closely related problem of determining the relationship between classical and operant conditioning (the covariation
between classically and operantly conditioned responses, and the effects

[3]One might be tempted to argue that relevant operant reinforcement could not take
place until the first CR had occurred in the presence of the CS. Therefore, classical conditioning that is uncontaminated by inadvertent operant reinforcement could be studied if
the experiment were terminated when the first CR occurs. This view can be questioned,
however, since the CR could have been influenced by operant reinforcement of related responses before its first occurrence. Inadvertent shaping of the response might have taken
place.

of one on the other). If classical and operant conditioning never occurred together, it is obvious that much less interest in the analysis of
the effect of one upon the other would have arisen. If, for example, they
could not occur together, we would not have become so interested in the
hypothesis that classically conditioned emotional responses motivate
operant responding. Therefore, the fact that the procedures for producing the two types of conditioning are not mutually exclusive forces us to
consider the relationship between the two types of conditioning. At the
same time, this fact makes it difficult to analyze the relationship, just as
it makes it difficult to compare the two types of conditioning.

It would be most helpful if these problems of defining, comparing,
and relating classical and operant conditioning were solved, and the operant-classical dichotomy could be employed as a solid frame of reference for the analysis of autonomic conditioning. Unfortunately, as the
above brief discussion of these problems indicates, this is not the case.
Therefore it will be necessary to grapple with these problems as the
chapter proceeds.

C.   The Analysis of the Response

The discussion of the special status of autonomic responses indicated
that they were assigned certain unique properties in relation to classical
and operant conditioning. Autonomic responses were assumed to be
amenable to classical conditioning procedures and refractory to operant
conditioning procedures. In addition, Mowrer (1947) suggested that autonomic responses mediated skeletal responses in avoidance conditioning. While these properties can be considered in isolation, they are better
understood when treated within a more general framework for analyzing
the changes in responses during conditioning.

As in the previous section, we shall take as our starting point an analysis of the basic relationship between the effective component of a conditioning procedure and the behavior change which it produces. Once
information on this relationship is available, we can focus in more detail
on the stimuli (both conditioned and reinforcing) or on the changes in
behavior that occur during conditioning.

Much interest has been expressed in the stimulus. For example, reduction experiments have been carried out to specify which features of the
conditioned stimulus control the conditioned response, and to determine
which aspects of the experimental procedure and of behavior are responsible for selecting the effective stimuli from the welter of stimuli impinging on the organism during conditioning (Kamin, 1967; Miles, 1965).
This concern, in turn, has stimulated interest in the theoretical analysis

of the mechanisms underlying stimulus-selection, as illustrated in recent treatments of attention in discriminative conditioning (Trabasso & Bower, 1968).

In research on autonomic conditioning, there has been a great deal of concern with a similar analysis of the response. Given that we can specify the changes in behavior produced by the effective component of the conditioning procedure, we can ask the following series of questions.

The first question concerns the *selection* of the conditioned response. What features of the conditioning procedure and of behavior determine that one particular response (or set of responses) will be conditioned from among the many that could be conditioned in a given experimental situation? We might ask, for example, what variables would we manipulate to produce the operant conditioning of one response as opposed to some other response? The obvious answer is to pair one response with the reinforcer, but not the other response. Other variables (or groups of interacting variables) might also be employed to select responses. One example is deprivation. In this case, reinforcement would follow both responses but the animal would be deprived only when one response was made. The latter, however, is not a particularly practical suggestion since it is difficult to deprive a subject when one response occurs but not when another occurs in a single brief experimental session. This discussion of response selection has been limited to operant conditioning, in which there seems to be agreement that the usual method for selection of the response is to make the reinforcer follow the chosen response. In classical conditioning, however, it is more difficult to specify the factors involved in response selection, as will be shown in Section IV.

The second question concerns the shared properties of conditioned responses. Can we classify responses that can be conditioned by a particular procedure separately from those that cannot on the basis of some independent criterion? Is it true, for example, that autonomic responses cannot be operantly conditioned? The data presented in the next section force us to question this proposition.

We can also classify responses in terms of their relative *ease of conditioning* and ask what features lead to poor or to better conditioning. Although research on this question has focused on the features of the procedure in the past, research on the properties of the response that interact with the procedure to produce optimal conditioning is also important. In operant conditioning, when the procedure is kept constant (except for the change required to select different responses), what properties of a response lead to the faster conditioning of some responses than others? Furthermore, in classical conditioning, when several responses are conditioned by the same procedure, what properties of a response lead to differences in the rate of conditioning among the responses?

The fourth and final question concerns the *internal processes* underlying changes in the organization of behavior that are produced by the conditioning procedure. Hypotheses concerning such mechanisms attempt to account for the sequential and concurrent relationships among responses during conditioning. They also provide an account of the sequence of events between the application of a particular conditioning procedure and the occurrence of a given response.

Traditionally, the consideration of such internal processes has been avoided in discussions of the research on conditioning. The present author is sympathetic to this tradition. Our knowledge of the actual neurophysiological mechanisms underlying changes in the organization of behavior is still limited; therefore, our speculations about such mechanisms will inevitably be both naïve and inadequate. Unfortunately, however, these speculations about underlying processes are implicit (if not explicit) in the thinking that lies behind much of the research on autonomic conditioning. Therefore, it seems advisable to deal with them explicitly.

The phrase "internal processes" opens a Pandora's box of actual and hypothetical neural processes that might control the organization of behavior. In this analysis the possibilities will be somewhat limited, however, since we will be concerned mainly with effector processes. In other words, we will be concerned more with the outflow to muscles, and the neutral processes immediately involved in producing such an outflow, than with sensory processes.

Mediational mechanisms, in which the occurrence of one response is supposed to produce a second response, are most commonly postulated to account for the organization of behavior in conditioning. A number of varieties of mediational hypotheses can be identified. The first and simplest hypothesis is that changes in one response are produced by changes in another response because of some innate prewired connection between the primary response and the mediated response. For example, it has been suggested that autonomic changes during conditioning are produced by skeletal movements; the skeletal movement has been conditioned, and the autonomic change is produced by built-in reflex connections between neural structures involved in skeletal and autonomic behavior. Skinner (1938) has proposed these mediational hypotheses to account for the apparent operant conditioning of autonomic changes, and Smith (1954, 1964, 1967) has proposed them to account for the apparent classical conditioning of autonomic responses. In addition, the obvious interconnections between changes in the autonomic system, particularly the relationships between sympathetic and parasympathetic re-flexes would fall into this category.

A second type of mediational hypothesis bases the relationship between the two responses on some form of conditioning. The responses are regarded as chained, so that feedback from the primary response acts as a CS for the mediated response. Chaining of this sort can be homogenous (between two operantly or two classically conditioned responses), or heterogenous (between an operantly conditioned response and a subsequent classically conditioned response, or vice versa). Heterogenous mediation is of primary concern in this chapter.[4] Skinner (1938) suggested that autonomic changes which were apparently operantly conditioned could be produced by the operant conditioning of a skeletal response whose feedback acts as a CS for some classically conditioned autonomic change. The opposite relationship is suggested by Konorski (1948), in which feedback from a classically conditioned response is supposed to act as a CS for a subsequent operant response. This last example is very similar to Mowrer's (1947) view described earlier, in which autonomic responses were assumed to control subsequent operant behavior. This type of mediating hypothesis, however, should be treated separately from those types suggested by Konorski, since Mowrer assigns motivational and emotional properties to the mediating response, in addition to its function as a CS.

There are, of course, many hypotheses which will account for the organization of behavior during conditioning, which do not involve the mediation of one response by another. The simplest example is provided by those theories which assume that the signalling motivational and emotional effects of a classically conditioned CS on operant responding do not depend on the classically conditioned response but rather on some central mediating motivational and/or cognitive state (Rescorla and Solomon, 1967). Although such hypotheses will be discussed in this chapter, the hypotheses in which responses do the mediating will be employed as a starting point since they have played such a prominent role in the past.

These questions provide a framework for studying the properties of conditioned responses. While other questions might naturally have been asked, these particular questions were chosen because they focus attention on some of the crucial issues which have arisen in research on autonomic conditioned responses.

---

[4]Homogeneous chaining is of interest in interoceptive conditioning when feedback from one autonomic change acts as a CS for a second classically conditioned response.

D.   Conclusion

According to the above discussion, the starting point for comparing and relating classical and operant conditioning and for the analysis of the autonomic response is the description of the effective component of the conditioning procedure, and of the changes produced by it. An attempt will be made to provide such a description for operant and classical autonomic conditioning, respectively, in the next two sections. In addition, the analysis of the response will be discussed for each type of conditioning. Before going on to this, one final point should be made.

Those interested in the classical-operant distinction have also been concerned with the distinction between uniprocess and multiprocess theories of conditioning. Are there two (or more) forms of learning, or is there only one form? The question has been purposely avoided in this chapter. Until the different effects of the pairing of CS and US and of the pairing of response and reinforcement can be described precisely and compared, it is impossible to demonstrate convincingly that there is one process (which would be shown if their effects and underlying neural processes were identical) or two processes (which would be demonstrated if their effects and underlying neural processes were different in some fundamental way). As will be indicated in subsequent sections, we are still far from being able to make such comparisons. Therefore, the question of whether there are one or two learning processes is one from which we can turn away with little guilt. The purpose of this chapter is less ambitious. It is simply to analyze autonomic conditioning with the

---

[5]Even if the effects of pairing CS and US are different from those of pairing R and S^R, this still does not justify the belief that two different learning processes are involved. This point can best be illustrated in the following manner. Pairing CS and US and R and S^R are only two of the possible relationships that may occur among stimuli, responses and reinforcers in a given conditioning situation. Other relationships such as the time interval between successive reinforcements can be manipulated. It does not seem reasonable to postulate a different learning process for each case in which we discover that the effect of a particular empirical relationship between stimuli, responses and reinforcers is different from the effect of other relationships between these events. Therefore, the mere fact that different empirical conditioning procedures have different effects does not justify the postulation of different learning processes. Some further criterion must be established to indicate when differences are to be considered fundamental.

Looking at the other side of the coin, one could treat all operant conditioning as a form of classical conditioning i.e., in operant conditioning the CS is feedback from the response and this CS is paired with the reinforcer (Mowrer, 1960). Similarly, one could suggest that all response changes in classical conditioning are really produced by inadvertent operant reinforcement. Even if this is done, the distinction between pairing CS and US and pairing response and reinforcer is valid. One could still ask whether these two relations among stimuli, responses and reinforcers have similar or different effects.

hope of determining whether some of our beliefs about the properties of conditioned autonomic responses and the effects of different conditioning procedures are correct.

III. OPERANT AUTONOMIC CONDITIONING

A. Introduction

Current research on the operant conditioning of autonomic responses has been devoted to two problems. The first is to determine whether changes in autonomic responding can be attributed to the effect of pairing the response and reinforcer. The second problem is to determine the response mechanism underlying such changes in autonomic responding if they occur. Are the autonomic changes produced directly by the operant conditioning procedure, or are they mediated by the operant conditioning of a skeletal response which in turn produces a change in autonomic activity? These two possibilities are outlined in Figure 1. The top row gives the procedure that the experimenter carries out in which the rein-

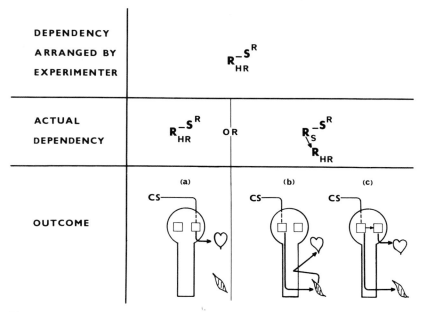

Fig. 1. Operant conditioning procedure, dependencies that might occur when this procedure is employed, and possible outcomes of these operations. R_{HR}, heart rate response; R_s, skeletal response; S^R, reinforcer.

forcement is made dependent on a response (heart rate is employed as an example of an autonomic response). In the next row, the empirical dependencies that might be occurring are presented. Either an autonomic change is operantly reinforced, or a skeletal response is operantly reinforced, and leads to a change in heart rate. The bottom row represents diagrams designed to indicate the outcome of the operant conditioning procedure. According to the first hypothesis (a), the autonomic change is conditioned directly. The activation of neural centers that control heart rate produces an operant heart rate response. In the second hypothesis (b), a skeletal response is operantly conditioned, tnd this response produces feedback stimuli which elicit an autonomic change. The activation of neural centers that control skeletal movement produces overt skeletal movement, and feedback from such skeletal movement produces a change in heart rate. According to the third hypothesis (c), central neural processes that control skeletal movement are operantly conditioned, and these processes produce a change in heart rate. The activation of neural centers controlling movement directly produces a change in heart rate. The actual occurrence of movement is not necessary. In the discussions of mediation by central movement processes, no attempt will be made to deal with these neural processes in terms of the available neurophysiological data and concepts. This omission makes these references to neural processes appear to be naïve, which one naturally wants to avoid. Nevertheless, at this primitive stage of research on the problem, it seems reasonable to avoid a detailed analysis of the neural mechanisms that might be involved. One point should be made, however. Neurophysiological evidence consistent with the hypothesis of mediation by central processes intimately associated with skeletal movement does exist. Autonomic responses occur when skeletal motor centers are stimulated and overt movement is prevented by curare (Landau, 1953; Wall & Davis, 1951). Although additional hypotheses can be suggested, these three are the ones usually considered in attempts to explain the effect of operant conditioning procedures on autonomic responses. The two mediational processes could, of course, occur at the same time. Therefore, the question is not to decide which occurs, but whether one process is sufficient alone.

Why should attention have been focused on the two problems of control by operant reinforcement and underlying mediational mechanisms? The first problem needs no discussion as it is the obvious starting point for research on operant autonomic conditioning. The reasons for concern with the second problem, however, are not as obvious. There is no doubt that it would be interesting to know whether unmediated operant control can be achieved over autonomic responses. One might argue, however, that this problem is no more important than others involved in the analysis of the response. For example, the problem of determining the properties of the response that lead to optimal conditioning should also be important. It is usually assumed that if autonomic responses can be operantly conditioned at all, they are more difficult to condition than skeletal responses. If the properties of autonomic responses which make them difficult to condition by operant procedures can be identified, perhaps the procedures can be adjusted to overcome these difficulties.[6] Why, then, should there be a concentration on the problem of the mediation of autonomic changes by operantly conditioned skeletal responses to the exclusion of other problems? The answer seems to be that research on mediation is presumed to be of crucial theoretical importance. If direct operant control of autonomic responses could be demonstrated, we could no longer assume that autonomic responses were sensitive only to classical conditioning procedures, and that they were useful in distinguishing between operant and classical conditioning. Therefore, theories such as Mowrer's would have to be modified if autonomic responses were under the control of operant conditioning procedures. If, however, direct operant conditioning could not be demonstrated, we could assume that autonomic responses were sensitive only to classical conditioning procedures, and theories such as Mowrer's could be maintained. According to his view, mediated autonomic responses would not be classified as operantly conditioned responses. Kimmel (1967) reflects this attitude in his review of the literature on operant autonomic conditioning. He treats mediation as a "procedural problem," and describes autonomic conditioned responses mediated by skeletal responses as "artifactual." The correctness of this interpretation of the meaning of experiments on mediation will be discussed after the data on these two problems have been considered.

B. Is Autonomic Behavior Controlled by the Operant Conditioning Procedure?

Although the belief that autonomic responses cannot be operantly conditioned has been in circulation since the 1930's, the evidence supporting this belief has been surprisingly sparse. Experiments by Mowrer

[6]Skinner (1938) has suggested that autonomic responses do not normally lead to changes in the environment and, therefore, are not correlated with reinforcement during the normal development of the organism. Transfer from previous operant conditioning would not be available, therefore, to assist in operant conditioning of autonomic responses as is the case for other responses. It has also been suggested that autonomic responses do not provide feedback which assists the subject in knowing that he has performed the correct response (Brener & Hothersall, 1966). It would seem, however, that feedback from reinforcement itself should be enough to accomplish this goal if the reinforcement ratio is 1 to 1.

(1938) and Skinner (1938) seem to be the only early references indicating the failure of operant autonomic conditioning. Skinner's (1938) description was only cursory:

> I have attempted to condition vasoconstriction of the arm in human subjects by making a positive reinforcement depend upon the constriction. The experiments have so far yielded no conclusive result, but there are many clinical observations that seem to indicate conditioning of this sort (Skinner, 1938; p. 112).

Mowrer (1938) failed to demonstrate the operant conditioning of the galvanic skin response (GSR) because of technical difficulties which prevented him from beginning the experiment, rather than any demonstrated insensitivity of the GSR to operant procedures.

> In an experiment recently conducted by the writer, an attempt was made to determine whether human beings learn to make a galvanic skin response to a flash of light of five seconds duration more readily and more consistently (a) when the light is invariably followed by a brief electric shock (of 200 milliseconds duration) or (b) when the light is followed by shock only if a response does not occur within the five-second interval during which the light is on . . . However, it soon became evident that it was useless to carry out the experiment as originally planned, for it was noted during the early stages of the study that the subjects almost always showed a sizable galvanic response to the light on its first presentation, before the shock had ever been presented (Mowrer, 1938; pp. 62–63).

This early evidence of the inability to condition autonomic responses was not impressive. Furthermore, no additional light was cast on the problem during the next twenty years. According to Kimmel (1967), no papers on the topic were published. This lack of data did not, however, inhibit the robust theoretical activity mentioned earlier.[7]

[7] It is not only the lack of evidence concerning a failure of operant autonomic conditioning that makes the persistence of this hypothesis surprising, but also the data on the successful operant conditioning of respondents (among which are usually classed most autonomic responses). The probability of consummatory and instinctive responses to the stimuli that usually elicit them has been modified by operant dependencies (Hogan, 1968; Thompson & Sturm, 1965; Williams & Teitelbaum, 1956). One could argue, of course, that the instinctive and consummatory responses which have come under operant control are no longer the same responses as the original respondent. For example, Goodrich (1966) implies this possibility when he questions whether one can assume that voluntary blinking which results from instructions to blink is the same as blinking controlled by operant reinforcement and involuntary blinking.

In the last few years, a spate of papers on successful operant autonomic conditioning has appeared. If the present rate of publication continues, the preceding twenty years of silence will be more than compensated for. While most of these experiments employed human subjects [see Kimmel (1967) for a review of the human literature], a number of experiments employed animals as subjects (Banuazizi, 1968; Black, 1966, 1967; DiCara and Miller, 1968a,b,c; DiCara and Weiss, 1968; Fromer, 1963; Miller, 1967; Miller and Banuazizi, 1968; Miller and Carmona, 1967; Miller and DiCara, 1967; and Trowill, 1967).

The first question of interest in considering this group of studies is whether autonomic behavior can be operantly conditioned. Will the pairing of an autonomic response and a reinforcer lead to an appropriate change in the probability of the autonomic response when possible confounding variables are controlled? In other words, will the effective component of the operant procedure (see Section I,B) account for changes in autonomic responding? One might expect experimental designs for answering this question to be relatively straight-forward. This is not the case, however. There has been considerable disagreement over the appropriate choice of control groups, and a number of alternative control procedures have been suggested.

1. Control Procedures

Three major types of control procedures have been proposed for determining whether a given behavior change is produced by operant conditioning.

a. The free reinforcement procedure. The first control procedure is a presentation of the S^R that is not dependent on the response. Consider an operant conditioning situation in which food reinforcement is employed. An experimental group reinforced for the operant response would be compared with a control group that received a series of food presentations not associated with any particular response. In an operant situation in which a CS is employed, a group reinforced for the operant response in the presence of the CS would be compared with a group receiving presentations of food in the presence of the CS which were not associated with the occurrence of the response. (In the latter case, the control procedure is essentially a classical conditioning procedure because the S^R is associated with a CS.) The justification for this type of control is straightforward. If the pairing of response and reinforcement is important, then the experimental groups should perform better than the control group, since the pairing occurs only for the experimental group. This control procedure has been criticized, however, because the pattern and number of reinforcements are not necessarily the same for both groups. In the experimental group, food reinforcement is given only when the operant response occurs; in the control group, food is presented according to a predetermined schedule. The control group could conceivably receive a different number and different temporal pattern of reinforcements than the experimental group. If this is the case, any difference between control and experimental groups could be attributed to these factors rather than to the effect of the pairing of response and reinforcement.

   b.   *The yoked control procedure.* A second type of control procedure, the yoked control procedure, was designed to circumvent this difficulty. In this procedure, the experimenter arranges a dependency between the S^R and response in the experimental group, but not in the control group. Each subject in the control group is paired with a partner in the experimental group, and reinforcement is presented to the control subject whenever a response by the experimental partner produces reinforcement. This procedure guarantees that the control subject receives the same number and temporal pattern of reinforcements as his yoked experimental partner, and in this manner, satisfies the objection to the first control procedure. This procedure, however, has been criticized by Church (1964), who argues very convincingly that the subjects in the experimental group may perform better than the subjects in the control group, even though there is *no* effect of the pairing of response and reinforcement. Church points out that the S^R may have many effects, in addition to its effect as an operant reinforcer. It may sensitize the animal to other stimuli, increase motivation, or act as a US for classical conditioning. He demonstrates that individual differences in these extraneous effects of reinforcers could lead to superior performance by the experimental group, even when there is no effect of the pairing of response and reinforcement. Because of this possibility, an ambiguity exists in interpreting data which use yoked controls.

   A further criticism of yoked control procedures is their dependence on the rate of operant responding before reinforcement begins (Black, 1967). If the operant level of responding in the yoked control group is very high, then the response may occur so frequently that it will be inadvertently followed by the reinforcer. Both experimental and control groups would then be subjected to very similar conjunctions between response and reinforcement. If, on the other hand, the operant response level is zero, it is obvious that no response will be made in the experimental group, and the reinforcement will not be presented to either group. Again, no between-group differences would be expected. The yoked design is appropriate, therefore, only if the rate of response to be reinforced falls within some intermediate range. Because of these two difficulties, yoked control group designs will often prove to be inappropriate.

c. *The bidirectional control.* A third control procedure, the bidirectional control, has been designed to avoid the difficulties which arose in the first two types. The rationale for this bidirectional control procedure is the following. We have assumed that both classical and operant conditioning effects can occur in any conditioning situation. Therefore, the results of any conditioning experiment can be partitioned into those effects produced by classical conditioning and those produced by operant conditioning. If we find a conditioning situation in which the classical conditioning procedure is the same in two groups of subjects, but the operant conditioning procedure is different, then a difference in response between the groups must be attributed to the effects of the operant conditioning procedure. (Nonassociative variables such as the number of reinforced presentations must also be kept constant in both groups.) One conditioning situation which seems to meet this requirement is to make the operant reinforcement dependent on different responses in the two groups, while attempting to keep the pairings of CS and S^R constant. For example, one group could be operantly reinforced for increasing the rate of a given response, while another group could be reinforced for decreasing the rate of that response. If a difference existed between the two groups in the rate of the reinforced response, it could be attributed to the effects of the pairing of response and reinforcer, provided, of course, that the pairing of CS and US remained the same in the two groups.

This latter requirement could produce problems since it is obviously difficult to keep the values of variables that control classical conditioning or nonassociative effects constant across the two groups. A group trained to increase the rate of a response may differ from a group trained to decrease the rate of a response with respect to some variable such as number of pairings of CS and S^R. This problem would not be serious if one found no correlation between number of pairings of CS and S^R and the direction of the response in the two groups. Similarly, if a parametric experimental analysis of the effect of pairing CS and US on the direction of the response revealed that the classically conditioned CR was undirectional, the differences between groups could not be attributed to classical conditioning. If, on the other hand, the CR was found to be an increase in rate under one set of experimental conditions and a decrease under another, the danger that group differences were produced by classical conditioning is more serious. Unfortunately, heart rate, the response most extensively studied in research on autonomic operant conditioning, falls into this category (See Section IV,D,1).

A final point about bidirectional control procedure concerns the inter-action between classical and operant effects. If both classical and oper-ant procedures affect the same response, then they can act antagonistically or synergistically. Suppose the classical conditioning procedure acts to increase the rate of a response. In this case, it will be more difficult to operantly condition decreases in this response than in-creases. If the classical conditioning effect is particularly strong, then one might fail to condition decreases operantly altogether. Therefore, the failure to operantly condition either an increase or a decrease in re-sponse rate does not imply that the operant conditioning procedure can-not control behavior. The antagonistic effect of classical conditioning may have suppressed the effect of the operant conditioning. Such inter-ference might have been avoided by changing the conditions of the ex-periment so that the effect of the extraneous variable would be less intense. Sheffield (1965), for example, found that he could not condition dogs to refrain from salivation using food reinforcement. Miller and Carmona (1967), on the other hand, changed to water reinforcement, and successfully trained dogs to increase the rate of salivation or to re-frain from salivating. Some classically conditioned salivary response elic-ited by the food US may have interfered with the training to refrain from salivation, and this classical conditioning response may not have occurred when water was employed. The failure to operantly condition a response under a particular set of experimental conditions does not nec-essarily imply that the response cannot be operantly conditioned.

In summary, while all three control designs are beset by difficulties of one sort or another, the bidirectional design seems to hold the most promise for demonstrating that operant procedures influence behavior.

2. The Experimental Results.

A number of recent experiments have been reported in which aversive reinforcers were employed to operantly condition autonomic responses (Banuazizi, 1968; Black, 1967; DiCara & Miller, 1968b,d,e,f; DiCara and Weiss, 1968; Fromer, 1963).

Fromer (1963) attempted the avoidance conditioning of vasomotor responses in the rabbit. He employed three control groups in addition to the experimental group. One of the control groups received classical pairings of CS and US, and the other two groups were yoked controls. A discrimination procedure was employed. Although all groups acquired a conditioned response, there were no significant differences among the groups. This experiment, then, failed to demonstrate the operant conditioning of vasomotor responses. DiCara and Miller (1968a,c), on the other hand, have recently demonstrated vasomotor conditioning in the curarized rat using positive reinforcement.

DiCara and Miller (1968b) have also carried out research on operant heart rate conditioning. They trained one group of 6 rats to increase heart rate, and another group of 6 rats to decrease heart rate to avoid shock while curarized. Three different types of conditioning trials were employed. The first type of trial was the "avoidance-shock" trial. In this type of trial, a flashing light, CS, was turned on. If the rat achieved a criterion heart rate within five seconds of CS onset, the CS was turned off and shock was avoided. The criterion for successful avoidance was established in the following manner. The average heart rate for approximately one second was the unit of measurement. A heart rate level achieved on the average of once every five seconds was found before the experiment began. This was the original criterion level. The criterion was made 2% faster in the increase group (and 2% slower in the decrease group) each time the rat began meeting the previous criterion within 3 sec. If the rat failed to reach the criterion heart rate within 5 sec, a series of brief pulses of shock at 2-sec intervals was presented. Shock and CS were terminated when the rat achieved the criterion heart rate level. Every tenth avoidance trial was a test trial. The CS was presented for a fixed period of 5 sec, during which the avoidance response had no effect. After the 5-sec period, the usual avoidance contingencies were in effect. The second type of trial employed was the "safe" trial. A 5-sec tone was presented and was not followed by shock. The third type of trial was the "blank" trial. On this trial, heart rate was recorded in a 5-sec period during which no stimuli were presented. One hundred of each of the three types of trials were presented in an irregular order, separated by a mean intertrial interval of 30 sec.

Two types of evidence for conditioning were obtained in this experiment. First, there was a significant increase in the overall level of heart rate for the group reinforced for an increase in heart rate, and a significant decrease in the overall level of heart rate for the group reinforced for a decrease. Second, there was evidence of discriminative conditioning. The heart rate for rats reinforced for increases was higher, and the heart rate for rats reinforced for decreases was lower, during the avoidance CS than during the blank trials. The heart rate on the safe trials was also significantly different from that on the blank trials, but in the opposite direction to the response during the avoidance CS. These results are illustrated in Figure 2. They suggest that the operant conditioning procedures did have an effect on heart rate; further, that a clear discrimination was established in each case between the stimulus leading to avoidance and the safe signal. Similar results have been obtained in subsequent experiments on heart rate conditioning, in curarized rats (DiCara & Miller, 1968e; DiCara & Weiss, 1968).

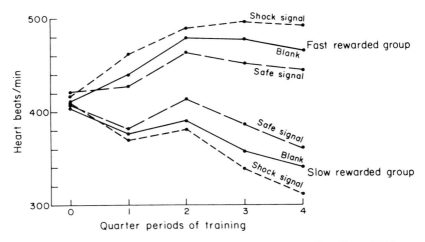

Fig. 2.   Heart rate changes during avoidance training (DiCara & Miller, 1968b).

Black (1967) also used a bidirectional control design to operantly condition heart rate in curarized dogs. One group was trained to increase heart rate to avoid shock; another group was trained to decrease heart rate to avoid shock. Before receiving heart rate avoidance training under curare, some of the dogs were given pretraining in the normal state similar to that in the experiments by Trowill (1967), Miller and DiCara (1967), and Miller and Banuazizi (1968). Nine dogs were conditioned to press a pedal to avoid shock in the presence of a white noise CS in the normal state. The remaining 6 dogs were simply subjected to a series of presentations of the CS in the normal state.

After pretraining, the dogs were curarized employing a medium level of curarization. At this level, little or no overt movement was observed, although electromyographic responding did occur. Nine dogs were then trained to increase heart rate to avoid shock (6 with pedal press avoidance pretraining in the normal state, and 3 without such pretraining). Six dogs were trained to decrease heart rate to avoid shock (3 with pedal-press pretraining and 3 without).

The avoidance conditioning procedure for increases was the following. (A similar procedure was employed for decreases.) On each trial, the maximum heart rate during 20 sec of the intertrial interval was determined just prior to the onset of the white noise CS. This rate was employed as the criterion level. After CS onset, the dogs were reinforced by

CS termination and avoidance of shock for maintaining heart rate above the criterion level for 6 sec. If no avoidance occurred after CS onset, the dogs were given a series of brief pulsed shocks which continued until the appropriate response occurred. Each dog was trained to a criterion of 20 consecutive avoidances. If the dog did not reach this criterion of 20 consecutive avoidances within 150 trials, the conditioning session was terminated.

There was a significant increase in the number of avoidances from the first 20 to the last 20 training trials for dogs in both pretraining groups. It would seem, then, that the operant conditioning procedure controlled behavior. The dogs reinforced for increases, however, were conditioned more rapidly than the dogs reinforced for decreased heart rate. Only 2 out of 6 dogs in the decrease group met the criterion of 20 consecutive avoidances within 150 trials, while 8 out of 9 in the increase group met the criterion within 150 trials.

Since the dogs in the decrease group took longer to condition than those reinforced for increases, the different direction of conditioned response in the two groups might be attributed to the different numbers of shocks or CS-shock pairings, e.g., few shocks might lead to an increase in heart rate and many shocks to a brief increase followed by a decrease. This does not seem likely since the 2 dogs which received the most shock failed to make a decelerative CR.

Examples of operantly conditioned heart rate responses from the Black (1967) experiment are presented in Figure 3. Two examples of operantly conditioned heart rate increases and two examples of operantly conditioned decreases are shown. These examples lead one to ask whether responses in the increase group are really different from responses in the decrease group. One might argue that all dogs were making the same response—an increase followed by a decrease. In the increase group, the CS was terminated early, and the later component of the response may not have had a chance to appear, as it did in the decrease group. If this conjecture is correct, then the duration of the increase component ought to be similar in both groups. This was not the case. The duration of the increase for dogs trained to accelerate was significantly greater than the increase for dogs trained to decelerate. Therefore, although the two responses may be similar in form, they are certainly not identical in this experiment. Although Miller and his associates did not provide analyses which permit one to determine whether the responses in their experiment were different, the examples which they did present suggest that they were. Furthermore, tonic changes in intertrial heart rate in the DiCara and Miller experiment (1968b) could not be explained by the occurrence of the same phasic response during the CS.

These experiments (Black, 1967; DiCara and Miller, 1968b,e; DiCara

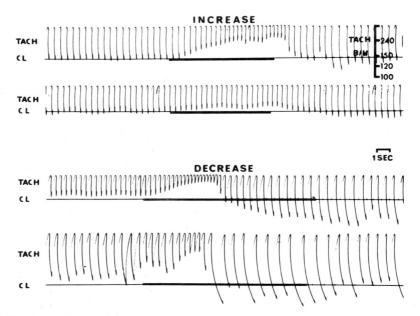

Fig. 3. Tachographic examples of heart rate avoidance responses. Two examples for dogs trained to increase heart rate to avoid shock, and two examples for dogs trained to decrease heart rate to avoid shock. Presentation of the CS is indicated by solid horizontal line; CL: criterion level.

and Weiss, 1968) seem to demonstrate the operant conditioning of increases and decreases in heart rate. The only serious disagreement in their results is in the effect of the operant conditioning procedure on the intertrial heart rate. DiCara *et al.* found a significant increase in intertrial heart rate in the group reinforced for increasing heart rate, and a significant decrease in intertrial heart rate in the group reinforced for decreasing heart rate. Black found a significant increase in intertrial heart rate in *both* groups. Whether this difference in responses can be attributed to differences in species employed or to procedures is not yet established.

The operant conditioning of two autonomic responses in addition to heart rate has been demonstrated using aversive reinforcers. DiCara and Miller (1968d) employed a procedure to condition systolic blood pressure responses similar to that which they employed to condition heart rate. They were able to condition an increase in overall level of blood pressure in one group and a decrease in overall level in another group. There was, however, no evidence of discriminative responding to the CS, *i.e.*, the blood pressure level on CS trials and blank trials did not differ.

Banuazizi (1968) used a somewhat different method to operantly condition intestinal contraction and relaxation in deeply curarized rats. Two
groups of rats were used, one reinforced by shock avoidance for intestinal contraction, and the other reinforced by shock avoidance for intestinal relaxation. Each group was subjected to three types of conditioning
trials: avoidance trials, blank trials, and safe trials. On avoidance trials,
the CS remained on for 1 min. In the contraction group, the rat avoided
shock when the intestinal motility was above a certain criterion level,
and received a series of pulsed shocks 1 sec apart when intestinal motility was below the criterion level. In the relaxation group, the reinforcement dependencies were reversed. On safe trials, no shocks were
presented, and on blank trials no stimuli were presented. Successful operant conditioning both of relaxation and of contraction was obtained to
the CS. The rats maintained the state of intestinal motility during the CS
that led to shock avoidance.

In summary, experiments using aversive reinforcement seem to demonstrate the operant reinforcement of autonomic responses. The generality of these results is enhanced since positive results were obtained with
three operant conditioning procedures, three responses, and two species.

C. The Mechanism Underlying the Response Change

The next problem is the analysis of the mechanism underlying operantly conditioned autonomic responses. The various mechanisms which
have been of most concern in the past are outlined in Figure 1. In the
following discussion, an attempt will be made to determine which of
these mechanisms provides the most plausible account of operant autonomic conditioning. This will be done by considering in detail the two
proposed mechanisms using the mediation hypothesis (Figure 1(b) and
(c)).

1. Mediation by Overt Skeletal Responses

Several experiments have attempted to rule out the possibility of mediation by overt skeletal behavior (Figure 1b) by employing curare-like
drugs to paralyze the skeletal musculature (Banuazizi, 1968; Black, 1966,
1967; DiCara and Miller, 1967a–f; DiCara and Weiss, 1968; Miller,
1967; Miller and Banuazizi, 1968; Miller and DiCara, 1967; Trowill,
1967).

Trowill (1967) and Miller and DiCara (1967) reported that under curare, all overt movement dropped out and successful operant conditioning of heart rate took place. They concluded that overt movement did

not mediate operantly conditioned heart rate responses. This conclusion, however, can be questioned. The curarization procedure might not have prevented all muscle activity, even though all obvious movement had disappeared. If this were the case, vestigial responses of the skeletal musculature could have been inadvertently reinforced and could have mediated changes in heart rate. In order to check on occurrences of muscle activity under curare, electromyographic activity was measured in experiments by Banuazizi (1968), and DiCara and Miller (1968b). Di-Cara and Miller reported successful operant conditioning of heart rate and Banuazizi reported successful operant conditioning of intestinal contractions under complete or deep curarization when neither electromyographic activity nor overt movement occurred. These results lead one to reject the hypothesis of mediation of heart rate changes by overt movement.

Black (1967), working with dogs, reported somewhat different results. The procedure employed was essentially the same as that in the experiment described in Section III,B,2. Black found that heart rate accelerations occurred without EMG and movement under deep curarization. Under deep curarization, however, the heart rate response was smaller and less stable from trial to trial, than under medium curarization (when EMG activity but no actual movement occurred). The dogs often failed to avoid shock under deep curarization. One could argue that this effect of curare on heart rate was produced by the blocking of EMG. This does not seem likely, however, since some dogs showed a disruption of conditioned heart rate while EMG was continuing. The most reasonable explanation of these results is that curare had a direct effect on peripheral cardiac nerves (probably at synapses in peripheral autonomic ganglia), in addition to its effect on the skeletal neuromuscular junction. In order to check on this hypothesis, Black studied the effects of direct stimulation of the cardiac nerves under different dose levels of curare. Three dogs were operantly conditioned to increase heart rate while under medium curarization, and then were given gradually increased doses of curare until they reached a level of deep curarization. During the transition from medium to deep curarization, further avoidance conditioning trials were presented. In addition, electrodes that had been chronically implanted on peripheral cardiac nerves prior to the experiment were employed to stimulate these nerves periodically during the transition from medium to deep curarization. Data on two dogs are shown in Figure 4. In one dog (A), the stimulating electrodes were implanted on the vagus and two levels of stimulation were employed. The other dog (B) had electrodes implanted on a predominantly sympathetic nerve near the caudal cervical ganglion.

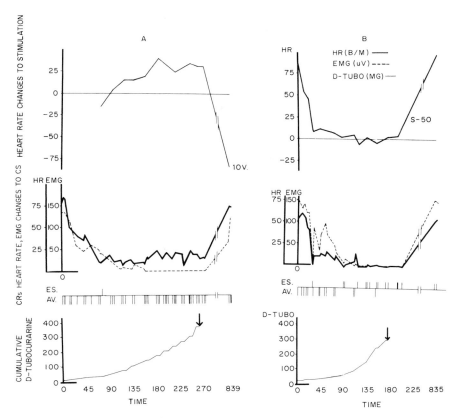

Fig. 4. Transition from medium to deep curarization following avoidance training to accelerate heart rate under medium curarization. Upper graphs present response to direct stimulation of peripheral cardiac nerves. Heart rate measure is the difference between heart rate during stimulation and the heart rate immediately preceding onset of stimulation. In graph A, the vagus nerve was stimulated. In graph B, a predominantly sympathetic nerve near the caudal cervical ganglion was stimulated. Middle graphs present data on heart rate and EMG. Heart rate measure is the difference between heart rate during CS and the heart rate immediately preceding CS onset. EMG measure is the maximum EMG response during CS. Lower graph is cumulative record of the amount of d-tubocurarine injected. The arrow in the bottom graph indicates end of injections. Vertical marks between middle and lower graphs give points at which acquisition trials were presented. Marks below horizontal lines represent avoidances; marks above represent nonavoidances. Time is in minutes.

These two dogs displayed a diminution in the magnitude of heart rate and EMG responses to the CS as curarization became deeper. In one dog (Figure 4A), the EMG disappeared while the heart rate response to the CS continued. In the other dog (Figure 4B), both heart rate and

EMG responses to the CS dropped out together. Recovery from curarization led to a recovery of EMG and heart rate responses to the CS.

Parallel heart rate changes occurred in the response to the CS and in the response to the stimulation of the cardiac nerves. In one dog, the stimulation of the vagus, which initially produced a deceleration in heart rate, was attenuated during the transition to deep curarization, and then recovered as the effects of curare wore off, just as the heart rate response to the CS was attenuated and recovered (Figure 4A). In fact, a reversal occurred in the response to vagal stimulation under deep curarization. An increase, rather than a decrease, was observed. This reversal occurred because the vagus contains both sympathetic and parasympathetic components, and the latter seem to be more readily blocked by d-tubocurarine in this dog. Not only did the dog show a reversal when the vagus was stimulated, but it was also the only dog whose heart rate acceleration to the CS did not deteriorate under deep curarization. The sympathetic component seemed to be particularly immune to d-tubocurarine in this dog, and permitted a response to direct stimulation and to the CS under deep curarization.

In the second dog, stimulation of an apparently sympathetic location was attenuated during the transition to deep curarization and then recovered just as the response to the CS first attenuated and then recovered (Figure 4B). In this dog, the response to the CS disappeared completely, as did the response to direct stimulation. Apparently, the sympathetic components were not immune to the effects of d-tubocurarine in this case.

In summary, Black (1967) found an attenuation of the heart rate response to direct stimulation[8] parallel to the attenuation of the heart rate response to the CS during the transition from medium to deep curarization. Furthermore, the heart rate change to the CS occurred only when direct sympathetic stimulation had an effect. This result is consistent with the view that the conditioned heart rate increase is a sympathetically controlled response.

These data support the hypothesis that difficulties in performing an operantly conditioned heart rate response under deep curarization could stem from the blocking action of curare on peripheral autonomic synapses and not from the prevention of skeletal responding. Operantly conditioned heart rate responses do occur independently of overt movement, and these responses would probably be seen stably in all dogs if

---

[8] In the dogs described in the text, the peripheral autonomic nerves were not cut. Similar attenuation of the heart rate response to direct stimulation was observed in anesthetized acute preparations in which the vagus was severed between the stimulating electrodes and the brain.

d-tubocurarine did not have the unfortunate property of blocking peripheral autonomic synapses in some dogs. These conclusions are in agreement with those reached by Miller and his associates working with deeply curarized rats. The reason that Black ran into difficulty with deep curarization and Miller and his associates did not is not clear. Some species differences or differences in procedure may account for the different results.

2. Mediation by Central Movement Processes

Although we can reject the mediation of operantly conditioned heart rate by changes in overt movement (Figure 1b), two of the alternative explanations of operant heart rate conditioning described in Figure 1 remain. Perhaps autonomic responses can be directly conditioned (Figure 1a); or perhaps they depend on central movement processes rather than on overt movement alone (Figure 1c). Experiments which employ curare must be indecisive with respect to this latter hypothesis, since curare only serves to block the overt responses and leaves the central state unaffected.

How are we to decide between these two alternatives? Two approaches have been suggested. The first is obvious and has been employed extensively (Kimmel, 1967). If central movement processes produce heart rate changes, we should find activity in central structures associated with movement, as shown in Figure 1c. If the subject is not curarized, activity in these central structures will lead to overt movement. Therefore, a relationship should exist between overt skeletal movement and heart rate when movement can occur, if the hypothesis of central mediation is valid. If such functional relationships are not found, this central mediation hypothesis can be rejected.

The second approach depends on the analysis of the relations among autonomic responses during operant conditioning. If the same central movement process were mediating two autonomic responses, they should change in a parallel manner during conditioning. If, however, a given autonomic response is operantly conditioned and parallel changes do not occur simultaneously in a second autonomic response, and vice versa, we could not maintain that a single central movement process is mediating both autonomic changes. Rather, we would have to argue for the occurrence of a mediating process unique to each autonomic response. The more demonstrations of operant conditioning of unrelated autonomic responses, the more we would have to postulate different mediating central movement processes that affect certain autonomic responses independently of others. It seems reasonable to believe that the likelihood of a large number of such unique central mediating processes is small. Therefore, if we could find a number of cases in which a given autonomic response could be operantly conditioned without parallel changes in other autonomic responses, the central mediation hypothesis would become much less convincing. These approaches to the problem of central mediation are discussed in the following two subsections.[9]

a.   Autonomic–skeletal relationships. Black (1967) has presented data relevant to the relationship of EMG to heart rate. These data came from the experiment described earlier using bidirectional control procedures. EMG was recorded from the forelimbs and shoulder of dogs. Movement of the forelimbs was also measured. These sites were chosen since the avoidance response on pretraining was pressing a pedal with the forelimbs. In the nine dogs trained to increase heart rate under medium curarization, two types of relationships between EMG responding and heart rate increases were observed. Two examples of conditioning trials which illustrate these relationships are shown in Figure 5. The majority of

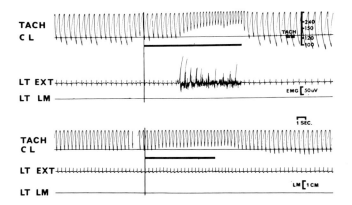

Fig. 5.   Two examples of heart rate and EMG responses for dogs trained to increase heart rate. TACH: tachographic recording of heart rate. CL: criterion level of heart rate. LT EXT: EMG from left foreleg extensor muscle. LT LM: movement of left foreleg.

"It is interesting to note in passing that little of the research on mediation has involved the analysis of the temporal relationship between the mediated and mediating responses. This is somewhat surprising since the sequential pattern of responding should provide very useful information. If response A precedes B in time, it is very unlikely that B mediates A. The reason for the lack of sequential analyses is probably the difficulty in identifying the time at which an autonomic response begins, as Shapiro and Miller (1965) have pointed out.

heart rate avoidance responses were accompanied by EMG (532 out of 588 trials), one of which is illustrated in the top example. Less than 10% were unaccompanied by EMG, one of which is shown in the bottom example. Only 2 of the 9 dogs made more than one response of the latter type. Furthermore, those heart rate responses accompanied by EMG activity were significantly greater in magnitude than those responses unaccompanied by EMG in the 2 dogs.

The type of responses which occurred during heart rate deceleration are shown in Figure 6. All avoidances were accompanied by an EMG response during the initial acceleration of heart rate, and a cessation of EMG during the later deceleration. In some cases, the EMG activity began before CS onset; in others, it began after CS onset. Whatever the occasion of this small burst of EMG, heart rate deceleration was always associated with its cessation.

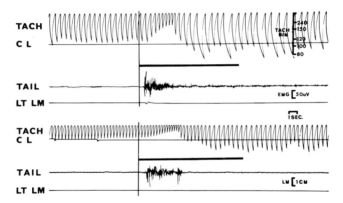

Fig. 6. Examples of two heart rate responses for dogs trained to decrease heart rate, showing correlated changes in EMG. TACH: tachographic recording of heart rate. CL: criterion level of heart rate. TAIL: EMG recorded from tail. LT LM: movement of left foreleg.

The result that heart rate changes were accompanied by EMG tends to support the hypothesis that heart rate changes are produced by central movement processes. Nevertheless, one would still like to understand why the few exceptions to the association of heart rate and EMG occurred. Black (1967) suggested that those exceptions occur when partial curarization blocks small amplitude EMG responses associated with small increases in heart rate. The fact that the heart rate response was of small amplitude when no EMG was occurring supports this hypothesis. In order to check on this further, Black trained 6 dogs in the normal state to maintain EMG below a criterion level in order to avoid shock. It was expected that dogs that made very small EMG responses would increase heart rate, and that dogs that refrained from EMG completely would not. The results were more complicated than expected. The heart rate response depended not only on movement during the CS, but also on pre-CS movement. Examples of records from 2 dogs in Figure 7 illustrate this point. If a great deal of muscle activity existed during the

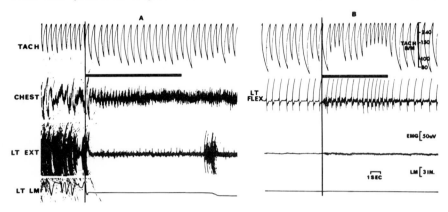

Fig. 7. Examples of trials for two dogs trained in normal state to maintain EMG activity in the left leg below a criterion level. Presentation of CS is indicated by solid horizontal line. TACH: tachographic record of heart rate; CHEST: EMG from chest; LT FLEX: EMG from left foreleg flexor muscle; LT EXT: EMG from left foreleg extensor muscle; LT LM: movement of left foreleg.

pre-CS period, and little during the CS period, then there tended to be a decrease in heart rate during the CS period. If there was no muscle activity during the pre-CS period, and again little activity during the CS period, the heart rate increased. The latter response is very similar to the type thought to have occurred under curare. This result suggests that heart rate increases under curare could have been produced by low level activity in central movement centers; the activity being so low that curare would prevent it from producing any EMG.

In Black's experiments, changes in heart rate were associated with specific patterns of movement as well as with generalized struggling. This fact may explain why accelerative heart rate avoidance conditioning was faster than decelerative heart rate avoidance conditioning. It seems reasonable that a simple increase in muscle activity is easier to condition than an increase followed by a cessation of muscle activity. If this is so, then one would expect that accelerative heart rate responses (associated with a simple increase in EMG) would be easier to condition than decelerative heart rate responses (associated with an increase in EMG followed by a cessation of EMG).

Recently DiCara and Miller (1968e,f) and DiCara and Weiss (1968) have studied the correlation between heart rate and skeletal responding in rats using a somewhat different approach. One group of rats was first trained to increase heart rate and another group of rats to decrease heart rate using essentially the same procedure as that employed in the paper described earlier (DiCara and Miller, 1968b). After the rats recovered from curarization, the appropriate CS was presented and measurements were made during the intertrial interval of heart rate, skeletal activity and respiration. In the normal state, there was no difference in heart rate between the groups trained to increase and decrease heart rate just before CS presentations began. However, there was a difference in skeletal activity and respiration: the increase group showed less activity and a higher respiration rate. After a series of presentations of CS alone there were significant differences in heart rate between the two groups. The heart rate of the increase group was significantly higher than the heart rate of the decrease group. At the same time, the differences between the two groups with respect to skeletal activity and respiration rate decreased. After these CS presentations operant heart rate avoidance training in the normal state was carried out, and it led to an accentuation of heart rate differences between groups, and a further decrease in differences in skeletal activity and respiration.

DiCara and Miller suggest that these results indicate a lack of correlation between skeletal responses and heart rate changes—a reasonable interpretation. There is a possibility, however, that a more detailed analysis might reveal some correlation between these responses. This possibility is made more likely by the data of DiCara and Weiss (1968) which indicate a positive relationship between operant heart rate conditioning under curare and subsequent skeletal avoidance responding in the normal state. Rats trained to decrease heart rate under curare learned to run to avoid shock more quickly in the normal state than those trained to increase heart rate.

In summary, the experiments of Black (1967) and DiCara and Weiss (1968) suggest that skeletal responding and heart rate are related (however complicated the relationship between the two may turn out to be). The results of these experiments are consistent with the hypothesis of mediation of heart rate changes by central movement processes, whereas the findings of DiCara and Miller (1968e) do not seem to support such mediation.

b. Autonomic–autonomic relationships. DiCara and Miller (1968d) trained rats under curare either to increase or to decrease systolic blood pressure to avoid shock using a procedure similar to that described by DiCara and Miller (1968b). While significant changes in blood pressure occurred in the appropriate direction, no significant changes in heart rate or rectal temperature occurred during training. There was no significant correlation between overall changes in baseline levels of heart rate and blood pressure from the beginning to the end of the experiment.

Similar results have been obtained in research employing positive electrical brain stimulation as the operant reinforcement. Miller and Banuazizi (1968) operantly conditioned heart rate increases and decreases and observed changes in intestinal contractions. They also conditioned intestinal contractions and relaxation and observed concomitant changes in heart rate but found no clear-cut correlation between the two responses when groups were compared. Similar results were obtained by DiCara and Miller (1968a,c) for peripheral vasodilation. They showed that increases or decreases in vasodilation of the tail could be conditioned without correlated changes in heart rate (although rectal temperature was correlated with vasodilation). In a second experiment, these authors demonstrated that vasomotor responses in one ear could be conditioned independently of those in the other ear. Miller and DiCara (1968) found that changes in the rate of urine formation and in the rate of blood flow through the kidney could be operantly conditioned without correlated changes in heart rate, blood pressure, and vasomotor responses in the tail.

These results are inconsistent with the hypothesis that a single skeletal response mediates operantly conditioned autonomic changes. The same response cannot mediate unrelated responses. They also indicate that if one wants to maintain mediational hypotheses, a variety of mediating skeletal responses with unique autonomic effects must be postulated. For example, one would have to argue that certain skeletal responses mediated heart rate change, but not gastrointestinal activity, and that others mediated gastrointestinal activity but not heart rate responses. However implausible such mediating responses may appear, they are nevertheless a possibility. One could argue, of course, that the issue could be resolved, once and forever, by measuring skeletal responses as well as autonomic responses during the operant conditioning of a given autonomic response. In theory, one would have to measure all skeletal responding, and this is obviously very difficult. Nevertheless, the measurement of some skeletal muscle activity in these experiments might be useful.

Further research will obviously be needed on this issue since the data on the relationship of skeletal responding to autonomic responding lead to a conclusion that is different from the data on relations among autonomic responses. The former suggest that mediation occurs; the latter indicate that its occurrence is unlikely and that if it does occur, it is very complex. It must be admitted, however, that whatever the outcome of this research, correlational data can never be completely convincing. Even if a relationship between the central movement processes and autonomic responses is found, it may be coincidental. Also, one may not find a relation among autonomic responses, because one does not measure the appropriate response properties in enough detail. This problem could be avoided if one were able to condition autonomic responses while central movement processes were controlled in the same way that overt movement is controlled by curare. One possible method for achieving this goal is to attempt to condition more complex responses, *i.e.*, a heart rate acceleration accompanied by no change in movement (Black, 1967).

D. Discussion

The data presented above were concerned with two problems. First, can changes in autonomic responses be attributed to the effective component of the operant conditioning procedure? Second, is this conditioning direct, or is it the result of mediation by operantly conditioned skeletal responses? The answer to the first question is positive. Operant procedures were found to affect autonomic responses when other variables are controlled. The second question is more difficult to answer, since it turns out that a number of different types of mediation are possible.

The research using complete curarization rules out mediation involving overt skeletal movement. Furthermore, the possibility of mediation by vestigial skeletal responses in these curare experiments is remote, since no skeletal movement was recorded during curarization. Even if vestigial movement did occur, the difference between such skeletal responses under curare and skeletal responses in the normal state is so great that it is difficult to see how the movement under curare could be similar enough to the movement in the normal state to have the same mediating functions.

A second form of mediation of the autonomic change is by central movement processes associated with overt skeletal responses. Some data on autonomic–skeletal relationships support this possibility; other data do not. The data on autonomic-autonomic relationships are clear-cut, however; they indicate that the same central movement process cannot mediate all operantly conditioned autonomic changes. If a single central movement process were mediating all autonomic changes, responses should have changed in a parallel manner during operant conditioning, and this was not the case.

If one were to attempt to retain a mediational hypothesis in the face of such data, one would have to argue that different central movement processes mediate different autonomic responses. Therefore, the choice is not between direct operant conditioning of autonomic responses and simple mediation, but between direct operant conditioning and a very complex sort of mediation in which different mediating responses produce different patterns of autonomic change.

The data have been discussed up to this point as though the alternatives were mutually exclusive. This may not be correct. It may be that different strategies can be employed by an animal to produce the autonomic change, depending on the particular conditioning procedure employed. In one situation, the autonomic response may be changed directly; in others, it may be mediated. For example, it may be that the procedure employed by Black required the subject to make a much more difficult response than that employed by DiCara and Miller. In the former experiment, the dog was required to maintain an autonomic change for 6 sec, and in the latter, for 1 sec. Furthermore, DiCara and Miller employed a shaping procedure and Black did not. This difference in procedure may have led to the use of mediational strategy in the one case, and none in the other. In short, a given autonomic change may be involved in several different complexly interacting feedback control systems, each of which may be activated by different conditions, involve different central processes, and have a different function in the economy of the organism. Cardiovascular changes are involved in the relatively limited system regulating the movement of the skeletal musculature, and may also be involved in the more extensive system which we label "emotional arousal," to mention only two examples. If operant conditioning brings one of these systems into play in one case and not in another, different central processes could occur in the two situations, even though the behavior change was the same, and different patterns of mediation would be observed. If this hypothesis is correct, one ought not to be as concerned with whether mediation occurs, but rather with determining which experimental procedures produce mediation and which do not for a particular pattern of autonomic responding.

Although the discussion so far has concentrated on mediation, the data in this section are also relevant to other questions concerning the analysis of response classification (see Section II,C). It is obvious that one must reject the classification scheme based on the position that autonomic responses are not controlled by the operant conditioning procedure. In fact, it seems that all responses can be affected by the operant conditioning procedure. Therefore, rather than attempt to classify responses in terms of whether they can be conditioned operantly or classically, one might attempt to classify them in terms of their relative ease of conditioning. Such a classification would be particularly useful if the properties of behavior which lead to rapid or slow conditioning could be identified and manipulated experimentally. If, for example, responses which conditioned slowly lacked feedback, some artificial source of feedback could be added. Furthermore, criteria for classification other than the distinction between autonomic and skeletal responding might prove to be more successful in the long run. Breland and Breland (1966) have pointed out, for example, that responses in certain species are easy to operantly condition using a wide variety of conditioned stimuli and reinforcers, whereas responses in other species are limited to the reinforcing situations in which they occur naturally. The same distinctions may hold for responses within a given species. Salivation was operantly conditioned when water reinforcement was employed (Miller and Carmona, 1967), but not when food reinforcement was used (Sheffield, 1965). Therefore, it may provide an example of a response which is more limited in its range of applicability than some other responses. If the properties of the response which determine its range of applicability can be identified, then a more useful classification may be established.

In those cases where mediation does not seem to occur, questions concerning the variables controlling the relative ease of conditioning arise. One can regard the autonomic and skeletal responses made in a given situation as components of a complex set of feedback systems (*i.e.*, homeostatic systems which maintain autonomic responding at a certain level). When autonomic responses are operantly reinforced, one has changed the control system so that a new baseline level of responding is achieved and maintained. Is the usual method of operant reinforcement enough to do this, or is more required in certain cases? DiCara and Miller (1968f) failed to condition heart rate increases in normal subjects who were naïve, even though they conditioned increases in both curarized subjects who were naïve and in normal subjects who had been previously trained under curare. Therefore, one might ask whether the curare procedure is more than a simple control for overt movement in infrahuman subjects. Curare, because of its additional direct effect on the autonomic nervous system, may block those parts of the system which might prevent operant reinforcement from changing the baseline level of the system in the normal state. If this conjecture is correct, the sensitivity of responses to modification by operant reinforcement would depend on the role of that response in the various self-regulative feedback systems in which it was involved. If the response that one wanted to change is part of a system which was relatively immune to outside influence, operant reinforcement might be easier if some of the regulating variables in the system were prevented from having their effect during the course of conditioning.

The questions dealt with in the previous two paragraphs reflect the obvious fact that the effects of operant reinforcement depend on the properties of the response to be reinforced. Since we know so little about these properties (many discussions of operant reinforcement blandly assume that the choice of the response to be conditioned is arbitrary), it might be more profitable at the present time to emphasize research on this problem rather than on the problem of mediation. Two further reasons may be given for reducing our concern about the problem of mediation.

As pointed out in Section II, the view is held by many that if mediation is demonstrated, theories can be maintained which propose that autonomic responses can be directly conditioned only by classical procedures. While this statement is true, the power of these theories is reduced even if operantly conditioned autonomic responses are mediated rather than directly conditioned. Suppose one observed a change in some autonomic response during a conditioning experiment. Could one use this autonomic response as a measure of classical conditioning? Even if one accepts the mediation hypothesis, the answer must be negative since the autonomic change could have been produced by the operant conditioning of some mediating response as well as by classical conditioning. Therefore, one would not be able to employ the autonomic response to differentiate between operant and classical conditioning or to act as a measure of classically conditioned responses during operant conditioning. The demonstration of mediation, then, does not really protect these theories as much as might be supposed.

The second reason for questioning the widsom of focusing so much attention on the problem of mediation is that a point of diminishing returns may have been reached in this type of research. The study of mediation is extremely difficult when one becomes involved in the analysis of central processes. The meaning of the phrase "central movement processes" is clear. These processes were assumed to occur when impulses which lead to movement were being sent out from the brain, and movement would have taken place if the impulses had not been blocked at the neuromuscular junction. There is the possibility, however, that other kinds of central states can be operantly conditioned, and can produce autonomic responses. For example, the occurrence of emotional states is assumed to produce autonomic changes. If one could operantly condition these central emotional states, they too could mediate autonomic responses. In order to check on this possibility, one has to distinguish conditioned central *movement* states from conditioned central *emotional* states, and these in turn from other central states that also directly control autonomic reactions. (The variety of central states that might be operantly conditioned and that might lead to autonomic responses is obviously much greater in human than in infrahuman subjects.) Dealing with a single central state is difficult enough, let alone measuring three different types of central states. At this point, then, it might be wiser to limit the consideration of mediation to skeletal movement and its associated central movement processes and to work on other questions concerning the analysis of the response which are, after all, important. Such an approach could provide more useful information about the organization of behavior and the mechanisms underlying behavior changes in operant autonomic conditioning than some over-fastidious concern with the problem of mediation.

IV. CLASSICAL CONDITIONING OF AUTONOMIC RESPONSES

A. Introduction

The literature on the classical conditioning of autonomic responses differs from that on the operant conditioning of autonomic responses not only in content but also in extent and goals. Few studies have been carried out on the operant conditioning of autonomic responses, as we have seen, and these are concerned with the problems of attributing changes in autonomic responding to the effects of the pairing of response and reinforcer and of determining the response mechanism underlying this change. On the other hand, many studies exist on the classical conditioning of autonomic responses, and these have been concerned with a wide variety of problems. Furthermore, even though more research on more problems has been carried out on the classical conditioning of autonomic responses than on their operant conditioning, more serious disagreements seem to exist over fundamental issues in the case of classical conditioning. Some question has arisen as to the identification of the experimental procedure necessary and sufficient for classical conditioning, and even more about what behavioral change to the CS is produced by this effective component of the classical conditioning procedure. The traditional Pavlovian stimulus substitution hypothesis, for example, states that classical conditioning procedures lead to an increase in the probability of responses to the CS that are produced by the same neural centers as the responses to the US. A second hypothesis states that the US determines the classically conditioned response. Each US has associated with it certain responses which will be conditioned, and these may or may not resemble the UR. In contrast to the stimulus substitution position, this view implies that one cannot identify which responses can be classically conditioned until after some conditioning with a given US in a given experimental situation has been carried out. Another hypothesis states that no behavior is reinforced by the pairing of CS and US; rather, it is the pairing of R and S^R that accounts for the reinforcement of responses during classical conditioning. Finally, the problem of describing the behavioral change in classical conditioning is exacerbated by the view that the classical conditioning procedure does not affect responses directly; rather, it is supposed to produce changes in central motivational or cognitive states which, in turn, influence responses. Because of these disagreements, the experimental procedure and the resulting behavioral change will be discussed before considering the analysis of the response.

B.   The Essential Features of the Classical Conditioning Procedure

The experimental procedure necessary to produce classical conditioning is usually specified as follows: a CS and US must be paired in temporal contiguity with the CS preceding the US. Disagreements with this hypothesis can be divided into two types: those concerned with the choice of reinforcer and those concerned with the relationship between CS and reinforcer.

1.   The Reinforcer

The basic question concerns the event with which the CS must be paired: is it the US or the UR elicited by the US? The results of experiments on salivary conditioning when the UR is blocked indicate that the classical conditioning of salivation can take place when the salivary UR is prevented from occurring by atropine (Crisler, 1930; Finch, 1938). These results agree with informal observations on heart rate conditioning under curare by Black, Carlson, and Solomon (1962), who found that conditioned cardiac responses were observed after recovery from curarization even though the heart rate response was blocked inadvertently during conditioning under curare. Skeletal responses to the US were also prevented under curare, and were observed in the presence of the CS after recovery from curarization. The occurrence of the UR, therefore, is not necessary for conditioning, although some central movement processes could be involved when the UR is blocked peripherally.

Furthermore, the occurrence of the UR does not guarantee that conditioning will occur. A light US elicits a pupillary contraction but does not produce classical conditioning (Young, 1965). Pilocarpine elicits a salivary response but may not produce conditioning: Young (1965), Crisler (1930), and Kleitman (1927) found no conditioning, but Finch (1938) did report some slight evidence of pilocarpine conditioning. Kimble (1961) and Young (1965) suggest that these failures occurred because the US did not involve higher central nervous system processes in producing the UR.

In summary, the UR seems to be neither necessary nor sufficient for classical conditioning to occur. All that seems to be necessary is the occurrence of the appropriate type of US.

A further question concerns the properties of the US. Is US onset or US termination the crucial variable? (Research on this problem is limited to those discrete USs such as shock for which onset and termination can be easily manipulated.) In one line of research on this problem (Wegner and Zeaman, 1958), heart rate conditioning was studied in human subjects. The interval between CS onset and US onset was held constant, while the duration of the US was varied. If US termination was the important variable, the conditioning should have been slower with the longer US because the interval between CS onset and US termination was longer. No such differences were found. Therefore, it was concluded that the interval between CS onset and US onset was important, and that US onset was the crucial reinforcer. This conclusion can be questioned. The measures of conditioning may have been unaffected by the interval between CS onset and US termination, not because the CS–US onset interval was important, but because the particular CS–US termination intervals employed were not sufficient to produce differences in rate of conditioning. Church and Black (1958), for example, have shown no difference between CS–US onset intervals of 5 and 20 sec in the speed of heart rate conditioning of dogs.

Miller (1963) has questioned the research on US duration on different grounds. He argued that a major decrease in the drive state associated with the US could have occurred well before the termination of the US. If this were so, variations in the duration of the US would be irrelevant. While this argument is difficult to deal with empirically, another approach to this problem, proposed by Mowrer (1960), suggests that it is not correct. Mowrer asserted that both US onset and US termination can act to produce conditioning, but that each leads to the conditioning of different responses. According to this hypothesis, the onset of the US is the important variable for CSs that precede the US. (It is possible, of course, that both US onset and US termination produce conditioning to a CS that precedes the US. The conditioning produced by US termination would presumably be much weaker than that produced by US onset.) Experiments such as those of Mowrer and Aiken (1954), in which stimuli paired with shock onset have effects different from those paired with shock termination, lend some credence to this view.

In summary, it would seem that it is the US rather than the UR with which the CS must be associated; and further, the present evidence suggests that US onset rather than US termination is crucial when the CS precedes the US.

2. The Relationship between CS and US

The second major disagreement with the hypothesis that classical conditioning is produced by pairing CS and US in temporal contiguity concerns the specification of the relationship between CS and US. This disagreement is more difficult to deal with than the preceding one. The main alternative to the usual hypothesis argues that classical conditioning depends on what is going on not only during the CS but also during the non-CS period.[10] Lashley (1942) and Lashley and Wade (1946), for example, have suggested that discrimination training is necessary in order to produce conditioning. An association will be formed between the CS and US only when the subject is able to compare two stimuli, one of which is paired with the US, and one of which is not. (Since the CS in classical conditioning is paired with the US, and the intertrial stimulus condition is not paired with the US, classical conditioning involves a discrimination training procedure. Therefore, little practical difference exists between Lashley's position and the original one.) More recently, Prokasy (1965) and Rescorla (1967) have presented analyses of the essential condition for Pavlovian conditioning in the same tradition as Lashley's. (The hypothesis developed by Egger and Miller (1962) to deal with secondary reinforcement can also be classified with these positions.) Prokasy described conditioning in terms of the dependencies between CS and US, and in doing so, focused attention on the probability of the US occurring during the intertrial period when the CS is absent. (This intertrial period will be called the $\overline{\text{CS}}$ period.) Rescorla argued further that the essential operation for producing classical conditioning is that the probability of the US in the presence of the CS (Pr(US/CS)) must be greater than the probability of the US in the absence of the CS

[10]The difference between "during the CS" and "during the non-CS" is perfectly clear when delayed conditioning procedures are employed in which the US is presented during the CS. In trace conditioning procedures, however, the US is presented after a brief CS has terminated. Therefore, the contrast is between events which occur just after the CS and those which do not. It is obvious, however, that as the time interval between the CS and US increases, there is no a priori method for determining when the US stops occurring after the CS and begins to take place in the non-CS period.

$(Pr(US/\overline{CS}))$. This can be considered a more general form of Lashley's position and will be called the dependency position. This position is contrasted with the contiguity view which states that the essential condition for classical conditioning is the pairing of CS and US in temporal contiguity (called the "pairings" position by Rescorla). The main difference between the two views is that the dependency position includes events that occur in the absence of the CS among the experimental operations that are considered necessary for producing classical conditioning.[11]

Rescorla has suggested the following experimental design for distinguishing between the contiguity and dependency positions. Suppose one compares two groups of subjects in which the $Pr(US/CS)$ is the same, but the $Pr(US/\overline{CS})$ is different. The response to the CS ought to be the same in both groups if the contiguity view is correct, but different if the dependency view is correct. Rescorla (1966) has provided evidence which supports the dependency position. Kremer (1968), on the other hand, has provided data which do not support it. He found that the magnitude of conditioned suppression did not depend on the relationship between $Pr(US/CS)$ and $Pr(US/\overline{CS})$ alone. However, too few experiments exist to permit a clear-cut choice between these alternative views at present.

There is no doubt that some modification in the simple contiguity notion will have to be made as further evidence accumulates. Kamin's (1967) research makes this point clear. In his experiments, rats were first trained to bar-press for food reinforcement, and were then subjected to a classical conditioning procedure while bar-pressing. They were classically conditioned to a simple CS (S_1). Further training was carried out to a compound CS consisting of two elements, S_1 and S_2. This training produced a suppression of bar-pressing in the presence of the compound. Later, S_1 and S_2 were presented alone, and the amount of suppression in the presence of each was measured. No conditioned suppression occurred to S_2. Control subjects without prior training to S_1 did suppress to both S_1 and S_2 when each was presented alone. Prior training to S_1 seemed to block the development of conditioning to S_2 when the compound was presented. Kamin (1967), after a long series of experiments designed to determine what factors were responsible for blocking, concluded that the "blocking experiment demonstrates very clearly that the

[11]We have not dealt with the problem of inhibition in this discussion in order to emphasize the contrast between contiguity and dependency views. The analysis of inhibition seems to bring the two views closer together. In the contiguity view, it has been suggested that inhibition of a CS will not develop until excitation to that CS or to a similar CS has been established. Terrace (1966), for example, has argued that some excitatory responding to the inhibitory stimulus must occur before it can become inhibitory. In this sense, inhibition depends not just on what is going on during the inhibitory CS, but rather on the contrast between the inhibitory stimulus and an excitatory stimulus.

mere contiguous presentation of a CS element and a US is not a sufficient condition for the establishment of a CR. The question, very simply, is: what has gone wrong in the blocking experiment? What is
deficient?'' (Kamin, 1967: p. 24). It is obvious that more research will be
required before the specification of the experimental operation for Pavlovian conditioning can be stated as precisely as one would like.

C.   Is Autonomic Behavior Controlled by the Classical Conditioning Procedure?

The general problem considered in this section is the determination of
the changes in behavior which are produced by the pairing of CS and
US when the effects of other variables are controlled. Of primary concern, of course, is determining whether changes in *autonomic* responses
can be attributed to the effects of pairing CS and US. In order to provide a clear answer to this question, control groups that are appropriate
for ruling out the effects of confounding variables must be employed.
Different control groups will be appropriate for ruling out different alternatives. These controls can be divided into two major classes. One
class is concerned with ruling out the possibility of nonassociative effects
of the CS, the US, or some extraneous variable. The second class is concerned with ruling out inadvertent operant conditioning effects.

1.   Control Procedures for Nonassociative Effects

Rescorla (1967) has provided a thorough analysis of the adequacies
and inadequacies of designs used to deal with the first type of control
problem. He classifies the control designs in this manner: CS-alone,
novel CS, US-alone, backward conditioning controls, explicitly unpaired
controls, discrimination controls, and random controls. The first three
designs control for the nonassociative effects of only one of the two
stimuli employed in classical conditioning. Therefore, they are inadequate because they leave the effects of the other stimulus uncontrolled.
The adequacy of the backward conditioning design depends on the particular theory of conditioning. It will obviously not be a satisfactory
control if it is assumed that excitatory conditioned connections are established to the backward CS. (If it is believed that inhibitory connections are established to a backward CS, the comments made about the
subsequent designs will also apply to the backward design.)
The three final control procedures require more discussion. In the discrimination control design, responding to a CS paired with the US (the
CS+) and a CS not paired with a US (the CS−), is compared for each

subject. The only difference between CS+ and CS− is the pairing of the CS+ with the US. The effects of extraneous variables are presumed to be the same for each stimulus. Therefore, it is argued that any difference in responding between CS+ and CS− must be attributed to the effect of the pairing of CS+ and US. In the explicitly unpaired control procedure, the experimental group ($Pr(US/CS) > 0$; $Pr(US/\overline{CS}) = 0$) is compared to a group in which CS and US are presented but never paired with each other ($Pr(US/CS) = 0$ and $Pr(US/\overline{CS}) > 0$). The justification for this procedure is much the same as for the discriminative control procedure. Any difference between experimental and control groups is attributed to the pairing of CS and US, because the two groups are considered to be identical in every other respect.

Rescorla has criticized these two procedures because they do not permit an exact assessment of excitatory and inhibitory effects of the CS. In both designs, the CS paired with the US is compared with a CS *not* paired with the US. Therefore, according to Rescorla, differences in the response rate of the two CSs could be attributed to the establishment of inhibition to the control CS, just as easily as to the establishment of excitation to the experimental CS. Rescorla argues further that the random control (in which $Pr(US/CS) = Pr(US/\overline{CS})$ and the probability of USs within each stimulus period is constant) does not suffer from these difficulties; it should provide a more adequate baseline for assessing the effects of the coupling of CS and US, because it gives a true zero point with respect to excitatory and inhibitory effects. In addition, he states that the random control has a further advantage over the other control designs in that it "holds constant between the experimental and control procedures all of the factors extraneous to the CS–US contingency without demanding that we be able to specify in advance what factors might be operating (p. 74, Rescorla, 1967)."

These two apparent advantages of the random control design can be questioned. First, it is not clear how the random control design is *a priori* better than the other two designs in dealing with factors "extraneous to the CS–US contingency." In fact, it seems easier to control for nondependency factors such as total number of shocks in the explicitly unpaired design than in the random design, because the former makes fewer restrictions on the number of stimulus presentations. For example, in the random design, the number of shocks during the $\overline{CS}$ is determined by the probability of shock during the CS. No such restriction is made for the explicitly unpaired design. Actually, the main advantage of the random design, if one understands Rescorla's argument correctly, is that it controls for CS–US dependency factors which the discrimination and explicitly unpaired designs do not.

Second, the justification for the view that the random control provides a zero baseline may also be questioned. Prokasy (1965) pointed out when he was writing in 1963, that nothing was known about the random control procedure. Since that time, only limited data on this procedure have become available. Given the present state of knowledge, the justification for the belief that the random control group will establish a true zero point is not provided by data but by Rescorla's theory about the nature of conditioning. Rescorla argues that two classes of states (or properties of the CS or responses to the CS) can be classically conditioned: excitatory and inhibitory. These states are determined by the relationship between $Pr(US/CS)$ and $Pr(US/\overline{CS})$. Assume that the probability of the US is constant over the duration of each stimulus presentation. If $Pr(US/CS) > Pr(US/\overline{CS})$, the CS will become excitatory and the $\overline{CS}$ inhibitory. If $Pr(US/CS) < Pr(US/\overline{CS})$, the CS will become inhibitory and the $\overline{CS}$ excitatory. Finally, if $Pr(US/CS) = Pr(US/\overline{CS})$, the CS will have a zero effect. The subject will learn that the CS is irrelevant. Therefore, the random control will provide the required zero baseline.

If it were true that the conditional probabilities ($Pr(US/CS)$ and $Pr(US/\overline{CS})$) were the only associative variables controlling the excitatory and inhibitory properties of the CS, this argument would be convincing. However, other associative variables influence the excitatory and inhibitory properties of the CS. Consider the temporal contiguity between the CS and US. Suppose one were to condition three groups of subjects in which the parameters were identical to those in the three groups described above, except for one difference: the duration of the CS period is made extremely long. This would result in a longer average CS–US interval. One might expect less conditioning to the CS than to the $\overline{CS}$, because the average CS–US interval would be long and the average $\overline{CS}$ interval short. The temporal contiguity of CS and US would interact with the conditional probabilities of the US to determine the excitatory and inhibitory effects conditioned to the CS. If one admits that excitatory and inhibitory states are controlled by such associative variables in addition to the conditional probabilities of the US, it is obvious that one cannot insure a true zero point by making $Pr(US/CS) = Pr(US/\overline{CS})$.[12] Also, excitation and inhibition will not be necessarily symmetrical, as seems to be required by Rescorla's position.

Rescorla's arguments, therefore, for the superiority of random control design over the other designs are not convincing. The random control is

---

[12]This problem is exaggerated if the effects of these other variables change during the course of conditioning. If this happens, the random control group could change its character as a function of number of trials. If more conditioning occurs to the CS than to the $\overline{CS}$ at first, the CS would become excitatory before becoming irrelevant.

useful, however, for the specific purpose of examining the effects of dependencies between CS and US. This question is important by itself, so that, although the random procedure may not provide an all-purpose control, it does have important functions.

Since one cannot determine the procedure that will produce a true zero baseline *a priori,* one is naturally led to ask if some acceptable empirical criterion for a zero baseline can be established. One obvious possibility is to compare an explicitly unpaired control group with a control group receiving only CS presentations. If no difference exists between the response to the CS in these two groups, while both differ from an experimental group in which CS and US are associated, one might be willing to accept the view that the CS in the explicitly unpaired group was at the zero baseline. (It must be insured that it is possible for the level of response in the explicitly unpaired group to diminish below the level of the CS alone group; otherwise, the similarity of the two groups would be spurious.) Schneiderman, Smith, Smith, and Gormezano (1966) and Cohen and Durkovic (1966) presented data on heart conditioning in which the appropriate control procedures were carried out. No difference was found between CS-only and explicitly unpaired control groups.

In summary, the discrimination and explicitly unpaired control procedures are useful in determining whether the pairing of CS and US has an effect. (In this context, pairing of CS and US refers to the establishment of either excitatory or inhibitory states.) The random controls can be used to determine whether the dependency between CS and US has an effect. If the contiguity view is correct, obviously the random control will not be useful for other purposes. None of the procedures alone provides an *a priori* true zero baseline from which excitatory and inhibitory effects can be measured.

2. Control Procedures for Inadvertent Operant Reinforcement

While control procedures which rule out nonassociative effects of CS and US are relatively satisfactory, the control procedures designed to rule out operant effects during classical conditioning are far less adequate. Since relatively little work has been done on this problem, the following discussion will be more speculative and tentative than one would like.

a. The bidirectional design. In the section on operant autonomic conditioning, the bidirectional control was suggested as the most appropriate for holding classical conditioning constant during operant conditioning. Can this bidirectional control design be adapted to hold operant effects constant during classical conditioning? In order to do this, a situation must be arranged in which a difference between two groups in the effective classical conditioning procedure (the pairing of the CS and US) can produce a difference between the groups in behavior, while the effective operant conditioning procedure (the pairing of the response and reinforcement) is held constant in the two groups. The first requirement, then, is to find some variation in the parameters of the classical conditioning procedure which will produce differences between the two groups. The obvious possibility is to vary the US. Food and positive brain stimulation, for example, produce different conditioned responses in the rat; the former produces an increase in heart rate, the latter a decrease in heart rate. The second requirement is to keep the effective operant conditioning procedure constant in the two groups. In order to do this, it must be ascertained that the difference in the effective classical conditioning procedure is not one which will also act as a difference in the effective operant conditioning procedure. Therefore, if two USs are employed, we must be sure that they will have the same power to reinforce operant responses. Also, we must maintain the same dependency between the response and the US in the two groups. This latter requirement seems to be impossible. In any operant reinforcement experiment, the presentation of reinforcement is dependent on the occurrence of the response. Response probability in the two groups must be the same if the operant reinforcement dependency is to be the same. The two groups will differ, however, with respect to the probability of the response if the classical conditioning procedure produces differences in behavior. Therefore, the operant reinforcement dependencies cannot be maintained the same in the two groups unless the pairing of CS and US is having no differential effect.

   b.   Comparison designs. In the bidirectional design, the attempt was made to determine whether a behavior change could be attributed to the pairing of CS and US by varying the effective component of the classical conditioning procedure, and at the same time trying to keep the effective component of the operant reinforcement procedure constant. Another approach to the isolation of classical conditioning effects is based on the direct contrast between the effects of operant and classical conditioning.[13] This approach is a weaker version of the bidirectional design. Instead of controlling operant reinforcement, we will attempt to demonstrate that the pairing of CS and US has an effect above and beyond that produced by pairing response and reinforcer.

[13]This same comparison procedure could be employed to study operant conditioning independent of classical conditioning. It was not considered in Section III. B because it was not necessary.

This approach can best be illustrated by some examples. Suppose that an aversive US is made dependent on a particular response in the presence of a given CS. According to our expectations concerning the action of operant punishment, this procedure should result in a decrease in the rate of any response on which the aversive US is made dependent. Therefore, if control is exerted by the operant procedure, the response should decrease in probability. If, however, the response does not decrease in probability, and further, if this unexpected result is related to the pairing of CS and US, it seems reasonable to conclude that there is some effect of pairing CS and US that cannot be attributed to operant reinforcement.

A similar approach can be employed with a US that is a positive operant reinforcer. If we make a positive reinforcer dependent on refraining from making a response, the probability of that response ought to decrease according to our expectations concerning the action of operant reinforcement. If, however, the probability of the response does not decrease to a low stable level, but changes as a function of the pairing of CS and US, again it seems reasonable to conclude that there is some effect of pairing CS and US that cannot be attributed to operant reinforcement.

Comparison designs differ from standard classical conditioning procedures only by the explicit use of operant reinforcement. Two requirements must be met in carrying out these comparison designs. First it must be demonstrated that the outcome of the experiment is different from that which would be produced by pairing a particular response and reinforcer. Second, it must be shown that this difference can be attributed to the pairing of CS and US, and not to some extraneous variable or to additional sources of operant reinforcement. The first of these requirements is usually satisfied by an appeal to our previous knowledge of operant conditioning. The second, however, is more difficult than might be anticipated. Relevant information concerning the effects of the inadvertent operant reinforcement is often difficult to obtain and to apply. For example, consider the belief that the aversive stimuli decrease the probability of operant responses which they follow. This is not always the case. They also produce an increase in responding, and these increases in responding to shock seem to be under the control of operant dependencies, at least in some cases (Kelleher & Morse, 1964). Even when shock is inescapable, responses may be operantly conditioned to decrease the intensity of the shock, its duration, or the disturbing effects of the UR which it elicits (Wagner, Thomas, & Norton, 1967). Therefore, an increase in the rate of a response which precedes an aversive reinforcer does not necessarily imply that the pairing of response and reinforcer was not controlling behavior. Some subtle operant dependencies may have been in effect. A similar problem arises in dealing with the procedure in which subjects are trained to refrain from responding. In this procedure, we assume that a failure to operantly condition a subject to refrain from responding indicates that operant reinforcement is not having its usual effect. The further assumption, that this failure to observe an effect of operant reinforcement can be attributed to the pairing of CS and US, may be incorrect. For example, the previous history of the subject may have involved a great deal of operant reinforcement for making the response and little for refraining from the response. Transfer from this previous history might have led to the difficulty in attempting to train refraining from the response.

The previous two examples make it clear that one must have a precise knowledge of the effects of the operant conditioning procedure and of the previous history of the subject with reference to that procedure in order to know that an operant reinforcer is not having its usual effect and that additional sources of operant reinforcement are not controlling the response.

We may be tempted to try to avoid these difficulties by appealing to previous knowledge of classical conditioning. This approach, however, begs the question. We cannot appeal to previous knowledge of classical conditioning, unless some other control procedure has already permitted us to obtain this knowledge by isolating some of the effects of the pairing of CS and US.

It is obvious from this discussion that a wide variety of comparison designs can be suggested, depending mainly on our ingenuity in finding contrasts between operant and classical conditioning. If the present discussion is correct, however, the success of these designs will depend more on our interpretations of a particular set of results than on the compelling logic of the experimental procedure.

  c. *Transfer designs.*The analysis of the bidirectional design implied that the effects of classical conditioning are best studied in situations that explicitly employ operant conditioning procedures. Otherwise, the effects of operant reinforcement could not be controlled. The same point is reflected clearly in the transfer design which has become popular recently and which is closely related to the bidirectional design (Rescorla & Solomon, 1967; Trapold, 1966). In this design, the attempt is made to separate classical and operant conditioning procedures, and to assess the effects of the classical operation by studying its influence on ongoing operant responding. Two groups of subjects are operantly conditioned to perform a response in the presence of a given CS (CS_1) in stage 1. In stage 2, the two groups are removed to a different situation, and are classically conditioned to a CS (CS_2) which is different from the CS_1. There is usually a difference between the two groups in some parameter of the classical conditioning procedure. Finally, in stage 3, the two groups of subjects are returned to the original situation. The CS_2 is presented while the subject makes the operant response in the presence of CS_1. The effects of classical conditioning are measured by determining the effect of CS_2 on the operant response.

It could be argued, in an attempt to justify this design, that the crucial operant response has been made the same in both groups in stage 1. Therefore, any difference in the effect of the CS on the operant response in stage 3 must be attributed to differences in the classical conditioning procedure carried out in stage 2. This analysis is not quite correct. As pointed out earlier, both classical and operant dependencies can occur in any conditioning situation. Therefore, operant components could have been the effective ones in stage 2. If the effects of operant conditioning were different in the two groups in stage 2, the difference in behavior observed in stage 3 would have been produced by the operant rather than the classical dependencies. Therefore, this design is open to criticism. One could maintain that operant conditioning does not occur in stage 2, because the subject is usually removed to a new environment where the operant response cannot be made. Even in such cases, relevant operant conditioning is still possible. Responses different from the original operant response but similar enough to show transfer can be inadvertently shaped. Such operant shaping might even occur in curarized subjects. Black (1958), for example, found that presentations of a CS-alone under curare decreased the rate of avoidance responding to that CS in the normal state. The obvious explanation of this result is that classically conditioned fear was extinguished during the presentations of the CS under curare. Another possibility is that the dogs were operantly reinforced for refraining from movement by CS termination. This latter explanation is supported by a recent experiment (Black, 1967), in which operant conditioning of "refraining from movement" in curarized dogs transferred to affect overt behavior in the normal state. DiCara and Weiss (1968) provide further evidence supporting the possibility of transfer of operant conditioning from the curarized state to the normal state. Rats were first operantly conditioned to increase or decrease heart rate under curare. Subsequent tests in the normal state indicated that rats trained to increase heart rate made fewer skeletal avoidance responses than rats trained to decrease heart rate.

The possibility of inadvertent operant reinforcement in stage 2 is much greater for autonomic than for skeletal responses, since we cannot prevent the occurrence of the autonomic responses by removing the subject to a new environment, as we can with many skeletal responses. This feature of skeletal responses will be less important, however, if the transfer from operant reinforcement of autonomic responses to skeletal responses (DiCara and Weiss, 1968) is general.

These criticisms of the transfer design depend on the interpretation of a particular result in terms of inadvertent operant reinforcement during stage 2. Certain results, which do not easily lend themselves to such an interpretation, are discussed in detail in Section IV,C,1. Whatever degree of success the transfer design has, it is not particularly useful for studying directly classically conditioned autonomic responses, since the measure of conditioning in the transfer design is a change in some operantly conditioned response.

It is obvious from this discussion that the procedures for determining the effect of pairing the CS and US when the effects of operant dependencies are controlled do not seem to be well formulated. The only design which seems to hold some promise for the study of directly conditioned autonomic responses is the comparison design, and this is difficult to employ.

3. Research Data on Nonassociative Effects

When we are dealing with several different autonomic responses, the amount of concern varies as to whether changes in autonomic responding can be attributed to the effect of pairing CS and US independent of the nonassociative effects of stimulus presentations. In recent research on salivary classical conditioning in which an aversive US was employed (Colavita, 1965; Fitzgerald, 1963, Ost and Lauer, 1965; and Warstler and Ost, 1965), there were no controls for nonassociative effects of the CS. (The considerable body of research on differential salivary conditioning, beginning with Pavlov (1927) and continuing to the present (Ellison, 1964; Ellison and Kònorski, 1966), makes it clear, however, that nonassociative effects alone cannot account for the development of the salivary conditioned response.) In heart rate conditioning, on the other hand, many current experiments using aversive reinforcers employ controls for nonassociative effects. Fitzgerald (1963), Fitzgerald, Vardaris, and Brown (1966), Fitzgerald, Vardaris, and Teyler (1966), and Fitzgerald and Walloch (1966) employed backward controls. (In these experiments, the CS followed the US by a considerable period of time. This long period between the US and the subsequent CS brings this procedure close to that of the explicitly unpaired control procedure.) Cohen and Durkovic (1966), Holdstock and Schwarzbaum (1965), Schneiderman et al. (1966) and Yehle, Dauth, and Schneiderman (1967) employed explicitly unpaired controls. Black (1965), de Toledo and Black (1966), Dykman, Mack, and Ackerman (1965), Parrish (1967), and Smith and Stebbins (1965) employed a discrimination procedure. In every case, the performance to the CS associated with the US was superior to that of the control CS or the CS−

The experiments of Schneiderman *et al.* (1966) and of Cohen and Durkovic (1966) may be singled out for special mention. In both of these, CS-alone control groups were trained, in addition to the explicitly unpaired controls. In both cases, the effect of the explicitly unpaired CS was no different from that of the CS-alone. This suggests that no development of inhibitory property to the explicitly unpaired CS occurred.

Although little work has been done on other responses, it also shows effects that cannot be attributed to simple presentations of stimuli. Examples are electrodermal responses (Holdstock & Schwarzbaum, 1965; Roberts & Young, 1968) and blood pressure (Dykman, *et al.*, 1965). In general, these are clear-cut examples of the classical conditioning of a number of autonomic responses which cannot be attributed to the non-associative effects of stimulus presentations.

4. *Research Data on Operant Effects*

The analysis of data on the effects of pairing CS and US when the effects of operant reinforcement are controlled is difficult. First, transfer designs are not relevant to the present discussion. They measure the effects of the CS on the changes in the baseline of some on-going operantly conditioned response, while we are interested in the changes which develop in the presence of the CS without explicit previous operant conditioning. Second, the results of comparison designs are hard to interpret. Consider, for example, research in which an aversive US is employed to punish an autonomic response. As pointed out in the previous section, decreases in the probability of autonomic responses have been produced by making an aversive US dependent on the response. Banuazizi (1968), for example, produced a decrease in the rate of gastrointestinal contractions by making shock dependent on those contractions, and vice versa. At the same time, a classical conditioning procedure increases the probability of autonomic response such as heart rate, salivation and gastrointestinal activity, even though they are followed by the aversive stimulus. Why does an increase rather than a decrease occur in the latter case? We must first ask whether the increase is produced by inadvertent positive operant reinforcement which overrides the effect of punishment. Is the situation similar to leg flexion, for exam-

ple, where the classically conditioned flexion response seems to be operantly reinforced by a reduction in the amount of postural imbalance
produced by shock? (See Section IV,D.) This question cannot be answered with respect to autonomic responses without more data. Suppose
for the moment that there is no positive operant reinforcement counter-
acting the punishing effects of shock. We still cannot conclude that the
increase in the autonomic response is influenced by the pairing of CS
and US. Suppose, for example, that the effect of the US onset was to
punish certain skeletal responses during the CS–US interval. In this case,
as Gibson (1952) has shown, very variable skeletal behavior would occur. The subject would make one skeletal response for a while, then shift
to another, and so on. These shifts would be interspersed with periods of
inactivity. Since heart rate changes can be produced by any skeletal response, the heart rate increase may be a by-product of shifting skeletal
behavior that is controlled by operant punishment. In this case, the
heart rate response to the CS would not be under the direct control of
the classical procedure.

A similar analysis can be made of those experiments that demonstrate
the inability to condition operantly a subject to make a response or to
refrain from making a response. Breland and Breland (1961) reported a
number of examples of the former type. In general, they found that if a
CS resembles a goal object it was difficult to maintain certain operantly
conditioned responses which were incompatible with the response that
occurred to the goal object in the normal sequence of consummatory
behavior. For example, pigs tend to root out food. While they can be
trained to retrieve a token (presumably resembling a small piece of food)
and drop it into a container, it is difficult to maintain this response.
The incompatible rooting response seems to intervene. An example of
the second type is the failure to condition operantly refraining from licking reported by Patten and Rudy (1967). In this case, operant reinforcement did not seem to have its usual effect. Before we can attribute these
failures of operant conditioning to the classical conditioning of interfering responses, however, we must again provide evidence that failure is
produced by the pairing of CS and US. In the example provided by Breland and Breland it seems reasonable to believe that classical conditioning produced the interfering response. Yet a question arises as to
whether this is simple classical conditioning. The effect seems to depend
on the properties of the CS. If some CS which did not resemble the goal
object had been employed, it seems likely that the interfering response
would not have occurred. In the Patten and Rudy experiment the rats
continued to lick even though licking was never reinforced. One explanation of this persistance is that the subject had been operantly reinforced

for making the response, and transfer from this previous history of operant reinforcement interfered with the operant conditioning of refraining from responding. Furthermore, even if this possibility is ruled out, the persistance of the response is still difficult to attribute to the effects of pairing CS and US. If the occurrence of the persisting response prevents the animal from being operantly reinforced, it also prevents the CS and US from being paired frequently. If the persistance of the response is greater than that which would be expected on the basis of a few intermittent pairings of CS and US, simple classical conditioning will not provide an explanation of the results either.

While the previous two examples involve certain difficulties of interpretation, the second seems more convincing than the first with respect to the demonstration of classical conditioning effects. Certain examples such as the classical conditioning of nausea (which is discussed in the next section) also seem to fall into this category. Unfortunately, experimental analyses designed to rule out the effects of inadvertent operant reinforcement, and to provide evidence that the pairing of the CS and US is controlling the response, are not sufficient at present. The point of this discussion is, therefore, *not* that the pairing of the CS and US has no effect when other relationships and variables are controlled. Rather, such effects have not been demonstrated adequately. It is not clear whether this lack of evidence should be attributed to the inadequacies of the experimental procedures, the lack of relevant experiments, or to the actual failure of the pairing of CS and US to influence responses to the CS in the way that we expect.

The foregoing analysis of the control of operant reinforcement depends on the interpretation of the results of particular experiments which differ in both subject matter and design. One is always uneasy that the difficulties in interpretation raised are niggling and, perhaps, implausible, and further, that some particularly convincing demonstration has been missed. Some comfort is provided by disagreements which exist over the changes in behavior produced by the pairing of CS and US. If the data were more clear-cut, it seems unlikely that such disparate views could be put forward about both the change in behavior produced by classical conditioning, and the problems of response selection and classification which will be discussed in the next two sections.

D. Response Selection

In this section, two hypotheses will be considered. The first is the stimulus substitution hypothesis, which in its simplest form, states that a

CS will acquire the power to elicit responses originally elicited by a US. According to the stimulus substitution view, therefore, response selection is achieved by choosing a US which elicits the appropriate responses. If one accepts the position that stimulus substitution applies only to built-in or innate unconditioned responses, one can choose the CR simply from a knowledge of the URs which a particular US elicits. If, on the other hand, one accepts the view that stimulus substitution applies to operantly conditioned responses to the US (Logan & Wagner, 1965), the analysis of response selection is more complicated. (An example of an operantly conditioned response to a US is the escape response to shock that has been operantly reinforced by shock termination (Solomon & Brush, 1956).) In this case, one cannot predict the CR from the general knowledge of the URs elicited by a given US. One must also have information about a given subject's previous history with a US in order to know the operantly conditioned responses that it elicits.

The second hypothesis is that the US determines the CR. Each US has associated with it a set of CRs that will be conditioned, and these may or may not resemble the UR.

The adequacy of the stimulus substitution hypothesis will be determined by the similarity of the responses to the CS and the responses to the US. The data do not support the hypothesis. In rats, the unconditioned heart rate response to shock, for example, is an increase in rate; the conditioned response, however, is sometimes an increase in rate and sometimes a decrease in rate. For example, in research on the rat, conditioned increases in heart rate have been reported by Black and Black (1967), and Fehr and Stern (1965); conditioned decreases have been reported by de Toledo and Black (1966), Fitzgerald *et al.* (1966), Holdstock and Schwartzbaum (1965) and Parrish (1967); and both increases and decreases have been reported by Block-Rojas, Toro, and Pinto-Hamuy (1964), and McDonald, Stern, and Hahn (1963). Similar differences in direction of the CR have been reported in the dog (Black, 1965). This comparison between conditioned responses and the URs suggests that the CR is not a copy of the UR. Before accepting this conclusion, however, one must consider the possibility that the form of a response may change with the intensity of the eliciting stimuli. The response to a very weak US may be a decrease in heart rate, and the response to a very intense US may be an increase in heart rate. This does not seem to be the case. Lang and Black (1963), and Church, Lolordo, Overmier, Solomon and Turner (1966) found that the UR to the shock was an increase in heart rate for both low and high intensity shocks. Therefore, the argument can be rejected.

If the US determines which responses will be selected, the CR for a given US ought to be the same (de Toledo, 1968). The data on heart rate conditioning do not support this hypothesis. The same US can lead either to accelerations or decelerations of heart rate. As a result, it is clear that the US *alone* does not account for the selection of a particular conditioning response. Other variables must be taken into consideration. Therefore, while this hypothesis might eventually lead to the development of some rule for response selection, at present it is still inadequate.

Another possible explanation of these data, which is consistent with the stimulus substitution hypothesis, is that the heart rate increase that is identical to the UR is classically conditioned, and that the heart rate decrease is produced by the contaminating effects of operant reinforcement. This possiblility arises because it is difficult to control for operant effects in research on the effects of pairing CS and US. The position taken with respect to this hypothesis will depend on whether the view is accepted that the relationship between the effective component of the classical conditioning procedure and the behavior changes which it produces provide the starting point for an analysis of classical conditioning, or whether additional assumptions about the type of response amenable to classical conditioning could be made. If we take the former position, we would have to admit that we are not sure whether the difference between CR and UR was produced by operant reinforcement. There will be ambiguity, therefore, as to whether the stimulus substitution hypothesis is correct. If we take the latter position, this ambiguity can, of course, be avoided. It can simply be assumed that only URs can be classically conditioned, and can be concluded that any other behavioral change *must* have been produced by inadvertent operant reinforcement. We would then label increases in heart rate as classically conditioned, and attribute decreases to operant reinforcement. While the latter position has the advantage of avoiding ambiguity, it has the unfortunate disadvantage of probably being wrong. It does not seem likely that those responses to the CS that do not resemble the UR are all produced by inadvertent operant conditioning, while those responses that resemble the UR are produced by classical conditioning. For example, the data presented in Section III,B indicate that operant conditioning of both accelerations and decelerations in heart rate occurred. It is not clear why operant conditioning should lead to decelerative responses only, especially when these are the most difficult to condition by operant procedures.

These results suggest that stimulus substitution alone will not account for response selection in classical conditioning. A disconcerting question then arises as to whether the hypothesis of stimulus substitution should be rejected altogether.

Suppose we were to take an extreme position and entertain the hypothesis that stimulus substitution did not occur at all. Is there evidence which would convince us that we were wrong? The simple demonstration of similarity between CR and UR is not enough. A coincidence between the two responses could have occurred by chance, particularly if the alternative values which each response could assume were few. For example, the changes in heart rate that can occur are limited. The heart rate can increase, decrease, or show some combination of these two patterns. Since only a limited number of changes can occur in the direction of the heart rate response to the CS and the US, it is possible that coincidences in the form of a response between the two could occur by chance. Therefore, we have to demonstrate not only that the CR and UR are similar, but also that the probability of their being the same by chance is very low.

The simplest strategy for achieving this goal is to compare several USs, each of which elicits a clearly different pattern of the response. If the CRs match the URs in each case, we would be much more likely to accept some notion of stimulus substitution. We have already pointed out that the heart rate CR does not seem to follow the heart rate UR. There are other examples, however, involving the cardiovascular system which seem to demonstrate a matching between CR and UR that is at first glance unlikely. For example, different drugs clearly have different effects on the electrocardiogram, according to Bykov (1959). He has presented data which seem to indicate that the CR to each of these drugs matches the UR very precisely. Unfortunately, the evidence is anecdotal, and it is difficult to determine how close the match between CR and UR really is. Much of the work on autonomic responses suffers from this defect. Furthermore, because of the limitations in the number of different patterns of autonomic responses that normally occurs, it is difficult to find USs which will elicit markedly different patterns of response in the autonomic nervous system. Jenkins (1968) has carried out experiments on pecking in the pigeon which are much more convincing than most of the research on autonomic responding. He paired a neutral stimulus (the lighting-up of a key) with food reinforcement in some animals, and water reinforcement in others. The CR to the key established with a food US was very different from the CR to the key with a water US. The food CR resembled the pecking response in picking up grain, while the water CR resembled the sucking movements typical of drinking.

Another, perhaps simpler strategy is to consider USs which elicit rare patterns of behavior. Accidental similarity between CR and UR would be very unlikely in such cases. Unfortunately, most of the simple autonomic responses usually studied would not fall into this category. Examples are provided, however, by complex reflexes such as nausea and instinctive patterns of responding. For example, Thompson and Sturm (1965) reported on the classical conditioning of aggressive displays in Siamese fighting fish. A mirror reflection of the S elicited a complex aggressive display involving four very distinct components: fin erection, undulating movements, gill cover erection, and frontal approach. Each of these components was conditioned to the CS, and each was conditioned at a different rate. Components of the courtship display of the Japanese quail are also classically conditioned at different rates (Farris, 1967). In the latter experiment, the components which were most likely to occur on any given unconditioned courtship display and which occurred first during ontogentic development were the first to condition.

The evidence presented in the previous two paragraphs does suggest, then, that stimulus substitution occurs. The question still remains, however, as to whether this stimulus substitution is a basic process itself or simply an example of some other more fundamental process. For example, just as operant reinforcement could be used as a *deus ex machina* to account for differences between CR and UR, so can it be used to account for similarities. Two requirements must be met to demonstrate that inadvertent operant reinforcement will account for the similarities between CR and UR. First, one must show that operant reinforcement was controlling the response to the CS. Second, one must determine why the inadvertently operantly conditioned CR was one that resembled the response elicited by the US rather than some other response. Leg flection conditioning provides an example which seems to meet these requirements. Wagner *et al.* (1967) and Thomas (1967) have presented convincing evidence that operant reinforcement leads to the occurrence of flection responses to the CS. The flection response permits the dog to make postural adjustments which prevent it from being thrown off balance by the US. If the dog is allowed to stand in a position in which the US does not produce imbalance, flection conditioning does not occur. These results suggest that the similarity between the flection CR and the flection UR is produced by operant rather than classical conditioning. In this example it is clear how operant reinforcement could produce a conditioned response that resembled the UR. It is not clear from the available data, however, how such an analysis can account for the results of Thompson and Sturm (1965), Farris (1967), or Jenkins (1968).

In summary, stimulus substitution is not sufficient to account for the selection of classically conditioned responses. One does not have to agree with this conclusion if he accepts the position that all CRs which do not resemble the UR are inadvertently operantly reinforced. The latter possibility, however, does not seem to be a likely one. At this point we are naturally led to ask whether stimulus substitution takes place at all. It is very unlikely that the similarity between CR and UR observed in some experiments could have occurred by chance, and this suggests that stimulus substitution does occur. Again, we may ask whether stimulus substitution ought to be treated as a separate phenomenon or as a form of some more fundamental process such as operant reinforcement. In some cases, such as leg flection, the possibility that operant reinforcement was involved seems to be reasonable. In other cases, it is less so. The issue, however, is still far from being resolved.

In conclusion, the data do not provide compelling evidence for any of the hypotheses concerning response selection in classical conditioning except, of course, for those hypotheses which state that one cannot give a general rule for selecting classically conditioned responses.

E.   Response Classification in Classical Conditioning

In this section, we will deal with attempts to find features shared by responses that can be classically conditioned in contrast to those that cannot. Such a classification provides information that is useful in attempting to account for response selection, because it limits the range of alternative responses that must be considered. Even though one will not be able to describe how the response is selected, one will still be able to rule out certain responses from consideration because they belong to the class of responses that cannot be classically conditioned.

We will first discuss the hypothesis that only autonomic responses can be classically conditioned,[14] and we will then consider two other distinctions—one between emitted and elicited responses and the other between voluntary and involuntary responses. The latter are closely related to a classification based on the stimulus substitution hypothesis (*i.e.*, that only URs can be classically conditioned).

Two preliminary points must be mentioned. First, the evaluation of a classification scheme requires the comparison of different responses during classical conditioning, *i.e.*, of autonomic and skeletal responses, of emitted and elicited responses, and so on. The most efficient method for making such comparisons is to measure different responses during the same classical conditioning experiment. We are limited to the same experiment; otherwise, we could not be sure whether a difference between

[14]An opposite hypothesis has been proposed by Smith (1954, 1964, 1967). He has suggested that only skeletal responses are conditioned, and that autonomic responses are artifacts of the occurrence of the skeletal responses. This hypothesis is discussed on page 73.

responses occurred because of some trivial differences in the parameters of two different conditioning experiments or because of some features of the response itself. Therefore, the present discussion will be limited to experiments in which the responses to be compared were measured in the same conditioning situation.

Second, most classifications refer to both operant and classical conditioning. They state that responses with property A can be classically conditioned and responses that do not have property A can be operantly conditioned. In the present discussion we will be concerned with classical conditioning only. It is worth repeating in passing, however, that the usual classifications do not apply to operant conditioning. The data of the previous section demonstrated that both autonomic and skeletal responses, and both emitted and elicited responses (see footnote 8) are controlled by the effective component of the operant conditioning procedure.

1.   The Autonomic–Skeletal Distinction

Several experiments provide data relevant to the hypothesis that only autonomic responses can be classically conditioned. (In all of the experiments to be referred to, there were control procedures for the nonassociative effects of stimulus presentations.) Dykman et al. (1965) measured heart rate, blood pressure, general activity, and flection responses concurrently in dogs, and found that all responses were conditioned. Similarly, Jaworska, Kowalska, and Soltysik (1962) classically conditioned heart rate and flection discriminations in dogs. The conditioning of heart rate and respiration has been demonstrated in fish (Otis, Cerf, and Thomas, 1957), pigeons (Cohen and Durkovic, 1966), and dogs (Fitzgerald and Walloch, 1966). Heart rate and the response of the nictitating membrane in rabbits (the latter, according to Gormezano (1965), is a skeletal response in rabbits) were conditioned during the same procedure by Meredith and Schneiderman (1967), and by Vandercar and Schneiderman (1967). De Toledo and Black (1966) and Parrish (1967) demonstrated the discriminative classical conditioning of heart rate and suppression of bar pressing, and Young (1968) demonstrated the classical conditioning of electrodermal responses and suppression of bar pressing. Finally, Holdstock and Schwartzbaum (1965) classically conditioned heart rate, GSR, and suppression of EMG in rats.

In all of these experiments both skeletal and autonomic responses were changed during the same classical conditioning procedure. There were, of course, differences between autonomic responses and skeletal responses in speed of conditioning, pattern of change during the CS, etc.

These will be discussed in the next section. The only point that needs to be made here is that when several autonomic responses are compared, differences among them are found; similarly, when several skeletal responses are compared differences among them occur. The differences between autonomic responses treated as one class and skeletal responses as another class seem to be no greater than those within each class. The responses do not seem to be categorized according to autonomic–skeletal distinction.

How can we maintain the hypothesis that skeletal responses are not affected by the classical conditioning procedure in the face of these data?[15] The lack of controls for inadvertent operant reinforcement provides one answer. We could argue that the CR was autonomic, and that the changes in the skeletal response during classical conditioning were produced by inadvertent operant reinforcement. This latter alternative is not particularly convincing, given the close relationship between certain autonomic responses and skeletal behavior, and the sensitivity of both to operant procedures.

2.   The Emitted–Elicited and the Voluntary–Involuntary Distinction

The data did not fall neatly into place for the autonomic–skeletal distinction, nor do they seem to do so for the emitted–elicited or voluntary–involuntary distinctions. The research described in the section on stimulus substitution does not support the hypothesis that only involuntary responses to a US or responses elicited by that US are classically conditioned. One could suggest in reply to this point that the response need not be elicited by the particular US employed in a given conditioning situation; the response could be elicited by some other stimulus. Since operant responding is presumably not elicited, this suggestion does not account for the ability of the classical CS to modulate ongoing operant behavior unless, of course, one assumed that such modulating effects were produced by interfering or facilitating conditioned involuntary responses. As the discussion in Section IV indicates, there do seem to be some exceptions to the position that all of the effects of a CS can be

[15]Given these data, one wonders how the hypothesis that only autonomic responses could be classically conditioned was ever seriously considered. The main experimental basis for the hypothesis seems to be research begun in the 1930's on the comparison between avoidance and classical conditioning procedures (Brogden, Lipman, & Culler, 1938; Gibson, 1952; Hunter, 1935; Scholsberg, 1934, 1936; Sheffield, 1948). Many of these experiments showed not only that the avoidance procedure was superior to the classical procedure, but also that stable classical conditioning of skeletal responses failed to occur. Why there is a failure of classical conditioning of skeletal responses in some situations and not in others is an important problem and must be dealt with. A similar problem arose in dealing with the effects of an aversive operant reinforcer on heart rate.

explained in terms of the interfering or facilitating effects of elicited responses.

Distinctions between emitted and elicited responses or voluntary and involuntary responses suffer from an additional difficulty, not shared by the autonomic-skeletal distinction. Not only do the data fail to support the classification, but also the criteria for making the classification are often ambiguous. When a response is made in the presence of a stimulus, it is difficult to decide whether an elicited response or an emitted response has come under stimulus control. An analysis of the previous conditioning history of the subject could provide an answer to this question, but the pertinent information is not usually available.[16]

The problems in classifying responses as voluntary or involuntary are even greater. The commonsensical notion is that one can perform or inhibit a voluntary response intentionally but one cannot make or inhibit an involuntary response intentionally. This approach is reflected in research on eyelid conditioning. If a response can be made or inhibited to a signal on the basis of instructions given before the signal is presented, it is classified as voluntary. If previous instructions have no effect on the power of the stimulus to elicit the response, it is considered to be involuntary. Hebb (1966) employed a different set of criteria since he was concerned mainly with animal behavior and obviously could not employ instructions. He suggested that involuntary responses are more completely under stimulus control than voluntary responses, and that involuntary responses are mediated by simpler neural mechanisms than voluntary responses. This distinction is, of course, identical to that made between reflexive behavior and voluntary behavior, and is very similar to Skinner's distinction between elicited and emitted responding.

One could avoid this miasma, of course, by employing the operant-classical distinction to define voluntary and involuntary responding. Galanter (1966) has suggested that responses that can be modified by their consequences are voluntary, and responses that cannot be modified by their consequences are involuntary. If one infers that only the latter can be classically conditioned, the number of responses in this category becomes very small as more data accumulate on the operant conditioning of autonomic and instinctive behavior patterns.

---

[16]In comparing emitted and elicited responses, the distinction has been made between the power of the CS to *elicit* responses such as salivation, and to *modulate* ongoing operant responses such as bar pressing. This choice of terminology may be misleading. The contrast is not really between the elicitation of certain responses as opposed to the modulation of the rate of other responses. The heart rate is, after all, modulated by the CS in a manner similar to bar pressing. The use of this distinction suggests that the contrast is between the power of the CS to elicit or modulate responses not operantly conditioned, and the power of the CS to elicit or modulate operantly conditioned responses.

The above discussion indicates that no simple criterion is available for classifying responses that can be classically conditioned (or for that matter, for classifying responses together that can be operantly conditioned). Obvious exceptions can be found for each classification scheme. Because of the difficulty in controlling for inadvertent operant reinforcement, one could maintain that such exceptions were produced by it. This position, however, is not convincing. As was the case in operant conditioning, classification based on the relative ease of conditioning may be more successful. What features are shared by responses which are conditioned quickly or slowly in a given situation? How do these features interact with the conditioning procedure to influence the rate of conditioning? Answers to questions such as these might lead to a better understanding of the properties of the response and to a more useful classification than the attempt to group responses that can be conditioned separately from those that cannot.

F.   The Response Mechanism in Classical Conditioning

This section is concerned with the processes that underlie the change in behavior presumably produced by the classical conditioning procedure. Two issues will be considered in dealing with this problem. First, we may ask whether the autonomic response is classically conditioned directly or mediated by some other conditioned response. This is the same question that was asked about operant responses in Section III and illustrated in Figure 1. Second, we can ask whether the classical conditioning procedure has a direct effect on any response. The discussion has proceeded to this point as though there were agreement that the classical conditioning procedure affects neural structures intimately connected with the occurence of responses. The position can be taken, however, that motivational or cognitive internal states are classically conditioned and that these states affect central movement processes which produce the response. ("Motivational states" rather than "cognitive states" will be discussed because these have played the most prominent role in recent theoretical treatments.) According to this view, the classical conditioning procedure affects neural processes one step back, so to speak, from those controlling the response. If we assume a one-to-one relationship between the states and the particular conditoned responses as Mowrer (1947) seems to, the position that states are conditioned does not introduce additional complications. If, however, there is an assumption that responses are controlled by other variables in addition to the conditioned state, further complexities are introduced into the analysis of how the classical conditioning procedure controls behavior.

1. The Mediation of Autonomic Responses in Classical Conditioning

The questions that will be considered are whether autonomic responses are conditioned directly, or whether they are mediated either by overt skeletal movement or by central processes associated with movement. These alternatives are illustrated in Figure 1. Smith (1954, 1964, 1967) has supported the mediational hypotheses, and Shearn (1961) and Obrist and Webb (1967) have discussed these possibilities for the heart rate response in particular.

a. *Mediation by overt responses.* Data on autonomic conditioning in completely curarized subjects suggest that the overt skeletal response is not necessary for autonomic conditioned responses to occur.[17] Black (1965) and Black and Lang (1964) studied classical heart rate conditioning in dogs whose skeletal musculature was paralyzed by *d*-tubocurarine chloride. They also measured EMG in order to be certain that no muscle activity could occur. Heart rate responses to the CS were observed when no concurrent EMG activity took place. Yehle *et al.* (1967) employed a similar procedure in research on the classical conditioning of heart rate and blood pressure in the rabbit. Flaxedil was employed to produce paralysis of the skeletal musculature, and EMG was recorded in order to monitor muscle activity. An experimental group in which CS and US were paired was compared with a control group in which CS and US were explicitly unpaired. A comparison of the experimental and control groups indicates that conditioned heart rate decelerations and blood pressure elevations occurred in completely curarized subjects. It would seem that the hypothesis which postulates that overt movement is necessary for autonomic conditioned responses during a classical conditioning procedure can be rejected.

As Smith (1967) has pointed out, however, it is always possible that some miniscule overt response occurred in these experiments and mediated the autonomic response. As the evidence accumulates, the likelihood of this possiblity seems less and less. Furthermore, if the skeletal response were important, one would expect a large difference between the autonomic response in the normal state when skeletal activity can occur, and the autonomic response in the curarized state when skeletal activity is greatly reduced. This expectation was not fulfilled. Although there were differences between heart rate responses in the normal and

[17]Other experiments on classical conditioning of autonomic responses under curare give results similar to those described in the text (Black *et al.*, 1962; Gerall & Obrist, 1962; Leaf, 1964). These experiments were not dealt with since they did not monitor EMG activity to make certain that paralysis was complete.

curarized states, it is surprising how few they were (Black, 1965; Yehle, et al. 1967).

   b.   *Mediation by central movement processes.* The possibility that autonomic responses are mediated by central processes associated with movement is more difficult to deal with since most of the relevant evidence is indirect, *i.e.,* based on correlational studies similar to those on central mediational explanations of operant autonomic conditioning.

   Obrist and Webb (1967) carried out a detailed correlational analysis of heart rate and general motor activity during classical aversive conditioning in dogs. They found a positive relationship between the magnitudes of the two responses: the greater the heart rate acceleration to the CS, the more the skeletal activity. Similar results have been reported in other studies. Lang and Black (1963) reported that changes in the intensity of a shock US led to parallel changes in general activity and heart rate in dogs. High intensity shocks produced less activity and greater frequency of heart rate decelerations. Santibanez, Saavedra, and Middleton (1963) reported that when cats stopped moving during the CS, heart rate decelerations began to occur. In a later paper, Santibanez, Saavedra, and Tisler (1965) found no difference in magnitude of heart rate change to the CS between restrained and unrestrained cats. The authors concluded that the view that the heart rate response was a postural artifact must be discarded. This conclusion may be questioned, however. It is based on the assumption that restrained and unrestrained cats show large differences in amount of skeletal behavior. This may not be the case. Block-Rojas, Toro, and Pinto-Hamuy (1964) studied the effects of removal of the neocortex on classically conditioned heart rate responses and movement in the rat. Neodecortication prior to conditioning resulted in less movement and a greater number of heart rate decelerations to the CS in experimental animals than in normal controls. A relationship between decreases in motor activity and heart rate deceleration may account for these results rather than the hypothesis which the authors favor, *i.e.,* a dissociation between autonomic and skeletal responses. (Why the four rats which received extensive avoidance training prior to classical conditioning did not show this relationship is not clear.) Finally, Young (1968) has reported a close correlation between electrodermal activity and suppression of bar pressing.

   Similar correlations have been reported between heart rate and respiration. Obrist and Webb (1967), in the study described above, and Fitzgerald and Walloch (1966) found magnitude of heart rate acceleration and amplitude of respiration to be significantly positively correlated in the dog. Cohen and Durkovic (1966) reported a significant positive correlation between respiratory rate and cardiac acceleration in the pigeon. Santibanez et al. (1963) reported informally that whenever heart rate decelerations occurred in cats, a decrease in both rate and amplitude of respiration occurred; Otis et al. (1957) reported similar results for fish. Finally, Yehle et al. (1967) found heart rate decelerations to be correlated with increases in respiratory rate and a decrease in respiration amplitude in the rabbit.

These results suggest a close positive correlation between heart rate and skeletal activity. Some data, however, do not seem to support this conclusion. Smith and Stebbins (1965) report no correlation between respiration and heart rate changes. Unfortunately, their analysis is not detailed enough to permit one to account for the differences between this experiment and those which report positive results. (For example, often when quantitative data are given, only measures of rate or of amplitude of respiration are presented, even though both seem to be required.) Furthermore, the relationship between heart rate and conditioned leg flection responses does not seem to be close (Dykman et al., 1965; Jaworska et al., 1962; Obrist & Webb, 1967; and Soltysik & Jaworska, 1962). Soltysik and Jaworska found that either omitting the US or increasing its intensity affected the leg flection response but not heart rate. Although no correlational data are presented, and different response measures are employed in each experiment, the Dykman et al., and Obrist and Webb experiments reported that conditioned leg flection responses developed after heart rate, while Jaworska and Soltysik concluded that flection was conditioned first. Even though we may not be sure which response was conditioned first, it is clear that the two responses are not closely related. The response of the nictitating membrane also seems to be uncorrelated with changes in heart rate. Vandercar and Schneiderman (1967) have demonstrated that the percentage of nictitating membrane responses decreased with longer CS–US intervals (the range of the CS–US intervals was from .25 to 6.75 sec), while the percentage of heart rate responses was the highest at an intermediate (2.25 sec) CS–US interval.

One striking example of an apparent failure to observe a relationship between autonomic and skeletal responses during classical conditioning is provided by the research on conditioned heart rate and suppression of bar pressing in rats (de Toledo, 1968; de Toledo & Black, 1966; Parrish, 1967). In these experiments, rats were first trained to press a lever on a variable interval schedule of food reinforcement. Classical conditioning was then carried out with a shock US while the subject was bar-pressing. The effects of the classically conditioned CS on the rate of bar pressing and heart rate were measured. The results for the de Toledo and Black (1966) experiment are shown in Figure 8. The heart rate deceleration

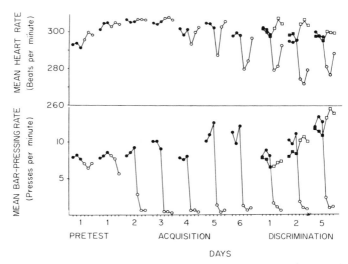

Fig. 8. Mean heart rate and mean bar-pressing rate as functions of conditioning days. Solid symbols show the mean rate for each of three consecutive 1-min periods before CS onset. Open symbols show the mean rate for each of three consecutive 1-min periods during presentation of the CS. Circles represent data for the CS+; squares represent data for the CS−.

conditioned after suppression of bar pressing and there was no relationship between the two responses in speed of conditioning.[18] Furthermore, while positive correlations between amount of suppression of bar pressing and amount of heart rate deceleration occurred on early trials, these disappeared as conditioning progressed. Subsequently, de Toledo (1968) has shown that the relationship between heart rate suppression varied with the parameters of the conditioning situation. With a white noise CS interrupted three times per second, heart rate deceleration and suppression of bar pressing were conditioned at roughly the same rate. With a white noise CS interrupted fifteen times per second, the two responses were less closely correlated with respect to speed of conditioning. Furthermore, in the latter condition, the relationship between the responses varied as a function of shock intensity—lower shocks produced a better correlation.

The lack of correlation between heart rate and certain skeletal responses does not necessarily imply that heart rate and skeletal behavior are

[18]There is disagreement about the correlation of heart rate and bar-pressing suppressions when monkeys are employed as subjects. Goldberg and Schuster's (1967) results are similar to those found in the experiments on rats. Stebbins and Smith (1964) found an increase in heart rate during suppression.

unrelated. The responses which do not seem to be highly correlated with heart rate such as suppression of bar pressing, the nictitating membrane response, and leg flection, all measure very restricted forms of skeletal behavior. Other measures of skeletal responding which are more inclusive and which measure amplitude of response (such as general activity) seem to be much more closely related to heart rate. The work of Obrist and Webb (1967), in particular, supports this statement. They found a strong positive correlation between general activity and heart rate, but little correlation between flection and heart rate. The one clear exception to this generalization is provided by Holdstock and Schwartzbaum (1965) who compared the effects of low and high intensity shock USs on classical conditioning in the rat. They found that low shock produced *greater* heart rate deceleration than high shock, and that no differences existed between shock intensity groups in magnitude of EMG activity. This result was replicated by de Toledo (1968) in two of her groups. In further research carried out in our laboratory, de Toledo demonstrated a close relationship between changes in general activity (measured by a stabilimeter) and changes in heart rate, even though there was no significant correlation between EMG of the neck and heart rate. These results suggest that the measure of EMG in the Holdstock and Schwartzbaum experiment may have been inappropriate.

The positive correlation between heart rate and general skeletal activity during the CS is consistent with the hypothesis that heart rate is mediated by central movement processes. Even if we can account for the exceptions to this generalization, a basic problem is left unsolved. Heart rate is related only to certain patterns of skeletal movement. Both heart rate and the measures of movement with which it seems to be correlated are uncorrelated with other skeletal responses. Although a simple mediational hypothesis might account for the occurrence of heart rate changes, it does not deal with this lack of correlation among skeletal responses. For example, what leads to the difference between the nictitating membrane response on the one hand, and general activity on the other? This problem has not been analyzed adequately. Similarly, not enough data exist on the correlation among different autonomic responses during aversive conditioning in animal subjects.

Positive correlations have been observed between autonomic responses in some cases. Smith and Stebbins (1965) found a positive correlation between blood flow and heart rate in monkeys during a conditioned cardiac acceleration. Yehle et al. (1967) found that blood pressure increased during cardiac decelerations in the rabbit. These authors interpret the latter result as indicating that the primary response to an aversive CS was a blood pressure increase and that this produced a heart rate deceleration as a secondary response. This interpretation, however, is not consistent with the results of Mack, Davenport, and Dykman (1961), which indicate that both heart rate and blood pressure increased during the initial stages of the conditioned response and that blood pressure then decreased before heart rate. In other experiments, however, there is an apparent lack of relationship. An examination of the data of Holdstock and Schwartzbaum (1967) indicates that the relationship between electrodermal and heart rate responses is not close. Shock intensity seemed to affect heart rate but not the electrodermal response, and the magnitude of the electrodermal response decreased from session to session. However, the latter result may be due to some difficulty in measuring the electrodermal response because it is notorious even among autonomic responses for its susceptibility to measurement artifacts (Roberts, 1967). Finally, Dykman *et al.* (1965) found that blood pressure discriminations were much less stable than heart rate discriminations to the same CS+ and CS−. Although too few data are available to permit us to describe the general organization of autonomic responding during classical conditioning, they suggest that the same complex pattern of correlation and lack of correlation exists among autonomic responses as among skeletal responses.

In summary, while much of the data are consistent with the hypothesis of mediation of heart rate by central movement processes, they do not support a simple mediational hypothesis for all changes in autonomic responding during classical conditioning. More complex hypothesis about the processes underlying the pattern of response to the CS in classical conditioning must be suggested because of the apparent lack of concurrent correlation among different skeletal responses and among different autonomic responses, as well as between the two types of responses. Although the available data provide some constraints, there still is a great deal of latitude in framing such "more complex" hypotheses. Furthermore, as in operant conditioning, there may be different strategies that a subject can employ to produce a change in a given autonomic response during classical conditioning. Since work on this problem is only in the beginning stages, a precise modification of the processes underlying the response change in classical conditioning will have to wait until more data are available.

    c. The conditioning of central states. In this section, the hypothesis that the classical conditioning procedure leads to the acquisition by the CS of the power to elicit central motivational states will be discussed briefly. According to this hypothesis, the pairing of CS and US produces changes in central motivational states rather than in the neural system directly controlling responses (Bindra, 1968; Rescorla & Solomon, 1967). If this hypothesis is correct, the effects of classically conditioned motivational states should be the same as those produced by unconditioned motivational states. Therefore, if the CS was conditioned to elicit a motivational state similar to that produced by food deprivation, it should produce effects similar to those of hunger drive and/or hunger incentive-motivation, it should elicit innate responses typical of hunger, it should increase the rate of responses previously operantly conditioned in the presence of hunger, and its termination should act as an operant reinforcer.

This hypothesis can be compared with the one that states that the classical conditioning procedure simply leads to the acquisition by the CS of the power to elicit specific responses. The contrast between these two hypotheses is not sharp. The specific response hypothesis is usually stated in a manner which leads to many of the same predictions as the central state hypothesis, and vice versa. For example, in attempting to account for the effects of classical conditioning on operant responding, feedback from specific classical conditioned responses is often assumed to augment relevant drive states, to act as a CS for operant responses, or both (Spence, 1956). Therefore, both the specific response and the central state hypothesis could predict that the presentation of the CS will increase the level of motivation, elicit certain specific responses, and change the rate of operantly conditioned responses. While the two hypotheses can lead to similar predictions, they differ in one obvious respect. According to the specific response hypothesis, the effects of the CS depend on the occurrence of specific CRs; on the other hand, the central state hypothesis indicates that some effects of the CS do not depend on the occurrence of specific CRs. In order to distinguish between the two, therefore, we must determine whether the effects of the CS are correlated with the occurrence of specific CRs. One source of evidence comes from research in which classically conditioned responses are measured at the same time as the effects of the CS in modulating operant responding. If specific classically conditioned responses are necessary for the various motivational, cueing, and incentive effects of the CS on operant responding, there should be a correlation between the specific CRs and the changes in operant responding produced by the CS. Some relevant data were discussed in the previous section, and more are reviewed in Section VI. While the results are as complex as expected, certain responses presumed to be classically conditioned are uncorrelated with the effects of the CS on operant responding. The results, then, are consistent with the central state hypothesis, at least for the classically conditioned responses studied to date.

Even if one does not measure specific CRs, another line of evidence raises the question as to whether specific CRs will account for the effects usually attributed to central states. The effects of the CS may be produced by the facilitating effects of compatible CRs, or by the interfering effects of incompatible CRs. Suppose, for example, that a classically conditioned CS produced a decrease in rate of some ongoing operantly conditioned response. According to the specific response hypothesis, we could maintain that this effect was produced by response interference, *i.e.*, the CS elicited a response which was incompatible with the operant response. According to the central state view, we could argue either that the CS produced a change in a central motivational state which directly influenced the operant response, or that it produced a change in a central motivational state which led to some specific classically conditioned response, which in turn interfered with the operant response. When we attempt to deal with hypotheses concerning compatible and incompatible responses, the research design most appropriate for this purpose seems to be the transfer design described earlier in Section IV,C,2,b. It has been suggested by Jenkins (1968), for example, that the ability of the CS to modulate a group of apparently unrelated operant responses such as bar pressing, running, or jumping could provide evidence for the central state view. The basis for this belief is that it does not seem likely that a single set of CRs could interfere with or facilitate all of the different operant responses in the same way. This argument will be convincing only if the operant responses are such that the transfer effect from a single set of classically conditioned responses would necessarily be different (*e.g.*, the operant of making a response as contrasted with the operant of refraining from making that response).

Another case which seems difficult to account for in terms of response interference or facilitation alone is provided by research in which the same CS has very different effects on a given operant response depending on the operant reinforcer. Rescorla (1966) has shown that a CS+ associated with shock can enhance the rate of an ongoing skeletal avoidance response, and that a CS− not paired with shock can lead to a decrease in the rate of the avoidance response. Parrish (1967) has presented data (unfortunately, not in a transfer design) which indicate that a CS+ associated with shock diminishes the rate of ongoing skeletal positively reinforced responses, and that the CS− enhances the rate. Since CSs and USs were the same in these experiments, the CRs were most likely the same. If the ongoing skeletal operant responses can be considered as similar, it is difficult to see how interference or facilitation by classically conditioned responses could account for the data. How can a given CR facilitate a given operant response in one case, and interfere with the same operant response in another case? Therefore, it would seem reasonable that some factor other than the interaction between responses must be involved.[19]

These data provide some support for the hypothesis that classical conditioning affects central motivational states which influence responses. Whatever the final decision with respect to the viability of this hypothesis, it is clear that it does not add much toward the explanation of the relationships or lack of relationships among CRs described in the previous section. If we accept a simple central motivational state hypothesis, all responses affected by the state ought to change in a parallel fashion as the state changed during conditioning. This does not seem to be the case. The same criticisms of the hypothesis which states that a single skeletal conditioned response mediates all autonomic changes also applies to the hypothesis that a single central classically conditioned motivational state controls these autonomic responses. More complex hypotheses relating central motivational states (along with other variables) to classically conditioned responses must be considered.

G. Discussion

In many of the discussions of conditioning that appeared in the literature, the assumption has been made (implicitly if not explicitly) that classical conditioning is a simpler, better understood, and more fundamental phenomenon than operant conditioning. Attempts by Spence (1956) and Mowrer (1960) to explain operant conditioning in terms of classical conditioning reflect this point of view. The discussion of classical conditioning in the present chapter does not support this assumption. The description of the experimental procedure in classical conditioning has provoked controversy. More important, little agreement exists as to the effect of this procedure. The first and most serious problem is that

---

[19]Such transfer experiments are difficult to interpret because of the wide variety of relationships that may exist between the classically conditioned CRs and the responses of the operant conditioning situation. Not only must one consider similarities and differences between the CR and the operant response as in the text, but one must also consider similarities and differences between the CR of the classical conditioning situation and CRs inadvertently classically conditioned in the operant situation. The CRs produced by the food during positive operant reinforcement differ from those produced by shock during operant avoidance conditioning. The CRs elicited by the superimposed CS that had been paired with shock could have interfered with the food CRs and facilitated the shock CRs. These, in turn, could have affected the operant response. This argument provides an account of the results described in the text in terms of the interaction of specific responses. It depends on the control of concurrent operant responses by classically conditioned responses, and the evidence presented in this section and in Section VI, suggests little support for such control.

we have not described the effects of pairing CS and US that are independent of the confounding effects of operant reinforcement. Furthermore, we have no rule which states how the conditioned response is selected from the many responses that could be conditioned. Stimulus substitution does not provide an answer, nor does the classification of responses that can be classically conditioned separately from those that cannot. Finally, we have not developed adequate explanations of the processes that underlie the relationships among CRs. Mediation of autonomic responses by overt skeletal responses can be ruled out. Similarly, simple mediation of all autonomic changes by some simple central movement process or central motivational process is not acceptable. More complex hypotheses are required, but, unfortunately, no convincing ones seem to be available. Classical conditioning, therefore, is more a phenomenon which requires analysis than a fundamental process that can be used in explanation of other changes in behavior.

We might even go so far as to ask whether we ought to regard what has been called classical conditioning as a single phenomenon. We can discern at least two fairly different conceptions of classical conditioning in the current literature. One conception deals with classical conditioning as a procedure which leads to the acquisition by a CS of the power to modulate ongoing operant responding. The second conception is of an experimental procedure which produces the conditioning of specific responses to a CS. It is not surprising that a particular experimental procedure has different effects on behavior. If, however, the effects are unrelated, there is no need to treat them as components of some unitary phenomenon. The two conceptions of classical conditioning are usually related to each other by assuming that the acquired powers of the CS to influence a variety of operantly conditioned responses depends on interference or facilitation by specific classically conditioned responses. The hypothesis which suggests that central motivational states are classically conditioned implies that the power of the CS to influence ongoing operant behavior is unrelated in part to the classical conditioning of specific responses and vice versa. If this lack of relationship is confirmed, it might be wise to treat these two effects separately. This may be an especially sensible approach if it turns out that one is more able to carry out properly controlled experiments on the power of the CS to influence ongoing operant behavior using transfer designs than on the classical conditioning of specific responses.

These problems in dealing with classical conditioning stem in large part from our inability to devise adequate control procedures for ruling out the inadvertent effects of operant reinforcement during research on classical conditioning. This, however, is not the only source of difficulty. Another seems to be our unwillingness to admit that the problems discussed above make any difference. Concern over these problems is not new, as the comments of Bitterman (1962), Kimble (1961, 1966), Rescorla and Solomon (1967) and Schoenfeld (1966) testify. This concern, however, seems to have had little impact. On the one hand, we are aware of the problems, and on the other, we continue to describe classical conditioning as a simple, well-understood phenomenon. It is unfortunate that a consideration of classical conditioning phenomena seems to inspire one with the confidence of understanding, when this may not be the case.

Whatever the solution to the problems of analyzing classical conditioning, it is clear that autonomic responding does not open a special window on the process of classical conditioning. Skeletal responses, as well as autonomic responses, are affected by the classical conditioning procedure. In fact, changes in one autonomic response (heart rate) may be mediated by changes in central movement processes that control skeletal responding during classical conditioning. (It is important to note, however, that not all the available evidence supports a simple mediation hypothesis for autonomic responses.) Furthermore, it has been suggested by Kamin (1965) that the modulation of the ongoing operant skeletal responses by a classically conditioned CS provides a more sensitive measure of classical conditioning than autonomic responding to the CS. One wonders, of course, whether the effect of the CS in modulating operantly controlled autonomic responses might be equally sensitive.

V. THE COMPARISON OF CLASSICAL AND OPERANT CONDITIONING

No attempt will be made to make a detailed comparison of classical and operant conditioning. Some comments will be made, however, which bring together the points made in the previous discussions concerning the differences between classical and operant autonomic conditioning.

First, the experimental procedures are obviously different. In one case, the procedure is pairing CS and US; in the other case, it is pairing response and reinforcement. Second, in operant conditioning, the bidirectional control design permitted the description of changes in behavior produced by the effective component of the operant conditioning procedure. In classical conditioning, however, we do not seem to have found a truly satisfactory method for describing the effects of pairing CS and US while controlling the effects of operant conditioning. Third, in operant conditioning a statement of how responses are usually selected is built into the description of the experimental procedure. In classical conditioning, on the other hand, ambiguity exists as to how responses are selected.

While these differences are important, they are not sufficient for an adequate comparison. In addition, it is necessary to establish whether any *empirical* differences in the effects of the two experimental procedures occur, and to describe them precisely. What differences exist in the way in which changes in the same (see footnote 3, page 15) parameters of the classical and operant conditioning situations influence behavior? What responses are sensitive to variations in the parameters of one of the procedures, and not to the other? Are there differences in the processes underlying the response? If mediation occurs, is it the same in both classical and operant conditioning? Is the hypothesis correct that operant conditioning is a procedure which effects responses directly, whereas classical conditioning has effects in addition to the conditioning of particular responses to the CS?

Attempts to answer these questions fall into two major categories: those in which a classically conditioned group of subjects is compared to an operantly conditioned group, and those in which concurrent classical and operant conditioning are compared within a given group of subjects.

The interpretation of the first type of experiment contains many pitfalls. We have to be certain, first of all, that differences between groups were not produced by some irrelevant variable. For example, if the response employed in the classical group is different from that in the operant group, differences between groups could be produced by differences in properties of the response, rather than by any difference between the classical and operant conditioning procedures. Similarly, if there is some difference in a procedural variable, the difference between groups may be attributed to the effects of changing a parameter on either classical or operant conditioning alone, rather than to a difference between the two types of conditioning. Even in those cases in which between-group comparisons seem to have produced a clear-cut difference between the two types of conditioning, the distinction has not stood up well. For example, it has been proposed that intermittent reinforcement leads to greater resistance to extinction than continuous reinforcement in operant conditioning, but not in classical conditioning (Kimble, 1961). After a number of failures, recent research has been reported which demonstrates partial reinforcement effects in the classical conditioning of heart rate in dogs

(Fitzgerald, 1963, 1966; Fitzgerald *et al.* 1966) and conditioned suppression of bar pressing in rats (Hilton, 1967). Furthermore, the partial reinforcement effect does not seem to have been necessarily produced by inadvertent operant reinforcement in these experiments, as Wagner, Siegal, and Fein (1967) have suggested. Hilton (1967) concludes that:

> The most parsimonious assumption we could adopt for the present would be that the PRE (partial reinforcement effect) either has very similar mechanisms for both types of conditioning procedures *or* that both PREs are, fundamentally, attributable to one form of conditioning. The one form of conditioning might be either a "Pavlovian" or an "instrumental" process, irrespective of the type of experimental procedure. The total evidence available, in any event, does not justify an attempt to distinguish classical from instrumental conditioning on the ground that PRE affects the two forms of conditioning in different ways (Hilton, 1967; p.87).

The second type of design in which a comparison is made between classical and operant conditioning within a single group of subjects was discussed in Section IV,C,2 on comparison designs. As pointed out there, whereas the data do point to different effects of classical and operant conditioning, the interpretation of the data is difficult.

All of these problems make one hesitant about attempting to compare classical and operant autonomic conditioning. Nevertheless, it does seem clear that the hypothesis that autonomic responses can be classically conditioned but not operantly conditioned can be rejected. A weaker hypothesis, that autonomic responses can be classically conditioned more easily than they can be operantly conditioned can be proposed. Classical autonomic conditioning does seem to take place more rapidly than operant autonomic conditioning, and there are many more successful demonstrations of the former. One would like to attribute this difference in ease of conditioning to the properties of autonomic responses, but before this can be done, certain other possibilities must be ruled out. It is possible that these results may have occurred simply because there has been greater interest in classical autonomic conditioning, which in turn led to more effective training methods and to more successful experiments. Since research on the properties of autonomic responses which affect their speed of operant training is only beginning, a choice among these alternative explanations of the current results cannot be made at present.

VI.   AUTONOMIC CHANGES DURING THE OPERANT
CONDITIONING OF SKELETAL RESPONSES

A.   Introduction

As pointed out in Section II, one of the major reasons for carrying out research on autonomic changes during the operant conditioning of skeletal responses has been the desire to measure simultaneously classical and operant conditioning. The assumption behind this approach is that only autonomic responses reflect the effects of classical conditioning. The research described in the earlier sections of this chapter does not support this assumption. If the operant conditioning of autonomic responses is accepted (either directly or mediated by skeletal responding), then the autonomic response cannot be considered automatically as an indicator of classical conditioning effects. Therefore, the *a priori* grounds for believing that autonomic responses will provide an accurate measure of classical conditioning during operant conditioning are not strong.

While the attempt to measure classical conditioning during operant conditioning seems to have been the most popular reason for carrying out this research (and, ironically, the least justified), it is not the only one. Even though the research may not provide a great deal of information on the simultaneous measurement of classical and operant conditioning, it will provide information on the concurrent changes in several response systems during operant conditioning. Such information on the similarities and differences in the way the responses change during the operant conditioning is important by itself, and also has obvious relevance to the psychosomatic problems described earlier.

The relevant research can be broken down into two classes. The first class attempts to determine the role of autonomic responding during operant conditioning by blocking or interfering with the autonomic nervous system. The second class of experiments consists of studies in which autonomic responses are measured during operant skeletal conditioning.[20] After the data have been described, some of the issues raised in this introduction will be reconsidered.

---

[20]The measurement of autonomic responses during the conditioned suppression procedure was discussed in Section IV It could just as easily have been classified with the experiments of the present section, since autonomic responses were measured during operant reinforcement of bar pressing. The basis for the decision to treat conditioned suppression earlier was the following. In conditioned suppression experiments a separate classical conditioning procedure was carried out with a CS and US that could be different from the operant discriminative stimulus and reinforcer. In contrast, the experiments of the present section employ only the operant procedure. Classical conditioning is assumed to occur to the discriminative stimulus. In short, the experiments of the previous section employed explicit classical conditioning procedures, while those of the present section do not.

B. The Experimental Data

1. Blocking of the Autonomic Nervous System

Wynne and Solomon (1955) employed surgical techniques to block peripheral sympathetic activity. They found that the sympathectomized dogs acquired an avoidance response, but did so somewhat more slowly than control dogs. Similar results were obtained by Auld (1951) and Arbit (1958), who employed tetraethylammonium to block sympathetic reactions. More recently, Wenzel and Jeffrey (1967) also found poorer acquisition of avoidance in immunosympathectomized mice. Immunosympathectomy was accomplished by injecting an antiserum into newborn mice. This antiserum is supposed to produce permanent destruction of most of the sympathetic ganglia. These results indicate that peripheral sympathetic activity is not necessary for the operant avoidance conditioning of skeletal responses. Overton (1964) has also demonstrated that rats do not learn to respond differentially to the blocked and unblocked states of the autonomic nervous system. The responses of the autonomic nervous system do not seem to provide CSs for subsequent operant responses.

Although parasympathetic activity is more difficult to block than sympathetic activity, the available data (Wynne & Solomon, 1955) are in accord with the results for a sympathetic blocking. The research on autonomic blocking, therefore, does not support the peripheralist view that autonomic responses are necessary in operant conditioning. We could, of course, try to salvage such a peripheralist view by arguing that blocking was only partial and that the poorer performance of blocked groups reflects this fact (Arbit, 1958). The same case was made earlier in curare experiments, and can be discounted for the same reasons. If the overt autonomic response controls operant responding, it does not seem reasonable that so little effect on operant responding should occur when gross changes in the overt autonomic response and its correlated feedback are made.

2. Autonomic Measurement during Operant Skeletal Conditioning

Heart rate is the autonomic change most intensively studied during operant aversive conditioning. In research on aversive control, changes in heart rate have been typically measured during avoidance conditioning (Black, 1959, 1965, 1967; Black & Dalton, 1965; Carlson, 1960; de Toledo & Black, 1964; McCleary, 1954; Miller, Banks, & Caul, 1967; Perez-Cruet, Tolliver, Dunn, Marvin, & Brady, 1963; Soltysik, 1960; Soltysik & Kowalska, 1960; Stern & Word, 1962; and Wenzel, 1961; Werboff, Duane, & Cohen, 1964).

In all of these experiments, the heart rate change to the CS during avoidance conditioning was an acceleration. Wenzel (1961), however, did find a slight deceleration just after CS onset, followed by an acceleration just before and during the skeletal avoidance response. The heart rate acceleration to the CS seems to have been acquired more rapidly than the skeletal avoidance response (Black, 1959). During the early stages of avoidance training, avoidance occurred on some trials and not on others. The heart rate change during the CS was higher on avoidance trials than on nonavoidance trials (Black, 1959; Stern & Word; 1962). Furthermore, the heart rate response was higher during avoidance responses than during intertrial responses (Stern & Word, 1962).

In these experiments, the CS was terminated when the avoidance response occurred. The heart rate acceleration to the CS usually continued for several seconds after the avoidance response and termination of the CS (Black, 1959; de Toledo & Black, 1964; and Stern & Word, 1962). Futhermore, de Toledo and Black (1964) found that a group of subjects which learned to avoid quickly displayed a longer continuation of heart rate acceleration after CS termination than a group which learned slowly. Soltysik and Kowalska (1960) found considerable variability among dogs after CS termination: one dog continued to accelerate, two dogs decelerated rapidly, and one dog decelerated slowly. The acceleration after CS termination also seems to be related to the amount of training. Black and Dalton (1965) observed that both the heart rate acceleration to the CS and the duration of the acceleration after CS termination were reduced with overtraining. They also found that the heart rate response was correlated with the duration of the CS. When the duration of the CS was prolonged, the duration of the heart rate change was also prolonged. Soltysik and Kowalska (1960) observed similar effects of CS duration.

While stable heart rate response occurred during avoidance training and seemed to be related to the occurrence of the CS and the avoidance response, more variable data were found during extinction. Black (1959) found that the heart rate extinguished before the avoidance response, and that the rate of extinction of the two responses was not similar. Soltysik (1960) found that the two extinguished at much the same rate. Carlson's (1960) data are similar to Soltysik's, as far as can be ascertained.

Other experiments have been performed which indicate a clear dissociation between the heart rate and the skeletal avoidance response. Black (1959) first trained a group of dogs to avoid shock in the normal state. The dogs were then curarized and the avoidance CS was presented alone under curare. The animals were allowed to recover and the extinction of the avoidance response was studied. He found that presentations of the CS under curare led to extinction of the avoidance response in the normal state. This effect was measured by comparing the experimental group which received extinction trials under curare with a control group which did not. There was no difference, however, in the cardiac response to the CS after recovery from curarization. In this case, the procedure under curare produced a difference in the avoidance response but not in the cardiac response. Wenzel (1961) has also reported a dissociation of heart rate and avoidance response. She trained cats to avoid shock by pressing a lever. Heart rate responding to the CS for the avoidance response was measured. Reserpine injections diminished the heart rate response insignificantly but did decrease the probability of avoidance quite drastically. Werboff *et al.* (1964) employed two different extinction procedures in rats. In one procedure, the avoidance responses terminated the CS, and in the other, the CS remained on for a fixed period of time. They found that rats receiving the fixed duration CS showed a lower level of avoidance responding during extinction than the rats which could terminate the CS. The opposite result occurred with heart rate. Rats receiving the fixed duration CS showed a higher heart rate response to the CS during extinction than rats which could terminate the CS.

While the relation between the avoidance response and heart rate seemed close in some cases but not in others, the relation between heart rate and vigor of activity was in general quite close. (This finding is similar to the results on heart rate and skeletal behavior in classical conditioning.) Black (1959) found that the relation between amount of activity and heart rate increase was closer than the relation between the occurrence of avoidances and heart rate increases. Also, the prolongation of the heart rate response after the termination of the CS described previously seems to have been associated with vigor of skeletal movement. Black and Dalton (1965) observed that the amplitude and duration of movement and of electromyographic activity during and after the CS diminish with overtraining as does the heart rate acceleration. The magnitude and duration of the heart rate change seem to covary with the magnitude and duration of skeletal activity.

One of the most striking examples of the close relationship between skeletal movement and heart rate is found in a recent paper by Webb and Obrist (1967). They first classically conditioned dogs using a light CS and food reinforcement. The dogs were then placed on a complex schedule of operant reinforcement in which 10 pedal presses were followed by onset of the CS, followed by food if the dog refrained from responding for 14 sec. during the CS. They found a close relation between bar pressing, general body movement, and heart rate. The heart

rate and general body movement increased during the bar-pressing period and decreased during the subsequent period when the dog was required to refrain from movement. The only point at which the three
responses were not completely parallel occurred just after CS onset. For
two dogs there was a brief burst of general activity not accompanied by
an increase in heart rate. These data from a positive reinforcement situation are very similar to the results shown in Figure 6 obtained by Black
(1967) in a situation that employed aversive reinforcers. In this case, the
changes in heart rate also paralleled the changes in amplitude of skeletal
movement.[21]

These results indicate a very close relationship between heart rate
changes and amplitude and duration of general skeletal activity during
avoidance conditioning. The relationship was much closer than that
between the heart rate changes and the occurrence of particular avoidance responses. Not all heart rate changes, of course, were concomitant
with changes in movement. Stern and Word (1962), for example, reported that heart rate increases occurred in rats during the early stages
of conditioning when no skeletal movement occurred. The Black (1959),
Werboff et al. (1964), and Wenzel (1961) experiments could also provide
exceptions to the relation. Unfortunately, no data exist on general activity in these experiments. Thus, while exceptions (and possible exceptions)
do exist to the relation between magnitude of general activity and heart
rate, they are few.

C. Discussion

The present data do not support the two-factor theories of avoidance
conditioning which postulate that autonomic responses reflect the classical conditioning processes assumed to influence operant responding.
First, data on autonomic blocking do not support the hypothesis that
the peripheral autonomic response is necessary. Second, studies on concurrent measurement of responses do not support the hypothesis that the
autonomic response provides an index of some classically conditioned
emotional state. Rescorla and Solomon (1967) have also concluded that
the data from concurrent measurements do not support two-factor theo-

[21]McCleary (1960) has demonstrated that classically conditioned heart rate responses and
generalized activity (the latter response was referred to incidentally) show interocular transfer under a wider variety of conditions in the goldfish than avoidance responses. Unfortunately, heart rate, activity and avoidance were not measured during the same experimental
procedure. If one discounts the possibility that some procedural difference produced this
result, McCleary's data provide an example of a relationship between activity and heart
rate but not between avoidance and heart rate.

ries, and attribute this lack of support to the lack of consistent results in research on concurrent measurements. While one can agree with the conclusion, one cannot agree with the reasons for it. There seems to be considerable agreement as to the form of the heart rate response and its relationship to general activity during avoidance conditioning. In this last instance it is not so much variability or even a lack of a general relation between autonomic changes and the avoidance response which is damaging to two-factor theories, as the failure to find the type of relationship which they postulate at certain crucial points in the conditioning process. For example, a problem arises for two-factor theories in interpreting continued heart rate activity after CS termination. The reduction of the classically conditioned emotional state is assumed to play a major role as a source of reinforcement in two-factor theories: either as a form of drive reduction reinforcing the operant avoidance response (Mowrer, 1947; Solomon & Wynn, 1954) or as a US leading to the conditioning of "relief" responses to feedback from the avoidance response (Mowrer, 1960), or as a conditioned inhibitor which produced a decrease in the magnitude of the drive state (Soltysik & Kowalska, 1960). If these theories are correct, a rapid drop in the heart rate response following CS termination might be expected, and should accompany rapid avoidance learning. The data described above do not support this expectation, particularly during the early stages of learning.[22]

One has two choices at this point. One could reject the two-factor theory or argue that heart rate responses are not adequate measures of classical conditioning during operant conditioning. If one accepts the latter alternative, a question naturally arises as to whether some other autonomic response could provide a better measure. The data on classical salivary conditioning suggest that this may be the case. Ellison and Konorski (1964) measured salivation in a situation very similar to that employed by Webb and Obrist (1967) for heart rate, and found very different results. Ellison and Konorski first paired a CS with food (CS_1). A second CS (CS_2) was then introduced preceding CS_1. Nine lever presses during CS_2 led to the presentation of the CS_1, and food followed 8 sec later. The only difference between the two procedures was that Webb and Obrist required that no responses occur between the CS_1 and food, while Ellison and Konorski made no such requirement. In the Ellison and Konorski experiment, salivation and bar pressing were inversively related. Salivation occurred almost exclusively during CS_1, and bar pressing almost exclusively during CS_2. In the Webb and Obrist (1967)

---

[22]*Editor's note:* See also a discussion differentiating relief and relaxation by Denny, Chapter 4, this volume.

experiment, heart rate and bar pressing were directly related. The relationship between heart rate and lever pressing is very different from that between salivation and bar pressing. Salivation does not seem to be a simple artifact of bar-pressing activity and, therefore, might be a more satisfactory measure of classical conditioning.

Although salivation might be more satisfactory than heart rate because it is not as easily affected by the skeletal response, it is still open to doubt whether it is really a classically conditioned response. A response is not necessarily classical just because it changes in a way which is different from a particular operant response. Salivation and lever pressing might have developed the observed relationship to each other because they were affected differently by operant reinforcement. Ellison and Konorski (1966) argued that this problem in the interpretation of their results can be avoided by varying a parameter of the conditioning situation that will presumably affect classically and operantly conditioned responses in different ways. If the autonomic response were to change according to the laws of classical conditioning and if the skeletal response were to change according to the laws of operant conditioning, some justification would have been provided for the use of autonomic responses to measure classical conditioning effects during operant conditioning. This approach can be questioned. For the appeal to differences between the laws of classical and operant conditioning to be acceptable, we must have obtained some data which establish a reliable difference between the two types of conditioning. Such data do not seem to be available at present for many of the situations in which we are interested. Therefore, the use of autonomic responses to measure classical conditioning during the operant conditioning of skeletal responses is not satisfactory. This, of course, does not deny that the analysis of the factors which lead to a difference in the way heart rate and salivation are related to operant skeletal responses is both interesting and important. The point is that it is not a simple matter to show that a given autonomic response is under the control of the effective component of the classical conditioning procedure in these experiments.

There is a further dilemma for two-factor theorists which would exist even if the above problems were not serious. On the one hand, researchers look for a difference between autonomic and skeletal responses in order to justify the use of the autonomic response as an index of classical conditioning. (This is the basis for the appeal to the laws of conditioning discussed above.) On the other hand, they look for a positive relation between autonomic responses and skeletal operant responses in order to justify the hypothesis that the autonomic response motivates the operant response. *Therefore, the more successful they are in demonstrating the independence of the autonomic and skeletal responses in order to justify using the autonomic response to measure classical conditioning, the more they provide evidence which contradicts two-factor theories.*

The experiment by Ellison and Konorski (1966) described earlier illustrates this point. Because salivation and bar pressing occurred at different points during the trial, they concluded that salivation reflected the effect of the classical conditioning procedure. If this conclusion is correct, then salivation cannot measure the classically conditioned motivation for bar pressing, since it occurs at a different time. We can resolve the dilemma by postulating two kinds of classical conditioning effects: one motivating the operant response, and closely related to it in time; another occurring before food reinforcement indicating the anticipation of food (a consummatory effect), and not necessarily temporally related to the operant response. These two classically conditioned effects— motivational and consummatory—are familiar ones and are often discussed in the literature. If, however, more types of separation between responses presumed to be classically conditioned and those presumed to be operantly conditioned are found, the danger arises that the attempt to patch up two-factor theories will lead to the postulation of an unwieldly array of classically conditioned states that are related to operant behavior in different ways.

It would seem, then, that the measurement of autonomic responses during operant conditioning may not provide much information on the relationship between classical and operant conditioning at present. Nevertheless, even though the study of autonomic responses during the operant conditioning of skeletal responses may not be relevant to the testing of two-factor theories of learning, it does have relevance both to the understanding of the complex pattern of changes in behavior that occur as a function of operant reinforcement, and to the study of psychosomatic problems.

One further comment should be made about this last point. Most of our attention in this discussion has been focused on phasic autonomic changes during the CS. We have not been concerned with changes throughout the conditioning period, and with generalizations to new situations. It is obvious that in psychosomatic research, the major concern is with long-lasting, rather than short-lasting changes, and with changes that generalize widely. Research on which autonomic changes are measured during operant responding under complex schedules of reinforcement should provide relevant information. This research has been carried out in positive reinforcement situations (Morse, Kelleher, &

Herd, 1967; Shapiro & Miller, 1965; and Williams, 1965) and therefore will not be discussed here.

VII. CONCLUSION

In the introduction of this chapter, we focused attention on two issues: the comparison of operant and classical conditioning and the analysis of the conditioned response. In this chapter, we pointed to serious unsolved problems in each of these issues, and suggested that research on autonomic conditioning will help to deal with only a small portion of them.

In Section II, we stated that we would not be concerned with whether classical and operant conditioning involved the same or different learning processes; a more limited goal was set. Of the relationships between stimuli, responses, and reinforcers that occur in conditioning situations, the pairing of CS and US is considered to be essential for producing classical conditioning, and the pairing of response and reinforcer is considered to be essential for producing operant conditioning. Our goal was to analyze the effects of each while controlling the other, to compare their effects, and to study their interaction. Even this more limited goal, however, turned out to be more difficult to achieve than had been expected. One difficulty was the lack of relevant data. Another was our apparent inability to deal with classical conditioning separately from operant conditioning. In operant conditioning, the bidirectional control design seemed to be adequate for determining whether a particular response is changed by the effective component of the operant conditioning procedure. In classical conditioning, however, the control procedures for studying the effective component of the classical procedure do not seem to have been developed to the same extent. These difficulties could be largely circumvented if autonomic responses provided an uncontaminated measure of classical conditioning. Unfortunately, this does not seem to be the case.

Research on the second issue, the analysis of the response, has only begun in operant autonomic conditioning. The data indicate that autonomic responses are under the control of the effective component of the operant conditioning procedure. The role of mediating skeletal responses and their associated central processes in producing autonomic changes, however, has not been completely determined. The overt skeletal response is not necessary for operant autonomic conditioning. Also, mediation of all autonomic conditioned responses by a single central movement process is an inadequate hypothesis. However, complex mediation by central movement processes remains a possibility in some cases. While it is still too early to draw a conclusion, heart rate, the response most thoroughly analyzed, may be mediated under certain experimental procedures but not under others. In addition, other autonomic responses such as gastrointestinal activity seem to be less open to mediational effects than heart rate. A resolution to some of these problems concerning mediation should be available in the near future. It would be unfortunate, however, if research were limited to the analysis of mediation to the exclusion of other important problems such as response selection, and the identification of response properties related to their relative ease of conditioning.

In classical conditioning, the data provide fewer clear-cut answers to questions concerning the analysis of the response, even though considerably more research has been carried out. The changes in behavior produced by the effective component of the classical conditioning procedure have not been described adequately. Furthermore, there seems to be no simple rule for stating which responses will be selected by the pairing of a particular CS and US; the traditional notion of stimulus substitution is not adequate alone. Nor do we have any simple method for dealing with the properties of the response. We cannot classify responses that can be classically conditioned separately from those that cannot; in particular, classical conditioning does not seem to be limited to autonomic responses. In addition, the problem of the processes underlying the response to the CS needs further research. A great deal of the data is consistent with the view that the heart rate response is mediated by central movement processes. This view does not hold for all autonomic responses, however, since the relations among certain skeletal responses and among certain autonomic responses are not close. Therefore, the hypothesis that autonomic changes are mediated by a single central movement process is not adequate to account for the relationships among responses during classical conditioning, nor is the hypothesis that the responses are controlled by a single classically conditioned central motivational state. Finally, there seems to be disagreement as to whether it will be more profitable to consider the pairing of CS and US as a procedure which affects responses directly, or as a procedure which influences cognitive or motivational states which in turn affect behavior.

While research on autonomic conditioning does not seem to provide unique information on many issues concerned with analyzing the response or with comparing and relating classical and operant conditioning, such research is still both important and informative. The analysis of how autonomic responses can be changed during conditioning is relevant for those generally interested in the functioning of the autonomic nervous system, and, more specifically, in the analysis of psychosomatic disorders. Furthermore, research on autonomic conditioning is pertinent to our understanding of how the organization of behavior changes during conditioning. In most conditioning experiments, only a single measure of responding is taken. In these cases, the justification for studying a new response is usually that it has unique properties and will, therefore, provide information that would not be obtained otherwise (see Section II). If, however, we consider that the change in organization of behavior produced by a conditioning procedure is an important topic, we must obviously study a number of responses during conditioning. The justification for working on a particular type of response, in this case, is not so much its unique properties (although the impoitance of these is not denied), as its functional role in the organized pattern of conditioned responding. Autonomic changes are components of many organized patterns of responding in which we are interested. Therefore, a major reason for studying autonomic conditioning is its relevance to our understanding of the organization of the conditioned behavior, rather than its special relevance to the analysis of classical conditioning, the measurement of classically conditioned emotional states, the comparison of classical and operant conditioning, or the study of their relationship. In short, it might be more profitable to focus on how autonomic and skeletal responses are organized during conditioning than to worry about testing theoretical notions concerning classical and operant conditioning which are either outmoded or better studied by some other means.

ACKNOWLEDGMENTS

The preparation of this chapter was supported by funds from Research Grant No. 81 from the Ontario Mental Health Foundation, and by Research Grant No. APY-42 from the National Research Council of Canada. I thank C. Batenchuk for his assistance in carrying out the research, Mrs. H. Santa-Barbara for her assistance in the preparation of the paper, and L. de Toledo, H. Jenkins, D. Reberg, L. Roberts and W. vom Saal for their helpful comments. Work on this chapter was completed in the fall of 1968. The literature that has appeared after that date, therefore, is not covered.

REFERENCES

Arbit, J. Shock motivated serial discrimination learning and the chemical block of autonomic impulses. *Journal of Comparative and Physiological Psychology*, 1958, **51**, 199-201.

Auld, F. The effects of tetraethylammonium on a habit motivated by fear. *Journal of Comparative and Physiological Psychology*, 1951, **44**, 565-574.

Banuazizi, A. Modification of an autonomic response by instrumental learning. Unpublished Ph.D. dissertation, Yale University, 1968.

Bindra, D. Neuropsychological interpretation of the effects of drive and incentive–motivation on general activity and instrumental behavior. *Psychological Review*, 1968, **75**, 1–22.

Bitterman, M.E. Techniques for the study of learning in animals: analysis and classification. *Psychological Bulletin*, 1962, **59**, 81–93.

Black, A.H. The extinction of avoidance responses under curare. *Journal of Comparative and Physiological Psychology*, 1958, **51**, 519–524.

Black, A.H. Heart rate changes during avoidance learning in dogs. *Canadian Journal of Psychology*, 1959, **13**, 229–242.

Black, A.H. Cardiac conditioning in curarized dogs: the relationship between heart rate and skeletal behavior. In W.F. Prokasy (Ed.), *Classical conditioning*. New York: Appleton, 1965.

Black, A.H. The operant conditioning of heart rate in curarized dogs: Some problems of interpretation. Paper presented at the Seventh Annual Meeting of the Psychonomic Society, St. Louis, October, 1966.

Black, A.H. Heart rate conditioning in curarized animals: what is operantly conditioned. Invited address at the 75th Annual Meeting of the American Psychological Association, Washington, D.C., September, 1967.

Black, A.H., Carlson, N.J., & Solomon, R.L. Exploratory studies of the conditioning of autonomic responses in curarized dogs. *Psychological Monographs*, 1962, **76**, No. 29.

Black, A.H., & Dalton, A.J. The relationship between the avoidance response and subsequent changes in heart rate. *Acta Biologiae Experimentalis*, 1965, **25**, 107–119.

Black, A.H., & Lang, W.H. Cardiac conditioning and skeletal responding in curarized dogs. *Psychological Review*, 1964, **71**, 80–85.

Black, R.W., & Black, P.E. Heart rate conditioning as a function of interstimulus interval in rats. *Psychonomic Science*, 1967, **8**, 219–220.

Block-Rojas, S., Toro, A., & Pinto-Hamuy, T. Cardiac versus somatic-motor conditioned responses in neocorticate rats. *Journal of Comparative and Physiological Psychology*, 1964, **58**, 233–236.

Breland, K., & Breland, M. The misbehavior of organisms. *American Psychologist*, 1961, **16**, 681–684.

Breland, K., & Breland, M. *Animal behavior*. New York: Macmillan, 1966.

Brener, J., & Hothersall, D. Heart rate control under conditions of augmented sensory feedback. *Psychophysiology*, 1966, **3**, 23–28.

Brogden, W.J., Lipman, E.A., & Culler, E. The role of incentive in conditioning and extinction. *American Journal of Psychology*, 1938, **51**, 109–117.

Bykov, K. *The cerebral cortex and the internal organs*. Moscow: Foreign Languages Publishing House, 1959.

Cannon, W.B. *Bodily changes in pain, hunger, fear and rage*. (2nd ed.) New York: Appleton, 1929.

Carlson, N.J. Primary and secondary reward in traumatic avoidance learning. *Journal of Comparative and Physiological Psychology*, 1960, **53**, 336–341.

Church, R.M. Systematic effect of random error in the yoked control design. *Psychological Bulletin*, 1964, **62**, 122–131.

Church, R.M., & Black, A.H. Latency of the conditioned heart rate as a function of the CS-US interval. *Journal of Comparative and Physiological Psychology*, 1958, **51**, 478–482.

Church, R.M., LoLordo, V.M., Overmier, J.B., Solomon, R.L., & Turner, L.H. Cardiac responses to shock in curarized dogs: effects of shock intensity and duration, warning signal, and prior experience with shock. *Journal of Comparative and Physiological Psychology*, 1966, **62**, 1–7.

Cohen, D.H., & Durkovic, R.C. Cardiac and respiratory conditioning, differentiation and extinction in the pigeon. *Journal of the Experimental Analysis of Behavior,* 1966, **9,** 681–688.

Colavita, F.B. Dual function of the US in classical salivary conditioning. *Journal of Comparative and Physiological Psychology,* 1965, **60,** 218–222.

Crisler, G. Salivation is unnecessary for the establishment of the salivary conditioned reflex induced by morphine. *American Journal of Physiology,* 1930, **94,** 553–556.

Dalton, A. Hippocampal electrical activity and operant conditioning in the dog. Unpublished Ph.D. dissertation, McMaster University, 1968.

deToledo, L. Changes in heart rate and skeletal activity during conditioned suppression in rats. Unpublished Ph.D. dissertation, McMaster University, 1968.

deToledo, L., & Black, A.H. Heart rate changes during avoidance conditioning in rats. Paper presented at the Canadian Psychological Association Meetings, 1964.

deToledo, L., & Black, A.H. Heart rate: changes during conditioned suppression in rats. *Science,* 1966, **152,** 1404–1406.

DiCara, L.V., & Miller, N.E. Instrumental learning of peripheral vasomotor responses by the curarized rat. *Communications in Behavioral Biology,* 1968, Part A, **1,** 209–212. (a)

DiCara, L.V., & Miller, N.E. Changes in heart rate instrumentally learned by curarized rats as avoidance responses. *Journal of Comparative and Physiological Psychology,* 1968, **65,** 8–12. (b)

DiCara, L.V., & Miller, N.E. Instrumental learning of vasomotor responses by rats: learning to respond differentially in the two ears. *Science,* 1968, **159,** 1485–1486. (c)

DiCara, L.V., & Miller, N.E. Instrumental learning of systolic blood pressure responses by curarized rats: dissociation of cardiac and vascular changes. *Psychosomatic Medicine,* 1968, **30,** 489–494. (d)

DiCara, L.V., & Miller, N.E. Transfer of instrumentally learned heart-rate changes from curarized to noncurarized state: implications for a mediational hypothesis. *Journal of Comparative and Physiological Psychology,* 1968, in press. (e)

DiCara, L.V., & Miller, N.E. Heart rate learning in the noncurarized state, transfer to the curarized state, and subsequent retraining in the noncurarized state. *Physiological Behavior,* 1968, in press. (f)

DiCara, L.V., & Weiss, J.M. Effect of heart rate learning under curare upon subsequent noncurarized avoidance learning. Paper presented at the meetings of the Eastern Psychological Association, April 1968, Washington, D.C.

Dykman, R.A., Mack, R.L., & Ackerman, P.T. The evaluation of autonomic and motor components of the nonavoidance conditioned response in the dog. *Psychophysiology,* 1965, **1,** 209–230.

Egger, M.C., & Miller, N.E. Secondary reinforcement in rats as a function of information value and reliability of the stimulus. *Journal of Expimental Psychology,* 1962, **64,** 97–104.

Ellison, G.D. Differential salivary conditioning to traces. *Journal of Comparative and Physiological Psychology,* 1964, **57,** 373–380.

Ellison, G.D., & Konorski, J. Separation of the salivary and motor responses in instrumental conditioning. *Science,* 1964, **146,** 1071.

Ellison, G.D., & Konorski, J. Salivation and instrumental responding to an instrumental CS pretrained using the classical conditioning paradigm. *Acta Biologiae Experimentalis (Warsaw),* 1966, **26,** 159–165.

Farris, H.E. Classical conditioning of courting behavior in the Japanese quail, *coturnix coturnix japonica. Journal of the Experimental Analysis of Behavior,* 1967, **10,** 213–218.

Fehr, F.S., & Stern, J.A. Heart rate conditioning in the rat. *Journal of Psychosomatic Research*. 1965, **8**, 441–453.

Finch, G. Salivary conditioning in atropinized dogs. *American Journal of Physiology*. 1938, **124**, 136–141.

Fitzgerald, R.D. Effects of partial reinforcement with acid on the classically conditioned salivary response in dogs. *Journal of Comparative and Physiological Psychology*. 1963, **56**, 1056–1060.

Fitzgerald, R.D. Some effects of partial reinforcement with shock on classically conditioned heart-rate in dogs. *American Journal of Psychology*. 1966, **79**, 242–249.

Fitzgerald, R.D., Vardaris, R.M., & Brown, J.S. Classical conditioning of heart-rate deceleration in the rat with continuous and partial reinforcement. *Psychonomic Science*. 1966, **6**, 437–438.

Fitzgerald, R.D., Vardaris, R.M., & Teyler, T.J. Effects of partial reinforcement followed by continuous reinforcement on classically conditioned heart rate in the dog. *Journal of Comparative and Physiological Psychology*. 1966, **62**, 483–486.

Fitzgerald, R.D., & Walloch, R.A. Changes in respiration and the form of the heart-rate CR in dogs. *Psychonomic Science*. 1966, **5**, 425–426.

Fromer, R. Conditioned vasomotor responses in the rabbit. *Journal of Comparative and Physiological Psychology*. 1963, **56**, 1050–1055.

Galanter, E. *Textbook of elementary psychology*. San Francisco, California: Holden-Day, 1966.

Gerall, A.A., & Obrist, P.A. Classical conditioning of the pupillary dilation response of normal and curarized cats. *Journal of Comparative and Physiological Psychology*. 1962, **55**, 486–491.

Gibson, E.J. The role of shock in reinforcement. *Journal of Comparative and Physiological Psychology*. 1952, **45**, 18–30.

Goldberg, S.R., & Schuster, C.R. Conditioned suppression by a stimulus associated with nalorphine in morphine-dependent monkeys. *Journal of the Expimental Analysis of Behavior*. 1967, **10**, 235–242.

Goodrich, K.P. Experimental analysis of response slope and latency as criteria for characterizing voluntary and nonvoluntary responses in eyeblink conditioning. *Psychological Monographs*. 1966, **80**, 1–34.

Gormezano, I. Classical conditioning. In J.B. Sidowski (Ed.), *Experimental methods and instrumentation in psychology*. New York: McGraw-Hill, 1965, Pp. 385–420.

Hebb, D.O. *A textbook of psychology*. (2nd ed.) Philadelphia, Pennsylvania: Saunders, 1966.

Hilton, A. Partial reinforcement of a conditioned emotional response. Unpublished Ph.D. dissertation, McMaster University, 1967.

Hogan, J.A. Fighting and reinforcement in the Siamese Fighting Fish *(Betta splendens)*. *Journal of Comparative and Physiological Psychology*. 1968, (in press).

Holdstock, T.L., & Schwartzbaum, J.S. Classical conditioning of heart rate and galvanic skin response in the rat. *Psychophysiology*, 1965, **2**, 25–38.

Hunter, W.S. Conditioning and extinction in the rat. *British Journal of Psychology*. 1935, **26**, 135–148.

James, W. What is an emotion? *Mind*. 1884, **9**, 188–205.

Jaworska, K., Kowalska, M., & Soltysik, S. Studies on the aversive classical conditioning. 1. Acquisition and differentiation of motor and cardiac conditioned classical defensive reflexes in dog. *Acta Biologiae Expimentalis*. 1962, **22**, 23–24.

Jenkins, H.M. Personal communication, 1968.

Kamin, L.J. Temporal and intensity characteristics of the conditioned stimulus. In W.F. Prokasy (Ed.), *Classical conditioning.* New York: Appleton, 1965. Pp. 118–147.

Kamin, L.J. Predictability, surprise, attention, and conditioning. Technical Report No. 13, Department of Psychology, McMaster University, 1967.

Kelleher, R.T., & Morse, W.H. Escape behavior and punished behavior. *Federation Proceedings,* 1964, **23,** 808–817.

Kimble, G.A. *Hilgard and marquis' conditioning and learning.* (2nd ed.) New York: Appleton, 1961.

Kimble, G.A. Classical and instrumental conditioning: one process or two? XVIII International Congress of Psychology, 1966, Symposium 4, 55–65.

Kimmel, H.D. Instrumental conditioning of autonomically mediated behavior. *Psychological Bulletin,* 1967, **67,** 337–345.

Kleitman, N. The influence of starvation on the rate of secretion of saliva elicited by pilocarpine and its bearing on conditioned salivation. *American Journal of Physiology,* 1927, **82,** 686–692.

Konorski, J. *Conditioned reflexes and neuron organization.* Cambridge, Massachusetts, Cambridge University Press, 1948.

Konorski, J., & Miller, S. On two types of conditioned reflex. *Journal of General Psychology,* 1937, **16,** 264–272.

Kremer, E. Pavlovian conditioning and the random control procedure. Unpublished M.A. thesis, McMaster University, 1968.

Landau, W.M. Autonomic responses mediated via the corticospinal tract. *Journal of Neurophysiology,* 1953, **16,** 299.

Lang, W., & Black, A.H. Cardiac conditioning in dogs as a function of US intensity and difficulty of differentiation. Paper presented at Eastern Psychological Association meetings, 1963.

Lashley, K.S. An examination of the "continuity theory" as applied to discriminative learning. *Journal of General Psychology,* 1942, **26,** 241–265.

Lashley, K.S., & Wade, M. The Pavlovian theory of generalization. *Psychological Review,* 1946, **53,** 72–87.

Leaf, R.C. Avoidance response evocation as a function of prior discriminative fear conditioning under curare. *Journal of Comparative and Physiological Psychology,* 1964, **58,** 446–448.

Lindsley, D.B. Emotion. In S.S. Stevens (Ed.), *Handbook of experimental psychology.* New York: Wiley, 1951.

Logan, F.A., & Wagner, A.R. *Reward and punishment.* Boston, Massachusetts: Allyn and Bacon, 1965.

Lorenz, K. Morphology and behavior patterns in closely allied species. In B. Schaffner (Ed.), *Group processes.* New York: Josiah Macy, Jr. Foundation, 1955, Pp. 168–220.

Mack, R.L., Davenport, O.L., & Dykman, R.A. Cardiovascular conditioning in dogs. *American Journal of Physiology,* 1961, **201,** 437–439.

Mandler, G. Emotion. In *New directions in psychology.* New York: Holt, 1962, Pp. 267–343.

McCleary, R.A. Measurement of experimental anxiety in the rat: an attempt. *Journal of Genetic Psychology,* 1954, **84,** 95–108.

McCleary, R.A. Type of response as a factor in interocular transfer in the fish. *Journal of Comparative and Physiological Psychology,* 1960, **53,** 311–321.

McDonald, D.G., Stern, J.A., & Hahn, W.W. Classical heart rate conditioning in the rat. *Journal of Psychosomatic Research*, 1963, **7**, 97–106.

Meredith, A.L., & Schneiderman, N. Heart rate and nictitating membrane classical discrimination conditioning in rabbits under delay versus trace procedures. *Psychonomic Science*, 1967, **9**, 139–140.

Miles, C.G. Acquisition of control by the features of a compound stimulus in discriminative operant conditioning. Unpublished Ph.D. dissertation, McMaster University, 1965.

Miller, N.E. Some reflections on the law of effect produce a new alternative to drive reduction. In M.R. Jones (Ed.), *Nebraska symposium on motivation*. Lincoln, Nebraska: University of Nebraska Press, 1963, Pp. 65–112.

Miller, N.E. Psychosomatic effects of specific types of training. Paper read at conference on Experimental Approaches to the Study of Emotional Behavior, at the New York Academy of Sciences, November, 1967.

Miller, N.E., Banks, J.H., & Caul, W.F. Cardiac conditioned responses in avoidance and yoked-control rats. *Psychonomic Science*, 1967, **9**, 581–582.

Miller, N.E., & Banuazizi, A. Instrumental learning by curarized rats of a specific visceral response, intestinal or cardiac. *Journal of Comparative and Physiological Psychology*, 1968, **65**, 1–7.

Miller, N.E., & Carmona, A. Modification of visceral response, salivation in thirsty dogs, by instrumental training with water reward. *Journal of Comparative and Physiological Psychology*, 1967, **63**, 1–6.

Miller, N.E., & DiCara, L.V. Instrumental learning of heart-rate changes in curarized rats: Shaping and specificity to discriminative stimulus. *Journal of Comparative and Physiological Psychology*, 1967, **63**, 12–19.

Miller, N.E., & DiCara, L.V. Instrumental learning of urine formation by rats: changes in renal blood flow. *American Journal of Psychology*, 1968, **215**, 677–683.

Morse, W.H., Kelleher, R.T., & Herd, J.A. Observations on blood pressure changes under various schedules of reinforcement. Paper presented at the Eastern Psychological Association meetings, Boston, 1967.

Mowrer, O.H. Preparatory set (expectancy) — a determinant in motivation and learning. *Psychological Review*, 1938, **45**, 62–91.

Mowrer, O.H. On the dual nature of learning — a re-interpretation of "conditioning" and "problem-solving." *Harvard Educational Review*, 1947, **17**, 102–148.

Mowrer, O.H. *Learning theory and behavior*. New York: Wiley, 1960.

Mowrer, O.H., & Aiken, E.G. Contiguity vs. drive-reduction in conditioned fear: temporal variations in conditioned and unconditioned stimulus. *American Journal of Psychology*, 1954, **67**, 26–38.

Obrist, P.A., & Webb, R.A. Heart rate during conditioning in dogs: relationship to somatic-motor activity. *Psychophysiology*, 1967, **4**, 7–34.

Ost, J.W.P., & Lauer, D.W. Some investigations of classical salivary conditioning in the dog. In W.F. Prokasy (Ed.), *Classical conditioning*. New York: Appleton, 1965.

Otis, L.S., Cerf, J.A., & Thomas, G.J. Conditioned inhibition of respiration and heart rate in the goldfish. *Science*, 1957, **126**, 263–264.

Overton, D.A. State-dependent or "dissociated" learning produced with pentobarbital. *Journal of Comparative and Physiological Psychology*, 1964, **57**, 3–12.

Parrish, J. Classical discrimination conditioning of heart rate and barpress suppression in the rat. *Psychonomic Science*, 1967, **9**, 267–268.

Patten, R.L., & Rudy, J.W. The Sheffield omission training procedure applied to the conditioning of the licking response in rats. *Psychonomic Science*, 1967, **8**, 463–464.

Patton, H.D. The autonomic nervous system. In T.C. Ruch *et al., Neurophysiology.* Philadelphia, Pennsylvania: Saunders, 1961. Pp. 220–233.

Pavlov, I.P. *Conditioned reflexes.* London and New York: Oxford University Press, 1927.

Perez-Cruet, J., Tolliver, C., Dunn, C., Marvin, S., & Brady, J.V. Concurrent measurement of heart rate and instrumental avoidance behavior in the Rhesus monkey. *Journal of the Experimental Analysis of Behavior,* 1963, **6,** 61–64.

Premack, D. Reinforcement theory. In D. Levine (Ed.), *Nebraska Symposium On Motivation.* Lincoln, Nebraska: University of Nebraska Press, 1965. Pp. 123–180.

Prokasy, W.F. (Ed.) *Classical conditioning.* New York: Appleton, 1965.

Rescorla, R.A. Predictability and number of pairings in Pavlovian fear conditioning. *Psychonomic Science,* 1966, **4,** 383–384.

Rescorla, R.A. Pavlovian conditioning and its proper control procedures. *Psychological Review,* 1967, **74,** 71–80.

Rescorla, R.A., & Solomon, R.L. Two-process learning theory: Relationships between Pavlovian conditioning and instrumental learning. *Psychological Review,* 1967, **74,** 151–182.

Roberts, L.E. Central, peripheral, and artifactual determinants of skin resistance in the mouse. *Journal of Comparative and Physiological Psychology,* 1967, **64,** 318–328.

Roberts, L.E., & Young, R.K. Conditioning of skin conductance, skin potential and the suppression of operant behavior in the restrained rat. Paper presented at the Eastern Psychological Association meetings, Washington, D.C., 1968.

Santibanez, H., Saavedra, Maria, A., & Middleton, S. Cardiac and respiratory concomitants in classical defensive conditioning in cats. *Acta Biologiae Experimentalis,* 1963, **23,** 165–170.

Santibanez, G., Saavedra, M.A., & Tisler, S. Further studies on conditioned bradycardia in cats. *Acta Biologiae Experimentalis,* 1965, **25,** 363–372.

Schlosberg, H. Conditioned responses in the white rat. *Journal of Genetic Psychology,* 1934, **45,** 303–335.

Schlosberg, H. Conditioned responses based upon shock to the foreleg. *Journal of Genetic Psychology,* 1936, **49,** 107–138.

Schlosberg, H. The relationship between success and the laws of conditioning. *Psychological Review,* 1937, **44,** 379–394.

Schneiderman, N., Smith, M.C., Smith, A.C., & Gormezano, I. Heart rate classical conditioning in rabbits. *Psychonomic Science,* 1966, **6,** 241–242.

Schoenfeld, W.N. Some old work for modern conditioning theory. *Conditional Reflex,* 1966, **1,** 219–223.

Shapiro, M.M., & Miller, T.M. On the relationship between conditioned and discriminative stimuli and between instrumental and consummatory responses. In W.F. Prokasy, *Classical conditioning.* New York: Appleton, 1965. Pp. 269–301.

Shearn, D. Does the heart learn? *Psychological Bulletin,* 1961, **58,** 452–458.

Sheffield, F.D. Avoidance training and the contiguity principle. *Journal of Comparative and Physiological Psychology,* 1948, **41,** 165–177.

Sheffield, F.D. Relation between classical conditioning and instrumental learning. In W.F. Prokasy (Ed.), *Classical conditioning.* New York: Appleton, 1965. Pp. 302–322.

Skinner, B.F. *The behavior of organisms: An experimental analysis.* New York: Appleton, 1938.

Smith, K. Conditioning as an artifact. *Psychological Review*, 1954, **61**, 217–225.

Smith, K. Curare drugs and total paralysis. *Psychological Review*, 1964, **71**, 77–79.

Smith, K. Conditioning as an artifact. In G.A. Kimble (Ed.), *Foundations of conditioning and learning*. New York: Appleton, 1967.

Smith, O.A., Jr. & Stebbins, W.C. Conditioned blood flow and heart rate in monkeys. *Journal of Comparative and Physiological Psychology*, 1965, **59**, 432–436.

Solomon, R.L., & Brush, E. Experimentally derived conceptions of anxiety and aversion. In M.R. Jones (Ed.), *Nebraska Symposium on Motivation*. Lincoln, Nebraska: University of Nebraska Press, 1956. Pp. 212–305.

Solomon, R.L., & Wynne, L.C. Traumatic avoidance learning: The principles of anxiety conservation and partial irreversibility. *Psychological Review*, 1954, **6**, 353–385.

Soltysik, S. Studies on the avoidance conditioning: II. Differentiation and extinction of avoidance responses. *Acta Biologiae Experimentalis*, 1960. **20**, 171–182.

Soltysik, S., & Jaworska, K. Studies on the aversive classical conditioning. 2. On the reinforcing role of shock in the classical leg flexion conditioning. *Acta Biologiae Experimentalis*, 1962, **22**, 181–191.

Soltysik, S., & Kowalska, M. Studies on the avoidance conditioning. I. Relations between cardiac (type I) and motor (type II) effects in the avoidance reflex. *Acta Biologiae Experimentalis*, 1960, **20**, 157–170.

Spence, K.W. *Behavior theory and conditioning*. New Haven, Connecticut: Yale University Press, 1956.

Stebbins, W.C., & Smith, O.A., Jr. Cardiovascular concomitants of the conditioned emotional response in the monkey. *Science*, 1964, **144**, 881–882.

Stern, J.A., & Word, T.J. Heart rate changes during avoidance conditioning in the male albino rat. *Journal of Psychosomatic Research*, 1962, **6**, 167–175.

Taub, E. & Berman, A.J. Movement and learning in the absence of sensory feedback. In S.J. Freedman (Ed.), *The neuropsychology of spatially oriented behavior*. Homewood, Illinois: Dorsey Press, 1968.

Terrace, H. Discrimination learning and inhibition. *Science*, 1966, **154**, 1677–1680.

Thomas, E. The role of postural adjustments in conditioning with electrical stimulation of the motor cortex as US. Unpublished doctoral dissertation, Yale University, 1967.

Thompson, T., & Sturm, T. Classical conditioning of aggressive display in Siamese fighting fish. *Journal of the Experimental Analysis of Behavior*, 1965, **8**, 397–403.

Trabasso, T., & Bower, G.H. *Attention in learning*. New York: Wiley, 1968.

Trapold, M.A. Reversal of an operant discrimination by noncontingent discrimination reversal training. *Psychonomic Science*, 1966, **4**, 247–248.

Trowill, J.A. Instrumental conditioning of the heart rate in the curarized rat. *Journal of Comparative and Physiological Psychology*, 1967, **63**, 7–11.

Vandercar, D.H., & Schneiderman, N. Interstimulus interval functions in different response systems during classical discrimination conditioning of rabbits. *Psychonomic Science*, 1967, **9**, 9–10.

Vanderwolf, C.H. Hippocampal electrical activity and voluntary movement in the rat. Technical Report No. 17, Department of Psychology, McMaster University, 1968.

Wagner, A.R., Seigel, L.S., & Fein, G.G. Extinction of conditioned fear as a function of percentage of reinforcement. *Journal of Comparative and Physiological Psychology*, 1967, **63**, 160–164.

Wagner, A.R., Thomas, E., & Norton, T. Conditioning with electrical stimulation of motor cortex: evidence of a possible source of motivation. *Journal of Comparative and Physiological Psychology.* 1967, **64,** 191–199.

Wall, P.D., & Davis, G.D. Three cerebral cortical systems affecting autonomic function. *Journal of Neurophysiology.* 1951, **14,** 507.

Warstler, H.E., & Ost, J.W.P. Classical salivary conditioning in the dog: effects of three US intensities. *Journal of Comparative and Physiological Psychology,* 1965, **60,** 256–259.

Watson, J.B., & Morgan J.J.B. Emotional reactions and psychological experimentation. *American Journal of Psychology.* 1917, **28,** 163–174.

Watson, J.B., & Rayner, R. Conditioned emotional reactions. *Journal of Experimental Psychology.* 1920, **3,** 1–14.

Webb, R.A., & Obrist, P.A. Heart-rate change during complex operant performance in the dog. Proceedings, 75th Annual Convention, American Psychological Association, 1967. Pp. 137–138.

Wegner, N., & Zeaman, D. Strength of cardiac CRs with varying unconditioned stimulus durations. *Psychological Review.* 1958, **65,** 238–241.

Wenzel, B.M. Change in heart rate associated with responses based on positive and negative reinforcement. *Journal of Comparative and Physiological Psychology.* 1961, **54,** 638–644.

Wenzel, B.M. & Jeffery, D.W. The effect of immunosympathectomy on the behavior of mice in aversive situations. *Physiology and Behavior.* 1967, **2,** 193–201.

Werboff, J., Duane, D., & Cohen, B.D. Extinction of conditioned avoidance and heart rate responses in rats. *Journal of Physomatic Research.* 1964, **8,** 29–33.

Williams, D.R. Classical conditioning and incentive motivation. In W.F. Prokasy (Ed), *Classical conditioning.* New York: Appleton, 1965. Pp. 340–357.

Williams, D.R., & Teitelbaum, P. Control of drinking behavior by means of an operant-conditioning technique. *Science,* 1956, **124,** 1294–1296.

Wynne, L.C., & Solomon, R.L. Traumatic avoidance learning: Acquisition and extinction in dogs deprived of normal peripheral autonomic function. *Genetic Psychology Monographs* 1955, **52,** 241–284.

Yehle, A., Dauth, G., & Schneiderman, N. Correlates of the heart-rate classical conditioning in curarized rabbits. *Journal of Comparative and Physiological Psychology.* 1967, **64,** 98–104.

Young, F.A. Classical conditioning of autonomic functions. In W.F. Prokasy (Ed.), *Classical conditioning.* New York: Appleton, 1965.

Young, R. Changes in skin conductance, skin potential and the suppression of operant behavior during CER conditioning in the restrained rat. Unpublished M.A. thesis. McMaster University, 1968.

CHAPTER 2

Behavioral Measurement of Conditioned Fear[1]

WALLACE R. McALLISTER and DOROTHY E. McALLISTER

Northern Illinois University
De Kalb, Illinois

I. INTRODUCTION: THE CONDITIONING, MEASUREMENT, AND DEFINITION OF FEAR

There seems to be little disagreement that the acquisition of fear, or anxiety, depends on classical (Pavlovian) conditioning procedures. That is, pairing a neutral stimulus (CS) appropriately with a painful or noxious stimulus (UCS) results in the conditioning of fear to the CS. Fear, typically, is considered to be an internal, unobservable response which must be measured indirectly through other, observable responses. Any change in an observable response which follows the presentation of the CS and which is the result of the appropriate pairing of the CS and noxious UCS can potentially be used to measure fear (Brown, 1961, pp. 144 *ff.;* McAllister & McAllister, 1965, pp. 172–174). Among the measures which have been employed for this purpose are various physiological responses such as the GSR, heart rate, and respiration, the change in rate of ongoing behavior such as bar pressing, shuttling, or ingesting, the learning of a response leading to the avoidance of a noxious stimulus or to the escape from fear, the change in performance of a response leading to conditioned (secondary) punishment, and the change in the magnitude of an unlearned response such as startle.

The assumption underlying the indirect measurement of fear is that a correlation exists between the magnitude of the measurable response and the magnitude of fear. This relationship may not be linear and it may differ for the various response measures. The measures may not, therefore, be highly correlated with one another, which is consistent with recent research showing that one measure may reflect fear, or differences in fear, when another does not (*e.g.,* de Toledo & Black, 1966; Over-

[1]This chapter was completed in February, 1969, while the authors were at Syracuse University.

mier, 1966; Parrish, 1967). Nevertheless, a defense, on either logical or theoretical grounds, can be provided for the use of each of the response measures mentioned as an index of fear. No single measure can be considered to be superior to the others in all respects. The specific responses involved (*e.g.*, bar pressing, hurdle jumping, changes in skin resistance, etc.) are not uniquely associated with fear; all occur under a wide variety of other conditions and can be affected by variables unrelated to fear. Therefore, fear cannot be defined in terms of a particular response measure. The only characteristic common to all the occasions in which the presence of fear is asserted seems to be the prior appropriate pairing of neutral and noxious stimuli (classical conditioning). For this reason, fear is best defined in terms of these antecedent conditions. With this definition, any of the various response measures may then be used as an index of the relative strength of fear. This type of definition makes fear a historical concept in the sense discussed by Bergmann (1957, pp. 64 *ff.*).

A problem for psychological theory is to account for the relationship between fear and its various indexes. A theoretical treatment based on Mowrer (1939) and Miller (1948, 1951) assumes that conditioned fear is an acquired drive and, thus, that it can motivate and its reduction can reinforce other behavior. It is also assumed that fear, as a response, can produce stimuli to which other responses may be learned or which may elicit innately associated responses (*e.g.*, crouching, freezing, withdrawing). With the additional assumption that fear as a drive has a general energizing role (Hull, 1943; Spence, 1956), it is possible, as shown in Section I,A, to account for the relationship between fear and each of the nonphysiological response measures mentioned above. In the ensuing discussion, this theoretical position will be adopted; some alternatives will be considered subsequently.

The use of physiological response measures as indexes of fear requires a different rationale. To use the conditioning of a response such as the GSR or the heart rate as a measure of fear is to use one classically conditioned response to measure another classically conditioned response. Such a procedure requires the assumptions that the two responses are conditioned concomitantly and that the laws of conditioning are the same for both. Logically, even skeletal responses which are conditioned by pairing neutral and noxious stimuli could be used to index fear. In fact, the use of classically conditioned activity as a basis for explaining avoidance learning in goldfish (Bitterman, 1965, pp. 13–14) may be interpreted as one such instance. On the other hand, the eyelid response, which is also conditioned by pairing neutral and noxious stimuli, is not normally used as an index of fear. In this case, it is known that the laws differ for the two responses. For example, the optimal CS–UCS interval is approximately .5 sec for the eyelid response, while for fear it seems to be much longer. (See Section II,A,2.) With GSR conditioning, the optimal CS–UCS interval has also been reported to be shorter than that for fear (Beecroft, 1966, pp. 66–73). Despite this, and despite the current question concerning the number and independence of conditionable GSR responses (*e.g.*, Lockhart, 1966), the use of this measure as an index of fear has not been limited. This state of affairs could reflect the belief that since both the GSR and fear are autonomic responses, the conditioning of one response must be accompanied by the conditioning of the other or that the GSR is a component of the fear response. In any event, the above considerations would seem to indicate that there is no generally applicable *a priori* rationale for the use of another classically conditioned response as a measure of conditioned fear.

In this chapter attention will be focused on aversive learning situations in which the conditioning of fear and its measurement are generally considered to be independent. Specifically, the interest will be in situations in which the noxious UCS is usually assumed to have its effect on the conditioning of fear but not *directly* on the measured response. Therefore, procedures such as those involved in avoidance learning, defense conditioning, and the conditioning of physiological responses will not be discussed systematically, even though their use leads to the conditioning of fear, since the measured responses are themselves elicited by the UCS and may be directly conditioned to the CS. Four measures of fear which ostensibly avoid these complications and with which this chapter is mainly concerned will be described in the following section. A discussion of some of the strengths and weaknesses of each measure, as well as a theoretical rationale for the use of each as an index of fear, will be included. Since the available research employing these measures has usually involved shock as the UCS and adult rats as *S*s, throughout this chapter these conditions will be understood to have been used unless otherwise indicated.

A. Measures of Fear

1. Learning to Escape Fear

This measure indexes fear through its effect on the learning of a response which permits escape from fear-eliciting stimuli. A typical procedure is first to administer a series of paired presentations of a neutral stimulus and shock in the grid side of a two-compartment box. This treatment results in fear being conditioned to the discrete CS and to the static apparatus cues (McAllister & McAllister, 1962b). Subsequently, *S* is permitted to escape from the fear-eliciting stimuli in the grid box to the adjacent safe box if the appropriate, to-be-learned response (hurdle jumping, wheel turning, bar pressing) is performed. No shock is administered during this instrumental learning phase of the experiment. Hence, the task may be characterized as learning to escape from fear, although in some instances fear is not escaped completely. For example, if the safe box is similar in some way to the grid box, an escape to it might only reduce, but not eliminate, fear. Theoretically, the escape response is motivated by fear and reinforced by the reduction of fear. The amount of fear is indexed by the difference in performance between a group treated as described above and an appropriate control group. (See Section I,B for a discussion of control procedures.) This technique has sometimes been called an acquired-drive paradigm.

In the literature, there has frequently been a failure to distinguish between learning to escape from fear and active avoidance learning. Although the two tasks share some common properties, their procedural differences have important consequences. In avoidance learning the classical conditioning of fear and the learning of the instrumental response occur concurrently. The onset of the CS is followed after an interval by the noxious UCS (classical fear conditioning), but if the to-be-learned instrumental response (hurdle jumping, bar pressing, panel pushing) occurs in the interval between the onsets of the CS and the UCS, the presentation of the UCS is prevented (avoided) and the CS and, hence, fear is terminated (escaped). If an avoidance response does not occur, S must make the response following presentation of the UCS, in which case the response allows escape from both the CS and the UCS. Both primary and secondary sources of motivation and reward (pain and fear and their reductions) are involved in the instrumental learning, and, therefore, this performance is not an unambiguous index of fear nor of the effect of fear-conditioning variables (cf. Kamin, 1957, p. 453). For example, the number of conditioning trials cannot be controlled since the number of shock presentations (as well as shock durations) is determined by S's performance. Even if fear conditioning precedes the beginning of avoidance training, an uncontrolled number of additional conditioning trials would occur during the initial training while escape responses were still being made. Similarly, the effect of variations in the CS–UCS interval cannot be clearly assessed with an avoidance-learning measure since there is a confounding between the length of the interval and the opportunity to make a response (Bitterman, 1965, p. 3).

In contrast, the escape-from-fear task, since it depends only on fear as a motivator and reinforcer, furnishes in this sense an uncontaminated index of fear and allows a clear distinction to be made between the conditioning and the measurement of fear. Thus, the effect of the manipulation of fear-conditioning variables can be unambiguously evaluated by holding the procedures of the measurement situation constant. It follows that with fear conditioning held constant, variables affecting the instrumental learning may be investigated.

The escape-from-fear measure can be interpreted as a measure of resistance to extinction. Since shock is never administered following the fear-conditioning trials, each exposure to the fear-eliciting stimuli during the instrumental learning is, effectively, an extinction trial. Apparently, the extinction of fear in this situation is relatively slow since the learning of the escape-from-fear response can occur and be maintained over many trials. It may be noted that extinction of fear also occurs in avoidance learning since shock is omitted on each occasion that an avoidance response is made. In this case, however, when the extinction of fear has proceeded to the point where avoidance responses are not made, shock is again administered and fear is reconditioned.

Early investigators employing the escape-from-fear paradigm have reported instances of poor learning or failures to learn (e.g., Brown & Jacobs, 1949; Miller, 1948; Solomon & Brush, 1956, p. 221). One suggested basis for such difficulties was the occurrence of freezing or crouching responses which interfered with making the instrumental response. Such immobility responses are generally held to be associated innately to the fear stimulus and, thus, would occur during the instrumental phase of the experiment when fear was elicited. It is also possible that a freezing or crouching response, elicited by the fear stimulus serving as the UCS, could be classically conditioned to the CS or environmental stimuli during fear conditioning and be directly elicited by them during the instrumental learning phase. A further possibility is that a freezing response could be learned instrumentally during classical conditioning. Such learning might be influenced by the type and intensity of shock used. McClelland and Coleman (1967) have reported that, except at high intensities, more freezing responses occur during the administration of constant current than constant voltage shock, the greatest effect being found with constant dc. Grasping the grid bars during presentation of constant current shock may minimize the amount of pain (Cornsweet, 1963, pp. 119–125). Accordingly, it would be more likely that freezing would occur as an instrumentally learned competing response when this type of shock is used.[2]

[2]Recent research by Blanchard and Blanchard (1969) directed toward a classification of various types of immobility responses and the conditions under which each occurs may ultimately permit a choice in a given situation between these several mechanisms. No attempt will be made in this chapter to distinguish between immobility responses.

Despite the plausibility of the above suggested mechanisms, caution should be exercised in attributing a failure to learn an escape-from-fear response to competing immobility responses. Thus far, criteria have not been established which distinguish between immobility and a simple failure to perform the to-be-learned response. It might be equally tenable to assume that a failure to learn the instrumental response is due to inadequate conditioning or measurement procedures. Ample evidence exists in the recent literature that, with appropriate procedures, competing responses do not prevent the efficient learning by rats (*e.g.*, Desiderato, Butler, & Meyer, 1966; McAllister & McAllister, 1965) or by fish (Brookshire & Hognander, 1968) of an instrumental response to escape fear-eliciting stimuli.

2. *Change in Performance Resulting from Conditioned Punishment*

This measure indexes fear through the effect on an instrumental response of a fear-eliciting stimulus which follows that response. It differs from the escape-from-fear measure by employing the effect of response-contingent conditioned punishment (increase of fear) rather than response-contingent conditioned reinforcement (decrease of fear) as the basis for measuring fear.

One prototype procedure based on Mowrer and Solomon (1954) and Mowrer and Aiken (1954) involves training a bar-pressing response with a positive reward and separately conditioning fear to a CS. Subsequently, in a free-responding situation, each bar press is followed not only by the positive reward but also by the presentation of the CS for a fixed duration. A variation of this procedure is to omit the positive reward when the punishing CS is introduced (Strouthes & Hamilton, 1959). Fear is indexed by the change in the number of bar-pressing responses, relative to that of an appropriate control group, occurring within a fixed interval of time after the introduction of the response-contingent CS (conditioned punisher).

A second method is to train a running response in a straight runway to a positive reward and separately to condition fear to a CS. Subsequently, the decrease in the speed of running resulting from the presentation of the CS in the runway, relative to performance with an appropriate control condition, is used as a measure of fear. During the punishment phase, the running response may be nonreinforced (*e.g.*, Anderson, Plant, & Paden, 1967) or may continue to be reinforced (*e.g.*, Strouthes, 1965). The CS is usually presented when the start-box door is opened, but, as a consequence of its location at or near the goal box, there is an increased exposure to the fear-eliciting stimulus (an increase in conditioned punishment) as S proceeds down the runway. A complication can arise if the punishing CS, for example a light, is placed in the alley prior to the goal box. In this case, if S reaches the goal box, the approach response up to the location of the CS would be punished, but beyond the CS it would be reinforced (by fear reduction). Hence, running speed may be maintained or increased, rather than decreased, when punishment is introduced, depending on the relative strength of punishment to that of reinforcement. Such a procedure, which is analogous to that used in studies of self-punitive or masochisticlike behavior involving shock (*e.g.*, Brown, Martin, & Morrow, 1964), would not provide an unambiguous measure of fear.

A third procedure using this measure is to administer fear-conditioning trials in the grid side of a two-compartment box. Following this, S is allowed a free choice between the grid side and the adjacent solid-floor safe side (*e.g.*, Campbell & Campbell, 1962, Experiment 1). Fear of the grid side is indexed by the amount of time S spends in the safe side as compared to performance obtained under an appropriate control condition. It would seem to be essential that with this procedure the behavior of S be monitored to insure that it is actually being affected by fear. Merely noting that S remains in the safe box does not indicate whether the grid-box stimuli are influencing this behavior or whether some other response (*e.g.*, sleeping) is occurring.

A theoretical explanation for the results expected in these situations involves a competition-of-response notion. Presumably, in the bar-pressing task, fear would be elicited by the CS and crouching and freezing responses, innately associated with the fear stimulus, would occur and would compete with the learned response. In the runway task, where the CS is continuously present, withdrawal responses elicited by the fear stimulus, perhaps augmented by crouching and freezing, would compete with the learned running response. A similar competition between an approach response and a withdrawal response based on fear occurs in the safe-grid box task since there is a tendency for Ss to prefer a box with a grid floor to one with a solid floor (Campbell & Campbell, 1962; McAllister, McAllister, & Zellner, 1966). It might also be expected in the latter two situations that, with training, a response of withdrawing from the locus of the fear-eliciting stimuli might be instrumentally learned since it is followed by a decrease in fear.

It is apparent that the adequacy of the measure of fear obtained in any of these prototype situations depends on the strength both of fear and of the opposing response tendency. That is, fear may not be indexed if its strength is too low relative to the strength of the opposing response. On the other hand, if the strength of the opposing response is weak relative to the strength of fear, performance may be zero. To avoid such ceiling effects and to permit the measurement of differential amounts of fear, the strength of the opposing response must be selected judiciously.

Certain complications can occur in interpreting the difference between experimental and control groups in the two conditioned punishment situations involving a positively reinforced response. In the prototype bar-pressing task, for instance, where free responding is allowed, a difference in performance between an experimental and a control group (*e.g.,* a backward-conditioning group) may reflect more than a difference in fear. If the bar-pressing response continues to be reinforced during the punishment phase, the decrease in responses in the experimental group due to conditioned punishment would reduce for this group, as compared to the control group, the number of positive reinforcements received during the fixed-duration test interval. As a result, the groups would eventually differ with respect to the strength of the bar-pressing response as well as of fear. This problem would probably be of less importance if asymptotic bar-pressing performance had been reached prior to the punishment phase. On the other hand, if positive reinforcement were eliminated when conditioned punishment was introduced, other problems would follow. In this case, the greater number of responses made by the control Ss would lead to a greater number of nonreinforcements and, hence, to more extinction of the bar-pressing response for them as compared to the experimental Ss. Since frustration can be expected to occur as a result of the failure to receive an anticipated reward (Amsel, 1958), more frustration would occur in the control than in the experimental group. Thus, the groups would differ with respect to the strengths of fear, frustration, and the bar-pressing response.

These complications might be circumvented if a discrete-trial procedure were employed. If the conditions were such that all Ss responded on each trial, the number of reinforcements or nonreinforcements and, therefore, the strength of the bar-pressing response and the amount of frustration would be equated between the groups. The effect of conditioned punishment would be evidenced in this case by differences in the latency rather than the rate of responding.[3] An increase in latency in the experimental group, relative to the control group, would require some anticipatory mechanism as an explanation. Such a mechanism might be

[3]The longer latencies of responding expected in the experimental group would, in the case where positive reinforcement was continued, introduce a difference between the groups in its delay, defined as the time from the beginning of the trial to the receipt of reinforcement. On the other hand, if positive reinforcement was discontinued, the delay of nonreinforcement and, hence, of frustration, would be greater in the experimental than in the control group. Depending on the importance of these factors, a difference in the strength of the bar-pressing response might occur.

the conditioning of fear to external or response-produced stimuli through higher-order conditioning or the direct conditioning of a crouching response to these stimuli with the stimulus from CS-elicited fear serving as the UCS.

Analogous complications in interpretation arise in the runway situation. Briefly, if the runway response continues to be reinforced after conditioned punishment is introduced, differences in its strength between the experimental and control groups may result. The control group would continue to be reinforced, but the experimental group would either not receive reinforcement, if the goal were not reached, or would have a greater delay of reinforcement. If extinction procedures were used, differences in the amount of frustration could occur if the control Ss but not the experimental Ss reached the goal. Such confounding, which arises from using multiple trials, would be obviated if the measure of fear involved only the first trial following the introduction of conditioned punishment.

Since an initial difference in fear is responsible for all of the above complications, they could be ignored and an effect of fear inferred provided the experimental and control groups differed appropriately. The use of such a gross index of fear, however, obscures the role of the other processes which can contribute to the performance difference. As discussed above, the effect of these complicating factors changes with training. Therefore, it would be particularly important to consider their effect, as well as the effect of fear, when interpreting differential trends in performance.

The conditioned punishment procedures bear a close relationship to those of passive avoidance or primary punishment (Mowrer, 1960, pp. 26–33) in the sense that in both cases a response is followed by an aversive stimulus. There are, however, procedural differences and theoretical considerations which suggest the wisdom of clearly distinguishing between them. As an example, consider the safe-grid-box situation arranged for passive-avoidance learning. In this case, each entry into the grid box would be followed by shock. As a result, fear would become conditioned to the stimuli produced by the response of approaching the grid box as well as to the grid-box stimuli. Subsequently, initiation of the approach response would produce fear-arousing cues which presumably would lead to freezing, crouching, or withdrawing. Termination of the response would eliminate these cues and reduce fear. Hence, S would learn not to approach or enter the grid box; shock would be passively avoided.[4] As in active avoidance, fear conditioning and the learning of

---

[4]Approach-avoidance conflict procedures in which shock is administered following the approach response (*e.g.*, Kaufman & Miller, 1949; Miller, 1959) would, according to this argument, be classified as passive avoidance.

the instrumental response (withdrawing from the grid box) occur concurrently. On the other hand, in the conditioned punishment situation, response-produced cues are not initially fear elicitors since the fear-conditioning trials are given prior to the test phase, and, thus, the response of approaching or entering the grid box is never followed by shock. Therefore, the important controlling stimuli are the external stimuli of the grid box rather than the response-produced cues. Since the approach responses are, however, punished by the arousal of fear (conditioned punishment), the response-produced cues could eventually, through higher-order conditioning, become fear elicitors.

3. Change in Rate of an Ongoing Response

This measure indexes fear by the effect of the presentation of a stimulus previously paired with shock on the performance of some ongoing response. It differs from the conditioned punishment measure in that the occurrence of the fear-eliciting stimulus is independent of S's response rather than being response contingent. Thus, only adventitiously would a response be followed by the onset of the CS.

In an early study using this measure (Estes & Skinner, 1941), hungry rats were first trained to bar press for food reinforcement. During subsequent bar-pressing sessions, tone-shock pairings were administered. It was found that the rate of bar pressing decreased during presentation of the tone. Similar suppression of ongoing consumatory behavior (drinking) has been reported (e.g., Leaf & Muller, 1965).

The paradigm used by Estes and Skinner has been called the CER (conditioned emotional response) procedure or the conditioned suppression procedure. These designations apparently came into use because the pairing of the CS with shock is assumed to result in the conditioning of an emotional response (fear or anxiety) to the CS, and the effect of CS presentation is usually a suppression of ongoing behavior. For two reasons the use of *CER* or *conditioned suppression* as labels for a method is unfortunate. In the first place, it is widely accepted that an emotional response is conditioned whenever neutral and noxious stimuli are paired, and clearly the suppression of ongoing behavior is only one of many measures which may be used to index such conditioning. In the second place, the procedure does not necessarily lead to the suppression of ongoing behavior, although this usually is the case when that behavior is maintained by positive reinforcement. There are circumstances, however, in which the rate of a positively reinforced response is enhanced by presentation of a fear-eliciting CS. In one instance (Herrnstein & Sidman, 1958), Sidman lever-pressing avoidance learning in monkeys was interspersed between two sessions in which a CS was paired with shock during lever pressing for food reinforcement. In the first of these two sessions, lever pressing was suppressed during CS presentations, but in the second, the rate of responding during the CS was greater than the baseline rate. Likewise, an enhanced rate of a food-reinforced bar-pressing response in rats during CS-shock pairings has been reported when prior shock-alone presentations were administered (Brimer & Kamin, 1963). Also, when the ongoing behavior is maintained by aversive stimulation, an enhanced rate of responding during presentations of a fear-eliciting CS has been reported with a Sidman shuttlebox avoidance response in dogs (*e.g.*, Rescorla & LoLordo, 1965) and a Sidman lever-pressing avoidance response in monkeys (Sidman, Herrnstein, & Conrad, 1957). (Theoretical explanations which may be applied to these enhancement effects are discussed in Sections I,C and II,B,4.)

Additional terminological confusion is evident in the literature because the term CER is used not only as a name for the procedure, but also as a description of, or sometimes as an explanation for, the obtained results. To avoid these various problems, CER will be considered here to be a synonym for fear or anxiety. *Conditioned suppression* will not be used to identify a method but only to describe a result, a practice consistent with the definition provided by Ferster and Skinner (1957).

A reasonable explanation for the suppression of positively reinforced ongoing behavior during the presentation of a fear-eliciting CS is the interference resulting from freezing or crouching responses elicited by the fear stimulus (Miller, 1951, p. 441). Presumably, the amount of interference covaries with the strength of fear. This may be called a competing response interpretation of conditioned suppression. It is obvious that in order to index adequately the effect of fear-conditioning variables, just as with the conditioned punishment measure, the strength of the ongoing behavior must be carefully selected. Ongoing behavior of great strength may mask differences in the amount of fear. Conversely, very weak ongoing behavior may be completely suppressed by any amount of fear.

One possibility which must be considered before attributing suppression of response rate to conditioned fear is that crouching or freezing responses may have been learned instrumentally to the CS during the fear-conditioning trials in the manner described in Section I,A,1. To the degree that this source of competing response affects ongoing performance, a rate change may not be an adequate index of fear. It would seem to be difficult ever to be sure that such instrumental responses are not present, at least to some extent. Nevertheless, with the type and intensity of shock held constant, the findings that manipulation of classical-conditioning variables affects the degree of suppression (*e.g.*, Kamin, 1965) and that these procedures sometimes lead to an enhancement of ongoing behavior argue against this interpretation being the whole story and suggest that fear does play an important role.

Consideration must also be given to the possibility that during the fear-conditioning trials the bar-pressing response would be punished sufficiently by chance coincidences of bar pressing and shock to bring about suppression. This latter complication can be eliminated by using an alternate procedure in which fear-conditioning trials are not administered while the operant response is being performed (*e.g.*, Ayres, 1966; Blackman, 1966; Kamin, Brimer, & Black, 1963; Libby, 1951). An additional virtue of such a procedure is that it may eliminate the possibility that variables other than those involved in the CS-shock pairings would affect the amount of fear conditioned. For instance, if identical CS-shock pairings were imposed on different operant baselines, different amounts of fear might be conditioned. That is, the stronger the operant response tendency the more likely it would be that a reinforced response would occur during the CS. The consequence might be a decrease in the amount of fear conditioned to the CS as a result of either counterconditioning or a decrease in the saliency of the CS. In addition, the shock may be differentially efficacious depending on the posture of the animal which could vary with operant response strength. Furthermore, the greater its strength, the more likely it is that an operant response would occur during the CS and be punished adventitiously by shock. For all of these reasons, there is much to recommend the separation of the conditioning of fear from the operant training. Wagner, Siegel, and Fein (1967) provide evidence that such a separate procedure can lead to consequences different from those obtained with the traditional procedure. (See Section III,B.)

4. Change in Magnitude of an Unlearned Response

This measure indexes fear by the effect of a fear-eliciting stimulus on the performance of an unlearned response. The general procedure is to condition fear by pairing a CS with a noxious UCS and then on test trials to substitute a reflex-eliciting stimulus (probe) for the UCS. The increase in the magnitude of the reflex in the presence of the CS, relative to that of a control condition, is the index of fear. This method was introduced by Brown, Kalish, and Farber (1951) who used a loud noise as the probe stimulus to elicit the reflex, a startle response. Spence and Runquist (1958) and Ross (1961) have used a puff of air as the probe stimulus for a reflex eyeblink response in human Ss. On the assumption that drive energizes unlearned tendencies as well as habits, it would be expected that the magnitude of the reflex would be enhanced when elicited in the presence of a fear-eliciting CS.

Recently, this interpretation of the startle-response data has been questioned by Kurtz and Siegel (1966). These investigators found an increased startle response when foot shock (used by Brown *et al.*), but not when back shock, was employed. They interpreted this finding to indicate that a postural adjustment adopted by *S*s receiving foot shock facilitated the startle response. They did not, however, rule out the possibility that with back shock a response antagonistic to the startle response was adopted. In this latter case, the energizing role of fear might be obscured. Taken together, the results of these two studies suggest that postural adjustments can be learned under either one or both of the shock conditions. Thus, the importance of considering the effect of postural adjustments (*e.g.*, crouching and freezing) on the other indexes of fear, as previously discussed, gains support.

B.   Control Groups

The appropriate pairing of the CS and the noxious UCS (*e.g.*, shock) which results in the conditioning of fear to the CS ordinarily involves a forward-conditioning procedure. That is, the onset of the CS precedes the onset of the UCS. Such conditioning occurs with a wide range of CS–UCS intervals but does not occur when the UCS precedes the CS by a sufficient length of time (backward conditioning) or when the stimuli are otherwise unpaired. The use of one of these latter procedures as a control condition insures equal presentations of the stimuli in both the forward-conditioning and the control group. Therefore, any observed difference in performance between the groups cannot be attributed to pseudoconditioning, sensitization, or habituation. In addition, control is provided by these groups for fear conditioned to static apparatus cues, as well as to extra-apparatus cues, which occurs whenever shock of sufficient intensity is administered. Such control is needed if the performance of a forward-conditioning group is to be interpreted as resulting from fear of the discrete CS.[5]

Since the effect of fear-conditioning variables is evaluated in terms of

[5]Accepting the general principle, as is done throughout this chapter, that fear is conditioned to all stimuli impinging on *S* at the time of application of shock does not deny the possibility that the amount of conditioning may depend on the previous experience of *S*. Certainly, in a given situation it is necessary to consider, for example, the effect of prior habituation to the CS (*e.g.*, Carlton & Vogel, 1967) or of the prior conditioning of fear to an element of a compound before the compound is paired with the noxious UCS (Kamin, 1968).

the manner in which fear affects some other response, it is often necessary to control for various factors inherent in the measurement situation
which might affect this evaluation. The specific factors which must be
considered depend on the particular measure used. For example, if the
measure of fear is the learning of a hurdle-jumping response to escape
fear, it is necessary to control for jumping that is due only to the inherent aversiveness of the CS or to exploratory tendencies. With a conditioned punishment measure involving a bar-pressing or a runway task,
as described in the prototype experiments, the possibility that presentation of the CS *per se* would disrupt performance must be ruled out.
Similar disruptive effects of the CS must be considered with the
change-in-rate measure. When the effect of fear on the magnitude of an
unlearned response is measured, control must be provided for changes in
the reflex response attributable to sensitization or to habituation to the
probe stimulus. The control groups described above can serve also to
rule out the effects of such factors, which otherwise might confound the
measurement of fear.

Recently, Rescorla (1967a) has discussed in some detail various control procedures used in studying classical conditioning and has drawn
the conclusion that none of those typically used, including those mentioned above, is adequate. This point of view is based on the contention
that the relevant factor in classical conditioning is not the pairing of the
CS and the UCS but rather the contingency between these stimuli
(Rescorla, 1966, 1967a). That is, the nature of the conditioning which
occurs is dependent upon ". . . the probability of a US occurring given
the presence of a CS (or given that the CS occurred at some designated
prior time), and the probability of a US occurring given the absence of
the CS . . . (Rescorla, 1967a, p. 76)." With respect to fear, the contingency view holds that a CS which predicts the occurrence of the UCS
will become an elicitor of fear, a CS which predicts the nonoccurrence of
the UCS will become an inhibitor of fear, and a CS which is nonpredic-
tive will neither elicit nor inhibit fear. The concept of inhibition invoked
by Rescorla appears to be the internal inhibition of Pavlov which consists of four types: extinctive inhibition, conditioned inhibition, differential inhibition, and the inhibition of delay (Rescorla & Solomon, 1967,
pp. 171 *ff.*).

In contrast, an alternative, more traditional view of conditioning
emphasizes the pairing of the CS with the UCS. According to this view,
a CS appropriately paired with shock automatically becomes an elicitor
of fear, but a CS does not become an inhibitor of fear simply by being
unpaired with the UCS. Rather, inhibition develops to such a CS only
through the process of nonreinforcement (extinction). This implies that

in order for a CS to become inhibitory it must first have acquired excitatory properties, either through direct conditioning or through stimulus generalization. Without such excitatory properties, a CS unpaired with shock would remain neutral, *i.e.*, would neither elicit nor inhibit fear.

These two views of conditioning dictate the use of different control conditions for evaluating the effect of CS–UCS presentations. From the traditional view, backward conditioning procedures or explicitly unpaired CS and UCS presentations would be adequate in most cases as control conditions. From the contingency view, however, such control conditions would be inappropriate since they are specifically designed to produce a contingency between the CS and the *absence* of the UCS. Hence, the CS would be expected to become inhibitory. To circumvent this problem, Rescorla proposed that another control procedure be adopted: a "truly random" presentation of the CS and the UCS. That is, the temporal relationship between the stimuli would vary by chance throughout the experimental session, implying that on some occasions the stimuli would be paired. Since, however, no contingency would exist between the CS and the UCS with this procedure, the CS would neither elicit nor inhibit fear because it would be irrelevant as a predictor of the UCS. Such a control group, according to his view, can provide a neutral base level against which to evaluate the amount of fear conditioned to the CS with a forward-conditioning procedure as well as the inhibition developed to the CS when it is explicitly unpaired with shock.

The basic empirical issue between the two viewpoints is whether or not a neutral stimulus explicitly unpaired with shock will become inhibitory without first becoming excitatory. According to the contingency view, it would; according to the traditional view, it would not. Several studies have provided evidence taken to support the contingency position. In two experiments, a series of unpaired CS and shock presentations was administered to dogs (Rescorla, 1966; Rescorla & LoLordo, 1965, Experiment 3). Subsequently, when the CS was presented during the performance of a previously learned Sidman shuttlebox avoidance task, a decrease in the avoidance rate occurred as compared to that of a "truly random" control group or to a pre-CS baseline. The explanation was that fear supporting the avoidance responding was inhibited by the CS. Similar inhibitory effects have recently been reported by Grossen and Bolles (1968) and by Moscovitch and LoLordo (1968). There are other data, however, which indicate that an unpaired stimulus may not become inhibitory. In an experiment by McAllister and McAllister (1962b), two groups of Ss received, in a white grid box, 35 trials consisting of a shock followed after 15 sec by a light, with an intertrial interval (ITI) of 2 min. Subsequently, without shock, Ss were allowed to jump a hurdle from a white grid box to a gray safe box. Although the light was presented in the grid box during hurdle training for one group and not for the other, performance of the groups did not differ. Learning of hurdle jumping in both groups was based on fear conditioned to the static apparatus cues; the CS remained neutral. This finding is consistent with the traditional view of conditioning. It is, however, inconsistent with the contingency view since the unpaired stimulus predicted a shock-free period during classical conditioning, which is the only condition specified as necessary for the development of inhibition, and yet it did not depress instrumental performance, *i.e.*, did not inhibit fear.

The discrepancy between the above studies with respect to whether an unpaired neutral stimulus becomes inhibitory may possibly be reconciled by considering the various procedural differences between the studies. One of these, the number of classical conditioning trials, seems particularly relevant. A large number of trials was administered in those studies finding inhibition and a relatively small number in the study which obtained no evidence for inhibition. If this basis for resolving the discrepant results proves to be correct, the trials variable would have to be incorporated into the contingency view. All of the results may, however, be accounted for with the traditional view if one considers that, although the CS is unpaired with shock, it is paired with apparatus cues which have become fear-eliciting through their pairing with shock. With sufficient trials, higher-order conditioning may occur so that the CS would also become fear-eliciting but, since shock never occurs in the presence of the CS, extinction of fear should eventually take place. Thus, through nonreinforcement, the CS should become inhibitory. This analysis implies that an unpaired CS may remain neutral with a small number of trials but become, with increasing trials, first excitatory and then inhibitory. Whether or not such a sequence of events occurs will require empirical verification.[6] The implication of this latter interpretation is that the control conditions typically used (*e.g.*, backward conditioning) may be inadequate only when certain numbers of classical conditioning trials are administered. It is, thus, at odds with the contingency view

---

[6]It is possible that a CS unpaired with shock during classical conditioning depresses instrumental performance based on fear as a result of an excitatory process rather than an inhibitory process as proposed by either the contingency or the traditional view. That is, the termination of the shock UCS could initiate a response of relaxation which, occurring in the presence of the unpaired CS, would become conditioned to it (*e.g.*, Denny & Weisman, 1964; Miller, 1951, pp. 451–452). During instrumental training the relaxation response elicited by the unpaired CS would, presumably, compete with the fear response and thereby degrade performance. This explanation would be consistent with the data under consideration if it is assumed that, with the procedures used in these experiments, a large number of trials is required to condition relaxation.

which considers such control groups inappropriate under all circumstances.

There is another set of studies which yields data pertinent to the difference between the contingency and the traditional position with respect to the development of inhibition and which implicates the number of conditioning trials as an important variable. The experimental design used in these studies provides that one stimulus (CS_1) is paired with shock and a second stimulus (CS_2) is paired with CS_1. With this paradigm, Rescorla and LoLordo (1965, Experiment 2) reported that the rate of Sidman shuttlebox avoidance responding in dogs decreased during the presentation of CS_2 as compared to the pre-CS baseline rate. Their interpretation was that this stimulus had become a conditioned inhibitor and thereby inhibited the fear supporting the avoidance response.[7] On the other hand, several studies using the same paradigm obtained second-order conditioning of fear rather than conditioned inhibition (Anderson, Plant, Johnson, & Vandever, 1967; Davenport, 1966; Kamil, 1968; McAllister & McAllister, 1964). In these cases, CS_2 became an elicitor, rather than an inhibitor, of fear.[8] The generality of these latter findings is indicated by the diverse indexes of fear used: a decrease in performance of a running response by conditioned punishment, the suppression of a positively reinforced bar-pressing response, and the learning of a hurdle-jumping response to escape fear.

Recently, Herendeen and Anderson (1968) have attempted a reconciliation of these discrepant findings. They have proposed that the relevant variable is the number of conditioning trials and have reported data

[7]The results of a study by Hendry (1967) were also interpreted as providing evidence for conditioned inhibition. During the performance of a food-reinforced bar-pressing response, noise-shock pairings and light-noise pairings were presented. Bar pressing was strongly suppressed during the noise presentations but only slightly suppressed during the light-noise presentations. Although the lesser amount of suppression in the presence of the light was attributed to the development of conditioned inhibition, the experimental design does not rule out the possibility that the results were due to external inhibition or to a stimulus generalization decrement.

[8]These empirical results are somewhat surprising in view of Pavlov's discussion (1927, pp. 33, 69) of the procedures which lead to the development of higher-order conditioning and of conditioned inhibition. Pavlov specified that the standard procedure for obtaining conditioned inhibition involved overlapping the presentations of CS_2 and CS_1 whereas in order to obtain higher-order conditioning a temporal gap between the presentations of the two stimuli was required. Ironically, none of the studies cited which reported second-order conditioning employed a temporal gap between the stimuli, and the one study demonstrating conditioned inhibition did not overlap the stimuli. Since Pavlov reported some exceptions to his specifications for obtaining the two phenomena, the current work could merely be viewed as such instances. It seems more likely, however, that Pavlov did not identify all of the relevant variables.

suggesting support for this view. That is, second-order conditioning is expected with a small number of trials; conditioned inhibition, with a large number. Shipley (1933) has previously made the same suggestion. A plausible explanation consistent with the traditional view of conditioning may be proposed here. Following the conditioning of fear to CS_1, its use as the functional UCS in the CS_2–CS_1 trials would be expected to result in the conditioning of fear to CS_2. However, since no primary reinforcement is present on these trials, extinction of fear should occur, *i.e.*, inhibition should develop to CS_1. When, with continued trials, CS_1 ceases to be a reinforcer for CS_2, inhibition should develop to the latter stimulus. Thus, the role of CS_2 first as an elicitor, and later as an inhibitor, of fear is understandable. As presently formulated, the contingency view of conditioning does not seem able to handle the fact of second-order conditioning.

Differential conditioning is another task in which the acquisition of inhibitory properties by a CS may be assessed. In this situation, two stimuli are presented, one paired with the UCS and the other unpaired. With a noxious UCS, the contingency view would predict that the paired stimulus would become an elicitor of fear and the unpaired stimulus, an inhibitor of fear. The same prediction would be made with the traditional view provided that fear conditioned to the paired CS generalized initially to the unpaired CS so that inhibition resulting from the nonreinforcement of the response to this stimulus could develop (Kimble, 1961, pp. 364 *ff.*). The results of an experiment by Bull and Overmier (1968) with dogs as *S*s, which used this procedure with tones for the paired and unpaired stimuli, are consistent with either view. However, the findings of LoLordo (1967) present a problem of interpretation for each position. During the performance by dogs of a Sidman panel-pressing avoidance task, an auditory stimulus was paired with a noxious UCS (either shock or a loud noise) while a visual stimulus occurred alone, or vice versa. Presentation of the unpaired stimulus led to a decrease in the rate of the avoidance response when the other stimulus had been paired with a shock but not when it had been paired with a loud noise. Since the paired stimulus under both UCS conditions became an elicitor of fear (as indexed by an increased avoidance rate), the failure under the loud-noise condition for the unpaired stimulus to become inhibitory is inconsistent with the contingency position. These findings may be considered to be congruent with the traditional view if it is assumed that the shock employed as the UCS was more aversive than was the loud noise (Campbell & Bloom, 1965). On this basis, one would expect greater fear conditioning to occur with the former UCS. Therefore, cross-modality stimulus generalization between the paired and unpaired stimuli might have occurred only under the shock condition. Alternatively, higher-order conditioning of fear to the unpaired stimulus might have occurred under the shock, but not under the loud-noise, condition if only in the former case was an adequate amount of fear of the apparatus cues present to serve as the functional UCS. Either of these mechanisms provides a basis for the unpaired stimulus to become initially a fear elicitor only under the shock condition. However, with the failure of primary reinforcement to occur in the presence of the unpaired stimulus, extinction of fear would result. Thus, through nonreinforcement, this stimulus would eventually become inhibitory.

Several studies using as a response measure the change in rate of a positively reinforced response also bear on the development of inhibitory properties by a CS. In a study by Hammond (1966), three tone-shock trials and three light-alone trials were administered on each of 15 days during the performance of a previously learned water-reinforced bar-pressing response. Following introduction of the shock, the baseline rate of bar pressing (in the absence of the stimuli) became depressed and then gradually recovered. This baseline suppression can be attributed to interfering responses produced by fear conditioned to the apparatus cues. With training, the response rate during tone presentations came to be depressed below the baseline rate, an effect expected because of the additional fear conditioned to the tone. During light presentations, the bar-pressing rate also was lower than the preshock level but showed less suppression than the baseline rate. This *relative* enhancement of performance during presentation of the light disappeared as the baseline rate recovered to its original level. Hammond's interpretation of this latter effect was that the light, by being explicitly unpaired with shock, became an inhibitor of fear. As fear of the apparatus cues extinguished with training, the light had progressively less fear to inhibit and, thus, the enhanced performance ceased to be demonstrated. This explanation is called into question by the data of Brimer and Kamin (1963). They found a similar enhancement of bar pressing over a depressed baseline during presentations of a stimulus which had never been contrasted with shock and which, therefore, according to the contingency view (Rescorla, 1967a, p. 78), would not have become an inhibitor of fear. Since this finding can be attributed to external inhibition (or to a stimulus generalization decrement), it seems parsimonious to account for Hammond's results in the same manner.

A similar enhancement effect reported by Ray and Stein (1959) is not readily attributable to external inhibition because of its occurrence after very extended differential conditioning. The development of some form of internal inhibition is more plausible. In this case, inhibition resulting from nonreinforcement (extinction) is implicated since tones were used for both the paired and unpaired stimuli and generalization occurred between them initially. These results, however, present an interpretative problem. It would be expected on the basis of other findings (*e.g.*, Hammond, 1966) that after extensive training fear of the apparatus cues would extinguish and baseline responding would recover. Whether or not this occurred is unknown; baseline data were not presented. If recovery had occurred, a critical question remains as to what was inhibited by the unpaired stimulus to allow for the enhanced performance. In a similar experiment using pigeons, where stable baseline responding was obtained, there was no enhancement of performance during presentation of the unpaired stimulus or other stimuli similar to it (Hoffman & Fleshler, 1964). The inference from these several studies, as well as others reported in Section II,B,4, is that enhanced performance occurs only when baseline responding is depressed. Because of the apparent importance of considering baseline data in evaluating inhibitory effects in these types of studies, it is difficult to assess the results of a second study by Hammond (1967), since such data were not reported. Complicating this analysis is the report by Hoffman, Fleshler, and Jensen (1963) of the enhancement phenomenon when baseline responding was normal. Here, a 1000-Hz tone was paired with shock during the performance by pigeons of a key-pecking response for a food reward. Subsequently, in the absence of shock the amount of suppression to generalized stimuli was measured. With continued tests, the rate of responding in the presence of these stimuli was greater than the baseline rate. Although extinctive inhibition resulting from the nonreinforced test trials would be expected to develop to the generalized stimuli, the absence of a fear-depressed baseline again leaves unanswered the question of what could have been inhibited by these stimuli to allow for the increase in response rate. An obvious conclusion to be drawn on the basis of the above survey of experiments which used the change in rate of a positively reinforced response to study inhibitory effects is that at least some important variables operative in this situation have not yet been identified. Although the depression of the baseline seems to be particularly relevant, even it is not unambiguously related to the inhibitory phenomena reported.

Regardless of the ultimate resolution of the theoretical issues related to inhibition, the important point for the present concern with appropriate control conditions is that the available data demonstrate clearly that inhibition does not inevitably develop to a CS which is unpaired with a noxious UCS. Therefore, it must be concluded that control groups given backward conditioning or unpaired stimulus presentations are not necessarily inadequate. Nevertheless, the evidence that inhibition can, under some circumstances, develop to a CS which is unpaired with the UCS suggests the necessity for exercising caution in using these control procedures until the conditions under which they may be inadequate are more precisely delineated. On the other hand, it is also important to investigate the consequences of using a "truly random" control procedure. For example, it may be that when a small number of trials is given to experimental and control groups the chance pairing of the CS and UCS with a "truly random" procedure would have a measurable excitatory effect on behavior since it is known that fear may be conditioned in a few trials (Section II,A,1). In such a case, this control technique may be more inappropriate than those typically used. Also, recent evidence has indicated that, following "truly random" presentations of the CS and UCS, a previously learned positively reinforced bar-pressing response may either be completely suppressed (Seligman, 1968) or show no suppression at all (Rescorla, 1968b). Although these disparate results presumably depend on differences in the procedures employed, a specification of the relevant factors has yet to be made. In any event, the "truly random" procedure does not seem to be a panacea for the control-group problem.

C. Some Theoretical Issues

There are two main theoretical problems involved in the types of studies under consideration: (a) the basis for the conditioning of fear and (b) the basis for the effects of fear, once conditioned, on other behavior.

The procedures used to condition fear—the appropriate contiguous presentation of a neutral and a noxious stimulus—are not a matter of controversy. However, a theoretical dispute exists concerning the mechanism by which the conditioning occurs. The issue involved is whether mere contiguity of the stimuli is sufficient for the occurrence of conditioning or whether a reinforcing state of affairs, usually specified either as the termination of the UCS or as drive reduction, is also necessary. Some of the experimental and theoretical problems involved in testing these alternatives and reviews of pertinent studies are available in several sources (e.g., Bolles, 1967, pp. 321–323; Champion, 1961; Damianopoulos, 1967; Dua & Champion, 1968; Furedy, 1967; Kimble, 1961, pp. 273–274; Strouthes, 1965) and will not be repeated here. It should be pointed out that the reliance sometimes placed on the results of Mowrer and Aiken (1954) and Mowrer and Solomon (1954) as providing clear-cut evidence against the drive reduction position has been shown by Brown (1961, pp. 339–348) in a carefully reasoned argument to be unwarranted. At the present time, it seems best to consider the issue unresolved.

The absence of a compelling theoretical account of the manner in which fear is conditioned does not preclude an attempt to understand the effect of fear on other behavior. It is, of course, this second theoretical problem which has been of concern in the previous sections. There, for expository purposes, the theoretical positions of Miller and the early one of Mowrer were used as a basis for rationalizing the use of the several measures of fear. Here the tenets of that position will be contrasted with some alternatives.

The view proposed by Schoenfeld (1950) holds that the pairing of a neutral CS with a noxious UCS (classical conditioning) results in the conditioning to the CS of those responses elicited by the UCS (*e.g.*, autonomic responses and involuntary muscular responses). It is assumed that this procedure leads to the CS acquiring the property of depressing ongoing operant behavior as in the Estes–Skinner situation, although no rationale for such an effect is supplied. Furthermore, the pairing of the stimuli results in the acquisition by the CS (as well as by other external or proprioceptive stimuli) of negative secondary reinforcing properties. For Schoenfeld, it would be the termination of the secondary aversive stimuli, and not the reduction of fear, which would be a reinforcer. In experimental situations where the termination of the CS is the operation for reducing fear, predictions concerning performance from the Schoenfeld and from the Mowrer–Miller approach would be identical. Under this circumstance, it might seem that the elimination of the concept of fear would be parsimonious. There are, however, several considerations which commend its use.

Classical conditioning is normally understood to be a process by which an originally neutral CS acquires the capacity to elicit some response as a result of its pairing with the UCS. Since the acquired aversiveness of the CS postulated by Schoenfeld is assumed to be the result of classical conditioning, it seems reasonable that the mechanism underlying the aversiveness is some conditioned response, which can be called fear. Furthermore, the formerly neutral CS, which is assumed to acquire aversiveness following conditioning, does not itself change. If a light, it remains a light; if a tone, a tone. Rather, what changes, as a result of conditioning, is the manner in which *S* responds to the stimulus. It seems appropriate to assume that this response is the conditioned fear response.[9]

[9]Despite the presentation of a similar argument, Anger (1963, p. 480) has rejected the use of the fear concept.

The results of Solomon and Turner (1962), which may be interpreted to indicate that fear can serve a mediating role in affecting behavior, offer a compelling argument for the use of the fear concept. In this study, dogs were trained to press a panel to avoid a shock, the CS being the termination of a light. Then, following administration of curare to eliminate skeletal responses and their proprioceptive feedback, differential classical fear conditioning trials were given. During this phase one tone was paired with shock and another tone was presented in the absence of shock. Following recovery from curare, the panel-pressing responses to the tones and to the original CS were measured in the absence of shock. Performance to the original CS remained at about the level reached before the curarization. A panel-pressing response to the tone which had been paired with shock under curare occurred on the very first trial in five of the six *S*s. For both of these stimuli the response occurred to a greater extent throughout the test trials than it did to the tone not paired with shock under curare. The Mowrer–Miller theory can readily account for these results. Presumably, during the initial learning of panel pressing, fear would become conditioned to the original CS, and the response-produced cue from fear would become associated with the instrumental panel-pressing response. Under curare, fear would become conditioned to the tone which was paired with shock, but not to the other tone. During the test phase, the former tone should elicit fear with its response-produced cue, which in turn should mediate panel pressing at the outset of training because of the association learned initially between the fear-produced cue and the instrumental response. It is difficult to see how these results could be accounted for merely in terms of the reinforcement provided by the termination of a conditioned aversive CS, in accordance with Schoenfeld's theory, since the instrumental response occurred on the first trial before reinforcement could have had an opportunity to affect performance.

A mediational interpretation can also account for the immediate transfer of an instrumental response to a fear-eliciting CS as found in dogs by Overmier and Leaf (1965) and in rats by May (1948; see Miller, 1951, p. 440). The findings of Leaf (1964) with dogs can probably be similarly explained, although first-trial data were not presented. Additionally, the increase in Sidman shuttlebox avoidance responding in the presence of a CS previously paired with shock, as reported by Rescorla and LoLordo (1965), yields to a mediational interpretation. In the first phase of the experiment, the Sidman avoidance response was acquired. The learning of this task demands that *S*, with no external warning stimulus, make the shuttle response prior to a scheduled shock in order to avoid it. Typically, the response occurs temporally close to shock onset. Such learning is presumably based on fear conditioned to internal cues produced by the shuttle response. Since only the long-term traces of these response-produced cues are closely associated with shock, they would be expected to elicit more fear and, therefore, to be more likely to produce the avoidance response than would the short-term traces (*cf.* Anger, 1963; Mowrer & Keehn, 1958). During this training the shuttle response would become associated with the fear stimulus. In the second phase of the experiment, fear was classically conditioned to a tone. Subsequent presentation of the tone resulted in an increase in the rate of the shuttle response, presumably because the mediating fear response was elicited more frequently when the tone was present than when it was absent and, thus, the fear stimulus could more often elicit the instrumental response. Assuming that the obtained effect occurred on the initial test trial, an assumption which does not seem unreasonable, an explanation based on the termination of a conditioned aversive CS appears inadequate.

An interpretation involving the energizing role of fear, which may be offered for each of these studies as an alternative to the mediation hypothesis, would be equally repugnant to Schoenfeld, as well as to others (*e.g.*, Bolles, 1967; Dinsmoor, 1954, 1955). Specifically, this explanation would hold that in the studies of May, Leaf, Overmier and Leaf, and Solomon and Turner the instrumental response would be associated during the learning phase with the environmental stimuli and during the test phase this association would be energized by the fear produced by the CS. In the Rescorla and LoLordo study it may be assumed that the internal stimulus traces produced by the shuttle response lie on a generalization gradient. Elicitation of the shuttle response by a short-term (generalized stimulus), rather than the long-term, trace would be expected if drive were increased by a fear-producing CS.

The reluctance of some theorists to accept the motivating role of fear seems to be part of the more general position which rejects the notion that drive energizes behavior and instead emphasizes the role of reinforcement. One factor contributing to the espousal of this position may be the difficulty in aversive learning situations of clearly separating the energizing role of drive from that of reinforcement. For example, there is usually a perfect positive correlation between the amount of reinforcement (fear reduction) ensuing from the termination of a fear-eliciting stimulus and the amount of fear elicited. The same problem is often present when shock is used. This difficulty in evaluating the drive-energization hypothesis can be avoided by using situations in which drive is manipulated without a concomitant change in reinforcement. Studies of the combination of drives, such as those of Amsel (1950) and Ley (1965), are of this type. The conclusion from both studies, that a primary appetitive drive added to fear facilitates instrumental performance, is consistent with the drive-energization hypothesis. Since in both cases the only reinforcement, fear reduction, was kept constant, dispensing with the drive interpretation would require the substitution of some mechanism other than reinforcement to account for the results. One solution might be that increased activity normally elicited by hunger or thirst would facilitate the instrumental behavior, but then the problem remains as to how the increased activity becomes appropriately channeled.

The evidence usually cited as support for the energizing role of fear is the finding of Brown *et al.* (1951) that fear increased the magnitude of a startle response. This interpretation, as described in Section I,A,4, has been called into question by Kurtz and Siegel (1966), who provided evidence that the obtained facilitation may have resulted from postural adjustments. Nevertheless, the data of Spence and Runquist (1958) and Ross (1961), which showed in humans an increased eyeblink reflex in the presence of fear, support its energizing role. In these studies, muscular adjustments probably were unimportant. Other data, at least indirectly, suggest that fear may be energizing. For instance, the increased startle response observed under hunger (Meryman, 1952) or frustration (Wagner, 1963) conditions, which are unlikely to affect postural adjustments, suggests that these manipulations have an energizing role, and, thus, it does not seem unreasonable to assume that fear acts similarly.

Recently, Bolles (1967) has rejected the conception of fear as an acquired drive. His view is based specifically on his contention that the best evidence for it, the learning of a "new" response (one arbitrarily chosen by the experimenter) lacks empirical verification (Bolles, 1967, p. 315).[10] He maintains that the only responses which can be learned in a fearful situation are those which are part of S's innate defensive repertory: in the rat these are withdrawing, freezing, or cowering (Bolles, 1967, pp. 406–409). On this basis, learning a hurdle-jumping response to escape fear is possible because it is consistent with the innate withdrawal tendency. However, other "new" or "nondefensive" responses such as bar pressing, wheel turning, or key pecking cannot be learned as fear-escaping responses. Bolles claims that when bar pressing or wheel turning occur and lead to an escape from fear (Miller, 1948) they are not instrumental but rather are adventitiously made in the process of withdrawal. Also, bar-press escape and avoidance responses are said to result from S's freezing on the bar and then pressing the bar as part of a star-

[10]This argument does not imply that responses *per se* are learned. Responses are not learned; rather, learning consists of the formation of an association between a stimulus and a response already in the organism's repertory.

tle reaction to the shock or to the CS. Before this analysis can be accepted, it would seem to be imperative that some criteria be established to allow a determination as to whether the responding is instrumental or innate. In any event, it would seem that Bolles' explanation of bar-press avoidance cannot account for the learning of a Sidman bar-press avoidance response since with this procedure a CS is not presented (Sidman, 1966). Nor can it account for the good discriminated bar-press avoidance learning obtained by Fantino, Sharp, and Cole (1966) and by Christophersen and Denny (1967). In the first case, Ss began each trial at a distance from the bar; in the second case, a discrete-trial procedure was used in which the CS and the bar were presented simultaneously. Therefore, in neither study can the avoidance response be attributed to a reflexive reaction to the CS. His view also cannot encompass the learning of a key-pecking Sidman avoidance response in pigeons reported by Azrin (1959) or the learning by rats of a "nosing" response to escape shock (e.g., Milby, 1968). It would, thus, seem that the evidence presented by Bolles does not constitute a convincing basis for dismissing the notion of fear as an acquired drive. His treatment does point up the importance of considering the manner in which innate defense responses may interfere with or interact with the to-be-learned response.[11]

Thus far, the theoretical treatment of the manner in which fear affects the learning of a fear-escaping response has been primarily concerned with accounting for the demonstration of the phenomenon. No attempt has been made to consider the manner in which traditional learning variables such as the magnitude, shift, and percentage of reward might operate. The Mowrer–Miller theory can be elaborated to include these variables in a manner analogous to Spence's incentive theory of appetitive learning (1956). It will be presented here by considering its application to the learning of a hurdle-jumping response to escape fear.

The source of motivation for the instrumental learning is the fear conditioned to the CS and to the apparatus cues in the start box of the hurdle-jumping apparatus through their pairing with shock. Reinforcement is contingent upon the reduction of fear which occurs following the escape into the safe box. Presumably, the reduction of fear is accompanied by a response of relaxation or relief (Denny & Weisman, 1964; Mowrer, 1960) which becomes conditioned to the stimuli present, namely, the cues of the safe box and proprioceptive cues resulting from the hurdle-jumping response. Through stimulus generalization, cues present in the start box would come to elicit relief in a fractional form. This anticipation of relief (incentive motivation), together with the strength of

[11]*Editor's note:* See Chapter 3 by Bolles, this volume, for additional discussion of these issues.

drive (fear) and the strength of the hurdle-jumping habit, would determine performance.

Many escape-from-fear studies may be accounted for in terms of the simple motivating and reinforcing properties of fear and do not require the introduction of the notion of relief. This would be true of studies varying magnitude of reward (fear reduction). Nevertheless, in one such study reported in Section II,B,3 (W.R. McAllister & D.E. McAllister, 1967), the theory has been applied to explain the manner in which the theoretical variables, drive and incentive motivation, combine. Other data reported in Section II,B,3, which show in an escape-from-fear task slower extinction following partial than continuous reinforcement, *i.e.,* the partial reinforcement effect (PRE), seem to demand for explanation a more complex analysis which includes some anticipatory mechanism such as conditioned relief. In explaining these data, the added assumption that disconfirmation of anticipated relief results in frustration is required. On a nonreinforced trial in which fear reduction and, hence, relief is prevented, frustration would occur and would become conditioned to the cues present in the safe box. With trials, it would be expected that, through stimulus generalization, conditioned frustration would come to be elicited in the start box. Hurdle jumping would, thus, be learned by a partially reinforced group to a stimulus complex including the stimulus produced by frustration. Such experience with frustration would be absent during acquisition in a continuously reinforced group. However, following introduction of continuous nonreinforcement (extinction), conditioned frustration would eventually occur in the start box in the continuously reinforced Ss. The frustration-produced stimulus would modify the stimulus complex to which the hurdle-jumping response had been learned and lead through stimulus generalization to a performance decrement. In addition, the frustration stimulus would presumably introduce responses incompatible with the hurdle-jumping response and thereby facilitate extinction.[12] The introduction of continuous nonreinforcement would not have these same effects in the partially reinforced Ss in which conditioned frustration and frustration-produced

[12]This theoretical analysis is complicated by consideration of the research, briefly described in Section IV, pp. 167–168, which suggests a functional similarity between the stimuli produced by fear and frustration. On this basis, one might not predict a decrement in the performance of the continuously-reinforced Ss when the frustration stimulus occurs in extinction. That is, since hurdle jumping would have been learned to the fear stimulus, the frustration stimulus, if similar, might be expected to elicit this response instead of the incompatible responses. That such stimulus generalization, if it occurs, is not complete is indicated by the results of the experiment shown in Figure 3 which illustrate a PRE. Obviously, clarification of the theoretical issues raised by the results of these several studies will require additional research.

competing responses had occurred in the start box during acquisition when the hurdle-jumping response was being reinforced (partially). Under these conditions, hurdle jumping would be learned to the frustration stimulus and could compete successfully with frustration-elicited responses. Thus, in extinction the decremental effects of frustration would be mitigated in this group. It follows that the continuously reinforced group would extinguish more rapidly than the partially reinforced group. This treatment is analogous to that often used to explain similar results obtained in appetitive-learning situations (Amsel, 1958).

The elaborated theory would also be required to explain the effect of shifts in reward if in an escape-from-fear task the results obtained were similar to those of appetitive learning. No such studies seem to be available in the literature. Recently, however, Woods (1967) studied shifts in reward in an instrumental escape conditioning task and has proposed a theory similar to that described above to account for his results.

It should be noted that a number of investigators have speculated about the role which positive components play in aversive learning tasks (e.g., Denny & Weisman, 1964; Margules & Stein, 1968; Miller, 1963; Mowrer, 1960; Schoenfeld, 1950). In general, however, these treatments have been concerned primarily with avoidance learning.

II. VARIABLES INFLUENCING THE CONDITIONING AND THE MEASUREMENT OF FEAR

Considering fear to be a classically conditioned response implies that its acquisition is influenced by the variables which affect other conditioned responses. Some of the pertinent data obtained in investigations using the four measures of fear being considered in this chapter are summarized in Section II,A. Mention has been made in the previous discussion that changes in the response indexing fear might reflect the effect of factors inherent in the measuring situation rather than, or in addition to, fear. Studies which have specifically manipulated measurement variables while holding fear conditioning constant are discussed in Section II,B.[13]

Most investigators who have manipulated fear-conditioning variables have used a discrete CS and have focused, in interpreting the results, on fear conditioned to it. This is true despite the ample evidence that fear is also conditioned to static apparatus cues whenever sufficiently strong

[13]Several recent reviews of the empirical literature or of theoretical issues pertinent to the present chapter are available (Beecroft, 1967; Bolles, 1967; Davis, 1968; Goldstein, 1962, 1968; Lyon, 1968).

shock is administered. For example, in the original study by Miller (1948) demonstrating the learning of a response to escape fear and in a study by Meryman (1952) which measured fear through its effect on a startle response, a discrete CS was not used; the only stimuli eliciting fear were the apparatus cues. Other evidence pointing to the importance of this source of fear has been obtained with a change-in-rate measure (*e.g.*, Annau & Kamin, 1961; Brimer & Kamin, 1963; Hammond, 1966; Hendry & Van-Toller, 1965; Hunt & Brady, 1955; Tapp, 1964), with shuttlebox avoidance conditioning (Brush, 1962), and with one-way avoidance conditioning (Baum, 1965).

Relatively little systematic work has, however, been devoted to a determination of the manner in which these two sources of fear are jointly involved in the conditioning and the measurement of fear. In one study dealing with this problem (McAllister & McAllister, 1962b), two groups of Ss were given forward classical fear-conditioning trials with a discrete CS. Subsequently, fear was indexed by an escape-from-fear measure (hurdle jumping) with the discrete CS being present for one group and not for the other. Both groups learned, but the group with the discrete CS learned significantly better. A question can be raised as to whether the inferior performance, which occurred without the discrete CS, resulted from using a compound CS during conditioning but not during hurdle training (stimulus generalization decrement), or whether it was due to the simple removal of one fear-eliciting component. Data bearing on this issue, obtained in this laboratory as part of a larger study (unpublished), is contained in Figure 1. There it may be seen that the

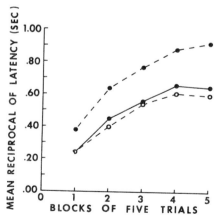

Fig. 1. Speed of hurdle jumping as a function of trial blocks when both conditioning and hurdle training involved a discrete CS (CS-CS; solid circle, dashed line), when the discrete CS was present only during conditioning (CS-NCS; open circle, dashed line), and when the discrete CS was never presented (NCS-NCS; solid circle, solid line).

performance of the CS–CS group, which was both conditioned and given hurdle training with a discrete CS, was markedly superior to that of the CS–NCS group, which was conditioned with the CS and given hurdle training without it. This latter group did not differ from the NCS–NCS group for which the discrete CS was not used in either part of the experiment. These data suggest that conditioning of fear did not occur to the compound *per se* but rather to the components, the discrete CS and static apparatus cues, and that the two sources of fear combined additively. The implication of this study, along with those cited above, is clear: In the interpretation of the results of any study involving fear conditioning, consideration must be given to the possible role of fear conditioned to static apparatus cues in addition to that conditioned to the discrete CS.

A. Conditioning Variables

1. *Number of Conditioning Trials*

It would be expected, in keeping with the body of evidence in the literature pertaining to other classically conditioned responses, that the strength of fear would increase with the number of conditioning trials. Relevant data are available from experiments involving both between-Ss and within-S comparisons.

a. Between-Ss comparisons. When the conditioning of fear occurs prior to its measurement, between-Ss comparisons are required to evaluate the effect of the variable. With this method an increasing monotonic relationship between fear and the number of conditioning trials (1, 3, 9, and 27) has been obtained by Kalish (1954) with an escape-from-fear measure and by Kamin *et al.* (1963) with a change-in-rate measure. Desiderato (1964a) using an escape-from-fear measure obtained evidence of fear conditioning with 25 CS–UCS pairings but not with 3 pairings. Other data, partially consistent with these findings, have been reported by Goldstein (1960) and Gwinn (1951) with an escape-from-fear measure and by Libby (1951) with a change-in-rate measure. Goldstein's data indicated an increase in fear from 1 to 3 conditioning trials and a nonsignificant reversal with 9 and 20 trials, at least at low levels of shock. However, the relationship obtained with a high-shock condition was monotonic when fear was indexed by the final levels of instrumental performance. On the other hand, Gwinn found an increase in fear from 4 to 16 trials with weak but not with strong shock. The data reported by Libby demonstrate a monotonic increasing relationship up to 40 trials and a reversal at 80 trials. No significant effect of variations in the number of trials was obtained by Mathers (1957) and by Miller and Lawrence (cited in Miller, 1951, p. 447) with an escape-from-fear measure, by Strouthes and Hamilton (1964) and Strouthes (1965) with a conditioned punishment measure, and by Leaf and Muller (1965) with a change-in-rate measure. However, the trend of some of these latter results is in the expected direction. It should be noted that the studies of Gwinn and of Miller and Lawrence did not employ a discrete CS; learning was based only on fear of apparatus cues.

No simple reconciliation of these disparate findings is possible. The wide variations among the studies in the measures used as well as the particular conditions and procedures employed preclude meaningful comparisons among all of the studies. Nevertheless, some of the discrepancies might be understood in terms of some general conclusions which can be drawn from the overall results. It appears that fear may be conditioned in a few trials. Therefore, if the conditions of an experiment are such that fear approaches an asymptote with the fewest number of trials employed, additional trials would not be expected to have an effect. One such condition would be the use of a strong shock as the UCS. On this basis it is possible to account for the Gwinn but not for the Goldstein data.

Another consideration, which applies particularly to the escape-from-fear situation, rests on the findings described above which indicate that fear conditioned to the CS and to the apparatus cues combine to influence performance. Increasing the number of conditioning trials would be expected to increase the strength of fear to both sources. However, because fear of the apparatus cues could extinguish during the ITI, this source of fear might begin to decrease in strength as trials increased, particularly with a long ITI and a weak shock. The consequence would be that the relative contribution of the two sources of fear would vary as conditioning was continued and might yield the same total amount of fear despite differences in the number of trials. Conceivably, even though fear of the CS continued to increase, the total amount of fear might eventually decrease. Possibly the discrepancy between the results of Kalish and of Goldstein can be accounted for in these terms. Since fear of the apparatus cues was extinguished in all of Kalish's groups, it could play no role. However, Goldstein interpreted the data of his control group to indicate that the performance of all of his groups may have been influenced by fear of apparatus cues and suggested the possible effect of this source of fear on his results.

Other factors which may be responsible for failure to obtain expected differences in performance with increases in the number of conditioning trials may be mentioned. With change-in-rate or conditioned punishment measures, the ongoing behavior or competing behavior, if sufficiently strong, might override the effect of increases in fear (*e.g.,* Strouthes, 1965). It might also be that desensitization occurs with increasing numbers of shocks, that when fear is overlearned extinction is more rapid, that competing responses such as crouching are more strongly learned with increasing trials, or that a discrimination between the conditioning and test phases occurs with a large number of trials. To pursue the ramifications of these many alternatives seems premature in the absence of empirical data which would allow clear choices among them.

    b.   Within-S comparisons. When the conditioning of fear and its measurement proceed concurrently, the evaluation of the effect of the number of conditioning trials is based on a within-*S* comparison. Brown *et al.* (1951) found an increase in the strength of fear in the presence of the CS, as indexed by the amplitude of a startle response, with increases in the number of conditioning trials (a typical "learning curve"). Most studies using a change-in-rate measure have reported greater suppression of bar pressing (evidence for increased fear) with increases in CS–UCS pairings (*e.g.,* Estes & Skinner, 1941; Kamin, 1965; Tapp, 1964) and have found that fear conditioning occurred within a relatively few trials. Recently, however, Hendry and Van-Toller (1965) and Millenson and Hendry (1967) have reported that as conditioning was continued beyond about 50 trials the suppression of bar pressing progressively decreased. The extent of recovery was related to the intensity of the shock. With strong shock, only partial recovery occurred while with weaker shock recovery was almost complete. This alleviation of suppression with trials was attributed, at least in part, to the marked tendency for suppression to become restricted mainly to the interval just prior to shock. The most obvious explanation of this effect is in terms of inhibition of delay. That is, the inhibition of fear occurring in the early portion of the CS would allow for the increase in the operant response rate. That suppression also decreased in the latter portion of the CS–UCS interval as training was extended under the weak-shock condition suggests that processes other than inhibition of delay were also involved. One possible explanation is that as the operant response continued to be reinforced (strengthened) it offered relatively more competition to the fear-elicited responses occurring throughout the CS. Also, as the operant response was made in the presence of the CS, perhaps as a result of inhibition of delay, and was reinforced, it could have been learned instrumentally to the CS or to the fear stimulus. Another possibility is that the occurrence of reinforced bar presses during the CS served to countercondition fear of the CS. Desensitization to the UCS could also have taken place with extended exposure to shock. It remains for future investigation to determine whether and to what extent these processes, or possibly others, operate to alleviate conditioned suppression during extended training.

There is also evidence indicating that the conditioning of fear to apparatus cues increases with shock presentations and occurs within a few trials. This relationship is apparent in the study by Meryman (1952) in which the amplitude of the startle response increased with the number of shocks. Likewise, progressive decreases in the baseline rate of responding with increases in the number of shocks reported in numerous studies using a change-in-rate measure (e.g., Annau & Kamin, 1961; Brimer & Kamin, 1963; Hammond, 1966; Hendry & Van-Toller, 1965; Hunt & Brady, 1955; Tapp, 1964) may be attributed to competing responses elicited by fear conditioned to the apparatus cues. Some of these studies (e.g., Hammond, 1966; Hendry & Van-Toller, 1965) show, with continued training, a recovery of the baseline rate of responding in the absence of the CS. Such recovery might be expected since fear elicited by apparatus cues alone was never reinforced and, hence, could extinguish, either through the development of inhibition or through counterconditioning. It is also possible that fear of the apparatus cues remains but that the occurrence of reinforced operant responses in the presence of this fear results in the conditioning of the operant response to the fear stimulus.

2. CS–UCS Interval

The temporal interval between the onsets of the CS and UCS is one variable determining the strength of classical conditioning (Beecroft, 1966, pp. 66–73; Kimble, 1961, pp. 155–160). Generally, performance increases to a maximum and then declines as the CS–UCS interval increases. Only a few studies using the fear response have systematically investigated this relationship with a delayed-conditioning procedure. Libby (1951) employed CS–UCS intervals of 0, 1, 4, 7, 10, 20, or 30 sec and measured fear by the degree to which the CS subsequently depressed a food-reinforced bar-pressing response. The amount of conditioned fear increased as the CS–UCS interval was lengthened up to 7 sec and then leveled off. There was some suggestion that less fear was conditioned with intervals longer than 20 sec. Using CS–UCS intervals of .5, 5, and 500 sec, Murfin (1954) found that the amount of conditioned fear, as indexed by the learning of a hurdle-jumping response, was maximum for the 5-sec interval. Some fear was conditioned at .5 sec, but conditioning was essentially nil at 500 sec. A study by Stein, Sidman, and Brady (1958) allows for several within-S comparisons of the effect of the CS–

UCS interval on the conditioning of fear, as indexed by the amount of suppression of an ongoing response. Their data are consistent with the conclusion that the amount of fear that is conditioned decreases as the length of the CS–UCS interval increases beyond 30 sec, but the procedures, which will be elaborated in Section II,A,5, prevent an unequivocal interpretation. Lyon (1963) has reported similar results with a key-pecking response in pigeons. As the CS–UCS interval was increased from 100 to 200 to 300 sec for each of two *S*s, less suppression of key pecking (less fear) was exhibited. Again, these results must be considered only as suggestive since the procedures used forced a concomitant variation in ITI, and the total number of preceding shocks differed for the three CS–UCS conditions.

These data suggest that the function relating conditioned fear to the CS–UCS interval with delayed-conditioning procedures is curvilinear, as is the case with other classically conditioned responses. The decreasing wing of this function may, however, be more protracted than is typically found. That is, fear has been conditioned with CS–UCS intervals of many minutes duration when the experimental conditions (*e.g.*, shock level, ITI) were appropriate (*e.g.*, Annau & Kamin, 1961; Stein *et al.*, 1958). It may be that this conclusion should be restricted to the change-in-rate measure since Murfin found no learning at a 500-sec CS–UCS interval with an escape-from-fear measure. However, this latter finding is possibly attributable to the inclusion by Murfin of an extinction procedure prior to hurdle jumping.

With trace conditioning procedures, two experiments have failed to find evidence that the amount of fear conditioned varies with the length of the interval between the onsets of the CS and the UCS. Strouthes (1965) used a .30-sec CS and a CS–UCS interval of either .30, .85, or 1.95 sec. Leaf and Leaf (1966) employed CS–UCS intervals of either 10, 20, 30, 40, 50, or 60 sec with a CS of 10-sec duration. The measure of fear used by Strouthes was the degree to which the CS, presented in a runway, interfered with a well-learned running response, while Leaf and Leaf employed the recovery from suppression of a drinking response during presentation of the CS. In both studies, the group conditioned with the shortest CS–UCS interval, which actually did not involve a trace procedure, showed more fear than any of the trace-conditioned groups, which did not differ among themselves. These failures to find an effect of the CS–UCS interval among the trace groups may possibly be related to the fact that in both cases the testing situation involved extending the duration of the CS. As a consequence, the stimulus which was contiguous with shock during conditioning (the trace of the CS) was never presented during the test for any of the trace groups. This factor may have prevented the measurement of differences in fear which actually were present.

On the other hand, results with trace conditioning consistent with those found with delayed conditioning have been reported by Ross (1961). First, fear was conditioned in human Ss by pairing a light CS with shock delivered to the fingers. The CS, of .25-sec duration, was used with CS–UCS intervals of either .5, 2, 5, or 10 sec. Subsequently, a puff of air to the temple (probe stimulus) was delivered following CS presentations. Fear was indexed by the amount of increase in the amplitude of the eyeblink reflex to the probe stimulus relative to that of a control group. The typical curvilinear relationship was found; maximum conditioning occurred with the 2- and 5-sec CS–UCS intervals. Performance was poorer, although not significantly so, with the 10-sec interval, while no evidence for conditioning was found with the .5-sec interval.

Other relevant data have been reported by Kamin (1965). His measure of fear in one series of studies was the amount of suppression of a food-reinforced bar-pressing response by a 60-dB CS. With CS–UCS intervals of 61.5 to 180 sec, and with a trace interval (termination of CS to onset of UCS) of at least 60 sec, the amount of fear conditioned decreased as the length of the CS–UCS interval increased. Little or no conditioning occurred with the 180-sec interval. This finding held for several different durations of the CS. When a 180-sec CS–UCS interval was used with short (.5- or 5-sec) trace intervals, conditioning occurred, although the amount was less than that obtained with a delayed-conditioning group with the same CS–UCS interval. The poorer conditioning obtained with the trace procedure was eliminated when a stronger CS (80 dB) was employed with a .5-sec trace interval. Apparently, the trace interval can be bridged more effectively with a stronger CS. Kamin provides other data permitting a direct comparison of the trace and delayed conditioning procedures. With a constant 61.5-sec CS–UCS interval and with a CS of 1.5-sec duration in the trace group, good conditioning, equal for the two procedures, was obtained. On the other hand, with a 180-sec CS–UCS interval, and a 1.5-sec CS in the trace group, the delayed procedure led to good conditioning, although inferior to that with the 60-sec CS–UCS interval, but the trace procedure did not.

The foregoing findings indicate that with trace conditioning there is a curvilinear relationship between the CS–UCS interval and fear similar to that obtained with delayed conditioning. These functions differ, however, in that with the trace procedure fear is not conditioned with a long CS–UCS interval unless the trace interval is sufficiently short or the CS is sufficiently strong. This latter effect can be understood if it is assumed

(a) that an afferent process begins with CS onset, changes with the duration of the CS, and following CS termination, its trace gradually decays with time, and (b) that conditioning occurs to the afferent process or its trace present at the time of UCS presentation. Thus, with a long trace interval or a weak CS, the trace of the afferent process may be completely dissipated so that conditioning would fail to occur.

Other data consistent with the above assumptions have been reported. Bitterman (1965) found that the amount of classically conditioned activity in goldfish was greatest near the time at which the UCS had occurred during training. A similar result has been obtained by Siegel (1967) using a probe-stimulus technique. Following the conditioning of fear to a tone of 4.5-sec duration, with a 4-sec CS–UCS interval, a startle stimulus was presented during test trials at various times following the presentation of the tone. The maximum startle magnitude was found at 4 sec, with smaller startle reactions occurring at both shorter and longer intervals (stimulus generalization decrement). This demonstration of the temporal dimensionality of the afferent process provides support for the usual interpretation of the inhibition of delay phenomenon. Initially, in a fear-conditioning situation, the afferent process occurring early in the CS–UCS interval should show fear-eliciting properties because of stimulus generalization from the afferent process contiguous with the UCS to which fear becomes conditioned. Since such early responses would be nonreinforced, inhibition would be expected to develop with sufficient training. Therefore, one might expect a CR eventually to occur only in the interval just preceding the UCS. The results of Hendry and Van-Toller (1965) and Millenson and Hendry (1967), described in Section II,A,1,b, are consistent with this reasoning, as are those of Rescorla (1967b, 1968a).

The finding of good delayed conditioning with CS–UCS intervals of several minutes duration may be somewhat surprising in view of the results usually obtained with other classically conditioned responses such as the eyelid response. A moment's reflection should dispel the surprise. Fear can be conditioned to static apparatus cues. Evidence that such is the case has been adduced on several occasions in previous sections of this chapter. Since such conditioning does occur, it would be expected that fear also would be conditioned to a discrete CS of long duration. In fact, the explanatory problem would be to account for any instance in which such conditioning failed to occur.

In the above discussion, attention was focused on temporal arrangements of the stimuli in which the onset of the CS preceded that of the UCS (forward conditioning). Typically, it is not expected that conditioning will occur when a backward arrangement, UCS preceding the CS, is used. There have been, nevertheless, several instances in which fear has ostensibly been conditioned with a backward sequence of stimuli. Specifically, following conditioning in which the termination of the UCS preceded the onset of the CS by 15 or 20 sec, learning of an escape-from-fear response has been reported (Goldstein, 1960; W.R. Mc-Allister & D.E. McAllister, 1962a, 1967). Such learning, however, does not represent true backward conditioning, *i.e.*, conditioning of fear to the discrete CS. Rather, as has been demonstrated by McAllister and McAllister (1962b), the learning is based on fear conditioned to static apparatus cues.

On the other hand, when the termination of the UCS is coincident with the onset of the CS, the results are less clear cut. Mowrer and Aiken (1954) administered such a treatment in one apparatus and then in a different apparatus presented the CS when *S* pressed a bar to obtain a food reward. Since this procedure (conditioned punishment) led to a greater suppression of the bar-pressing response than occurred in a control group, backward conditioning of fear to the CS seems to be indicated. These results are similar to those obtained by Champion and Jones (1961) who found that when shock was administered to human *S*s 750 msec before the onset of a tone, the GSR became conditioned to the tone. They argued that because of its long latency, the GSR would actually occur following the onset of the CS. Thus, the conditioning would be in the usual forward direction. If accepted, the implication is that the empirical variable should be specified as the CS–UCR instead of the CS–UCS interval. Since the fear response appears to have a long latency (Ross, 1961), the same interpretation can be offered for the results of Mowrer and Aiken. The failure of Kamin (1963) to obtain evidence, with a change-in-rate measure, for backward conditioning with this temporal arrangement of stimuli may possibly be attributable to differences in experimental conditions. Kamin used a .5-sec or 1-sec shock and a 3-min CS while Mowrer and Aiken used a 10-sec shock and a 3-sec CS. The purported evidence of backward conditioning reported by Singh (1959) cannot be seriously considered because of technical flaws, several of which have been pointed out by Kamin (1963).

3.   CS Intensity

The most extensive investigation of the effect of CS intensity in fear conditioning has been conducted by Kamin (1965) using as the index of fear the amount of suppression of a food-reinforced bar-pressing response. Increases in the intensity of either a white noise CS or a light CS led to increases in the amount of suppression. This relationship held true

with the auditory CS for both delayed and trace conditioning procedures, although a weak CS, sufficient to suppress performance with delayed conditioning, was ineffective with trace conditioning. The latter
result presumably occurred because the weak stimulus provided a trace
of insufficient strength to bridge the trace interval.

In the usual investigation of the effect of CS intensity there is a confounding between this variable and the concomitant variation in the
magnitude of the stimulus difference between the CS and the background stimuli. Either factor could account for the better performance
obtained with an intense, as compared to a weak, CS. Two studies reported by Kamin bear on this question. In one, the CS was an increase
in the intensity of white noise to 80 dB from background levels of 0, 45,
50, 60, or 70 dB. In the other, the CS was a decrease in the background
level from 80 dB to 0, 45, 50, 60, or 70 dB. Within each study, the
amount of suppression increased with increases in the amount of stimulus change. With the largest stimulus changes, performance did not differ between the increase and decrease procedures. With the smaller
stimulus changes, however, a CS involving an increase in intensity led to
greater suppression than did a CS involving an equal decrease in intensity. Thus, the amount of suppression appears to be affected by both the
magnitude of the stimulus change and the intensity of the stimulus coincident with the UCS. The possible effect of a third factor, the direction
of the stimulus change *per se,* cannot be ruled out on the basis of these
experiments.

4. UCS Intensity

The variation of UCS intensity yields the most consistent results of all
the variables manipulated in the types of studies under consideration.
An increasing monotonic relationship between shock intensity and the
amount of fear conditioned has been obtained in a large number of
studies involving various index responses. Thus, such a relationship has
been observed with an escape-from-fear response (Goldstein, 1960;
Gwinn, 1951; W.R. McAllister & D.E. McAllister, 1962a, 1967; Miller
& Lawrence [cited in Miller, 1951, p. 448]), with a change-in-rate measure (Annau & Kamin, 1961; Hendry & Van-Toller, 1965; James &
Mostoway, 1968; Millenson & Hendry, 1967) and with conditioned punishment (Anderson, Plant, & Paden, 1967; Strouthes & Hamilton, 1964).

These typical findings may be contrasted with the inverse relationship
obtained between intensity of shock and performance in shuttlebox
avoidance learning (*e.g.,* Levine, 1966; Moyer & Korn, 1964). In the face
of the impressive evidence cited above, this latter finding certainly can-

not be attributed to less fear being conditioned with high than with low shock. Most likely the effect is due to an interaction between shock intensity and the shuttle procedure. Possibly the increased fear of apparatus cues occurring with strong shock results in relatively less reinforcement for the shuttle response, despite a greater fear of the CS, than is the case with weaker shock.

5. *Intertrial Interval*

Systematic data pertaining to the effect of the ITI on the conditioning of fear as indexed by the types of measures of concern in this chapter is almost nonexistent. Data provided by Brimer and Dockrill (1966) suggest that conditioning of fear is better with distributed than with massed trials (1 or 2 vs. 4 CS–UCS pairings in a two-hour session). Among the few other relevant studies is that of Stein *et al.* (1958) which varied both the CS–UCS interval and the ITI. During a training session of set duration, in which a bar-pressing response was reinforced with a water reward on a variable-interval schedule, a series of CS-shock pairings was superimposed on the operant behavior. The degree to which the CS suppressed bar pressing was the response measure used. A given session was divided into a fixed proportion of CS-on and CS-off periods, the termination of the CS always being accompanied by a shock. Sessions were continued with a given CS–UCS interval (CS on) and ITI (CS off) until the degree of suppression had stabilized Then, one or both of these temporal variables were changed, and training was again continued until a new stable level of suppression was reached. Each of five Ss received successively a different sequence of treatments. If the stable level of performance obtained with each set of conditions can be assumed not to have been affected by transfer from previous treatments, several within-S evaluations of the effect of the CS–UCS interval and of the ITI are possible. Specifically, with ITI held constant, the following comparisons between CS–UCS intervals can be made: ½ vs. 4, 1 vs. 5, 2 vs. 5, 2 vs. 10, and 2 vs. 5½ vs. 9 min. Similarly, comparisons can be made between the following ITI values with the CS–UCS interval constant: 2 vs. 16, 2 vs. 24, 5 vs. 15, ½ vs. 7 vs. 15, and 28 vs. 50 min. Greater suppression (more fear) was found within each of the several comparisons for the shorter CS–UCS interval and for the longer ITI.

The interpretation offered by Stein *et al.* was that suppression occurred only to the extent that ceasing to respond during the CS did not lead to a marked loss of positive reinforcements. Since each session was of a fixed duration, it is apparent that with ITI also fixed, suppression would result in the loss of more reinforcements with a long, as compared to a short, CS–UCS interval. Also, with a fixed CS–UCS interval, if suppression occurred, more reinforcements would be lost with a short, as compared to a long, ITI. With both variables, the results were consistent with the hypothesis. Carlton and Didamo (1960) tested this interpretation by varying the ITI while holding constant the CS–UCS interval and allowing each experimental session to continue until an equal number of reinforcements was received. They found, as did Stein *et al.*, that the greatest suppression occurred with the longest ITI. Since suppressing during the CS under these conditions could not result in a loss in the total number of reinforcements, they suggested the alternative hypothesis that suppression occurs only when it does not result in a sufficient decline in the reinforcement *rate*.

The foregoing findings are also consistent with the hypothesis that the two variables under consideration have their effect through influencing the amount of classically conditioned fear in the direction which would be expected on the basis of results obtained in other learning situations. Thus, better conditioning should occur with greater distribution of trials and, within the range studied, with the shorter CS–UCS intervals. A complicating factor for any interpretation is that the procedures used in these experiments resulted in large variations in the number of CS-shock trials which were confounded with the manipulated variables. For example, with a constant CS–UCS interval and a fixed length of session, a short ITI inevitably leads to a greater number of conditioning trials than a long ITI. Likewise, with a constant ITI, the number of trials would increase as the CS–UCS interval decreased. This circumstance suggests the possible relevance to these data of the finding that suppression decreases with extended numbers of conditioning trials (*e.g.*, Hendry & Van-Toller, 1965). Thus, it would be predicted that the greater number of conditioning trials occurring with the shorter ITI's would result in less suppression, as obtained. The fact that the alleviation-of-suppression notion is not consistent with the effect of the CS–UCS interval might suggest the overriding importance of this latter variable.

An obvious conclusion to be drawn on the basis of the above discussion is that in this type of study a procedure which separates the conditioning of fear from its measurement, such as that used by Libby (1951), Ayres (1966), and Blackman (1966), is required to ascertain clearly the effects of these variables on the conditioning of fear.

6. Percentage of Reinforcement

Since the conditioning of fear depends upon CS–UCS pairings, it would be expected that better conditioning of fear would occur under continuous than under partial reinforcement. Available data, although sparse, appear to support this generalization.

Geller (1964) using goldfish and Brimer and Dockrill (1966) using rats measured the change in rate of food-reinforced lever pressing as a function of the percentage of reinforcement used in superimposed fear-conditioning trials. In both cases, the development of suppression of lever pressing was faster (indicating more fear) for continuously, as opposed to partially, reinforced Ss. With continued training, suppression was complete regardless of reinforcement conditions in both studies, a finding probably attributable to a ceiling effect on the index response rather than on fear. Using the same response measure in a within-S design, Willis and Lundin (1966) found that, after extended training, the amount of suppression and, hence, of fear, was directly related to the percentage of shock reinforcement (10, 50, and 90%). Wagner *et al.* (1967) reported that with a startle-response measure acquisition of fear was greater following 100% than 50% reinforcement. In this study, because test trials were employed, these percentage values are nominal; both groups were partially reinforced.

B.   Measurement Variables

1.   Retention Interval

To avoid ambiguity, it is essential that the retention of fear not be confounded with the retention of the response used to index fear, a state of affairs which can occur when the index response is learned prior to the retention interval. For example, when fear is acquired in an escape or avoidance learning task, the retention interval could have its effect on fear, on the index response, or on both.[14] Relatively few studies circumvent this problem. Of these, the reported results have ranged from an increase of fear over time (incubation), to perfect retention, to a loss of fear.

The data relating to incubation have been reviewed recently (D.E. McAllister & W.R. McAllister, 1967), and the conclusion was drawn that the phenomenon has not yet been convincingly demonstrated. Near perfect retention of fear has been reported up to 42 days in adult rats with a conditioned punishment measure (Campbell & Campbell, 1962,

[14]A similar objection might be leveled against using the change in rate of a positively reinforced response as a measure of fear since normally the index response (*e.g.*, bar pressing) is learned prior to the retention interval. However, with this measure no problem exists if the operant baseline rate does not change over time or if it is retrained to its original level before the retention test. If baseline responding changes equally over various retention intervals, the *relative* retention of fear may be adequately indexed.

Experiment 1), for several years in pigeons with a change-in-rate measure involving a key-pecking response both to a CS and to generalized stimuli (Hoffman, Selekman, & Fleshler, 1966a), for 90 days with a change-in-rate measure using an appetitively reinforced bar-pressing response in adult rats (Gleitman & Holmes, 1967), and up to 24 hr in adult rats with an escape-from-fear measure (Desiderato et al., 1966; McAllister & McAllister, 1963). With the latter measure, however, a loss of fear has been obtained with a 47-hr retention interval (McAllister & McAllister, 1968), which is in sharp contrast with the findings obtained with the other measures. In this latter study, four groups of Ss received fear-conditioning trials with a tone CS followed after either 23 or 47 hr by hurdle-jumping training. Within each delay condition one group was trained with the CS and the other without it (NCS). The pattern of results allows an interpretation which offers some reconciliation with the other findings. It was found that the magnitude of the loss of fear between the 23-hr and 47-hr CS groups was approximately the same as that between the two NCS groups. Since the latter loss can represent only forgetting of fear of apparatus cues, it is reasonable to attribute the loss in the CS groups to the same source. Possibly this loss may be due to the extinction of fear of the grid box resulting from some similarity between it and the home cage. Accepting the above argument allows the assumption that forgetting of fear of the CS did not occur and eliminates the apparent discrepancy with the results of Hoffman et al. and Gleitman and Holmes who used measures unlikely to be affected by fear of apparatus cues. However, a problem remains in reconciling the results with those of the Campbell and Campbell study where performance was based only on this source of fear. One possible solution is to attribute the discrepancy in results to differences in sensitivity of the response measures. That is, little fear may be required to inhibit completely the approach response used by Campbell and Campbell and, thus, a loss of fear if it occurred may not have been measured. On the other hand, a hurdle-jumping, escape-from-fear response may be sensitive to small losses of fear. The solution may lie elsewhere, however, since Campbell and Campbell (Experiment 3) have reported that when 24 hr intervene between two 30-min test sessions, a loss of fear occurred. Therefore, their report of perfect retention up to 42 days based on a 1-hr test period is called into question. If the performance loss between the two 30-min periods is the result of extinction of fear occurring in the first 30 min, a similar extinction effect would be expected to have been measured during the final half of the 1-hr period. Alternatively, if some variable associated with the placement in the home cage between the two 30-min sessions was responsible for the loss of fear, it would be expected that the delay groups of Experiment 1 would have been similarly affected. A resolution of the inconsistency found with the Campbell and Campbell measure is obviously needed before meaningful comparisons with other indexes of fear can be made.

2. *Stimulus Similarity*

Performance of a positively reinforced response has been shown to be suppressed, not only by a CS previously paired with shock, but also to a lesser extent by similar (generalized) stimuli. The amount of suppression, reflecting the amount of fear elicited, has been found in pigeons (Hoffman & Fleshler, 1961) and in rats (Desiderato, 1964b) to be directly related to the degree of similarity between the original CS and the generalized stimulus. A stimulus generalization gradient has also been reported with a hurdle-jumping, escape-from-fear measure (Desiderato, 1964a) and with a conditioned-punishment measure (Rohrbaugh & Riccio, 1968). Other data have indicated that in pigeons fear of generalized stimuli summates (Hoffman, Selekman, & Fleshler, 1966b).

Generalization gradients have been reported in several differential conditioning studies using the change in rate of a positively reinforced response as the index of fear in pigeons (Hoffman & Fleshler, 1964) and in rats (Ray & Stein, 1959; Winograd, 1965). An evaluation of such data must, of course, consider the generalization both of fear resulting from CS-shock pairings and of inhibition of fear resulting from failure to reinforce the response to the negative stimulus. Evidence for the generalization of the inhibition of fear is presented in Section III,C.

In the previous studies, the temporal interval between the conditioning of fear and the test for generalization was not manipulated. This variable has, however, been shown by both Desiderato *et al.* (1966) and McAllister and McAllister (1963,1965) to determine importantly whether fear will be elicited by generalized stimuli. The data from these studies, along with those from other experiments which also used hurdle jumping as the index of fear, are summarized in Figure 2. In preparing this figure, all available data were gathered in which a group tested with a 23–24-hr postconditioning delay (PCD) could be compared to at least one other group treated identically except for the PCD. To eliminate differences in levels of performance between experiments due to different values at which other variables had been held constant, the performance of each 23–24-hr group was used as a base. That is, the mean performance of this latter group was subtracted from the mean performance of the group(s) with which it could be legitimately compared. In each case the measure of performance was the mean speed of hurdle jumping over the

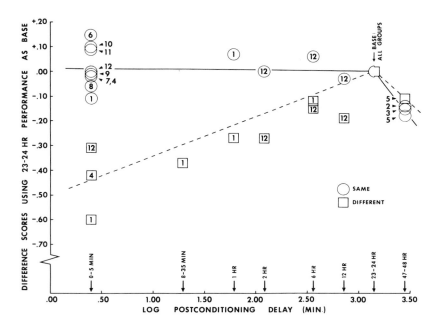

Fig. 2. Difference scores obtained by subtracting performance (mean speed of hurdle jumping over 25 trials) of 23–24-hr postconditioning delay base groups from performance of groups tested at shorter or longer delays under same or different stimulus conditions.

first 25 trials. The resulting difference scores are plotted in the figure as a function of minutes of PCD transformed to log units. A zero value for a comparison group indicates that its performance was equal to that of its base group. Negative and positive values represent speeds of hurdle jumping slower or faster, respectively, than that of the base group. In the figure, each circle represents a difference score obtained from groups given conditioning and hurdle jumping in the same stimulus situation. Each square represents a difference score obtained from groups conditioned in one stimulus situation and given hurdle training in a different, but similar, stimulus situation. The choice of the 23–24-hr group as a base for comparison with other PCD groups was dictated by the fact that at this PCD no significant difference in performance was ever found within an experiment between the same and different stimulus conditions. Points labeled with the same number at different PCD intervals within the same or the different treatment represent comparisons with the same base value. When the same number is employed for both treatments, it indicates that these data were obtained in the same experiment.[15] The lines drawn in the figure join the 23–24-hr base with the mean of the difference scores obtained with the 0–5-min and the 47–48-hr PCD for the same (solid line) and the different (dashed line) treatments.

It is clear that, when conditioning and hurdle jumping take place under the same stimulus conditions, performance does not change with PCD intervals up to 24 hr. Apparently, the amount of fear available to motivate and reinforce hurdle jumping does not vary over this temporal range. On the other hand, when the stimulus situation differs between the two phases of the experiment, there is a marked stimulus generalization decrement immediately after conditioning, indicating that the amount of fear present is small. The tendency for performance to increase progressively with PCD up to 24 hr suggests a corresponding increase in the amount of generalized fear. Beyond 24 hr, regardless of the stimulus condition, hurdle-jumping performance decreases, indicating a loss of fear. As discussed in Section II,B,1, this loss may be attributed to a forgetting of the fear conditioned to the apparatus cues rather than that conditioned to the CS.

The generality of the relationship between stimulus similarity and PCD illustrated in Figure 2 is attested to by the correspondence in results of the studies labeled 1, 4, and 12. In these studies the same results were obtained despite the fact that three different hurdle-jumping apparatuses were employed, and the data were collected independently in two different laboratories using rats which differed with respect to sex and strain.

The increase with PCD in the amount of fear elicited by generalized stimuli requires explanation. An account in terms of the incubation of fear is clearly contraindicated by the data presented in Figure 2. If fear simply increases spontaneously over time, it would be expected that performance under the same condition would have shown an increase similar to that found under the different condition. Obviously, such was not the case. Any plausible interpretation must take into account the interaction between PCD and the similarity condition. One hypothesis (McAllister & McAllister, 1963, 1965) assumes that Ss are responding to a psychophysical dimension along which lie the conditioning and hurdle-jumping situations. Assume

---

[15]An exception is that, for those points designated 1, data collected in separate, procedurally identical experiments were combined. Data for the fifth trial block of the different stimulus condition for these combined experiments have been published (McAllister & McAllister, 1965, p. 180). The data labeled 1 for the same stimulus condition, combined for Figure 2, have been reported separately (McAllister & McAllister, 1965, pp. 176, 182). Other published data are those indicated by numbers 2 and 3 (McAllister & McAllister, 1968) and by number 12 (Desiderato et al., 1966). All other data were obtained from unpublished studies conducted in this laboratory. Group means are based on 8 Ss for the points labeled 12; the number of Ss ranges from 15 to 48 for the other points.

that this dimension can be scaled by comparing the conditioning stimulus situation with the other stimuli along the dimension. If such a scaling procedure utilized different temporal intervals between exposures to the two stimulus situations compared, a difference in the number of jnd's might be expected. Presumably, a larger number of jnd's would be obtained with a short delay between exposures than with longer delays. As applied to the data under discussion, the number of jnd's separating the conditioning and hurdle-jumping situations would be large with a short, and small with a long, retention interval. Thus, little stimulus generalization of fear would occur immediately following conditioning and, consequently, hurdle-jumping performance would be poor. The decrease in the number of jnd's with longer delays would lead to greater generalization of fear and increasingly better hurdle jumping. Some independent supporting evidence for this hypothesis, obtained with human Ss, has been reported (McAllister, McAllister, & Franchina, 1965).

The specification of the dimension (or dimensions) defining the same-different variable in Figure 2 differs among the experiments since the stimulus conditions were not manipulated in the same manner in all instances. In the experiment designated 12 in the figure (Desiderato et al., 1966), the brightness of the grid box was varied between conditioning and hurdle jumping. The Ss were administered light-shock pairings in a grid box with white walls and were subsequently given hurdle training with the light CS presented in this box (same stimulus condition) or in the same box with black walls (different stimulus condition). The data indicated by 1 were obtained when different, but similar, apparatuses were used for conditioning and hurdle jumping. In this case it was hypothesized that some differences in the interior cues between the conditioning box and the start box of the hurdle apparatus led to the generalization effect (McAllister & McAllister, 1963). Such stimulus differences within the apparatus cannot be readily invoked to account for the data obtained in the experiment designated 4. Although in this instance different apparatuses were used for conditioning and hurdle jumping, the construction of the boxes was such that the interior differences were negligible. In this situation evidence has been presented indicating that visual and auditory extra-apparatus cues provide at least a partial basis for the stimulus generalization decrement (McAllister & McAllister, 1966). Other evidence demonstrating that the presence or absence of visual extra-apparatus cues can interact with PCD to affect hurdle-jumping performance differentially has been published (McAllister & McAllister, 1965, pp. 183–186). In sum, it appears that the generalization effect is based on the utilization by S of whatever cues are available to permit a discrimination between the conditioning and the hurdle-jumping situations.[16]

3. Amount and Percentage of Reinforcement

On the assumption that reinforcement (or reward) variables in appetitive and aversive learning situations operate in the same manner, it would be expected that the learning of an instrumental response leading to an escape from fear would depend on the amount of reinforcement (fear reduction). An attempt to study this variable by conditioning different amounts of fear and permitting escape to a fear-free environment, although allowing a variation in the amount of reinforcement, would unfortunately confound that variable with the strength of drive (fear). A satisfactory procedure must hold fear constant while allowing changes in the amount of fear reduction. One such method would be to manipulate the degree to which the fear-eliciting stimuli, i.e., the discrete CS or apparatus cues, are changed following an escape-from-fear response. For instance, in a hurdle-jumping situation after fear is conditioned in a white box, Ss could be trained to jump a hurdle either to a white or to a gray safe box. The greater fear reduction occurring with a gray safe box should lead to better performance. Unpublished data from this laboratory support this prediction. Similar results obtained with analogous procedures in avoidance conditioning tasks have been reported (Bower, Starr, & Lazarovitz, 1965; Knapp, 1965).

Another method of manipulating the amount of reinforcement is based on the finding that fear is elicited by novel stimuli (e.g., McAllister et al., 1966). Thus, a safe box of a hurdle-jumping apparatus which had not been explored prior to hurdle training would, presumably, elicit more fear than one which had been explored. Therefore, with the amount of fear conditioning in the start box held constant, greater reinforcement (fear reduction) and, hence, better performance of a hurdle-jumping response would be expected when the safe box is familiar than when it is novel. This reasoning has been tested at four different levels of fear (W.R. McAllister & D.E. McAllister, 1967). At each of the two highest levels, the results were consistent with expectations; better performance was obtained with high than with low reward. At the lowest level of fear, no learning occurred under either reward condition indicating that insufficient fear was present to serve as a basis for learning. However, at a somewhat higher level of fear, learning did occur when

[16]Editor's note: Additional discussion of this problem can be found in Chapter 7 by Brush.

the safe box was familiar (high reward), but not when it was novel (low reward). The fact that equal fear was conditioned in both of these latter groups, but was indexed only when the reward condition was appropriate, points up the importance for the measurement of fear of having adequate knowledge of the relevant variables in the measuring situation.

A more complete understanding of the effect of reinforcement variables on instrumental behavior motivated by fear would be provided by investigations of shifts in reward and of percentage of reward. Data pertaining to the manipulation of the former variable do not seem to be available in the literature, but one study (unpublished) conducted in this laboratory involving the latter variable may be mentioned. Two groups of Ss were administered 35 light-shock pairings in a white grid box and on the next day were given 40 hurdle-jumping trials in the absence of shock. During the first 20 hurdle-jumping trials, the percentage of reinforcement differed between the groups. One group was. reinforced on each trial (100%) while the other received reinforcement on a random half of the trials (50%). In this case, the reinforcement consisted of the reduction of fear which occurred with the escape from the white grid box with the CS to an identical safe box without the CS. On a nonreinforced trial the CS was also presented in the "safe" box following the hurdle-jumping response, thus preventing fear reduction. The effect of this difference in treatment on the acquisition of the instrumental response is shown in Figure 3 by the performance on trial blocks 1-4. Speed of hurdle jumping was significantly faster in the 100% than in the

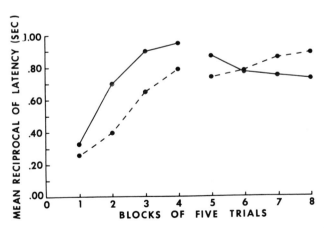

Fig. 3. Speed of hurdle jumping during acquisition with continuous (100%; solid line) or partial (50%; dashed line) reinforcement (trial blocks 1-4) and during extinction (trial blocks 5-8).

50% group. For both groups the last 20 hurdle-jumping trials were non-reinforced. On these extinction trials, shown in Figure 3 as trial blocks 5–8, a significant interaction was obtained. The performance of the 100% group declined with the introduction of continuous nonreinforcement, while that of the 50% group was maintained. This demonstration of the PRE with instrumental behavior based on fear is explicable in terms of the incentive theory described in Section I,C, on pp. 130–132.

4. Special Issues with the Change-in-Rate Measure

It can be assumed that the degree to which a fear-eliciting CS suppresses the performance of an ongoing positively reinforced response depends both on the strength of the ongoing behavior and on the strength of fear. A strong tendency to bar press or key peck for a food reinforcement would be less affected (suppressed) by the competing behavior (crouching or freezing) elicited by fear than would a weak tendency. Therefore, with fear conditioning held constant, any variable which affects the strength of ongoing behavior could be expected to affect, in turn, the amount of suppression. Data supporting this contention are available. Geller (1960) has reported results which show that less suppression occurred during both the acquisition and extinction of fear with a stronger operant response (based on food deprivation and milk reinforcement) than with a weaker one (based on water deprivation and water reinforcement). Similarly, Hoffman and Fleshler (1961) presented data suggesting that fear elicited by generalized stimuli suppressed key pecking in pigeons less when the motivation (defined in terms of body weight loss) for a food reward was high than when it was low. In addition, Vogel and Spear (1966) found that suppression of drinking during presentation of a CS previously paired with shock was less with a 32% sucrose solution (high reward) than with a 4% solution (low reward).

Another way of varying strength of the operant response is through the manipulation of the schedule of reinforcement. Brady (1955) first trained his Ss to lever press for water reinforcement and then presented CS-shock pairings during the operant training. Performance during this initial training was used to obtain six groups of Ss matched both for strength of lever pressing and for amount of fear conditioning. Subsequently, a different schedule of water reinforcement was administered to each group over a period of 60 days with neither the CS nor shock being presented. Three types of ratio schedules, two types of interval schedules, and one continuous schedule were employed. Each group developed stable performance consistent with its reinforcement schedule, the ratio groups showing faster response rates than the interval groups. The effect of the CS on performance under each of the six schedules was then evaluated by presenting the CS without shock once daily for 11 days. Complete suppression of the lever-pressing response occurred in all groups during the first CS presentation. Thereafter, the amount of suppression decreased rapidly for the three ratio-schedule groups, and much more slowly for the remaining three groups. By the eleventh test trial, performance of all of the groups was similar; none showed appreciable suppression.

Brady interpreted these results to indicate that the rate of extinction of fear depends upon the schedule of reinforcement for the lever-pressing response. Such an account of the results is plausible if a counterconditioning theory of extinction is adopted. Thus, the stronger the lever-pressing tendency, the more likely that a reinforced lever-pressing response would occur when the CS was presented during the fear-extinction trials and the greater the opportunity for the counterconditioning of fear. An explanation of this sort seems required if fear is defined in terms of the response measure (amount of suppression). Defining fear in terms of antecedent conditions allows, however, an alternate interpretation in which it is assumed that the extinction of fear depends only on the number of nonreinforced CS presentations. On this basis, extinction of fear should occur equally in all groups. The more rapid loss of suppression in the ratio groups, as compared with the other groups, would be accounted for simply as the result of their stronger lever-pressing response competing more successfully with the fear-elicited crouching response as fear extinguished.

A study by Lyon (1963) showing that the amount of suppression of a key-pecking response in pigeons varied with the reinforcement schedule for the operant response is consistent with this latter interpretation. During both the acquisition and the extinction of fear, less conditioned suppression was obtained with a VI-1 min schedule than with a VI-4 min schedule. The two schedules were presented in an alternating sequence for 10 min each. Since the CS paired with shock was the same under the two schedules and a within-S design was used, it is reasonable to assume equal fear under the two schedules. Thus, the data may be interpreted as resulting from the stronger response tendency associated with the VI-1 min schedule competing more successfully with the fear-elicited responses than the weaker response tendency of the VI-4 min schedule.

In both the Brady and the Lyon studies, the stronger response tendency (inferred from the greater rate of responding), which led to less suppression, may be attributed to a differential frequency of reinforcement. However, both Lyon (1965) and Blackman (1966) have proposed that response rate itself might affect suppression even if reinforcement were held constant. To test this proposition experimentally, Lyon trained three pigeons on a multiple VI-3 FR-50 schedule and presented CS-shock pairings during the VI phase. Subsequently, the rate of responding during the VI component was successively increased through changing the FR phase first to a FR-75 and then to a FR-100 schedule (behavioral contrast). Despite the increased response rate during VI performance, no change was observed in the amount of suppression; the suppression was complete in each instance. Lyon's interpretation was that the amount of conditioned suppression does not depend on the baseline response rate. Blackman (1966) contended, however, that a ceiling effect may have been responsible for Lyon's failure to obtain differences in suppression. He found, in two studies which used yoking procedures to vary the baseline while controlling the frequency of reinforcement, that the amount of conditioned suppression was greater for a high, than for a low, baseline response rate. Further corroboration of this finding was obtained using a pacing procedure (Blackman, 1967a). Although it appears that the controversy about this series of studies has yet to be settled by the participants (Blackman, 1967b; Lyon, 1967), an attempt at a reconciliation of the disparate findings will be made here. It is suggested that the critical determinant of the relationship between the two dependent variables, rate of responding and degree of response suppression, is the technique used to manipulate the operant rate since fear conditioning (CS–UCS pairings) is held constant in these studies. When increases in frequency of reinforcement lead to increases in operant response rate, it may be assumed that a high rate represents a stronger response tendency than does a low rate. It would then be expected that a lesser amount of suppression would occur with a high, than with a low, rate, since the stronger operant response would compete more effectively with the fear-elicited responses. On the other hand, when frequency of reinforcement is controlled and response rate is manipulated by other techniques (behavioral contrast, yoking, or pacing), there may be no necessary relationship between the strength of the operant response tendency and the rate of responding. For example, when a slow rate of response is shaped by the reinforcement contingency, it does not necessarily mean that the tendency to make that response is weaker than when a fast rate of response is similarly shaped (Blackman, 1967a). In fact, since the slower response rate is associated with a greater *relative* frequency of reinforcement (fewer responses required per reinforcement) than the fast rate, it might be reasonable to assume a stronger tendency to make the response in the former case. On this basis, less suppression would be predicted with the slow baseline response rate. Thus, Blackman's data are not inconsistent with the competition-of-response interpretation of conditioned suppression.

Another measurement problem associated with schedules of positive reinforcement has been pointed up by the results obtained by Lyon (1964) and Lyon and Felton (1966). These studies indicated that when a key-pecking response by pigeons was reinforced on a FR-100, FR-150, or FR-200 schedule, the extent of suppression of this behavior occurring with the presentation of a fear-eliciting CS depended on the point in the chain of responses at which the CS was introduced. In the early stages of the FR run, presentation of the CS led to suppression of key pecking. When the CS was presented in the later stages of the FR run, key pecking continued during the CS until the reinforcement was received, and then suppression occurred. This pattern of responding was not always found with a FR-50 schedule, S sometimes continuing to respond following the reinforcement. In the case of a FR-25 schedule little suppression occurred regardless of when the CS was presented, and S typically continued responding following a reinforcement. One explanation of these findings is based on the fact that there is a tendency, when long FR schedules are employed, for a cessation of operant responding to occur after a reinforcement. It can be assumed that the tendency to make the operant response is weak at this point and, therefore, it does not compete successfully with the fear-elicited responses, while the stronger operant response tendency, which develops as the number of preceding responses in the chain increases, offers more competition. Since, with short FR schedules, operant responding tends to continue after a reinforcement, it may be assumed that response strength can be sufficient throughout a short ratio run to compete successfully. Resulting variations in the amount of observed suppression with the different FR schedules and at various points within a ratio run are, therefore, consistent with the competing-response interpretation of suppression. Another explanation of these findings is based on the goal gradient hypothesis (Kimble, 1961, pp. 140 ff.) which assumes an increasing strength of response with nearness in time or space to reinforcement. In fact, this hypothesis can be considered to provide the mechanism underlying the previous interpretation. These considerations clearly indicate that if the effect of fear-conditioning variables is to be indexed with a change-in-rate measure employing a FR schedule, careful control of the locus of introduction of the CS in the ratio run must be exercised.

In the research discussed so far in this section, consideration has been directed to the manner in which the index of fear (suppression) was affected by changes in the baseline rate of the ongoing response due to variations in motivation, reward, and type and schedule of reinforcement. It is important to note, however, that the procedure for conditioning fear, which is then to be evaluated by baseline rate changes, itself alters the rate of responding. That is, the introduction of shock as the

UCS in fear conditioning decreases the baseline rate (*e.g.*, Annau & Kamin, 1961; Hammond, 1966; Hendry & Van-Toller, 1965; Hunt & Brady, 1955; Tapp, 1964), presumably as a result of the elicitation of competing responses by fear conditioned to the situational or apparatus cues. The amount of this fear could be measured by comparing the suppressed baseline performance to a stable baseline performance obtained prior to the introduction of shock. Usually, however, the interest is in the suppression which occurs in the presence of the discrete CS, which is measured by obtaining a ratio of the rate of responding during the CS and the rate occurring in a comparable interval just prior to the presentation of the CS. Since the comparison baseline rate is itself affected by fear, the use of a suppression ratio, while serving as an index of the fear conditioned to the discrete CS, does not normally serve as a measure of the total amount of fear present in the situation. Data provided by Brimer and Kamin (1963) indicate the importance of considering fear of apparatus cues when using the change-in-rate measure to index fear of the CS. Several groups of rats were first trained to bar press for food reinforcement on a VI-2.5 min schedule. Over the next several days a series of shock presentations, which differed for the groups in the pattern of shock intensities, was superimposed on the operant behavior. It was found that the shock-alone presentations depressed the operant barpressing rate, the effect being directly related to the intensity of shock. On subsequent days, CS-shock pairings were introduced during the barpressing sessions. At the outset of these sessions, the groups with the lower operant rates of responding showed, during the CS, an increased rate of bar pressing as compared to their baseline rate. This enhancement tended to be directly related to the degree of depression of the baseline. With continued CS-shock pairings, the usual suppression of bar pressing to the CS developed. Since low baseline rates in and of themselves do not result in enhanced (supernormal) responding during the CS (*e.g.*, Leaf & Muller, 1964) some other explanation is required. A reasonable interpretation is that the CS served as an external inhibitor of the fear classically conditioned to the apparatus cues (or produced a stimulus generalization decrement) and, hence, allowed for the increase in operant responding which continued until fear became conditioned to the CS.

It follows that the presentation of an external inhibitor would produce supernormal responding only after fear of the apparatus cues had been conditioned. Evidence supporting this contention is provided by Hammond (1966). Only after baseline performance of a bar-pressing response had been depressed by tone-shock pairings did the presentation of a light result in supernormal responding. Furthermore, as the bar-pressing baseline rate recovered, indicating extinction of fear of the apparatus cues, performance ceased to be enhanced during presentation of the light. In addition, Kamin (1963) has reported that presentation of a CS paired in a backward order with shock did not elicit fear but rather resulted in an enhanced rate of bar pressing. This effect occurred, however, only after the administration of several shocks which presumably conditioned fear to the apparatus cues.

On the basis of this analysis, it would be expected that the operation of a stimulus as an external inhibitor would be prevented by extinction of fear of the apparatus cues. The third experiment of Brimer and Kamin (1963) provides relevant data. Following shock-alone presentations, which again markedly depressed baseline performance, two different extinction-of-fear procedures were introduced, neither of which involved CS or shock presentations. For one group the treatment consisted of five additional bar-pressing sessions. For the second group, it involved placing S in the apparatus with the bar and food cup blocked off with a false wall. Complete recovery of baseline performance occurred in the bar-pressing group, which would be expected if the procedure led to the development of inhibition or to the counterconditioning of fear of the apparatus cues. In the other group, baseline performance showed only a partial recovery, indicating incomplete extinction of fear, which is in keeping with exposure of this group to a generalized stimulus situation. After the extinction procedures, presentation of a white noise (external inhibitor) increased the rate of bar pressing relative to the baseline rate only in the group in which some fear of the apparatus cues still remained. Corroborating data are provided by Ayres (1966). He interpolated a baseline recovery period (bar pressing in the absence of shock) between CS-shock pairings and the test for conditioned suppression. Presentation of an extraneous stimulus during the test phase did not result in supernormal responding.

The above discussion indicates the important role that fear of apparatus cues can play when fear is indexed with a change-in-rate measure. Several techniques are available which can eliminate the possible confounding of this source of fear if such is desired. Basically, these procedures involve the administration of the CS–UCS pairings either outside of the experimental situation or prior to extended operant recovery training (free of CS or shock presentations) sufficient to insure extinction of fear of the apparatus cues. If the subsequent test for fear of the CS uses an extinction procedure (CS-alone presentations), further conditioning of fear to the apparatus cues could not occur (*e.g.*, Ayres, 1966; Blackman, 1966; Brady, 1955; Libby, 1951).

III. EXTINCTION PHENOMENA

Empirically, extinction refers to a decrement in a learned response resulting from the continued presentation of the eliciting stimulus in the absence of reinforcement. Fear, as a classically conditioned response, would be expected to extinguish in the same manner as other responses. Various theories proposed to account for extinction have been discussed and compared by Kimble (1961, pp. 281–327). These theories can be classified according to whether the basic process involved is assumed to be one of inhibition, of counterconditioning (interference), or their combination. As applied to fear, inhibition theory would hold that extinction procedures result in the development of an inhibitory state which would progressively diminish the occurrence of the conditioned fear response. On the other hand, counterconditioning theory would hold that the extinction procedure allows the opportunity for the learning of an antagonistic, competing response which would come to replace the conditioned fear response. This competing response could be one of relaxing or resting (e.g., Denny & Weisman, 1964; Hull, 1943, pp. 281–284; Miller, 1951, pp. 451–452). Usually there is no basis for selecting one of these alternative explanations over the other.

The necessity for measuring fear indirectly requires that, in studying its extinction, caution be exercised in attributing differences in an index response to differences in fear. That is, it is important to insure that the correlation between fear and its index response is maintained during extinction. When it is not, a problem of interpretation arises, which can be illustrated with an experiment by Page (1955). Following the conditioning of a one-way locomotor avoidance response, a control group was given extinction training involving only the omission of shock. The experimental group received, prior to the same extinction training, five trials in which the locomotor response was blocked. Faster extinction of the avoidance response occurred in the experimental group. In a second part of the experiment, food was placed in the shock compartment, and the Ss, now hungry, were allowed to enter it from the safe box. It was found that the experimental group showed longer latencies than the control group in approaching the food, suggesting greater fear of the grid box. Thus, extinction of the avoidance response occurred faster in the group which by the second measure actually had more fear. Apparently, avoidance performance during extinction did not accurately index fear. The explanation offered by Page was that during the blocked trials an instrumental response antagonistic to the avoidance response was learned and facilitated extinction. That is, the avoidance response, and not fear, was counterconditioned. The possibility of such antagonistic responses being learned would seem to be maximal when the conditioning of fear takes place during avoidance learning or escape-from-shock learning and when extinction involves the blocking of the already learned instrumental response. The use of procedures in which the conditioning and extinction of fear occur prior to the opportunity to perform the index response might eliminate or minimize such learning and provide a more unambiguous method of studying the extinction of fear. One such example is the experiment of Kalish (1954) in which an escape-from-fear measure was employed. Even in this case, however, the possibility should be given careful consideration that the learning of responses antagonistic to the index response plays a role.

The remainder of this section will be devoted to a discussion of selected variables related to the extinction of fear: the number of nonreinforced trials, the percentage of reinforcement during the conditioning of fear, and the generalization of extinction effects.

A.   Number of Nonreinforced Trials

An evaluation of the effect of the number of extinction trials cannot be clearly made in a situation in which S's behavior determines the amount of exposure to the CS. For example, with the escape-from-fear measure the speed with which the instrumental escape response is made on a given trial will determine the duration of exposure to the fear-eliciting stimuli and, hence, the amount of extinction. This problem was handled by Kalish (1954) and Murfin (1954) through the use of a between-Ss design in which the conditioning of fear and the subsequent manipulation of the amount of extinction occurred prior to measuring fear with the learning of a hurdle-jumping response. The extinction procedure differed between these two studies. Kalish administered either 0, 3, 9, or 27 extinction trials in which the CS was presented alone for 5 sec. In Murfin's experiment, five extinction trials were given to all Ss, but the duration of the CS was varied, being either 1.5, 6, or 501 sec. The results in both cases indicated that the amount of extinction increased with the degree of exposure to the CS.

Two other investigations using an escape-from-fear response studied the extinction of fear of the apparatus cues rather than of the discrete CS (McAllister & McAllister, 1962b, Experiment 2; Nelson, 1966, Experiment 1). In both cases, fear conditioning was followed by a period of exposure to the apparatus cues in the absence of shock. As expected, this procedure led to the extinction of fear; learning to escape from the grid box to a safe box was slower than in a nonextinguished group. Brimer and Kamin (1963, Experiment 3) with a change-in-rate measure have also demonstrated that fear of the apparatus cues extinguishes with either of two types of exposure to these cues in the absence of shock. (See Section II,B,4, p. 158.) Nelson also varied the extinction treatment by including a group which was allowed to eat during the exposure period. This group showed more extinction of fear than the nonextinguished group but less than the group merely exposed to the apparatus cues in the absence of food. Nelson concluded that eating in a fear-evoking situation does not countercondition fear as has been widely held. Rather, according to his argument, extinction of fear occurs simply as a result of exposure to the fear-arousing stimuli. The food group showed less extinction of fear, as indicated by faster escape behavior, than the no-food group, presumably because eating reduced the amount of exposure to the feared cues. However, an alternative explanation may be offered. The difference in escape speed between the groups may not have been due to a difference in fear but instead to a difference in frustration because food was removed from the apparatus prior to the escape training. Evidence that this type of instrumental learning can be based upon frustration is presented in Section IV, pp. 165–167. The other studies of Nelson, used as support for his exposure hypothesis (Nelson, 1966, Experiment 2; 1967), involved the conditioning of fear during the learning of an escape-from-shock response and the use of blocking during extinction for some of the groups. As indicated above in the discussion of the Page study, such procedures may confuse the extinction of fear with the extinction of the escape response. In addition, in one of the experiments (Nelson, 1966, Experiment 2) the presence during extinction, for some of the groups, of an empty food cup from which Ss had been accustomed to eat, and the absence of the cup for all of the groups during the test phase, could have introduced differential amounts of frustration. Therefore, the interpretation of the obtained differences as due solely to the extinction of fear is probably unwarranted.

With measures of fear in which S's behavior does not affect the length of his exposure to the CS, the progress of the extinction of fear resulting from nonreinforcement can be evaluated with the use of a within-S design. The expected change in the index response with continued nonreinforced trials, reflecting the extinction of fear, has been demonstrated with a startle-response measure (Brown et al., 1951) and with a change-in-rate measure for generalized stimuli (e.g., Desiderato, 1964b; Hoffman et al., 1966a) as well as for a CS (e.g., Annau & Kamin, 1961; Ayres, 1966; Blackman, 1966; Brady, 1955; Lyon, 1963). Extinction has also been reported, with a change-in-rate measure, to increase progressively as the CS is extended beyond its usual length for some arbitrary duration (Estes & Skinner, 1941; Libby, 1951).

The general conclusion which can be drawn from the studies cited here is that fear does extinguish with nonreinforcements and that sometimes it does so in a relatively few number of trials. However, as pointed out above with respect to the Page study, because of the indirect measurement of fear, caution must be exercised before concluding on the basis of the performance of the index response that fear is completely extinguished. An illustration of the same point is provided by the analysis in Section II,B,4, pp. 153–154, of the extinction data of Brady (1955).

It should be noted that the spontaneous recovery of conditioned fear has been observed (Brown *et al.*, 1951; Estes & Skinner, 1941) as well as the spontaneous recovery of fear of novel stimuli (W.R. McAllister & D.E. McAllister, 1967).

B. Percentage of Reinforcement

Contradictory results have been obtained in investigations of the effect of percentage of reinforcement during classical fear conditioning on the resistance of fear to extinction. Geller (1964) has reported a failure to obtain the PRE (slower extinction following partial than continuous reinforcement) using as the index of fear the change in rate of bar pressing in goldfish. In fact, he found that the partial group showed faster extinction than the continuous group. Wagner *et al.* (1967) found no PRE in rats using the amplitude of the startle response as a measure of fear. Neither did they find a PRE with a change-in-rate (bar pressing) measure when the usual procedure was altered so that bar pressing was prevented during the fear-conditioning sessions (except for the final one) by the insertion of a Plexiglas shield in front of the bar and food cup. However, they did obtain the PRE when the traditional procedure of administering fear-conditioning trials during bar pressing was employed. This result is consistent with that of Brimer and Dockrill (1966) and of the unpublished studies reported by Geller (1964). Taken together, these results could be interpreted to indicate, as suggested by Wagner *et al.*, that the PRE is not a phenomenon associated with classical fear conditioning. Rather, in the instances in which the PRE has been reported with a change-in-rate measure, it may be attributed to some aspect of the instrumental training involved in the measurement of fear. This account is, however, called into question by data presented by Hilton (1969) who measured the PRE with a change-in-rate measure following classical fear conditioning administered in the traditional manner (bar-in) as well as with the separate procedure in which the bar was removed during the fear-conditioning sessions (bar-out). Within each of these procedures, the CS–UCS interval was manipulated, being either 30 sec or 3 min. Using a trials-to-extinction measure, the PRE was obtained under all conditions except the 3-min condition with the bar in, where the means for the partial- and continuous-reinforcement groups were very similar. The failure to find the PRE in this instance is contrary to the findings reported by Brimer and Dockrill and by Geller (unpublished data) who employed similar conditions. Hilton's 30-sec groups may be compared to those of Wagner *et al.*, who also used this CS–UCS interval. The studies agree in finding a PRE with the bar-in condition but disagree with respect to findings with the bar-out condition where the PRE was obtained by Hilton but not by Wagner *et al.* A reconciliation of these disparate findings may result from investigations of the relevance of the many procedural differences between the studies (*e.g.*, equated trials versus equated reinforcements, amount of operant training, schedule of positive reinforcement, number and spacing of fear-conditioning trials, intensity of shock).

C. Generalization of Extinction Effects

A study by Porter (1958) provides evidence that the effects of the extinction of fear generalize. He administered, in a grid box, 30 fear-conditioning trials with a forward sequence of stimuli (FC) to four groups of rats. The onset of a 5-sec CS of 116.4 fc was followed after 4 sec by a 1-sec shock. For another group the stimuli were presented in a backward order (BC) in which the shock was followed after 15 sec by the CS. On the next day all five groups were returned to the grid box for 62 min during which time 20 extinction trials (shock omitted) were given to three of the FC groups. Extinction consisted of the presentation of the original CS to one of the groups and of a generalized stimulus of either 5.4 or 25 fc to the other two groups. No stimuli were presented during the extinction phase to the other FC group (nonextinguished control) or to the BC control group. The treatments were evaluated in terms of the speed with which *S* jumped a hurdle to a safe box to escape the original CS. The results are presented in Figure 4, where the groups, except for the BC group (control), are identified by the intensity of the light presented during extinction.

That fear of the CS is not conditioned with BC procedures and that the extinction procedure eliminated fear of the apparatus cues are indi-

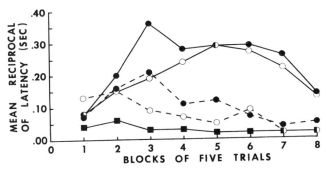

Fig. 4. Speed of hurdle jumping as a function of trial blocks following various fear-extinction procedures. Intensity of light presented to each group during extinction: 0 fc (solid circle, solid line); 5.4 fc (open circle, solid line); 25.0 fc (solid circle, dashed line); 116.4 fc (open circle, dashed line); control (solid square).

cated by the failure of the BC group (control) to learn. Thus, it may be assumed that the ordering of performance of the other four groups reflects only the amount of fear elicited by the original CS. The superior performance of the 0 fc group, indicating the presence of the greatest amount of fear, would be expected since for this group the extinction treatment did not involve presentation either of the CS or of generalized stimuli. For the three experimental groups administered the differential extinction treatments, performance was poorer the more similar the extinction stimulus was to the original CS. Presumably, the inhibition of fear resulting from the unpaired presentations of the 5.4 and 25 fc stimuli generalized to the CS in different amounts. A test of the rank ordering of the grand means of the five groups (Jonckheere, 1954) was significant, thus supporting the foregoing analysis.

IV. SIMILARITY OF FEAR AND FRUSTRATION

Recent evidence has indicated that conditioned frustration is similar to conditioned fear in the sense that both can motivate and reinforce, as well as disrupt, other behavior. The motivating effect of conditioned frustration has been demonstrated most clearly by Wagner (1963) with a startle-response measure. The Ss were first given partially reinforced runway training during which a CS was presented to the experimental Ss on each nonreinforced trial. Control Ss did not receive the CS in the runway but were given equal exposure to it while in their retaining box. Subsequently, in a stabilimeter, a startle stimulus was delivered in the presence of the CS. The magnitude of the startle response was significantly greater in the experimental than in the control group. Theoretically, a failure to obtain an expected reward in the runway would lead to the elicitation of primary frustration and eventually, for the experimental Ss, to the classical conditioning of frustration to the CS. Although equal frustration would be expected to occur in the control Ss, the absence of the CS in the runway would preclude such conditioning. On the assumption that conditioned frustration is motivating, it would be expected that the amplitude of the startle response in the presence of the CS would be greater in the experimental than in the control group, as obtained. The similarity between the analysis of these results and that provided by Brown *et al.* (1951) to account for the energizing effect of conditioned fear is apparent.

Although Wagner (1963) has provided evidence with a shuttlebox task that the reduction of conditioned frustration is reinforcing, the most convincing data have been obtained by Daly (1969). In her study, four experimental groups were given runway training with a 15-pellet reward, following which the reward was shifted for two groups to 1 pellet and for the other two groups to 0 pellets (extinction). During the shift trials, a CS (light) was presented in the goal box for one group under each reward condition but not for the other. Four control groups were used. Two received a 1-pellet reward in the goal box throughout all runway training, while the other two groups received 0 pellets. One control group under each reward condition received the CS in the goal box on the trials corresponding to the shift phase of the experimental groups while the other did not. Subsequently, hurdle-jumping training was administered in which S was permitted to jump from the goal box of the runway into a discriminably different adjacent box. On each of these trials S was placed in the goal box with the same reward and CS conditions which had prevailed during the runway shift phase.

The results are presented in Figure 5. In the caption the groups are designated according to the reward and stimulus conditions occurring during the shift and hurdle-jumping phases of the experiment. The presence or absence of the discrete CS is indicated, respectively, by CS and NCS, whereas the number of pellets received is represented by 0 or 1. Since the performance of the four control groups did not differ significantly, their grand mean is plotted, and the range of their means indicated by the vertical lines. It is apparent that the experimental procedures led to differential learning of the hurdle-jumping response.

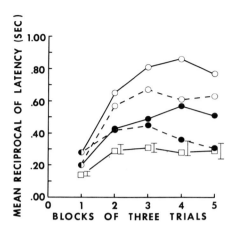

Fig. 5. Speed of hurdle jumping based on conditioned frustration as a function of trial blocks. Magnitude of reward (0 or 1 pellet) and presence (CS) or absence (NCS) of a discrete CS during frustration conditioning and hurdle jumping: 0 CS (open circle, solid line); 0 NCS (open circle, dashed line); 1 CS (solid circle, solid line); 1 NCS (solid circle, dashed line); controls (open square). (Data supplied by H.B. Daly.)

Performance was significantly superior under the 0-pellet as compared to the 1-pellet condition and under the CS as compared to the NCS condition.

That significantly better learning of hurdle jumping occurred in the experimental than in the control groups provides evidence that escape from frustration-eliciting stimuli is reinforcing. The difference in performance with respect to the reward variable is presumably due to a greater amount of primary frustration occurring during the runway shift trials with the 0-pellet, relative to the 1-pellet, reward. As a consequence, a greater amount of frustration would be conditioned under the 0-pellet treatment and would furnish a greater source of reinforcement for the learning of hurdle jumping. (These manipulations leading to different amounts of primary frustration are analogous to varying the intensity of the UCS in fear conditioning.) It may be assumed that frustration is conditioned to all stimuli present when primary frustration occurs. On this basis, the apparatus cues of the goal box would become elicitors of frustration in all of the experimental groups. The discrete CS would provide an additional source of frustration in the CS groups. Thus, the superior performance of these latter groups may be attributed to the greater frustration reduction occurring following the hurdle-jumping response. The striking similarity of these results to those obtained with comparable procedures in a fear-conditioning situation can be seen by a comparison of the present data with those shown in Figure 1. There it may be seen that better learning of hurdle jumping occurred when fear had been conditioned both to a discrete CS and to the apparatus cues (CS–CS group) than when conditioning was to the apparatus cues alone (NCS–NCS group).

The disruption of other behavior by conditioned frustration may be best illustrated with the data of Amsel and Surridge (1964). Presentation in a runway of a light previously paired with nonreward was found to decrease running speed. Presumably, frustration produced by nonreward became conditioned to the light and subsequently was elicited when the light was presented in the runway. The frustration stimulus would be expected to evoke responses incompatible with the running response and lead to its disruption. Obviously, this effect of frustration is similar to that of conditioned fear obtained when the conditioned punishment measure is used with the prototype runway task.

The recent findings of Leitenberg, Bertsch, and Coughlin (1968) can be taken to indicate that frustration can act to suppress ongoing behavior in the same manner as fear. They found that presentation of a CS previously paired with a time-out from positive reinforcement depressed the rate of a food-reinforced bar-pressing response. This effect can be interpreted to indicate that frustration occurred when positive reinforcement was withdrawn, became conditioned to the CS, and later allowed for the elicitation of responses incompatible with bar pressing.

The discussion thus far in this section has indicated that each of the four measures of fear being considered in this chapter has also been used to index frustration; the effects of fear and frustration on other behavior in each case have been parallel. In addition to this similarity, there is the added possibility that the stimuli arising from these emotional responses are functionally equivalent. That is, a response learned to one of these stimuli may be elicited by the other, although, perhaps, with a stimulus generalization decrement. Several studies have provided supporting data for this notion. For example, Brown and Wagner (1964) found that a group partially reinforced with food in a runway situation later, when punishment (shock) and food were presented in the goal box on each trial, showed a smaller decrement in running speed than did a group which had previously received 100% food reinforcement. In another comparison, two groups were given food reinforcement on each runway trial, and, in addition, one received punishment (shock) on half of these trials. Subsequently, when food and shock were no longer presented in the goal box, the previously punished group showed a smaller decrement in running speed than did the unpunished group. The explanation of these data assumes the development of conditioned frustration as a result of partial reinforcement and of conditioned fear as a result of punishment. Presumably, these conditioned responses would come to occur in the start box and runway and provide stimuli to which the running response could become associated. To the extent that these fear and frustration stimuli are functionally equivalent, the running response learned to one would be expected to be maintained by the presence of the other, as was found.

Further support for this hypothesis has been obtained by Franchina (1965). His Ss were first trained to traverse a runway while hungry under either a 50% or 100% reinforcement schedule. Then during extinction, shock of either 0-, 30-, or 70-V was administered in the goal box. It was hypothesized that the difference in extinction performance between the nonshocked and the shocked groups (0- versus 30-V or 0- versus 70-V) trained with partial reinforcement would be smaller than the comparable differences for the continuously reinforced groups. The rationale was that during original training the running response would become associated with the frustration stimulus in the 50% groups but not in the 100% groups. Therefore, if fear was later aroused in these groups and if there is some similarity between the fear and frustration stimulus, the running response should be maintained only in the shocked groups trained with 50% reinforcement. Reliable evidence favoring this hypothesis was obtained under the 30-V shock condition with the runway speed measure.

V. SUMMARY AND SOME IMPLICATIONS

In this chapter an attempt was made to present the current status of the concept of fear from a consistent viewpoint. Fear was considered to be a classically conditioned response, defined in terms of the prior appropriate pairing of neutral and noxious stimuli. Since fear is unobservable, it may be measured only by its effect on other observable responses. Because of this state of affairs it is necessary, in studying fear, to maintain a clear conceptual separation between the fear response and the response used as its index. Therefore, the discussion was restricted mainly to four index responses which permit such a distinction. These measures were designated as learning to escape fear, change in performance resulting from conditioned punishment, change in rate of an ongoing response, and change in magnitude of an unlearned response.

The theoretical rationale which was used to account for the effect of fear on the various index responses assumes that fear is an acquired drive with general energizing properties and that its decrease is a reinforcer. In addition, the theory assumes that fear has stimulus properties; that is, stimuli produced by the fear response may elicit other responses, either innately or through learning. A discussion was included of an extension of this theory which assumes that relief, conceived of as a response occurring when fear is reduced, is conditioned to the stimuli present. In fractional form, relief can occur as an anticipatory response. The disconfirmation of anticipated relief is presumed to lead to frustration effects analogous to those found in appetitive learning situations.

The tenets of this theory were applied to explain the results of studies investigating a number of variables relevant to the conditioning and extinction of fear, as well as to its measurement. Consideration was given to the control procedures required in order to attribute changes in the index response to conditioned fear.

The one finding which may, perhaps, have the broadest implications for studies of aversive learning is that whenever sufficiently strong shock is appropriately administered fear is conditioned to all stimuli impinging on S. The term "free shock" is thus misleading since conditioning of fear to ubiquitous static situational cues occurs. This basic principle may be applied to explain various phenomena observed in avoidance learning situations, for example, the greater difficulty of learning a shuttlebox, as compared to a one-way, avoidance task (e.g., Theios, Lynch, & Lowe, 1966). With the shuttlebox procedure shock is administered in both compartments and fear would be conditioned to the apparatus cues of each. The avoidance response would be reinforced by the decrease in fear resulting from the termination of the CS. In the one-way task, however, shock is delivered, and fear would be conditioned to the apparatus cues, in only one compartment. Hence, the avoidance response would be reinforced by the decrease of fear from two sources: the apparatus cues and the CS. The greater reinforcement thereby occurring in the one-way task would be expected to lead to more rapid learning. Some attempts to capitalize on the efficacy of the one-way task, while retaining a shuttling procedure, have involved rotating the apparatus so that the response is unidirectional (e.g., Lubar & Perachio, 1965). The better performance obtained with this modified one-way task, as compared to the two-way task, cannot be attributed to differences in reinforcement resulting from the decrease in fear of apparatus cues since the tasks are identical in this respect. Fear conditioned to extra-apparatus cues can, however, provide the basis for differential amounts of reinforcement with the two procedures. By reasoning analogous to that above, the decrease in this source of fear would be greater with the modified one-way task and, hence, can account for the superior learning with it relative to the two-way task.

The further finding that fear of apparatus cues, but not of the CS, may be forgotten with time might account for some instances in which shuttlebox avoidance learning has been reported to improve with the length of the intersession interval (*e.g.,* Webster & Rabedeau, 1964). The above examples illustrate the manner in which basic knowledge concerning fear, obtained with the relatively simple tasks considered in this chapter, may be of aid in clarifying the processes involved in more complex learning situations. Such an analytic approach in other instances may likewise increase our understanding of aversive learning.

ACKNOWLEDGMENTS

Preparation of this chapter was supported in part by research grant MH-12978 from the National Institute of Mental Health, Public Health Service. The authors are indebted to Charles Abrams, W. Keith Douglass, Joseph J. Franchina, Ottalie McClymont Price, and Roy B. Weinstock for aid in the collection and analysis of much of the unpublished data reported in this chapter and to these individuals, as well as to Dr. Helen B. Daly, for helpful discussions and comments. A special debt is owed to W. Keith Douglass for careful preparation of the figures and to Suzanne Seigal for dedicated secretarial assistance.

REFERENCES

Amsel, A. The combination of a primary appetitional need with primary and secondary emotionally derived needs. *Journal of Experimental Psychology.* 1950, **40**, 1–14.

Amsel, A. The role of frustrative nonreward in noncontinuous reward situations. *Psychological Bulletin.* 1958, **55**, 102–119.

Amsel, A., & Surridge, C.T. The influence of magnitude of reward on the aversive properties of anticipatory frustration. *Canadian Journal of Psychology.* 1964, **18**, 321–327.

Anderson, D.C., Plant, Carol, & Paden, P. Conditioned suppression of a running response as related to competing responses, drive, and basal skin resistance level. *Journal of Comparative and Physiological Psychology.* 1967, **63**, 282–287.

Anderson, D.C., Plant, Carol, Johnson, D., & Vandever, Jaylynne. Second-order aversive classical conditioning. *Canadian Journal of Psychology.* 1967, **21**, 120–131.

Anger, D. The role of temporal discriminations in the reinforcement of Sidman avoidance behavior. *Journal of the Experimental Analysis of Behavior.* 1963, **6**, 477–506.

Annau, Z., & Kamin, L.J. The conditioned emotional response as a function of intensity of the US. *Journal of Comparative and Physiological Psychology.* 1961, **54**, 428–432.

Ayres, J.J.B. Conditioned suppression and the information hypothesis. *Journal of Comparative and Physiological Psychology,* 1966, **62**, 21–25.

Azrin, N.H. Some notes on punishment and avoidance. *Journal of the Experimental Analysis of Behavior,* 1959, **2**, 260.

Baum, M. "Reversal learning" of an avoidance response as a function of prior fear conditioning and fear extinction. *Canadian Journal of Psychology.* 1965, **19**, 85–93.

Beecroft, R.S. *Classical conditioning.* Goleta, California: Psychonomic Press, 1966.

Beecroft, R.S. Emotional conditioning. *Psychonomic Monograph Supplements,* 1967, **2** (4, Whole No. 20).

Bergmann, G. *Philosophy of science.* Madison, Wisconsin: University of Wisconsin Press, 1957.

Bitterman, M.E. The CS–US interval in classical and avoidance conditioning. In W.F. Prokasy (Ed.) *Classical conditioning: A symposium.* New York: Appleton, 1965. Pp. 1–19.

Blackman, D. Response rate and conditioned suppression. *Psychological Reports,* 1966, **19,** 687–693.

Blackman, D. Effects of response pacing on conditioned suppression. *Quarterly Journal of Experimental Psychology,* 1967, **19,** 170–174. (a)

Blackman, D. Conditioned suppression: Comments on Lyon's reply. *Psychological Reports,* 1967, **20,** 909–910. (b)

Blanchard, R.J., & Blanchard, D. Caroline. Crouching as an index of fear. *Journal of Comparative and Physiological Psychology,* 1969, **67,** 370–375.

Bolles, R.C. *Theory of motivation.* New York: Harper, 1967.

Bower, G., Starr, R., & Lazarovitz, Leah. Amount of response-produced change in the CS and avoidance learning. *Journal of Comparative and Physiological Psychology,* 1965, **59,** 13–17.

Brady, J.V. Extinction of a conditioned "fear" response as a function of reinforcement schedules for competing behavior. *Journal of Psychology,* 1955, **40,** 25–34.

Brimer, C.J., & Dockrill, F.J. Partial reinforcement and the CER. *Psychonomic Science,* 1966, **5,** 185–186.

Brimer, C.J., & Kamin, L.J. Disinhibition, habituation, sensitization, and the conditioned emotional response. *Journal of Comparative and Physiological Psychology,* 1963, **56,** 508–516.

Brookshire, K.H., & Hognander, O.C. Conditioned fear in the fish. *Psychological Reports,* 1968, **22,** 75–81.

Brown, J.S. *The motivation of behavior.* New York: McGraw-Hill, 1961.

Brown, J.S., & Jacobs, A. The role of fear in the motivation and acquisition of responses. *Journal of Experimental Psychology,* 1949, **39,** 747–759.

Brown, J.S., Kalish, H.I., & Farber, I.E. Conditioned fear as revealed by magnitude of startle response to an auditory stimulus. *Journal of Experimental Psychology,* 1951, **41,** 317–328.

Brown, J.S., Martin, R.C., & Morrow, M.W. Self-punitive behavior in the rat: Facilitative effects of punishment on resistance to extinction. *Journal of Comparative and Physiological Psychology,* 1964, **57,** 127–133.

Brown, R.T., & Wagner, A.R. Resistance to punishment and extinction following training with shock or nonreinforcement. *Journal of Experimental Psychology,* 1964, **68,** 503–507.

Brush, F.R. The effects of intertrial interval on avoidance learning in the rat. *Journal of Comparative and Physiological Psychology,* 1962, **55,** 888–892.

Bull, J.A., III, & Overmier, J.B. Additive and subtractive properties of excitation and inhibition. *Journal of Comparative and Physiological Psychology,* 1968, **66,** 511–514.

Campbell, B.A., & Bloom, J.M. Relative aversiveness of noise and shock. *Journal of Comparative and Physiological Psychology,* 1965, **60,** 440–442.

Campbell, B.A., & Campbell, Enid H. Retention and extinction of learned fear in infant and adult rats. *Journal of Comparative and Physiological Psychology*, 1962, **55**, 1–8.

Carlton, P.L., & Didamo, Pauline. Some notes on the control of conditioned suppression. *Journal of the Experimental Analysis of Behavior*, 1960, **3**, 255–258.

Carlton, P.L., & Vogel, J.R. Habituation and conditioning. *Journal of Comparative and Physiological Psychology*, 1967, **63**, 348–351.

Champion, R.A. The acquisition and extinction of the fear response. *Australian Journal of Psychology*, 1961, **13**, 23–38.

Champion, R.A., & Jones, J.E. Forward, backward, and pseudoconditioning of the GSR. *Journal of Experimental Psychology*, 1961, **62**, 58–61.

Christophersen, E.R., & Denny, M.R. Retractable-bar avoidance. *Psychonomic Science*, 1967, **9**, 579–580.

Cornsweet, T.N. *The design of electric circuits in the behavioral sciences.* New York: Wiley, 1963.

Daly, Helen B. Learning of a hurdle-jump response to escape cues paired with reduced reward or frustrative nonreward. *Journal of Experimental Psychology*, 1969, **79**, 146–157.

Damianopoulos, E.N. S–R contiguity and delay of reinforcement as critical parameters in classical aversive conditioning. *Psychological Review*, 1967, **74**, 420–427.

Davenport, J.W. Higher-order conditioning of fear (CER). *Psychonomic Science*, 1966, **4**, 27–28.

Davis, H. Conditioned suppression: A survey of the literature. *Psychonomic Monograph Supplements*, 1968, **2** (14, Whole No. 30).

Denny, M.R., & Weisman, R.G. Avoidance behavior as a function of length of nonshock confinement. *Journal of Comparative and Physiological Psychology*, 1964, **58**, 252–257.

Desiderato, O. Generalization of acquired fear as a function of CS intensity and number of acquisition trials. *Journal of Experimental Psychology*, 1964, **67**, 41–47. (a)

Desiderato, O. Generalization of conditioned suppression. *Journal of Comparative and Physiological Psychology*, 1964, **57**, 434–437. (b)

Desiderato, O., Butler, Barrie, & Meyer, C. Changes in fear generalization gradients as a function of delayed testing. *Journal of Experimental Psychology*, 1966, **72**, 678–682.

de Toledo, Leyla, & Black, A.H. Heart rate: Changes during conditioned suppression in rats. *Science*, 1966, **152**, 1404–1406.

Dinsmoor, J.A. Punishment: I. The avoidance hypothesis. *Psychological Review*, 1954, **61**, 34–46.

Dinsmoor, J.A. Punishment: II. An interpretation of empirical findings. *Psychological Review*, 1955, **62**, 96–105.

Dua, J.K., & Champion, R.A. Contiguity and reinforcement in classical fear conditioning. *Australian Journal of Psychology*, 1968, **20**, 1–9.

Estes, W.K., & Skinner, B.F. Some quantitative properties of anxiety. *Journal of Experimental Psychology*, 1941, **29**, 390–400.

Fantino, E., Sharp, D., & Cole, M. Factors facilitating lever-press avoidance. *Journal of Comparative and Physiological Psychology*, 1966, **62**, 214–217.

Ferster, C.B., & Skinner, B.F. *Schedules of reinforcement.* New York: Appleton, 1957.

Franchina, J.J. Effects of percentage of reward and intensity of shock on performance during extinction. Unpublished doctoral dissertation, Syracuse University, 1965.

Furedy, J.J. Aspects of reinforcement through UCS offset in classical aversive conditioning. *Australian Journal of Psychology*, 1967, **19**, 159–168.

Geller, I. The acquisition and extinction of conditioned suppression as a function of the base-line reinforcer. *Journal of the Experimental Analysis of Behavior*, 1960, **3**, 235–240.

Geller, I. Conditioned suppression in goldfish as a function of shock-reinforcement schedule. *Journal of the Experimental Analysis of Behavior*, 1964, **7**, 345–349.

Gleitman, H., & Holmes, P.A. Retention of incompletely learned CER in rats. *Psychonomic Science*, 1967, **7**, 19–20.

Goldstein, M.L. Acquired drive strength as a joint function of shock intensity and number of acquisition trials. *Journal of Experimental Psychology*, 1960, **60**, 349–358.

Goldstein, M.L. Aversive conditioning methodology in animal research. *Psychological Reports*, 1962, **11**, 841–868.

Goldstein, M.L. Physiological theories of emotion: A critical historical review from the standpoint of behavior theory. *Psychological Bulletin*, 1968, **69**, 23–40.

Grossen, N.E., & Bolles, R.C. Effects of a classical conditioned 'fear signal' and 'safety signal' on nondiscriminated avoidance behavior. *Psychonomic Science*, 1968, **11**, 321–322.

Gwinn, G.T. Resistance to extinction of learned fear-drives. *Journal of Experimental Psychology*, 1951, **42**, 6–12.

Hammond, L.J. Increased responding to CS- in differential CER. *Psychonomic Science*, 1966, **5**, 337–338.

Hammond, L.J. A traditional demonstration of the active properties of Pavlovian inhibition using differential CER. *Psychonomic Science*, 1967, **9**, 65–66.

Hendry, D.P. Conditioned inhibition of conditioned suppression. *Psychonomic Science*, 1967, **9**, 261–262.

Hendry, D.P., & Van-Toller, C. Alleviation of conditioned suppression. *Journal of Comparative and Physiological Psychology*, 1965, **59**, 458–460.

Herendeen, D., & Anderson, D.C. Dual effects of a second-order conditioned stimulus: Excitation and inhibition. *Psychonomic Science*, 1968, **13**, 15–16.

Herrnstein, R.J., & Sidman, M. Avoidance conditioning as a factor in the effects of unavoidable shocks on food-reinforced behavior. *Journal of Comparative and Physiological Psychology*, 1958, **51**, 380–385.

Hilton, A. Partial reinforcement of a conditioned emotional response in rats. *Journal of Comparative and Physiological Psychology*, 1969, **69**, 253–260.

Hoffman, H.S., & Fleshler, M. Stimulus factors in aversive controls: The generalization of conditioned suppression. *Journal of the Experimental Analysis of Behavior*, 1961, **4**, 371–378.

Hoffman, H.S., & Fleshler, M. Stimulus aspects of aversive controls: Stimulus generalization of conditioned suppression following discrimination training. *Journal of the Experimental Analysis of Behavior*, 1964, **7**, 233–239.

Hoffman, H.S., Fleshler, M., & Jensen, P. Stimulus aspects of aversive controls: The retention of conditioned suppression. *Journal of the Experimental Analysis of Behavior*, 1963, **6**, 575–583.

Hoffman, H.S., Selekman, W., & Fleshler, M. Stimulus aspects of aversive controls: Long term effects of suppression procedures. *Journal of the Experimental Analysis of Behavior*, 1966, **9**, 659–662. (a)

Hoffman, H.S., Selekman, W.L., & Fleshler, M. Stimulus factors in aversive controls: Conditioned suppression after equal training to two stimuli. *Journal of the Experimental Analysis of Behavior,* 1966, **9,** 649–653. (b)

Hull, C.L. *Principles of behavior.* New York: Appleton, 1943.

Hunt, H.F., & Brady, J.V. Some effects of punishment and intercurrent "anxiety" on a simple operant. *Journal of Comparative and Physiological Psychology,* 1955, **48,** 305–310.

James, J.P., & Mostoway, W.W. Conditioned suppression of licking as a function of shock intensity. *Psychonomic Science,* 1968, **13,** 161–162.

Jonckheere, A.R. A distribution-free k-sample test against ordered alternatives. *Biometrika,* 1954, **41,** 133–145.

Kalish, H.I. Strength of fear as a function of the number of acquisition and extinction trials. *Journal of Experimental Psychology,* 1954, **47,** 1–9.

Kamil, A.C. The second-order conditioning of fear in rats. *Psychonomic Science,* 1968, **10,** 99–100.

Kamin, L.J. The gradient of delay of secondary reward in avoidance learning tested on avoidance trials only. *Journal of Comparative and Physiological Psychology,* 1957, **50,** 450–456.

Kamin, L.J. Backward conditioning and the conditioned emotional response. *Journal of Comparative and Physiological Psychology,* 1963, **56,** 517–519.

Kamin, L.J. Temporal and intensity characteristics of the conditioned stimulus. In W.F. Prokasy (Ed.) *Classical conditioning: A symposium.* New York: Appleton, 1965. Pp. 118–147.

Kamin, L.J. "Attention-like" processes in classical conditioning. In M.R. Jones (Ed.) *Miami symposium on the prediction of behavior, 1967: Aversive stimulation.* Coral Gables, Florida: University of Miami Press, 1968. Pp. 9–31.

Kamin, L.J., Brimer, C.J., & Black, A.H. Conditioned suppression as a monitor of fear of the CS in the course of avoidance training. *Journal of Comparative and Physiological Psychology,* 1963, **56,** 497–501.

Kaufman, Edna L., & Miller, N.E. Effect of number of reinforcements on strength of approach in an approach-avoidance conflict. *Journal of Comparative and Physiological Psychology,* 1949, **42,** 65–74.

Kimble, G.A. *Hilgard and Marquis' conditioning and learning.* New York: Appleton, 1961.

Knapp, R.K. Acquisition and extinction of avoidance with similiar and different shock and escape situations. *Journal of Comparative and Physiological Psychology,* 1965, **60,** 272–273.

Kurtz, K.H., & Siegel, A. Conditioned fear and magnitude of startle response: A replication and extension. *Journal of Comparative and Physiological Psychology,* 1966, **62,** 8–14.

Leaf, R.C. Avoidance response evocation as a function of prior discriminative fear conditioning under curare. *Journal of Comparative and Physiological Psychology,* 1964, **58,** 446–449.

Leaf, R.C., & Leaf, Susan R.P. Recovery time as a measure of degree of conditioned suppression. *Psychological Reports,* 1966, **18,** 265–266.

Leaf, R.C., & Muller, S.A. Effect of CER on DRL responding. *Journal of the Experimental Analysis of Behavior,* 1964, **7,** 405–407.

Leaf, R.C., & Muller, S.A. Simple method for CER conditioning and measurement. *Psychological Reports,* 1965, **17,** 211–215.

Leitenberg, H., Bertsch, G.J., & Coughlin, R.C., Jr. "Time-out from positive reinforcement" as the UCS in a CER paradigm with rats. *Psychonomic Science,* 1968, **13,** 3–4.

Levine, S. UCS intensity and avoidance learning. *Journal of Experimental Psychology*, 1966, **71**, 163–164.

Ley, R. Effects of food and water deprivation on the performance of a response motivated by acquired fear. *Journal of Experimental Psychology*, 1965, **69**, 583–589.

Libby, A. Two variables in the acquisition of depressant properties by a stimulus. *Journal of Experimental Psychology*, 1951, **42**, 100–107.

Lockhart, R.A. Comments regarding multiple response phenomena in long interstimulus interval conditioning. *Psychophysiology*, 1966, **3**, 108–114.

LoLordo, V.M. Similarity of conditioned fear responses based upon different aversive events. *Journal of Comparative and Physiological Psychology*, 1967, **64**, 154–158.

Lubar, J.F., & Perachio, A.A. One-way and two-way learning and transfer of an active avoidance response in normal and cingulectomized cats. *Journal of Comparative and Physiological Psychology*, 1965, **60**, 46–52.

Lyon, D.O. Frequency of reinforcement as a parameter of conditioned suppression. *Journal of the Experimental Analysis of Behavior*, 1963, **6**, 95–98.

Lyon, D.O. Some notes on conditioned suppression and reinforcement schedules. *Journal of the Experimental Analysis of Behavior*, 1964, **7**, 289–291.

Lyon, D.O. A note on response rate and conditioned suppression. *Psychological Record*, 1965, **15**, 441–444.

Lyon, D.O. CER methodology: Reply to Blackman. *Psychological Reports*, 1967, **20**, 206.

Lyon, D.O. Conditioned suppression: Operant variables and aversive control. *Psychological Record*, 1968, **18**, 317–338.

Lyon, D.O., & Felton, M. Conditioned suppression and fixed ratio schedules of reinforcement. *Psychological Record*, 1966, **16**, 433–440.

Margules, D.L., & Stein, L. Facilitation of Sidman avoidance behavior by positive brain stimulation. *Journal of Comparative and Physiological Psychology*, 1968, **66**, 182–184.

Mathers, B.L. The effect of certain parameters on the acquisition of fear. *Journal of Comparative and Physiological Psychology*, 1957, **50**, 329–333.

May, M.A. Experimentally acquired drives. *Journal of Experimental Psychology*, 1948, **38**, 66–77.

McAllister, Dorothy E., & McAllister, W.R. Second-order conditioning of fear. *Psychonomic Science*, 1964, **1**, 383–384.

McAllister, Dorothy E., & McAllister, W.R. Incubation of fear: An examination of the concept. *Journal of Experimental Research in Personality*, 1967, **2**, 180–190.

McAllister, Dorothy E., & McAllister, W.R. Forgetting of acquired fear. *Journal of Comparative and Physiological Psychology*, 1968, **65**, 352–355.

McAllister, Dorothy E., McAllister, W.R., & Zellner, D.K. Preference for familiar stimuli in the rat. *Psychological Reports*, 1966, **19**, 868–870.

McAllister, W.R., & McAllister, Dorothy E. Postconditioning delay and intensity of shock as factors in the measurement of acquired fear. *Journal of Experimental Psychology*, 1962, **64**, 110–116. (a)

McAllister, W.R., & McAllister, Dorothy E. Role of the CS and of apparatus cues in the measurement of acquired fear. *Psychological Reports*, 1962, **11**, 749–756. (b)

McAllister, W.R., & McAllister, Dorothy E. Increase over time in the stimulus generalization of acquired fear. *Journal of Experimental Psychology*, 1963, **65**, 576–582.

McAllister, W.R., & McAllister, Dorothy E. Variables influencing the conditioning and the measurement of acquired fear. In W.F. Prokasy (Ed.) *Classical conditioning: A symposium*. New York: Appleton, 1965. Pp. 172–191.

McAllister, W.R., & McAllister, Dorothy E. Factors influencing inter-apparatus discrimination. Paper presented at the meeting of the Psychonomic Society, St. Louis, October 1966.

McAllister, W.R., & McAllister, Dorothy E. Drive and reward in aversive learning. *American Journal of Psychology*, 1967, **80**, 377–383.

McAllister, W.R., McAllister, Dorothy E., & Franchina, J.J. Dependence of equality judgments upon the temporal interval between stimulus presentations. *Journal of Experimental Psychology*, 1965, **70**, 602–605.

McClelland, W.J., & Colman, F.D. Activity and different types of electric shock stimuli. *Psychonomic Science*, 1967, **7**, 391–392.

Meryman, J.J. Magnitude of startle response as a function of hunger and fear. Unpublished master's thesis, State University of Iowa, 1952. Cited by J.S. Brown, *The motivation of behavior*. New York: McGraw-Hill, 1961. Pp. 152–154.

Milby, J.B., Jr. Delay of escape conditioning as a function of two kinds of secondary reinforcement stimulus conditions. *Psychonomic Science*, 1968, **11**, 5–6.

Millenson, J.R., & Hendry, D.P. Quantification of response suppression in conditioned anxiety training. *Canadian Journal of Psychology*, 1967, **21**, 242–252.

Miller, N.E. Studies of fear as an acquirable drive: I. Fear as motivation and fear-reduction as reinforcement in the learning of new responses. *Journal of Experimental Psychology*, 1948, **38**, 89–101.

Miller, N.E. Learnable drives and rewards. In S.S. Stevens (Ed.) *Handbook of experimental psychology*. New York: Wiley, 1951. Pp. 435–472.

Miller, N.E. Liberalization of basic S-R concepts: Extensions to conflict behavior, motivation, and social learning. In S. Koch (Ed.) *Psychology: A study of a science*. Vol. 2. New York: McGraw-Hill, 1959. Pp. 196–292.

Miller, N.E. Some reflections on the law of effect produce a new alternative to drive reduction. In M.R. Jones (Ed.) *Nebraska symposium on motivation, 1963*. Lincoln, Nebraska: University of Nebraska Press, 1963. Pp. 65–112.

Moscovitch, A., & LoLordo, V.M. Role of safety in the Pavlovian backward fear conditioning procedure. *Journal of Comparative and Physiological Psychology*, 1968, **66**, 673–678.

Mowrer, O.H. A stimulus-response analysis of anxiety and its role as a reinforcing agent. *Psychological Review*, 1939, **46**, 553–565.

Mowrer, O.H. *Learning theory and behavior*. New York: Wiley, 1960.

Mowrer, O.H., & Aiken, E.G. Contiguity vs. drive-reduction in conditioned fear: Temporal variations in conditioned and unconditioned stimulus. *American Journal of Psychology*, 1954, **67**, 26–38.

Mowrer, O.H., & Keehn, J.D. How are intertrial "avoidance" responses reinforced? *Psychological Review*, 1958, **65**, 209–221.

Mowrer, O.H., & Solomon, L.N. Contiguity vs. drive-reduction in conditioned fear: The proximity and abruptness of drive-reduction. *American Journal of Psychology*, 1954, **67**, 15–25.

Moyer, K.E., & Korn, J.H. Effect of UCS intensity on the acquisition and extinction of an avoidance response. *Journal of Experimental Psychology*, 1964, **67**, 352–359.

Murfin, F.L. The relationship of fear to the CS-UCS interval in acquisition and the CS-duration in extinction. *Dissertation Abstracts*, 1954, **14**, 2413.

Nelson, F. Effects of two counterconditioning procedures on the extinction of fear. *Journal of Comparative and Physiological Psychology*, 1966, **62**, 208–213.

Nelson, F. Effects of chlorpromazine on fear extinction. *Journal of Comparative and Physiological Psychology*, 1967, **64**, 496–498.

Overmier, J.B. Instrumental and cardiac indices of Pavlovian fear conditioning as a function of US duration. *Journal of Comparative and Physiological Psychology*, 1966, **62**, 15–20.

Overmier, J.B., & Leaf, R.C. Effects of discriminative Pavlovian fear conditioning upon previously or subsequently acquired avoidance responding. *Journal of Comparative and Physiological Psychology*, 1965, **60**, 213–217.

Page, H.A. The facilitation of experimental extinction by response prevention as a function of the acquisition of a new response. *Journal of Comparative and Physiological Psychology*, 1955, **48**, 14–16.

Parrish, Jan. Classical discrimination conditioning of heart rate and bar-press suppression in the rat. *Psychonomic Science*, 1967, **9**, 267–268.

Pavlov, I.P. *Conditioned reflexes*. London, and New York: Oxford University Press, 1927.

Porter, L.G. Generalization of fear and of the inhibition of fear. Unpublished doctoral dissertation, Syracuse University, 1958.

Ray, O.S., & Stein, L. Generalization of conditioned suppression. *Journal of the Experimental Analysis of Behavior*, 1959, **2**, 357–361.

Rescorla, R.A. Predictability and number of pairings in Pavlovian fear conditioning. *Psychonomic Science*, 1966, **4**, 383–384.

Rescorla, R.A. Pavlovian conditioning and its proper control procedures. *Psychological Review*, 1967, **74**, 71–80. (a)

Rescorla, R.A. Inhibition of delay in Pavlovian fear conditioning. *Journal of Comparative and Physiological Psychology*, 1967, **64**, 114–120. (b)

Rescorla, R.A. Pavlovian conditioned fear in Sidman avoidance learning. *Journal of Comparative and Physiological Psychology*, 1968, **65**, 55–60. (a)

Rescorla, R.A. Probability of shock in the presence and absence of CS in fear conditioning. *Journal of Comparative and Physiological Psychology*, 1968, **66**, 1–5. (b)

Rescorla, R.A., & LoLordo, V.M. Inhibition of avoidance behavior. *Journal of Comparative and Physiological Psychology*, 1965, **59**, 406–412.

Rescorla, R.A., & Solomon, R.L. Two-process learning theory: Relationships between Pavlovian conditioning and instrumental learning. *Psychological Review*, 1967, **74**, 151–182.

Rohrbaugh, M., & Riccio, D.C. Stimulus generalization of learned fear in infant and adult rats. *Journal of Comparative and Physiological Psychology*, 1968, **66**, 530–533.

Ross, L.E. Conditioned fear as a function of CS-UCS and probe stimulus intervals. *Journal of Experimental Psychology*, 1961, **61**, 265–273.

Schoenfeld, W.N. An experimental approach to anxiety, escape and avoidance behavior. In P.H. Hoch and J. Zubin (Eds.) *Anxiety*. New York: Grune & Stratton, 1950. Pp. 70–99. (Republished: Hafner, 1964.)

Seligman, M.E.P. Chronic fear produced by unpredictable electric shock. *Journal of Comparative and Physiological Psychology*, 1968, **66**, 402–411.

Shipley, W.C. An apparent transfer of conditioning. *Journal of General Psychology*, 1933, **8**, 382–391.

Sidman, M. Avoidance behavior. In W.K. Honig (Ed.) *Operant behavior: Areas of research and application*. New York: Appleton, 1966. Pp. 448–498.

Sidman, M., Herrnstein, R.J., & Conrad, D.G. Maintenance of avoidance behavior by unavoidable shocks. *Journal of Comparative and Physiological Psychology*, 1957, **50**, 553–557.

Siegel, A. Stimulus generalization of a classically conditioned response along a temporal dimension. *Journal of Comparative and Physiological Psychology*, 1967, **64**, 461–466.

Singh, S.D. Conditioned emotional response in the rat: I. Constitutional and situational determinants. *Journal of Comparative and Physiological Psychology*, 1959, **52**, 574–578.

Solomon, R.L., & Brush, Elinor S. Experimentally derived conceptions of anxiety and aversion. In M.R. Jones (Ed.) *Nebraska symposium on motivation, 1956*. Lincoln, Nebraska: University of Nebraska Press, 1956. Pp. 212–305.

Solomon, R.L., & Turner, Lucille H. Discriminative classical conditioning in dogs paralyzed by curare can later control discriminative avoidance responses in the normal state. *Psychological Review*, 1962, **69**, 202–219.

Spence, K.W. *Behavior theory and conditioning*. New Haven, Connecticut: Yale University Press, 1956.

Spence, K.W., & Runquist, W.N. Temporal effects of conditioned fear on the eyelid reflex. *Journal of Experimental Psychology*, 1958, **55**, 613–616.

Stein, L., Sidman, M., & Brady, J.V. Some effects of two temporal variables on conditioned suppression. *Journal of the Experimental Analysis of Behavior*, 1958, **1**, 153–162.

Strouthes, A. Effect of CS-onset UCS-termination delay, UCS duration, CS-onset UCS-onset interval, and number of CS-UCS pairings on conditioned fear response. *Journal of Experimental Psychology*, 1965, **69**, 287–291.

Strouthes, A., & Hamilton, H.C. Fear conditioning as a function of the number and timing of reinforcements. *Journal of Psychology*, 1959, **48**, 131–139.

Strouthes, A., & Hamilton, H.C. UCS intensity and number of CS-UCS pairings as determiners of conditioned fear R. *Psychological Reports*, 1964, **15**, 707–714.

Tapp, J.T. Strain differences in the acquisition of a conditioned emotional response. *Journal of Comparative and Physiological Psychology*, 1964, **57**, 464–465.

Theios, J., Lynch, A.D., & Lowe, W.F., Jr. Differential effects of shock intensity on one-way and shuttle avoidance conditioning. *Journal of Experimental Psychology*, 1966, **72**, 294–299.

Vogel, J.R., & Spear, N.E. Interaction of reward magnitude and conditioned fear on the consummatory response. *Psychonomic Science*, 1966, **5**, 263–264.

Wagner, A.R. Conditioned frustration as a learned drive. *Journal of Experimental Psychology*, 1963, **66**, 142–148.

Wagner, A.R., Siegel, Linda S., & Fein, Greta G. Extinction of conditioned fear as a function of percentage of reinforcement. *Journal of Comparative and Physiological Psychology*, 1967, **63**, 160–164.

Webster, C.D., & Rabedeau, R.G. The effect of intersession interval in shuttle-box conditioning of the guinea-pig. *Psychonomic Science*, 1964, **1**, 73–74.

Willis, R.D., & Lundin, R.W. Conditioned suppression in the rat as a function of shock reinforcement schedule. *Psychonomic Science*, 1966, **6**, 107–108.

Winograd, E. Maintained generalization testing of conditioned suppression. *Journal of the Experimental Analysis of Behavior,* 1965, **8,** 47–51.

Woods, P.J. Performance changes in escape conditioning following shifts in the magnitude of reinforcement. *Journal of Experimental Psychology,* 1967, **75,** 487–491.

AVOIDANCE LEARNING

CHAPTER 3

Species-Specific Defense Reactions

ROBERT C. BOLLES

University of Washington
Seattle, Washington

I. INTRODUCTION

There is something fundamentally wrong with our traditional interpretations of avoidance learning. There is probably also something basically
wrong with the way in which avoidance experiments have traditionally
been conducted. Consider the following contrasting pair of studies.
Maatsch (1959) found that rats could learn in a single trial to jump out
of a box where they had been shocked. On the other hand, when
D'Amato and Schiff (1964) tried to train rats to press a bar to avoid shock
they found that only 3 of their 24 Ss attained even a modest level of
proficiency in 1000 trials. Other research, which we will consider shortly,
indicates that although there were many differences in procedure between these two studies, much of this difference between 1-trial learning
and 1000-trial failure to learn must be attributed to the requirement of
different avoidance responses in the two cases.
Perhaps it is not surprising that jumping out of a box should be much
easier to learn as an avoidance response than pressing a bar, but if we
expect such a difference, then we would hope that our current theories
of instrumental or operant learning would predict it and indicate why it
occurs. However, our major theoretical statements of animal learning
principles seem to be concerned with other matters since they contain no
hint that the choice of the response is such an important parameter.
They might attribute the poor acquisition of the bar press response to a
low operant level. But this is an inadequate explanation because some of
the D'Amato and Schiff Ss made hundreds of responses and still failed
to learn to respond consistently. The response occurred, the presumed
reinforcement contingency was applied, but little or no learning was
found. It seems that either (1) we do not yet know what the effective
reinforcing events are, so that we do not know how to arrange for their
effective application, or (2) whatever the effective reinforcing contingencies are in avoidance learning, they simply are not effective in strength-

ening some responses in some situations. In this chapter, I hope to convince the reader that we are actually beset by both of these difficulties, *i.e.*, that the effective reinforcement contingencies in avoidance learning are not what they are usually assumed to be, and that there is, in fact, a rather limited class of responses that can serve effectively as avoidance responses. Let us consider first the problem of the response.

Learning theorists are naturally reluctant to recognize limits on the generality of their theories, and more than one theorist has gone to considerable trouble to encompass the phenomena of avoidance behavior. Certainly this is an important goal. The destiny of Pavlovian conditioning theory no doubt hinged in considerable part upon the classic papers of Hull (1929) who showed that it could account for avoidance learning and of Mowrer (1947) who showed that it could not. Perhaps equally important for the drive-reduction hypothesis of reinforcement were the papers of Mowrer (1939) showing how it explained avoidance learning and of Schoenfeld (1950) showing how it did not.

Today we may place less faith in the general systematic positions than we used to, but we are no less inclined to try to generalize our favorite assumptions. Thus, the widespread and largely successful application of various versions of reinforcement theory has gradually inclined us to see no limits to it. We have become inclined to believe that we may choose any animal, choose any response in its repertoire, and strengthen that response as much as we please by the appropriate application of a suitable reinforcer. Of course some allowance is made for the fact that learning is faster and more certain in some situations than in others, but this is treated not as a question of principle but only as a matter of technique. With sufficient diligence, the use of automated equipment and a few tricks included in the preliminary training we can train Ss to do almost anything. Such confidence in the powers of reinforcement may be justified in some cases (even though it detracts from the credit that belongs to a dazzling display of diligence, equipment, and tricks), but its application to avoidance behavior inspires little confidence. Applied to the aversive case, our principles of reinforcement have resulted in little practical success, not much ability to predict behavior, and almost no understanding of the behavior involved.

The trouble is that the difference between the speed of learning to jump out of a box and the speed of learning to press a bar is a huge difference, vastly larger than can be produced by manipulating any of the usual array of experimental variables—including the events that are supposed to reinforce avoidance. This difference cannot be dismissed as a mere technical matter and there seems to be nothing in our bag of tricks that can get rid of it. We are proposing therefore that since the response requirement looms as such a large factor it should be made fundamental. It should be recognized as a first principle in avoidance learning.

As indicated elsewhere (Bolles, 1967; Bolles, Stokes, & Younger, 1966), the learning of an avoidance response (R_a) is greatly facilitated if it is chosen to be one of S's innate defense reactions. Here, we will go one step further and argue that *an R_a can be learned only if it is a species-specific defense reaction (SSDR)*, or at least that it is very much like one of the animal's SSDRs. Let us see how far the SSDR hypothesis can go toward accounting for the importance of what R_a is required of the animal.

It is clear that the responses which are the easiest for the rat to learn in aversive situations (excepting perhaps the fear reaction itself) are those that take it out of the situation. Our first assumption then has to be that taking flight is one of the rat's SSDRs. The rat does, in fact, withdraw from stimulus events, and particularly geographical locations, that elicit fear. If a rat is forcibly placed in a frightening situation, then it will leave if it can do so. If the rat gets itself into a frightening situation, then it retreats in a species-specific manner from whence it came. A large part of the daily activity of the rat in the wild involves tracing and retracing escape routes in its territory with the result that should the occasion arise it will be able to take flight very quickly and effectively.

If an experimental S is placed in a distinctive box and shocked a few seconds after a door is opened to an adjoining no-shock region, it will learn in very few trials to leave the shock box immediately upon being put there. This is the experimental paradigm of the "one-way" avoidance situation where the R_a is rapidly acquired, performed quite consistently, and is quite resistant to extinction (*e.g.*, Clark, 1966; Theios, 1963). One-way avoidance learning can sometimes be demonstrated after a single trial (*e.g.*, Maatsch, 1959). Santos (1960) reports that one-way avoidance of shock is acquired as rapidly as escape from shock; in fact, avoidance learning is so dependable in the one-way situation that no escape contingency is necessary. Here we find extremely rapid learning which is like avoidance in that S eliminates situational cues that have been paired with shock by leaving the situation. There are a number of similar reports of rapid learning from "acquired drive" studies as well as avoidance studies (Denny in Chapter 4 of this volume describes some examples).

If an R_a which provides for a clean flight from the situation is readily acquired, we might also expect some moderate degree of learning of R_as that provide for a less clean leave-taking. The shuttlebox is a situation of this type since it permits S to leave its position but requires returning to a location where it has just previously been shocked. The shuttlebox introduces an element of conflict because both sides of the apparatus elicit fear and the tendency to flee. Somewhat poorer acquisition should be expected than in the one-way situation and this is precisely what is reported (*e.g.*, Theios & Dunaway, 1964).[1] Typically, some proportion of the experimental group fails to learn (*e.g.*, Brush, 1966; Kamin, 1959), and Ss that do learn the response are likely to be performing at a level of only 60 to 90% after 100 trials.

Considerably faster acquisition and better performance levels than these are usually reported in running wheel studies where the rat can run *as though* it were getting away but where it is not actually altering its location. In the running wheel nearly all rats acquire the R_a and performance approaches 100% within 40 trials or so (Bolles *et al.*, 1966). The situations which involve equivocal flight-taking R_as provide a means of checking the SSDR hypothesis and making it more explicit. Unfortunately, there is relatively little data suitable for that purpose at the present time. We can only conclude that these R_as, and particularly the R_a required in the shuttle box, are ambiguous: they are neither obviously SSDRs nor obviously not SSDRs. They occupy some middle ground that needs to be more carefully defined.

The rat has also been trained extensively in nonlocomotory situations where, in fact, flight is impossible. The investigator selects some "convenient, arbitrary piece of behavior" or operant, but what the selection invariably comes down to is pressing a bar or turning a small paddle wheel. The rat is notoriously poor at acquiring both of these responses as R_as (D'Amato & Schiff, 1964; Meyer, Cho, & Wesemann, 1960; Myers, 1959; Smith, McFarland, & Taylor, 1961).

Many Ss apparently never learn, as we noted above, and many more show a dropout effect in which a partially learned R_a begins to disintegrate after a few hundred trials (Anderson & Nakamura, 1964; Coons, Anderson, & Myers, 1960). The full extent of the difficulty is probably not apparent because failures to learn generally do not appear in the literature. We can only guess at the number of aspiring students of behavior who have undertaken to train rats to press a bar or engage in some other task to avoid shock, and who have given up after finding few Ss able to learn. (The first discriminated bar-press avoidance seems to have been reported as late as 1959 by Myers.) A further unfortunate consequence is that if the aspirant does not give up entirely, he may confine his study to a shuttlebox where the level of achievement is likely to be more encouraging. Due publication of his results in the shuttlebox is

---

[1]*Editor's note:* See also Theios' chapter (Chapter 5) for an analysis of two-way avoidance in terms of 2 one-way habits.

likely only to reinforce the widespread belief that of course the rat can learn to avoid. The myth persists that the rat can learn any response, and we end up with serious ignorance about the actual range of responses that can serve the rat effectively as R_as.

In the last few years there have been a number of attempts to alter the bar-press situation so as to facilitate the acquisition of this response. Some of these attempts have been remarkably unsuccessful (e.g., Chapman & Bolles, 1964; D'Amato & Schiff, 1964; Meyer et al., 1960). But D'Amato has discovered that using discontinuous shock, i.e., brief pulses rather than continuous shock, produces considerable improvement (D'Amato & Fazzaro, 1966; D'Amato, Keller, & DiCara, 1964). Minimizing shock intensity seems to help (Bolles & Warren, 1965a; D'Amato & Fazzaro, 1966), as does using the longest possible CS–US interval (Bolles, Warren, & Ostrov, 1966). So does "shaping" the response (Feldman & Bremner, 1963; Keehn & Webster, 1968). But while all of these effects appear to be genuine and rationally explicable, none of these experimental manipulations makes the R_a easy to learn. Even under optimum conditions, bar pressing is a much more difficult R_a to acquire than running in a shuttle box.

From time to time we are told that the difficulty arises because the rat tends to freeze and to hold onto the bar (Feldman & Bremner, 1963; Meyer et al., 1960). We may suppose, incidentally, that because freezing is such a characteristic part of the frightened rat's response repertoire, it too is an SSDR. Thus we find that the rat's defensive repertoire contains two quite different responses: taking flight and freezing. Now, rather than viewing freezing while holding onto the bar as a decremental factor, a competing response which interferes with the acquisition of bar pressing, it can be argued that the rat is only able to press the bar at all because it freezes. In a typical instance what we observe is that the shock comes on and stays on while S frantically jumps and scratches and runs around in the box. Then it runs into the bar. The shock stops and so does the rat. (The rat has a remarkable tendency to stop whatever it is doing immediately upon shock termination.) It freezes in whatever posture and in whatever location it happens to be in when the shock stops. Then when the next shock comes on the rat is right there, the probability of hitting the bar again is much higher, and what counts is that it is in a position to make a very short latency escape response. Within 50 trials the rat will be terminating the shock with a latency in the order of .05 sec (Bolles & McGillis, 1968). By freezing on the bar the rat is able to execute an extremely rapid escape response (R_e) which limits the duration of shock to a value that does not disrupt its freezing behavior. Any other response topography is likely to lead to slower escape responses, i.e., longer shocks, and consequent disruption of that topography

(Campbell, 1962; Migler, 1963). In short, this procedure is the best possible technique for training the rat to freeze on the bar. Since freezing is part of its natural defense repertoire, the animal is trapped in the performance of this behavior. Keehn (1967) has shown that the rat is very good at "learning" to hold the bar down continuously. It can be argued that since holding the bar down requires a less delicate touch than initiating a new press, it is more rapidly acquired because it is more compatible with freezing.

The rat can further reduce shock duration by partial execution of the response, i.e., by depressing the bar part way. When this occurs we should expect to start getting intertrial responses, some of which would avoid shock and produce a further reduction in the total amount of shock. However, the low levels of performance and the instability of the behavior so often found in this situation suggest that responses of this sort provide a poor starting point for establishing more substantial levels of performance. It is only after a number of "freezing trials" that some rats begin to initiate responses characterized by a relatively long latency, a clean topography and increased variability. The fact that some rats ultimately acquire such behavior poses a challenge to the SSDR hypothesis since the bar-press response can scarcely be construed as an SSDR. The challenge can be met at this time only by making a set of assumptions. These are, first, that the rat must go through a phase in which it freezes on the bar, second, it must go through a phase in which it minimizes shock partly by making adventitious R_as but mostly by making very quick R_es. Third, it is then necessary to assume that a critical stage is reached in which fear begins to dissipate and as it does the restriction upon S's response repertoire relaxes so that S can not only flee and freeze, it can also bar press. The transition cannot be made too quickly because, by the first assumption, freezing has to occur to keep S at the bar. It is a precarious situation and the transition is uncertain. Indeed, our assumptions are uncertain, but perhaps no more uncertain than whether in any given instance the rat will acquire the response. This assumed dissipation of fear and broadening of the response repertoire with continued training will be discussed further later. The emphasis here is upon the early acquisition of R_a, and the point of the argument is that the available data from bar press situations is not wholly inconsistent with the SSDR hypothesis.

Just as the rat frequently makes its first bar press R_as in the effort to get out of the box, so it tends to make the first wheel turning R_as while attempting to get out through the window the wheel is mounted in. On subsequent trials the situation is the same as in the bar press apparatus: S freezes attempting to hold onto the wheel. Because the wheel tends to turn when a little pressure is put on it, S has to readjust its paws onto the next rung and thereby generates a number of inter-trial responses, some of which serve to avoid shock. We have observed that essentially the same pattern occurs, although the topography of the response is a little different, when the rat is required to jump up on a pole suspended from the ceiling in order to escape and/or avoid shock.

In all of these cases, the response which is said to be a conditioned operant can be considered to be simply a slight modification of S's freezing behavior. If the typical S learns anything in such situations it is to freeze while holding onto the manipulandum. Experimental procedures which minimize bar holding by punishing it sometimes facilitate performance (Feldman & Bremner, 1963; Brush, 1964a; Jones & Swanson, 1966) but they do not necessarily do so (Bolles & Warren, 1965b; Anderson, Rollins, & Riskin, 1966).

To summarize the argument so far: there is a clear alternative to the prevailing view that R_a can be any response in S's repertoire. The alternative hypothesis states that the R_a is either a defense reaction or some very slight topographic modification of a defense reaction. The rat appears to have two such reactions, namely, fleeing and freezing. These are in a sense the only responses available to the frightened rat and we cannot profitably require it to learn any more than to do one rather than the other in any aversive situation. If we require a running R_a, in a shuttlebox for example, the rat quickly learns it because this SSDR is already quite strong and only freezing competes with it. On the other hand, if we require bar pressing, then learning is uncertain because, to begin with, this R_a requires freezing in a particular location and with a particular posture, and this SSDR is in competition with all other freezing behavior and all of S's flight behavior.

We must note that many animals, including the rat, have a particularly interesting defense reaction which is not really defensive at all but offensive. If a rat is shocked it will exhibit certain unconditioned reactions to the shock such as jumping, running, or flinching, depending upon the intensity (Kimble, 1955; Trabasso & Thompson, 1962). This behavior appears to be largely under the control of the prevailing shock stimulation; S appears to be stimulus bound. But Azrin and Ulrich and their collaborators have shown that if another animal is introduced into the situation there is a sudden and complete alteration in behavior: S will attack the other animal (see especially Azrin, Hutchinson, & Hake, 1967). Two aspects of this interesting phenomenon are relevant here. One is that the precise nature of the animal's repertoire when being aversively stimulated is more a function of other environmental stimuli than might be thought. The defensive repertoire is not inflexible by any means; it is highly adaptable to specific environmental constraints. In different apparatus S's behavior may consist mostly of running, jumping, or scratching at the floor. If a pathway for flight is available S is likely to find it. If no escape route is available S is likely to freeze, but it may attack another animal that is present, and it may attack even if there is no other animal; it may bite at the bar or the grid floor or the walls of the apparatus. Flight, freezing, and attack are all rather broad classes of behavior rather than specific responses with fixed topographies.

The second conclusion is that an animal such as the rat has three rather than two responses in its defense repertoire: it can leave the situation, it can freeze, or it can attack. It is entirely conceivable that the stance of the rat in front of the bar or in front of the paddle wheel has as its prototype the attack response or the threat reaction. Such an analysis is suggested by the findings (Bolles, unpublished) that bar-press avoidance is facilitated by having the bar about 3 in. above the floor rather than much closer, and by putting shock on the bar itself rather than leaving it uncharged.

Up to this point, we have been primarily concerned with demonstrating that the chief factor determining how readily an R_a is learned is what the R_a is. By now there should be no question about either the main effect—some R_as are enormously easier to learn than others—or that the effect is intrinsic in the responses involved. We have tried to show how the SSDR hypothesis provides an explicit interpretation of this effect, and have reviewed in a rather cursory manner a few illustrative experiments. Now we shall have to take a closer look at the experimental literature to test the viability of the SSDR hypothesis. The argument must also become a little more complicated because of the fact that the response requirement effect shows up not only as a main effect, *i.e.*, in how fast learning occurs, it also shows up in a number of interactions. That is, the effects of other experimental treatments on avoidance learning also depend upon what response is required of S. The following sections will be concerned with the difficult question of what reinforces avoidance behavior. We will find that the contingencies which have historically been afforded the greatest importance, *i.e.*, the escape contingency and the CS-termination contingency, appear to have rather limited generality, and that, in fact, their effectiveness appears to depend primarily upon what R_a is chosen to be.

II. AVOIDANCE STUDIES

Three factors may be cited as logically potential sources of reinforcement for avoidance behavior. These are:

The Escape Contingency. If S fails to avoid the US (usually shock) on a given trial, it is given the opportunity to escape, usually by making the same response (R_e) as would have avoided it (R_a).[2] At one time, during the 1930s, the escape contingency was incorporated into avoidance studies because it was thought to be necessary; according to Pavlov, R_a was the conditioned form of R_e. Subsequently, the escape contingency has been used for reasons of expediency; it is widely thought that R_a will be more readily learned if the same response has been previously established as an R_e.

The CS-Termination Contingency. The occasion for making a successful R_a is usually marked by a signal, a warning stimulus, a CS. The original use and the terminology flow from a now discarded Pavlovian orientation. But for reasons that have nothing to do with Pavlov, termination of the CS began to be made contingent upon R_a. It is now very widely believed that this contingency is the principal source of reinforcement. This belief has become so fundamental in some quarters that when R_a is acquired in the absence of an explicit CS-termination contingency, internal proprioceptive stimuli have been hypothesized and the reinforcement of R_a attributed to their termination. Thus, a functional CS is assumed to be provided by the proprioceptive feedback from making responses other than R_a.

The Avoidance Contingency. Avoidance experiments are defined by the fact that shock is withheld following R_a, but until rather recently few investigators attributed any potency to this defining contingency. This situation is now changing, however, as we will see later.

The typical avoidance study includes all three of these contingencies and it is therefore impossible to assess their individual contributions to the acquisition of R_a. Fortunately there have been a number of studies that have partially isolated one or another of these contingencies, and we shall now turn our attention to them.

---

[2] A note on terminology: "CS" will be used to denote the stimuli paired with shock and, sometimes, "US" to refer to shock. This terminology fits since these are conditioned and unconditioned stimuli, at least as far as the fear response is concerned; and these designations are well established. But CR and UR cannot be accepted for the avoidance and escape responses, as the former cannot be assumed to be a conditioned form of the latter, nor to be conditioned to the CS, nor can the UR be assumed to be an unconditioned response to the US without begging the very questions raised here. We will use R_a and R_e.

A.   Avoidance Studies with R_a Different from R_e

The optimum technique for assessing the reinforcing effects of the different contingencies would be to use them independently to establish different independent responses. Ideally, we would make shock avoidance contingent upon one response, R_a, CS-termination upon a second response, R_{cs}, and shock escape contingent upon a third response, R_e. A properly counterbalanced experiment of this type would answer most of our questions about the sources of reinforcement in the avoidance situation. The closest approach to this ideal design is the classic study by Mowrer and Lamoreaux (1946). Their Ss were trained in a shuttlebox and while one group was required to run from one side to the other in the usual manner to avoid shock, the other group was required to jump up in the air. These groups were then split so that for half the Ss R_e was the same as R_a (homogeneous conditions), while for the other subgroup R_e was the other response (heterogeneous conditions).

Figure 1 shows a breakdown of the Mowrer and Lamoreaux data for the four subgroups. The original analysis of the data involved pooling Ss with the heterogeneous response requirement and showing that they did learn to avoid. It would appear then that the escape contingency is not a necessary feature of avoidance acquisition. This is what Mowrer and Lamoreaux were trying to show. But there is a more interesting feature of their data. Notice that all Ss with the running R_a learned the response quite rapidly and approached perfect performance whether or not running was also the R_e. Mowrer and Lamoreaux's conclusion is entirely justified as far as the running Ra is concerned. But the situation

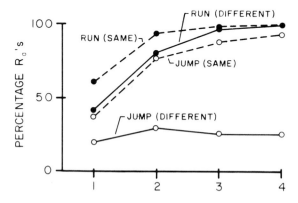

Fig. 1. Acquisition of R_a for Ss jumping or running. Different groups either had the same or different R_e. (From Mowrer & Lamoreaux, 1946.)

with the jumping R_a is quite different. Here, R_a was only acquired by the group for which jumping was also the R_e.

The marked asymmetry between jumping and running, *i.e.*, the interaction between this variable and homogeneous versus heterogeneous conditions, would appear to invalidate the implication usually drawn from the Mowrer and Lamoreaux study that because R_a need not be the same as R_e it can be any operant in S's repertoire. Their results are consistent, though, with the hypothesis that if R_a is an SSDR (running), then the escape contingency adds little to its strength, but if R_a is not an SSDR (jumping), then the escape contingency may be necessary if it is to be established. The efficacy of CS termination (which was the contingency to which Mowrer and Lamoreaux attributed reinforcement since they did not consider the possibility that avoidance itself might be reinforcing) would appear to be a statistical artifact of pooling subgroups and not a general principle.

This early study has, surprisingly, been followed by only a few other reports of attempts to train two different R_as and R_es. Boren (1961) trained rats to escape shock by pressing one lever and to avoid it by pressing another. Unfortunately for our understanding of avoidance acquisition, the data Boren reported were obtained after very extensive training. There is the additional problem of whether the two responses were different. It is not clear that pressing one bar or pressing another involves two responses; it could be one response under the control of two rather complicated sets of temporal and situational stimulus patterns. The S may have learned mainly a temporal discrimination since the commonly reported "post-shock bursts" of responding occurred predominantly on the escape bar while subsequent post-burst responses occurred predominantly on the avoidance bar. Bower (1965) has reported a dismal failure of rats to learn in a T maze to go one way to escape and the other to avoid.

In a design more like Mowrer and Lamoreaux's, Bixenstine and Barker (1964) attempted to train rats in a shuttlebox to run to avoid and to press a bar to escape. Their Ss showed extremely poor levels of avoidance behavior. The only learning occurred under those conditions in which R_e led to delayed termination of shock. With delay of shock termination, which compromised the efficacy of R_e, Ss were able to acquire the different R_a. Unfortunately, the interpretation of their results is obscured by the lack of symmetry in the experimental design. There was no condition under which Ss had a press R_a and a run R_e. This difficulty, plus the low level of avoidance performance obtained under conditions which should have produced results comparable to those of Mowrer and Lamoreaux, limit any possible conclusions.

Keehn (1959a) trained a rat in the wheel to run for the R_a and to turn around for the R_e. Within just a few minutes S was running almost continuously. But the lack of symmetry in the experimental design again limits the possible conclusions to what we already knew from Mowrer and Lamoreaux: the rat does not need an escape contingency to learn a running R_a.

The unsatisfactory state of the evidence on the acquisition of different avoidance and escape responses finally prompted us at the University of Washington to undertake a systematic study of the problem (Bolles, 1969). Rats were trained in a running wheel, and different groups were required to avoid shock either by running, by turning around in one spot, or by rearing up on their hind legs. These groups were further divided so that for some subgroups R_e was the same response whereas for others R_e was one of the other two responses. Thus there were nine groups in all, three with homogeneous conditions and six with heterogeneous response requirements. The results are shown in Figure 2.

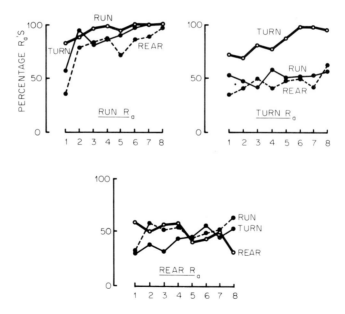

Fig. 2. Percentage of R_as by 10-trial blocks for nine groups required to run, turn, or rear to avoid shock and to run, turn, or rear to escape it. Labels on individual groups' data refer to the R_e requirement. (From Bolles, 1969).

The data can be pooled to show significant overall differences attributable to different R_as; some R_as are much easier to learn than others. They can also be pooled to show a significant overall superiority of homogeneous over heterogeneous conditions, but this conclusion would be too conservative. The impressive finding is the interaction between R_a and R_e requirements. Thus, if the rat can run to avoid, then it learns to do so regardless of the escape contingency. There were reliable differences among these three groups but they were small in magnitude compared with the differences attributable to different R_as, and in all cases the running R_a was rapidly acquired. On the other hand, none of the groups with the rearing R_a showed any learning in 80 trials, even with the assistance of the escape contingency. In the case of the turning-around response, modest learning occurred under homogeneous conditions but none under the heterogeneous conditions. The contribution of the escape contingency to avoidance learning appears to depend entirely upon what R_a happens to be.

It should be noted that these three responses were selected for study because they all had high operant rates in the situation, and they all occurred between 40% and 50% of the time on the first block of trials. In spite of this high operant rate, and the use of the CS-termination contingency for all Ss, some groups failed to learn. Sometimes the customary reinforcement contingencies simply do not work.

Perhaps it is too much to require the rat to learn two mutually exclusive responses—one to avoid and one to escape shock. The data indicate that such two-response learning cannot be obtained with many combinations of responses. There is considerably more information available on the reinforcement problem from studies in which R_a is acquired in the absence of any explicitly required R_e.

B.   Avoidance Studies without R_e

The rat should certainly be able to learn to run out of a place where shock is imminent without prior training to escape the shock. Marx and Hellwig (1964) trained two groups of Ss in a one-way situation. One group was run under ordinary escape conditions in which R_e was running into an adjoining compartment. The second group was placed in the same apparatus and allowed 3 sec to run away before the door was closed and a severe inescapable shock was administered. The latter Ss, who could avoid shock but not escape it, learned the R_a quite quickly, although not as quickly as the other group learned the R_e. In this situation, as in other one-way avoidance and some of the "acquired drive" situations, acquisition is so precipitous that one must wonder in what sense any instrumental learning is being demonstrated. If leaving the situation is the top response in the hierarchy of SSDRs, then S really has nothing more to learn once fear has become conditioned to situational cues. It is also interesting to note that when Ss fail to learn flight responses they fail because they have learned to freeze.

A similar type of analysis can be applied to running wheel avoidance where, again, running is evidently a preeminent defense reaction of many animals. Sheffield (1948) has shown that guinea pigs will learn to avoid shock in running wheels when the shock is presented for so brief an interval (.1 sec) as to make it inescapable. Bolles *et al.* (1966) have reported that rats also show considerable proficiency at a wheel-running R_a when shocks are of minimal duration. The Bolles *et al.* study seems to be the only published attempt to isolate experimentally all three of the contingencies usually involved in avoidance learning tasks. It was a factorial design in which shock either had to be escaped or was too short to be escaped, the CS either terminated with R_a or was prolonged for 10 sec, and shock was either avoidable or unavoidable. The percentage of R_as in the the first 100 trials for each group is given in the right-hand side of Table 1. It is apparent that the avoidance contingency is more important than either the escape contingency or the CS-termination contingency in this situation. The shuttle box produced somewhat different results, however (see the left-hand side of Table 1). In the shuttlebox the

TABLE I

Percentage of R_as in Two Different
Kinds of Apparatus as a Function of
Whether S Could Avoid the US (A),
Escape Shock (E), or Terminate the CS (T)[a]

Available contingencies	Apparatus	
	Shuttlebox	Wheel
A E T	70	85
A E	40	75
A T	37	79
E T	31	38
A	15	62
E	9	26
T	10	48
None	15	28

[a]From Bolles, Stokes & Younger, 1966.

three contingencies appear to have approximately equal and additive effects upon the strength of R_a. Again, the relative importance of the events that are supposed to reinforce R_a varies with what R_a happens to be.

Church and Solomon (1956) introduced an avoidance procedure that almost abolishes the escape contingency: shock is terminated after a delay of several sec. following R_e. Dogs were tested in a shuttlebox, and although R_e was seriously disrupted, there was relatively little effect upon R_a. However, Kamin (1959) has reported disruption of avoidance with rats under these conditions (see Section IV).

Something very like avoidance without escape has also been studied in the bar-press situation. It was reported independently by Hurwitz (1964) and D'Amato and his associates (Biederman, D'Amato & Keller, 1964; D'Amato et al., 1964) that bar-press avoidance behavior is more readily obtained with intermittent shock than with continuous shock. D'Amato et al. report that the more intermittent the shock, at least to the point where it is on 0.2 sec and off 2.0 sec, the easier R_a is to learn. Both D'Amato and Hurwitz use shocks that are too brief to permit an operant R_e; S does not really turn the shock off but simply stops the series. To this extent there is no escape contingency.[3] D'Amato usually starts his Ss with continuous shock, but this initial training phase is concluded before R_a has gained much strength. The superior acquisition of R_a under these conditions implies that in some manner the usual escape contingency with continuous shock disrupts the bar-press R_a. D'Amato has speculated that the stimulus settings for escape and avoidance are more alike in the case of discontinuous shock than they are in the case of continuous shock since, most of the time, only the CS is present. Therefore the "pseudo-escape" response should generalize more readily to the avoidance situation than the usual R_e does. Alternatively, it might be supposed that continuous shock provides too much stimulation, or arousal, or fear to permit proficient avoidance behavior; intermittent shock may be simply a low average intensity shock. In any case, there is an interesting question of how the inter-shock pseudo-escape response is maintained. What is the source of reinforcement?

[3]All shock scramblers introduce some intermittency into the US, and some commercial scramblers introduce a lot (Bolles, 1966), so the continuity of shock is at best a relative matter. The question is further complicated by the report of D'Amato et al. that a preponderance of R_es occurs during shock-on. We also know that the rat can turn off shock within .05 sec if it freezes on the bar (Bolles & McGillis, 1968). We therefore not only have a new relativistic dimension of shock continuity, but also the puzzle of how such short latency R_es can be reinforced by shock termination if they are not operant but are as reflexive as they seem to be. Perhaps the escape contingency is not as effective in this situation as is usually assumed, and perhaps it is most effective in producing freezing on the bar.

Does the escape contingency always interfere with a bar press R_a? The answer is no, not necessarily. Hearst and Whalen (1963) gave rats several hundred trials with both avoidance and escape contingencies, and then withdrew the escape contingency leaving S only able to avoid. Avoidance behavior (which had only reached about 25%) collapsed completely. It should be noted, however, that when the US was inescapable its duration was 15 sec. Its occurrence must have produced gross behavior which broke up the usual pattern of freezing on the bar, thereby eliminating R_a. Hearst and Whalen's own explanation, that the effect was due to an excess of emotionality with the greater amount of shock, is probably not false but incomplete.

Finally, we may cite a study by Malott, Sidley, and Schoenfeld (1963) in which rats were trained to avoid and/or escape brief intermittent shocks spaced every 1.5 sec, and then tested in the absence of the escape contingency. Little systematic effect was found either upon response rate or upon the overall shock rate. Thus, we can find instances in which removal of the escape contingency either facilitates bar-press avoidance, destroys it, or leaves it unaffected. No direct comparison of these different studies is possible, however, because of the different procedures used and the fact that in some cases early acquisition was being investigated whereas in others only the maintenance of a learned response is reported. There is no reason to suppose that the same associative mechanisms are involved, and probably the different effects do involve quite different mechanisms.

C. Sidman Avoidance

One of the most interesting avoidance learning situations is that discovered by Sidman (1953). Sidman's procedure involves a series of very brief inescapable shocks which occur perhaps every 5 sec (the S–S interval). Although S cannot escape individual shocks, it can break the sequence and postpone the next shock for perhaps 30 sec (the R–S interval) by pressing a bar. Ordinarily no CS is given. The theorist is therefore faced with a rather interesting problem: Since S does not escape the US, nor terminate a CS, there appears to be no way in which any reinforcement contingency can make contact with its behavior so as to reinforce R_a. Nonetheless, R_a is acquired, sometimes with great facility.

Basically, there are two schools of thought about how to explain the phenomenon. One is based on the assumption that S does, in fact, make use of the only available reinforcement contingency, avoidance of shock. The question then becomes how to specify what avoidance means in behavioral terms. What explanatory mechanisms are required to make sense of the notion that the rat can avoid? The earliest suggestion (Schoenfeld, 1950; Sheffield, 1948; Sidman, 1953) was that avoidance meant freedom from punishment. The S must end up pressing the bar because R_a is safe, at least for 30 sec, whereas all other responses are shocked within 5 sec. More recently, Sidman (1962) has proposed that the source of reinforcement in this situation is the reduction in shock frequency that R_a produces. The S is differentially reinforced over a period of time for that behavior which leads to differential rates of shock. The trouble with these hypotheses is that the acquisition of bar pressing is frequently precipitous in the early stages of training and its extinction is generally extremely slow (Sidman, 1955). If we think of all possible responses having to be gradually reduced to near-zero strength the freedom from punishment hypothesis seems rather far fetched. But it appears much more plausible if we think of the severe restriction that fear puts on S's repertoire, *i.e.*, if we think of S only being able to freeze or to seek escape from the situation. The initial train of shocks produces a high level of activity incompatible with freezing. Leaf (1965) and Stone (1966) have shown that short S–S intervals facilitate acquisition. One of S's early encounters with the bar will lead to some accidental presses, the intershock interval is thereby increased to the point where S can freeze on the bar, and there he is! Operant bar presses will gradually emerge as freezing becomes gradually better differentiated and especially as S's success at the bar reduces shock density to levels that reduce fear and its limitation of the response repertoire. Some reinforcement mechanism is still needed, however, to explain the continued gradual improvement in performance, and it is at this point that the second school of thought offers some promising possibilities.

The second approach to the problem is based on the assumption that there must be an effective CS whose termination reinforces R_a. The problem is to find or hypothesize an appropriate CS since there is none in the observable environment. Anger (1963) has suggested that there may be internal stimulus consequences of having recently pressed the bar; there may be a trace which changes discriminably as the response recedes into the past. The effective CS is the "old" trace. Immediately following R_a the trace is new, and since new traces are never paired with shock they remain relatively unaversive. But as the end of the R–S interval draws near, the trace becomes increasingly like that which has been paired with shock and it is therefore increasingly aversive. The R_a is reinforced by the substitution of safe "new" traces for aversive "old" ones. This conception, originally formulated by Mowrer & Keehn (1958) with the additional provision that fear and a diminution in fear were involved, appears to be well able to account for the very gradual improvement that occurs with continued training long after S has reduced shock frequency to a low value. Sidman's shock density hypothesis would require that S be able to distinguish and be differentially reinforced by, *e.g.*, one shock per hour as against two shocks per hour. Anger's hypothesis requires only that S be able to discriminate the consequences of having responded 20 sec previously from the consequences of having responded 10 sec previously.

An interesting aspect of acquisition is that rats will frequently show a very sudden onset of responding at a rate of about 500 presses/hr, a rate which may change only a few percent with 100 hr of additional training. The details of the behavior do change, however. Initially, most responses are apparently elicited by shock, since they come in bursts during and immediately after a shock. After a postshock burst S usually stops responding until the next shock comes on. The acquisition of responses located well into the R–S interval, which result in the continual postponement of shock, are acquired slowly as the postshock bursts slowly disappear. Thus, there are two critical phases of acquisition to account for: one is the sudden appearance of postshock bursts, and the other is the gradual development of temporal discrimination.

Keehn (1963) has argued that even though shock is inescapable it may be that R_a is maintained by superstitious shock-escape responses. He shortened the shock progressively so as to remove any possible adventitious escape contingency, and R_a showed a progressive deterioration. Although such a mechanism may operate here, the evidence is not conclusive. For one thing, under the briefest shocks Keehn used (.05 sec), S may have been deprived not only of the opportunity to escape but also of the need to escape, or avoid. Specifically, fear may have dropped out. Bolles (unpublished) studied the acquisition of Sidman avoidance in three groups for which shock duration was fixed at .3 sec but for which there were different consequences of short latency responses. For one group, responses during shock were effective in producing avoidance, for another group the usual requirement was imposed so that no responses during shock were permitted to be effective, while for the third group, no responses initiated for .5 sec after shock onset were effective. No differences in acquisition among the three groups were found, which suggests that Sidman's original conjecture was correct, and that his procedure does really permit the acquisition of an R_a in the absence of any escape contingency, real or adventitious. It appears that Sidman (1953) may have been correct in supposing that the important contingency is actually the avoidance of shock.

One vexing problem is that many Ss fail to learn Sidman avoidance (Weismann, 1962). There are investigators who have never been able to get it in any Ss. Hence the mechanisms that are proposed to account for the acquisition of the R_a also have to be able to account for frequent failures to learn. It is a rather fascinating puzzle, practically speaking, because E has no means at his disposal to permit shaping up the response except by basically altering the procedure. Sidman (1966) explains these individual differences by invoking a factor of "attention." He says that in cases where S fails to acquire R_a, S was "probably not attending to the downward movement of the lever as the critical element of the avoidance response, but rather to some other aspect of its behavior that was imperfectly correlated with the lever pressing" (Sidman, 1966, p. 454). Indeed, it would seem that the fundamental difficulty of bar-press Sidman avoidance is that this R_a is not part of S's SSDR repertoire.

It has apparently been known for some time that, in contrast with discriminated bar-press avoidance, the acquisition of Sidman avoidance can be considerably improved by the introduction of an escape contingency, *i.e.*, by using shock that is long enough that R_e can shorten it. Stone (1966), who has carefully reviewed the evidence on Sidman acquisition and arrived at an account similar to the present one, proposes, however, that the effect of the escape contingency is merely to get S onto the bar. It is also known that once R_a is established, it can be considerably strengthened by the introduction of a CS which precedes a scheduled shock by a few seconds. Under the CS condition S comes to restrict R_a almost entirely to times when the CS is on (Sidman, 1955).

In his most recent discussion, Sidman (1966) has noted that lengthening the R–S interval reduces response rate but has an even greater effect in reducing shock rate, and can be said therefore to make R_a more efficient. The length of the R–S interval appears to have no effect upon the acquisition of the behavior, however.

Using a Sidman avoidance procedure in a running wheel situation, Keehn (1967) demonstrated extremely rapid acquisition and an extremely high level of performance after a single short session. Running is an SSDR. Similarly, neither Rescorla and LoLordo (1965) nor Grossen and Bolles (1968) report trouble in getting dogs or rats to perform in a shuttlebox with Sidman's procedure. The speed with which dogs learn ordinary "discriminated" avoidance in the shuttlebox (Solomon, & Wynne, 1953) suggests that jumping a hurdle may be an SSDR for the dog. The study of Sidman avoidance in situations other than the Skinner box promises to shed new light on the behavioral mechanisms involved.

D.   Conclusions

There is one other relationship between R_e and R_a that can be considered. Suppose conditions are arranged to maximize the transfer of R_e to the avoidance situation. Specifically, what would be the consequences of selecting as an R_a precisely that reaction which is the unconditioned response to the shock? Turner and Solomon (1962) addressed themselves to this question using human Ss and a movement of the big toe as both R_e and R_a. Electrodes on the ankle produced a very short latency reflexive toe movement, and the question was whether this movement could be learned as an R_a. A number of groups were run under different instructions and stimulation conditions, but we need not be concerned with a full account of the experiment; the surprising and important finding was that under instructions which minimized voluntary responding (withholding the information that this was an avoidance experiment), it was impossible to condition the short latency, reflexive toe movement R_a. Those Ss who did learn to avoid by making the required movement responded slowly and, presumably, voluntarily. The results force us to the conclusion that in spite of the appeal of the Pavlovian conditioning conception in which a reflexive reaction, elicited by the US, is supposed to become automatically conditioned to a CS that is paired with the US, this simply does not happen in avoidance learning. The simplest (although probably somewhat oversimple) way to state the case is that an R_a cannot be acquired if it is an unconditioned reflex to shock.

Further support for this hypothesis comes from a study by Warren and Bolles (1967), who trained a wheel-running R_a in rats. Three groups were run which differed according to whether shock was administered on nonavoidance trials to the hind feet, the front feet, or all four feet. The most obvious but incorrect hypothesis (following the procedure and findings of Fowler & Miller, 1963) would be that Ss shocked in the hind feet should lurch forward as a reflexive reaction to the shock, and then since this response is compatible with the forward-running R_a, these Ss should have an advantage in learning to run. On the other hand, Ss shocked in the front feet, who recoil backward as a reflexive reaction to shock, should have considerable difficulty acquiring the incompatible forward-running R_a. The results came out in the opposite direction: Ss showed better acquisition of the running R_a if that response was *incompatible* with the unconditioned reaction to shock. Here again the acquisition of R_a was hindered rather than facilitated by a compatible but reflexive R_e.

To gather up a number of loose ends from this section, it can be said that there are well-established cases in which the escape contingency fails to provide any positive transfer to the R_a, and in some cases the transfer appears to be negative. Negative transfer has been found in bar-press situations, at least once in the shuttlebox, and in the running wheel. Certainly the bulk of the evidence that has been cited supports the conclusion that avoidance behavior can be acquired, and quite readily, in the absence of any escape training. It is mainly just in the shuttlebox situation that the escape contingency contributes importantly to the acquisition of R_a.

TABLE II

Illustrative Experiments Showing How Rapidity of Avoidance Learning Is a Function of R_a and R_e

Avoidance response, R_a	Escape response, R_e					
	Key[d]	Same as R_a	Key	Different from R_a	Key	None possible
R_a takes S away One-way Running wheel	++	Theios (1963)	++	Keehn (1959a) Bolles (1969)	++	Santos (1960) Marx & Hellwig (1964) Sheffield (1948) [a]Keehn (1959b)
Ambiguous Shuttle box	+−	Mowrer & Lamoreaux (1942)	−	Mowrer & Lamoreaux (1946) Bixenstine & Barker (1964)	−	Bolles et al. (1966) Kamin (1959)
R_a keeps S there Bar press	−	Myers (1959) D'Amato & Schiff (1964) Coons et al. (1960) Bolles (1969) c	−	Boren (1961) Bolles.(1969)	+	[a]Sidman (1953) [b]D'Amato et al. (1964) Hurwitz (1964) c

[a]No CS

[b]Discontinuous US

[c]Other studies could be cited

[d]Positive results in terms of rapid learning of RA (see text for explanation).

We have also discovered the overriding importance of the response requirement. If R_a is an SSDR, particularly if it permits S to leave the situation, then R_a will be readily acquired, and neither the escape contingency nor the CS-termination contingency will add very much. This interaction between R_a and R_e is summarized in Table 2. The columns of the table characterize avoidance training procedures according to whether R_e is the same as R_a (the standard procedure), different from R_a, or not possible, presumably, because there is no explicit escape contingency. The rows break down avoidance training procedures according to whether R_a permits S to leave the situation, requires S to remain in the situation, or is ambiguous in this respect. There is probably a continuum for the R_a variable, with the one-way apparatus at one extreme, and the bar-press situation near the other. The shuttlebox is the most common example of the ambiguous situation.

The pattern of positive results with respect to how fast R_a is learned corresponds rather well with what would be expected from the SSDR hypothesis. The top row is all strongly plus, the middle row is rather indifferent, although the escape contingency appears to assist learning, and the bottom row is strongly minus except for the unique case of bar-press avoidance, which appears to proceed better without the escape contingency. These relations, especially those involving comparisons across columns, must be rather tentative because of the meager amount of available data.

III. ACQUIRED DRIVE STUDIES

The so-called acquired drive paradigm is much like the avoidance paradigm, enough so that we cannot afford to ignore some representative studies. Two features define the procedure:

1. A stimulus, the CS, is paired with shock. This pairing is inevitable since shock cannot be avoided, although sometimes it is made escapable.

2. The S is tested with the CS alone, in the absence of shock, to see if its termination will reinforce some criterion response. We may call this response an R_a, although since there is no more shock S is not really avoiding it.

The rationale underlying these procedures is that initially fear, which is the acquired drive, becomes conditioned to the CS when it is paired with shock. Subsequently it is possible to reinforce any operant R_a selected from S's repertoire by making CS termination (and reduction of the conditioned fear) contingent upon its occurrence. The rationale is the same as that of avoidance studies, and the procedures are the same too except that (1) CS–US pairings all come in an early block of trials instead of occurring on nonavoidance trials, and (2) there is no avoidance contingency. From what we have already seen of avoidance learning, we may anticipate that R_a will be readily acquired if it is an SSDR, and acquired only with difficulty otherwise.

A. Studies with R_a the Same as R_e

Consider first the situation in which there is an R_e during the CS–US pairing trials, and it is the same response as R_a. This is, in effect, escape training followed by extinction of R_e. The question is not whether the CS-termination contingency reinforces a new response, but whether it helps maintain the old one. In the first such experiment May (1948) trained rats in a shuttlebox to leap over a hurdle to the other side to escape shock. These escape trials were interspersed with CS–US pairing trials on which R_e was prevented. (The intermixture of trials was used to prevent freezing from becoming the predominant response to the CS.) In subsequent tests shock was omitted and CS termination was made contingent upon R_a (which had been R_e). Although no trial by trial data are given, so we do not know how fast R_e was extinguishing, there was a high incidence of hurdle jumping, and the appropriate control groups indicated that the response was being controlled by the CS. However, the level of performance was not impressive in terms of the standards set by more recent studies, quite possibly because testing was conducted in a shuttlebox where S could not effectively flee. Mathers (1957), using a paddle-wheel turning response, which is definitely not part of S's defensive reaction repertoire, found rapid extinction of R_e in a study similar to May's.

The results are quite different when R_a provides for an unequivocal flight from the situation. Clark (1966) could report almost perfect execution of R_a after four CS–US pairing and escape trials. Part of Clark's success may be attributable to his use of simultaneous presentation of CS and US. Other Ss given the usual 10-sec CS–US interval performed at 42% whereas the simultaneous Ss were at 98%. Controls were run to demonstrate that the response was in fact controlled by the CS, *i.e.*, Ss given only the CS or only the US performed at 15% and 20%, respectively. Such controls have become commonplace, and they are desirable for showing that R_a is, in fact, under the associative control of the CS. However there are other cues present, namely, environmental and apparatus cues, which have also been paired with the US, and which might therefore be expected to evoke R_a in the absence of the nominal CS. Indeed, several experimenters (*e.g.*, Edmonson & Amsel, 1954; Maatsch, 1959; Page, 1955) have found that R_a can be acquired and maintained over many trials without any explicit CS being used. Since this effect appears to be limited to situations in which S runs from a place where it has been shocked to a place where it has never been shocked, it makes sense from the SSDR point of view.

B. Studies with R_a Different from R_e

The most powerful test of the reinforcement hypothesis would involve the use of different responses for R_a and R_e to index separately the reinforcing effects of the CS-termination contingency and the escape contingency. There is no avoidance contingency in the acquired drive procedure, and so it cannot confound the other two.

Miller (1941, 1948) can be credited with almost doing the crucial experiment in what was, interestingly, the first acquired drive study. Miller confined rats to a white box, and gave them a series of brief shocks to condition fear to the environmental cues. Then a door was opened leading to an adjoining black box, and S was given a series of shocks which had to be escaped by running into the black box. A series of pretest trials was then run to make sure that upon being placed in the white box, S would promptly run into the black box without being shocked. At this point Miller had confirmed what May had found: an old R_e could be maintained by the termination of cues (apparatus cues in this case) that had been paired with shock. But Miller then ran a series of test trials in which the door to the black box was closed, and S was required to learn a new R_a, turning a paddle wheel, in order to open the door and leave the white box. The new R_a was acquired, although a lot of Ss dropped out by freezing.

There is something ironic in the fact that this study, the second oldest experiment cited in this chapter, presents the most serious challenge to the SSDR hypothesis. Indeed, it presents us with a major crisis. While it is easy to argue that leaving the white box was an SSDR, it is a little late to maintain that this is also true for turning a paddle wheel. Still, it is likely that the first R_as occurred while S was attempting to scratch its way out through the door or climb out through the window the wheel was mounted in. (The wheel was immediately adjacent to the door.) There is also some question whether the effective reinforcement in Miller's study was the *acquired* aversiveness of the white box. Miller gave his Ss initial preshock exposure to the apparatus, and found that there was no preference for the black side. However, Allison, Larson, and Jensen (1967) have demonstrated that while rats normally show little preference for black boxes over white ones, *frightened* rats show a very strong preference for black boxes. Allison *et al.* could not even overcome this preference by shocking Ss in the black box; it was still preferred to a white box. The implication is that if Miller had run a comparable group from black to white there would have been little maintenance of R_e and undoubtedly no acquisition of R_a.

Finally, there is a real possibility that R_e and R_a were not as different as is usually supposed; R_a may not have really been a "new" response. Miller almost acknowledges this when he suggests that learning would proceed faster if during initial R_e training we were to introduce "a hurdle approximately 2 in. high over which the animals have to climb, thus introducing components of standing up and reaching into the initial response. This should favor the subsequent occurrence of wheel turning . . . ." He also suggests that we might "connect the door to an electronic relay so that it will fall when touched and require the animals to touch it in order to make it fall . . ." (Miller, 1948, p. 92). Admitting that the acquisition of R_a will be facilitated by making it similar to R_e, one may speculate about how similar they can be and still provide a test of the hypothesis that they can be different! There seem to be real grounds for doubting that Miller has shown either that R_a can be any response in S's repertoire, or that R_a is reinforced by the termination of cues that have been paired with shock.

There are very few other acquired drive studies with R_a different from R_e, but Robinson (1961) has reported an elaborate experiment part of which provides the necessary design features. Rats were first trained with ordinary procedures to avoid shock in a shuttlebox. Then the door was closed and Ss learned a new R_a, bar pressing, to terminate the CS. The US was no longer presented. Here the new R_a was clearly different from the old R_a, and a variety of control groups demonstrated that the new R_a was governed by the CS. But there are two difficulties in the interpretation of Robinson's results. First, the new R_a was not pressing the bar but holding it down; releasing it turned the CS back on immediately. Thus, S could freeze and keep the CS off. Second, S showed almost perfect execution of the new R_a right from the beginning of training, a finding which also suggests that S was freezing. Moreover, the bar-holding sessions were only 5 min long; freezing in the absence of shock might be expected to persist throughout a period this short. If Robinson's Ss were freezing, then it hardly seems necessary to invoke any reinforcement mechanisms to account for his results.

Trapold, Blehert, and Sturm (1965) attempted to replicate Robinson's study, and did replicate the results that have been cited. The same interpretation might be applicable, but it should be noted that Trapold *et al.*

obtained relatively slow acquisition of the response and reported having to shape it. Thus in their study the response may have been an operant and not just the result of freezing.

Another investigation of the acquisition of an R_a different from R_e was reported by Bolles and Tuttle (1967). Two groups of rats were trained in a shuttlebox to escape shock, one by running and the other by rearing up on the hind legs. All Ss were then required to make the other response (rearing or running) to terminate the CS in the absence of shock. Control groups were run under the same conditions, either running or rearing to escape shock, and then tested with the CS to determine if the other response could be reinforced; the difference was that at the time of testing the CS was novel to the controls: it had not been previously paired with shock, or even previously presented. The acquisition of the new R_a by the four groups is shown in Figure 3. The four "delayed" groups were corresponding groups for whom CS termination was delayed for 10 sec after the occurrence of R_a.

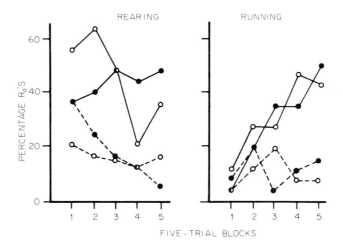

Fig. 3. Acquisition of R_a based on CS termination as a function of immediacy of CS termination and prior CS pairing with shock. Key: (solid circle, solid line) paired immediate termination; (open circle, solid line) unpaired immediate termination; (solid circle, dashed line) paired delayed termination; (open circle, dashed line) unpaired delayed termination. (From Bolles & Tuttle, 1967).

If we look just at the performance of the experimental groups we find considerable support for the hypothesis that CS termination is a reinforcer. It appears to provide maintenance of rearing, which was initially a strong response, and good acquisition of running, which was initially weak. However, the performance of control Ss for whom the CS was novel was not significantly different. It seems unlikely that the CS (an 80 dB white noise) was inherently very aversive, and more likely that the data illustrate some type of pseudoconditioning phenomenon. Similar effects have been previously reported in acquired drive studies (*e.g.*, Baron, 1959; Grossberg, 1962), although other investigators (*e.g.*, May, 1948) appear to have gotten CS-termination effects over and above pseudoconditioning effects. It is also interesting that Bolles and Tuttle observed acquisition only in the case of the running R_a. Running is an SSDR.

No other investigations using this paradigm seem to have been reported, but it might be possible that there have been investigations that have not been reported because, like the Bolles and Tuttle, Baron, and Grossberg studies, they yielded negative results. The evidence as it stands is equivocal; some of it is consistent with the fear-reduction-CS-termination hypothesis advanced by Miller and others, but some of it is not. The chief uncertainty surrounding these studies is whether the "new" response is, in fact, a new response, or whether its occurrence is already dictated by S's prior learning in the test situation.

If fear is elicited by the test situation, then we should expect rapid acquisition of an R_a that is compatible with S's SSDRs. There are no experimental reports involving R_as that take S out of the situation except for Miller's study where there is some question about the definition of R_a. Then in the few studies that have required R_as that clearly do not allow leaving the situation, the results are rather negative. This latter case provides a particularly tough test of the reinforcement hypothesis, however, because not only does it require the acquisition of an R_a which is actively in competition with R_e, it also requires an R_a that is in competition with the S's SSDRs. But if the response requirement is weakened, *e.g.*, by the seemingly minor detail that bar holding rather than bar pressing is permitted so that R_a is more compatible with freezing, then S acquires it with no difficulty (Robinson, 1961).

C. Studies without R_e

There is much more information available from situations in which R_a acquisition has been investigated following a series of *inescapable* shocks, *i.e.*, where no explicit R_e is allowed. It has been well established that when Ss are shocked in one box they will quickly learn to jump into an adjoining box (Goldstein, 1960; Kalish, 1954; McAllister & McAllister,

1962a, 1962b, 1963) and stay there if given the opportunity to do so (Campbell & Campbell, 1962). The acquisition of R_a is so dependable under these conditions that some experimenters take it for granted and simply measure resistance to extinction (Gwinn, 1951; Kurtz & Pearl, 1963). The occurrence of R_a is frequently used to monitor S's fear. Thus, the number of prior CS–US pairings is varied for different groups, and the investigator looks to see if the subsequent strength of the R_a varies accordingly (Desiderato, 1964; Goldstein, 1960; Gwinn, 1951; Kalish, 1954). Apparently fear does increase with the number of pairings, but on the other hand, too many inescapable US presentations tends to promote freezing, which may later predominate in the test situation. (Perhaps it would be better to vary the number of CS–US pairings while holding the number of USs constant.) The effect of US intensity on fear conditioning has also been investigated this way (Goldstein, 1960; Gwinn, 1951; McAllister & McAllister, 1962b). A positive relationship has always been found here, so far. And the effects of different CSs on fear conditioning have been investigated (Desiderato, 1964; Fromer, 1962.)

Underlying all of this work is the assumption that the strength of R_a is directly related to the strength of fear. This assumption is, strictly speaking, probably not justified. For example, Goldstein (1960) and McAllister and McAllister (1962a, 1962b, 1963) have reported that R_a may be considerably stronger on the second day of testing than it was on the first day immediately after US presentation. Are we to conclude that fear increases with time after fear conditioning? McAllister and McAllister (1962b) have suggested that following a series of shocks a condition is produced that is something like Amsel and Maltzman's (1950) "emotionality." This emotionality is hypothesized to be something other than fear itself. It is supposed to be more transient than fear and to dissipate in a few hours. This emotionality state is also assumed to be the source of certain unconditioned reactions, specifically, freezing. Now if it is assumed further that the emotionality condition is not at full strength immediately after shock, but increases for an hour or two before it begins eventually to dissipate, then it could provide an explanation of the poor performance that has been reported in a number of aversive situations when S is tested an hour or two after being shocked (Brush, 1964b; Desiderato, 1964; Kamin 1957a). This effect, the Kamin effect, is discussed further in Chapter 7 by Brush, Chapter 4 by Denny and Chapter 2 by McAllister and McAllister.

Apart from the question of whether the strength of R_a can be properly taken as an index of the strength of fear, there is the further question of whether it is realistic to believe there is no R_e in these situations.

Can we assume that just because S is confined in the apparatus and cannot make an R_e that has been defined and authorized by the experimenter it will not learn some unauthorized response, perhaps a postural adjustment, that minimizes shock or its aversiveness? Perhaps S learns to freeze during a series of inescapable shocks because moving around makes the shocks more painful (Campbell & Masterson, 1969). Alternatively, perhaps S makes abortive escape attempts during inescapable shock, and these responses are conditioned to the CS and reinstated by it on subsequent test trials. The conditioning of such fractional escape responses could help explain why S is so good at escaping from the situation when later given the opportunity to do so. Kent, Wagner and Gannon (1960) and Wagner (1964) have attempted to test this possibility by giving CS–US pairings in a situation which not only confined S but which literally prevented all bodily movement. Under restricted conditions Ss were stuffed into boxes only $1\frac{5}{8} \times 1\frac{7}{8} \times 5\frac{3}{8}$ in. When subsequently tested in a normal hurdle box, the restricted Ss did not learn the jumpaway R_a whereas unrestricted Ss did (Kent et al, 1960). Wagner (1964) also obtained a significant decrement with Ss restricted during the CS–US pairings, but his restricted Ss learned the R_a too, perhaps because he made the mistake of giving them shocks in a box identical to the test box before administering shock in the restricted situation.

Finally there is the important question of whether the CS is relevant. Is R_a really under any associative control by the CS or really reinforced by its termination? There are three lines of evidence which suggest that the CS may be relatively unimportant in the acquisition of a flight-taking R_a. First of all, many of the effects that have been discussed here have been found without the use of a specific stimulus being paired with shock (Campbell & Campbell, 1962; Gwinn, 1951; Fromer, 1962; McAllister & McAllister, 1962a). In these cases, situational cues have to carry the burden of being the effective CS which S terminates by leaving the situation. Second, it is possible to get good acquisition of R_a with backward conditioning procedures, i.e., under conditions in which the CS is not paired with the US but presented 15 sec or so after the US (McAllister & McAllister, 1962a; Wagner, 1964). McAllister and Mc-Allister (1962a) reported one experiment in which S was confined to the test apparatus for one hour after CS–US pairing so that the fear conditioned to the situational cues would extinguish. Results are shown in Figure 4 for four groups given extinction or not, and given either forward or backward CS–US pairings.

This pattern of results suggests that situational cues and the CS contribute about equally to R_a, but in most of the McAllister and Mc-Allisters results the situational cues appear to be relatively more

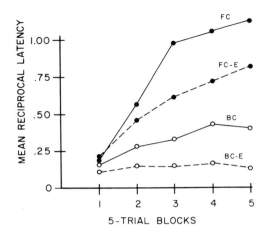

Fig. 4. Reciprocal latency of a running R_a for Ss given either forward or backward pairing of CS and shock, and either given one hour to extinguish fear of the apparatus or not. (From McAllister & McAllister, 1962a).

important. (See also Hearst, 1962, who found only small CS effects with monkeys in a CER situation.) McAllister and McAllister suggest that the atypical pattern shown in Fig. 4 may be due to the time course of the hypothetical emotionality condition described above. If this suggestion is valid, then the occurrence of R_a in this situation begins to appear to be a rather complex matter involving at least three different stimulus-motivation-response associations: CS-fear-R_a, situation-fear-R_a, and situation-emotionality-freezing. The role of situational cues in aversive learning is treated more fully by McAllister and McAllister in this volume, Chapter 2.

The third line of evidence which makes it difficult to attribute a decisive role to the CS is an effect discovered by Brown and Jacobs (1949). Brown and Jacobs gave CS–US pairings with an inescapable US, and then tested whether CS termination could be used to reinforce a hurdle jumping R_a. There was a fundamental difference between their procedure and the others discussed in that their CS–US pairings were given on *both* sides of the apparatus, *i.e.*, both sides of the hurdle. The purpose was evidently to condition fear equally to all parts of the test apparatus so that if acquisition of R_a was found it could be attributed to the reinforcing effect of CS termination alone. Two experiments are reported using these conditions which require R_a to be more like shuttling than like running away. In the first experiment Brown and Jacobs observed no acquisition of R_a but they did in the second. There were several parameters of the situation that were changed in the second experiment: the

CS and the US were both made intermittent, and S was made hungry. But perhaps the crucial parametric change, the variable which made the ambiguous shuttle-type of situation more like a to-be-escaped-from situation, was the introduction of a door which was opened when the CS came on. Learning here evidently depends upon a delicate balance of a number of subtle factors, however, since Grossberg (1962) duplicated the Brown and Jacobs' procedures, including the door, and found no learning and no difference in performance between experimental and control Ss.[4]

Perhaps the most elegant test of the CS-termination hypothesis would be an acquired drive study (so there was no avoidance contingency) with inescapable shock (so there was no escape contingency), and with the operation of some manipulandum as the criterion R_a (so that CS-termination would not be confounded with leaving the situation). Pseudoconditioning controls should be run to demonstrate that the R_a is really controlled by the CS. Using just these procedures, Baron (1959) found no sign of R_a acquisition, but only various kinds of pseudoconditioning effects. Dinsmoor (1962), using a somewhat more complex procedure, however, has reported appropriate maintenance of bar-press behavior. A series of well-spaced shocks was presented while a tone was on. The series of shocks and/or the CS could be terminated but only on a VI-30-sec schedule. Control procedures indicated that S was responding to the CS and not just to shock. Of course, a considerable amount of prior unspecified training was given, which clouds the question of acquisition somewhat.

D.   Conclusions

As with the studies of genuine avoidance learning, it is possible to analyze the procedures of these acquired drive or pseudo-avoidance experiments according to the nature of R_a and R_e. Table 3 gives a breakdown of the experiments according to whether the CS-US pairing stage of training provides for an R_e which is the same as the R_a subsequently to be acquired, an R_e which is different from R_a, or no explicit R_e. The rows of the table distinguish among cases in which R_a clearly enables S to get away, clearly requires S to stay put, or is ambiguous in this respect. The ambiguous category includes the shuttle box type of studies and the study of Miller (1948), whose Ss ultimately got away, but had to paddle a wheel to do so.

[4]*Editor's note:* See also Chapter 6 by Seligman, Maier, and Solomon, this volume, Section II,A,1.

TABLE III

Illustrative Experiments Showing How Learning in Acquired
Drive Situations Is a Function of R_a and R_e

Avoidance response, R_a	Escape response, R_e					
	Key	Same as R_a	Key	Different from R_a	Key	None possible
R_a takes S away. One-way	++	Clark (1966) [a]Edmunson & Amsel (1954) [a]Page (1955) [a]Maatsch (1959)	?		++	[a]Gwinn (1951) Kalish (1954) Goldstein (1960) [b]Kent et al. (1960) [a]Campbell & Campbell (1962) [c]
Ambiguous Shuttle box	+	May (1948)	−+	Miller (1948) Bolles & Tuttle (1967)	−+	Brown & Jacobs (1949) Grossberg (1962)
R_a keeps S there Bar Press	−	Mathers (1957)	−	Robinson (1961) Trapold et al. (1965) Bolles & Tuttle (1967)	−	Baron (1959) Dinsmoor (1962)

[a]No CS.

[b]Restrict all responding.

[c]Other studies could be cited.

[d]Positive results in terms of rapid learning of R_a (see text for explanation).

To hazard a few summary statements: it could be said that Table 3 is quite similar to Table 2, but that there are some interesting differences. These differences presumably attest to the fact that the avoidance contingency itself has some importance. Comparing the lower right-hand cell of the two tables, it is apparent that in the absence of an escape contingency bar-pressing behavior is much more readily acquired if there is an avoidance contingency. In the avoidance learning situation, shocks that result from failures to avoid continue to modify S's behavior, while in the acquired drive situation all behavior is punished and S ends up freezing. Freezing then prevails later and R_a is not acquired.

Table 3 indicates the overriding importance that has to be attributed to whether R_a permits S to leave the fear-arousing situation. If S cannot flee, it fails to learn; if S can flee, it quickly learns to do so. In neither case does the nature of R_e seem to make much difference. The ambiguous situation yields ambiguous results. This is the area in which there is the greatest need for further information, because at the present time it is not clear where the line should be drawn between leaving the situation and staying there, or where the pluses turn into minuses, or what the critical variables are that either permit or prevent S from learning R_a. Outside of this narrow ambiguous region, however, it is obvious that the most important single consideration is whether the response to be learned permits S to leave the fear-arousing situation.

IV. THE CS-TERMINATION CONTINGENCY

The evidence we have reviewed so far indicates that when S cannot leave the situation, the CS-termination contingency is insufficient to produce reinforcement of R_a, and that in situations where S can leave the situation, R_a is established so quickly that the additional contribution of CS termination to the learning is hard to demonstrate. The crucial test should be in the ambiguous situation, but unfortunately the data now available do not compel us either to accept or reject the idea that CS termination can be a source of reinforcement. The evidence suggests, however, that if it is a reinforcer, it must have a subtle impact upon R_a relative to some of the other factors we have discussed. The purpose of the present brief section is to note some additional difficulties with the CS-termination hypothesis.

Kamin (1956) compared the acquisition of R_a in four groups of rats trained under the following conditions: one group could avoid shock and terminate the CS in the usual manner, one group could neither avoid shock nor terminate the CS, and the other two groups could either terminate the CS or avoid shock but not both. All Ss had the escape contingency (plus termination of the accompanying CS) following a failure to avoid. The results suggest that both termination of the CS and avoidance of the US are significant factors in the acquisition of R_a, and that these two factors are of about equal importance and are independent, *i.e.*, they do not interact. These results are sometimes cited as demonstrating two independent sources of reinforcement (*e.g.*, Solomon & Brush, 1956). However, Kamin's own analysis put the burden of reinforcement entirely upon CS termination. He argued that Ss which terminated the CS but could not avoid shock would have done better were it not for the fact that the nonfunctional R_a was inevitably followed by shock, *i.e.*, punished. On the other hand, Ss that were only able to avoid and could not terminate the CS, did in fact have the CS-termination contingency, but it was delayed (the CS was arranged to go off 5 sec after R_a occurred). Kamin's ability to predict the results of the same type of study with a different interstimulus interval (Kamin, 1957b) makes this interpretation rather attractive, and of course it is entirely consistent with the "traditional" interpretation of avoidance learning.

However the results reported by Bolles *et al.* (1966), described in Section II, 5, p. 196, indicate that there are two limitations on the generality of Kamin's conclusion. First, there are really three potential reinforcement contingencies rather than two, and all three of them appear to have approximately equal importance in the shuttlebox. Second, this pattern may be limited to the shuttlebox, since Bolles *et al.* found a very different pattern in the running wheel (see also Mogenson, Mullin, & Clark, 1965). In the running wheel avoidance was by far the biggest factor, termination of the CS was smaller but still significant, and the escape contingency was negligible.

There are other phenomena which flow naturally from the assumption that CS termination is reinforcing. One is the finding (Biederman *et al.*, 1964; McAdam, 1964; Whittleton, Kostansek & Sawrey, 1965) that avoidance is learned more readily if S is permitted to run away from the CS than if it has to approach it in executing R_a. Another phenomenon is that reported by Bower, Starr, and Lazarovitz (1965). They found that the facility of R_a acquisition was positively related to the amount of change in the CS that the R_a produced. A third effect, found with rats in shuttlebox avoidance by Mowrer and Lamoreaux (1942) and Black (1963), is that a trace procedure leads to poorer learning than the normal delay procedure. (We can thank Pavlov for the terminology: "delay" means that the CS fills the CS–US interval while "trace" means that the CS is momentary, terminating before US onset and usually before R_a occurs.) A fairly serious decrement is found with the trace procedure, and this is what would be expected if S is deprived of the CS-termination contingency. It is a little embarrassing, though, that any acquisition of R_a can be found without CS termination.

Perhaps some of these effects can be accounted for by considering other functions of the CS besides the hypothetical reinforcing function of CS termination. For one thing, the CS is a stimulus; it is, in fact, the stimulus to which we are usually trying to condition R_a. The CS is a discriminative stimulus in the sense that if R_a occurs in its presence, then something will happen (the CS stops), but if the R_a occurs in the absence of the CS, *e.g.*, before the CS–US interval has begun, R_a will have no effect upon the environment. And of course with both the trace procedure and Kamin's prolonged-CS procedure nothing happens when R_a occurs. Shock may be avoided, but there is no immediate stimulus consequence of responding. Thus we may think of the CS as having an informational function. The termination of the CS tells the animal that it has done something, it has changed the situation. D'Amato *et al.* (1968) have suggested that it tells S that shock has been avoided.

If the decrement found with both the trace procedure (short CS) and Kamin's procedure (long CS) are due to loss of information rather than loss of reinforcement, then it ought to be possible to eliminate the decrements by introducing a new stimulus, one that is never paired with shock, whenever R_a occurs. This technique, originally used by Keehn and Nakkash (1959), has recently been applied to the bar-press R_a by D'Amato *et al.* (1968) and to the shuttlebox and running-wheel situations by Bolles and Grossen (1969). In all of these situations the introduction of a "feedback" stimulus contingent upon R_a nearly eliminated the decrements produced by withdrawing the CS-termination contingency, and it made little difference whether CS termination was prevented by using a trace procedure or Kamin's procedure.

Although these results provide striking support for the idea that an R_a-contingent cue, or feedback stimulus, facilitates the acquisition of R_a they do not require—they only suggest—that when the CS-termination contingency is available, it operates in the same way. Bolles and Grossen obtained some evidence for the second conclusion, however, by testing rats in several different situations, and finding that the size of the ameliorating effect of the feedback stimulus was roughly proportional to the size of the decrement produced by preventing CS termination. Thus, in a one-way runway neither effect was observed; in the running wheel both effects were small but statistically significant; both effects were much larger in the shuttlebox; and in the Skinner box the existence of one or the other contingency meant the difference between Ss being able or not being able to learn the R_a (Bolles & Grossen, 1969). It is apparent that the R_as which are the easiest to learn, *i.e.*, those that involve running, are the least dependent upon CS termination and are the least affected by the introduction of a feedback stimulus. Bolles and Grossen (1969) suggest that the reason for this, and the reason such R_as are rapidly acquired in the first place, is that these responses produce a larger amount of *intrinsic* feedback; they change Ss' location and they involve vigorous body movement. At the other extreme is the bar-press R_a which produces no change in environmental cues and requires minimal body movement. The bar press provides little intrinsic feedback and therefore its acquisition is slow and uncertain and highly dependent upon some form of extrinsic feedback, either that normally provided by CS termination or that introduced in our study by making another stimulus contingent upon its occurrence. In this view, CS termination is seen merely as a kind of response-produced stimulus change and not a very effective kind of stimulus change at that.

The CS-termination hypothesis has some troubles in addition to those that have already been mentioned. One trouble is that if the CS really does become aversive, then pairing it with another neutral stimulus ought to make the latter aversive. But the evidence indicates that such higher-order fears are either nonexistent or extremely ephemeral (e.g., McAllister & McAllister, 1964). Still more trouble for the CS-termination hypothesis comes from a series of studies beginning with Knapp, Kause, and Perkins (1959) which shows that when S is given unavoidable shocks, it prefers to have them come on immediately rather than after a delay, and prefers to have them preceded by a warning stimulus (CS) rather than to come on without warning (Lockard, 1963, 1965). Similar studies using human Ss have begun to indicate that the critical factor in such preferences is the *uncertainty* of the unsignalled shock, precluding S's getting ready for it (Badia, McBane, Suter, & Lewis, 1966; Cooke & Barnes, 1964; D'Amato & Gumenik, 1960; Perkins, Levis, & Seymann, 1963).

Perhaps the same type of phenomenon is involved in what might be called the double avoidance procedure, *i.e.*, a procedure in which S can prevent the onset of the CS by responding in an interval just before its scheduled onset: the S can avoid both the US and the CS by responding at the right time. All of the evidence from double avoidance situations indicates that S does not avoid the CS. Quite the contrary, the pre-CS incidence of inter-trial responses drops to zero, and S comes to respond exclusively in its presence; S appears to rely upon it (Keehn, 1959b; Sidman, 1955; Sidman & Boren, 1957). (See also Sidman's 1966 review.) The discriminative or associative properties of the CS appear to be much more important in these situations than its aversive properties.

The various associative and informational functions of the CS merit much more intensive investigation; they have been consistently bypassed in the rush to jump on the reinforcement bandwagon. Indeed, the assumption that it must be CS termination that reinforces R_a has become so well embedded that we are all somewhat at a loss when we discover that it may not be true. The facts seem to force two conclusions upon us, however. One is that we still have to determine precisely what part the CS does play in avoidance behavior. And the second is that avoidance behavior obtains its strength primarily from sources other than CS termination.

V. WHAT IS LEFT?

It remains only for us to summarize, to point out a few rather general principles to bolster our outmoded theories, and to suggest some new research directions.

One thing that we can discern is that the avoidance response is definitely not merely a generalization of the learned escape response. Under some experimental conditions, *e.g.*, rats running in a shuttlebox, the escape contingency appears to be important, but this may be a peculiarity of the rat or the shuttlebox; the situation may be quite different for other Ss and other apparatus.

It is also clear that the effective avoidance response is not just an operant; it is not just an arbitrarily selected response that has been given a lot of reinforcement. We have seen that the most important single parameter in avoidance learning is the choice of R_a. All real organisms come into all real experimental situations with a host of previously learned and innate S–R connections, and in the case of avoidance behavior these connections are probably largely innate; they are probably specific to a given species, and it is probably because of these defensive reactions that animals survive. When rats are frightened they sometimes freeze, sometimes run away, and occasionally attack. As a consequence, it is extremely easy to teach a rat an R_a that takes it out of the frightening situation, and it is also possible, but a little trickier, to teach it an R_a that is compatible with freezing. Although data are lacking, it seems that it would be easy to teach the rat an R_a that was compatible with attack or offensive behavior. Still limiting ourselves to the rat, probably all aversive situations are conflictful since the two most important predispositions, to run away and to freeze, are incompatible. This conflict is overtly evident in a shuttle box. But it is resolved in the bar-press situation which is arranged so that freezing pays off, and in situations like the running wheel and the one-way apparatus in which taking flight pays off.

It would seem that if R_a must be an SSDR, then it can only be "learned" in the limited sense that all other defense reactions disappear because they are ineffectual. The weakening of ineffectual SSDRs may be effected by the escape contingency, but at least in some situations it is done mainly by the avoidance contingency itself. Thus if the rat is in a Skinner box, abortive flight will be consistently punished by the unavoided shock and it ends up freezing on the bar. If it is in a situation that requires a locomotory R_a, then freezing will be consistently punished by unavoided shock and it ends up running. The difficulty of acquiring a given R_a therefore turns out to be primarily a function of how difficult it is to suppress S's other SSDRs in the situation. This interpretation implies that the acquisition of an R_a, especially when it is rapidly acquired, is due in large part to the avoidance contingency, a view which for various reasons has been suggested by several recent writers (e.g., D'Amato et al., 1968; Herrnstein & Hineline, 1966; Keehn, 1966).

Additional flexibility in S's response repertoire can arise in a different manner, and such flexibility is evidently needed if S can sometimes learn to press a bar with proficiency. The key, I believe, was suggested by Solomon and Wynne (1954) in the form of what they termed the Anxiety Conservation principle. They observed that in the case of a well-learned avoidance response, a response which is so strong that S is receiving virtually no more shocks, the latency of R_a is very short, shorter than the fear response. Thus, the avoidance response appears to be occurring in the absence of fear, and it is only when S for some reason fails to make a short latency R_a that it begins to show overt signs of emotionality. In short, S appears to be not only avoiding shock but avoiding fear as well! At this point, of course, the traditionalist has a new dilemma because he must now explain the motivation and the reinforcement of the response by devices other than the traditional fear and fear reduction. Neither Solomon and Wynne nor any subsequent writer has offered any serious suggestions for the new dilemma. No matter how the maintenance of R_a is explained, however, it seems reasonable to suppose that there will be a dissipation of fear with continued improvement in avoidance behavior (Kamin, Brimer, & Black, 1963). We may assume that there will also be a correlated expansion of S's response repertoire, e.g., the rat will be able to do things other than freeze or run away. Thus, it may be possible for freezing (while holding onto the bar) to merge or be molded or be shaped gradually into operant bar pressing. Although how the molding and reinforcement and maintenance of R_a in the later stages of training occur remains an open question, it seems likely that the processes are different from those involved in the original development of R_a, which is our present concern.

Fear has been a recurrent concept. The reader may have noted that we have been scrupulously careful in not formally attributing functional properties to fear, nor even in defining it. A great deal has been found out about fear and fear conditioning, as the reader will discover by going through this volume, but here we have attributed to it only two behavioral properties. One is that it is conditionable, so that it is produced by stimuli that have been paired with shock. The second property is simply that it limits S's response repertoire to a very restricted set of species-specific defense reactions. It is not necessary to postulate anything going on in the autonomic nervous system, nor, of course, to deny that there are interesting events occurring there. Specifically, it is not necessary to make any assumptions about the motivating function of fear or the reinforcing function of fear reduction. There is sufficient lawfulness in avoidance behavior itself that it is not necessary to look elsewhere for devices to explain it.

Some New Directions

Although there is a fair amount of research using different animals in avoidance situations, not much of this work stems from a comparative point of view. What we tend to find is that fish can learn to avoid, which is true of dogs, rats, cats, pigs, and hamsters. It is rather more interesting to discover that turtles can also learn avoidance. It is much more interesting to discover that the turtle's avoidance was in a different type of situation from the shuttlebox that was common to all the other animals. Very little of the research, of course, has paid much attention to the ecological defense problems faced by a given species. Although any naturalist would expect avoidance behavior in dogs to differ from avoidance behavior in rats, one can search endlessly through the experimental journals for a direct, or even an indirect (*i.e.*, across experiments) comparison of these two well-studied species. Thus, Solomon and his students have discovered that dogs can move a head panel to avoid shock, but has such a response ever been reported, or even investigated in rats? Granda, Matsumiya, and Stirling (1965) reported turtles learning a head retraction R_a. But Granda *et al.* do not tell us whether they started their investigation of the turtle with this unique response, or whether they ended up with it in desperation after having tried everything else with no avail. Granted that head retraction is a defense reaction of the turtle, does it also freeze? And if so, can such freezing be shaped into bar pressing? Do turtles take flight, and if so, can this behavior be shaped into shuttle box avoidance? Granda *et al.* do note that in early trials there was generalized bodily withdrawal, but they do not go on to tell us whether such behavior can serve as a prototype for a leave-taking R_a. In short, what we need as much as anything else are descriptions of negative findings.

The situation was better many years ago when James (1937) described in some detail his difficulty in getting classical aversive conditioning in the opossum. From his report we can make a good guess what responses can and cannot serve as R_as for this animal. Ader and Tatum (1963) have described a unique trans-species type of experiment using humans that were run without being given any verbal instructions. Humans, it seems, are not very smart under these conditions!

A need for negative data is also suggested by the peculiar lack of a-voidance data on birds. The SSDR hypothesis would suggest that birds would have great difficulty in learning to peck a key to avoid shock, unless such behavior appeared in the context of an attack response. It is possible that hundreds of investigators have attempted avoidance training in chickens, pigeons, crows, and the like, and been unable to get acquisition of any of the required responses. If this is the case it would be extremely helpful to know about it; the mere lack of relevant research reports provides little comfort. Only two avoidance studies with birds have been reported that the author knows of. One with pigeons (Graf & Bitterman, 1963) is also unusual in that S was allowed to make any response whatever which produced a movement of the floor sufficient to be detected by an electronic device. Most Ss were able to learn to avoid shock, and it is of some interest to note that the only response described by Graf and Bitterman was the well-known barnyard threat reaction involving hunching of the wings, lowering of the neck, and stamping of the feet. However, Krieckhaus and Wagman (1967) reported that chickens were quite able to learn avoidance in a shuttlebox.

In contrast with the Graf and Bitterman results, Greene and Peacock (1965) found that rats were exceedingly poor at learning to be active when any movement (as detected by an ultrasonic movement detector) would effect avoidance. Greene and Peacock failed to report what the animals did learn, or what they were doing when they were being active. On the other hand, when Bindra and Anchel (1965) made avoidance contingent upon lack of movement in rats, we can be sure that the response was freezing. Bindra and Anchel found that this behavior was learned in the sense that the experimental Ss showed less movement than yoked controls that received the same shock. The latter, apparently, froze quite a bit also.

The comparative literature that is available seems to be consistent with the SSDR hypothesis, e.g., James (1937) on the opossum, Pearl's work (1963) with four species of rodents, Winston, Lindzey, and Connor's (1967) comparison of albino and pigmented mice in passive and active avoidance, and two studies (Lockhart & Steinbrecher, 1965; Steinbrecher & Lockhart, 1966) comparing rabbits and cats. In the latter two studies, for example, Ss were required to avoid on a temporal schedule, during the last 15 sec of the 60-sec inter-trial interval. Rabbits were much less able than cats to acquire the temporal discrimination, a finding which is in keeping with the defensive behavior of the two animals. Flakus and Steinbrecher (1964) had previously demonstrated that rabbits perform quite well on a standard signalled avoidance task in a shuttle box, where the rabbit's hair-trigger, all-or-none flight behavior would pay off. Cats, on the other hand, perhaps because they are domesticated, or perhaps because they are predators, were better able to acquire the deliberate type of restraint required by the temporal discrimination task. Cats are also evidently quite proficient at running in a running wheel (Thompson, 1958). And it has been found that the rat is good at learning T-maze avoidance (Jacobs, 1963), which is consistent with the rat's ability to solve geographical problems in general, and at acquiring R_as that take it from fear-producing places.

There has been considerable interest recently in a modification of the old one-way avoidance box to the form of the simple runway. Curiously, the interest in this apparatus has been limited mostly to the question of whether R_e extinguishes more or less rapidly if the rat is punished in the previously safe goal box (Campbell, Smith, & Misanin, 1966; Eisen & Sawrey, 1967; Kintz & Bruning, 1967; Seligman & Campbell, 1965). The results of these studies clearly show that such punishment rapidly weakens R_a, and this result is usually contrasted with the vicious circle phenomenon (Brown, Martin, & Morrow, 1964) in which punishing an R_e retards its extinction. There is no conflict between the two results, however, if we consider the manner in which shock is administered during acquisition in the two situations. Campbell et al. (1966) have shown that if the punishing shock is administered in the goal box, so that S cannot run through it, then the running R_a is seriously disrupted, but if the punishment is given near the beginning of the runway, so that S must run onto it and is then reinforced by running off of it, then the running response may be facilitated. The results are only paradoxical from the point of view of the utilitarian assumption that shock is bad and therefore S ought to avoid it. If we consider the response elicited by the punisher, running forward in the one case and backing off in the other, then the results of Campbell et al. are perfectly consistent with those of Fowler and Miller (1963) and others demonstrating that S learns through punishment only that response which the punishment elicits (Bolles, 1967). In any case, the old-fashioned runway promises to be as useful a device in the study of defensive behavior as it has been in the study of appetitive behavior.

There have been a couple of studies in which R_a is part of a chain of responses to be learned. If S can learn a chain of responses to avoid shock, then some modification of the SSDR hypothesis would be required. The response chain that has been investigated (Fantino, Sharp, & Cole, 1966; Marx, 1966) is pressing a bar at one end of a shuttlebox after executing a running response. The Marx study is concerned with extinction phenomena, but the Fantino et al. paper sheds some interesting light on the acquisition of such chains. A group that was required to run across to the other side and press a bar to avoid shock achieved a high level of performance in a single session. An impressive finding. Various control procedures demonstrated that the effective CS was opening the door between the two compartments. It should be expected that the control group, which was confined to a single side and required merely to learn the bar press R_a, would learn it, but they did not. How can a chain of R_as be easier to learn than a single R_a? An explanation is suggested by the results obtained when conditions were switched so that instead of executing the chain, the experimental group merely had to perform the last response, *i.e.*, bar-pressing. An immediate and total deterioration of R_a was found. Evidently neither the nominal CS, nor the situational cues had attained any associative control over the bar press. It appears that running had become the cause of bar-pressing. One might suppose that Fantino's Ss never pressed the bar in any meaningful sense, but were running through the door and crashing into it. This surprising turn of events certainly does not mean that a chain of R_as cannot be acquired, but only that it has not yet been demonstrated.

Avoidance behavior appears to have been severed from the rest of behavior theory; many of the accepted explanatory devices appear to be no longer applicable. One of the problems in this area is that the theory of avoidance has lagged behind the development of the theories that have been proposed for appetitive behavior. Thus, the motivation of appetitive behavior is now largely treated in incentive terms while the aversive case continues to be treated in terms of the old-fashioned concept of drive. A variety of hypothetical anticipatory mechanisms, such as r_g, have been postulated to guide and/or motivate, and even reinforce appetitive behavior, but no counterparts of such mechanisms have been proposed for the aversive case. Perhaps the time has come when it would be profitable to apply some of the concepts of incentive motivation to the aversive case.[5]

But first it should be established that avoidance behavior is motivated in the technical sense that the probability or vigor of R_a increases with increasing aversiveness of the situation. It is entirely possible that even a weak shock provides more than enough fear to maintain R_a. Many animals' defense reactions have an all-or-none character so that what has to be accounted for is the associative control of the response rather than its motivation. A slight fear may be as hard to find as a slight pregnancy. The S either freezes (or leaves) or it does not, and the question is what stimuli control these behaviors, not how motivated are they.

[5]*Editor's note:* See also Chapter 4 by Denny, this volume, for another analysis relevant to this issue.

On the other hand, there are two rather slim lines of evidence to suggest that avoidance behavior really is motivated. One is the claim of Rescorla and Solomon (1967) that through differential classical conditioning procedures stimuli can be given the power to energize or to inhibit R_a in a graded manner.[6]

The second line of evidence that R_a is motivated in a formal sense (not just in the sense that fear "produces" avoidance) comes from studies of the effects of shock intensity on R_a. In the one-way avoidance and acquired drive situations involving flight, where R_a is the prepotent response, the evidence is for a uniform strengthening of R_a with increasing US intensity (e.g., Goldstein, 1960; Moyer & Korn, 1966.) In the shuttlebox and bar-press situations, the matter is more complicated. It seems fairly certain that the rate of acquisition of R_a is inversely related to shock intensity in these situations (Bolles & Warren, 1965a; D'Amato & Fazzaro, 1966; Johnson & Church, 1965; Levine, 1966; Moyer & Korn, 1964). The reasons for this relationship are still obscure; perhaps response competition can account for it. By contrast, D'Amato, Fazzaro, and Etkin (1967) have shown that once a bar-press R_a is established, it is maintained somewhat better with more intense shocks (see also Huff, Piantanida, & Morris, 1967). Thus, the evidence can be construed to support the motivation hypothesis. More compelling would be the demonstration of a Crespi effect in which rapid shifts in the strength of R_a followed shifts in momentary motivation conditions.

If a motivation mechanism is indicated, and particularly if it can be shown that the source of motivation is primarily governed by associative factors, then a case could be easily made for a negative incentive construct. The S would be expected to show conditioned anticipation of impending aversive events, and this anticipation could be attributed to an anticipatory escape response, r_e. If we think of r_g as the anticipatory form of the consummatory response, why shouldn't we treat r_e as an anticipatory defensive response? If we think of r_g motivating appetitive behavior, why not think of r_e motivating aversion? If we can conceive of defining hunger in terms of the readiness to eat, can we also begin to think of defining fear as the readiness to execute an escape response or some other SSDR?

[6]*Editor's note:* See also Chapter 6 by Seligman, Maier, and Solomon, this volume.

226   Robert C. Bolles

ACKNOWLEDGMENT

Prepared with support from grant GB-5694 from the National Science Foundation.

REFERENCES

Ader, R., & Tatum, R. Free-operant avoidance conditioning in individual and paired human subjects. *Journal of the Experimental Analysis of Behavior,* 1963, **6,** 357–359.

Allison, J., Larson, D., & Jensen, D.D. Acquired fear, brightness preference and one-way shuttlebox performance. *Psychonomic Science,* 1967, **8,** 269–270.

Amsel, A., & Maltzman, I. The effect upon generalized drive strength of emotionality as inferred from the level of consummatory response. *Journal of Experimental Psychology,* 1950, **40,** 563–569.

Anderson, N.H., & Nakamura, C.Y. Avoidance decrement in avoidance conditioning. *Journal of Comparative and Physiological Psychology,* 1964, **57,** 196–204.

Anderson, N.H., Rollins, H.A., & Riskin, S.R. Effects of punishment on avoidance decrement. *Journal of Comparative and Physiological Psychology,* 1966, **62,** 147–149.

Anger, D. The role of temporal discrimination in the reinforcement of Sidman avoidance behavior. *Journal of the Experimental Analysis of Behavior,* 1963, **6,** 477–506.

Azrin, N.H., Hutchinson, R.R., & Hake, D.F. Attack, avoidance, escape reactions to aversive shock. *Journal of the Experimental Analysis of Behavior,* 1967, **10,** 131–148.

Badia, P., McBane, B., Suter, S., & Lewis, P. Preference behavior in an immediate versus variably delayed shock situation with and without a warning signal. *Journal of Experimental Psychology,* 1966, **72,** 847–852.

Baron, A. Functions of the CS and US in fear conditioning. *Journal of the Comparative and Physiological Psychology,* 1959, **52,** 591–593.

Biederman, G.B., D'Amato, M.R., & Keller, D.M. Facilitation of discriminated avoidance learning by dissociation of CS and manipulandum. *Psychonomic Science,* 1964, **1,** 229–230.

Bindra, D., & Anchel, H. Immobility as an avoidance response and its disruption by drugs. *Journal of the Experimental Analysis of Behavior,* 1963, **6,** 213–218.

Bixenstine, V.E., & Barker, E. Further analysis of the determinants of avoidance behavior. *Journal of Comparative and Physiological Psychology,* 1964, **58,** 339–343.

Black, A.H. The effect of CS–US interval on avoidance conditioning in the rat. *Canadian Journal of Psychology,* 1963, **17,** 174–182.

Bolles, R.C. Shock density and effective shock intensity: a comparison of different shock scramblers. *Journal of the Experimental Analysis of Behavior,* 1966, **9,** 553–556.

Bolles, R.C. *Theory of motivation.* New York: Harper, 1967.

Bolles, R.C. Avoidance and escape learning: simultaneous acquisition of different responses. *Journal of Comparative and Physiological Psychology,* 1969, **68,** 355–358.

Bolles, R.C., & Grossen, N.E. Effects of an informational stimulus on the acquisition of avoidance behavior in rats. *Journal of Comparative and Physiological Psychology,* 1969, **68,** 90–99.

Bolles, R.C., & McGillis, D.B. The non-operant nature of the bar-press escape response. *Psychonomic Science,* 1968, **11,** 261–262.

Bolles, R.C., Stokes, L.W., & Younger, M.S. Does CS termination reinforce avoidance behavior? *Journal of Comparative and Physiological Psychology,* 1966, **62**, 201–207.

Bolles, R.C., & Tuttle, A.V. A failure to reinforce instrumental behavior by terminating a stimulus that had been paired with shock. *Psychonomic Science,* 1967, **9**, 255–256.

Bolles, R.C., & Warren, J.A., Jr. The acquisition of bar-press avoidance as a function of shock intensity. *Psychonomic Science,* 1965, **3**, 297–298. (a)

Bolles, R.C., & Warren, J.A., Jr. Effects of delayed UCS termination on classical avoidance learning of the bar-press response. *Psychological Reports,* 1965, **17**, 687–690. (b)

Bolles, R.C., Warren, J.A., Jr., & Ostrov, N. The role of the CS–US interval in bar press avoidance learning. *Psychonomic Science,* 1966, **6**, 113–114.

Boren, J.J. Isolation of post-shock responding in a free operant avoidance procedure. *Psychological Reports,* 1961, **9**, 265–266.

Bower, G.H. Unpublished study described in Ch. 6 of Atkinson, R.C., Bower, G.H., & Crothers, E.J. *An introduction to mathematical learning theory.* New York: Wiley, 1965.

Bower, G., Starr, R., & Lazarovitz, L. Amount of response-produced change in the CS and avoidance learning. *Journal of Comparative and Physiological Psychology,* 1965, **59**, 13–17.

Brown, J.S., & Jacobs, A. Role of fear in motivation and acquisition of responses. *Journal of Experimental Psychology,* 1949, **39**, 747–759.

Brown, J.S., Martin, R.C., & Morrow, M.W. Self-punitive behavior in the rat: facilitative effects of punishment on resistance to extinction. *Journal of Comparative and Physiological Psychology,* 1964, **57**, 127–133.

Brush, F.R. Discriminative avoidance training of rats. *Science,* 1964, **146**, 1599–1600. (a)

Brush, F.R. Avoidance learning as a function of time after fear conditioning and unsignalled shock. *Psychonomic Science,* 1964, **1**, 405–406, (b).

Brush, F.R. On the differences between animals that learn and do not learn to avoid electric shock. *Psychonomic Science,* 1966, **5**, 123–124.

Campbell, B.A., & Campbell, E.H. Retention and extinction of learned fear in infant and adult rats. *Journal of Comparative and Physiological Psychology,* 1962, **55**, 1–8.

Campbell, B.A., & Masterson, F.A. Psychophysics of punishment. In B.A. Campbell & R.M. Church (Eds.) *Punishment.* New York: Appleton, 1969.

Campbell, B.A., Smith, N.F., & Misanin, J.R. Effects of punishment on extinction of avoidance behavior: Avoidance-avoidance conflict or vicious circle behavior? *Journal of Comparative and Physiological Psychology,* 1966, **62**, 495–498.

Campbell, S.L. Lever holding and behavior sequences in shock-escape. *Journal of Comparative and Physiological Psychology,* 1962, **55**, 1047–1053.

Chapman, J.A., & Bolles, R.C. Effect of UCS duration on classical avoidance learning of the bar-press response. *Psychological Reports,* 1964, **14**, 559–563.

Church, R.M., & Solomon, R.L. Traumatic avoidance learning: The effects of delay of shock termination. *Psychological Reports,* 1956, **2**, 357–358.

Clark, R. A rapidly acquired avoidance response in rats. *Psychonomic Science,* 1966, **6**, 11–12.

Cooke, J.O., & Barnes, G.W. Choice of delay of inevitable shock. *Journal of the Abnormal and Social Psychology,* 1964, **68**, 669–672.

Coons, E.E., Anderson, N.H., & Myers, A.K. Disappearance of avoidance responding during continued training. *Journal of Comparative and Physiological Psychology,* 1960, **53**, 290–292.

D'Amato, M.R., & Fazzaro, J. Discriminated lever-press avoidance learning as a function of type and intensity of shock. *Journal of Comparative Physiological Psychology*, 1966, **61**, 313–315.

D'Amato, M.R., Fazzaro, J., & Etkin, M. Discriminated bar-press avoidance maintenance and extinction in rats as a function of shock intensity. *Journal of Comparative and Physiological Psychology*, 1967, **63**, 351–354.

D'Amato, M.R., Fazzaro, J., & Etkin, M. Anticipatory responding and avoidance discrimination as factors in avoidance conditioning. *Journal of Experimental Psychology*, 1968, **77**, 41–47.

D'Amato, M.R., & Gumenik, W.E. Some effects of immediate versus randomly delayed shock on an instrumental response and cognitive processes. *Journal of the Abnormal and Social Psychology*, 1960, **60**, 64–67.

D'Amato, M.R., Keller, D., & DiCara, L.V. Facilitation of discriminated avoidance learning by discontinuous shock. *Journal of Comparative and Physiological Psychology*, 1964, **58**, 344–349.

D'Amato, M.R., & Schiff, D. Long-term discriminated avoidance performance in the rat. *Journal of Comparative and Physiological Psychology*, 1964, **57**, 123–126.

Desiderato, O. Generalization of acquired fear as a function of CS intensity and number of acquisition trials. *Journal of Experimental Psychology*, 1964, **67**, 41–47.

Dinsmoor, J.A. Variable-interval escape from stimuli accompanied by shocks. *Journal of the Experimental Analysis of Behavior*, 1962, **5**, 41–48.

Edmonson, B.W., & Amsel, A. The effects of massing and distribution of extinction trials on the persistence of a fear-motivated instrumental response. *Journal of Comparative and Physiological Psychology*, 1954, **47**, 117–123.

Eisen, C.L., & Sawrey, J.M. Extinction of avoidance behavior: CS presentations with and without punishment. *Psychonomic Science*, 1967, **7**, 95–96.

Fantino E., Sharp, D., & Cole, M. Factors facilitating lever-press avoidance. *Journal of Comparative and Physiological Psychology*, 1966, **62**, 214–217.

Feldman, R.S., & Bremner, F.J. A method for rapid conditioning of stable avoidance bar pressing behavior. *Journal of the Experimental Behavior*, 1963, **6**, 393–394.

Flakus, W.J., & Steinbrecher, B.C. Avoidance conditioning in the rabbit. *Psychological Reports*, 1964, **14**, 140.

Fowler, H., & Miller, N.E. Facilitation and inhibition of running performance by hind- and forepaw shock of various intensities. *Journal of Comparative and Physiological Psychology*, 1963, **56**, 801–805.

Fromer, R. The effect of several shock patterns on the acquisition of the secondary drive of fear. *Journal of Comparative and Physiological Psychology*, 1962,**55**, 142–144.

Goldstein, M.L. Acquired drive strength as a joint function of shock intensity and number of acquisition trials. *Journal of Experimental Psychology*, 1960, **60**, 349–358.

Graf, V., & Bitterman, M.E. General activity as instrumental: Application to avoidance training. *Journal of the Experimental Analysis of Behavior*, 1963, **6**, 301–305.

Granda, A.M., Matsumiya, Y., & Stirling, C.E. A method for producing avoidance behavior in the turtle. *Psychonomic Science*, 1965, **2**, 187–188.

Greene, J.T., & Peacock, L.J. Response competition in conditioned avoidance. *Psychonomic Science*, 1965, **3**, 125–126.

Grossberg, J.M. Pseudoconditioning, drive reduction, and the acquired fear-drive hypothesis. *Psychological Record*, 1962, **12**, 299–308.

Grossen, N.E., & Bolles, R.C. Effects of a classical conditioned 'fear signal' and 'safety signal' on nondiscriminated avoidance behavior. *Psychonomic Science*, 1968, **11**, 321–322.

Gwinn, G.T. Resistance to extinction of learned fear-drives. *Journal of Experimental Psychology*, 1951, **42**, 6–12.

Hearst, E. Concurrent generalization gradients for food-controlled and shock-controlled behavior. *Journal of the Experimental Analysis of Behavior*, 1962, **5**, 19–31.

Hearst, E., & Whalen, R.E. Facilitating effects of D-amphetamine on discriminated-avoidance performance. *Journal of Comparative and Physiological Psychology*, 1963, **56**, 124–128.

Herrnstein, R.J., & Hineline, P.N. Negative reinforcement as shock-frequency reduction. *Journal of the Experimental Analysis of Behavior*, 1966, **9**, 421–430.

Huff, F.W., Piantanida, T.P., & Morris, G.L. Free operant avoidance responding as a function of serially presented variations of UCS intensity. *Psychonomic Science*, 1967, **8**, 111–112.

Hull, C.L. A functional interpretation of the conditioned reflex. *Psychological Review*, 1929, **36**, 498–511.

Hurwitz, H.M.B., Method for discriminative avoidance training. *Science*, 1964, **145**, 1070–1071.

Jacobs, B., Jr. Repeated acquisition and extinction of an instrumental avoidance response. *Journal of Comparative and Physiological Psychology*, 1963, **56**, 1017–1021.

James, W.T. An experimental study of the defense mechanism in the opossum, with emphasis on natural behavior and its relation to mode of life. *Journal of Genetic Psychology*, 1937, **51**, 95–100.

Johnson, J.L., & Church, R.M. Effects of shock intensity on nondiscriminative avoidance learning of rats in a shuttle box. *Psychonomic Science*, 1965, **3**, 497–498.

Jones, E.C., & Swanson, A.H. Discriminated lever-press avoidance. *Psychonomic Science*, 1966, **6**, 351–352.

Kalish, H.I. Strength of fear as a function of the number of acquisition and extinction trials. *Journal of Experimental Psychology*, 1954, **47**, 1–9.

Kamin, L.J. The effects of termination of the CS and avoidance of the US on avoidance learning. *Journal of Comparative and Physiological Psychology*, 1956, **49**, 420–424.

Kamin, L.J. The retention of incompletely learned avoidance response. *Journal of Comparative and Physiological Psychology*, 1957, **50**, 457–460. (a)

Kamin, L.J. The effects of termination of the CS and avoidance of the US on avoidance learning: An extension. *Canadian Journal of Psychology*, 1957, **11**, 48–56. (b)

Kamin, L.J. The delay-of-punishment gradient. *Journal of Comparative and Physiological Psychology*, 1959, **52**, 434–437.

Kamin, L.J., Brimer, C.J., & Black, A.H. Conditioned suppression as a monitor of fear of the CS in the course of avoidance training. *Journal of Comparative and Physiological Psychology*, 1963, **56**, 497–501.

Keehn, J.D. On the non-classical nature of avoidance behavior. *American Journal of Psychology*, 1959, **72**, 243–247. (a)

Keehn, J.D. The effect of a warning signal on unrestricted avoidance behaviour. *British Journal of Psychology*, 1959, **50**, 125–135. (b)

Keehn, J.D. Effect of shock duration on Sidman avoidance response rates. *Psychological Reports*, 1963, **13**, 352.

Keehn, J.D. Avoidance responses as discriminated operants. *British Journal of Psychology,* 1966, **57,** 375–380.

Keehn, J.D. Running and bar pressing as avoidance responses. *Psychological Reports,* 1967, **20,** 591–592.

Keehn, J.D., & Nakkash, S. Effect of a signal contingent upon an avoidance response. *Nature,* 1959, **184,** 566–568.

Keehn, J.D., & Webster, C.D. Rapid discriminated bar-press avoidance through avoidance shaping. *Psychonomic Science,* 1968, **10,** 21–22.

Kent, N.D., Wagner, M.K., & Gannon, D.R. Effect of unconditioned response restriction on subsequent acquisition of a habit motivated by "fear." *Psychological Reports,* 1960, **6,** 335–338.

Kimble, G.A. Shock intensity and avoidance learning. *Journal of Comparative and Physiological Psychology,* 1955, **48,** 281–284.

Kintz, B.L., & Bruning, J.L. Punishment and compulsive avoidance behavior. *Journal of Comparative and Physiological Psychology,* 1967, **63,** 323–326.

Knapp, R.K., Kause, R.H., & Perkins, C.C., Jr. Immediate versus delayed shock in T-maze performance. *Journal of Experimental Psychology,* 1959, **58,** 357–362.

Krieckhaus, E.E., & Wagman, W.J. Acquisition of the two-way avoidance response in chicken compared to rat and cat. *Psychonomic Science,* 1967, **8,** 273–274.

Kurtz, K.H., & Pearl, J. The effects of prior fear experience on acquired drive learning. *Journal of Comparative and Physiological Psychology,* 1960, **53,** 201–206.

Leaf, R.C. Acquisition of Sidman avoidance responding as a function of S-S interval. *Journal of Comparative and Physiological Psychology,* 1965, **59,** 298–300.

Levine, S. UCS intensity and avoidance learning. *Journal of Experimental Psychology,* 1966, **71,** 163–164.

Lockard, J.S. Choice of a warning signal or no warning signal in an unavoidable shock situation. *Journal of Comparative and Physiological Psychology,* 1963, **56,** 526–530.

Lockard, J.S. Choice of a warning stimulus or none in several unavoidable shock situations. *Psychonomic Science,* 1965, **3,** 5–6.

Lockhart, R.A., & Steinbrecher, C.D. Temporal avoidance conditioning in the rabbit. *Psychonomic Science,* 1965, **3,** 121–122.

Maatsch, J.L. Learning and fixation after a single shock trial. *Journal of Comparative and Physiological Psychology,* 1959, **52,** 408–410.

Malott, R.W., Sidley, N.A., & Schoenfeld, W.N. Effects of separate and joint escape and avoidance conditioning. *Psychological Reports,* 1963, **13,** 367–376.

Marx, M.H. Differential resistance to extinction of escape and avoidance conditioning. *Psychological Record,* 1966, **16,** 449–456.

Marx, M.H., & Hellwig, L.R. Acquisition and extinction of avoidance conditioning without escape responses. *Journal of Comparative and Physiological Psychology,* 1964, **58,** 451–452.

Mathers, B.L. The effect of certain parameters on the acquisition of fear. *Journal of Comparative and Physiological Psychology,* 1957, **50,** 329–333.

May, M.A. Experimentally acquired drives. *Journal of Experimental Psychology,* 1948, **38,** 66–77.

McAdam, D. Effects of positional relations between subject, CS and US on shuttle box avoidance learning in cats. *Journal of Comparative and Physiological Psychology,* 1964, **58,** 302–304.

McAllister, D.E., & McAllister, W.R. Second-order conditioning of fear. *Psychonomic Science*. 1964, **1**, 383–384.

McAllister, W.R., & McAllister, D.E. Role of the CS and of apparatus cues in measurement of acquired fear. *Psychological Reports*. 1962, **11**, 749–756. (a)

McAllister, W.R., & McAllister, D.E. Post conditioning delay and intensity of shock as factors in the measurement of acquired fear. *Journal of Experimental Psychology*. 1962, **64**, 110–116. (b)

McAllister, W.R., & McAllister, D.E. Increase over time in the stimulus generalization of acquired fear. *Journal of Experimental Psychology*. 1963, **65**, 576–582.

Meyer, D.R., Cho, C., & Wesemann, A.F. On problems of conditioned discriminated lever-press avoidance responses. *Psychological Review*, 1960, **67**, 224–228.

Migler, B. Bar holding during escape conditioning. *Journal of the Experimental Analysis of Behavior*. 1963, **6**, 65–72.

Miller, N.E. An experimental investigation of acquired drives. *Psychological Bulletin*. 1941, **38**, 534–535.

Miller, N.E. Studies on fear as an acquirable drive: I. Fear as motivation and fear-reduction as reinforcement in the learning of new responses. *Journal of Experimental Psychology*. 1948, **38**, 89–101.

Mogenson, G.J., Mullin, A.D., & Clark, E.A. Effects of delayed secondary reinforcement and response requirements on avoidance learning. *Canadian Journal of Psychology*. 1965, **19**, 61–73.

Mowrer, O.H. A stimulus-response analysis of anxiety and its role as a reinforcing agent. *Psychological Review*. 1939, **46**, 553–565.

Mowrer, O.H. On the dual nature of learning: a reinterpretation of "conditioning" and "problem solving." *Harvard Educational Review*. 1947, **17**, 102–148.

Mowrer, O.H., & Keehn, J.D. How are intertrial "avoidance" responses reinforced? *Psychological Review*. 1958, **65**, 209–221.

Mowrer, O.H., & Lamoreaux, R.R. Avoidance conditioning and signal duration—a study of secondary motivation and reward. *Psychological Monographs*. 1942, **54**, (Whole no. 247).

Mowrer, O.H., & Lamoreaux, R.R. Fear as an intervening variable in avoidance conditioning. *Journal of Comparative Psychology*. 1946, **39**, 29–50.

Moyer, K.E., & Korn, J.H. Effect of UCS intensity on the acquisition and extinction of an avoidance response. *Journal of Experimental Psychology*, 1964, **67**, 352–359.

Moyer, K.E., & Korn, J.H. Effect of USC intensity on the acquisition and extinction of a one-way avoidance response. *Psychonomic Science*. 1966, **4**, 121–122.

Myers, A.K. Avoidance learning as a function of several training conditions and strain differences in rats. *Journal of Comparative and Physiological Psychology*. 1959, **52**, 381–386.

Page, H.A. The facilitation of experimental extinction by response prevention as a function of the acquisition of a new response. *Journal of Comparative and Physiological Psychology*. 1955, **48**, 14–16.

Pearl, J. Avoidance learning in rodents: A comparative study. *Psychological Reports*. 1963, **12**, 139–145.

Perkins, C.C., Jr., Levis, D.J., & Seymann, R. Preference for signal-shock vs. shock-signal. *Psychological Reports*. 1963, **13**, 735–738.

Rescorla, R.A., & LoLordo, V.M. Inhibition of avoidance behavior. *Journal of Comparative and Physiological Psychology*. 1965, **59**, 406–412.

Rescorla, R.A., & Solomon, R.L. Two-process learning theory: Relationships between Pavlovian conditioning and instrumental learning. *Psychological Review,* 1967, **74,** 151–182.

Robinson, H.B. Persistence of a response in the apparent absence of motivation. *Journal of Experimental Psychology.* 1961, **61,** 480–488.

Santos, J.R. The influence of amount and kind of training on the acquisition and extinction of avoidance responses. *Journal of Comparative and Physiological Psychology.* 1960, **53,** 284–289.

Schoenfeld, W.N. An experimental approach to anxiety, escape and avoidance behavior. In P.H. Hock & J. Zubin (Eds.) *Anxiety.* New York: Grune & Stratton, 1950.

Seligman, M.E.P., & Campbell, B.A. Effect of intensity and duration of punishment on extinction of an avoidance response. *Journal of Comparative and Physiological Psychology.* 1965, **59,** 295–297.

Sheffield, F.D. Avoidance training and the contiguity principle. *Journal of Comparative and Physiological Psychology.* 1948, **41,** 165–177.

Sidman, M. Two temporal parameters of the maintenance of avoidance behavior by the white rat. *Journal of Comparative and Physiological Psychology.* 1953, **46,** 253–261.

Sidman, M. Some properties of the warning stimulus in avoidance behavior. *Journal of Comparative and Physiological Psychology.* 1955, **48,** 444–450.

Sidman, M. Reduction of shock frequency as reinforcement for avoidance behavior. *Journal of the Experimental Analysis of Behavior,* 1962, **5,** 247–257.

Sidman, M. Avoidance behavior. In W.K. Honig (Ed.) *Operant behavior: Areas of research and application.* New York: Appleton, 1966.

Sidman, M., & Boren, J.J. A comparison of two types of warning stimulus in avoidance situation. *Journal of Comparative and Physiological Psychology.* 1957, **50,** 282–287.

Smith, O.A., Jr., McFarland, W.L., & Taylor, E. Performance in a shock-avoidance conditioning situation interpreted as pseudo-conditioning. *Journal of Comparative and Physiological Psychology.* 1961, **54,** 154–157.

Solomon, R.L., & Brush, E.S. Experimentally derived conceptions of anxiety and aversion In M.R. Jones (Ed.) *Nebraska Symposium on Motivation,* 1956, **4,** 212–305.

Solomon, R.L., & Wynne, L.C. Traumatic avoidance learning: Acquisition in normal dogs. *Psychological Monographs,* 1953, **67,** (Whole No. 354).

Solomon, R.L., & Wynne, L.C. Traumatic avoidance learning: The principles of anxiety conservation and partial irreversibility. *Psychological Review,* 1954, **61,** 353–385.

Steinbrecher, C.D., & Lockhart, R.A. Temporal avoidance conditioning in the cat. *Psychonomic Science,* 1966, **5,** 441–442.

Stone, G.C. Some factors that influence acquisition of free-operant avoidance behavior. *Psychological Reports,* 1966, **18,** 383–396.

Theios, J. Simple conditioning as two-stage all-or-none learning. *Psychological Review,* 1963, **70,** 403–417.

Theios, J., & Dunaway, J.E. One-way versus shuttle avoidance conditioning. *Psychonomic Science,* 1964, **1,** 251–252.

Thompson, R.F. Primary stimulus generalization as a function of acquisition level in the cat. *Journal of Comparative and Physiological Psychology.* 1958, **51,** 601–606.

Trabasso, T.R., & Thompson, R.W. Shock intensity and unconditioned responding in a shuttle box. *Journal of Experimental Psychology.* 1962, **63,** 215.

Trapold, M.A., Blehert, S.R., & Sturm, T. A failure to find a response persisting in the apparent absence of motivation. *Journal of Experimental Psychology,* 1965, **69,** 538–540.

Turner, L.H. & Solomon, R.L. Human traumatic avoidance learning: Theory and experiments on the operant-respondent distinction and failures to learn. *Psychological Monographs,* 1962, **76,** (Whole No. 559).

Wagner, M.K. Restriction of the unconditioned response and its effect upon the learning of an instrumental avoidance response. *Psychological Reports,* 1964, **15,** 803–806.

Warren, J.A., Jr., & Bolles, R.C. A reevaluation of a simple contiguity interpretation of avoidance learning. *Journal of Comparative and Physiological Psychology,* 1967, **64,** 179–182.

Weismann, A. Nondiscriminated avoidance behavior in a large sample of rats. *Psychological Reports,* 1962, **10,** 591–600.

Whittleton, J.C., Kostansek, D.J., & Sawrey, J.M. CS directionality and intensity in avoidance learning and extinction. *Psychonomic Science,* 1965, **3,** 415–416.

Winston, H., Lindzey, G., & Connor, J. Albinism and avoidance learning in mice. *Journal of Comparative and Physiological Psychology,* 1967, **63,** 77–81.

CHAPTER 4

Relaxation Theory and Experiments

M. RAY DENNY

Michigan State University
East Lansing. Michigan

I. THE THEORY IN GENERAL

The theoretical background for analyzing escape-avoidance behavior in terms of relaxation has been called elicitation theory (Denny, 1966, 1967; Denny & Adelman, 1955) or elicitation hypothesis (Bolles, 1967; Maatsch, 1954). By and large, this approach is a comprehensive theory of behavior which borrows heavily from Hull, Guthrie, Tolman and Skinner and represents an attempt to integrate these neo-behavioristic schools. On the contemporary scene, there are certain similarities between this theory and Premack's (Bolles, 1967; Premack, 1959).

In regard to learning, the theory is a monistic, contiguity position which emphasizes that a particular response must occur consistently and to the relative exclusion of other responses in order to be learned: many variables that help mediate learning are those that commonly minimize or eliminate competing responses. As such, the theory bears definite similarities to Guthrie's position (1952) but differs in several basic respects: (a) reinforcers are given a central role as consistent elicitors of approach response; (b) the removal of an elicitor (UCS) from a learned sequence also consistently elicits a characteristic class of response (also mediates learning); (c) no assumption is made regarding one trial or all-or-none learning (incremental learning is the preferred assumption, but, in accord with Guthrie, it is also assumed that additional stimulus elements become conditioned to the response on successive occasions); and (d) extinction effects are the resultant of pitting the original response tendency against antagonistic tendencies (counter-conditioning but *no* unhooking of the original response is assumed).

The theory avoids positing hypothetical concepts or intervening variables and depends upon a continual, detailed analysis of stimulus and response for the explanation and prediction of behavior. The main *abstract* concepts employed are stimulus (S) and response class (R) and the relationship between them, response tendency (S-R). Quite specifically, these constucts are the only ones involved in the statement of S-R laws and thus the only concepts which are assumed to be needed in an S-R behavior theory. Thus many referents which ordinarily participate in the definition of an intervening variable are involved in defining S, R, and S-R. For example, the concept of drive collapses into deprivation conditions which contribute heavily to the definition of such Ss as food or water and their incentive value (S-R). And the concept of fear or anxiety becomes an R with distinctive stimulus accompaniments or response aftereffects.

In order to present a complete but brief picture of the theory, definitions mainly of S, R, and S-R; two corollaries of the acquisition postulate, which is paraphrased above; and two other postulates which are not covered elsewhere are presented in outline form. Or, the reader may go directly to p. 239.

A. Concepts, Corollaries, and Postulates

1. Definitions

   a. *Definition of stimulus (S).* As a concept, S is inferred from a number of referents. Briefly stated, S is defined (a) when some object or event (including behavioral events), (b) acting through the afferent neural pathways, is (c) potentially capable of eliciting an R, in (d) a particular class of organisms. By afferent is meant, for the time being at least, all neural structures in the peripheral and central nervous system which are clearly *not* efferent (for primitive organisms without an afferent system, the whole organism is presumably involved); by potentially capable is meant that R has been reliably elicited in the life history of some representative members of the organism in question; by elicitation is meant that R is contingent upon an immediately antedating S.

   (a) Kinesthetic and other interoceptive stimuli cannot be identified with objects but can be inferred from specific behavioral or physiological events; the removal of an object such as food is an event rather than an object or a form of physical energy, and this event helps define certain stimulus classes (the secondary elicitation hypothesis).

   (b) Although physiologists use the term stimulus to refer to an agent which directly activates a muscle or motor neuron, psychologists have typically reserved the term innervation for this process. This usage is supported by the fact that the laws of behavior for innervation are often not the same as for elicitation by a stimulus, that is, when the afferent NS is involved.

(c) Defining S in terms of R seem circular, but this is not the case at all. The S in an S-R law is defined independently of this R, just as R is defined independently of this S. Some R at some time or another, however, has had to be contingent upon this S before S could be classified as such. Frequencies, wavelengths, and intensities that are never responded to, are simply not Ss, for the class of organism in question.

Fundamentally, this definition simply reflects the way S is used in the description of experimental procedures in psychological research. The definition implies once an S always an S, whether on occasion it elicits an R or not. As a concept with a constant meaning, S can therefore enter into lawful statements with R (In a scientific law the concepts involved must have a constant meaning). When R is predictable from an S-R law and yet fails to occur in the presence of S, this has no bearing on the definition of S. It simply means that strong, competing Ss or other relevant variables are present and need to be taken into account when explaining the observed behavior.

b. Definition of response (R). In theory, response class is inferred from three sets of referents: (a) a set of response occurrences for (b) a particular class of organisms where the identification of the response class is primarily based on (c) some recurrent aspect of the stimulus situation. For example, if a rat (b) is running East (a) *toward a place* where it has previously found food (c), then R is classified as approach. If the same running behavior (a) is observed in the rat (b) when there is an electrified grid to the West (c) then R is classified as escape. The presence of the word "bar" in the response class, "bar-pressing rate," is a pointed example of the use of stimulus like concepts to define response class. In the theory, overt response occurrences are necessary to infer a particular response class, but this does not mean that the response class must itself represent overt behavior. Perception, thinking, relaxation, etc. are all legitimate response classes which, in human beings, are typically inferred from verbal report. The task of classifying response in lower animals is somewhat more complex but logically equivalent.

A fourth defining referent of response class is often a set of mathematical operations. We speak of the mean latency or median amplitude of response or its probability of occurrence; such operations clearly denote the abstract nature of the concept of response.

c. Definition of response tendency (S-R). The property of a stimulus (S) to elicit a response (R) is called a response tendency (S-R).

2. Corollaries of the Acquisition Postulate

a. Corollary 1. If conditioning is to occur to a particular CS, the eliciting value of the CS at some time or another must be greater than the eliciting value of other concurrent Ss (possible competing cues). Up to a low suprathreshold value at least, the greater the eliciting value of the CS the faster the conditioning. That the organism makes an initial orienting response to the CS appears to be almost a prerequisite for conditioning to occur to this S (Sokolov, 1963; Maltzman & Raskin, 1965), and some CSs are better than others (Smith, McFarland & Taylor, 1961; Spence, Haggard, & Ross, 1958).

b. *Corollary 2.* The greater the response involvement with respect to the elicited, to-be-learned response (frequently response involvement can be equated with the eliciting value of the US) the better the conditioning (Colavita, 1965; Jaynes, 1950; Spence *et al.,* 1958). It appears impossible, for example, to condition a single, isolated reflex such as pupillary contraction whereas it is entirely possible to condition pupillary dilation where it is part of a larger response complex (Young, 1958; Gerall, Sampson, & Boslov, 1957).

3. Elicitation Postulate

a. *The satiation hypothesis.* By definition, all Ss elicit R. But with continued or repeated presentation all Ss lose or partially lose the property to elicit R as a decay function of the duration or frequency of presentation. The slope of this decay function varies with the nature and intensity of S, *i.e.,* some Ss (food for hungry animal, shock, etc.) are more resistant to adaptation (satiation) than other classes of S. With the passage of time S recovers its capacity to elicit a response.

b. *The elicitation hierarchy.* At any moment in time all Ss impinging upon an organism are arranged in an elicitation hierarchy. The Ss continually exchange places in the hierarchy because of (a) stimulus satiation effects, (b) changes in the physical intensity of a stimulus, (c) changes in deprivation level, (d) the use of set-producing instructions (in human beings), and (e) basic associative changes (acquisition and extinction).

4. Stimulus Generalization Postulate

Stimulus generalization is the transfer of S-R from one stimulus complex to another. The magnitude of the generalization is a direct function of the proportion of effective stimulus elements common to the situations under consideration. Thus prior to differential training when only a limited number of effective elements are likely to be changed when switching from one stimulus complex to another, transfer is practically complete; *i.e.,* the gradient of generalization is relatively flat. If the altered element(s) is(are) made discriminative so that the remaining elements become nondifferential or irrelevant then the gradient of generalization for the discriminative elements becomes relatively steep, as of the type specified by Hull (1943). In other words, typical generalization gradients are the result of discrimination training which places the brunt of response specification (stimulus control) on a particular stimulus.

Because a number of stimulus elements typically share stimulus control (or are effective) some change in the total stimulus situation can often produce decrement in performance (generalization decrement). One main source of inhibition, including both the phenomena of forgetting and experimental extinction, is generalization decrement.

5. Some additional definitions

a. Stimulus element. An *element* is any unanalyzable part of a stimulus complex.

b. Stimulus change. A *change* in a stimulus element can occur along one or more of the following parameters: Spatial or temporal arrangement, some quantifiable dimension, and presence or absence.

c. Effective stimuli. Effective stimulus elements are those elements which are exclusively conditioned to the response in question.

B. The Theory and Instrumental Learning

The workings of the theory can be illustrated by analyzing instrumental reward learning in lower animals. Such an analysis involves the same sort of thinking that is present in analyzing escape-avoidance behavior and should facilitate this later task. Instrumental learning, which is traditionally interpreted in terms of the operation of a reinforcement principle, is retranslated within the theory into a Pavlovian or classical conditioning model. A critical aspect of the analysis is that the unconditioned response which mediates the instrumental learning is the response of approaching the incentive (food, water, etc.) rather than the response of ingesting it (the possibility that approach to the sight and smell of familiar food has been strengthened through learning early in the life history of the organism is in no way precluded by the term unconditioned response). The conditioning that is assumed to be going on in an instrumental situation differs from that of a traditional classical conditioning experiment in a number of ways: (a) the UR of approach involves the whole organism rather than representing an isolated reflex and is long-lasting rather than short-lived (there may be other URs and other CRs such as fractional consummatory responses; they are simply assigned a lesser role); (b) the series of higher order conditionings ("backchaining") which is presumably involved in instrumental conditioning is protected from extinction effects because the incentive (US) is neither delayed nor omitted with respect to terminal approach; and (c) the CS is typically not a single aspect but all the elements of the current stimulus situation. (In discrimination training, learning is slow and resembles the learning in a typical classical conditioning experiment using a unitary CS.) All of these differences imply rapid instrumental learning, as demanded by the experimental data in the area.

All of this can be explicated in detail by describing how a rat learns to turn right in a T-maze. Let us assume a small piece of familiar food is at the end of the right alley, no food is on the left, and S is hungry. Exploratory-approach is sooner or later elicited in S by the novel stimuli of the alley, and this locomotor behavior eventually brings S to the goal area. Figure 1 presents a symbolic representation of the conditioning that presumably goes on in such a T-maze after this has happened. The conditioning begins with Step A and proceeds alphabetically, as presented. One thing that is immediately apparent is that T-maze learning is not really very simple; it is often called simple, but it is really a complex sequence of learned responses: all responses presumably have to be built up gradually in an indirect, backward fashion.

The omnipresent unconditioned response of approach to food—i.e., before the animal can eat the food it has to approach it—is represented by a solid line in Figure 1, the conditioned associations by dots and dashes (dashes alone represent the later, weaker associations). In instrumental approach learning, withdrawal from the nonreinforced end of a T or Y is assumed to be a relevant class of unconditioned response which is conditioned to the cues on the incorrect side (Denny & Dunham, 1951; Lachman, 1961). This aspect is not adequately covered in Figure 1 in order to keep the drawing uncluttered.

In this figure, S^1 is a CS that represents that part of the goal box which immediately precedes the region where the food is presented and is close enough in time to be conditioned to the approach response which is unconditionally elicited by S^R. Thus the first response learned in the T-maze is to approach the food tray as soon as entering the goal box. This is the double-dash and double-dot connection between S^1 and $R_{approach}$ in part A in the lower portion of Figure 1. It is critical for learning that S make a definite approach response to the food tray. In fact, it only needs to be hungry (food-seeking) while in the goal box, i.e., *after* a right turn has been made (Mendelson, 1966). After the initial

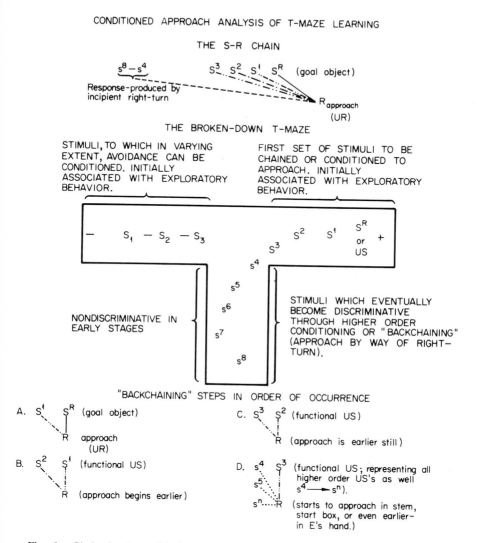

Fig. 1. Chained or conditioned approach analysis of T-maze learning (elicitation theory).

approach response there is an increase in the probability of selecting the reinforced side on the succeeding trial, regardless of how soon the food was eaten after S first approached it (Denny & Martindale, 1956).

As soon as S^1 has acquired adequate eliciting value, it then serves as a functional US, eliciting approach in close temporal contiguity with S^2. Next, S^2 becomes a functional US. Since S^2 closely follows S^3 in time, S^3 acquires conditioned approach value and becomes a functional US. At this point, the analysis is much the same as described by Tolman years ago, namely, that the rat learns to go to a particular place. According to the present analysis, Tolman's description is accurate only in the early stages, when approach has only been conditioned to S^1, S^2, or S^3. During this early stage, the rat makes a number of errors and displays considerable vicarious trial and error (VTE) or looking-back-and-forth behavior at the choice point; with continued trials VTE diminishes.

The chain continues to develop, involving response-produced kinesthetic stimuli which are represented in Figure 1 by s. So after S^3, s^4 becomes a functional US, and then s^5 and so on all the way back to wherever stimuli remain discriminative. Thus the typical, well-trained rat starts to turn as soon as it leaves the start box. At this point in learning, it is legitimate to call the learned response a right-turn response. Prior to this stage, the rat learns to *approach cues* on the right side of the maze; this is different from the response class of *turning* right, which is controlled largely by kinesthetic stimuli. Not until the chain has built back to s^4 do the stem stimuli (s^8–s^4) start to become discriminative, specifying a right turn before the rat has arrived at the choice point (note the centrifugal swing of s^8–s^4 in Figure 1). In short, the rat finally learns to approach the food *by way of* a right turn. In much the same way, a rat in a Skinner box learns to approach the food tray *by way of* a bar press. In the bar-pressing situation an early discrimination for the rat to learn is to approach the food tray *after* a bar press, instead of reapproaching the tray *after* eating a pellet. With continued backchaining, the sight of the bar *after* the rat has eaten the food pellet becomes the S^D (CS) for approaching the bar. This in turn initiates the bar press whose attendant stimuli then elicit approach to the food tray, and the chain is complete.

One implication of this analysis is that instrumental (operant) conditioning differs from classical (respondent) conditioning mainly with respect to the origin of the S^D (CS) for the next response in the chain. The organism, through its own responding, supplies the S^D in an instrumental situation, while the experimenter (environment) supplies the CS in classical conditioning. This of course means that the relevant S^Ds in instrumental learning are often proprioceptive-tactual stimuli. According to the present theory, such stimuli are usually initiated by exploratory-manipulatory behavior which is elicited by the novel aspects of the stimulus situation (emitted behavior for Skinner). Obviously, the responses which need to occur are those of approaching the goal and approaching and manipulating the manipulandum (or traversing an alley).

When these instrumental responses fail to occur, the competing responses (R_c) are habituated by exposing S continuously to the situation; and,
if necessary, special methods of shaping and prompting (fading) are in-
stituted so that the required R eventually occurs.

One example of the usefulness of this analysis is to apply it to the
learning of observing responses (OR) as first described by Wyckoff
(1952). The OR is usually considered a paradox: Why should an animal
learn to make an OR (e.g., peck a particular key, press a treadle, or turn
right rather than left in a T-maze, etc.) just to find out whether the next
set of responses in the chain is going to be reinforced or not? Since the
final operant series is always available and is reinforced, say, 50% of the
time irrespective of whether OR occurs, why doesn't the animal bypass
the OR? Nothing is gained except a little advance "information." The
present analysis says that learning an OR is essentially the same as
learning any instrumental response. The backchaining going on in learning an instrumental response automatically includes the next earlier response in the sequence whenever this response is followed by an S^D
(functional US for the next operant), provided an alternative route consistently leads to an S^Δ or a nondifferential stimulus. The S^Δ consequence defines the conditioning that goes on in ordinary instrumental
learning, while the nondifferential stimulus as a consequence defines the
conditioning of an OR. Conditioning of the OR, like instrumental learning, proceeds readily even though the OR may produce an S^D fairly infrequently (the partially reinforced bar press only occasionally produces
the click of the food magazine). What is more important are the consequences of failing to make the OR. If this happens, the chain is broken:
the succeeding set of responses in the chain is not *immediately* followed
by a discriminative stimulus but by proprioceptive-tactual-visual stimuli
which are irrelevant, stimuli that are correlated equally often with reinforcement and nonreinforcement.

One assumption in this analysis is that the next R following the OR is
not going to be immediately reinforced, for example, by the noise of the
food magazine. Wyckoff's pigeons were on a 30-sec FI following the
OR; and Bower, McLean, and Meacham's (1966) were on at least a
10-sec FI schedule. Thus "noise" as a functional US could not by itself
effectively bridge the time gap between the start of the operant series
(e.g., pecking a colored key) and the occurrence of noise-elicited approach to the food hopper. Given a delay, the OR is needed so that the
intermediate S^D, when it occurs, overlaps the succeeding S^D (functional
US), building and preserving the chain. Without a delay between the OR
and the reinforcement of the final operant, the OR and its S^D consequences are nonfunctional. Lutz and Perkins (1960) found that a delay

of at least 3 sec near the end of the chain was necessary for the development of an OR and that 3 sec was as good as 81 sec. This finding strongly supports the entire backchaining analysis; without it most of what has been said so far would be disconfirmed.

C. The Theory and Experimental Extinction

The elicitation hypothesis grew out of data and observations which were initially made while rats were being extinguished (Denny, 1946; Maatsch, 1951; Denny and Dunham, 1951). In an instrumental approach situation, after $R_{approach}$ had been fairly well established under continuous reinforcement, it was regularly noticed that new and vigorous Rs appeared with the omission of the goal object (frustration-instigated behaviors) and that $R_{withdrawal}$ soon tended to replace $R_{approach}$. This was interpreted to mean that the backchaining of competing responses (R_c) starts in the goal area and works forward in the behavior sequence to the start region—much like the conditioning of approach, except that extinction can be mediated much more by stimulus generalization because it is nonspecific. According to the procedures used and data obtained (Maatsch, 1951), R_c was being conditioned to the current stimulus situation solely through contiguity and consistency considerations; the net effect was the extinction of $R_{approach}$. We then reasoned that perhaps all learning takes place in the same fashion—through the consistent elicitation of a characteristic R in close temporal association with S.

Several years later, Denny & Adelman (1955) extended the original notion about the eliciting effects of omitting food or water so that the omission of *any* consistent elicitor (US), including the omission of aversive stimuli such as shock, constituted an eliciting state of affairs. We called this postulate secondary elicitation because a learned behavior sequence (conditioned anticipation) had to be established to some minimal level *before* the omission was itself an elicitor (US). The Rs elicited by secondary elicitation were typically antagonistic to the original response (R_0). With the positing of secondary elicitation, we now had a general theory to handle all extinction phenomena within the context of counterconditioning or interference learning. When formalized, the extinction postulate was expressed as follows:

The inhibition of performance which is *not* due to generalization decrement is the result of competing response tendencies (S-R_c) being conditioned to stimulus situations which are *similar* to the one of original conditioning. The S-R_c pitted against the original response tendency (S-R$_0$) produces singly, or in vector summation, a resultant reduction in S-R$_0$ as a direct function of the relative strength and degree of incompatibility of S-R$_c$. No unhooking of R, no *absolute* weakening of S-R$_0$, and no intrinsic inhibition (inhibitory drive state) are posited. The conditioning of R$_c$ during extinction is commonly, though not always, produced by secondary elicitation.

The cues present in extinction autmatically differ from those of acquisition because the omission of the US (reinforcement) elicits responses, largely emotional, which have distinctive stimulus accompaniments and aftereffects. Such stimulus aftereffects diminish with the passage of time and make it possible to derive spontaneous recovery and related effects without having to posit temporary inhibitory states; such aftereffects also help in the explanation of certain partial reinforcement effects (PRE).

Because stimulus aftereffects diminish with time, it is generally assumed that a shift from acquisition to extinction conditions constitutes a stimulus change only when all trials are relatively massed. However, it is also possible to posit a cue difference at the start of an extinction trial even when all trials are spaced at least one day apart. During each of the early spaced extinction trials, an emotional response is consistently being elicited by frustration (secondary elicitation for the omission of a positive incentive) and through conditioning is coming forward in the behavior sequence. Thus, after a number of extinction trials, a set of new emotion-produced stimuli would prevail at the start of a trial, say in the start box of a runway, and represent a stimulus change from acquisition to extinction. The principle invoked here does not differ appreciably from the one used by Amsel (1958) in his explanation of partial reinforcement effects. For Amsel, the emotional component, r$_f$, is conditioned to the start box cues, and its stimulus accompaniment, s$_f$, is conditioned to the response of running, mediating a PRE even when highly spaced trials are involved.

An important implication of secondary elicition for the acquisition of an original approach response is that it is important for an animal to complete the chain with a consummatory response, not because eating or drinking is satisfying à la Thorndike's law of effect, but because alternative (nonapproach) responses will be elicited if the incentive is removed or inaccessible. In a recent study by Mendelson (1967) it was found that rats will make themselves thirsty by bar-pressing for intracranial stimulation when water is available to drink. This finding makes a similar point in quite a different way: approach to water occurs by way of learning an instrumental response which produces a drive (thrist), not by a response which satisfies or reduces a drive. According to elicitation theory such learning takes place because the occasional thirst-producing bar presses initially made by an exploring S result in consistent approaches to water. Backchaining or conditioning of water-approach then occurs to stimuli earlier in the behavior sequence, and thus "detour approach," approaching water via instrumental bar pressing, is established.

The published studies which most clearly support the present interpretation of experimental extinction are those by Adelman and Maatsch (1955, 1956). Rats were given 36 reinforcements in a runway and then extinguished under three separate conditions: allowed to jump out of the goal box onto a 2-in. ledge; allowed to recoil from the goal box and retrace; stayed in goal box (regular extinction). The results indicated that extinction occurs most rapidly when the response (R_c), which is elicited by frustration, is directly incompatible with R_o: the recoil group extinguished fastest and the jump-out group slowest. A number of approximate replications of the Adelman & Maatsch study by other investigators, however, have failed in varying degrees to replicate these results, and the generality of the original finding has been questioned (Haggard, 1959; Bacon, 1967; and Theios and Bower, 1964). In this connection, it should be pointed out that none of the replications above satisfy the theory, as applied to the original experimental paradigm, in that they used a homogeneous runway (the details of the theory, however, were not readily available when these replications were conducted). The results of the one study which also used a homogeneous darkened surround (Haggard, 1959) disagreed completely with the Adelman and Maatsch results; the one in which the goal area was wider and at right angles to the main alley showed the most agreement (Bacon, 1967). In a fourth study with *distinctive* runway sections, a running-escape group performed like the jump-out group of the original study (Barrett & Carlson, 1966).

In the Adelman & Maatsch experiment, we were extremely careful to make the start box, alley, and goal box highly distinctive. Otherwise, any R_c could readily generalize to any other section of the runway, and at that point in the chain R_o and R_c could be incompatible and produce extinction effects. In the sense in which it was being tested, the elicitation hypothesis required that R_c be *conditioned* to the original chain, *starting* in the goal area: In accord with this dictum, a jump-out escape (R_{Jo}) during extinction could be tacked on to the end of the original running response ($R_{approach}$) and not be incompatible with $R_{approach}$ and not cause extinction. (Even so, Adelman & Maatsch made sure to put a glass cover over the high-walled start box to prevent the occurrence of

R_{JO} there—*i.e.*, through minimal stimulus generalization). Conversely, a recoil-running response which is conditioned discriminatively to the instrumental chain is going to be directly incompatible with R_0 and cause extinction. Whereas, a recoil-running response which is *not* conditioned discriminatively (which is not clearly oriented as to direction) might well prolong extinction rather than facilitate it: S simply learns to run, period.

One final point should be emphasized. Jump-out learning (Adelman & Maatsch, 1955) is consistently interpreted in secondary sources as being an example of learning through frustration reduction. This is a dubious interpretation. The evidence for such learning is scanty (Amsel, Ernhart, & Galbrecht, 1961; Amsel & Hancock, 1957; Amsel & Prouty, 1959; Amsel & Ward, 1954; Wagner, 1963) and can be readily reinterpreted in terms of the eliciting value of frustration. Furthermore, studies of Adelman and Maatsch (1956) represent an attempt to elucidate this point by showing that the R_{JO} which was directly elicited by an empty food dish was learned significantly faster than an R_{JO} which was reinforced with familiar food on the ledge to which a hungry S jumped. According to the theory, an R_{JO} that has been directly elicited by frustration does not have to backchain from the ledge to the floor of the goal box and thus should be learned faster than a food reinforced R_{JO}. The full implication of this aspect of their work seems to have been ignored. Anyone who adheres to a frustration reduction interpretation is claiming that a type of learning for which a veritable mountain of evidence exists (learning through food reinforcement) can lose ignominiously to a type of learning for which the amount of evidence approximates the mass of a gnat's eyebrow. If it is so easy to get good learning via frustration reduction, how does one account for the fact that it is so hard to accumulate acceptable evidence in support of the frustration reduction hypothesis? In our laboratory, Maatsch's M.A. thesis (1951), which started the elicitation theory, provided an early set of negative results for a test of this hypothesis but by no means the last (Sutey, 1967).

D. The Theory as Applied to Escape-Avoidance Behavior

One reason for having spent so much time on the intricacies of instrumental approach behavior is that instrumental escape and avoidance involve a similar analysis. The analyses are parallel in basic detail. Let us examine a prototypic situation in which S first learns to escape and then learns to avoid [a one-way or hurdle box, a jump-out apparatus (Figure 2), a shuttlebox, discrete bar-press avoidance, etc.].

Just as the organism must be in a special state (hungry, thirsty, etc.)

before the positive incentive can be a good elicitor of approach and mediate instrumental reward learning, so must the organism be in a special state before escape-avoidance learning can take place. This is the state of being agitated or emotional and regularly occurs with the initial presentation of the aversive stimulus (AS). With this and further presentation of AS, the associated stimulus situation (CS) comes to elicit a similar state (fear) in the organism and thus qualifies as a conditional aversive stimulus (CAS).

According to the theory, once the agitated state is present, *then* either the removal or omission of AS or the removal of the CAS has distinct response consequences. These consequences have been identified behaviorally in special escape-avoidance experiments which will be reported in detail later. The more recently isolated response seems to occur only after the termination of AS and is called short-latency "relief." In rats, and as tested, the effect begins approximately 5 sec after the cessation of shock and almost disappears within the next 10 or 15 sec. This response seems to correspond closely with the postshock effect in heart rate as investigated in dogs by Church, LoLordo, Overmier, Solomon, and Turner (1966). When shock is terminated, heart rate rapidly decreases within 10 sec to a rate below the preshock rate and then slowly returns to normal. Even though different species are involved, the temporal characteristics of these two phenomena are remarkably similar and each has been independently labeled "relief." The other response is long-latency relaxation which was originally posited in 1955 (Denny & Adelman) and was suggested by Miller as early as 1951 (Miller, 1951). The onset of relaxation seems to be 25–40 sec post-CAS or post-AS, and the minimal optimal duration is about 150 sec, at least for rats trained with a wide range of shock intensities.[1]

Like two-factor avoidance theory, the present analysis assumes that fear is soon conditioned to the shock situation, but unlike two-factor theory, the removal of CAS is not supposed to be *immediately* reinforcing. Learning, as always, is mediated by response, and the response in question can have a long latency. And since the learning is *instrumental,* as when escape terminates shock or avoidance prevents shock, then the US or UR that mediates the conditioning (backchaining) must be at the very end of the behavior sequence, functioning as a goal.

In other words, the crucial UR in escape-avoidance learning is the consistently elicited response that occurs in the safe region or safe period, following the removal of AS or CAS. In this connection, it is inter-

[1]*Editor's note:* See also Chapter 3 by Bolles, Chapter 1 by Black, and Chapter 6 by Seligman, Maier, and Solomon for additional treatments relevant to these notions.

esting to point out that the S-R operations in escape-avoidance learning are considered to be the reciprocal of instrumental approach. In approach learning, the approach component is elicited by the available incentive, while the withdrawal component—avoiding the wrong alley or avoiding the water dipper until after the bar has been depressed—is elicited by the omission of the incentive or S^D. In avoidance learning, the approach component is elicited by the absence of AS or CAS, while withdrawal or escape is originally elicited by the presence of AS.

In much the same way that the incentive elicits approach while S is in the goal box of a T-maze, it is assumed that the removal of AS or CAS can elicit approach-type behavior while S is in the nonshock (safe) region. This UR is called relaxation-approach because after S begins to relax, it begins to approach (look at, investigate, manipulate, etc.) the stimuli that constitute the nonshock region or time period.

Since relaxation, and possibly relief, is said to be a prerequisite for making $R_{approach}$, though this is mainly assumed rather than backed up by data, the question arises as to why the backchaining of approach takes priority over the backchaining of relaxation (relaxation typically manifests itself later, bringing about extinction effects). Presumably, $R_{approach}$ is compatible with S's emotional state while S is in the shock region, provided S is not freezing extensively, and $R_{approach}$ can therefore come forward in the sequence in the same backchaining fashion as described for the T-maze. Thus the point in the chain is reached where S approaches the safe region prior to the onset of shock. At this point it can be asserted that S is learning to avoid. Relaxation, on the other hand, is directly incompatible with the agitated state of S while S is in the shock region and only gradually "fights" its way back in the chain, to produce extinction effects.

In sum, escape is reinforced by shock termination plus the removal of CAS, and this conditioning brings about avoidance. When it occurs, avoidance may be "reinforced" by the removal of CAS or just because it is consistently elicited—just because it occurs without the occurrence of alternative responses. This analysis in no way precludes the learning of avoidance without the making of escape responses, i.e., solely on the basis of the removal of CAS, as found in experiments by Brown and Jacobs (1949), Kalish (1954), and McAllister and McAllister (1962, 1963). Typically, however, escape precedes avoidance and helps mediate the learning of avoidance.

The role of S's initial attempts to escape during avoidance learning needs to be examined. In the theory, these behaviors mainly supply the operant which finally gets the animal out of a box, across the midline, etc. (away from AS and CAS). Only when the early attempts to escape do not include the required operant or the elicited attempts are incompatible with the R that is elicited by the termination of the aversive US (Bolles and Seelbach, 1964) does the nature of the escape response become especially critical. This is because an escape-avoidance operant is learned mainly on the basis of what is elicited in the nonshock area or time period rather than in terms of what is directly elicited by shock. Long-lasting, consistently elicited escape responses doubtless do get directly conditioned to the situation, but these CRs are likely to be quite independent of the successful avoidance response. Such CRs would tend to come forward in the behavior sequence and are probably best represented by S's struggling in E's hand while it is being put back into the shock chamber at the start of a new trial. (This behavior tends to extinguish with the omission of the US, that is, as S continues to avoid.)

Evidence in favor of this sort of analysis has recently been supplied by Warren and Bolles (1967). Rats were shocked in a runway-wheel avoidance situation either on the hind feet, front feet, or all feet, and in all cases the avoidance response was running forward. According to the classical conditioning or contiguity theory of Sheffield (1948), where the avoidance response is assumed to be a replica of the response elicited by shock, the group which was shocked in the hind feet (and typically lurched forward) should learn faster than those which were shocked in the front feet (and typically backed up), but the reverse was found to be true. At first glance, these results might also seem to contradict the contiguity assumptions of the elicitation position, but in actual fact, as already indicated in part, they harmonize rather well. Warren and Bolles point out that Ss shocked on the front feet frequently turned around then ran forward in the same direction as they had recoiled. This means that this group not only made the appropriate operant but that more distinctive kinesthesis was involved in making this R than in the hind-foot shock group. If it is assumed that the operant is being learned by backchaining, then distinctive kinesthetic CSs are definitely going to facilitate the conditioning process, which is exactly what Warren and Bolles found. A direct test of this distinctive kinesthesis hypothesis in avoidance learning, to the author's knowledge, has not been made, as, for example, by using a weighted bar with a long excursion versus a light bar with a short excursion. In our laboratory, however, rats typically learn an 11-in. jump-out response in a mean of about 2 trials (Denny & Weisman, 1964) and take between 3 and 4 trials to learn the easier one-way running response.

Typically, escape and avoidance responses are a blend of each other so that the strength of R_{avoid} is based a great deal on the postshock reinforcement associated with escape, as has been clearly implicated in shuttle-box avoidance (Bolles, Stokes, & Younger, 1966). In fact, pure escape training typically yields an "avoidance" response. We often train Ss to "avoid" simply by using a solid block of 8 to 10 escape trials in a one-way or jump-out box, usually with nonshock periods that are about 150 sec long. "Avoidance" is then assessed in a no-shock extinction test (Denny & Dmitruk, 1967). With this technique S is never shocked for failing to respond quickly, yet during the test S typically responds with a very short latency, well below what would be required to avoid, for a mean of 25 to 30 trials. When such trials are highly massed (ITI of 10 or 15 sec) S escapes fairly well but learns to "avoid" very slowly or sometimes not at all (within the number of trials employed). In the theory, massed trials eliminate a clear-cut UR (relaxation-approach) in the safe region, and thus approach toward the safe place cannot be effectively conditioned to the stimuli of the shock chamber. Consequently, the learning of R_{avoid} is markedly impeded.

In many ways the present analysis is like other contemporary treatments of avoidance learning; for example, as a Skinnerian one simply reads negative reinforcement for shock termination and secondary negative reinforcement for removal of CAS. But there are also important differences. The emphasis of relaxation theorizing on temporal parameters such as ITI and length of nonshock periods (adequate opportunity for S to relax and approach) represents one main difference, but there are others, as exemplified below.

(a)   In the present analysis, the CS does not have to remain a conditioned fear stimulus throughout avoidance conditioning for avoidance to be strengthened and maintained. Fear is not conditioned solely to a specific CS, if there is one, but to the total shock situation which includes spatial as well as temporal cues. Thus loss of fear to CS does not mean loss of fear entirely, or even substantially. In any event, with continued backchaining, the CS or warning signal becomes primarily an S^D for the **appropriate operant, as has been suggested by Lockard (1963) and** Bolles *et al.* (1966). Once there is an established elicitor (S^D) for the appropriate operant, the S^D continues to function as such until R_c replaces Ro. Thus the results of Kamin, Brimer, and Black (1963) which showed that avoidance becomes stronger as fear of CS diminishes is congruent with the present position: If approach to the safe region is elicited without R_c also occurring, R_{avoid} continues to be learned and maintained. As soon, however, as relaxation effectively competes with S's total amount of fear, as soon as S begins to approach the cues of the shock region, R_{avoid} extinguishes. Similar effects (continuation of acquisition and failure to extinguish after the removal of reinforcement) can be arranged for instrumental approach learning by minimizing the elicitation and conditioning of R_c. If a rat makes only one bar press per day during both acquisition and extinction (no accumulation of R_c or frustration effects) and the bar is removed immediately after it is depressed and is thus *absent* during extinction when S visits the empty food tray (no conditioning of R_c directly to the bar), S-$R_{bar\ press}$ can become stronger during early extinction trials and fail to show any tendency to extinguish in 125 trials (Denny, 1959).

(b)   It is embarrassing to traditional two-factor theory that trace conditioning can proceed quite well even though the CS (conditioned fear stimulus) often terminates prior to the occurrence of the instrumental R (Kamin, 1954). Early in acquisition this happens on each escape trial and continues to happen on at least half the avoidance trials when a trace CS with a duration no longer than 2 sec is used, as has been found by Church, Brush, & Solomon (1956). The embarrassment results from the fact that "reinforcement through fear reduction" occurs in the "wrong" place, before R instead of immediately after R. In the present analysis, this is irrelevant; that which is critical is occurring at the very end of the chain (relaxation-approach).

Using the theory in a rather speculative manner, let us examine trace conditioning of R_{avoid} (the $R_{approach}$ component of relaxation-approach) in the shuttlebox procedure which resembles one-way avoidance (Solomon and Wynne, 1953). Here the CS occurs alternately in each chamber and thus temporarily defines safe versus shock regions (Ss are typically dogs). On early trials, fear is conditioned to the internal and external stimuli which precede shock and which are similar to the stimuli that are present throughout the CS–US interval. Fear thus promptly generalizes to the stimuli which *immediately* follow the trace CS; and fear which is then contiguous with the CS, gets conditioned to the CS: Such backchaining is presumably dependent upon the fact that fear persists and continues to overlap the US as it continues to backchain. If fear, as it was backchaining and moving forward in the sequence, were short-lived rather than long-lasting it would *not* be followed immediately by the US and would extinguish. That is, conditions of extinction such as those of McAllister (1953) would prevail, and backchaining would cease (a 2-sec delay of the airpuff US brings about the extinction of a transient eyelid CR).

With the continued backchaining of fear, the interval between the trace CS and the US of shock becomes filled with discriminative fear-produced stimuli. These cues are present when S avoids and thus support the rapid *generalization* and backchaining of R_{avoid} to the discriminative point in time when the trace CS is presented. Trace conditioning of R_{avoid} proceeds rapidly as long as the CS–US interval is not too long. With a very long CS–US interval, say 40 or more sec, the trace CS would *also* be directly associated with a nonshock period (relaxation) and would probably not become discriminative with respect either to fear or to safety (avoidance would be slow to develop or would not occur specifically to the CS (Kamin, 1954)). In fact, the backchaining of R_{avoid} explains why almost any CS, as in the Kamin, *et al.* study (1963), would typically lose its fear value in the later stages of avoidance training. Instead of remaining a CS for fear, the CS plus R_{avoid} feedback stimuli eventually become the cue for approaching safety.

(c)   This same sort of analysis also explains why very long CS–US intervals with delayed or overlapping CS can yield rapid avoidance learning (Brush, Brush, & Solomon, 1955). In our laboratory, the rat learns jump-out avoidance in only 5 or 6 trials when shock is administered 80 sec after CS onset, *i.e.*, 80 sec after S is put in the lower box. On the first trial or so, fear is presumably conditioned to the portion of the CS which is contiguous with shock. Because fear is long-lasting and overlaps shock and is thus protected from potential extinction effects, it quickly generalizes and backchains to the initial portion of the CS. The CS is similar throughout its course, and the fear-produced cues early in the CS–US interval strongly resemble the fear-produced cues that are present later in the interval, *i.e.*, those initially associated with R_{escape}. Therefore mainly through stimulus generalization, R_{escape} quickly moves forward in the sequence and becomes R_{avoid}, conditioned to the CS, with an asymptotic latency of about 2½ sec, a latency that is typical of long CS–US avoidance intervals (delayed and trace). That is, under these conditions, R_{avoid} is probably elicited only after a modicum of fear has also been elicited (after approximately 2½ sec have elapsed).

The most relevant and exciting evidence in support of several points that have been made in the last few pages is available in an unpublished study by Cole and Wahlsten (1967). In this study there was a direct comparison between classical and instrumental components of avoidance conditioning in the dog, even, in a few instances, in the same animal. Foreleg flexion was conditioned with the dog standing restrained on all four feet and with a front paw strapped to a response lever. A 2-in. elevation of the leg was required to record a response. Two groups, classical and avoidance, of 10 dogs each, received 50 trials per day with a 2-sec CS–US interval, .5-sec shock duration, and a variable 1-min ITI. For classical training, the tone CS preceded the .5-sec shock by 2 sec, and CS and US terminated simultaneously. Leg flexion had no effect on either stimulus. For instrumental training there was the same temporal sequence of CS and US, but a leg flexion during the CS–US interval prevented onset of the US and terminated the CS. A response during the US did not terminate the shock. All Ss were run for at least 5 days beyond asymptote.

Late in training, the two contingencies resulted in quite different forms of responding with respect to the distribution of latencies. The classical dogs gave almost all of their CRs just prior to shock onset, while avoidance Ss usually responded in less than a second after CS onset. Early in training there were no differences in the distributions of latencies. The avoidance group was initially like the classical, and the backchaining shift to shorter latencies was gradual. When conditions were reversed for the two groups the same gradual change in latencies took place, as if the dog had to learn and relearn two quite different responses for the classical and avoidance conditions. As would be expected, more CRs occurred with the avoidance contingency than with the classical.

The interpretation that is placed on these data is as follows. The directly elicited leg-flexion in the classical group cannot move forward in the behavior sequence because it is a short-lived R that would no longer overlap the US (shock) as it tended to move forward; short latency variations in the CR would extinguish before they got started. The latency data of Cole and Wahlsten indicate abortive shifts of the classical CR toward shorter latency, but these all but disappear in later training. In avoidance, however, the critical US is not the shock but the *nonshock* period, and the UR is long-lasting relaxation-approach where the CR and its attendant stimulation is just an early component of the appropriate route to the goal. Thus CR-approach can readily come forward and still overlap the US or its functional counterpart. This was especially true in the design used by Cole and Wahlsten because the CS (conditioned aversive stimulus) terminated with the CR if the CR anticipated shock (This aspect of the procedure probably heightened the obtained effect, but should not have been absolutely critical). Any further shortening of the avoidance latency than that observed by Cole and Wahlsten was limited by the onset of the CS; the period prior to onset is an $S^\triangle$ for shock.

During early training the functioning US (shock) was the same for both the classical and avoidance conditions (a leg flexion during the US did not terminate shock in either case which means that relief was never discriminatively associated with leg flexion during this early period). Concomitantly, the distributions of latencies were identical. Not until CR's occurred a few times in succession, mediating a nonshock period that was around 150 sec or longer, would this new US (the nonshock period) become clearly operative for the avoidance Ss (with a variable ITI of 1 min, even a single avoidance might result in a nonshock period of 150 sec, e.g., an ITI of 60 sec preceding the CS and an ITI of 90 sec following the avoidance CR). At this point the CR would begin to back-chain and produce the separate distribution of latencies for the avoidance group.

E.   The Theory as Applied to the Extinction of Escape-Avoidance Behavior

The theory states that extinction results from the pitting of one or more response tendencies against S-R_0 in a stimulus situation which is more or less like the original acquisition situation. When aversive stimuli are involved in acquisition and the aversive stimulus is omitted in extinction, R_c is very likely to be relaxation, elicited by the omission of the aversive stimulus (secondary elicitation). The main reason for excluding "relief" from R_c is that the evidence to date indicates relief occurs only after the termination of AS. This particular point is quite tentative because tests for relief have not been conducted following a large number of conditioning trials with a high level shock. But just because extinction can take place with very short ITIs or nonshock periods does not necessarily implicate short-latency relief. There is the clear possibility of a cumulative effect. When shock is omitted many trials in succession, a long nonshock period accumulates over trials and can mediate extinction solely through relaxation.

The R_0 complex against which R_{relax} is pitted is presumably some combination of R_{fear} and the instrumental act (R_{escape} or R_{avoid}). R_{relax} is assumed to be directly incompatible with R_{fear} and only opposed in varying degrees to the instrumental act, depending upon its nature (e.g., R_{relax} would be more directly antagonistic to R_{jo} than to an exploratory-like response such as $R_{shuttle}$). This implies that the extinction effect from R_{relax} will increase with the extent to which fear-produced cues are attached to R_{avoid}, as discussed above. In other words, some fear must be present during both terminal avoidance and extinction in order to exploit the inhibitory effects of relaxation. Some fear is assumed following conventional escape training, but, doubtless, it is possible to arrange an extended learning situation so that terminal avoidance and thus extinction is relatively free of fear-produced cues. In such a case, R_{relax} is probably not directly incompatible with R_0 and thus resistance to extinction should be high (the relevant R_c here might simply be general exploratory behavior in a calm S); in the case where S is fearful throughout training but not during extinction, then R_c has already preempted R_0, and extinction should be more or less immediate, as found by Reynierse (1966).

In the extinction of avoidance, relaxation will typically originate in the safe situation and generalize or backchain to the original shock situation: Even with short confinements in the safe situation, S spends more time there than in the original shock situation. In fact, the backchaining of long-lasting relaxation from the safe to the shock situation (extinction effects) will often start during avoidance trials, especially with long non-shock confinement periods and after a 100% avoidance level has been reached (data related to this point will be presented later). If, on the other hand, S were *forced* to remain in the original shock region well beyond its response latency (Page & Hall, 1953; Page, 1955; Carlson & Black, 1960; Weinberger, 1965) then relaxation could originate there and speed up extinction.

Extinction following pure escape training in which there is both a safe and a shock place would also probably originate in the safe place, for early in extinction S does not stay in the original shock area long enough for R_c to occur. In an escape paradigm without a safe place, relaxation would occur with or after the first few omissions of shock and would be directly conditioned to the total situation. Ordinarily, such extinction would be rapid, because R_{escape} is strongly conditioned to fear-produced cues which will drop out when R_{fear} is extinguished by R_{relax}, but this is also probably why extinction is *not* immediate (with the omission of shock the extinction situation is markedly different from the acquisition situation and extinction is facilitated through generalization decrement (Sheffield and Temmer, 1950; Jones, 1953; Santos, 1960)). That is, two factors, fear and generalization decrement, help regulate the extinction of R_{escape}, with fear-cues maintaining early responding. If fear (R_0) is very strong, then of course extinction is prolonged, except possibly where R_c is freezing rather than relaxing as described below.

It also appears that freezing can be the R_c that mediates the extinction of avoidance, even when extinction is defined in terms of shock omission (Bagné, 1968). In his M.A. research, Bagné gave rats 12 massed avoidance acquisition trials (ITI = 30 sec) in an all-white one-way avoidance box, followed in certain groups by either two escapable shock trials or 2 inescapable shock trials, followed immediately by massed extinction trials for all groups. Under these conditions he found that·a sizable minority of the Ss in all groups seemed to extinguish by freezing. These Ss were distinguished from "relaxers" not only in regard to overt behavior but in regard to the fact that extinction was both sudden and relatively quick. For the "freezers," short latencies prevailed right up to the point when S suddenly extinguished; and their freezing behavior at this point seemed especially reminiscent of the freezing observed in rats showing the decremental Kamin effect (Denny & Ditchman, 1962). Freezers always extinguished early in a session (50 extinction trials defined a daily session, and all such Ss extinguished within either 0–3, 50–56, or 100–102 extinction trials). Possibly the warm-up effect at the beginning of each day's session which is typical of wheel-turn avoidance is a related phenomenon (Reynierse, Zerbolio, & Denny, 1964). That is, freezing probably produces the poorer initial wheel-turn performance present in certain Ss.

In Bagne's study, intersession effects (Brush, 1963; Brush, Myer, & Palmer, 1964; Kamin, 1957) definitely seemed to accentuate the dichotomization between freezers and relaxers, since most of the freezers extinguished the day following the acquisition series somewhere within the range of 50–56 trials. According to Brush et al. (1964), the greatest decremental effect with a 30-sec ITI should occur, as it did, after about a 24-hr delay. On the other hand, relaxers extinguished anywhere within a session and many took over 200 trials to extinguish. These Ss typically looked about, groomed, and actively explored as their latencies gradually increased over many trials.

Reynierse (1966) also found immediate extinction in many Ss when extinction trials were first presented 24 hr after all Ss had reached the acquisition criterion of 3 successive avoidances in a simple one-way avoidance box. And it is inviting to speculate whether the two effects (Bagné and Reynierse) have a similar basis, though this would seem to be fairly unlikely. Reynierse's study was different from Bagné's in many ways, and the interpretation originally given was opposite to the freezing hypothesis of Bagné. The most telling difference was the fact that the trials in Reynierse's experiment were relatively well spaced (ITI = 2 min), which means that any effect of intersession interval would be maximal after a delay of 1 hr rather than 24 hr. And in Reynierse's critical group, training was terminated on the trial after S reached criterion (24 hr later these Ss extinguished rapidly and sometimes immediately), while the two groups which, 24 hr later, did *not* show sudden or rapid extinction were given either 20 additional acquisition trials or one additional acquisition trial about 40 min after meeting criterion, which, if anything, made them more like the Ss of Bagné which received the first set of 50 extinction trials the same day as the 12 acquisition trials.

According to the interpretation offered by Reynierse, S is still fearful during training when training only lasts a few trials, but one day later S is relatively relaxed (large change in internal, response-produced stimuli from end of acquisition to start of extinction); thus because of generalization decrement S extinguishes abruptly. If, however, S is given additional trials after reaching criterion, *i.e.*, after attaining a more relaxed condition, then there is much less generalization decrement when tested 24 hr later and thus greater resistance to extinction. The interesting finding was that a single trial placed 40 min after the criterion run was just about as effective in prolonging extinction as 20 trials which spanned the same time period. In any event, it appears that the avoidance as well as the escape paradigm can involve stimulus (cue or CS) change with the shift from acquisition to extinction conditions, with a concomitant decrease in resistance to extinction.

II. EXPERIMENTS

The present emphasis that extinction (relaxation) typically originates in the safe situation is critical since the theory of extinction and its application to escape-avoidance behavior stands or falls on this assumption. On the other hand, from either a cognitive or drive-reduction view, extinction could just as well originate in the original shock region. Since S no longer gets shocked there why should it respond?

Hence, the first point that we attempted to establish in our research on escape-avoidance behavior was that the origin of extinction effects was in the safe region—at the end of the chain where S *first* starts to relax (Denny, Koons & Mason, 1959). In this study the principle of stimulus generalization was pointedly exploited. Rats were given avoidance training to jump out of a foot cube box into another similar box or on to a large, open platform which was maximally dissimilar to the shock box. This jump-out apparatus, as well as later versions, was specifically designed to prevent S from seeing the safe area until *after* it had responded. The importance of this precaution will soon be made clear. The CS for S was simply being placed into the unique shock box prior to the delivery of shock; the CS-US interval was 5 sec; S was confined for 3 min in the safe area on each trial during both acquisition and extinction; and two successive R_{JO}s within less than 5 sec defined the acquisition criterion.

The main hypothesis was that groups which were extinguished with a safe chamber that was similar to the shock chamber would extinguish faster than groups which had a safe chamber that was dissimilar to the shock area. With a long nonshock period, relaxation presumably occurs in the safe area and generalizes to a similar shock region but not to a dissimilar shock region, provided S cannot see the safe region while still in the shock chamber. If, on the other hand, extinction were to originate in the shock region the similarity of the safe to the shock region should make little difference in rate of extinction (all groups are exposed to the identical shock region throughout the experiment). The hypothesis was strongly confirmed. Like-region groups extinguished in a mean of 22.6 trials, unlike-region groups in 97.6 (Extinction criterion was two successive 15-sec latencies).

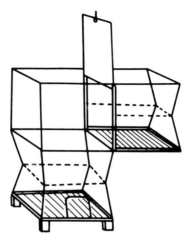

Fig. 2. The jump-out box apparatus.

The next study (Knapp, 1960, 1965) had three aims. First, it was a replication of Denny *et al.* (1959) to rule out the possibility that an open platform was intrinsically more reinforcing for a rat than an opaque box and had thus produced the obtained results. This was accomplished by using a jump-out box (Figure 2) in which dissimilar upper and lower chambers could be used interchangeably and compared with both pairs of similar chambers. Otherwise, the basic procedure was the same as Denny *et al.,* (1959). The original finding was upheld. Second, it was a test of the hypothesis that dissimilar boxes facilitate the acquisition of one-way avoidance even when S cannot view the safe chamber while in the shock box. The argument is based upon fear generalizing from the shock area to a similar safe area and competing with relaxation-approach, and upon relaxation-approach generalizing from the safe area to a similar shock area and competing with fear in the shock box. The acquisition hypothesis was clearly supported: The mean number of trials to criterion was 4.88 and 3.35 for the like and unlike groups, respectively ($p < .01$). The third aspect of Knapp's doctoral dissertation (1960) was the most informative even though it led to nonsignificant results. It was informative because we had been premature in our assumption about the time course of relaxation. During both acquisition and extinction one-half of the *S*s had a constant 90-sec safe period (ITI) and one-half a variable ITI with a mean of 90 sec (5, 25, or 240 sec). This manipulation hinted that 90 sec was too short for complete relaxation to occur. The clue for this came primarily, though not exclusively, from the acquisition data where it was noticed that some *S*s of the constant 90-sec ITI group took an excessive number of trials to learn, though not quite enough to yield a significant difference, whereas none of the variable ITI *S*s did. By the fourth 240-sec ITI trial, all of these had learned. A few good relaxation trials seemed to do the trick.

The next experiment was directed at exploring the time course of relaxation. How long does it take the rat to relax completely after the termination of shock or the removal of CAS? What is the minimal interval for the maximum pay-off? Weisman's M.A. thesis (Denny & Weisman, 1964) gave us this information for both acquisition and extinction in a situation in which very few trials were involved, that is, before the relaxation interval could be shortened appreciably through conditioning (backchaining). In the jump-out apparatus (Figure 2) length of confinement in the upper safe area during acquisition was varied in separate groups (10, 45, 90, 150, or 225 sec) with the remainder of the constant 230-sec ITI spent on an open platform (remaining procedure like Knapp's). After criterion, the 5 groups of 10 *S*s each were reassembled and an equal number from each acquisition confinement condition were assigned to each extinction confinement condition (10, 45, 90, 150, 225 sec), again with a constant 230-sec ITI. To facilitate predictions the shock and safe areas were different during acquisition and similar during extinction. The results for acquisition are depicted in Figure 3 and for extinction in Figure 4. The minimal optimal interval for relaxation seemed to be of the order of 150 sec since acquisition was equally rapid for the 150- and 225-sec groups. In general, the results were as anticipated: The longer nonshock confinement intervals yielded better learning and faster extinction except for the anomolous 10-sec group. Here the extinction results were especially deviant in that the 10-sec group extinguished more rapidly than the 45- and 90-sec groups. We then argued that relaxation in the 10-sec group which spent a long 220 sec on the open platform could backchain from the platform to the safe box and then generalize to the shock box to produce fast extinction.

This possibility was checked by running two new groups, a 10- and a 90-sec confinement group, whose ITI remainders were interrupted every 40 sec by placing *S* in a different place. For both groups this manipulation was supposed to break up the tendency to relax and disrupt the backchaining of any relaxation that still might occur. But this should

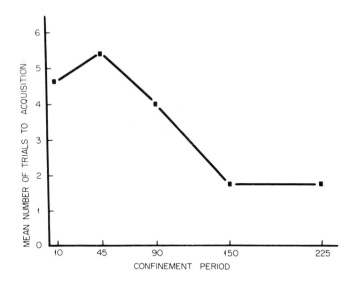

Fig. 3. Acquisition as a function of duration of confinement in the nonshock box.

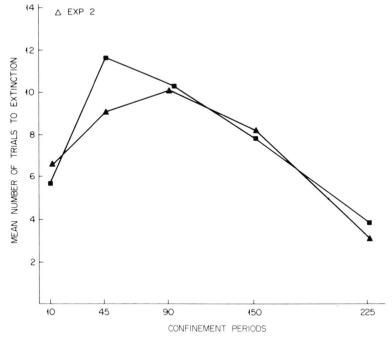

Fig. 4. Extinction as a function of duration of confinement in the nonshock box during both acquisition and extinction. (■) acquisition confinement; (▲) extinction confinement.

only have made a difference in the performance of the 10-sec group since only its ITI remainder was long enough to mediate much relaxation (>150 sec). Thus, the new 10-sec group should take longer to extinguish than the original 10-sec group, but there should be no significant difference between the old and new 90-sec groups. The results conformed to this pattern precisely: the means for the two 90 sec groups were identical, and trials to extinction for the new 10-sec group was a linear extrapolation of the 90-, 150-, and 225-sec data points (Exp. 2 point in Figure 4).

This interpretation demands that a 10-sec group should both learn and extinguish quite slowly if the total ITI were approximately 10 sec. A small side study on this point with 10Ss was quite conclusive; the mean number of trials to the acquisition criterion approximated 20 instead of the 4 or 5 required with the 230-sec ITI, and the number of trials to the extinction criterion was typically around 100. (Frequently, side studies like this one, which by themselves are usually unpublishable, are carried out to increase the total confidence level.)

Another side study in connection with Weisman's M.A. research was a variation in which the shock and safe regions were different rather than similar during extinction. Here the prediction was rather indeterminate: the longer S stays in the safe area the greater is the independent approach value of the safe region, but the longer S stays the greater is the amount of relaxing or potential extinction effect via backchaining. And happily, those were the results obtained—unpublishable "mishmash"!

About this time the research emphasis shifted for a while toward investigating acquisition phenomena. Specifically, we were able to show in separate studies that the rat can learn both two-choice and "go/no go" discriminations when the differential reinforcement is the relative amount of time spent in each of two nonshock chambers. In all cases, the discriminative stimuli were brightness and position, which covaried (*e.g.,* black chamber on the right versus white chamber on the left). One important aspect of these studies is that they help clarify the interpretation of the relaxation variable in the acquisition of avoidance. It is quite conceivable that one would accept the notion that the rat relaxes in the nonshock chamber but be unwilling to accept the interpretation that relaxation-approach *is* the reinforcing event. For example, in the Denny & Weisman study a relaxed rat might learn faster than a not-so-relaxed rat (shorter nonshock period) because the relaxed animal would freeze less when placed in the shock box at the beginning of a trial. Thus without the competing freezing response, S jumps sooner and avoids more often. In a two-choice situation, however, differential reduction of freezing *cannot* explain S's learning to prefer one chamber over another. That S simply is not freezing at the start of a trial can hardly bias S's subsequent choice one way or the other.

The two-choice situation was explored in Experiment 3 of Denny and Weisman (1964). The experimental group, when avoiding or escaping shock in the striped shock chamber, was permitted to stay 100 sec in the black (white) chamber on the right and only 20 sec in the white (black) on the left. The control group spent only 20 sec in each chamber, but after going to the longer ITI side, the side in which the experimental group spent 100 sec, the controls stayed an additional 80 sec in a clear plastic box, making the temporal consequences of a response the same for both groups. The experimentals clearly learned to prefer the 100-sec side, while the controls did not develop an appreciable preference for this side (see Figure 5). The development of such a preference is reminis-

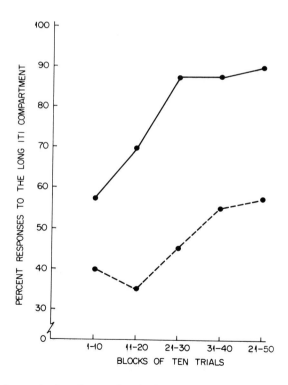

Fig. 5. Development of preference for the long confinement compartment. (---) control group; (——) experimental group.

cent of the magnitude of reward studies in which S learns to go to the side of the T-maze which contains the larger food incentive (Festinger, 1943; Denny & King, 1955, Hill & Spear, 1963). Analagously, the two-choice data help argue that long nonshock confinement is an important reinforcing event in avoidance learning.

Another study, done about the same time (Reynierse, Weisman, & Denny, 1963), also argues convincingly against the freezing hypothesis and controls for the extra handling that the control Ss received on the long ITI side in the study above. In this modest experiment two groups of 4 rats each were run in a one-way avoidance box. One group spent 100 sec in the white nonshock chamber and then 20 sec in the black shock chamber on each trial prior to CS onset (buzzer plus raising of the guillotine door); for the other group these time relations were reversed. The latter group (20 sec in the nonshock box and 100 sec in the shock box) made significantly fewer avoidances over a six-day period (Figure 6). In this study, relaxation-approach is presumably doing double-

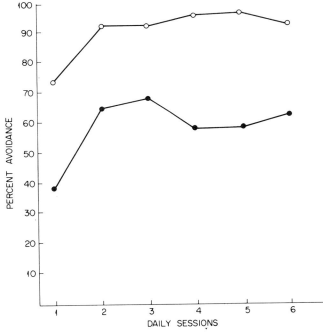

Fig. 6. Mean percent avoidance for groups spending either 20 sec or 100 sec of a 120-sec intertrial interval on the shock side. (O) 20-sec shock compartment; (●) 100-sec shock compartment.

duty in producing the obtained results: Confinement for 100 sec in the shock chamber tends to bring about extinction of fear or reduction in avoidance because S *begins* to relax there; and, in the other group, confinement for 100 sec in the safe side increases the positive approach value of this side and thereby facilitates avoidance. In contradiction to the differential freezing hypothesis, the group which was more likely to undergo extinction of freezing in the shock box while confined there for 100 sec without shock was the slower learning group.

Weisman, Denny, & Zerbolio (1967), using 17 groups and a total of 112 rats, extended this research to a type of "go/no-go" discrimination problem. As above, their results fail to fit the freezing hypothesis and, in addition, shed some light on the "double-duty" interpretation of Reynierse *et al.* In Weisman *et al.* (1967), responses in a shuttlebox with distinctive black and white chambers (S_1 and S_2) typically led to different nonshock confinement periods (ITIs) for $S_1 \rightarrow S_2$ than for $S_2 \rightarrow S_1$. In three different experiments the ITI differentials for the S_1 and S_2 chambers varied in independent groups from 0 to 190 sec, with the minimum time in a chamber in any group being 10 sec and the maximum 390 sec. Over 120 trials, 60 in each direction, all groups in which the differential was greater than zero avoided more often in the direction of the chamber with the longer ITI. For all values of S_1 and S_2, the proportion of avoidances in the S_1 direction ($R_1/(R_1 + R_2)$) was directly proportional to the proportion of time spent in the S_1 chamber ($S_1/(S_1 + S_2)$), as shown in Figure 7. Since the same sort of linear relationship has been observed in both multiple and concurrent schedules using varying amounts or densities of positive reinforcement (Herrnstein, 1961; Reynolds, 1961; Shettleworth & Nevin, 1965), it can be argued analogously that nonshock confinement reinforces shuttlebox avoidance.

This brings up another side study which tested the limits of the proportionality law. A group of four rats was run with S_1 = 600 sec and S_2 = 200 sec ($S_1/(S_1 + S_2)$ = 600/800 = .75) which means, if the law holds for extreme values, that $R_1/(R_1 + R_2)$ should equal approximately .7 (See Figure 7). Because running a solid block of 120 trials with a 600-sec ITI in one chamber would require more than 18 continuous hours of running time, each S was run six successive days, 20 trials per day. Otherwise, the procedure was identical to Weisman *et al.* (1967). Even with the small N, the results were convincing: no S developed a preference for either chamber, and $R_1/(R_1 + R_2)$ was .49 rather than .7 or thereabouts. The law, in other words, does not seem to hold for extreme confinement intervals, which also is the case for extreme values in the food reinforcement situation (Reynolds, 1963). The limitation on the proportionality law seems to be due to the fact that very long intervals tend to have an extinction-like

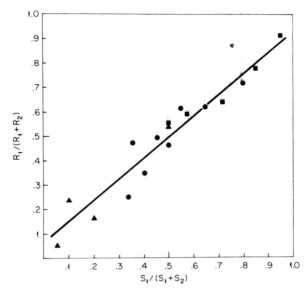

Fig. 7. Proportion of avoidances toward S_1 as a function of the proportion of total nonshock confinement time associated with the S_1 chamber. (■) Experiment 1, (▲) Experiment 2; (●) Experiment 3.

effect during the acquisition series, as mentioned in the theory section and as will be referred to again later. This interpretation is suggested by relatively poor performance (45% avoidance over 120 trials) which peaked on the fifth rather than the sixth day and by the fact that one S tended to extinguish after day 2 and another leveled off there.

Incidentally, wild rats (F_1 stock) prefer the chamber associated with the longer nonshock confinement interval (180 vs. 30 sec.) to at least the same degree as domestic rats (Boice, Denny, & Evans, 1967). Even more recently, it has been found that domestic rats, mice, gerbils, and kangaroo rats are similarly affected by the length of the nonshock confinement interval (Boice, Boice, & Dunham, 1968).

In the Weisman *et al.* shuttlebox discrimination study, one of the better avoiding groups for R_1 and R_2 combined was $S_1 = S_2 = 200$ sec. One implication here is that spending a long time in one chamber does not mediate better avoiding in the direction of the longer confinement chamber *solely* because of the extinction of fear in the longer confinement side. Theoretically, the extinction of fear in the long side could impede avoidance toward the short confinement side and, in part at least, account for the preference for approaching and staying in the longer confinement side. But extinction of fear in the $S_1 = S_2 = 200$-sec group would mean that both chambers become neutral, and such a state of affairs could hardly account for good avoidance in this group. Only strong, positive approach to each chamber accounts for good avoidance in both directions.

In several ways, a perusal of the performance curves of the various groups in Weisman et al. (1967) seems to reveal the operation of both of the explanatory factors that were suggested by Reynierse et al. (1963) for the role of long nonshock confinement, an extinction effect and an avoidance effect. For example, one line of evidence for an extinction effect is that the percentage of avoidance, regardless of direction, was less among all four groups for which the shorter confinement side was 200 sec (200 versus 230, 290, 350 and 390) than for 200 versus 200 and for several other groups such as 150 versus 60, 100 versus 10, and 200 versus 50. (According to the theory, relaxation has a dual function, mediating extinction as well as the approach component of avoidance. Approach is optimized by a 150-sec nonshock period, but longer periods mean more relaxation (R_c) and thus more extinction.) Further evidence for the interpretation that extinction may accompany acquisition was observed by Denny and Weisman (1964) where it was found that subsequent extinction was significantly facilitated if long nonshock confinement periods prevailed during acquisition (Figure 4). This was independent of the length of nonshock confinement during the extinction session (the implication is that long nonshock confinement during acquisition gave Ss which had such treatment a head start on extinguishing). A similar, though nonsignificant trend, was also observed by Weisman, Denny, Platt, and Zerbolio (1966). For the control groups only, note that the 240-sec data point in Figure 9 represents fewer responses to extinction than is the case for all other confinement values (all values refer to length of nonshock confinement during *acquisition* of jump-out avoidance; during extinction length of confinement was the same for all groups).

An interesting side light of the shuttlebox study of Weisman et al. (1967) was that the learning of the 105- versus 105-sec group was especially poor when compared with the data on standard shuttlebox learning in which comparable ITI's (60 to 120 sec) were used. For Weisman et al., the obvious relevant difference in procedure seemed to be that standard shuttleboxes are typically homogeneous rather than one compartment white and the other black. Yet direct comparisons with data in the literature and with other standard shuttlebox data were not legitimate. In Weisman et al. (1967), a guillotine door was used between trials, all 120 trials were administered in a solid block on one day, and other possible

apparatus and situational differences were undoubtedly present. Therefore, we replicated the procedure, apparatus, and subject population for
three ITI conditions in which $S_1 = S_2$ (10 versus 10 sec: 105 versus 105
sec and 200 versus 200 sec) except that a homogeneous shuttlebox was
used, all white for half the Ss of each subgroup ($N = 8$) and all black
for the other half (Denny, Zerbolio, & Weisman, 1969). The results were
clear-cut; all three homogeneous shuttlebox groups, regardless of color,
performed better, at least early in training, than their ITI counterparts
with the distinctive black and white chambers; and the homogeneous 10-
versus 10-sec and 105- versus 105-sec groups were markedly and significantly superior throughout (Figure 8). It may be recalled that this is
opposite to the results obtained when using distinctive chambers in a
one-way avoidance situation (Knapp, 1965).

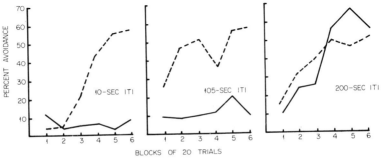

Fig. 8. Shuttle-box performance as a function of homogeneous (---) versus heterogeneous (——) box (black & white chambers) for three different intertrial intervals.

One possible interpretation of this finding relates to the relaxation
variable and the signal for safety. According to the theory, for S to exhibit good shuttlebox performance, place cues must be irrelevant for indicating when to relax. Each S learns that there is a safe *period* not a
safe *place i.e.*, S learns to relax after shuttling and after the warning signal terminates, but not in a particular compartment. When the box is
homogeneous, brightness cues are already irrelevant and the acquisition
of shuttle-avoidance is thereby facilitated. That the heterogeneous 200-
sec group seemed to learn about as well as the homogeneous 200-sec
group (Figure 8) probably means that the black and white chambers,
given an optimal 200-sec relaxation period (> 150 sec), are acquiring
equal and sizable approach value during the early *escape* trials so that
when S *avoids,* one color (chamber) does not immediately and markedly
win out over the other and thereby cause S *not* to avoid (not to leave
this positive chamber) on the subsequent trial. On the other hand, with

the shorter ITIs, S will very likely not avoid after having avoided because only when S avoids does the accumulated nonshock period have an opportunity to mediate the conditioning of approach, which if attached to a specific brightness cue (chamber) should mean that S would stay and get shocked there on the next trial, undoing the avoidance training. Essentially, such a series of events would be repeated again and again every time S avoided, and learning would be impeded accordingly. It would seem that other theories of avoidance would have greater difficulty in interpreting these findings, because what goes on in a particular place or across time is not given the same emphasis as is the case in relaxation theory.

III. CONDITIONED RELAXATION

The next phase of research took off in several new directions. The dominant direction concerned the conditioning of relaxation or relaxation-approach to neutral stimuli (Weisman et al., 1966; Zerbolio, 1965, 1968). Since the theory posits that relaxation is a response and that characteristic, consistently elicited responses get conditioned, it was clearly incumbent upon us to demonstrate, at least indirectly, that relaxation is conditionable. In fact the whole backchaining analysis of avoidance learning and extinction assumes first that, starting in the safe situation, each cue along the way is being conditioned to the response of approaching the safe situation and later that relaxation is similarly conditioned to this same set of cues, eventually chaining to the original shock situation and mediating extinction. Thus the analysis demands clear-cut evidence that relaxation and relaxation-approach can be conditioned. In a sense, such evidence is available in the discrimination studies which show that the color and position of a particular chamber gain control over behavior and differentially elicit approach, but more direct tests were in order.

The first attempt to condition relaxation was only partially successful (Experiment 1, Weisman et al. 1966). The jump-out apparatus with clear plastic boxes (Figure 2) was used and the CS for conditioning relaxation was a shielded flashing 10-W light attached to the exterior of the upper, safe chamber, about 1 in. above the floor. During 20 avoidance acquisition trials (CS–US interval for avoidance = 10 sec), two experimental groups and one control were presented with the flashing light while in the upper box for a 160 sec nonshock period (US for relaxation). Two other generalization decrement control groups did not see the flashing light until extinction. During extinction, one experimental group was presented with the light in the lower as well as in the upper chamber and the other experimental group received the light only in the lower box (original shock chamber). The control that had seen the light during acquisition continued to see it only in the upper box. One of the other two controls had the light presented in both boxes and one had it only in the lower box. Confinement in the upper chamber was again 160 sec for all groups. The hypothesis for the experimental groups was that introducing the CS in the original shock region would elicit relaxation at the start of a trial and thereby facilitate extinction.

Only the experimental group which had the light in both the lower and upper chambers during extinction extinguished significantly faster than the controls. Presumably, any conditioned relaxational properties that may have been attached to the light in the other experimental group quickly extinguished when the light was presented only in the original shock box. Thus the evidence was somewhat inconclusive.

The sequel (Experiment 2, Weisman *et al.* 1966) exploited what is known about secondary reinforcement for a positive incentive, namely, that discrimination training enhances the secondary reinforcement effect. We also placed a greater burden on the CS during the test phase by reducing the nonshock period in the upper chamber to 20 sec during extinction. The discriminative procedure consisted of giving 10 avoidance trials in which an experimental S spent only 20 sec in the upper chamber without the flashing light being present ($S^\triangle$ trials) and 10 avoidance trials in which the flashing light consistently accompanied the "longer" nonshock period in the upper box (S^D trials). In this parametric study, the "longer" periods for separate groups were 20, 60, 110, 170 or 240 sec; S^D and $S^\triangle$ trials were presented in a Gellermann order. The control groups received the same schedule of short and long nonshock periods but were never presented with a light during acquisition, only during extinction, where for all groups (experimental and control) the light was presented only in the original shock chamber. The parametric design made it possible to rule out flashing light, *per se,* as a critical variable. For in the experimental groups with the 20-, 60- and 110-sec nonshock confinement periods, the light, though presented in the same fashion as in the longer nonshock confinement groups, had no facilitative effect during extinction (Figure 9).

All groups learned about equally well, and the results for extinction are summarized in Figure 9. The light clearly and significantly facilitated extinction of avoidance in the experimental groups with the 170- and 240-sec nonshock confinement periods. All other comparisons were not statistically significant. Thus the results provided good, initial support for the phenomenon of conditioned relaxation and reaffirmed the

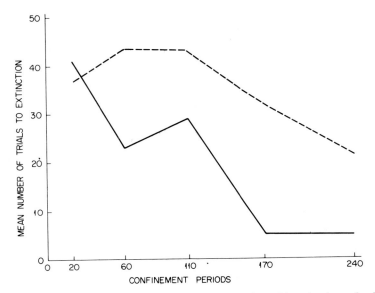

Fig. 9. Mean number of trials to extinction as a function of length of nonshock confinement during acquisition for both control and experimental conditions (Experiment 2). (---) control; (——) experimental.

long-latency aspect of relaxation. When Ss from the 170- and 240-sec experimental groups were observed during these early extinction trials, their overt behavior often conformed to the conditioned relaxation interpretation. Coincident with the flashing light, the typical S soon began to look around and explore rather than jump.

As already implied, conditioned relaxation-approach may be basically the same as the concept of secondary reinforcement (the positive value acquired by a neutral stimulus which has been paired with the termination of shock) as first studied by Barlow (1952) and Smith and Buchanan (1954). The point to make in this connection is that viewing the phenomenon in terms of long-latency relaxation appears to resolve the controversy as to whether this type of secondary reinforcement is a bona fide phenomenon or not (Beck, 1961). Earlier investigators such as Nefzger (1957) who failed to find a secondary reinforcing effect associated with shock termination were viewing the matter in terms of *immediate* shock reduction. The nonshock period in Nefzger's experiment was only 15 sec—not an adequate length of time for relaxation to occur. But when long intertrial intervals, long time-outs from avoidance, or other long nonshock periods have been used, associated stimuli definitely appear to acquire positive properties (Dinsmoor & Clayton, 1963; Evans, 1962; Murray & Strandberg, 1965; Sidman, 1962; Verhave, 1962; Weisman *et al.* 1966).

It also seems reasonable to view conditioned relaxation as the converse of CER or conditioned suppression. Conditioned relaxation is assessed by the capacity of the CS to reduce fear (suppress avoidance) and CER by the capacity of the CS to increase fear (suppress instrumental approach). Even so, the approach component of conditioned relaxation-approach would be determined less equivocally if the associated CS could be shown to mediate avoidance learning (approach to the safe area) as well as facilitate extinction. A portion of Zerbolio's Ph.D. research (1965, 1968) represents the initial attempt to assess conditioned relaxation-approach in this manner.

In this study, rats of the experimental group ($N = 12$) were shocked for 1 sec (2 mA) in a distinctive black and white diagonally striped box and then transported by hand to the black (white) chamber of a one-way box (CS) and confined there without shock for 150 sec (US). After five such trials S was given three additional trials in which the shock was omitted in the striped box. Control groups either stayed in the one-way chamber for only 30 sec and spent 120 sec on an open platform or were not shocked in the striped box. Handling was in all cases equated across groups. After these eight trials, all groups were given avoidance training in the one-way box either toward or away from their particular pretraining confinement chamber. Nonshock confinement in this phase was 30 sec for all groups. The experimental subgroup which was run *toward* the original confinement chamber reached the acquisition criterion of 3 successive avoidances in a mean of 1.5 trials, the experimental subgroup which was learning to run *away* from the original confinement side required a mean of 8.5 trials to reach criterion. Four control groups did not differ from each other or as to direction run but they differed significantly from the two experimental subgroups. Their pooled mean to criterion was 4.7 trials.

The most obvious interpretation of these findings is that approach was indeed conditioned to the cues of the specific postshock, post-fear chamber that the experimental Ss had been confined in and that this approach was related to long-latency relaxation because a 30 sec stay in this chamber in the shocked controls was ineffectual. In subsequent research, it became clear that Zerbolio's choice of 5 exposures to strong shock followed by 3 exposures to the conditioned aversive stimulus was especially fortuitous in tapping the long-latency relaxation effect rather than short-latency relief, but more of this later.

A. The Onset of Relaxation

Another phase of the research on conditioned relaxation was to use the phenomenon as a tool for determining the point of onset of relaxation for a rat under typical post-shock conditions. At this point in the chronology of our research, the *minimal optimal* duration of relaxation was fixed at about 150 sec (Denny & Weisman, 1964; Weisman *et al.*, 1966) but onset was an open question. According to the theory, relaxation, in addition to relief, can help mediate escape-avoidance learning even though the nonshock interval is considerably less than 150 sec, say, 20–60 sec long. Relaxation is presumably taking place to some extent with these shorter intervals and may become conditioned to the early cues of the postshock period so that the latency of functional relaxation-approach becomes shorter and shorter. Thus learning situations which involve many trials seem to show relaxation-like effects when all non-shock periods are under 150 sec in duration. A learned preference for the compartment that is associated with the *longer* interval has occurred, for example, when the longer interval was 40 sec and the shorter was 10 (Weisman *et al.*, 1967) and when the longer was 100 sec and the shorter was 20 (Experiment 3 of Denny and Weisman, 1964; Reynierse *et al.*, 1963). In fact, as already discussed, performance over the long run can be better with shorter nonshock intervals than with longer ones because of the sizable extinction effects which seem to be associated with long nonshock (relaxation) periods.

Thus for a better understanding of relaxation and how it may function, it was also critical to identify its onset. To this end, CS probes of 15-and 30-sec duration were introduced throughout a 185-sec nonshock period. The rationale was that onset would be identified fairly well by optimal CS placement. The CS which just precedes and overlaps relaxation onset should yield the best conditioning of relaxation. The CSs used were a mild buzzer (74 dB with a 45 dB ambient level) and the flashing light (Weisman *et al.*, 1966). The buzzer CS proved to be more convenient and did not initially inhibit performance (avoidance) in the control group. In fact, buzzer without prior conditioning had the tendency of slightly potentiating a response at the beginning of extinction, which was ideal for measuring conditioned inhibitory effect to the buzzer-CS. Eight 15-sec habituations to the buzzer always preceded training in both the experimental and control groups.

With the buzzer CS, the following procedure was finally adopted. The apparatus was a 36 in. one-way box with a 18 in. black chamber and an 18 in. white chamber, with a central guillotine door above a 2½ in. high hurdle. One half the Ss were run toward white, one half toward black. All 8 acquisition trials were escape trials, and time spent in the safe region was always 185 sec. On each acquisition trial, S stayed in the shock side 5 sec before a shock of .8 mA was delivered; simultaneously the guillotine door was raised and S was free to escape across the hurdle to the safe side. The buzzer CS always began a given number of seconds (0 -145) postshock, *i.e.,* after S had crossed the hurdle and the guillotine door had been lowered; during acquisition the CS (probe) lasted 15 sec. During extinction the buzzer CS was no longer paired with the safe period but occurred simultaneously with the placement of S into the shock chamber; 5 sec later the door was raised as in acquisition; and the CS terminated when S crossed the hurdle or after 30 sec, whichever was sooner. Two such 30-sec trials in succession defined extinction. The safe box confinement time was 20 sec for all Ss during extinction.

The purpose of using distinctive chambers was to minimize the generalization of conditioned relaxation from the safe chamber to the original shock chamber and, vice versa, to minimize the generalization of fear from the shock chamber to the safe chamber. Theoretically, the first instance of generalization would obscure the measurement of any conditioning to the buzzer CS, and the second would attenuate the conditioning of relaxation, as such. When, in fact, a homogeneous one-way box was tried, little conditioning of relaxation was observed to accrue to the buzzer.

In our earliest studies of relaxation onset, a 30-sec probe CS was used, and the optimal CS placement interval was found to be 30–60 sec postshock. An analysis of variance yielded a significant overall effect across the intervals used; and specific comparisons indicated that the CS in the 30–60 postshock interval produced significantly better conditioning than when the CS was in the 60–90 postshock interval and than the control condition when no CS was present during acquisition.With the subsequent use of a 15-sec probe, the 25–40-sec postshock placement was found to be optimal, with 0–15 being second best and not significantly less effective in facilitating extinction than the 25–40-sec interval. This latter finding led to the use of probes of 5-sec duration within the 0–15 sec range and to some extent beyond. In this way, short-latency "relief" was first identified.

B. The Conditioning of Relief

In order to study conditioned relief independently of the conditioning of relaxation, only very short postshock intervals (10–15 sec) could be used. Therefore, a rat was given a combination of escape and "avoidance" training with the following double E (escape) double A (modified avoidance) pattern of trials, EE, AA, EE, AA, . . . , for a total of at least 16 trials, 8E and 8A. The E trials were as described above in the paradigm for conditioning relaxation except that the safe-box confinement interval during acquisition was 10 or 15 sec rather than 185 sec. Immediately after removal from the safe side, S was placed in the shock side for the next trial. The second E trial of a pair was the same as the first except that it was followed by a modified avoidance trial (A). On an A trial, S was never shocked; if S did not cross the hurdle within 10 sec after the door was raised (15 sec after being introduced to the shock compartment), then it was gently boosted over the hurdle to the safe side (previous research had indicated that boosting produced better "avoidance" learning than other alternatives tried). The Ss which did not eventually cross the hurdle in less than 10 sec on A trials were discarded (an infrequent event). As on E trials, S remained in the safe compartment for only 10 or 15 sec, but the buzzer CS was omitted during the A trials.

The main purpose of using the "double E, double A" paradigm instead of a solid block of escape trials was to make the buzzer CS irrelevant with respect to what happened on the subsequent trial. If massed escape trials with a 10-sec postshock period were used, the buzzer would presumably acquire aversive properties as readily as it would acquire positive properties, for the termination of the buzzer would be followed 5 sec later by shock on the next trial. But, with the "double E, double A" design, the buzzer CS was *consistently* paired with a specific postshock period and both its presence and its absence, on the subsequent trial, were followed half the time by shock and half the time by non-shock—an ideal definition of an irrelevant stimulus.

Another advantage of the EE,AA paradigm for measuring the short-latency effect was that A trials permitted a "continuous" measure of the "avoidance" habit so that the strength of avoidance could be assessed prior to onset of extinction. This is important because S could also extinguish quickly during the extinction test trials for never having learned to "avoid" very well to begin with. With the EE,AA schedule, a slow learner could be given further trials and a nonlearner could be discarded.

With the EE,AA method, the 0–5-sec postshock stimulus yielded no conditioning, but both 5–10- and 10–15-sec postshock probes showed a considerable conditioning effect, as did the 5–15 sec probe when tried. When, however, the postshock safe box interval was increased just enough to accommodate probes from 15–20, 20–25, and 15–25 sec, there was virtually no conditioning effect. And even when the 185-sec postshock interval was used there was no conditioning effect for probes placed 25–30-, 30–35- and 35–40-sec postshock. A probe of 5-sec duration within the optimal conditioned relaxation interval (25–40 sec) was inadequate, presumably too short to catch the more variable relaxation onset, coming either too soon or too late for many Ss for good conditioning to occur (only a very few Ss seemed to show the conditioned relaxation effect with the 5-sec probe). But such a finding provided additional support for asserting two independent events, relaxation and "relief." In other words, short-latency "relief" seems to be relatively constant in its onset and duration, as well as short-lived.

The next phase of research dealt with determining whether relief could occur postfear as well as postshock. In this same series of experiments, it was possible to determine whether relaxation could be conditioned solely on the basis of the removal of CAS (all postfear elicited relaxation). To test for exclusive postfear effects, the buzzer CS was introduced during A trials rather than during E trials, and the same EE,AA paradigm was used except that the EE,AA series was preceded by a solid block of 6 escape trials. With these additional escape trials, the shock chamber was assumed to acquire conditioned aversive properties before the onset of the initial set of A trials. The buzzer CS was *only* introduced after S left the CAS (shock chamber) on the A trials.

When trials for conditioned "relief" were given with both 5 and 10 sec probes in the 5–15 postfear interval, the safe period was either 10 or 20 sec on all acquisition trials. In neither case was there a sign of a conditioned effect during the extinction test period. Thus relief seems to occur only after the termination of a primary aversive stimulus.[2,3]

The research at this time also included testing for post-fear conditioned relaxation (15-sec probe CS presented only on A trials); the optimal 25–40 sec CS placement period was used, plus a variety of post-fear confinement intervals (50, 90, 150 and 185 sec). The postshock confinement interval on E trials was in each case 10 sec. Conditioned relaxation was clearly evident when the safe interval was 150 and 180 sec but was not in evidence for 50 and 90 sec. In short, relaxation is not readily conditionable post-fear unless relaxation is complete. With such a paradigm, the data served as a control for possible habituation, sensitization, and other extraneous conditioning effects that might be alternatively suggested to explain conditioned relaxation effects.

The finding that the postfear interval needs to be 150 sec long before

[2]A very recent study by Braud (1968) implies that some degree of relief does occur after the removal of CAS but that the latency here is extremely short, 1 sec or less, which is presumably why it was missed in our research.

[3]*Editor's note:* See also Chapter 1 by Black, this volume.

relaxation can be conditioned is in keeping with recent research on conditioned approach in which we attempted to replicate and extend Zerbolio's work. In this research, the rat was shocked (2 mA) on all 8 trials in the striped external chamber rather than receiving 5 shocks followed by 3 short exposures to the external chamber without shock. This made a decided difference. Controls which spent only 30 sec in one chamber of the one-way box postshock plus 120 sec on an open platform, performed just about the same as experimental Ss which spent 150 sec postshock in the one-way chamber. Presumably, the first five trials in Zerbolio's experiment set up sufficient fear to the external chamber for the removal of the chamber itself to mediate relaxation; and, given a 150-sec nonshock period, relaxation could be conditioned on the last three trials to the associated stimuli and produce a differential conditioned effect in the experimental group. Presumably, with the 8-shock procedure, relief was equally well operative in both the control and experimental groups on all eight trials, and thus there was little difference between the 30-sec and 150-sec nonshock groups. In any event, it does not appear that postshock effects can be equated across the board with postfear effects. In many of the earlier avoidance studies that were reported, these two sets of effects are inextricably confounded. Incidentally, an exact replication of Zerbolio's method yielded essentially his results.

One specific implication of the concept of short-latency relief that might be mentioned is that it can be used to explain so-called vicious circle or self-punitive behavior of rats in a runway when they are shocked in an intermediate portion of the sequence during extinction (Brown, Martin, & Morrow, 1964; Melvin & Martin, 1966). Ss so shocked are more resistant to extinction than nonshocked controls (both groups learn originally to escape shock in the start area and intermediate region by running to a safe box). Presumably relief, which occurs only postshock, would continue to be operative in the safe area in the punished animals and would reinforce running. Since Brown, Anderson, and Weiss (1965) have demonstrated that vicious circle behavior occurs even with a 20-sec ITI, short-latency relief is especially applicable as an explanatory concept. But immediate reduction of pain-shock is also implicated.

Delprato and Denny (1968) have recently completed a study, however, which points its finger at short-latency relief and at the same time casts doubt on other interpretations of the effect. According to the data on conditioned relief, nothing positive is occurring in the first five seconds postshock. Therefore, a shocked S which is removed from the goal area before 5 sec has elapsed and put into a completely different environment during the ITI should not show increased resistance to extinction relative to an S held in the goal for more than 5 sec. Delprato and Denny ran a total of 48 rats in four groups, two shocked (Sh) and two nonshocked (NSh), each with a 30-sec and a 2-sec goal confinement group (Sh 30, Sh 2, NSh 30, and NSh 2). The ITI for all groups during extinction was 62 sec, 30 sec of which was spent in the start area. During acquisition all Ss spent 16 sec in both start and goal areas on each trial (ITI). As can be seen from Figure 10, Sh 30 showed increased resistance to extinction whereas Sh 2 did not; the interaction was statistically significant.

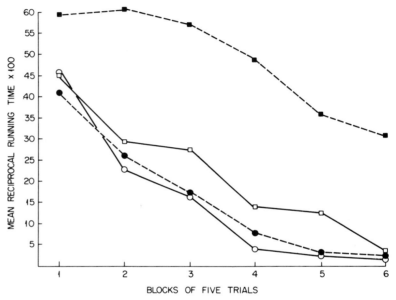

Fig. 10. Mean running speeds during extinction over 6 blocks of 5 trials, as a function of punishment and length of goal confinement. (○) NSh 2; (●) NSh 30; (□) Sh 2; (■) Sh 30.

The research on conditioned relaxation and conditioned relief so far reported, mainly studies in which probe stimuli were used, was largely preparatory to an extensive parametric investigation of these phenomena. Even though a large number of subjects were used in this early research, the focus was on finding the techniques and intervals which worked, and the results have been presented accordingly. This tack also means less redundancy when presenting the terminal studies following. From this point forward then, the data, as yet unpublished and often not completely collected, will be presented in a more formal, quantitative fashion.

One of these large parametric studies used the EE,AA paradigm with the 6 initial escape trials and investigated relaxation solely "postavoidance." Conditioned relaxation, assessed by subsequent facilitation of extinction, was studied as a function of the number of CS pairings with the 25–40 sec postfear interval (the period during an A trial which began 25 sec after S entered the safe region and which ended 15 sec later). A total of 80 albino rats were used in 8 independent groups, with an equal number of males and females in each group. The number of .8 mA shocks delivered during training was 14 for all groups. The groups differed only in the number of times an "avoidance" was followed by the buzzer CS: 0, 2, 4, 6, or 8 times. The 2, 4, and 6 pairings posed the problem as to where the pairings should come in the series of 8 A trials. This was at least temporarily resolved by having two subgroups for the 2, 4, and 6 pairings, one of which had the pairings at the start and the other at the end, *e.g.*, one subgroup with pairings on A trials 1–4 and the other subgroup with pairings on A trials 5–8 (See Figure 11).

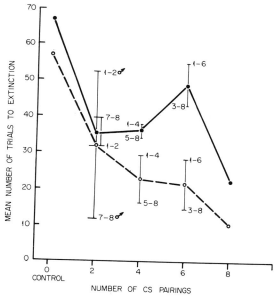

Fig. 11. Resistance to extinction of one-way responding as a function of the number of CS pairings of buzzer with the 25–40 sec postfear period during acquisition. During extinction the buzzer was presented for 12 sec in the original shock chamber prior to an opportunity to respond. (●) female; (○) male.

In order to increase sensitivity to a buzzer CS having only a few pairings, the CS during extinction came on 12 sec before the door was raised and before S could respond. The extinction criterion used for the data presented in Figure 11 was two latencies out of three greater than 10 sec, the avoidance interval during acquisition. This criterion, as opposed to two successive 30 sec latencies, helped eliminate extreme scores and tapped an early effect.

In Figure 11, the horizontal bars at the ends of the fine vertical lines represent the mean values for the groups that had the pairings at either the beginning or end of the series of 8 A trials, and the dots represent the means of each of these two groups as well as the means of the 0 and 8 groups. At first glance the conditioning curve of the males is as expected, showing a progressive decrease in trials to extinction as number of pairings increases, but a closer look at Figure 11 reveals that most of the effect over trials on which CS-relaxation pairings occurred can best be interpreted as the development of conditioned fear over E trials, this rather than a progressive development of conditioned relaxation.

This interpretation is based upon the fact that all male groups which had at least two relaxation conditioning trials *after* 14 fear-conditioning shock trials extinguished quickly and in about the same number of trials, irrespective of the number of "relaxation conditioning" trials which preceded the accumulation of 14 shock trials. For example, group 2 (7–8), males which received only two pairings of CS with relaxation, extinguished almost as quickly as the male group which had 8 pairings of CS with relaxation.

For the experiment's main objective, it seems that an insufficient number of escape trials (fear conditioning trials) preceded the EE,AA schedule. But the results also clearly imply that fear must be strongly established before relaxation is optimally elicited by the removal of CAS. Presumably, conditioned relaxation will be an increasing function of the number of pairings of the buzzer CS with the 25–40-sec safe interval once fear of the shock area has been well established. We simply do not yet have the data to tell. The strong conditioning effect with pairings on each of the 8 A trials that had been observed earlier when only 6 E trials had preceded the EE,AA sequence was what misled us to think that 8 E trials prior to any A trials would be enough aversive conditioning.

In this same experiment, the female groups were anomalous as usual, with one of the more striking bits of irregularity being that, for 2 pairings, groups 1-2 and 7-8 were reversed from the rest of the data for all comparable subgroups (Figure 11). Here more research rather than more speculation is needed.

Since it appears that substantial post-CAS conditioning of relaxation can occur in only two trials, it is worth noting that this harmonizes with the interpretation above of Zerbolio's experiment (1965, 1968), namely, that most of the relevant conditioning of relaxation-approach in his study took place during the last three conditioning trials (6, 7, and 8) when only the CAS was presented and removed (For Zerbolio, five prior shock or fear conditioning trials rather than 14 such trials were probably sufficient because he used 2 mA shock rather than .8 mA).

A parallel parametric study investigated conditioned relief as a function of the number of CS pairings, with number of shocks held constant. And for the first time, conditioned relief was evaluated in terms of its possible approach value. This was accomplished by a variation of the Zerbolio technique in which S was always shocked (1 mA) for 1 sec, 60 sec after having been placed in the black and white striped shock chamber. The S was then placed immediately into one of the distinctive all white or all black chambers of the one-way box which had an appropriately colored cardboard insert over the grid. On conditioning or experimental trials (E), S remained in this chamber 15 sec, and was then removed and placed on an open platform for 5 sec, after which it was returned to the shock chamber for the next trial. On nonconditioning or control trials (C), S remained in the chamber only 5 sec and stayed on the open platform 15 sec. A 60-sec period on the open platform intervened between the eighth or last trial and the beginning of one-way avoidance training. The Ss were always trained in the direction of the earlier confinement chamber (black or white), and any conditioned effect was presumably bolstered by using only a 15 sec safe period during avoidance training. Five separate groups, to date 32 males and 32 females, were given varying combinations and permutations of the C and E trials, 0E-8C (zero E and 8 C trials), 2E 6C, 4E 4C, 6E 2C and 8E 0C. In three of these main groups (2E, 4E, and 6E), subgroups comprising at least two Ss each were run in such a way that all ordinal positions in the series of 8 trials were equally often represented by E trials.

The mean number of shocks required to reach the acquisition criterion of three successive avoidances (crossing the low hurdle to the safe chamber within 5 sec) appears in Figure 12. In the combined group (males plus females), a progressive development of conditioned relief is rather satisfactorily depicted with the maximum conditioned effect falling at 6 pairings with the CS. For males the upswing (less effect) after 8 pairings seems to be an artifact due to fear chaining back from the external shock chamber, through the open platform, and finally arriving in the chamber of the one-way box by the end of the shock series (7 and 8th pairings). Actually, this interpretation was initially suggested by S's behavior: With each successive shock in the shock chamber S showed fear (agitated jumping behavior) sooner and sooner until by the 5th or 6th

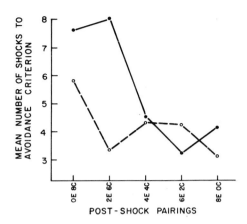

Fig. 12. Mean number of shocks received during one-way avoidance training as a function of number of prior postshock intervals of 15-sec duration (E) that *S* spent in the chamber to which it was finally trained. C refers to only a 5-sec stay in this chamber. (○) female (●) male and female combined.

shock it strongly resisted being put into the shock box (where it was shocked 60 sec later). This interpretation was tentatively checked with a few *S*s by introducing a 15-sec time buffer on trials 5, 6, and 7 between leaving the open platform and being introduced to the shock box. Such a buffer seemed to produce the expected monotonic function, that is, more conditioned effect with the 7th and 8th pairings. It is also relevant to mention that the subgroup of 2E 6C which had the 2E trials at the end of the shock series contributed most to the *lack* of a conditioned effect at two pairings.

The data are also presented in Figure 13 in terms of the mean latency of the first three acquisition trials (all *S*s had at least three trials). The same peculiar upswing at six pairings that occurred with the other measure and in the previous study is prominently present in the female *S*s. Basically, these data reflect the same trends as the mean number of shocks to criterion, including the upswing in the males at 8 pairings. Tentatively at least, it appears that conditioned relief can be positive and can help mediate the approach component of avoidance learning.

The final study to be reported in the area of conditioned relaxation is nonparametric and incomplete, but it still represents a full-scale test of the hypothesis that the Zerbolio effect (conditioned relaxation-approach) can be obtained solely on the basis of postfear pairings; or, that a combination of postshock and postfear pairings as originally employed is not essential. A total of 112 male and female albino and hooded rats, pre-

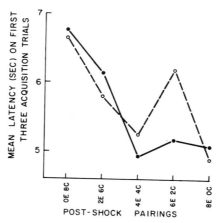

Fig. 13. Mean latency of the first three acquisition trials in one-way avoidance as a function of the number of prior postshock intervals of 15-sec duration that S spent in the chamber to which it was finally trained. (O) female Ss; (●) male and female Ss combined.

dominantly male hooded to date, have so far been used. The conditioning procedure which finally evolved is rather complicated. All Ss first received 2 min of habituation in both chambers of the one way box. Then all Ss received five massed fear conditioning trials to the striped shock chamber with a 5-sec CS–US interval and a strong 2-mA shock of 1-sec duration. Between each trial S was held in E's arm for 10 sec, and CS onset was being put back into the shock box. This was followed by three blocks of three relaxation conditioning trials. A fear conditioning booster trial was interpolated between the first and second block and the second and third block, making a total of 7 fear conditioning trials and 9 relaxation conditioning trials. In order to eliminate short-latency relief effects a period of 90 sec on an open platform separated a shock trial from the first relaxation conditioning trial of a block.

A relaxation conditioning trial consisted of placing S in the striped, fear-provoking chamber for 6 sec (no shock present), removing S and placing it consistently either in the white or black chamber of the one-way box where S stayed for 180 sec, and finally placing S on the open platform for 30 sec. Control Ss were treated exactly the same except that, postfear, S spent the first 180 sec on the open platform followed by 30 sec in the one-way chamber. On the two relaxation conditioning trials which were followed by a booster shock, an additional 30 sec buffer on the open platform ended the control group's trial so that experimental and control were always alike in terms of how soon confinement in the one-way chamber was followed by shock. Otherwise the chamber could become negative in the controls and help produce the effect. In the control Ss, one could also question whether 30 sec in the one-way chamber directly preceding placement in the striped box (nonshock trial) might not establish second-order conditioned fear to the one-way chamber and thereby produce less approach value for this chamber than in the experimental group. As will soon be seen, the data clearly refute this possibility as an explanation of the obtained results, though Ss are presently being run with a slight procedural variation to control this factor as well. In the final set of one-way avoidance trials, shock was reduced to 1mA and confinement in the safe chamber was only 15 sec.

For the purpose of a statistical analysis for this chapter, groups in process were balanced for color of confinement chamber, direction run (toward or away from this chamber), treatment (experimental versus control), and were assigned the same proportion of males, females, hooded and albino. In this way a grand $2 \times 2 \times 2$ analysis of variance was possible ($N = 14$ in each group). This preliminary analysis was based on the number of shocks to a criterion of three successive avoidances. The means for groups trained toward the confinement chamber were 3.7 and 6.2 for the experimental and control groups, respectively. The means for groups trained to avoid the confinement chamber were 9.4 and 7.8, respectively. These yielded a significant F for direction ($F = 14.4$; $p = .001$) and a significant direction x treatment interaction ($F = 4.7$; $p < .05$); that is, there was a conditioned effect that was largely limited to the experimental group. There was also a borderline effect for color of confinement, suggesting that running *away* from white when it is positive is harder than running *away* from black when it is positive.

The data were also analyzed in terms of the number of Ss in a group that avoided on the very first avoidance trial. In the experimental-toward groups, 15 out of 28 avoided on the first trial, while only 5 did so in the away groups, yielding a x^2 of 4.5 ($p < .05$). In the controls, 5 Ss and 7 Ss avoided on the first trial in the toward and away groups, respectively. This last comparison is unique in that it shows the operation of the conditioned approach effect in a new learning situation prior to any administration of shock. To some, this may represent a critical consideration.

A refutation of the explanation in terms of the second-order conditioning of fear in the controls includes (a) the large difference between the toward and away groups in the experimental condition; (b) a tendency for the earlier confinement chamber to be positive during the one-way trials even in the controls; and (c) the strong positive effect in the experimental-toward group as reflected by 15 Ss avoiding on the first trial of one-way training which is never true of Ss without prior relaxation conditioning.

Finally, it should be pointed out that several other investigators have presumably been working with the same set of variables and phenomena and have obtained similar results. They simply have used other rubrics than conditioned relaxation, conditioned relief, or relaxation-approach to describe their work (Rescorla and LoLordo, 1965; Rescorla, 1967; de Toledo & Black, 1967). And in the same general vein, there are the recent studies of Biederman, D'Amato, and Keller (1964); Kurtz and Shafer (1967); and Brush (1962), to mention a representative few.

C. Relaxation-Produced Stimuli

As is true of any response, relaxation presumably has its characteristic stimulus accompaniments, *i.e.,* internal response-produced stimuli which are distinctively different from the response-produced stimuli associated with fear (Reynierse, 1966). Let us look at a typical avoidance learning experiment in which S may fail to avoid after it has learned to avoid. The assumption here is that S tended to relax on this trial, which means that there were relaxation-produced stimuli present. Ordinarily, when S relaxes to the extent that it fails to avoid, it gets shocked or punished and escapes to the safe region. This means that the relaxation-produced stimuli, since they were paired once with shock, have become conditioned aversive stimuli. Thus if S, which has been punished for failing to avoid, starts to relax on some subsequent trial, the conditioned aversive stimuli are reinstated and the avoidance response recurs; that is, S no longer continues to relax and extinction is prevented.

Using the jump-out box (Figure 2), Denny and Dmitruk (1967) tested this hypothesis, namely, that the punishment of a single failure to avoid increases resistance to extinction. The CS–US interval was 10 sec and after the criterion of three successive avoidances was reached S was extinguished. For the experimental groups, the first part of the extinction session was a special situation in which the first long-latency response, namely, a failure to avoid within 20 sec was immediately followed by shock. On this trial, S was allowed to escape to the upper chamber. All trials succeeding this punished one were regular extinction trials in which no shock was present. Each experimental animal had a control match-mate which had performed like the experimental animal up to this point and was shocked on the same extinction trial as its experimental match, except that the shock occurred immediately upon being placed in the lower chamber rather than 20 sec later. There was also a control group which was never shocked during extinction. The results were clear-cut: The experimental group took a mean of 199 trials to extinguish, the shocked controls 69 trials, and the nonshocked controls 43. In a different way, the data which are presented in Figure 14 also strongly support the hypothesis. Here, the latencies for 4 typical experimental animals on the last 25 extinction trials preceding the extinction criterion are graphically compared with the latencies of their control match-mates. Fluctuating latencies characterize the experimental Ss but not the controls: Once a control S starts to relax (exhibit long latency) it continues to do so and promptly extinguishes; once an experimental S has a long latency (punished relaxation) there is a marked reduction in latency on subsequent trials.

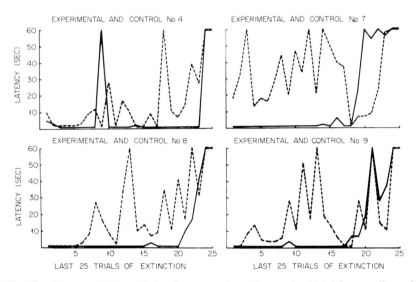

Fig. 14. Topographical analysis of response latencies on the 25 trials preceding criterion of extinction, for four typical pairs of Ss. Solid and broken lines represent control and experimental Ss, respectively.

Follow-up research was then carried out using an escape paradigm during original acquisition trials rather than an avoidance paradigm. That is, S was shocked immediately upon being placed in the lower chamber and allowed to escape. In the avoidance paradigm, all Ss acquired R_{JO} in the stimulus context of *not* being shocked immediately upon being placed on the shock box, which meant that the controls could have suffered greater generalization decrement on the immediate punishment trial than the experimental group did on the delayed punishment trial. In the escape paradigm, the reverse was true and the factor was controlled: any effects of generalization decrement were biased against the experimental group (delayed shock for the first time on the punishment trial). When a number of intervals for defining failure to "avoid" were employed for separate groups; namely, 0, 5, 10, 20, 40, 80, 120, 180 and 320 sec, it was found that the optimal interval for producing increased resistance to extinction was the 10-sec interval. These data are presented in Figure 15 in log units. Male rats which were punished for a 10-sec delay took a mean of over 400 trials to extinguish, whereas shocked male controls (0 interval) took approximately 40 trials. Punishing a 5-sec delay also markedly and significantly increased resistance to extinction, but punishing very long delays, that is over 40 sec, did not. This probably means that in order for relaxation-produced stimuli to be effective conditioned aversive stimuli they must be *incipient* relaxation-produced stimuli. As is true in all conditioning, the CS–US interval cannot be too long if good conditioning is to occur. With the shorter intervals (5 and 10 sec) relaxation-produced stimuli are followed very soon by the US, shock.

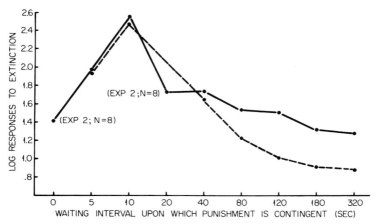

Fig. 15. Log mean responses to extinction, postpunishment, as a function of the interval during which S was required to wait in the original shock chamber, postacquisition, before receiving the single shock-escape trial (punishment). Solid line, male, $N = 3$; dashed line, female, $N = 3$.

One implication of these data is that they provide an explanation for extreme resistance to extinction of avoidance behavior, possibly even neurotic fixations. A good example of extreme resistance to extinction is provided by the experiments of Solomon and Wynne (1953, 1954) using dogs in a modified shuttlebox. These investigators used a stringent acquisition criterion of ten avoidances in a row, and nearly all dogs failed to avoid at least once after having avoided at least once previously. According to the present analysis, almost all their dogs were punished for relaxing during the original acquisition session. The CS–US interval used was typically 10 sec, the same interval used by Denny and Dmitruk in their avoidance paradigm and the same punished interval that gave an optimal effect with the escape paradigm. When possible interspecies differences and apparatus differences are ignored, there is a striking similarity between the Solomon and Wynne and the Denny and Dmitruk experiments.

There is also a possible parallel with the studies on experimental neurosis in cats (Masserman, 1943; Wolpe, 1958). Typically in such studies, a hungry animal is severely shocked in a box whenever it attempts to eat from a particular place, or it receives an occasional shock over a 5–10-min period. The point here is that if the shocks are fairly well spaced or S is shocked every time it attempts to eat, then S is presumably in a relatively relaxed state when the shocks are administered. Hence S is being repeatedly punished for relaxing, and it makes good sense that S remains continually afraid while in the situation no matter how long it stays in the chamber in which it no longer gets shocked—one of the main objective criteria of experimental neurosis. According to the theory, the best way to extinguish avoidance or fear is to make the animal wait in the original shock chamber until eventually it relaxes. In this way relaxation is directly conditioned to the cues of the original shock chamber, and fear or escape-avoidance behavior soon extinguishes. If, however, fear is conditioned to relaxation-produced stimuli this course of events would be disrupted and, according to this analysis, so-called neurotic behavior would ensue.

Thus it is possible to speculate wildly that the cues responsible for at least some varieties of generalized or free floating anxiety in the human being may be relaxation-produced stimuli. For example, a young child may have been severely scolded or punished by his father, and after a passage of time, *i.e.*, after beginning to relax, the child may approach the father and be met by a gruff, anxiety-provoking retort, "What in the hell do you want, kid?" If this sequence of events were to happen a number of times the clear possibility exists for conditioning generalized anxiety (conditioning fear to relaxation-produced stimuli). In other words, every time our hypothetical individual begins to feel calm or relaxed, he begins to feel anxious.

The theory suggests a possible therapeutic method for modifying generalized anxiety, assuming the foregoing analysis is to some extent appropriate. In rough outline, the method would consist of increasing anxiety way above the base level, using strong electric shock or some other extreme technique, so that it is *inevitable* that the generally anxious individual would eventually relax after the removal of the aversive stimulus. During the recovery or relaxation period everything would be made as pleasant and positive as possible for the subject. This would ensure a sizable relaxation response without accompanying relaxation-produced stimuli being punished. A large number of such trials would be given. Such a counter-conditioning procedure should eventually bring about the extinction of the conditioned aversive properties that may have been acquired by relaxation-produced stimuli. At least an experimental analogue of generalized anxiety and the suggested therapeutic technique should not be too difficult to devise for work with rats or cats in order to test these hypotheses.

IV. SUMMARY OF EXPERIMENTS

Research during the past few years appears to have isolated two critical events in the acquisition and extinction of escape-avoidance behavior in rats: short-latency "relief" and long-latency relaxation. The short-latency effect seems to occur postshock (not after the removal of a conditioned aversive stimulus) and is essentially limited to a period which begins 5 sec after shock removal and ends 10 to 15 sec later; *i.e.*, the effect is present with very short ITIs or nonshock intervals. The long-latency effect can occur after the removal of either an aversive or a conditioned aversive stimulus; the onset of relaxation seems to be 25–40 sec after said removal, but it is not complete until a nonshock period of about 150 sec has elapsed. Pairing a neutral stimulus (CS) with either of these completed events (periods) yields a conditioned effect which can be evaluated by the subsequent facilitation of extinction or by the rate of acquisition of a new avoidance response. The CS which appropriately follows an escape or avoidance response during acquisition facilitates the extinction of this response when the CS is placed so that it precedes this response during a subsequent extinction series. Such a CS facilitates the acquisition of a new avoidance response when it is associated with the safe region in the new avoidance situation and hinders acquisition when associated with the shock region of the new avoidance situation.

ACKNOWLEDGMENT

Most of the research from our laboratory has been supported by grants from the National Science Foundation, GB 238, GB 2964, and GB 4517.

REFERENCES

Adelman, H.M., & Maatsch, J.L. Resistance to extinction as a function of the type of response elicited by frustration. *Journal of Experimental Psychology*, 1955, **50**, 61–65.

Adelman, H.M., & Maatsch, J.L. Learning and extinction based upon frustration, food reward, and exploratory tendency. *Journal of Experimental Psychology*, 1956, **52**, 311–315.

Amsel, A. The role of frustrative nonreward in noncontinuous reward situations. *Psychological Bulletin*, 1958, **55**, 102–119.

Amsel, A., Ernhart, C.B., & Galbrecht, C.R. Magnitude of frustration effect and strength of antedating goal factors. *Psychological Reports*, 1961, **8**, 183–186.

Amsel, A., & Hancock, W. Motivational properties of frustration: III. Relation of frustration effected to antedating goal factors. *Journal of Experimental Psychology*, 1957, **53**, 126–131.

Amsel, A., & Prouty, D.L. Frustrative factors in selective learning with reward and nonreward as discriminanda. *Journal of Experimental Psychology*, 1959, **57**, 224–230.

Amsel, A., & Ward, J.S. Motivational properties of frustration: II. Frustration drive stimulus and frustration reduction in selective learning. *Journal of Experimental Psychology*, 1954, **48**, 34–47.

Bacon, W.E. Resistance to extinction as a function of mode and time of removal from goal box. *Psychonomic Science*, 1967, **8**, 101–102.

Bagné, C. Escape variables and avoidance conditioning: Two extinction processes. Unpublished M.A. thesis, Michigan State University, 1968.

Barlow, J.A. Secondary motivation through classical conditioning: One trial nonmotor learning in the white rat. *American Psychologist*, 1952, **7**, 272. (Abstract)

Barrett, G.V., & Carlson, N.J. Effect of escape versus non-escape responses from the goal box during extinction. *Psychological Reports*, 1966, **19**, 447–454.

Beck, R.C. On secondary reinforcement and shock termination. *Psychological Bulletin*, 1961, **58**, 28–45.

Biederman, G.B., D'Amato, M.R., & Keller, D.M. Facilitation of discriminated avoidance learning by dissociation of CS and manipulandum. *Psychonomic Science*, 1964, **1**, 229–230.

Boice, R., Boice, C., & Dunham, A.E. Role of docility in avoidance: gerbils and kangaroo rats in a shuttle box. *Psychonomic Science*, 1968, **10**, 381–382.

Boice, R., Denny, M.R., & Evans, T. A comparison of albino and wild rats in shuttle box avoidance. *Psychonomic Science*, 1967, **8**, 271–272.

Bolles, R.C. *Theory of motivation.* New York: Harper, 1967.

Bolles, R.C. & Seelbach, S.E. Punishing and reinforcing effects of noise onset and termination for different responses. *Journal of Comparative and Physiological Psychology*, 1964, **58**, 127–131.

Bolles, R.C., Stokes, L.W., & Younger, M.S. Does CS termination reinforce avoidance behavior? *Journal of Comparative and Physiological Psychology*, 1966, **62**, 201–207.

Bower, G.H., McLean, J., & Meacham, J. Value of knowing when reinforcement is due. *Journal of Comparative and Physiological Psychology*, 1966, **62**, 184–192.

Braud, W.G. Diminution of suppression by stimuli associated with the offset of fear-arousing cues. *Journal of Comparative and Physiological Psychology*, 1968, **65**, 356–358.

Brown, J.S., Anderson, R.C., & Weiss, C.G. Self-punitive behavior under conditions of massed practice. *Journal of Comparative and Physiological Psychology*, 1965, **60**, 451–453.

Brown, J.S., & Jacobs, A. The role of fear in the motivation and acquisition of responses. *Journal of Experimental Psychology*, 1949, **39**, 747–759.

Brown, J.S., Martin, R.C., & Morrow, M.W. Self-punitive behavior in the rat: Facilitative effects of punishment on resistance to extinction. *Journal of Comparative and Physiological Psychology*, 1964, **57**, 127–133.

Brush, F.R. The effects of intertrial interval on avoidance learning in the rat. *Journal of Comparative and Physiological Psychology*, 1962, **55**, 888–892.

Brush, F.R. The effects of kind of prior training and intersession interval upon subsequent avoidance learning. *Journal of Comparative and Physiological Psychology*, 1963, **56**, 539–545.

Brush, F.R., Brush, E.S., & Solomon, R.L. Traumatic avoidance learning: the effects of CS-UCS interval with a delayed-conditioning procedure. *Journal of Comparative and Physiological Psychology*, 1955, **48**, 285–293.

Brush, F.R., Myer, J.S., & Palmer, M.E. Joint effects of intertrial and intersession interval upon avoidance learning. *Psychological Reports*, 1964, **14**, 31–37.

Carlson, N.J., & Black, A.H. Traumatic avoidance learning: The effect of preventing escape responses. *Canadian Journal of Psychology*, 1960, **14**, 21–28.

Church, R.M., Brush, F.R., & Solomon, R.L. Traumatic avoidance learning: The effects of CS-UCS interval with a delayed conditioning procedure in a free-responding situation. *Journal of Comparative and Physiological Psychology*, 1956, **49**, 301–308.

Church, R.M., LoLordo, V.M., Overmier, J.VB., Solomon, R.L., Turner, L.H. Cardiac responses to shock in curarized dogs: effects of shock intensity and duration, warning signal, and prior experience with shock. *Journal of Comparative and Physiological Psychology*, 1966, **62**, 1–7.

Colavita, F.B. Dual function of the US in classical salivary conditioning. *Journal of Comparative and Physiological Psychology*, 1965, **60**, 218–22.

Cole, M., & Wahlsten, D. Classical and instrumental components of avoidance conditioning. Presented at the Psychonomic Society meeting, Chicago, 1967.

Delprato, D.J., & Denny, M.R. Punishment and the length of nonshock confinement during the extinction of avoidance. *Canadian Journal of Psychology*, 1968, **22**, 456–464.

Denny, M.R. The role of secondary reinforcement in a partial reinforcement learning situation. *Journal of Experimental Psychology*, 1946, **36**, 373–389.

Denny, M.R. One bar-press per day: Acquisition and extinction. *Journal of the Experimental Analysis of Behavior*, 1959, **2**, 81–85.

Denny, M.R. A theoretical analysis and its application to training the mentally retarded. In N.R. Ellis (Ed.), *International review of research in mental retardation*, Vol. 2 New York: Academic Press, 1966.

Denny, M.R. A learning model. In W.C. Corning and S.C. Ratner (Eds.), *The chemistry of learning*. New York: Plenum Press, 1967.

Denny, M.R., & Adelman, H.M. Elicitation theory: I. An analysis of two typical learning situations. *Psychological Review*, 1955, **62**, 290–296.

Denny, M.R., & Ditchman, R.E. the locus of maximal "Kamin effect" in rats. *Journal of Comparative and Physiological Psychology*, 1962, **55**, 1069–1070.

Denny, M.R., & Dmitruk, V.M. Effect of punishing a single failure to avoid. *Journal of Comparative and Physiological Psychology*, 1967, **63**, 277–281.

Denny, M.R., & Dunham, M.D. The effect of differential nonreinforcement of the incorrect response in the simple T-maze. *Journal of Experimental Psychology,* 1951, **41,** 382–389.

Denny, M.R., & King, G.F. Differential response learning on the basis of differential size of reward. *Journal of Genetic Psychology,* 1955, **87,** 317–320.

Denny, M.R., Koons, P.B., & Mason, J.E. Extinction of avoidance as a function of the escape situation. *Journal of Comparative and Physiological Psychology,* 1959, **52,** 212–214.

Denny, M.R., & Martindale, R.L. The effect of the initial reinforcement on response tendency. *Journal of Experimental Psychology,* 1956, **52,** 95–100.

Denny, M.R., & Weisman, R.G. Avoidance behavior as a function of the length of nonshock confinement. *Journal of Comparative and Physiological Psychology,* 1964, **58,** 252–257.

Denny, M.R., Zerbolio, D.J., Jr., & Weisman, R.G. Avoidance learning in heterogeneous and homogeneous shuttle boxes. *Journal of Comparative and Physiological Psychology,* 1969, **68,** 370–372.

Dinsmoor, J.A., & Clayton, M.H. Chaining and secondary reinforcement based on escape from shock. *Journal of the Experimental Analysis of Behavior,* 1963, **6,** 75–80.

Evans, W.O. Producing either positive or negative tendencies to a stimulus associated with shock. *Journal of the Experimental Analysis of Behavior,* 1962, **5,** 335–337.

Festinger, L. Development of differential appetite in the rat. *Journal of Experimental Psychology,* 1943, **32,** 226–234.

Gerall, A.A., Sampson, P.B., & Boslov, G.E. Classical conditioning of human pupillary dilation. *Journal of Experimental Psychology,* 1957, **54,** 467–474.

Guthrie, E.R. *The psychology of learning.* New York: Harper, 1935. 2nd Ed., 1952.

Haggard, D.F. Experimental extinction as a function of the type of response elicited in the goal box. *Psychological Record,* 1959, **9,** 93–98.

Herrnstein, R.J. Relative and absolute strength of response as a function of frequency of reinforcement. *Journal of the Experimental Analysis of Behavior,* 1961, **4,** 267–272.

Hill, W.F., & Spear, N.E. Choice between magnitudes of reward in a T-maze. *Journal of Comparative and Physiological Psychology,* 1963, **56,** 723–726.

Hull, C.L. *Principles of behavior.* New York: Appleton, 1943.

Jaynes, J. Learning a second response to a cue as a function of the magnitude of the first. *Journal of Comparative and Physiological Psychology,* 1950, **43,** 398–408.

Jones, M.B. An experimental study of extinction. *Psychological Monographs,* 1953, **67,** No. 369.

Kalish, H.I. Strength of fear as a function of the number of acquisition and extinction trials. *Journal of Experimental Psychology,* 1954, **47,** 1–9.

Kamin, L.J. Traumatic avoidance learning: the effects of CS-UCS interval with a trace conditioning procedure. *Journal of Comparative and Physiological Psychology,* 1954, **47,** 65–72.

Kamin, L.J. The retention of an incompletely learned avoidance response. *Journal of Comparative and Physiological Psychology,* 1957, **50,** 457–460.

Kamin, L.J., Brimer, C.J., & Black, A.H. Conditioned suppression as a monitor of fear of the CS in the course of avoidance training. *Journal of Comparative and Physiological Psychology,* 1963, **56,** 497–501.

Knapp, R.K. The acquisition and extinction of instrumental avoidance as a function of the escape situation. Unpublished doctoral dissertation, Michigan State University, 1960.

Knapp, R.K. Acquisition and extinction of avoidance with similar and different shock and escape situations. *Journal of Comparative and Physiological Psychology*, 1965, **60**, 272–273.

Kurtz, P.S., & Shafer, J.N. The interaction of UCS intensity and intertrial interval in avoidance learning. *Psychonomic Science*, 1967, **8**, 465–466.

Lachman, R. The influence of thirst and schedules of reinforcement-nonreinforcement ratios upon brightness discrimination. *Journal of Experimental Psychology*, 1961, **62**, 80–87.

Lockard, J.S. Choice of a warning signal or no warning signal in an unavoidable shock situation. *Journal of Comparative and Physiological Psychology*, 1963, **56**, 526–530.

Lutz, R.F., & Perkins, C.C., Jr. A time variable in the acquisition of observing responses. *Journal of Comparative and Physiological Psychology*, 1960, **53**, 180–182.

Maatsch, J.L. An exploratory study of the possible differential inhibitory effects of frustration and work inhibition. Unpublished M. A. thesis, Michigan State College, 1951.

Maatsch, J.L. Reinforcement and extinction phenomena. *Psychological Review*, 1954, **61**, 111–118.

Maltzman, I., & Raskin, D.C. Effects of individual differences in the orienting reflex on conditioning and complex processes. *Journal of Experimental Research in Personality*, 1965, **1**, 1–16.

Masserman, J.H. *Behavior and neurosis*. Chicago, Illinois: University of Chicago Press, 1943.

McAllister, W.R. Adaptation of the original response to a conditioned stimulus. *Iowa Academy of Science*, 1953, **60**, 534–539.

McAllister, W.R., & McAllister, D.E. Postconditioning delay and intensity of shock as factors in the measurement of acquired fear. *Journal of Experimental Psychology*, 1962, **64**, 110–116.

McAllister, W.R., & McAllister, D.E. Increase over time in the stimulus generalization of acquired fear. *Journal of Experimental Psychology*, 1963, **65**, 576–582.

Melvin, K.B., & Martin, R.C. Facilitative effects of two modes of punishment on resistance to extinction. *Journal of Comparative and Physiological Psychology*, 1966, **62**, 491–494.

Mendelson, J. Role of hunger on T-maze learning for food by rats. *Journal of Comparative and Physiological Psychology*, 1966, **62**, 341–349.

Mendelson, J. Lateral hypothalamic stimulation in satiated rats: the rewarding effects of self-induced drinking. *Science*, 1967, **157**, 1077.

Miller, N.E. Learnable drives and rewards. In S.S. Stevens (Ed.) *Handbook of experimental psychology*. New York: Wiley, 1951.

Murray, A.K., & Strandberg, J.M. Development of a conditioned positive reinforcer through removal of an aversive stimulus. *Journal of Comparative and Physiological Psychology*, 1965, **60**, 281–283.

Nefzger, M.D. The properties of stimuli associated with shock reduction. *Journal of Experimental Psychology*, 1957, **53**, 184–188.

Page, H.A. The facilitation of experimental extinction by response prevention as a function of the acquisition of a new response. *Journal of Comparative and Physiological Psychology*, 1955, **48**, 14–16.

Page, H.A., & Hall, J.F. Experimental extinction as a function of the prevention of a response. *Journal of Comparative and Physiological Psychology*, 1953, **46**, 33–34.

Premack, D. Toward empirical behavior laws: I. Positive reinforcement. *Psychological Review*, 1959, **66**, 219–234.

Rescorla, R.A. Inhibition of delay in Pavlovian fear conditioning. *Journal of Comparative and Physiological Psychology*, 1967, **64**, 114–120.

Rescorla, R.A., & LoLordo, V.M. Inhibition of avoidance behavior. *Journal of Comparative and Physiological Psychology*, 1965, **59**, 406–412.

Reynierse, J.H. Effects of CS only trials on resistance to extinction of an avoidance response. *Journal of Comparative and Physiological Psychology*, 1966, **61**, 156–158.

Reynierse, J.H., Weisman, R.G., & Denny, M.R. Shock compartment confinement during the intertrial interval in avoidance learning. *Psychological Record*, 1963, **13**, 403–406.

Reynierse, J.H., Zerbolio, D.J., & Denny, M.R. Avoidance decrement: Replication and further analysis. *Psychonomic Science* 1964, **1**, 401–402.

Reynolds, G.S. Behavioral contrast. *Journal of the Experimental Analysis of Behavior*, 1961, **4**, 57–71.

Reynolds, G.S. Some limitations on behavioral contrast and induction during successive discrimination. *Journal of the Experimental Analysis of Behavior*, 1963, **6**, 131–139.

Santos, J.R. The influence of amount and kind of training on the acquisition and extinction of escape and avoidance responses. *Journal of Comparative and Physiological Psychology*, 1960, **53**, 284–289.

Sheffield, F.D. Avoidance training and the contiguity principle. *Journal of Comparative Physiological Psychology*, 1948, **41**, 165–177.

Sheffield, F.D., & Temmer, H.W. Relative resistance to extinction of escape training and avoidance training. *Journal of Experimental Psychology*, 1950, **40**, 287–298.

Shettleworth, S., & Nevin, J.A. Relative rate of response and relative magnitude of reinforcement in multiple schedules. *Journal of the Experimental Analysis of Behavior*, 1965, **8**, 199–202.

Sidman, M. Time out from avoidance as a reinforcer: A study of response interaction. *Journal of the Experimental Analysis of Behavior*, 1962, **5**, 423–434.

Smith, M.P., & Buchanan, G. Acquisition of secondary reward by cues associated with shock reduction. *Journal of Experimental Psychology*, 1954, **48**, 123–126.

Smith, O.A., Jr., McFarland, W.L., & Taylor, E. Performance in a shock-avoidance situation interpreted as pseudoconditioning. *Journal of Comparative and Physiological Psychology*, 1961, **54**, 154–157.

Sokolov, Y.N. *Perception and the conditioned reflex*. (Pergamon Press) MacMillan, New York, 1963.

Solomon, R.L., & Wynne, L.O. Traumatic avoidance learning: Acquisition in normal dogs. *Psychological Monographs*, 1953, **67**, No. 4.

Solomon, R.L., & Wynne, L.O. Traumatic avoidance learning: the principles of anxiety conservation and partial irreversibility. *Psychological Review*, 1954, **61**, 353–385.

Spence, K.W., Haggard, D.F., & Ross, L.E. Intrasubject conditioning as a function of the intensity of the unconditioned stimulus. *Science*, 1958, **128**, 774–775.

Sutey, B.K. Frustration reduction or frustration elicitation as a reinforcing state of affairs. Unpublished M. A. thesis, Michigan State University, 1967.

Theios, J., & Bower, G.H. A test of the competing response-interference hypothesis of extinction. *Psychonomic Science*, 1964, **1**, 395–396.

de Toledo, L., & Black, A.H. Effects of preshock on subsequent avoidance conditioning. *Journal of Comparative and Physiological Psychology*, 1967, **63**, 493–499.

Verhave, T. The functional properties of a time out from an avoidance schedule. *Journal of the Experimental Analysis of Behavior,* 1962, **5,** 391–422.

Wagner, A.R. Conditioned frustration as a learned drive. *Journal of Experimental Psychology,* 1963, **66,** 142–148.

Warren, J.A., Jr., & Bolles, R.C. A reevaluation of a simple contiguity interpretation of avoidance learning. *Journal of Comparative and Physiological Psychology,* 1967, **64,** 179–182.

Weinberger, N.M. Effect of detainment on extinction of avoidance response. *Journal of Comparative and Physiological Psychology,* 1965, **60,** 135–138.

Weisman, R.G., Denny, M.R., Platt, S.A., & Zerbolio, D.J., Jr. Facilitation of extinction by a stimulus associated with long nonshock confinement periods. *Journal of Comparative and Physiological Psychology,* 1966, **62,** 26–30.

Weisman, R.G., Denny, M.R., & Zerbolio, D.J.,Jr. Discrimination based on differential nonshock confinement in a shuttle box. *Journal of Comparative and Physiological Psychology,* 1967, **63,** 34–38.

Wolpe, J. *Psychotherapy by reciprocal inhibition.* Stanford, California: Stanford University Press, 1958.

Wyckoff, L.B., Jr. The role of observing responses in discrimination learning. Part I. *Psychological Review,* 1952, **59,** 431–442.

Young, F.A. Studies of pupillary conditioning. *Journal of Experimental Psychology,* 1958, **55,** 97–110.

Zerbolio, D.J., Jr. Relaxation-mediated approach as a necessary component in simple avoidance learning. Unpublished doctoral dissertation, Michigan State University, 1965.

Zerbolio, D.J., Jr. Escape and approach responses in avoidance learning. *Canadian Journal of Psychology,* 1968, **22,** 60–71.

CHAPTER 5

Mathematical Models for Aversive Conditioning

JOHN THEIOS
University of Wisconsin

I. PRELIMINARY CONSIDERATIONS

A. Overview

Given the other theoretical approaches to aversive conditioning which have been presented in this volume, one might ask why a mathematical model approach is necessary or desirable. The reason is that written language may be vague and ambiguous to such an extent that the actual assumptions made by a theorist may be unclear or open to alternative interpretations. The logical consequences of the assumptions (the derivations or predictions) may also be ambiguous or obscure. In order to minimize vagueness and inexactness, scientists have traditionally turned to specifying their theories in mathematical terms, where, through standard mathematical logic, unambiguous and precise derivations can be made from the starting assumptions.

But what is a mathematical model? What is its purpose? Basically, as with any model, the main purpose of a mathematical model is description. A model builder does not attempt a complete description; but rather he attempts to model some aspects of the process or object of interest. For example, a model car usually only represents the stylistic features of the outer surface of the automobile, and not the detailed mechanical features of the drive train. It is obvious that physical models may vary considerably in the amount of detail they attempt to represent. The same is true of theoretical models.

Because theoretical models are only descriptions or representations of a limited number of aspects of a process, it goes without saying that they can never be true. They are only approximations and, as such, some models will be better, more complete approximations than others. The task of the scientist is to select or construct in light of the empirical evidence available, the theoretical model or process which most closely approximates that of the real system in which he is interested. He then directs his experimental research within the boundary conditions of that model, testing specific, unambiguous predictions from the model. In most cases, the predictions from the model will not fit the data in all its aspects. The points where the model is not predicting the data are of prime importance scientifically because they can indicate how the model can be improved or made more general. In short, the investigator starts with a restricted model and, as a result of repeatedly collecting new experimental evidence and revising the model in view of the new data, he progresses through a set of nested theoretical models, each model being a more general form of the preceding one. At some point in time, either the cumulative evidence inconsistent with the model will become so large or the current general model will become so unwieldy and mathematically cumbersome that the entire theoretical approach will be abandoned in favor of a simpler model which accounts for more of the details of the data. In the short history of research on avoidance conditioning, this cycle of theoretical development has gone through several phases. The original theoretical ideas of Mowrer (1939) and Miller (1948) about avoidance conditioning were first cast into the learning model of Hull (1943). As the Hull model proved too cumbersome to work with mathematically, the Mowrer–Miller ideas were incorporated into the simple, and mathematically elegant, two-operator linear learning model by Bush and Mosteller (1955). As data accumulated, it became obvious that the two-operator linear model could not adequately account for sequential properties in avoidance conditioning, and it was abandoned in favor of a radically different stochastic process, the finite state Markov chain (Theios, 1963; Theios & Brelsford, 1966a). Yet, the basic ideas of Mowrer (1939) and Miller (1948) still are found in the theoretical interpretations of the abstract Markov processes (*cf.* Theios & Brelsford, 1966a). The structure of the mathematical models has changed as dictated by data, but the main theoretical ideas are remarkably unmodified. Further, considering only the current Markov phase of the theoretical development, the form and interpretation of the models have undergone tremendous transformations, proceeding from quite restricted models to more and more general ones (Theios, 1963; Theios & Brelsford, 1966a, 1966b; and Theios, 1968). The details of the development of mathematical models for avoidance conditioning will be reviewed here following some preliminary terminological and notational considerations. In the final sections of this paper, some new theoretical suggestions will be made as a preliminary step to account theoretically for response latency.

It is difficult to predict how long the Markov phase of the theoretical development of avoidance conditioning processes will last. Eventually, new data inconsistent with the model will accumulate at such a rate that we most probably will be compelled to take off on an entirely different theoretical approach. In any event, it is the responsibility of investigators interested in avoidance conditioning to understand adequately the current theoretical models so that they will be able to recognize and discriminate data that is radically inconsistent with the models from data that is only inconsistent with a specific form or submodel of the general theoretical model.

B. Structure of Conditioning Experiments

Conditioning experiments have traditionally been conducted with more-or-less the same format, which is reviewed here for completeness. A sample of I individual subjects is tested on a total of N trials. It is convenient to let the subscript i be a subject index representing any arbitrary subject (the ith subject). Thus, the subscript i may take on the values 1, 2, 3, and so forth, up to I. The standard notation is $i = 1, 2, 3, \ldots , I$. In a similar manner, the subscript n is used to index trials, $n = 1, 2, 3, \ldots, N$. The within-trial structures of most learning experiments are similar because the trial begins by a stimulus (S_1) being presented to the subject, the organism eventually makes a response which is a member of a class of responses upon which the experimenter has made some outcome (a stimulus S_2) contingent, and then the outcome is presented.

Most aversive conditioning experiments are similar because similar physical stimuli are presented during each trial. In escape conditioning experiments, an aversive stimulus, the so-called unconditioned stimulus (S_u), is presented to start a trial. The S_u which is used in the experiment is selected to have the property that when it is applied to the subject he will move away from its source in a reasonably short time. The aversive stimulation is continued until the organism removes himself from the source of stimulation or until he makes a response in the class of responses which the experimenter has arbitrarily designated as "escape responses." The basic dependent variable in an escape experiment is the elapsed time from the onset of the S_u until the response criterion is met. The outcome of the trial is the removal of the aversive stimulation. Presumably, fast removal of aversive stimulation has more subjective utility to the organism than slow removal. Thus, the reward value of the outcome in an escape experiment is negatively correlated with the organism's response time.

In an active avoidance conditioning experiment, a trial begins with the presentation of a nonaversive stimulus, the so-called conditioned stimulus or S_c. After a prescribed length of time (the interstimulus interval,

ISI) an aversive S_u is applied to the organism. If the organism makes a criterional response before the application of the S_u, the outcome of the trial consists of the termination of the S_c. Termination of the S_c is generally considered to be a rewarding outcome. If the organism makes a criterional response after the application of the S_u (an escape response) the outcome of the trial consists of a termination of both the S_c and the aversive S_u. The dependent variables in an avoidance conditioning experiment are the latency or time of the response and the binary designation of whether the response enabled the subject to avoid or escape the S_u.

On each trial of the experiment one or more characteristics of S's response are recorded. The characteristics which the experimenter has chosen to record have traditionally been called the dependent variables of the experiment. However, in keeping with mathematical practice, we will refer to these characteristics as the response *random variables*. For example, in active avoidance conditioning the type of response (avoidance or escape) and the latency of the response may be recorded on each trial. There will thus be two random variables which may be designated as, say, X, and Y, respectively. The random variable $X_{i,n}$ would take on the value of zero or one depending upon whether subject i made an avoidance response or an escape response on trial n of the experiment. The random variable $Y_{i,n}$ may take on any positive real number corresponding to the elapsed time from the onset of the S_c on trial n until subject i's response exceeds a criterion set by the experimenter.

C.   Theoretical Response Probabilities and Expectations

It is almost universally assumed by learning theorists that on each trial each subject has a relatively stable theoretical distribution which specifies the probability of his emitting each of the possible values of the dependent variable. The response on trial n, e.g., $X_{i,n}$ is assumed to be a random sample from the underlying theoretical probability distribution. The theoretical probability distribution may be represented as $Pr(X_{i,n} = t)$, which is read "the probability that the random variable X sub i, n is equal to t." The letter t is an index representing the possible values which the random variable may assume. For example, if $X_{i,n}$ represents the binary classification of the responses into avoidance or escape responses, t would take on only the values of 0 and 1, respectively. On the other hand, if response latency were being measured to .1 sec accuracy, t would take on the values, 0, .1, .2, .3, ...

The major task facing learning theorists is that of determining how the theoretical response probability distribution $Pr(X_{i,n} = t)$ changes as a function of the stimuli, responses, and outcomes of the preceding sequence of trials. The mean or expectation of the theoretical response probability distributions is equal to

$$E(X_{i,n}) = \sum_t t \Pr(X_{i,n} = t), \qquad (1)$$

which should be read as the sum, over all possible t values, of t times the probability that $X_{i,n}$ takes on the value t. In the case of binary response classifications

$$E(X_{i,n}) = 0 \cdot \Pr(X_{i,n} = 0) + 1 \cdot \Pr(X_{i,n} = 1) = \Pr(X_{i,n} = 1). \qquad (2)$$

Thus, with binary response classifications, the expectation of the random variable is simply the theoretical probability of an escape response. In the literature, $\Pr(X_{i,n} = 1)$ has traditionally been represented as $q_{i,n}$.

The first research on application of a mathematical model to data from an aversive conditioning situation was performed by Bush and Mosteller (1955) who obtained data from the classic study by Solomon and Wynne (1953) who conditioned 30 dogs in a traumatic avoidance situation. The apparatus was a grid-floored shuttle box which consisted of two compartments separated by a barrier with a guillotine door over it. Each test began with simultaneously turning off a light above the occupied compartment and raising the guillotine door. The S had 10 sec to enter the other compartment by jumping the barrier. If he did not jump over within 10 sec, shock was turned on until the S did jump over. The shock intensity was extremely high, a just subtetanizing level. Although the shock intensity was individually set for each S, it averaged about 10.0 to 12.5 mA. As soon as the S jumped over the barrier, the door was lowered. Each S was given 10 trials per day for a number of days. No S failed to avoid the shock following trial 25.

Bush and Mosteller (1955) classified the Solomon and Wynne (1953) experiment as having two subject-controlled outcome events. These were shock and no shock. These two events were contingent upon the response, either an escape (a jump latency 10 sec or longer) or an avoidance (a jump latency shorter than 10 sec). In this sense, the outcome events were controlled by the subjects' responses. Bush and Mosteller (1955) were interested in accounting for the sequence of escape and avoidance responses made by an individual dog over the first 25 conditioning trials. The sequence of responses can be designated as a random variable X which can take on only one of two values for each trial n. For each trial n, X_n takes on the value 1 if the dog failed to avoid and received shock. On the other hand, X_n takes on the value 0 if the dog successfully avoided the shock. Thus for any individual dog i, we have a sequence $(X_{i,n}) = (X_{i,1}, X_{i,2}, \ldots, X_{i,24}, X_{i,25})$ which indicates the responses the ith dog made on every trial n. For example, the sequence for the first dog was:

$$(X_{1,1}, X_{1,2}, \ldots, X_{1,25}) = (1, 1, 0, 1, 0, 1, 0, 0, 0, \ldots, 0, 0, 0).$$

It can be assumed that the sequence of responses made by a subject was generated by an underlying sequence of theoretical response probability values $(q_{i,n}) = (q_{i,1}, q_{i,2}, q_{i,3}, \ldots, q_{i,25})$. The value of $q_{i,n}$ represents the probability that the ith dog will fail to avoid on trial n. The first task for any mathematical model is to specify changes in $q_{i,n}$ over trials such that the entire set of sequences $(X_{i,n})$ has the highest probability of having been generated from a set of theoretical sequences $(q_{i,n})$. In most of the work in mathematical learning theory, the subject subscript i has been suppressed for convenience of notation by assuming a homogeneous sample of subjects. Thus, we will talk of X_n and q_n for a theoretical subject.

II. THE TWO-OPERATOR LINEAR MODEL

Bush and Mosteller (1955) assumed that there was an initial probability q_1 of the organism failing to avoid the shock on the first trial. For the Solomon and Wynne (1953) experiment, q_1 was a very high value, nearly 1.00. In actuality, no dogs jumped during 10 pretest trials when the S_c (light-off plus raised door) was presented for 2-min exposures. One of the 30 dogs did jump on the first training trial, before he had received shock. Thus, we have two estimates of the initial probability of a nonavoidance response. If we assumed that the 10 pretest trials from one day are comparable to the first trial of acquisition, then the proportion of nonavoidance responses is 329/330 which equals .997. Since the observed proportion of a given type of event in a stationary sequence is the maximum likelihood estimate of that event, .997 is the maximum likelihood estimate of q_1 under the hypothesis that the tendency to jump did not change over test trials or over the intersession interval of one day. For convenience, Bush and Mosteller assumed that q_1 was 1.00 since the estimate was so close to that value. However, one could argue that adaptation to the apparatus was not complete by the beginning of the pretest and that the dogs were more fearful on the pretest day and less likely to jump than on the first day of training where they were more adapted, less fearful, and more likely to jump. Under this type of hypothesis, the maximum likelihood estimate of q_1 can be obtained by considering the proportion of nonavoidance responses on the first trial of the conditioning session. The estimate is 29/30 which equals .967.

Bush and Mosteller (1955) further assumed that the application of the two outcome events of shock and no shock decreased the probability of a nonavoidance when the S_c was presented. Following a shock trial, the probability of a nonavoidance response was reduced according to the following equation:

$$q_{n+1} = \alpha_1 q_n \tag{3}$$

where α_1 is a fraction between zero and one. The theoretical interpretation of α_1 is that it is the shock parameter or operator which, when it is applied, reduces the probability of a nonavoidance response. The estimate of α_1 was about .9 which indicates that the probability of an escape response on trial $n + 1$ was only about 9/10 what it was on trial n if shock in fact occurred on trial n. Following an avoidance trial, the decrease in the probability of a nonavoidance response is governed by the following equation:

$$q_{n+1} = \alpha_0 q_n \tag{4}$$

where α_0 is in the interval from 0 to 1. The theoretical interpretation of α_0 is that it is the avoidance parameter or operator. The estimate of α_0 was about .8 which indicates that the probability of an escape response on trial $n + 1$ was only about eight-tenths what it was on trial n if the subject in fact avoided on trial n. It is interesting to note that according to the model, a comparison of $\alpha_0 = .8$ and $\alpha_1 = .9$ indicates that in terms of learning to avoid shock (lowering the probability of escape responses) the dogs learned more following successful avoidance responses than following shocked failures to avoid.

In general, the equation for the change in q_n as a function of the response-outcome is

$$q_{n+1} = \alpha_{(X_n)} q_n \tag{5}$$

for $X_n = 0$ or 1 (0 if subject avoided shock on trial n and 1 if subject escaped shock on trial n). Because of the two parameters α_0 and α_1, which operate on q_n to produce a new value q_{n+1}, this model of Bush and Mosteller is called a two-operator linear model. A linear equation has a general form of

$$Y = aX + b. \tag{6}$$

That the avoidance model has a linear form can be seen if we note that b, the intercept, has the value zero in Eq. (5).

The sequence of q_n values predicted by the two-operator linear model is a response dependent process. In general,

$$q_n = \alpha_{(X_{n-1})}\alpha_{(X_{n-2})}\alpha_{(X_{n-3})} \cdots \alpha_{(X_3)}\alpha_{(X_2)}\alpha_{(X_1)}q_1. \qquad (7)$$

Since we are only considering two response alternatives, and thus only two operators, Eq. (7) reduces to

$$q_n = \alpha_0{}^{S_n}\alpha_1{}^{(n-1-S_n)}q_1 \qquad (8)$$

where S_n is the sum or total number of the avoidance responses which the subject made on the first $(n - 1)$ trials.

Because Eq. (8) depends upon the number of avoidances the subject has made in n-1 trials, it must be computed for each subject individually. Although tedious to use by hand, Eq. (8) can easily be used recursively with the aid of a computer. An excellent elementary exposition of the two-operator linear model is given in Atkinson, Bower, and Crothers (1965).

Commuting Operators

An important thing to notice about Eq. (8) is that the two operators α_0 and α_1, *commute*. That is, the number of times the operator α_0 is applied is equal to the number of previous avoidance responses the subject has had, and the number of times the operator α_1 is applied is equal to the number of previous escape responses the subject has made. In other words, at any trial n, the theoretically expected probability of an escape response depends only on the number of previous avoidance responses and shocks the subject has received, and does not depend upon their order or sequence of occurrence. Although Bush and Mosteller (1955) achieved reasonable fits to a number of statistics of the data from the Solomon and Wynne (1953) study, these were usually averages or variances which are insensitive to sequential effects, so the commutativity of the operators was not tested. Although the complete sequential data from the Solomon and Wynne (1953) study have been published (Bush and Mosteller, 1955), powerful tests of the commutativity prediction cannot easily be made since there are only 30 sequences in total.

In order to assess the commutativity and other sequential properties of the two-operator model, we will consider a number of sets of response sequences from avoidance conditioning experiments which generated a hundred or more sequences. Let us consider only the first five trials of a conditioning experiment. The greatest amount of learning takes place on these early trials. Although the obtained proportion of avoidance responses was zero on the first trial, by the fifth trial the obtained proportion of avoidance responses was .65, .80, and .71 in separate experiments by Theios (1963), Brelsford (1967), and Coulson (1967). Consider an arbitrary sequence of responses on the first five trials of an experiment, $(X_1, X_2, X_3, X_4, X_5)$. The probability of obtaining the sequence is equal to the product

$$\Pr(X_1, X_2, X_3, X_4, X_5) = Q_1 \cdot Q_2 \cdot Q_3 \cdot Q_4 \cdot Q_5 = \prod_{n=1}^{5} Q_n \qquad (9)$$

where $Q_n = [X_n q_n + (1-X_n)(1-q_n)]$. The obtained and predicted frequencies of each of the 16 possible 5-trial response sequences are given in Table 1 for the rat avoidance experiments by Theios (1963), Brelsford

TABLE 1

Observed Response Sequences on First Five Trials and Predictions from the Two-Operator Linear Model

Sequence	Theios (1963)		Brelsford (1967)		Coulson (1967)	
12345	Pre.	Obs.	Pre.	Obs.	Pre.	Obs.
11111	9	14	5	10	24	29
11110	15	20	16	18	36	37
11101	10	8	7	9	14	21
11100	15	11	31	29	47	51
11011	2	4	1^a	4	6	2^a
11010	7	8	7	5	11	13
11001	11	0	12	5	23	9
11000	10	11	39	41	37	45
10111	0^a	3	0^a	4	0^a	1
10110	0^a	2	0^a	2	0^a	4
10101	2^a	4	1^a	1	2^a	0
10100	1^a	8	3	7	3	7
10011	6	0	2^a	1	6	3
10010	6	4	9	5	13	3
10001	2^a	3	7	1	7	2
10000	4	0	26	24	20	14
N	100	100	166	166	245	245
χ^2	68.9		23.9		49.6	
df	9		9		10	
p	< .001		< .01		< .001	
α_1	.79		.89		.79	
α_0	.77		.46		.46	

[a] In each χ^2 test, cells with expected frequencies of 2 or less were pooled together.

(1967), and Coulson (1967). In each of these three studies a one-way avoidance procedure was used rather than a shuttle procedure [cf. Theios and Dunaway (1964) and Theios, Lynch, and Lowe (1966)].[1] Since none of the 511 response sequences had an avoidance response on the first trial, the value of q_1 was taken *a priori* to be equal to 1.00. For each experiment, estimates of the values of the parameters alpha-sub-zero and alpha-sub-one were obtained by having a computer select values which minimized the chi square statistic between the obtained and predicted frequencies of the sequences. In each chi square test, the degrees of freedom are equal to the number of cells in the test minus 3 (1 for the frequency constraint and 2 for the two estimated parameters). As can be seen from inspection of Table 1, the two-operator model is not predicting the data well at all. The overall chi square of goodness of fit between the obtained and predicted sequences for the three studies is 142.4 with a total of 28 degrees of freedom. This indicates that the deviations of the predicted frequencies from the obtained frequencies are highly significant, $p < .001$.

Bush and Mosteller's (1955) two-commuting-operator model is beautiful from a heuristic standpoint because it separates and allows for differential effects of the two relevant events of Su and Sc termination. It also allows for the strong temptation to relate the model to two-factor theories of avoidance conditioning by identifying the two alpha parameters with the reinforcing events of pain reduction and fear reduction. Unfortunately, the two-operator model cannot accurately account for sequential effects in one-way avoidance conditioning with rats. The question of whether commuting operators can account for shuttle avoidance conditioning in dogs as originally suggested could perhaps be answered in the near future if a large number of shuttle response sequences obtained from dogs under relatively homogeneous acquisition conditions were made available in the general literature.

III. DISCRETE PERFORMANCE LEVEL MARKOV MODEL

The bulk of the avoidance conditioning data available in the literature that is amenable to analysis by mathematical models involves one-way

---

Each rat was placed in one side of a two-compartment box which had a grid floor. After some preliminary adaptation to the apparatus, each conditioning trial began with the simultaneous opening of the door between the compartments and the onset of a tone. If S did not run into the other compartment within a few seconds after the onset of the tone, he was shocked until he did so. After a period of time, the rat was replaced in the starting compartment and another trial was begun. Trials were run for each S until it acquired at least 10 consecutive nonshocked trials.

avoidance conditioning with rats. Given the results of the tests in Table 1, we really have no choice at the moment but to consider the two operator linear model as an inadequate approximation to the avoidance conditioning process. The first alternative theoretical approach was a Markov model suggested in an early paper (Theios, 1963). Although the model was originally interpreted in terms of a stimulus sampling process with only two stimulus elements (*cf.* Atkinson & Estes, 1963), the sampling interpretation has not led to fruitful predictions and has since been dropped from serious consideration. Coulson (1967) has succinctly described the process and pinpointed its problems as follows:

Theios first interpreted the Markov process in terms of stimulus sampling theory, visualizing the conditioning situation as containing only two relevant elements, both of which had to be conditioned to the avoidance response before it would occur with a probability of unity. In the [initial] N-state, neither of the elements is conditioned and the avoidance response does not occur. In the [intermediate] I-state only one of the elements is conditioned and the probability of the avoidance response is p. When both elements are conditioned the probability of an avoidance response is unity.

There are several problems inherent in the stimulus sampling interpretation. The foremost of these is that there is no way to identify the independent variables with which to manipulate the hypothetical elements. Another is that since p is greater than .5 (Theios, 1963; Theios & Brelsford, 1966a), one has to imagine that the element leading to the higher probability of avoidance is usually conditioned first. Thirdly, since both elements cannot be conditioned on a single trial (the process cannot go from [the initial state directly to the terminal state] and the probability of making 10 consecutive avoidances in [state] I is *very* small), the two-element interpretation predicts at least two errors for each protocol, a prediction which has not been empirically supported. In sum, the two-element model is neither empirically tenable nor has it provided the coordinating definitions necessary to mediate between theory and research. (Coulson, 1967, p. 12)

More reasonable interpretations can be given; one which is consistent with the data is as follows. Consider the events which occur on the early trials in an avoidance conditioning experiment: A warning stimulus S_c is turned on and a short time later an aversive stimulus S_u is applied to the subject which forces him to make an instrumental escape response R_{run}.

It is assumed that the subject starts the experiment in a naïve state in which the probability of an avoidance response is effectively zero. There are five parameters concerned with entrance to and exit from the various states assumed by the model:

1. Fear-Conditioning Parameter, c

On at least the first trial of the experiment, the aversive stimulus will be applied to the subject, and two sequences of events are assumed to occur. First, the aversive S_u, in addition to eliciting the instrumental escape response, will also elicit an emotional response r_e in the organism. A relatively permanent association between s_e, the stimulus consequence of r_e (fear), and the instrumental response R_{run} is innate, has already been learned, or is established in a relatively few trials (one or two for one-way avoidance conditioning with rats). Thus, s_e very quickly comes to elicit R_{run} with a probability of unity. The second and simultaneous sequence of events involves the formation of an association between the warning stimulus S_c, and the emotional response, r_e. The model assumes that the probability that these two sequences of events have both been realized following any paired S_c–S_u trial is a constant c. Thus, c is the probability that following a trial the subject will be fearful in the presence of S_c and make an appropriate response.

2. Direct Long-Term Storage Parameter, d

The association between S_c and r_e may not be permanent, however. The association may be stored directly in long-term memory with probability d just after it was formed. On the other hand, it may be stored in short-term memory with probability $1-d$. Because of trade-off relations among the parameters (cf. Greeno & Steiner, 1964) the parameter d may be set equal to zero for most applications of the model.

3. Short-Term Memory Loss Parameter, q

The S_c–r_e association may be lost from short-term memory with probability q during a fixed intertrial interval. The subject will make an avoidance response whenever the S_c–r_e association is in either long-term or short-term memory, but will fail to avoid (and thus will escape) whenever it is not so stored.

4. Long-Term Storage Parameter Following Errors, e

Following an escape response which results due to the loss of the S_c–r_e association from short-term memory, the association is reestablished and may be stored in long-term memory with probability e or again stored in short-term memory with probability $1-e$.

5. Long-Term Storage Parameter Following Successes, s

When an S_c-r_e association is in short-term memory, it may be transferred to long-term memory with probability s during the intertrial interval. Thus, the parameter s also represents the probability of storing the association in long-term memory following an early successful avoidance response.

Formally, the process described above constitutes a Markov process which has the following starting vector, transition matrix, and response probability vector:

$$
\begin{array}{c}
\begin{array}{ccccc}
 & L_{n+1} & S_{n+1} & F_{n+1} & N_{n+1} & \Pr(X_n = 0 \mid \cdot)
\end{array} \\
\begin{array}{c} L_n \\ S_n \\ F_n \\ N_n \end{array}
\left[
\begin{array}{cccc}
1 & 0 & 0 & 0 \\
s & (1-s)(1-q) & (1-s)q & 0 \\
e & (1-e)(1-q) & (1-e)q & 0 \\
cd & c(1-d)(1-q) & c(1-d)q & 1-c
\end{array}
\right]
\left[
\begin{array}{c}
1 \\ 1 \\ 0 \\ 0
\end{array}
\right]
\end{array}
\qquad (10)
$$

$$\Pr(L_1, S_1, F_1, N_1) = (0, 0, 0, 1).$$

The starting vector gives the probability of the subject starting the process on trial 1 in each of the four states, and in this particular instance the vector indicates that the subject can only start in the naive state, N_1. The transition matrix has four rows and four columns, labeled L, S, F, N, corresponding to the four states of the process, respectively: long-term memory, short-term memory, forgotten, and naïve. The four states have been given trial number subscripts for clarity. The expression in any individual cell of the transition matrix gives the conditional probability of the process being in the column state on trial $n+1$ given that it was in the row state on trial n. The response probability vector indicates the conditional probability of an avoidance response for each of the row states. A detailed mathematical analysis of the model in Eq. (10) has been presented in Theios and Brelsford (1966a).

Unlike the two-operator linear model, the four-state Markov model requires marked sequential dependencies in the response sequences. Sequential data from the first five trials of the experiments by Theios (1963), Brelsford (1967), and Coulson (1967) are given in Table 2 along

TABLE 2
Observed Response Sequences on First Five Trials and Predictions from the Markov Model

Sequence 12345	Theios (1963) Pre.	Obs.	Brelsford (1967) Pre.	Obs.	Coulson (1967) Pre.	Obs.	Ident.
11111	15	14	13	10	39	29	29
11110	12	20	17	18	33	37	37
11101	6	8	6	9	10	21	18
11100	12	11	28	29	45	51	53
11011	5	4	4	4	5	6	4
11010	7	8	7	5	12	13	16
11001	5	0	3	5	4	9	8
11000	11	11	43	41	55	45	46
10111	2^a	3	2^a	4	2^a	1	0^a
10110	3	2	4	2	4	4	1^a
10101	2^a	4	1^a	1	2^a	0	1^a
10100	5	8	9	7	13	7	7
10011	2^a	0	1^a	1	2^a	3	1^a
10010	4	4	2^a	5	4	3	3
10001	3	3	1^a	1	1^a	2	2^a
10000	3	0	26	24	16	14	20
N	100	100	166	166	245	245	245
χ^2	5.9		8.4		23.2		9.0
df	9		7		8		4
p	.74		$>.25$		$>.01$		$>.05$
c	.52		.67		.48		(.14, .35, .52, .56)
d	$.00^b$		$.00^b$		$.00^b$		.55
q	.52		.58		.63		.58
e	.23		.37		.54		.68
s	.00		.41		.26		$.00^b$

[a]In each χ^2 test cells with predicted frequencies of 2 or less were pooled.

[b]Parameter was set equal to zero by assumption.

with predictions (rounded to integers) from the Markov model. For each experiment only 16 possible sequences of the first five trials are predicted since the model (and the data) require that the response on the first trial be a failure to avoid. Four parameters are estimated for each experiment $(c, s, q,$ and $e)$. The parameter d was arbitrarily set equal to zero by assumption. This means that an S_c-r_e association must first be stored in short-term memory before it can be transferred to long-term memory. For each experiment, the parameter values were selected so as to minimize the χ^2 statistic between predicted and obtained frequencies. In each χ^2 test all cells with predicted frequencies of two or less were pooled. The degrees of freedom for each test are the number of cells minus one, minus the number of estimated parameters. There is insufficient evidence to reject the fit of the Markov model to the data from the Theios (1963) and Brelsford (1967) studies. However, the Coulson (1967) data deviate significantly from the predictions, in spite of the fact that the predictions follow the profile of the data reasonably well, at least much better than the predictions from the two-operator linear model which were given in Table 1.

Detailed inspection of the Coulson (1967) data revealed that the assumption of the Markov model which requires the parameter c to be constant and independent of the trial number was not reasonable and that this was causing most of the misfit of the Markov model. Agreement between predictions of the Markov model and the Coulson (1967) data can be obtained by considering an identifiable states representation of the Markov process similar to that suggested by Greeno (1968). The only change in the process is that the subject's initial run of failures to avoid is treated as a single state in which the probability of leaving state N on trial n is c_n for $n = 1, 2, 3, \ldots$ and the parameter s is assumed to have the value zero. The transition matrix for the identifiable process is

$$
\begin{array}{c}
\\
L_n \\
S_n \\
F_n \\
N_n
\end{array}
\begin{array}{cccc}
L_{n+1} & S_{n+1} & F_{n+1} & N_{n+1} \\
\left[\begin{array}{cccc}
1 & 0 & 0 & 0 \\
0 & 1-q & q & 0 \\
e & (1-e)(1-q) & (1-e)q & 0 \\
dc_n & (1-d)c_n & 0 & 1-c_n
\end{array}\right]
\end{array}
\begin{array}{c}
\Pr(X_n = 0 \mid \cdot) \\
\left[\begin{array}{c}
1 \\
1 \\
0 \\
0
\end{array}\right]
\end{array}
\tag{11}
$$

$$\Pr(L_1, S_1, F_1, N_1) = (0, 0, 0, 1).$$

Following methods given in Greeno (1968) and Greeno and Steiner (1964), maximum likelihood parameter estimates are easily obtained from any set of data assuming an identifiable states process such as that given in (11). The maximum likelihood estimates of the parameters based on the Coulson (1967) data are $c_1 = .14$, $c_2 = .35$, $c_3 = .52$, $c_4 = .56$, $d = .55$, $q = .58$, and $e = .68$. The high value of the parameter d indicates that over half of the subjects had response sequences which were truly discrete, an initial string of escape responses followed by a criterion run of 10 consecutive avoidance responses. The predictions of the identifiable states Markov process are given in the last right-hand column of Table 2. The χ^2 of 9.0 with 4 degrees of freedom is not significant and most of its size is contributed by the cells with the very small expected frequencies. The interpretation of the increasing values of

c_n as a function of n is that the effectiveness of the shock as an S_u increased as a function of successive applications, at least for the first few trials. In actual practice, an equation specifying the changes in c_n as a function of n would replace the list of c_n values which are given here. The equation would probably have three parameters, an initial starting value, a rate of increase and an asymptote. For example, the following equation would probably do a reasonable job of characterizing c_n in the Coulson (1967) data where $0 < a < 1.0$:

$$c_n = c - (c - c_1)a^{n-1}. \tag{12}$$

In Figure 1 the overall discrepancies between the sequential predictions of the two-operator linear model and the Markov model may be compared relative to the pooled data from the three studies.

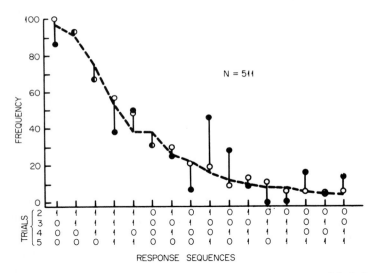

Fig. 1. Observed frequencies (dashed line) of response sequences on trials 2 through 5 pooled from the avoidance conditioning studies by Brelsford (1967), Coulson (1967), and Theios (1963) and predictions from the two-operator linear model (closed circles) and the Markov model (open circles). In the response sequences, a 1 represents an escape response (error) and a 0 represents a successful avoidance response. The sequences have been ordered on the basis of their frequency of occurrence. The solid lines indicate the deviations of the predictions from the data.

A.   Uniqueness of Parameters

Consider the set of possible binary response sequences in an experiment having a fixed number of trials. Every well-defined mathematical learning model specifies a probability or a likelihood for each of the sequences in the set of possible sequences. This will be called the probability distribution over the set of sequences. A model is said to be identifiable and its parameters are unique if every different combination of parameter values specifies a different, unique probability distribution over the set of sequences. In a highly technical and mathematical paper, Greeno (1968) has shown that the model represented in Eq. (10) is not identifiable. Roughly speaking, an arbitrary value between zero and one can be chosen for one of the parameters d, e, or s, and there exist values for the remaining parameters of the process which will specify the same probability distribution over the set of response sequences. This is an unpleasant state of affairs since it indicates that there are virtually entire planes in the four-dimensional probability space, any point of which will represent an optimal set of parameter estimates for a given set of data. This means that the values of a particular set of parameter estimates may have little psychological meaning since many other sets of parameter estimates could be found that would predict the data equally well. Greeno (1968) suggests that the way out of this problem is to impose an identifying restriction on one of the parameters, with the restriction being dictated on the basis of theoretical, psychological and physical considerations. In practice, this has been done by every investigator who has ever used a submodel of the model given in Eq. (10). In the original article, Theios (1963) assumed a number of restrictions dictated by the two-element sampling interpretation, namely, $d = 0$, $s = 0$, $e = c/2$, and $p = .5$. Any one of the first three restrictions would have been sufficient to render the model identifiable. Theios and Brelsford (1966a) considered a number of identifying restrictions, including a classical conditioning interpretation in which both d and e are set equal to zero and a memory storage interpretation in which s and e (and possibly d) are set equal to each other. Brelsford (1967) set s equal to zero, but this may be a bad choice for an identifying restriction because Coulson (1967) has shown that with $s = 0$, reasonable assumptions about response latency lead to the prediction that mean response latency in a criterion run of avoidance responses should be constant. This prediction is counter to fact because latency decreases during a criterion run of avoidance responses (Coulson, 1967). Permitting s to be larger than zero allows latencies during the criterion run to decrease. Along with the assumption that $d = 0$, McGinnis (1966) assumed that s was equal to e. This latter restriction probably is a bad one for avoidance conditioning, because it implies that the changes which take place in response probability are the same following intermediate escapes and avoidances, independent of the fact that the subject gets S_u on one type of trial and not on the other. The author's considered opinion is that the most reasonable identifying restrictions for avoidance conditioning are to set d equal to zero or d equal to e.

B. Two-Factor versus Memory Interpretation

Now that the basic feasibility of a Markov process as an approximation to avoidance conditioning has been shown, we turn to research directed at testing various theoretical interpretations and assumptions. A
long-term/short-term memory interpretation of the avoidance conditioning process was given earlier. An alternative theoretical interpretation of
the avoidance conditioning process is that the animal first must become
aroused or activated through fear conditioning and then must learn an
instrumental response which eliminates the S_c and thus fear. These notions are represented in the Markov process by assuming that fear conditioning has probability c of taking place on each trial and instrumental
conditioning has probability e of occurring on each trial. In an experiment involving 262 rats, Theios and Brelsford (1966a) differentiated
between the two theoretical interpretations. The experimental manipulation used was that of trapping the experimental group subjects when
they failed to avoid, giving them a brief, unavoidable shock with no
opportunity to perform an instrumental escape response. The two-factor
conditioning interpretation predicts that the second transition parameter
of the process, e, should be decreased since the trapping operation
should interfere with the learning of the instrumental response which has
probability e of occurring on each trial following fear conditioning. The
first transition parameter c, should not be affected by trapping, however,
since c is the probability of classically acquiring a fear response and
trapping should not interfere with that. On the other hand, the memory
interpretation requires that trapping should decrease the value of the
first parameter, c, since the instrumental response component is assumed
to be learned very early in avoidance training. The second transition
parameter, e, should not be affected by trapping since it represents a
central process of storing an association in long-term memory. The results of the Theios and Brelsford (1966a) experiment were that trapping
decreased only the value of the first transition parameter, c, and did not
affect the value of the second parameter, e. In fact, it was not possible
to differentiate the trapped and nontrapped rats on the basis of their
sequences of responses following their first avoidance response. These
sets of sequences were almost identical, indicating that both groups of
rats had the same values of the parameters e, s, and q. This result gives
very strong support to the memory interpretation.

C. Manipulation of State Occupancy

In his 1967 study, Brelsford theorized that if the memory interpretation of the Markov model were correct, it should be possible to manipulate the subject's state, and hence its behavior, by manipulating the
presence or absence of fear, s_e, which is the effective stimulus for the
instrumental avoidance response. Brelsford first ran a large group of 166
rats from which he estimated the values of the parameters of the process
with the identifying restriction that $s = 0$. He then showed that the response sequences of this parameter estimation group were in accord with
a large number of predictions from the model. Specifically, it was not
possible to reject the goodness-of-fit of the following theoretical predictions: independence of responses between S's first avoidance and last
error; stationarity of the proportion of avoidance responses on trials
between S's first avoidance and last error; sequence of responses on the
first five trials of the experiment; mean learning curve; and the distributions of total errors, errors before the first avoidance, and trial of the
last error.

According to the memory interpretation, an organism fails to make an
avoidance response because the S_c fails to evoke an emotional response,
r_e. Brelsford (1967) theorized that if he were to run a group of Ss under
a condition where he turned off the shock S_u after the S's first avoidance
response, then a proportion X of the Ss should exhibit an indefinitely
long sequence of avoidance responses since they already would have
been absorbed at state L with the S_c-r_e association stored in long-term
memory. The remaining Ss, a proportion $(1-X)$, would not have had
the S_c-r_e association stored in long-term memory, and thus each should
eventually make an error. Further, since S_u will not be applied when
these subjects make an error, they should continue to make an indefinitely long sequence of errors since they are in state F where the probability of an avoidance response is zero and with shock turned off, the
parameter q should equal 1.00 and the parameter e should equal zero. If
after a long run of errors without shock, S_u again is applied after errors
until the next avoidance response, a proportion X' of the original proportion $(1-X)$ of the Ss should have an indefinitely long run of avoidance responses following the first reappearance of an avoidance
response. The remaining Ss, a proportion $(1-X')$ of the original $(1-X)$,
should eventually make an error which would be followed by an indefinitely long run of errors. This cycle of turning shock off following the
first avoidance response, and then turning it back on following a long
run of errors can be repeated until all subjects are in state L giving indefinitely long sequences of avoidance responses. Brelsford (1967) performed this repeated extinction-reacquisition experiment and found that

he could accurately predict the acquisition-extinction-reacquisition-etc. behavior of a group of 70 rats using parameter estimates from his first group of 166 rats.

1. Manipulation of the S_c–r_e Association

The memory interpretation assumes that errors following the first avoidance response are due to a failure of S_c to elicit r_e and its consequent s_e. Errors provide an S_c–S_u pairing and thus allow the S_c–r_e association to be reestablished. Brelsford (1967) hypothesized that if the S_c–r_e association were established and stored in long-term memory before the first avoidance response then there would be *no errors* following the first avoidance response. To test this prediction, he gave 20 rats (the preconditioning group) 20 classical conditioning S_c–S_u pairings before they were allowed to make an avoidance or escape response. He found that the preconditioning group made an average of only 1.1 errors before criterion, whereas the parameter estimation group made an average of 3.2 errors. Furthermore, no S in the preconditioning group had an error following its first avoidance response, as is required by the memory interpretation. Since the preconditioning manipulation insured that the S_c–r_e association already was made and stored in long-term memory, the fact that Ss took only about one trial to reach criterion indicates that the s_e–R_{run} association takes only about one trial to be learned. The mean learning curves are reproduced in Figure 2.

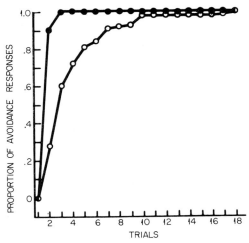

Fig. 2. Mean learning curves for (●) the preconditioning group ($N = 20$) and (○) the parameter estimation group ($N = 166$) from the Brelsford (1967) study. It should be noted that in the preconditioning group, 18 of the 20 rats made only one error, on the first trial, and the two other rats made errors only on the first two trials, and none thereafter.

2. *Manipulation of the r_e-s_e-R_{run} Chain*

The memory interpretation assumes that errors following the first avoidance response are never due to the absence of the s_e-R_{run} association, but are only due to the absence of the $S_{|c}$-r_e association. To test this assumption, Brelsford (1967) manipulated the r_e-s_e-$R_{|run}$ chain at various stages of learning by evoking r_e with a very brief (.1 sec) shock simultaneous with S_c onset. The assumption is that if the s_e-$R_{|run}$ association has been established, then a brief shock is very likely to result in the occurrence of r_e which should set off the chain r_e-s_e-R_{run}, resulting in an avoidance response. In one group of 70 rats, the no-error group, brief shock was given on each trial following the first avoidance response. Of the 70 Ss, 65 never made an error following the first avoidance response. The 5 Ss that made errors eventually ended up with a run of errors. Presumably, the brief shock was not sufficient to evoke r_e reliably for these few Ss.

Forty-three Ss were run in a one-error condition in which they were allowed to make one error following their first avoidance response before the brief shock was introduced. Of the Ss, 20 out of 43 did make one error, and of these 20, 19 went into a criterion of avoidance responses on the trial when the brief shock was introduced, as is required by the assumption that brief shock elicits r_e which sets off the r_e-s_e-$R_{|run}$ chain of behavior.

A control group against which the behavior of the no-error and one-error groups may be contrasted is a group of rats that had at least one error after their first avoidance response, who had the S_u shock turned off following their first avoidance, but who did *not* have the brief shock introduced after their first-error-after-their-first-avoidance-response. The Brelsford (1967) investigation included 40 such subjects which we will call the ten-error group since each of these rats eventually made ten consecutive errors.

In Figure 3, the behavior of the no-error group is contrasted to that of the ten-error group on the trial of and trials following each S's first avoidance response. The performance of the no-error group remains near 100% avoidance responses whereas the avoidance behavior of the ten-error group, which did not receive the brief shock, rapidly extinguishes. The solid lines in Figure 3 represent Brelford's (1967) predictions from the memory interpretation of the Markov model.

In Figure 4 the behavior of the one-error group is contrasted to that of the ten-error group on the trial of and trials following S's first error which occurred following an avoidance response. As can be seen, after the first error the behavior of the ten-error group remains at virtually zero percent avoidance responses, whereas the behavior of the one-error

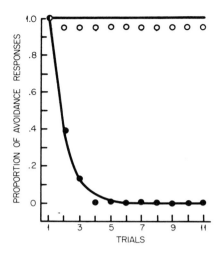

Fig. 3. Proportion of avoidance responses for (○) the no-error group ($N = 70$) and (●) the ten-error group ($N = 40$) on the trial of and trials following each S's first avoidance response in the Brelsford (1967) study. Predicted results (——); experimental results (○,●).

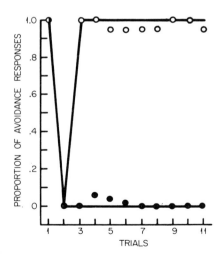

Fig. 4. Proportion of avoidance responses for (○) the one-error group ($N = 20$) and (●) the ten-error group ($N = 40$) on the trial of and trials following each S's first avoidance response in the Brelsford (1967) study. Predicted results (——); experimental results (○,●).

group jumped to virtually 100% avoidance responses after the introduction of the brief shock.

Brelsford (1967) also ran a control group in which he demonstrated that the simultaneous onset of $S_{|c}$ and the brief shock was not sufficient to support learning, and that the brief shock by itself did not unconditionally evoke running.

In summary, Brelsford (1967) was able to dramatically control Ss' behavior by experimentally manipulating physical variables which the memory interpretation links to the state-to-state transition parameters of the Markov process.

D.   Partial Reinforcement and Extinction

McGinnis (1966) has performed a series of experiments and subsequent mathematical analyses which shed much light on the avoidance conditioning process. In Experiment 1, McGinnis trained four groups of 10 rats each with shock probabilities (π) of .2, .4, .7 and 1.0 for at least 50 trials. Training was then followed by 150 extinction trials. Experiment 2 was essentially a replication with 20 Ss per group; π values of .1, .4, .7, and 1.0, at least 100 acquisition trials, and 200 extinction trials. In each experiment, shock was applied with probability π whenever S failed to respond to S_c within 5 sec.

The basic empirical results were that:

1.   The initial proportion of avoidance responses before the first shocked error was about .05.

2.   All groups reached the same asymptotic probability of avoiding, about .98.

3.   The average number of *shocked* errors was essentially the same for all groups regardless of the shock probability, π.

4.   All the groups extinguished at the same rate regardless of their acquisition π value.

5.   Only 30–50% of the subjects in each group extinguished in 150 to 200 trials.

E.   Stationarity: Effect of Initial and Asymptotic Avoidance Probabilities

An important, but overlooked observation which came out of both the Brelsford (1967) and Coulson (1967) studies was that control groups of 20 Ss that received 20 or 25 trials of $S_{|c}$ alone exhibited an overall avoidance probability of about .05. The Markov model in Eq. (10) requires that the initial probability of an avoidance response be absolutely zero. This deviation of the data from the boundary conditions of the model could cause problems, especially when questions of the predicted stationarity of the response probabilities on trials between the first avoidance response and last error were being considered. The Markov model predicts that *if* the probability of an avoidance response in the initial state, *N*, is *absolutely* zero and *if* the probability of an avoidance response in the asymptotic state, *L*, is *absolutely* unity, then the probability of an avoidance response on the intermediate trials between the first avoidance response and the last error should be a constant, P_I,

$$P_I = [(1 - q)(1 - s)]/[1 - qe - (1 - q)s] \qquad (13)$$

which is stationary and independent of the trial number. This stationarity prediction will not hold if either the probability of an avoidance response in state *N* is larger than zero or the probability of an avoidance response in state *L* is less than unity since on the average, even one success in state *N* would tend to add a large proportion of errors to the early part of the intermediate response sequence and one error in state *L* would tend to add a large proportion of successes to the later part of the intermediate response sequence. Although the hypothesis of stationary response probabilities could not be rejected on the basis of statistical tests in the Brelsford (1967), Coulson (1967), and Theios (1963) studies, the problem of the initial and asymptotic values is a sufficiently important theoretical issue that it cannot be ignored. On the basis of the Brelsford (1967), Coulson (1967), and McGinnis (1966) studies, it can be concluded that the initial probability of an avoidance response is not absolutely zero, but slightly higher, about .05.

McGinnis ran his rats 50 trials or more (Experiment 1) or 100 trials or more (Experiment 2) before giving them 150 (Experiment 1) or 200 (Experiment 2) extinction trials. The McGinnis experiments thus provide us with a large amount of asymptotic data to test the requirement that the asymptotic avoidance probability be 1.0. Estimates of the asymptotic probability of an avoidance response from the two McGinnis (1966) experiments were about .98. Thus, with the initial probability of an avoidance response equal to .05 and the asymptotic probability of an avoidance response equal to .98, we have no reason whatsoever to expect absolute stationarity of the response probability between the first avoidance response and the last error. Strictly speaking, the response probability vectors, and thus the models, presented in Eqs. (10) and (11) and in Theios (1963), Theios and Brelsford (1966a) and Brelsford (1967) are inapplicable to avoidance conditioning.

Many investigators have tested the stationarity prediction for rat avoidance conditioning and have been unable to reject it statistically (Theios, 1963; Bower & Theios, 1964; Theios & Dunaway, 1964; Ray, 1966a, 1966b, 1967; Isaacson & Olton, 1967; Theios & Brelsford, 1966a; Brelsford, 1967; and Coulson, 1967). The reasons for the failures to reject are themselves almost as numerous:

1. The use of a learning criterion (*e.g.*, 5, 10, or 20 consecutive) avoidance responses is almost universally used to determine when training stops. The asymptotic avoidance probability is so high that most *S*s will reach the learning criterion before they have a chance to make an asymptotic error. Thus, the use of a criterion stopping rule tends to bias the data in favor of the stationarity hypothesis. Polidora (1967) has commented on this problem.

2. In most avoidance conditioning situations with rats, the initial avoidance probability is so close to zero that relatively few *S*s will make an avoidance when in the initial state. Therefore, there are few occasions when the early part of the *intermediate* response sequence will contain errors actually made in the initial state.

3. One-way avoidance learning is typically very rapid and discrete. Many *S*s learn in a strictly all-or-none fashion with no responses between first avoidance and last error (*e.g.*, 26% in Theios, 1963; 64% in Theios & Brelsford, 1966; 20% in McGinnis, 1966; 53% in Coulson, 1967; and 30% in Ray, 1966a, 1966b). Many *S*s have only one response between the first avoidance and last error. Thus, the number of *S*s left to test the stationarity predictions is usually so small as to make the power of the test weak, again biasing the outcome of the test in the direction of the stationarity hypothesis.

In the McGinnis (1966) studies, where a performance criterion was not used to terminate training, most rats made at least one error very late in training after having more than 10 or 20 preceding consecutive avoidance responses. A stationarity test on this data, unrestricted by human impatience, would flatly reject the stationarity hypothesis. In view of these considerations, it is obvious that if we want to compare sequences of responses to predictions from theoretical models, we should *not* stop the learning process when a performance criterion is reached, but rather we should run each subject for a fixed and large number of trials to ensure that we get a reliable sample of asymptotic behavior.

IV. GENERAL MARKOV MODEL

A. Acquisition

In order for us to overcome the problems with stationarity, it is only necessary for us to change the response probability vector in Eq. (10) such that $\Pr(X_n = 0 | N_n) = p_N$, $\Pr(X_n = 0 | F_n) = p_F$, $\Pr(X_n = 0 | S_n) = p_S$, and $\Pr(X_n = 0 | L_n) = p_L$, where $0 < p_N, p_F < p_S, p_L < 1.0$. A detailed mathematical analysis of the model with these changes is presented in Theios and Brelsford (1966b). With respect to the error states, N and F, the generalized model changes only the probability of an avoidance response from zero to some value above but near zero. The memory states, S, and L are changed only by permitting the avoidance probabilities to be some value, less than but close to unity. The response probability vector of the general Markov process is as follows:

$$\Pr(X_n = 0 \mid L_n) = p_L$$
$$\Pr(X_n = 0 \mid S_n) = p_S$$
$$\Pr(X_n = 0 \mid F_n) = p_F \qquad (14)$$
$$\Pr(X_n = 0 \mid N_n) = p_N$$

The model given earlier in Eq. (10) can be obtained from this general model by assuming that p_N and p_F both equal zero and p_L and p_S both equal unity. It should be noted specifically that the general model does *not* require stationarity of the response sequences between the first avoidance and last error! This point is also discussed in Theios and Brelsford (1966b, p. 404).

McGinnis (1966) applied the general Markov model to his data and obtained very good fits for both of his experiments when he assumed that the shock probability π affected only the value of the parameter c and that all four of the groups in each experiment had the same values of the other parameters. To reduce the number of parameters, McGinnis (1966) assumed that $d = 0$ and that $s = e$. For sliding blocks of four trials, the obtained and predicted frequencies from McGinnis' Experiment 2 for each possible type of response sequence four trials long are presented in Table 3. The agreement between obtained and predicted frequencies was even closer for his Experiment 1.

Figure 5 presents the proportion of avoidance responses as a function of blocks of 10 trials for the four conditions of Experiment 2 along with the predictions from the general Markov model with only the parameter c varying across groups as a function of π. A similar fit was obtained for Experiment 1. It can be seen that the predicted mean learning curve becomes more and more S-shaped as the shock probability π, and thus the value of c, is decreased.

According to the memory interpretation of the general Markov model

TABLE 3

Frequency of response sequences in sliding blocks of four trials, predictions from the general model with one parameter varying across groups, and minimum χ^2 parameter estimates[a,b,c]

Sequence	Data	Pred.	Data	Pred.	Data	Pred.	Data	Pred.
0000	1558	1501	1351	1345	1290	1244	495	549
0001	48	50	49	47	37	45	35	23
0010	53	53	45	49	31	47	25	24
0011	9	15	22	16	17	16	23	12
0100	56	57	49	54	33	52	20	27
0101	7	16	10	16	18	16	29	12
0110	10	18	14	18	16	18	19	13
0111	8	12	24	19	24	23	47	56
1000	67	69	69	66	56	63	44	34
1001	14	18	18	18	12	18	14	13
1010	10	20	14	21	20	21	25	15
1011	7	14	15	21	22	25	42	57
1100	25	28	38	30	35	30	39	21
1101	9	16	19	24	24	29	36	60
1110	23	23	43	34	42	39	56	67
1111	36	30	160	162	263	252	991	955
χ^2	28.6		17.6		21.8		96.1	
π	1.0		0.7		0.4		0.1	
c	.320		.086		.058		.011	

[a]McGinnis (1966) Experiment 2 Acquisition Data.

[b]The use of sliding blocks of trials violates the χ^2 assumption of independence of observations. Therefore, the χ^2 values reported are to be interpreted only as measures of the weighted, squared error between the data and the predictions. Violation of independence generally results in a conservative bias in this type of test (*cf.* Holland, 1967).

[c]p_N = .050, p_I = .578, p_L = .980, s = .066

the shock S_u serves three functions. First, the pairing of S_c–S_u establishes the fear association S_c–r_e. Second, it forces the learning of the s_e–R_{run} association. Third, it provides an opportunity for an S_c–r_e association lost from short-term memory to be reestablished and stored back either in short-term or in long-term memory. Because the memory interpretation assumes that all three of the learning events take place on shocked-error trials and that either the loss of S_c–r_e from short-term memory or nothing takes place on avoidance trials, the prediction can be made that groups trained with different shock probabilities should have the same learning curves if all the nonshocked error trials are deleted from the response sequences. Figure 6 presents the mean learning curves for the four groups in Experiment 2 with the nonshocked error trials deleted. As can be seen, the curves are almost identical, giving

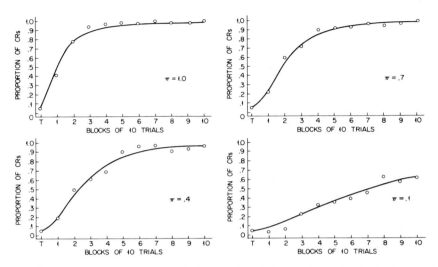

Fig. 5. Mean learning curves for the McGinnis (1966) Experiment 2. Obtained (○) and predicted (——) proportions of avoidance responses (CRs) in blocks of 10 trials as a function of π, the probability of shock on an error trial. (1) 1.0; (2) .7; (3) .4; (4) .1.

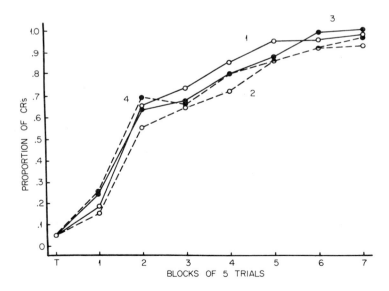

Fig. 6. Adjusted mean learning curves for the McGinnis (1966) Experiment 2. Proportion of avoidance responses (CRs) in blocks of 5 trials when nonshocked error trials have been deleted.

more support for the memory interpretation. The curves for Experiment 1 presented a picture similar to that of Figure 6.

McGinnis also made predictions from a modified two-element stimulus sampling model which permitted asymptotes less than unity and counterconditioning on nonshocked errors. This model is presented in detail in Section 6.5 of Atkinson *et al.*, (1965) as an attempt to explain extinction. The predictions of the modified stimulus sampling model fit the data less well than those of the general Theios and Brelsford (1966b) model for Experiments 1 and 2 both in acquisition and in extinction.

B. Extinction

To account for extinction, McGinnis reversed the general model and modified it with the following theoretical interpretation. As a result of performing the instrumental avoidance response a large number of times the organism may become fatigued with probability f, whereupon his avoidance probability drops from $p_{|L}$ to $p_{|F}$, where $1.0 \geqslant p_{|L} > p_{|F} \geqslant 0$. As a result of the fatigue, a response incompatible with the instrumental running response may become counterconditioned to the fear stimulus s_e. When this counterconditioning happens, the animal is extinguished and the avoidance probability drops to a very low value, $p_{|E}$, which is near zero.

The transition matrix and starting and response probability vectors for McGinnis's extinction model are

$$
\begin{array}{cc}
 & \begin{array}{ccc} L_{n+1} & F_{n+1} & E_{n+1} \end{array} \quad \Pr(X_n = 0 \mid \cdot) \\
\begin{array}{c} L_n \\ F_n \\ E_n \end{array} &
\begin{bmatrix} 1-f & f & 0 \\ 0 & 1-c' & c' \\ 0 & 0 & 1 \end{bmatrix}
\begin{bmatrix} p_L \\ p_F \\ p_E \end{bmatrix}
\end{array}
\tag{15}
$$

$$\Pr(L_1, F_1, E_1) = (1, 0, 0)$$

where $0 < f$, $c \lessgtr 1.0$ and $0 \leqslant p_E < p_F < p_{|L} \leqslant 1.0$, and the states L, F, and E stand for long-term memory, fatigued, and extinguished. Predicted and obtained frequencies of the various four trial response sequences for sliding blocks of four trials are given in Table 4 for the 200 extinction trials of Experiment 2. The agreement between the obtained and predicted frequencies for the 150 extinction trials of Experiment 1 was even closer than that of Experiment 2.

TABLE 4

McGinnis (1966) Experiment 2 Combined Extinction Data.
Frequency of Response Sequences in Sliding Blocks of Four Trials,
Predictions, and Minimum x^2 Parameter Estimates [a,b]

Sequence	Obtained	Predicted
0000	9745	9156
0001	183	246
0010	148	213
0011	62	63
0100	136	203
0101	35	35
0110	27	30
0111	73	82
1000	145	199
1001	27	28
1010	23	24
1011	39	49
1100	36	24
1101	27	38
1110	36	33
1111	5018	5338

$x^2 = 142.7$

[a] $p_L = .98$ $c' = .005$ $p_F = .383$ $s = .099$ $p_E = 0$

[b] The use of sliding blocks violates the x^2 assumption of independence of observations. Therefore, the x^2 value should be interpreted only as a measure of the weighted, squared error between the data and the predictions. Violation of independence generally results in a conservative bias in this type of test (*cf.* Holland, 1967).

C.   Finite Integer Analysis

In summary, we have amassed a large amount of data in support of the hypothesis that a general four-state Markov model interpreted in terms of short-term and long-term memory processes is a reasonable approximation to the avoidance conditioning of rats in a one-way response situation. Further, it has been shown that the initial probability of an avoidance response is not absolutely zero nor is the asymptotic avoidance probability absolutely unity. The use of a performance criterion to designate termination of training tends to foster the misconception that the asymptotic avoidance probability is unity. Given these two observations, we have shown that it is not reasonable to require a prediction of stationarity of the intermediate response probabilities from the Markov models, and as such, the typical statistical tests of stationarity are neither crucial, relevant, nor desirable as evidence bearing on the question of whether avoidance conditioning is a Markov process. For example, on the basis of the outcome of a stationarity test, Beecroft and Bouska (1967) concluded that the two-element sampling interpretation of the Markov model was inapplicable to their data on avoidance conditioning in a runway. On the other hand, a detailed examination of their raw data, which is presented in their article, indicates that the general model could probably be successfully applied to their data if the assumption were made that the asymptotic probability of an avoidance response was about .90 rather than 1.00. This is reasonable given the observation that the Beecroft–Bouska rats had only 3 sec to run a *6-ft long alley*. It is not unreasonable to expect the asymptotic latency or response time distribution to be such that .10 of its probability density falls above 3 sec. One would expect that the asymptotic avoidance probability would increase as the $S_{|c}$-$S_{|u}$ interval was increased. In view of these considerations, it is quite unreasonable to expect that the asymptotic avoidance probability will be unity invariantly across all experimental conditions, such as very short $S_{|c}$-$S_{|u}$ intervals.

What the general Markov approach requires is that underlying the subject's sequence of responses, there are only three, ordered, *theoretical*, avoidance probability values: $p_{\setminus}$, p_{I}, and $p_{|_L}$. Respectively, these correspond to the naive (unlearned), intermediate, and long-term memory (learned) states of the process. The intermediate state encompasses both short-term memory and temporary losses from short-term memory. The facts are that the theoretical probability values and the trials on which they are in effect will never be known exactly since they are unobservable random variables (*cf.* Greeno & Steiner, 1964). They can, however, be approximated by maximum likelihood decision criteria through methods discussed in Theios (1968a). The error in these estimates can be large, however, when applied to the short response sequences which characterize much avoidance conditioning data. The method discussed by Theios (1968a), called finite integer analysis, involves choosing for each subject two trials, i and j, such that the likelihood of the subject's sequence of avoidance and escape responses is maximized by assuming that: $p_{|N}$ is approximated by the proportion of avoidance responses on trials 1 to i; p_I is approximated by the proportion of avoidance responses on trials $i+1$ to j; $p_{|L}$ is approximated by the proportion of avoidance responses on trials after trial j. This technique merely breaks the S's response sequence into three segments where it is most likely that the avoidance probabilities within each segment are as homogeneous as possible. This can be seen clearly by considering a modified cumulative recorder which takes one step to the right when an S fails to avoid and takes one step up when he avoids. This type of cumulative record for a response sequence generated by the Markov process with three probability values ought to be approximated by three straight line segments with slopes of $p_N/(1-p_N)$, $p_I/(1-p_I)$, and $p_L/(1-p_L)$ respectively.[2]

As an example, consider five response sequences from the Beecroft and Bouska (1967) study which would probably cause the most trouble for a stationarity analysis. The cumulative records of these five response sequences are presented in Figure 7 and each has been fitted with three straight lines using a "least-squares-by-eye" method. Similar or identical break points would have been selected using Theios' (1968a) finite integer analysis. Obviously, three straight lines do give a reasonable approximation to these data, and from the standpoint of the Markov model, these are probably the most nonstationary subjects of the Beecroft and Bouska (1967) sample. A detailed examination of the records in Figure 7 shows that S 43 has an initial avoidance probability value greater than 0, 1 avoidance out of 14 trials for an individual maximum likelihood estimate of .07. Further, 3 of the Ss (69, 47, and 64) have asymptotic probability values less than 1, about .81, whereas the other 2 Ss have asymptotic levels of 1.00. The latter 2 Ss, however, had their training stopped after 10 consecutive avoidances, so we do not know whether they would have made further errors. On the basis of the McGinnis (1966) results, the strong suspicion is that they would have made further errors if training had been continued for a rather large number of trials.

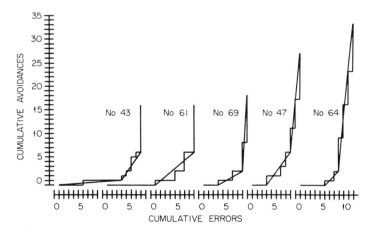

Fig. 7. Cumulative records of rats 43, 47, 61, 64, and 69 of the Beecroft and Bouska (1967) experiment. Three straight line segments have been fitted "by eye" to each record.

[2] I would like to acknowledge the fact that Colin G. McDiarmid introduced this type of analysis to me.

A complete finite integer analysis was performed on the Beecroft and Bouska (1967) data. The assumption was made that if the data were not characterized by three levels of performance, as required by the general Markov model, but by more levels, then one should be able to reject the hypothesis of three levels of performance in favor of a hypothesis that there are at least four levels of performance. A likelihood ratio test (Theios, 1968a; Lowe and Theios, 1968) indicated that the hypothesis of three levels of performance could not be rejected in favor of the hypothesis of four or more levels. For this type of test, Theios (1968b) has shown that -2 times the natural logarithm of the likelihood ratio is approximately distributed as the X^2 statistic with four degrees of freedom. If we let R represent this transformed likelihood ratio, the obtained average value of R was .7 and the largest was 2.27. A value of R equal to 4 or larger has probability of .6 of occurring by chance under the hypothesis that the data were really generated by a process with three discrete performance levels. Under the three-state hypothesis, the finite integer analysis indicated that the average avoidance probability in the initial state (p_N) would be .016, the average probability in the intermediate state (p_I) would be about .69 and the average avoidance probability in the terminal state (p_L) would be .995. Close inspection of the data, however, revealed that in 29 of the 30 rats, the third performance level was restricted to the criterion run of 10 avoidances. This fact suggests that the third performance level really was an artificial level created by the criterion stopping rule. To test this suspicion, a likelihood ratio test was performed between the hypothesis of only two discrete performance levels and the hypothesis of three levels. The average likelihood ratio transformation score (R) was 3.43, $(p > .5)$ and the largest R was 7.87 $(p > .1)$, indicating insufficient evidence to reject the hypothesis of only two avoidance probability values. Under the hypothesis of two discrete performance levels, the average initial avoidance probability (p_N) is .08, the asymptotic avoidance probability (p_L) is .9, and the average trial of transition from p_N to p_L is 8. In summary, data originally cited as being inconsistent with the restricted two-element stimulus sampling form of the Markov model have now been shown to be consistent with a simpler model which postulates only one jump in performance.

D. Homogeneity of Parameter Values

In all the applications of mathematical models to the avoidance data cited or presented here, it has been assumed that the sample of subjects was homogeneous with respect to the values of the parameters of the process. This is a difficult assumption to make because it is hard to believe that there would not be some individual differences in a sample of 100 or so rats or 30 mongrel dogs. Weitzman (1966) was concerned with the question of individual differences and looked at the Solomon and Wynne (1953) and Theios (1963) data with respect to individual differences in the parameters of the stimulus sampling interpretation of the Markov model. For the Theios (1963) data, he found that if there were individual differences in the single parameter c of the two-element sampling model, then the variance of the distribution was less than .001, negligible for practical purposes. We can strongly suspect that similar results would hold for the more general forms of the model considered in this paper in Eqs. (10), (11), and (14). Coulson (1967) theorized that if there were individual differences in his sample of 245 rats, then Ss that quickly learn the first stage (have a high value of c) would probably also quickly learn the second stage (also have a high value of e) and vice versa. With this state of affairs, there should be a positive correlation between the length of a S's initial run of escapes and the number of responses between his first avoidance and last escape.

> A correlation was made between number of responses before the first avoidance and number of *identifiable* trials in [the intermediate state] . . . The correlation thus derived was significant (r = .12, z = 1.88, $p < .05$, for a one-tailed test) but so low as to accord with the conclusions of Weitzman, among others, that individual differences, although possible in the closely controlled conditions which generate the data upon which mathematical models are usually based, are usually not of a high enough magnitude to be relevant [Coulson, 1967, p. 35].

The facts are that there is enough inherent variability in the stochastic process to permit what looks like gross individual differences in the response sequences.

E.   Lack of Transfer in Shuttle Conditioning

A most interesting finding of the Weitzman (1966) analyses was that if the shuttle-box behavior of each of the Solomon and Wynne dogs were separated into two sequences, one for responses from left to right and one for responses from right to left, then the two-element sampling model fit the data and there were no individual differences needed in the single parameter c. Predictions for the initial 5-trial response sequences were made from the model in Eq. (10) for the separate right-going and left-going responses of the 30 dogs in the Solomon and Wynne (1953) study. The observed and predicted sequences are presented in Table 5.

TABLE 5

Initial Split-Half Response Sequences from Solomon and Wynne (1953) Shuttle Study and Predictions from the General Markov Model[a]

Sequence	Observed	Predicted
11111	6	10
11110	11	8
11101	4	3
11100	13	11
11011	2	2[b]
11010	4	3
11001	2	1[b]
11000	9	13
10111	0	1[b]
10110	1	1[b]
10101	0	1[b]
10100	1	3
10011	1	1[b]
10010	1	1[b]
10001	0	0[b]
10000	5	6

[a] $c = .56$, $d = .16$, $e = .45$, $s = 0$, $q = .76$
$\chi^2(4) = 8.64$, $.10 > p > .05$

[b] These cells were pooled together for the test. The parameter s was set equal to zero by assumption.

The goodness-of-fit could not be rejected by a chi-square test, $\chi^2(4) = 8.68$, $.10 > p > .05$. This indicates that the dogs were learning the shuttle task as two independent problems, and there was no transfer from responding in one direction to responding in the other. Surprisingly, Isaacson and Olton (1967) have subsequently confirmed this observation for rats in a shuttle situation. They state:

We have reanalyzed our data reported in our two-way active avoidance problem as if animals were learning two separate problems, *i.e.*, the right to left problem and the left to right problem. From preliminary examination of the data it was clear that a multistage model such as discussed by Bower and Theios (1964) and Hilgard and Bower (1966) among others, was appropriate. According to such models, an animal enters the training situation with a low probability of making an avoidance response. After some period of training, it enters a second stage in which the probability of making an avoidance response is increased, but less than unity and is constant. The third stage occurs when the probability of an avoidance response, is, or approaches unity (Isaacson and Olton, 1967).

The findings that there is lack of transfer in the avoidance situation is further strengthened by an observation from my first avoidance experiment (Theios, 1963). Fifty rats were trained to avoid in one direction, *e.g.*, black to white and left to right (or vice versa). After 20 consecutive avoidance responses each S was given reversal learning, *e.g.*, run from white to black and right to left. The amazing observation was that there were no differences between original and reversal learning. For example, the Ss made an average of 4.8 errors during acquisition and 4.6 errors on reversal. Whether lack of transfer from one side of a shuttlebox to another is universal for rats, dogs, and other animals remains to be decided by future research as does the question of whether a Markov model can handle the separate halves of shuttle avoidance training.

V.   RESPONSE LATENCY

In my opinion, the most pressing problem facing mathematical models for learning is to account for changes in the shape of the response latency distribution as a function of trials. In general, the question of response latency has been almost universally neglected by mathematical learning theorists. To look only at dichotomized responses is to ignore most of the data, perhaps the most interesting part. In thinking about response latency in the avoidance situation, it seems obvious that the latency of avoidance responses should be separated from the latency of the escape responses, since the application of the S_u drastically changes the situation for the subject and almost forces the response with a rather short latency after its application. We thus will consider the two processes separately.

A.   Avoidance Latencies

Consider first the latency of the avoidance response. If we use the general Markov model with the response probability vector presented in Eq. (14) we can assume that there is a unique latency distribution associated with each of the four states of the process, N, F, S, and L. This method was outlined by Theios (1965a), Millward (1964), and by Suppes, Groen, and Schlag-Rey (1966). Let t be a response-time random variable and let $f_N(t)$, $f_F(t)$, $f_S(t)$ and $f_L(t)$ be the probability density functions for t in the various states. The avoidance probability in each of the states of the process is directly related to the avoidance latency distributions. With t as the avoidance latency random variable, let t' represent the length of the S_c–S_u interval. The integrals of the density functions for t from $t = 0$ up to $t = 't'$ will be the avoidance probabilities for Z indexing states, N, F, S, and L,

$$p_Z = \int_0^{t'} f_Z(t) \, dt. \tag{14a}$$

Since the avoidance latency distributions are truncated at t', the point of application of the S_u, they have to be normalized from 0 to t' so that their integral is unity. The normalization can be achieved by dividing the distributions by their integrals from 0 to t'. Let $g_Z(t)$ represent the normalized theoretical avoidance latency distribution for state Z, $Z = N,F,S,L$,

$$g_Z(t) = f_Z(t)/p_Z. \tag{16}$$

The theoretical distribution of avoidance latencies for a group of homogeneous subjects on trial n of an experiment is a simple probability mixture of the four normalized theoretical latency distributions (*cf.* Falmagne, 1965),

$$f_n(t) = g_N(t) \cdot \Pr(N_n) + g_F(t) \cdot \Pr(F_n) + g_S(t) \cdot \Pr(S_n)$$
$$+ g_L(t) \cdot \Pr(L_n) \tag{17}$$

where $\Pr(Z_n)$ is the probability of the process being in state Z on trial n, $Z = N, F, S, L$.

The form and parameters of the initial avoidance latency distribution, $f_N(t)$, could be estimated from an initial control session in which subjects were given unpaired S_c and S_u trials. The form and parameters of the asymptotic avoidance latency distribution, $f_L(t)$, could be estimated for individual subjects from a very large number of asymptotic trials. From a casual observation of latency distributions obtained in avoidance situations, it seems reasonable that the $f_N(t)$ distribution might be a normal or a gamma distribution with a relatively large number of steps and that the $f_L(t)$ distribution might be a generalized gamma with a relatively few number of steps (*cf.* McGill, 1963; McGill & Gibbon, 1965). If we do not wish to consider explicitly the forms of the theoretical latency distributions, the model makes a number of distribution-free predictions regarding average avoidance latency. Let $E_Z(t)$ be the expectation of the theoretical avoidance latency distribution of state Z, for $Z = N, F, S, L$,

$$E_Z(t) = \int_0^{t'} t\, g_Z(t)\, dt. \tag{18}$$

Then, the theoretical expectation of the latency of an avoidance response on trial n will be equal to

$$E_n(t) = E_N(t) \cdot \Pr(N_n) + E_F(t) \cdot \Pr(F_n)$$
$$+ E_S(t) \cdot \Pr(S_n) + E_L(t) \cdot \Pr(L_n). \tag{19}$$

An estimate of $E_N(t)$ can be taken as the mean avoidance latency on the first trial of the experiment since if all subjects are in state N on the first trial, then for the first trial Eq. (19) reduces to

$$E_1(t) = E_N(t). \tag{20}$$

If no subject avoids on the first trial of the experiment or during a pretest session without S_u, then $f_N(t)$ can be taken as zero. When this is the case, Eqs. (17) and (19) have to be normalized by dividing them by the sum of the probabilities of being in the states in which an avoidance response can occur. For example, if both $g_N(t)$ and $g_F(t)$ equal zero for all t, then Eq. (17) reduces to

$$g_n(t) = [g_S(t) \cdot \Pr(S_n) + g_L(t) \cdot \Pr(L_n)]/[\Pr(S_n) + \Pr(L_n)] \tag{21}$$

and Eq. (19) reduces to

$$E_n(t) = [E_S(t) \cdot \Pr(S_n) + E_L(t) \cdot \Pr(L_n)]/[\Pr(S_n) + \Pr(L_n)]. \tag{22}$$

Similarly, since as n becomes large, $\Pr(L_n)$ approaches unity, an estimate of the $E_L(t)$ can be obtained from the asymptotic mean response latency since

$$\lim_{n \to \infty} E_n(t) = E_L(t). \tag{23}$$

B. Escape Latencies

Latencies on escape trials can be handled in a manner similar to that used for avoidance latencies. For each state of the Markov process there is associated a theoretical distribution of escape times, conditional on an escape response being made. Denote the probability density functions for the escape times as $h_N(t)$, $h_F(t)$, $h_S(t)$, and $h_L(t)$, respectively. Each of the theoretical distributions would have zero density from $t = 0$ up to $t = t'$. The theoretical escape latency for a homogeneous group of subjects on trial n of an experiment is the simple probability mixture

$$h_n(t) = h_N(t) \cdot \Pr(N_n) + h_F(t) \cdot \Pr(F_n) + h_S(t) \cdot \Pr(S_n)$$
$$+ h_L(t) \cdot \Pr(L_n). \quad (24)$$

The form and parameter values of the initial escape latency distribution, $h_N(t)$, could be estimated from the obtained distribution of escape responses on the first trial of an experiment with homogeneous subjects. Most probably $h_N(t)$ could be approximated by some gammalike distribution with relatively large time constants and a dead time[3] from $t = 0$ up to $t = t'$. The form and parameter values of the asymptotic escape latency distribution, $h_L(t)$, could be estimated from the obtained asymptotic latency distribution of subjects given a large number of *escape* training trials. Presumably, $h_L(t)$ could be approximated by a generalized gamma distribution with a relatively few number of steps, relatively small time constants, and a dead time from $t = 0$ up to $t = t'$. A reasonable starting assumption would be that $h_S(t) = h_F(t) = h_L(t)$. Under that assumption, the theoretical escape latency distribution would reduce to

$$h_n(t) = h_N(t) \cdot \Pr(N_n) + h_L(t)[1 - \Pr(N_n)]. \quad (25)$$

where $$\Pr(N_n) = (1 - c)^{n-1}. \quad (26)$$

If it were assumed that the probability of an avoidance response were unity when the process was in the memory states S and L, then the escape latency distributions for those states would have no density and Eq. (24) would reduce to

$$h_n(t) = [h_N(t) \cdot \Pr(N_n) + h_F(t) \cdot \Pr(F_n)]/[\Pr(N_n) + \Pr(F_n)]. \quad (27)$$

Equation (27) can be tested easily since values for $\Pr(N_n)$ and $\Pr(F_n)$ can be obtained from analysis of the avoidance-error sequences (*cf.* Theios & Brelsford, 1966a, 1966b) and estimates of $h_N(t)$ and $h_L(t)$ are easily obtained from the mean initial and asymptotic escape latencies.

C. Response Latency on Trial n

It should be obvious now that the theoretical considerations given in

[3]A *dead time* in a latency distribution is an initial refractory period after the presentation of a stimulus during which responses are never observed to occur. The probability distribution has zero density during the dead time.

the preceding two sections can be mixed to yield the overall response latency. The response latency distribution on trial n, irrespective of whether an avoidance or an escape occurred, is equal to the simple probability mixture,

$$f_n(t) = g_n(t) \cdot \Pr(X_n = 0) + h_n(t) \cdot \Pr(X_n = 1) \qquad (28)$$

where $\Pr(X_{|n} = 0)$ is the theoretical probability of an avoidance on trial n and $\Pr(X_n = 1) = 1 - \Pr(X_n = 0)$ is the theoretical probability of an escape response on trial n,

$$\Pr(X_n = 0) = p_N \cdot \Pr(N_n) + p_F \cdot \Pr(F_n)$$
$$+ p_S \cdot \Pr(S_n) + p_L \cdot \Pr(L_n). \qquad (29)$$

Values for $\Pr(N_n)$, $\Pr(F_n)$, $\Pr(S_n)$, and $\Pr(L_n)$ can be obtained from the Markov process given earlier in Eq. (10).

D. Coulson's Latency Analysis

Coulson (1967) tested a number of latency assumptions for the Markov model presented in Eq. (10). He assumed that $f_N(t)$ and $f_F(t)$ were equal to zero for $t = 0$ up to $t = t'$. In other words, he assumed that the probability of an avoidance in the naive and forgotten states was equal to zero. He also assumed that the integrals of $f_S(t)$ and $f_L(t)$ from $t = 0$ up to $t = t'$ were both equal to unity. In other words, the probability of an avoidance response in the short-term and long-term memory states was assumed to be one. Under these assumptions, if the short-term to long-term memory transfer parameter, s, is taken to be zero, the model predicts that the mean avoidance latency for each trial of a criterion run of avoidances should be stationary and constant. The fact that the mean latencies in Coulson's (1967) criterion data decreased systematically indicates that the parameter s must have a value greater than zero. With the parameter e, the probability of transferring from state F to state L, set at zero he estimated s, the probability of transferring from state S to state L, to be about .26 from latency considerations alone and found a very similar estimate for s if only the dichotomous sequences of escapes and avoidances were considered. As an estimate of the expectation of $f_L(t)$, Coulson used .86 sec, the observed mean latency on the last trial of the criterion run of 10. As an estimate of the expectation of $f_S(t)$ Coulson used 2.19 sec, the observed mean latency of the first avoidance response of the criterion run, which also was equal to the mean of all the intermediate avoidance latencies between the first avoidance and last escape response. With Coulson's assumptions, the equation for the theoretically expected mean avoidance latency on the ith trial of the criterion run is

$$E_i(t) = E_S(t) \cdot (1 - s)^{i-1} + E_L(t)[1 - (1 - s)^{i-1}]$$

$$E_i(t) = (2.19)(.64)^{i-1} + (.86)[1 - (.64)^{i-1}].$$

(30)

For i from 1 to 10, the predicted values of $E_i(t)$ are 2.19, 1.70, 1.38, 1.18, 1.05, .97, .91, .88, .87, and .86 sec. Coulson (1967) states that, "The predicted values are so close to the observed data that a statistical test would supply little information."

Coulson's latency assumptions lead to the prediction that both the mean avoidance and the mean escape latencies on the intermediate trials between the subjects' first avoidance and last error should be stationary and equal to the expectations of $f_S(t)$ and $h_F(t)$, respectively. The mean avoidance and escape latencies decreased significantly over intermediate trials. This failure of the stationarity test for latencies can be taken to indicate that Coulson's assumptions about the probability of an avoidance response being zero for states N and F and unity for states S and L were not justified. A few long latency avoidance responses when in states N and F and a few failures to avoid when in states S and L could have permitted a large number of state N escape latencies and a large number of state L avoidance latencies to enter the stationarity analyses which are supposed to be restricted entirely to F and S state responses.

It is obvious that Coulson's (1967) latency analyses and the theoretical latency assumptions suggested in this paper represent only the initial steps in a much needed program of systematic analysis of latency mechanisms in avoidance conditioning. Most crucially, reasonable assumptions regarding the forms of the underlying theoretical distributions need to be arrived at through carefully executed normative studies. In terms of research strategy, it would seem best to start by attempting to account for the trial-by-trial changes in response latency which take place in simple escape learning before attempting to account for latency changes in the avoidance situation which includes the avoidance process as well as the escape process.

E. Analysis of Escape Latencies

Coulson and Theios (unpublished) performed a shock-escape experiment specifically to investigate latency changes. Using the two-compartment apparatus described by Theios and Brelsford (1966a), 100 rats were given 40 one-way shock escape trials with an intertrial interval of 30 sec. Each trial began with the raising of the door between the compartments and application of a 2.5 mA electric shock. The S was replaced in the shock compartment 15 sec after its escape response. Observation of the behavior of the Ss indicated that their responses on the first escape trial were characteristically different from all other escape responses. The mean escape latency on the first trial was unusually long, 4.8 sec. Invariably, a S's first response to the onset of shock was to bite the shock grid bars, which from the S's point of view had disastrous consequences. This rarely happened on subsequent trials, and the changes in latency from Trials 2–40 were very orderly. Presumably, the first trial problem could have been eliminated if the rats had been given a number of pretraining experiences with inescapable shock.

TABLE 6

Mean Escape Latencies

Trials	Predicted	Observed
2-6	1.65	1.60
7-11	1.10	1.05
12-16	.82	.74
17-21	.68	.68
22-26	.61	.62
27-31	.57	.59
32-36	.56	.56
37-40	.55	.54

For theoretical purposes, we will proceed with the following assumptions. On the first trial of the escape experiment, all Ss were in a naïve state in which the theoretical distribution of shock escape times had a large mean (4.8 sec) due to the fact that the Ss were prone to bite the bars. Following its first shock experience, every rat learned with probability 1 not to bite the bars and thus it moved to a second state in which the expectation of the theoretical escape latency distribution was equal to 1.98 sec, the obtained mean escape latency on the second trial. Following each escape response in the second state, the S had probability c of learning a more efficient escape response which had a theoretical latency distribution with an expectation of .54 sec, the obtained asymptotic escape latency. In other words, if we let t_2 represent the expected escape latency in the second state and t represent the expected latency in the asymptotic state, then following Eq. (25), the expected latency on trial n, for $n = 2, 3, \ldots, 40$, will be equal to

$$t_n = t_2(1 - c)^{n-1} + t[1 - (1 - c)^{n-1}]$$

$$t_n = t + (t_2 - t)(1 - c)^{n-1}. \tag{31}$$

As parameter estimates, $t_2 = 1.98$, $t = .54$, and $c = .14$ were chosen as giving a reasonable approximation to the actual data. The data and the predictions from Eq. (31) are given in Table 6 in blocks of 5 trials. It is difficult to imagine how the data points could be much closer to the predictions than they are now.

F. Analysis of Overall Response Latency

Using Coulson's (1967) data and his latency assumptions described in Section V,D, an analysis will be made of the mean response latency on Trial n of the avoidance conditioning experiment irrespective of whether or not the response was an avoidance or an escape. Training in the Coulson (1967) experiment was terminated when each rat reached a criterion of 10 consecutive avoidance responses. In order to avoid a systematic bias in response latency due to dropping out Ss that reached criterion, only the unbiased latency data from the first eleven trials will be considered in this analysis. When it is assumed that the avoidance probabilities are zero in states N and F and are unity in states S and L, then Eq. (28) becomes

$$f_n(t) = h_N(t) \cdot \Pr(N_n) + h_F(t) \cdot \Pr(F_n) + g_S(t) \cdot \Pr(S_n)$$

$$+ g_L(t) \cdot \Pr(L_n). \tag{32}$$

We can represent the expectations of the five theoretical distributions as t_n, t_N, t_F, t_S and t_L. According to the model of Eq. (10), the probabilities of being in the various states on trial n are

$$\Pr(N_n) = (1 - c)^{n-1} \tag{33}$$

$$\Pr(F_n) = q(1 - d)(\theta - c)^{-1}[(1 - c)^{n-1} - (1 - \theta)^{n-1}] \tag{34}$$

$$\Pr(S_n) = (1 - q)(1 - d)(\theta - c)^{-1}[(1 - c)^{n-1} - (1 - \theta)^{n-1}] \tag{35}$$

$$\Pr(L_n) = 1 - \Pr(N_n) - \Pr(E_n) - \Pr(S_n) \tag{36}$$

where $\theta = (1-q)s + qe$ and $n = 1, 2, 3, \ldots$. The expected response latency on trial n is just the simple probability mixture

$$t_n = t_N \cdot \Pr(N_n) + t_F \cdot \Pr(F_n) + t_S \cdot \Pr(S_n) + t_L \cdot \Pr(L_n). \tag{37}$$

An estimate of t_N = 6.96 sec was taken from the mean escape latency on the first trial of the experiment. An estimate of t_F = 6.19 sec was taken from the mean latency of all escape responses which occurred somewhere in the sequence after the first avoidance response. An estimate of t_S = 2.19 sec was taken from the mean latency of avoidance responses before the last escape response in each sequence. An estimate of t_L = .86 was taken from the asymptotic avoidance latency. Estimates of s, e, and q were taken as those that previously were used when considering the dichotomous responses presented in Table 2 of Section III. The parameter d was set equal to zero by assumption to render the model identifiable. You will recall that the parameter c caused trouble earlier in Section III when the sequences of avoidances and responses were considered. For the present latency analysis, a value of c = .39, along with the values for the other parameters given above, gave a reasonable description of the latency changes as can be seen in Figure 8. A value of c = .39, incidentally, is the average of the c estimates obtained from the identifiable states analysis described in Section III. In Figure 8 the obtained and predicted mean latencies are virtually identical except for one point.

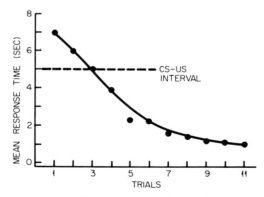

Fig. 8. Obtained and predicted mean response time (sec) as a function of trials in the Coulson (1967) avoidance conditioning experiment ($N = 245$). (●) experimental data; (——) theory.

VI. CHOICE REVERSAL UNDER AVERSIVE STIMULATION

A. Effect of Overtraining during Original Learning

Using a correction procedure, Theios (1965b) trained 100 rats to choose one of two arms of a T-maze in order to escape electric shock. A trial began with the simultaneous opening of the door of the starting compartment and application of shock to the grid floor of the maze. The trial ended when the S entered the correct, nonelectrified goal box. Four groups of 25 Ss each were given 0, 5, 15 or 35 additional trials of overtraining after they had reached a criterion of 5 consecutive correct choices. Choice reversal learning followed directly after each S's last acquisition trial, and it was found that overtraining systematically retarded reversal learning. The increase in errors made by the groups that received overtraining was entirely in the run of errors before the first correct choice. Using a criterion of 10 consecutive correct choices during reversal, the differences between the mean trials of the last error and mean total errors were essentially equal for all four groups as were the differences between mean total errors and mean number of errors before the first correct choice.

Theios (1965b) applied the two-operator linear model of Eq. (8) to the reversal data and found that in order to account for the systematic decrease in errors before the first correct choice, the assumption had to be made that the value of the error operator α_1 which applied following incorrect choices during reversal learning was systematically increased by overtraining during original learning. Permitting α_1 to increase, however, results in the prediction that the differences between the means of the trial of last error, total number of errors, and the number of errors before the first correct choice should increase systematically with overtraining. This was not true in the data, indicating that the two-operator linear model gives a less than adequate description of the shock escape reversal process.

On the other hand, the overtraining-reversal data can be easily accounted for by the Markov model given in Eq. (10). Applied to reversal of choice behavior, the model may be given the following interpretation. During original training, the subject is trained to choose consistently one of two mutually exclusive response alternatives (R_1 or R_2). In the shock escape situation, the aversive S_u provides the stimulus for the choice response. At the beginning of reversal training an S_u–R_1 association has been established and stored in long-term memory. During reversal S_u–R_1 is never followed by reinforcement (pain reduction through the removal of S_u), but the S_u–R_2 is always followed by reinforcement. Following any incorrect choice, an association may be formed between S_u and R_2 with probability c. With probability d the S_u–R_2 association may be stored directly in long-term memory, replacing the S_u–R_1 association. With probability $1-d$ the S_u–R_2 association may be stored in short-term memory. When the S_u–R_2 association is stored in short-term memory and the S_u–R_1 association is stored in long-term memory, the S_u will evoke R_1 with probability q and will evoke R_2 with probability $1-q$. Given that the S_u–R_2 association is in short-term memory, the probability that the S_u–R_2 association is transferred to long-term memory replacing the S_u–R_1 association is s following a successful choice and e following an error.

The model in Eq. (10) predicts that the differences between the expectations of the trial number of last error, total number of errors, and number of errors before the first correct choice are functions only of the parameters d, e, s, and q. Thus, it is possible to permit only the value of the parameter c to decrease with overtraining to account for the increasing number of errors before the first correct choice. The values of the other parameters may remain invariant with overtraining to obtain the expectation of identical behavior following the first correct choice for all the groups regardless of their overtraining experience. Theios (1965b) found that the Markov model in Eq. (10) did an excellent job of accounting for the data when the assumption was made that the value of the parameter c decreased as an exponential function of overtraining trials during original learning while the values of d, q, s, and e were invariant.

B. Effect of Successive Reversals

In a second experiment (Theios, 1965b) 3 rats were given 220 reversals of the shock escape choice task. Each daily experimental test began with an initial training session in which the S was run to the side of the maze opposite that to which he ran on the last reversal session of the previous day. The data from the initial training sessions of each day were not included in the analyses. At the beginning of any trial within a session, the entire floor of the maze was electrified except in one of the two goal boxes. The trial ended when the S entered the goal box which was not electrified. A session ended when the rat accumulated 10 consecutive correct choices. The next session began with the shock switched to the opposite goal box. Each S was given 10 reversal sessions in succession following the initial session of each day.

In applying the Markov model of Eq. (10) to the successive reversal data, Theios found that the estimates of the parameters c and d increased within the first 33 reversals to a value of 1.0 indicating that, after a while, it took only one error to establish the new S_u–R_2 association. The estimates of the parameter d increased from a value of zero to a value of over .76 during the 220 reversals. The increase in the estimates of d were described well by a simple negatively accelerated increasing exponential curve. The increases in d may be interpreted as indicating that with successive reversal experience, the newly established S_u-R_2 association begins to have a higher and higher probability of being stored directly in long-term memory, thus directly replacing the S_u-R_1 association and preventing it from competing with the newly acquired R_2 response. The estimates of the short-term memory process parameters q, s, and e remained relatively invariant as a function of successive reversals. Equation (10) fully accounted for the changes in the data as a function of successive reversals when it was assumed that c quickly increased to 1.0 and that d increased from 0 and approached 1.00 according to a negatively accelerated exponentially increasing function. In summary, after about 200 reversals, the Ss were acting like an on-off switch on over 70% of the reversal problems, perfectly switching their behavior as soon as they made one error. The most dramatic change in their behavior during the 220 reversals was the systematic development of the tendency to exhibit one-trial reversal learning.

VII.   CONCLUSIONS

Data have been cited which indicate that the two-operator linear model is an inadequate approximation to active avoidance conditioning and choice reversal in a shock escape T-maze. On the other hand, the general Markov model which requires discrete changes in performance has been shown to provide a reasonable description of the avoidance conditioning process in a large number of studies using rats as subjects. Interpretation of the discrete performance model in terms of short-term and long-term memory processes has proved fruitful because predictions which follow from the memory interpretation have been supported when experimental variables identified with the model's parameters have been manipulated. In avoidance conditioning, the initial avoidance probability is not absolutely zero nor is the asymptotic avoidance probability absolutely unity. As such, the discrete performance level model does not require stationarity of either the intermediate response probabilities or response latencies between the first avoidance and last error. It was pointed out that the use of stopping rules, such as a criterion of 10 consecutive correct responses, fosters the misconception that performance asymptotes are unity. It was urged that future researchers employ a fixed, fairly large number of trials in order to insure a good estimate of true asymptotic behavior.

Analyses were discussed which indicated that the inherent variability in the model's stochastic process is such as to permit great differences in speed of learning without assuming differences in individual learning rate in the samples of typical laboratory subjects. The model was applied to a situation in which shock occurred probabilistically when the subject failed to avoid. As predicted by the memory interpretation, nonshocked error trials had little effect on the conditioning process. The rats conditioned at the same rate if the nonshocked error trials were deleted from their response protocols. The basic notions of the Markov model were extended with reasonable success to account for extinction of an avoidance response.

Response latency in avoidance conditioning was discussed and the Markov model was extended to include a number of response latency assumptions. A few comparisons were made between predicted and observed changes in mean response latency. The preliminary results were encouraging. However, much more research is needed in the area of latency analysis. Finally, it was shown that in a shock-escape choice situation, manipulation of variables such as amount of overtraining and number of successive reversals had localized effects on just two of the parameters of the Markov process during reversal learning.

Although it was not discussed specifically in this chapter, the general Markov model has been applied very successfully to classical aversive eye-blink conditioning in rabbits (Theios and Brelsford, 1966b). In the classical situation, the discrete nature of the conditioning process is dramatically apparent since the acquisition of an eye-blink response in rabbits is much slower than the acquisition of an avoidance response in rats. In summary, a large mass of data exists which is consistent with the notion of discrete changes in performance during conditioning. At the moment, a viable theoretical alternative to the general Markov process has not yet appeared.

ACKNOWLEDGMENT

This research was supported by PHS Research Grant HD 03540-01 from the National Institute of Child Health and Human Development, Public Health Service. I would like to express my appreciation to John W. Brelsford, Jr., E. Grant Coulson, Rodney W. McGinnis, and Melvyn C. Moy without whose collaboration, data, research assistance, and programming skills this endeavor would have been impossible.

REFERENCES

Atkinson, R.C., Bower, G.H., & Crothers, E.J. *An introduction to mathematical learning theory.* New York: Wiley, 1965.

Atkinson, R.C., & Estes, W.K. Stimulus sampling theory. In R.D. Luce, R.R. Bush, and E. Galanter (Eds.) *Handbook of mathematical psychology, Vol. II,* New York: Wiley, 1963. Pp. 121–268.

Beecroft, R.S., & Bouska, S.A. Acquisition of avoidance running in the rat. *Psychonomic Science,* 1967, **9,** 163–164.

Bower, G.H., & Theios, J. A learning model for discrete performance levels. In R.C. Atkinson (Ed.) *Studies in mathematical psychology.* Stanford, California: Stanford University Press, 1964. Pp. 1–31.

Brelsford, J.W., Jr. Experimental Manipulation of state occupancy in a Markov model for avoidance conditioning. *Journal of Mathematical Psychology,* 1967, **4,** 21–47.

Bush, R.R., and Mosteller, F. *Stochastic models for learning.* New York: Wiley, 1955.

Coulson, E.G. Prediction of response latency by a Markov model for avoidance conditioning in rats. Unpublished M.A. Thesis, York University, Toronto, Ontario, Canada, 1967.

Falmagne, J.C. Stochastic models for choice reaction time with applications to experimental results. *Journal of Mathematical Psychology,* 1965, **2,** 77–124.

Greeno, J.G. Identifiability and statistical properties of two-stage learning with no successes in the initial stage. *Psychometrika,* 1968, **33,** 173–215.

Greeno, J.G., & Steiner, T.E. Markovian processes with identifiable states: General considerations and application to all-or-none learning. *Psychometrika,* 1964, **29,** 309–333.

Hilgard, E.R., & Bower, G.H. *Theories of learning.* (3rd ed.) New York: Appleton, 1966.

Holland, P.W. A variation on the minimum chi-square test. *Journal of Mathematical Psychology,* 1967, **4,** 377–413.

Hull, C.L. *Principles of behavior.* New York: Appleton, 1943.

Isaacson, R.I., & Olton, D.S. Further comment: Nonincremental avoidance behavior. *Psychonomic Science,* 1967, **9,** 445–446.

Lowe, W.F., Jr., & Theios, J. Likelihood ratio evaluation of M-state models applied to individual choice sequences of successive reversal learning. *Psychonomic Science,* 1968, **11,** 85–86.

McGill, W.J. Stochastic latency mechanisms. In R.D. Luce, R.R. Bush, and E. Galanter (Eds.), *Handbook of mathematical psychology,* Vol. I. New York: Wiley, 1963. Pp. 309–360.

McGill, W.J., & Gibbon, J. The general gamma distribution and reaction time. *Journal of Mathematical Psychology,* 1965, **2,** 1–18.

McGinnis, R.W. *Theoretical extensions of a Markov model for avoidance conditioning: Effect of probabilistic shock schedules on acquisition and extinction.* Ph. D. Dissertation, University of Texas, 1966. Available as Report No. 12, Conditioning Research Laboratory, Department of Psychology, University of Texas, Austin, Texas, 78712.

Miller, N.E. Studies of fear as an acquirable drive: I. Fear as reinforcement in the learning of new responses. *Journal of Experimental Psychology,* 1948, **38,** 89–101.

Millward, R. Latency in a modified paired-associate learning experiment. *Journal of Verbal Learning and Verbal Behavior.* 1964, **3,** 309–316.

Mowrer, O.H. A stimulus-response analysis of anxiety and its role as a reinforcing agent. *Psychological Review*, 1939, **46**, 553–564.

Polidora, V.J. Comment. *Psychonomic Science*, 1967, **8**, 391.

Ray, A.J., Jr. Shuttle avoidance: Rapid acquisition by rats to a pressurized air unconditioned stimulus. *Psychonomic Science*, 1966, **5**, 29–30. (a)

Ray, A.J., Jr. Non-incremental shuttle-avoidance acquisition to pressurized air US. *Psychonomic Science*, 1966, **5**, 433–434. (b)

Ray, A.J., Jr. Reply to Polidora: Continued evidence of non-incremental acquisition. *Psychonomic Science*, 1967, **8**, 391–392.

Solomon, R.L., & Wynne, L.C. Traumatic avoidance learning: Acquisition in normal dogs. *Psychological Monographs*, 1953, **67**, (4, Whole No. 354).

Suppes, P., Groen, G., & Schlag-Rey, M. A model for response latency in paired-associate learning. *Journal of Mathematical Psychology*, 1966, **3**, 99–128.

Theios, J. Simple conditioning as two-stage all-or-none learning. *Psychological Review*, 1963, **70**, 403–417.

Theios, J. Prediction of paired-associate latencies after the last error by an all-or-none model. *Psychonomic Science*, 1965, **2**, 311–312. (a)

Theios, J. The mathematical structure of reversal learning in a shock-escape T-maze: Overtraining and successive reversals. *Journal of Mathematical Psychology*, 1965, **2**, 26–52. (b)

Theios, J. Finite integer models for learning in individual subjects. *Psychological Review*, 1968, **75**, 292–307. (a)

Theios, J. Evaluation of the chi-square approximation of likelihood ratio transformation for a class of models having integer valued parameters. Paper presented at Mathematical Psychology Meetings, Stanford University, August 28, 1968. (b)

Theios, J., & Brelsford, J.W., Jr. Theoretical interpretations of a Markov model for avoidance conditioning. *Journal of Mathematical Psychology*, 1966, **3**, 140–162. (a)

Theios, J., & Brelsford, J.W., Jr. A Markov model for classical conditioning: Application to eye-blink conditioning in rabbits. *Psychological Review*, 1966, **73**, 393–408. (b)

Theios, J., & Dunaway, J.E. One-way versus shuttle avoidance conditioning. *Psychonomic Science*, 1964, **1**, 251–252.

Theios, J., Lynch, A.D., & Lowe, W.F., Jr. Differential effects of shock intensity on oneway and shuttle avoidance conditioning. *Journal of Experimental Psychology*, 1966, **72**, 294–299.

Weitzman, R.A. Statistical learning models and individual differences. *Psychological Review*, 1966, **73**, 357–364.

CHAPTER 6

Unpredictable and Uncontrollable Aversive Events

MARTIN E.P. SELIGMAN

Steven F. Maier[1] and Richard L. Solomon

University of Pennsylvania
Philadelphia, Pennsylvania

Aversive (painful or fearful) events occur frequently in the life histories of all organisms. We often attribute long-lasting behavior peculiarities, emotional illnesses, and anomalies of perception and thinking to such events. And yet we know that all organisms which have experienced painful or fearful events do not develop peculiarities, illnesses, and anomalies. Aside from genetic or constitutional variables which might lead to individual differences in reactivity to aversive stimuli, there are a host of environmental variables which· might help us to understand such individual differences. Two such environmental variables are the predictability and controllability of aversive events.

In this chapter we review some of the behavioral and physiological consequences of aversive events which are either unpredictable by a subject, or uncontrollable by him, or both. We find these two variables to be important ones, indeed. Unpredictable painful events turn out to be more distressing than are predictable ones. They generate more ulcers. They intensify subjective reports of painfulness and anxiety; and both people and animals choose, if given the choice, predictable painful events over unpredictable ones. Uncontrollable painful events can interfere with an organism's ability later to solve problems in order to escape or avoid these events. They can lead to a phenomenon we have labeled "helplessness." In this paper we discuss the current status of research and theory concerning these phenomena.

I. DEFINITION OF "PREDICTION" AND OF "CONTROL"

When E uses an aversive stimulus in order to control S's behavior, he

---

[1] Now at the University of Illinois

can arrange two sets of relations: (a) between a "neutral stimulus" and
the aversive event and (b) between a specific response and the aversive
outcome. In Pavlovian aversive conditioning, E typically arranges a relationship between CS and UCS such that the CS predicts either the occurrence of the UCS or its absence. An E interested in instrumental
aversive training (escape, avoidance, and punishment) on the other hand,
typically arranges for a response to produce, terminate, reduce, or prevent the aversive event. These, however, are not the only possible relations between CS and UCS or between responses and outcomes. CSs can
be arranged so that they predict neither the occurrence, nor nonoccurrence of the UCS: *i.e.*, the CSs and UCS can be in an *unpredictable* relation. Outcomes can be so arranged that they are neither produced,
terminated, reduced, or prevented by any response that S may make:
i.e., the outcomes are *uncontrollable* with respect to S's responding. After
defining our basic concepts, we shall describe the disruptive consequences that uncontrollable and unpredictable aversive events have on
behavior and shall review the theories which account for these effects.

Throughout this paper we will frequently use the terms "prediction"
and "control," so they require definition at the outset. E's arrangement
of the experimental events and *not* S's perception of them define these
concepts.

A.   Control and the Instrumental Training Space[2]

Learning theorists have usually viewed the relations between instrumental responding and outcomes to which S is sensitive in terms of the
conditional probability of a reinforcer following a response $p(RF/R)$,
which can have values ranging from 0 to 1.0. At 1.0, every response
produces a reinforcer (continuous reinforcement). At zero, a response
never produces a reinforcer (extinction). Intermediate values represent
various degrees of partial reinforcement.

One conditional probability, however, is an inadequate description of
the relations between response and outcomes about which S may learn.
Important events can sometimes occur when no specific response has
been made, and it would be a woefully maladaptive S that was insensitive to such a contingency. Rather than representing environmental contingencies as occurring along a single dimension, we think instrumental
training can be better described using a two-dimensional space, as shown
in Figure 1. The x-axis $p(RF/R)$ represents the traditional dimension,

[2] See Prokasy (1965, p. 209 *ff.*), Premack (1965, p. 123-180) and Rescorla (1967) for related discussions.

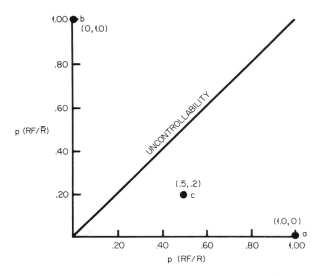

Fig. 1. The instrumental training space. The ordinate and abscissa represent the relationships between S's response and a reinforcer outcome. They are conditional probabilities, or contingencies, arranged by E. The 45° line represents a special condition, when the reinforcer is uncontrollable because $p(\text{RFT}/\text{R}) = p(\text{RFT}/\overline{\text{R}})$.

conditional probability of a reinforcer following a response. Orthogonal to the conditional probability of a reinforcer, given a response, is the conditional probability of a reinforcer occurring in the absence of that response ($p(\text{RF}/\overline{\text{R}})$). This dimension is represented along the y-axis. We assume that Ss are sensitive to variations along *both* dimensions conjointly, and the empirical meaning of this assumption is that systematic changes in behavior should occur with systematic changes along both dimensions. Thus S may learn the extent to which food occurs when it does *not* make a specific response along with learning the extent to which food occurs when it *does* make a specific response.

Consider a few examples. In Figure 1, point a (1.0, 0) is a case of continuous reinforcement: S is always reinforced for response R, and is never reinforced if it fails to make R. Point b (0, 1.0) is a case in which S is never reinforced for making the designated R, and is always reinforced for refraining from R (differential reinforcement of other behavior, DRO). Consider Point c (.5, .2): here S is reinforced 50% of the times that it makes R, but even if it fails to make R, it is reinforced 20% of the time.

The traditional training procedures arrayed along the x-axis have been thoroughly explored by many experimenters (e.g., Ferster & Skinner, 1957; Honig, 1966). The points in the training space which do not fall along the x-axis have not, however, been systematically investigated. Consider the points that lie along the 45° line, $(x, y$, where $x = y)$. Whether or not S responds, the density of reinforcement is the same. The conditional probability of a reinforcer occurring, given a specific response, *does not differ* from the conditional probability of reinforcement in the absence of that response. The reinforcer is independent of responding.

The concepts of controllability and uncontrollability are defined within this instrumental training space. Any time there is something S can do or refrain from doing that changes what it gets, it has control. Specifically, a response R, stands in a relation of *control* to a reinforcer, *RF,* if and only if

$$p(RF/R) \neq p(RF/\overline{R}). \tag{1}$$

Furthermore, when a response will not change what S gets, the response and reinforcer are independent. Specifically, a response, R stands in relation of *independence* to a reinforcer, RF, if and only if:

$$p(RF/R) = p(RF/\overline{R}). \tag{2}$$

When this is true of all responses (as in Pavlovian conditioning) S *cannot control* the reinforcer, and the outcome is defined as *uncontrollable.* Traditional operant experiments, in which some reinforcer is made contingent upon some specific response, and in which S acquires the response, can be interpreted to mean that S learns that his response controls the reinforcer. Moreover, we think that S can learn that it cannot control the reinforcer. Later in this paper we discuss some consequences of S's learning this.

B.   Prediction and the Pavlovian Conditioning Space

Parallel reasoning holds for Pavlovian conditioning. The traditional dimension is the conditional probability of a UCS, given a CS. But, obviously, UCSs can occur when no CS has preceded them. We then have a Pavlovian conditioning space analogous to the instrumental training space. This Pavlovian conditioning space consists of the conditional probability of a UCS, given a CS (p(UCS/CS)) and the conditional probability of that UCS in the absence of a CS (p(UCS/$\overline{CS}$)).

We think that Ss can learn about conjoint variations along both dimensions. Conditioning at points along the x-axis often produce a Pav-

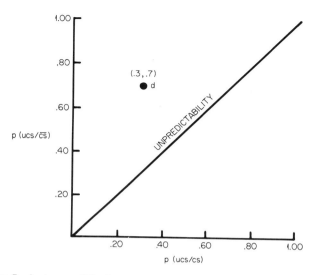

Fig. 2. The Pavlovian conditioning space. The ordinate and abscissa represent the relationships between CS and UCS. They are conditional probabilities, or stimulus contingencies, arranged by E. The 45° line represents a special condition, the unpredictability of Pavlovian reinforcement, because $p(\text{UCS/CS}) = p(\text{UCS}/\overline{\text{CS}})$.

lovian excitor (CS^+): here the CS predicts that the UCS will occur with some probability, but the UCS never occurs in the absence of the CS. Conditioning at points along the y-axis often produces a Pavlovian inhibitor (CS^-): here the CS predicts that the UCS will not occur although there is some probability that the UCS will occur in the absence of the CS. In many experiments (*e.g.*, differential conditioning) two explicit CSs are used. One stimulus may predict shock, the other, absence of shock. For these cases, we need two spaces, one for each CS, in order adequately to represent the operations.

Consider other points in the Pavlovian conditioning space. For example, point d (.3, .7) means: when the CS is on, the UCS occurs with a probability of .3, but when no CS is on, the UCS occurs with a probability of .7. Points along the x-axis, and to a lesser extent points along the y-axis, have been systematically studied by previous experimenters (*e.g.*, Pavlov, 1927, Beecroft, 1966). Later in this paper we focus on many studies along the 45° independence line.

The concepts of predictability and unpredictability are defined within the Pavlovian conditioning space: a CS predicts a UCS when its occurrence changes the probability of a UCS occurring, *i.e.*, a CS stands in a *predictive* relationship to a *UCS*, if and only if,

$$p(UCS/CS) \neq p(UCS/\overline{CS}).\qquad(3)$$

A CS is independent of a UCS when the UCS occurs with some constant probability whether or not a CS occurs, *i.e.*, a *CS* and a *UCS* are *independent*, if and only if:

$$p(UCS/CS) = p(UCS/\overline{CS}).\qquad(4)$$

Finally, a UCS is *unpredictable* if all CSs are independent of it.

We think that *S*s can learn that a UCS is unpredictable, and later in this paper we will discuss the consequences of their learning this.

We should note a possible relationship between predictability (Pavlovian contingencies) and controllability (instrumental contingencies). This possibility exists because the feedback from a response is a potential stimulus. Thus, if *S* can control an event by a response, it may be able to use the feedback from its response to predict that event. For instance, a rat that is punished with shock for pressing a bar *controls* shock, because it can change the probability of shock either by pressing or by not pressing. The exteroceptive and kinesthetic feedback from the movements which lead up to and include the bar pressing *predicts* shock. The absence of such feedback *predicts* no shock. However, the converse relation does not hold, *i.e.*, even if *S* can predict an event, it does not necessarily have the power to control it. Thus, if a CS predicts shock, there may or may not be anything *S* can do to modify the shock.

C. Summary

Using the concepts of an instrumental training space (Figure 1) and a Pavlovian conditioning space (Figure 2) we have defined controllability and predictability and their absence. We have not, however, exhausted the important contingencies under *E*'s control. For example, reinforcers can be arranged to depend on prior reinforcers rather than on responses alone (*e.g.*, adjusting schedules; see Ferster & Skinner, 1957). Similarly, in Pavlovian conditioning, UCS presentation can be contingent on prior UCS presentation and CSs can be contingent upon prior CS and UCS presentations. Obviously, a complete representation of the possible contingencies requires multidimensional contingency tables. What we have called the instrumental training space and Pavlovian conditioning space are over-simplifications of the important events *E* can impose on *S*. These spaces do, however, enable us to define uncontrollability and unpredictability, the two conditions which are the focus of our interest. In this chapter we will confine our discussion to the effects of uncontrollable and unpredictable aversive events, sometimes contrasting these effects with those of controllable and predictable aversive events.

II. UNCONTROLLABLE AVERSIVE EVENTS

A. Effects on Escape and Avoidance Responding

Inescapable and unavoidable shock is uncontrollable because no response S can make will affect the occurrence of shock. An experiment in which S receives inescapable and unavoidable shock can be described by a point along the line of independence in the instrumental training space. In this section we examine the effects of prior experience with inescapable and unavoidable shock on later acquisition of escape and avoidance responding. A naive S is first given inescapable and unavoidable electric shock and is then put into a situation where escape and/or avoidance (control) is possible. The data of interest are the characteristics of acquisition of the escape or avoidance responding. The experiments of this type differ widely with respect to the nature of the inescapable shocks, the situations in which the shocks are given, the time between the uncontrollable shock and the escape avoidance training, the topography of the escape or avoidance responses, and the species of experimental animal. Despite this variety, a consistent picture emerges if we classify the experiments according to the type of instrumental escape/avoidance training procedure used following exposure to uncontrollable shock. These different test situations can be divided into the following categories: (1) two-way shuttlebox escape/avoidance; (2) escape/avoidance by manipulation (*e.g.,* bar press, wheel turn, etc.); (3) one-way shuttlebox escape/avoidance; and (4) passive avoidance (punishment).

1. Two-way Shuttlebox Escape/Avoidance

A two-way shuttlebox is a chamber divided into two identical compartments, usually by a small hurdle. S must run or jump from one compartment into the other to escape or avoid shock. Shocks can occur in either compartment, so there is no *place* that is always safe, but the *response* of shuttling or jumping always leads to safety.

Overmier and Seligman (1967) and Seligman and Maier (1967) found the most dramatic effects of inescapable shock on two-way shuttlebox escape/avoidance. One group of dogs (experimental group) was strapped into a Pavlov harness and given 64 unsignalled, inescapable shocks. Each shock was 5 seconds long and 6.0 mA (very painful) in intensity. The dogs could not terminate the shock or postpone its onset. Another group of dogs (naive group) were strapped into the harness but not given any shock. Twenty-four hours later all dogs were given the opportunity to control shock in a very different apparatus. They received 10 trials of signaled escape/avoidance training in a shuttle box. The onset of a signal (CS) began each trial. If the dog jumped the barrier within 10 sec, the CS was turned off and no shock was presented. If the dog had not jumped by then, a 4.5 mA shock came on and stayed on until it jumped into the other compartment. Whenever the dog did not jump within 60 sec of CS onset, the trial ended.

The experimental group, which first received inescapable shock, was severely retarded in dealing with shock. Seven of these 8 dogs failed to escape on 9 out of 10 of the trials. The naive group escaped and avoided efficiently. Figure 3 shows the median latency of barrier jumping on each of the ten trials for the two groups. These data are typical: we have found that 63% of dogs pretreated with inescapable shock fail to escape within 50 sec of shock onset on 9 out of 10 trials ($n = 82$), whereas only 6% of naive animals fail ($n = 35$).

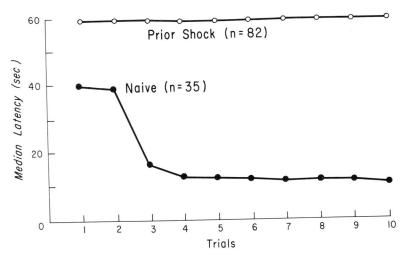

Fig. 3. The effects of uncontrollable shocks in the Pavlov harness on subsequent escape learning in the shuttle box. There is normal, rapid escape learning by 35 naive dogs which received no shocks in the harness. In contrast the median S of 82 dogs which received prior inescapable shocks in the harness, shows failure to escape shocks in the shuttle box. The arbitrary failure criterion was 50 sec of shock (a latency of 60 sec after onset of the S^D).

The behavior of the preshocked dogs was bizarre. When they received the *first* shock in the shuttlebox, they initially looked like the naive dogs: they ran about frantically, howled, defecated, and urinated. However, unlike naive dogs, they soon stopped running around and quietly whimpered until the trial terminated. After a few trials, they seemed to "give up" and passively "accept" the shock. On later trials, these dogs failed to make any escape movements at all. A few dogs would get up and jump the barrier, escaping or avoiding shock; yet, surprisingly, on the next trial such a dog would go back to taking shock. It did not seem to learn that barrier-jumping produced shock termination. We call such retardation of escape or avoidance, which results from prior exposure to uncontrollable shock, the "interference effect".

The interference effect does not depend on the use of particular shock parameters. Using dogs, Overmier and Seligman (1967) and Seligman and Maier (1967) found the interference effect with a variety of frequencies, densities, durations, and temporal distributions of inescapable shock. In addition, the interference effect occurs whether or not the uncontrollable shocks are preceded by a signal. Other similar results have been found in the dog by Carlson and Black (1960), Leaf (1964)[3], Overmier and Leaf (1965), and Overmier (1968).

The interference effect has also been found with rats in the two-way shuttlebox. Mullin and Mogenson (1963) gave separate groups different amounts of fear conditioning in a shuttlebox. Half of the shocks were given in each side. Fear conditioning, of course, means that the signalled shock occurs independently of responding. Twenty-four hours later, the groups received escape/avoidance training with the previous fear conditioning CS as the signal. The groups given fear conditioning were significantly slower at escaping shock than were the controls, but only on the first 5 trials. Furthermore, the more fear conditioning they had, the more slowly they escaped. Once efficient escape had emerged, the preshocked group learned to avoid more rapidly than did the controls. Also using rats, Weiss, Krieckhaus, and Conte (1968, Exps. I & II) found a decrement both in avoidance and in escape learning that resulted from prior fear conditioning. Anderson, Schwendiman, Packham, and Taylor, 1967, (Experiment IV) also found significant escape decrements in rats resulting from prior inescapable shock. Goldfish give parallel results (Behrend & Bitterman, 1963, Pinckney, 1967). In dogs, the effect is very large; *S* sits and takes the shocks. Rats and goldfish are merely *slower* at terminating the shock.

---

[3]Personal communication concerning the findings in this paper

When the test situation is a two-way shuttlebox, prior experience with uncontrollable shocks leads to poor escape from a *fear-arousing* CS as well as poor escape from shock itself. Brown and Jacobs (1949, Exp. I) gave one group of rats 40 fear-conditioning trials with a buzzer CS. A second group of rats received only the CS. All rats then received training in which jumping in a two-way shuttlebox from one compartment to the other terminated the buzzer. Shock did not occur in this phase of training. Remarkably, the shocked group was at first *slower* in jumping over the barrier to escape the buzzer than the group which had never been shocked. On later trials this relation reversed. Thus, when the response required is two-way shuttling, experience with uncontrollable shocks leads to an initial retardation in escaping both primary and conditioned aversive events.

2.   Manipulandum-Escape/Avoidance

In manipulandum-escape/avoidance, S must move some part of the environment (*e.g.*, a wheel or bar) rather than simply move itself within that environment (as in a shuttlebox). Prior uncontrollable shock retards the acquisition of manipulandum-escape/avoidance just as it retards two-way shuttling.

Dinsmoor and Campbell (1956a) gave one group of rats uncontrollable shock in a lever-press box while another group was just placed in the apparatus. All Ss then received shock which terminated whenever the lever was pressed. The rats which had had uncontrollable shock were slower to make their *first* escape and slower to *acquire* a stable escape response than were the nonshocked rats. This effect lasted through the whole test session. Dinsmoor and Campbell (1956b) and Dinsmoor (1958) have confirmed this finding with different temporal and shock parameters as have Nakamura and Anderson (1968) using a wheel-turn response. Similarly, Seward and Humphreys (1967) found that cats previously exposed to uncontrollable shock were slower to acquire a wheel-pawing response in order to escape and avoid shock than were either naive cats or cats previously exposed to escapable (controllable) shock. Thus, both two-way shuttlebox and manipulandum-escape/avoidance are retarded by prior experience with shock received independently of responding.

3.   One-Way Escape/Avoidance

A one-way shuttlebox is a chamber divided into 2 sides, usually by a hurdle. The two sides usually differ in appearance. For example, one side might be black and the other white, one might have a grid floor and the other a smooth floor. In this situation shock occurs in *only one* of the sides, so that one side is always safe and the other dangerous. To escape or avoid, S must get from the dangerous to the safe side. It is returned by E to the dangerous or "start" side before the next trial begins.

Surprisingly, although uncontrollable shock retards two-way shuttle box- and manipulandum-escape and avoidance, it either has no effect upon, or even slightly helps one-way avoidance. DeToledo and Black (1967) gave 3 groups of rats inescapable shocks in a one-way shuttle-box. One group was shocked in the "to-be-dangerous" side, another was shocked in the "to-be-safe" side, and the third group received half of its shocks in each side. A fourth group of rats was shocked in a different appatus. A control group received no shock and was merely confined to one side of the shuttlebox. Later, all groups were given one-way escape/avoidance training in the shuttlebox. The group given prior inescapable shocks in the dangerous side learned faster than the nonshocked controls. The group previously shocked in the safe side were worse than the nonshocked controls. But the group previously shocked on both sides, and the group shocked in a different apparatus, did not differ from nonshocked controls.

Similarly, Anderson (1966) found that prior uncontrollable shocks facilitated one-way signallized escape in rats. The inescapable shocks were administered while S was restrained in the "to-be-dangerous" side of the apparatus. Finally, Brookshire, Littman and Stewart (1961, Experiment I, Groups E IIa and E IIb) reported facilitation of avoidance and escape on early training trials by uncontrollable shock given to rats earlier in a highly dissimilar apparatus.

The response in a "jump-up" box is like one-way avoidance. In this apparatus, a rat is placed on the grid floor (the "start box") of a large chamber. Occasionally, a ledge onto which S can jump (the "goal box") is inserted into the chamber. If S jumps onto the ledge before the floor is electrified, it avoids shock. Baum's (1969) results using a jump-up apparatus, were like those for one-way avoidance. Rats which received inescapable shock on the grid floor, prior to avoidance training, later avoided better than did nonshocked controls. In fact, half of the pre-shocked Ss jumped to the ledge the very first time they were inserted, and they then avoided on every trial.

It will be recalled that shock which S cannot control will subsequently retard escape from a fear-arousing CS as well as from shock in a two-way shuttlebox (see Section II,A,1 above). This does not happen when

S escapes the fear CS by one-way responding. Brown and Jacobs (1949, Exp. II) repeated the experiment in which they found retarded escape-from-fear, with the following modifications: (1) fewer signal-shock pairings, (2) a change from steady shock to pulsating shock, (3) a change in the signal or CS from a buzzer to a tone-light combination, (4) introduction of an irrelevant hunger drive, and (5) *a change from two-way to one-way shuttle-responding.* As in the previous experiment, one group of rats was given CS-shock pairings and another was given only the CSs, with half of the presentations given in each side of the shuttlebox. The test was now one-way escape: CS onset occurred only while S was on the "dangerous" side of the shuttle box. Crossing to the "safe" side terminated the CS. S was then returned to the start side before the next CS presentation. As in the previous experiment, no shock was presented. The animals which had been given prior CS-shock pairings now responded *more quickly* than did the controls, from the very first trial on; whereas, with a two-way response for escape in the first experiment, they had responded more slowly on the first 5 trials.

Kalish (1954) found similar results, using continuous shock and food-satiated rats in a one-way shuttlebox. Furthermore, the facilitation increased with number of CS-shock pairings. It is likely, therefore, that the reversal of result found between Brown and Jacobs' Experiments I and II is attributable either to the change in the CS or to the change in the escape procedure from two-way to one-way. The type of escape training procedure is probably the more potent variable.

In summary, uncontrollable shocks retard subsequent one-way escape/avoidance only when they are administered in the side which will become the safe goalbox. If the shocks are given in the start box, escape/avoidance responding is facilitated; if given in a different apparatus, there is either no effect or a slight facilitation. Further, experience with a CS paired with uncontrollable shock facilitates one-way escape from that CS.

4. Passive Avoidance (Punishment)

In all of the situations that we have discussed (active escape/avoidance training), S made some designated response in order to escape or avoid. In passive avoidance training, S is required to *refrain* from making some designated response; it avoids shock by *not* doing something. The punished response is usually maintained by reward. A typical punishment procedure in which S is given both shock and food for bar pressing is procedurally a passive avoidance training situation; S avoids shock by not pressing the bar.

In general, Ss which first receive inescapable shocks acquire passive avoidance responding faster. Kurtz and Walters (1962) gave one group of rats uncontrollable shocks. A second group of rats was not shocked. Both groups were then trained to run in a runway to food. When both groups were subsequently given shocks as well as food in the goal box, the rats that had prior experience with inescapable shocks stopped running sooner. Similar findings have been reported by Anderson, Cole, McVaugh, (1968, Exps. I and II). Anderson and Paden (1966) have shown that facilitation of passive avoidance does not depend on the use of the same aversive stimulus in the two phases of the experiment. Their Ss learned to run a runway for food. One group was then "tumbled" in a rotating circular drum. The rats could not control tumbling. Another group was not "tumbled." Both groups were then given additional food training in the runway and were then shocked in the goal box. The "tumbled" group stopped running sooner than did the controls. Pearl, Walters, and Anderson (1964) obtained similar results using shock and loud noise in a bar-pressing situation. Thus, prior experience with uncontrollable aversive events probably facilitates the later acquisition of passive avoidance responses which prevent either the same or other aversive events.[4]

5. Summary

Our original question was: How do uncontrollable shocks affect the subsequent acquisition of responses that control shock? The answer depends on the kind of response S must make in order to control shock. Active two-way shuttlebox and manipulandum escape/avoidance are retarded by prior uncontrollable traumatic events. There is either a lack of effect, or a slight facilitation when the specific response is active one-way avoidance, unless S is exposed to uncontrollable shock on the side into which he must run later. Passive avoidance learning seems to be facilitated by uncontrollable shock.

B. Controllability, Distress, and Physiological Stress

We have reviewed the effects of uncontrollable shock on escape and avoidance responding. We now turn to the question of whether uncontrollable shocks are more distressing and stressful than controllable

---

[4]The generality of this conclusion may now be in doubt. Anderson, Schwediman, Packham, and Taylor (1967) have found the opposite effects of preshock on passive avoidance with Pullman and Holtzman rats. In addition, we should point out that McCulloch and Bruner (1939) had found that prior inescapable shocks produced subsequent slower discriminative learning in a situation where shock was used as the aversive stimulus. Whether discrimination learning under aversive control should be categorized as a type of passive avoidance learning is, however, questionable.

shocks.[5] Behavioral, physiological and subjective measures suggest that they are. Mowrer and Viek (1948) did the first experiment directed at this question. One group of rats was trained to escape shocks by rearing up on their hind legs. A second, yoked group received inescapable shocks of equivalent duration. Both groups were then offered food in the shock siuation. Ss that had received uncontrollable shocks refused food more frequently than did S which had received controllable shocks. Lindner (1968) has confirmed this result. If feeding inhibition is taken as an index of degree of distress, then uncontrollable shocks are more distressing than controllable shocks.

Hoffman and Fleshler (1965) trained pigeons to peck for food on a variable interval (VI) schedule. Then all Ss were presented with 4-min tones superimposed on the VI baseline. Nothing happened during the first 2 min of the tone. For one group of birds, the first peck occurring in the second 2 min of the tone was punished by a shock. If the bird did not peck during this 2-min period, the tone was terminated and no shock presented. Thus, Ss in this group could control shock: if S did not respond, shock would not occur. A second group of pigeons was yoked to these Ss. This group was given shock whenever the punished group was shocked. The yoked group could not avoid shock by not pecking. *Surprisingly, the yoked group pecked less during the first 2 min of the tone than did the punished group.* During the second 2 min of the tone, the punished group showed greater suppression than did the yoked group, since they could avoid by failing to peck. Furthermore, the yoked group pecked less than did the punished group when the tone was not present. Finally, the yoked Ss showed slower extinction of suppression than did the punished Ss. Hunt and Brady (1951, 1955) found similar results. If suppression outside the punishment period is taken as an index of distress, then uncontrollable shocks produce more distress than do controllable shocks.

If the breakdown of an easy, well-established, appetitive discrimination is taken as an index of distress, then we again arrive at the same conclusion. Hearst (1965) trained rats on successive discrimination for

[5]The use of these terms now needs some comment. Aversion and "aversiveness" is used to describe the psychophysical properties of shocks and the choice behavior of Ss relative to those properties. The term "distress" is used here to apply to the emotional effects of repeated aversive events, *i.e.*, their capacity to generate negative affect. Finally, the term "stress" is used to apply to the physiological consequences of repeated aversive events. Of course there may be strong relationships among these three dependent variables, but there is no reason why there must be. Thus, two psychophysically-identical shocks may yield different degrees of distress, or of stress, depending on their certainty, their immediacy, or their frequency. We are indebted to Byron A. Campbell for suggesting the use of the word "distress" as an attribute of the diffuse emotional reaction to aversive stimuli.

food reward. After the discrimination was well learned, one group of Ss (Experiment I) received signalled, uncontrollable shocks superimposed on the discrimination procedure. Another group (Experiment III) received signalled periods of controllable shocks superimposed on the discrimination. The latter group could avoid shock by not responding during the shock period. The discrimination was impaired for the group receiving uncontrollable shocks, but not for the other group. Here, too, uncontrollable aversive stimulation disrupted behavior more than controllable aversive stimulation.

However, Brady, Porter, Conrad, and Mason (1958), in their well-known "Executive Monkey" study, found different results. Monkeys which could avoid shock on a Sidman schedule developed massive stomach ulcers and died. In contrast, monkeys which did not have control over shock, and merely received shocks whenever the "executive" failed to avoid, did not develop ulcers. One can criticize this experiment on the grounds that the monkeys were not randomly assigned to groups. The experiment began with a pretest in which *all Ss* were given avoidance training. In each pair the *S* which acquired the avoidance response first was chosen as the executive. Sines, Clelland, and Adkins (1963) have found that rats which are susceptible to ulcers acquire an avoidance response faster than do controls. So it is possible that the "executive" Ss in the Brady *et al.* study were constitutionally more emotional and prone to ulcer formation than were their yoked partners. Furthermore, the results of Brady *et al.* have not been replicated with rats. Weiss (1968) has performed an experiment similar to that of Brady *et al.* and has obtained opposite results. One group of rats (Experiment I) was trained to escape and avoid shocks by jumping onto a platform. Another group (Experiment II) was trained to escape and avoid shocks by pressing a copper plate with its nose. Two other groups of rats were yoked to the escape/avoidance groups; they were shocked whenever their partners failed to avoid. Ss were randomly assigned to groups. Yoked Ss (1) lost weight, (2) developed larger and more frequent stomach ulcers, (3) defecated more, and (4) showed greater inhibition of drinking in the shock situation than did Ss that could escape and avoid. Thus, uncontrollable shocks produced more distress and physiological stress than did controllable shocks.

Similar results have been found with human Ss. Haggard (1943) found that Ss who could administer shock to themselves showed less anxiety, as measured by GSR, than did yoked Ss. Similarly, pain thresholds for heat are lower when *S* cannot control heat termination than when *S* can do so (Lepanto, Morney, & Zeahausern, 1965). Finally, Pervin (1963) found that Ss prefer shocks that thecn directly control to shocks that they cannot control. Therefore, the dimension of controllability affects the resultant emotional upset and physiological stress, as well as the subsequent acquisition of instrumental responses. Shocks which S cannot modify are more distressing and stressful than shocks with which S can cope, even though the physical stimuli are the same.

C. Explanation of the Effects of Uncontrollable Shocks

Many hypotheses have offered to explain the effects of prior experience with shock (preshock), but most of these hypotheses have been proposed to explain only a subset of the date we have described. Because we are searching for the most comprehensive explanation, we will consider the adequacy of each of these hypotheses as an explanation of the entire pattern of results.

1. Adaptation

This hypothesis holds that S adapts to shock during prior exposure to shocks and is therefore not motivated enough to escape or avoid in the later training situation. This hypothesis has been offered (e.g., MacDonald, 1946) as an explanation of instances in which interference results. Obviously, the adaptation mechanism cannot account for those instances in which either no effect or facilitation is the outcome. Moreover, the adaptation mechanism is an inadequate explanation, even in situations which result in interference:

(a) Adaptation to repeated, *intense* electric shocks has not been directly demonstrated (e.g., Church, LoLordo, Overmier, Solomon, & Turner, 1966).

(b) Even if adaptation occurs, it is unlikely to persist for the time periods that intervene between preshock and the escape/avoidance test.

(c) Overmier and Seligman (1967) and Seligman and Maier (1967) observed that their preshocked dogs did not "look" adapted: during the initial shocks of escape/avoidance training, the dogs howled, defecated, and urinated, and they appeared passive only on later trials, but evven then they jerked and whimpered with the shock.

(d) Overmier and Seligman (1967) have disconfirmed the adaptation hypothesis experimentally. They found that very intense shocks (6.5 mA with dogs) in the shuttle box did not reduce the interfering effects of prior inescapable shocks; the dogs howled more loudly, but they did not escape. If S fails to respond or responds slowly in the two-way shuttle-box only because shock is not motivating enough, then increasing the intensity of shock should produce responding.

(e) Seligman and Maier (1967) found that a series of *escapable* shocks received in a harness did not lead to interference with two-way barrier jumping, although the same shocks, if inescapable, produced interference. Both escapable and inescapable shocks should lead to the same degree of adaptation, but their effects are strikingly different.

(f) Dogs which first escaped shocks in a two-way shuttlebox and then received inescapable shocks in a harness continued to respond efficiently when returned to the shuttlebox (Seligman & Maier, 1967). There is no reason why prior escape training should reduce adaptation resulting from the series of inescapable shocks in the harness.

(g) Seligman, Maier, and Geer (1968) found that failure to escape in a shuttlebox, which resulted from prior experience with inescapable shocks, could be eliminated if E dragged the dog back and forth over the barrier during escape/avoidance trials. There is no reason why forcibly exposing S to the escape and avoidance contingencies should make the dog less adapted to shock.

(h) Finally, the increased stress and distress produced by inescapable shocks (Section B) is directly contrary to the adaptation hypotheses.

2. Sensitization

This hypothesis holds that preshock sensitizes S to later shocks. Consequently, during active avoidance training, S is "too motivated" to make organized responses in the test situation. However, during passive avoidance training, shock "hurts" more, and S is more reluctant to perform the punished response. Moreover, sensitization seems compatible with the enhanced distress caused by inescapable shock. This hypothesis, however, is inadequate to explain the interference effect in active avoidance learning. If, for example, prior inescapable shocks make S overmotivated, then reducing the shock intensity in the two-way shuttlebox should induce S to respond. Overmier and Seligman (unpublished data) found that the interference effect was not eliminated when the shock intensity used in the shuttle box was quite low (2.5 mA in dogs). In addition, arguments (e), (f), and (g) in Section 1 apply to the invalidation of the sensitization hypothesis as well as to the adaptation hypothesis.

3. Competing Motor Responses

Competing motor hypotheses occur in three simple and one complex form:

(a) The first version is based on competition from a response established by adventitious reinforcement. It states that some specific motor response happens to occur in close temporal contiguity with shock termination during inescapable shocks. This accidental pairing strengthens that particular response and makes it more likely that this response will be occurring at the moment of the next shock termination. This process would be expected to continue and so establish some strong motor response to shock. If this response is incompatible with the escape/avoidance response subsequently required, and if it is elicited by shock in that situation, then S should show interference with escape/avoidance learning. S should not perform the required response because it is engaging in this other behavior. On the other hand, if the superstitious response is not incompatible with the response required later, interference should not result. If the superstitious response is compatible with the escape/avoidance response, facilitation should occur.

Such a conception is inadequate. We have carefully observed dogs during their exposure to uncontrollable shocks and have not seen superstitious responding. More importantly, the argument itself contains flaws. First, because the accidently-acquired response is not specified in advance, there is no way of predicting whether prior inescapable shocks will cause interference, facilitation, or have no effect. Adventitious reinforcement arguments are generally applied *post hoc*. If interference is observed, one assumes that some unspecified response was incompatible. In short, this theory is not easily testable. Furthermore, even if some response is adventitiously strengthened by shock termination, and it increases in probability, it should be more likely to occur when shock goes *on* as well as when it goes *off*. Therefore, this response should be adventitiously punished as well as reinforced. Because the adventitious reinforcement concept does not suggest that reinforcement is more effective than punishment, it is not clear why uncontrollable aversive events should *establish* some specific motor response.

(b) The second simple version of response competition assumes that active responses are sometimes adventitiously punished by shock during exposure to inescapable shocks. The probability of active responding is thereby decreased, and S is less active in the subsequent test situation. The adventitious punishment concept has the same logical problems as does adventitious reinforcement: Its effect is usually stated *post hoc*. Furthermore, if active responding is punished by shock onset it should be reinforced by shock termination. Finally, if active responding should decrease, passive responding should increase; at this point, passive responding should be adventitiously punished and should yield an increase in active responding, and so on. The deduction based on the concept of adventitious punishment is as difficult to test as is the concept of adventitious reinforcement.

(c) The third simple version is not as loosely stated as the other two. It asserts that S reduces the "severity" of inescapable shock by making some specific motor response. This response then occurs later in the avoidance training situation when S is shocked. But under what circumstances will this response compete with, facilitate, or have no effect on the test response? Overmier and Seligman (1967) and Seligman and Maier (1967) delivered inescapable shocks through attached foot electrodes coated with electrode paste. It is therefore unlikely that S cound have modified electrical contact or resistance by any motor response in these experiments. It could, however, be argued that some pattern of movement or muscle tonus, such as standing motionless, may reduce the pain resulting from electric shock. Overmier and Seligman (1967) tested this possibility by administering shocks to dogs completely paralyzed by curare. Although these dogs could not move or modify muscle tonus during inescapable shocks, they subsequently failed, in the undrugged state, to escape shock in a two-way shuttlebox. Control animals, previously curarized, escaped normally when tested later in the undrugged state. So the interference effect is not due to the transfer of overt movements learned as a result of their pain-reducing characteristics. It is conceivable that that "severity" of shock can be reduced by S under curare paralysis, but the mechanism for such a process is obscure. Perhaps a "gating" mechanism can be controlled by the curarized S.

It should also be noted that the three simple competing motor response hypotheses do not account for the increased distress produced by uncontrollable shock.

(d) Weiss, Krieckhaus, and Conte (1968) proposed a more complex and more interesting hypothesis based on competing motor responses. They maintain that uncontrollable shocks affect later avoidance behavior through the classical conditioning of strong fear to the CS, rather than through instrumental reinforcement or punishment. Strong fear directly produces freezing, and S later freezes in response to the CS in escape/avoidance training, thus interfering with the required escape response. This assertion may be compatible with the increased distress of uncontrollable shock. Furthermore, it certainly applies to the interference effect when the preshock and instrumental training situations have CSs in common. But we have seen that prior uncontrollable shocks retard subsequent escape/avoidance learning even if the preshock and training situations are quite different. Nevertheless, either the shocks, or some stimulus consequence of S's reaction to shocks, may function as common stimuli. Weiss et al. offered strong support for this hypothesis. A group of rats was first given fear conditioning with a tone CS and shock UCS. They then received two-way shuttlebox escape/avoidance training with the same tone CS. Weiss et al. found the usual interference phenomenon. In addition, their preshock Ss showed a depression of movement during the very first presentation of the CS in the avoidance training situation. Finally, the amount of movement shown in response to the CS during fear conditioning was an excellent predictor of subsequent shuttlebox avoidance performance (correlation = +.83).

Weiss *et al.* (unpublished) argued that freezing should not occur and, hence, preshock should not interfere with one-way escape/avoidance performance: In one-way avoidance the problem is solved when S learns that shock occurs in one compartment and not in the other, because S *innately flees* from fear-producing places to safe places.[6] Thus, in one-way avoidance, when S is afraid, freezing is not the response highest in its response hierarchy. Fleeing to the safe side is. S freezes only if no safe place is in sight. In support of this interpretation, Weiss *et al.* found that the correlation between movement in response to the CS during fear conditioning and number of avoidances made in a *one-way* shuttlebox was only +.09. This same line of reasoning predicts that preshock should retard manipulandum-escape/avoidance performance and should facilitate passive avoidance performance. The Weiss *et al.* hypothesis is a powerful one, so that it will be discussed again later in the light of other findings.

4. *Emotional Exhaustion*

Does interference with escape and avoidance behavior occur because preshock produces an emotionally-exhausted organism? Because uncontrollable shocks produce more distress than do controllable shocks, one might expect greater emotional exhaustion after uncontrollable shocks. It is difficult for this hypothesis to account for those cases in which interference does not occur, but it might account for the interference effect in dogs because, in this case, the interference phenomenon *dissipates with time*. If only 24 hrs intervene between a single session of inescapable shocks in the Pavlov harness and the subsequent escape/avoidance training in the shuttlebox, interference results. Overmier and Seligman (1967) found that there was no interference effect in dogs when shuttlebox training came either 48, 72, or 144 hr after one session of inescapable shocks.[7] Emotional exhaustion which goes away with time might be me-

[6]*Editors note:* See Chapter 3 by Bolles, this volume.

[7]This time course may not exist in species other than the dog. Weiss *et al.* (1968), Brookshire *et al.* (1961), Anderson *et al.* (1968) have not found a time course in rats. Because the time course is such a striking phenomenon in dogs, we feel that extensive investigations of time parameters are needed for other species.

Recently Seligman and Groves (1970) demonstrated an interference effect in dogs that did not dissipate in time. Four, rather than one, sessions of inescapable shock were given in the harness, and the dogs tested in the shuttlebox one week later. These dogs showed profound decrements in escape and avoidance responding. Thus emotional exhaustion which dissipates in time cannot account for this nontransient interference.

diated by a temporary physiological state such as parasympathetic over-reaction (Brush, Meyer, & Palmer, 1963; Brush & Levine, 1965), adrenergic depletion, or sympathetic exhaustion. The parasympathetic over-reaction mechanism was proposed by Brush *et al.* (1963) to explain the Kamin Effect: the fact that retention of partially-learned avoidance responses yields a U-shaped function of passage of time. Rats performed better immediately after partial training than they did 3–6 hr later, but 24 hr later they performed as well as they had at the end of training. If, indeed, the time course of the interference phenomenon in dogs is the result of a mechanism such as that postulated to explain the Kamin Effect, we might expect a U-shaped time course for the interference effect. It seems important to note that Brush used inescapable shocks as one control condition and he did not observe the Kamin effect. Generalization across species may therefore be premature.

The hypothesis that preshock causes interference by producing emotional exhaustion is inadequate, however, even when restricted to the dog:

(a) the interference effect which is found in dogs can persist if inescapable shocks are repeated once. If a dog fails to escape in the shuttlebox 24 hr after repeated preshock, then it will fail to escape a month later (Seligman *et al.,* 1968).

(b) Prior experience with *escapable* shock does not produce interference (Seligman and Maier, 1967). Emotional exhaustion should be less after escapable shocks, because their emotional effect is less, but it should not be absent.

(c) Prior escape training in the shuttle box prevents the interfering effects of inescapable shocks (Seligman & Maier, 1967), but it should not be able to prevent emotional exhaustion.

(d) Seligman *et al.* (1968) have found that chronic failure to escape can be eliminated by dragging the dog across the barrier of the shuttle box during the CS and shock. There is no *a priori* reason why exposing S to the escape/avoidance contingencies should reduce emotional exhaustion.

5.   *Learned Helplessness*

McCulloch and Bruner (1939) trained rats in a brightness discrimination problem, wherein, in order to escape from a water tank, the Ss had to choose an escape alley that had no shock in it. Rats that had previously received 1000 sec of uncontrollable shocks made more errors in discrimination learning than did control Ss which had not previously been shocked. The authors speculated that a "new response to shock had been established in the shock treatment which inhibited the ordinary, violent, avoidance response" (McCulloch & Bruner, 1939, p. 335). Inhibition theory is not necessarily a response-competition theory, and so it is conceivable that this particular inhibition interpretation bears some resemblance to the helplessness hypothesis which we develop here. On the other hand, it may carry the same implications as did the competing response theories described above.

Seligman and Maier (1967) and Maier, Seligman, and Solomon (1969) proposed a view, more similar to Bruner and McCulloch's than to any of the above hypothesis. Central to this view is the fact that, during uncontrollable shocks, what S does and what happens to S are *independent*. For example, consider inescapable shocks. At first the dog is not merely the passive recipient of the shocks. It struggles, howls, turns its head, exerts pressure on the straps holding its legs, etc. However, none of these responses affect either the onset, termination, or duration of the shocks: the shocks are independent of all voluntary responding. We will assume that Ss learn about the outcomes of their acts: they can learn that some act produces reinforcers (acquisition), that withholding some act produces reinforcers (differential reinforcement of other behavior, DRO) or that some act no longer produces reinforcers (extinction). But when shock is uncontrollable, the relation between act and outcome is *not* one of these; rather it is one of *independence*.

We think that Ss can learn that their responses are independent of reinforcers. To learn that responding and the occurrence of reinforcers are independent, S would have to be sensitive to: (a) the conditional probability of a reinforcer given a specific response ($p(\mathrm{RF}/\mathrm{R})$), (b) the conditional probability of a reinforcer in the absence of that specific response ($p(\mathrm{RF}/\overline{\mathrm{R}})$), and (c) the conjoint variation of these probabilities. If S is sensitive to these three relations, then systematic variation through the instrumental training space (see Figure 1) should produce systematic changes in behavior.

Independence between responding and shocks is the special case in which the two conditional probabilities are equal. The logic of such a conclusion is as follows: assume that the time between the onset and termination of shock is divided into a series of intervals, each of duration Δt. In addition, assume that Δt is smaller than the minimum duration of any response that S can make. Thus, either one response or no response can be occurring during a single Δt, which can also contain shock termination as well as a response or the absence of a response. When shock is inescapable, there is a fixed probability that shock will terminate in any Δt. For example, if shock duration is constant, the probability of shock termination during a trial will be zero in all Δts except the last. For the last $\triangle t$, the probability will be one. Because S cannot affect this probability in any $\triangle t$, the *conditional* probability of shock termination, given the occurrence of any response, is equal to the *unconditional* probability of shock termination in that $\triangle t$. The conditional probability of shock termination in any $\triangle t$, given the nonoccurrence of any response, is also equal to the unconditional probability of shock termination. It follows that when the contingencies are such that shock is inescapable, the conditional probability of shock termination, given any response, is equal to the conditional probability of shock termination in the absence of that response.

How might this relation of independence between responses and shocks produce the interference phenomenon? (1) S makes active responses during exposure to inescapable shocks. (2) Because shock cannot be controlled, S learns that shock termination is independent of its behavior. (3) S's incentive for initiating active instrumental responses during a shock is assumed to be partially produced by its having learned that the probability of shock termination will be increased by these responses. When this expectation is absent the incentive for instrumental responding should be reduced. (4) The presence of shock in the escape/avoidance training situation should then arouse the same expectation that was previously acquired during exposure to inescapable shocks: shock is uncontrollable. Therefore, the incentive for initiating and maintaining active instrumental responses in the training situation should be low. Maier *et al.* (1969) have proposed the term "learned helplessness" as a label for these hypothetical expectational and incentive mechanisms.

In addition, learning that shock termination and responding are independent should interfere with the subsequent association of responding and shock termination, just as, in verbal behavior, learning A–B interferes with the later learning of A–C. More exposures to the new contingency should be required in order for S to learn that shock is controllable, because S has already learned that shock is uncontrollable. This is why we think preshocked dogs have difficulty acquiring escape and avoidance responding even after they once jump the barrier and terminate shock.

If we hold in abeyance a consideration of the puzzling time-course phenomenon, the "helplessness" hypothesis can help us to understand the two-way shuttlebox, manipulandum, and passive avoidance results. Uncontrollable shocks reduce the incentive for attempting active instrumental responses. Manipulandum and two-way shuttlebox escape/avoidance require active instrumental responses and so should be retarded. Passive avoidance required the suppression of such responding

and so should be facilitated. But why should one-way shuttlebox
escape/avoidance show either no effect or facilitation? In one-way avoidance training, shocks only occur in one compartment of the apparatus;
one side is dangerous and the other safe. In order to learn one-way
avoidance, S must merely acquire conditioned fear of one compartment
of the apparatus but not of the other. Once this stimulus conditioning has
occurred, S's problem is solved: it does not have to *learn* to flee from a
dangerous to a safe place when both are in view. According to this interpretation, *one-way avoidance learning is not response learning. It is place
learning. Running from a dangerous place to a safe place may be an innate
response* (see also Chapter 3 by Bolles, this volume). If one-way shuttlebox performance involves only Pavlovian discriminative fear conditioning (safe side and dangerous side), then the helplessness hypothesis de-
duces the absence of interference. Uncontrollable shocks reduce the
incentive for performing active instrumental acts, but if active instrumental acts are not involved, no effect should be found. If shocks occur
in the "to-be-dangerous" side, facilitation of escape/avoidance performance would be expected because S would have already acquired conditioned fear of the appropriate place. If this argument is correct, a typical
one-way avoidance training procedure, with the additional requirement
that S perform some active response (*e.g.*, bar press, wheel turn) to enter
into the safe side from the dangerous side, should now produce the interference effect. Levine, Chevalier, and Korchin (1956) have used this
procedure and found interference. Also, Allison, Larson, and Jensen
(1967) showed that rats are poor at escaping from a fear CS in a one-
way situation, when they are required to turn a treadle in order to get to
the safe side. Thus, the effect of prior uncontrollable shock *is* reversed
when an instrumental response requirement is added to the one-way
avoidance training situation.

   In addition, in accounting for the complete pattern of the effects of
preshock on escape and avoidance, the helplessness hypothesis is not
incompatible with the data on the enhanced distress produced by inescapable shock. If S can learn that shock is controllable or uncontrollable, it would not be surprising if learning that shock is uncontrollable
might cause more distress and stress than learning that shock is controllable.

D.   Three Tests of the Helplessness Hypothesis

1.   Escapable versus Inescapable Preshock

   Besides explaining the obtained effects of preshock, the helplessness hypothesis generates other predictions. For this hypothesis, it is not the aversive stimulation itself that causes interference but rather it is S's lack of control over the aversive stimulus. This prediction has been tested (Seligman & Maier, 1967). One group of dogs, the escape group, was trained in a harness to escape shock by pressing panels located on both sides of S's head. A yoked group received the same shocks as did the escape group but had no control over shock. A naive control group received no shocks in the harness. All Ss received 10 trials of two-way shuttle box escape/avoidance training, 24 hr after their treatment received in the harness. Figure 4 shows the median latency of barrier jumping, on each of the 10 trials, for each of the three groups. The escape group showed no deficit in escape/avoidance performance, whereas the yoked group showed significantly longer latencies than did the naive control group. Thus, one prediction of the helplessness hypothesis was confirmed. Failure to escape during escape/avoidance training was not

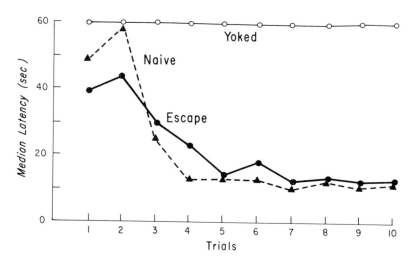

Fig. 4. The effects of matched escapable and inescapable shocks in the harness on later escape learning in the shuttlebox. Median escape latencies during shuttlebox training are shown for three groups of dogs: (a) those given escape training in the shuttle box as naive Ss, (b) those given prior escape training in the harness-panel press apparatus, and (c) those given prior inescapable shocks in the harness, their shocks matched in intensity, duration, and temporal distribution to the shocks actually received by the panel-press escape training group. The arbitrary criterion of failure to escape was 50 sec of shock (a latency of 60 sec from onset of the S^D).

produced by prior shock *per se,* but rather by *S*'s lack of control over prior shock.[8]

The "fear-freezing" hypothesis proposed by Weiss *et al.* (1968) does not deduce this finding easily. Escapable and inescapable shocks of equivalent duration and intensity should produce the same amount of conditioned fear and thus the same amount of freezing. *Fear* is traditionally defined as some conditionable part of *S*'s innate reaction to pain. Thus escapable and inescapable shocks should lead to the same amount of conditioned fear, unless one further assumes that the contingency between response and shock directly affects the distress produced by shock, which in turn controls the amplitude of conditioned fear. Even if one so argues that controllable shocks produce less conditioned fear than do uncontrollable shocks, controllable shocks should still produce *some* conditioned fear and therefore *some* subsequent freezing. But controllable shocks produced no interference at all in the Seligman and Maier experiment. But when one argues that uncontrollable shocks produce more conditioned fear than do controllable shocks, then one must still assume that *S* is sensitive to the fact that shock *is* uncontrollable. Thus, to make the "fear-freezing" argument adequate to the findings, one must accept the learning of independence between shock termination and responding which is the central thesis of the helplessness hypothesis.

2. The Immunization Procedure

The helplessness hypothesis suggests that prior experience with con-

[8]Maier (1970) provided more dramatic confirmation of the hypothesis. In response to the possible criticism that what is learned during uncontrollable trauma is not a set of helplessness, as we have proposed, but some motor response, like freezing, which antagonizes barrier jumping, Maier (1970) reinforced the most antagonistic response he could find. One group (passive–escape) of dogs had panels pushed to ¼ in. of the sides and top of their heads. Only by not moving their heads, by remaining passive and still, could these dogs terminate shock. Another group (yoked) received the same shocks in the hammock, but it was independent of responding. A third group received no shock. A response-learning source of helplessness predicts that when the dogs were later tested in the shuttlebox, the passive–escape group should be the most helpless since they had been trained explicitly to be still in the face of trauma. The helplessness hypothesis makes the opposite prediction: These dogs could control shock, albeit by being passive. Some response, even a competing one, was effective in producing relief, and they should not learn that responding doesn't matter. The passive escape group should not give up according to the helplessness hypothesis, and this is exactly what happened. The dogs in the yoked group were predominantly helpless in shuttlebox escape, and the naive controls escaped normally. The passive–escape group at first looked for "still" ways of minimizing shock in the shuttlebox. Failing to find these, they all began to escape and avoid. These results are clearly not compatible with Weiss' "fear-freezing" hypothesis. Thus it is not trauma *per se* that produces failure to escape but having learned that no response at all can control trauma.

trollable shocks should proactively interfere with S's learning that shock is *un*controllable and should also allow S to discriminate between the places where shocks are controllable and not controllable. Thus, the helplessness hypothesis predicts that one should be able to immunize Ss against the interfering effects of uncontrollable shocks. Seligman and Maier (1967) gave one group of dogs 10 trials of escape/avoidance training in the shuttlebox before treatment with inescapable shocks in the harness. Following exposure to inescapable shocks in the harness, the dogs escaped and avoided shocks normally when returned to the shuttlebox. Immunization must have been a result of the *controllability* of the initial shocks in the shuttlebox because initial experience with equivalent amounts of *uncontrollable* shocks in the shuttlebox did *not* prevent interference.

After an escape or avoidance response is well-learned, exposure to uncontrollable shocks in the same training situation can actually enhance escape and avoidance performance. For example, Sidman, Herrnstein, and Conrad (1957) trained monkeys to perform an avoidance response on a Sidman schedule. When performance was nearly perfect, Ss were exposed to occasional, unpredictable and uncontrollable shocks while they were performing the avoidance response. The response rate increased. Kelleher, Riddle, and Cook (1963) reported a similar finding in monkeys. Waller and Waller (1963) obtained this result in dogs. Baum (1965) also reported enhancement of a well-learned avoidance response in rats when they were exposed to inescapable shocks.

The effect of uncontrollable shocks therefore depends, at least in part, on the degree of control S has acquired *prior* to its being subjected to uncontrollable shocks. Sometimes, when S is only partially trained, and therefore has not achieved good control over shocks, the occurrence of inescapable shocks will then retard or interfere with subsequent escape and avoidance learning (for example, see: Anderson *et al.*, 1966; Anderson and Nakamura, Experiment II, 1964; Hearst and Whelan, 1963).

3. A Therapy Procedure

The helplessness hypothesis suggests a way to break up interference once it has occurred. If a dog fails to escape because it does not expect its active instrumental responding to lead to shock termination, forcibly exposing it to the escape/avoidance contingency should weaken this expectation and thus remove interference. Seligman *et al.* (1968) took three dogs that had repeatedly failed to escape, and during signalled shock trials they forcibly pulled them from one side of the shuttlebox (with barrier absent) to the other, thus terminating the CS and shock. After 20, 35, and 50 forcible exposures to the escape/avoidance contingency, each S began to respond on its own. The barrier was then replaced, and all Ss continued to respond successfully.

E.   A Difficulty for the Helplessness Hypothesis: Dissipation in Time

A major difficulty for the learned helplessness explanation is the work of Overmier and Seligman (1967) who found that dogs given prior experience with inescapable shocks do not show the interference phenomenon in two-way shuttlebox acquisition if 48 or more hours intervene between inescapable shocks and the training session. If this time course is a general phenomenon, how can it be explained? The helplessness hypothesis depends on *learned* tendencies and therefore does not predict the dissipation of interference effects in time. A supplementary explanation is that shocks, either controllable or uncontrollable, have a direct physiological or emotional effect which goes away with time. We have already argued (Section II,C,4) that this hypothesis, by itself, is inadequate. However, it is possible that emotional exhaustion is produced, not by pain *per se,* but by learning that S's behavior is ineffective in controlling a painful event. This seems plausible because inescapable shocks cause more distress than do equivalent numbers of escapable shocks (see discussion above, Section II,B). Emotional exhaustion might decay in time, thus partially accounting for the time course of the interference phenomenon. (See also footnote 7.)

On the other hand, when a dog is subjected to inescapable shocks on *two* successive occasions separated by 24 hr, the interference phenomenon lasts at least for one month. An explanation involving only a dissipating state of emotional exhaustion cannot explain this fact. Perhaps, like fear, a state of emotional exhaustion is conditionable. If so, exposure of S to the cues in the escape/avoidance training situation, a month after its previous failure to escape in that situation, might elicit the exhaustion state itself as a CR pattern. But can this kind of conditioning actually occur?

Alternatively, it might be argued that the interference effect results from the extinction of active responses during inescapable shock; then the subsequent *spontaneous recovery* of those extinguished, active attempts to escape might produce the time course. If, however, the time course of the interference effect should be shown to be nonmonotonic, *i.e.,* similar to the Kamin effect, then a spontaneous recovery explanation would be hard to support. In addition, spontaneous recovery, at least in appetitive situations, usually occurs in minutes, not over a period of two days. Finally, if one uses a spontaneous recovery argument, one should distinguish between extinction *procedures,* extinction *out-*

comes, and extinction *processes.* Administering shock independently of *S*'s behavior is not an extinction *procedure.* An extinction procedure for escape responding is one in which either no shock is presented or shock is turned on but does not terminate during the session. This follows from the definition of an extinction *procedure* as one in which the reinforcer is withdrawn from the situation. However, it is possible that inescapable shocks produce the same behavioral *outcomes* as do normal extinction procedures. It is also possible that the same *processes* are involved. Either removing aversive stimuli entirely from the situation or presenting them independently of *S*'s behavior might reduce incentive to initiate active responses. However, merely stating that inescapable shocks produce extinction of active responses is not an explanation. Unless a mechanism of extinction is described, the assertion is merely a restatement of the data. The helplessness hypothesis is not merely such a restatement of the data because it suggests a mechanism and generates deductions of its own.

F.   Summary

Uncontrollable shocks have several effects. They interfere with the later acquisition of responses that control shock in two-way escape/avoidance, and in· manipulandum escape/avoidance training situations. Uncontrollable shocks facilitate the later acquisition of passive avoidance responses, and either slightly facilitate or have no effect on later one-way avoidance learning. Uncontrollable shocks appear to cause more distress than controllable shocks. We have examined several explanations of these effects. None of them accounts for all of the findings. The theory, postulating learned helplessness, appeals to us because it has suggested several predictions which have been confirmed, and it seems more compatible with the available data than are competing explanations.

III.   UNPREDICTABLE SHOCKS

We have completed our discussion of the consequences of presenting uncontrollable aversive stimuli to organisms: we have seen that when shocks are presented along the 45° line of the instrumental training space, so that all responding is independent of shocks, adaptive behavior is often severely undermined. We now turn to experiments using conditions lying along the 45° line of the Pavlovian conditioning space. In these experiments shocks and CSs occur independently of one another, so that shocks are unpredictable.

Converging evidence suggests a generalization about experiments on both animals and humans using unpredictable and predictable shocks: unpredictable shocks are more aversive, distressing, and stressful than predictable shocks. A primary measure of aversiveness is choice, and animals and humans choose predictable over unpredictable shock. Distress can be measured subjectively, as well as by response suppression, and these measures show unpredictable shock situations to be more distressing than are predictable shock situations. Physiological measures of stress indicate the same thing.

A.   Predictable Shocks Are Preferred to Unpredictable Shocks

1.   Direct Choice

Lockard (1963) shocked rats on both sides of a two-compartment box. On the "predictable" side, each shock was preceded by a warning signal, while on the "unpredictable" side, shocks were not preceded by a signal. The rats could move freely from one side to the other. They progressively spent more of their time on the predictable shock side. Perkins, Levin, and Seymann (1963), and Perkins, Seymann, Levis, and Spencer (1966) using rats, and Pervin (1963) using humans, found similar results.

2.   Choice of Immediate over Delayed Shocks

When shocks occur immediately following a signal or an act, the termination of the signal or the performance of the act provides *exact* predictability of shock. If shock is delayed, predictability of the point in time at which shock will occur is less exact.

Knapp, Kause, and Perkins (1959) allowed hungry rats to take either of two paths to food. In each path there was a chamber in which the rats were held for 45 sec before being allowed to run on to food. Shocks occurred in both chambers. On one side, the rats received a shock as soon as they entered an "immediate" chamber. On the other side, shock occurred 45 sec after the rat entered a "delay" chamber. The rats preferred the "immediate" shock path.

D'Amato and Gumenik (1960), Cook and Barnes (1964), Badia, McBane, Suter, and Lewis (1966) and Badia, Suter, and Lewis (1967) have all demonstrated that human Ss show an analagous preference for immediate over delayed shocks.

3.   Choice of Response-Contingent versus Response-Independent Shocks

When a shock immediately follows a response, it is predictable. For example, if a rat is punished by shock for bar-pressing, then bar-pressing predicts shock, and not-bar-pressing predicts no-shock. A "yoked" rat, which receives response-independent shock, is given no such predictor. From this it follows that Ss should choose response-contingent over response-independent shocks, just as they will choose predictable over unpredictable shocks. Pervin (1963) reported this result in humans, but Rachlin and Herrnstein (1969) reported that pigeons did not strongly prefer punishment over response-independent shock. When the shock densities were equated, three out of their four birds, however, showed small preferences in the expected direction. Further exploration of this problem is needed.

B. Unpredictable Shocks Are More Distressing and Stressful than Predictable Shocks

Why do animals and humans choose predictable shocks over unpredictable shocks? One answer is that predictable shocks may cause less distress and physiological stress than unpredictable shocks. Behavioral, physiological, and subjective measures suggest that this may be so.

Azrin (1956) shocked pigeons that were key-pecking for food at either fixed (predictable) intervals (FI) or variable (unpredictable) intervals (VI). He measured suppression of pecking with these schedules of shock. VI shocks caused more suppression than did FI shocks, regardless of whether the birds were shocked for pecking or were shocked independently of pecking. If we assume that suppression of appetitive responding is a measure of fear, predictable shocks caused less fear than did unpredictable shocks. Similarly, Brimer and Kamin (1963) reported greater suppression of bar-pressing for food in rats receiving unsignalled shocks than in those receiving signalled shocks.

As emphasized previously, when shocks are response-contingent, they are more predictable than when they are response-independent, and we cited evidence (Section II,B) that response independent shocks result in more distress than do controllable shocks.

Physiological measures suggest that unpredictable shocks also are more stressful. Sawrey (1961) gave buzzers, lights, and shocks to two groups of rats. For one group, the light was always followed by a shock, and the buzzer was never followed by a shock. Thus shock was 100% reliably predicted by the light. These rats formed a mean of 1.83 ulcers. The other group received half of the lights followed by shocks and half of the buzzers followed by shocks. For this group, neither the buzzer nor the light was a 100% reliable predictor of shock. These rats formed a mean ot 5.50 ulcers. Similarly, Weiss (1968b) gave restrained rats signalled or unsignalled shocks through fixed tail electrodes. Shocks occurred once a minute for 19 hr. The rats that received unsignalled shocks showed higher rectal temperatures and formed larger ulcers than did the rats that received signalled shocks.

In contrast to these results, Paré (1964) and Brady, Thronton and deFisher (1962) reported slightly more weight loss in rats receiving predictable shocks than in rats receiving unpredictable shocks, and no significant differences in incidence of ulceration were found. We do not yet know the significant variables producing the discrepancies between these studies.

By-and-large, human Ss report that unsignalled shock *situations* are more distressing than are signalled shock *situations*. The evidence is not definitive, however, on whether the unpredictable shocks hurt more or whether the whole unpredictable shock situation is more anxiety-arousing. D'Amato and Gumenik (1960), Pervin (1963), and Badia *et al.* (1966, 1967) all reported that Ss say they dislike unpredictable shocks more than they dislike predictable shocks, and Hare and Petrusic (1967) found that long-delayed shocks are judged to be more intense than are less-delayed shocks.

Two prominent reasons Ss give for their preference are that with predictable shocks (a) they can relax when the signal is not present but they can never relax with unpredictable shocks, and (b) the signal allows them to "prepare for" shock, and so each shock hurts less. These two verbal reports embody the two theories of the effects of unpredictable shocks.

C.   Theories about the Emotional Attributes of Predictable and Unpredictable Shocks

1.   The Preparatory Response Hypothesis

In his experiments on the choice of predictable over unpredictable outcomes, Perkins suggested that a preparatory response occurs when outcomes are predictable, and the response makes the outcome more appetitive or less aversive. Thus, in the case of signalled food, S salivates when the signal comes on, and consequently the food tastes better than if it had been unsignalled and no preparatory salivation had occurred. In the case of signalled shock, S makes some response during the signal which reduces the pain of the shock; when shock is unsignalled the preparatory response cannot be made at the appropriate time. Similarly, in his experiments on the attenuation of the GSR unconditioned response to signalled shock, Kimmel (1965) has suggested that the signal allows S to make some preparatory response which lessens the pain of the shock.

The preparatory response hypothesis is consistent with much of the evidence that unpredictable shocks are more disturbing than are predictable shocks. So this hypothesis claims that Ss choose predictable shocks over unpredictable shocks because they *hurt* less. Ss choose immediate shocks over delayed shocks because they can time their preparatory responses more accurately with immediate shocks and thus render the shocks *less painful*. Unpredictable shocks are more disturbing because the *pain* produced by these shocks is greater.

Confirmation of this hypothesis requires E to show that pain is actually reduced by some preparatory response to a signal for shock. There is one line evidence, which, it has been claimed, provides this evidence. The Galvanic skin response (GSR) to shock, which is assumed to measure the pain-fear component of the unconditioned response (UCR) to shock, has been observed with both signalled and unsignalled shocks. It was found that the GSR to shock is larger if no CS precedes it. For example, Kimmel and Pennypacker (1962) presented human Ss with CSs followed by shocks. The GSR to shock became smaller and smaller over trials when shock was signalled. Then an unsignalled shock occurred, and the GSR increased. Lykken (1962) Kimmel (1965), Morrow (1966), and others, have all presented similar evidence. This effect has been interpreted to show a conditioned inhibition of the UCR to shock produced by the CS. Of interest to us is the possibility that the "conditioned inhibition" is caused by reduced painfulness of shocks when they are signalled.

The main evidence for the preparatory response interpretation of pain reduction is that the unconditioned GSR to shock is larger when a shock is unsignalled. We question the interpretation that this *necessarily* reflects decreased pain resulting from a preparatory response. Rather, we think that the increased GSR may reflect the arousal of an orienting response (OR) precipitated by breaking the consistent CS–UCS pairing, and not necessarily by increased pain and fear caused by shock.

Sokolov (1963) and others have gathered much evidence that the orienting response is reflected in increased GSR. Sokolov's findings show that when a stimulus pattern changes, S will show an orienting response. Increased GSR is one index of this orienting response. For example, it is commonly observed that when a novel tone is presented, S shows a large GSR. If the tone is sounded every 10 sec, the GSR gradually diminishes. If the tone is then omitted at one of the 10-sec intervals (changing the pattern of the stimulus situation), the large GSR *returns*. The data of Kimmel and his co-workers are consistent with the orienting response interpretation because their procedure always produced a change in a regularly-presented sequence. Consider, for example, the CS- omission data of

Kimmel and Pennypacker (1962): Here one can assume that an OR (GSR) occurs to the first shock when it is presented with the CS, and then habituates as the CS-shock pairings become less novel. Then, for the first time, E presents a shock without a CS, changing the stimulus pattern. The GSR (OR) returns to the shock. The pain-fear component of the UR may remain constant, but the OR (GSR) component changes. The same logic holds for the several other GSR studies of Kimmel and his collaborators. So it seems to us that the GSR data do not support the hypothesis that a signal preceding shock allows S to prepare for the shock and thereby reduce its intensity. Rather, these data seem to be subsumable under the traditional OR concepts of Sokolov.

The preparatory response explanation, moreover, is not easily testable, because the preparatory response is not an observable event. Recently, Perkins *et al.* (1966) found that even when rats were shocked through fixed electrodes on the ears (eliminating the pain-reducing effectiveness of those *peripheral* preparatory responses that change contact between S and grid bars) the rats still preferred signalled to unsignalled shock. Similarly, Weiss (1968b) has found that rats formed more ulcers with unpredictable shocks when the shocks were administered through a fixed tail electrode. Perkins *et al.* (1966) concluded that the preparatory response to signalled shock must be some unknown *central* event.

2.   A Safety-Signal Theory of the Effects of Unpredictable Shock

The preparatory response hypothesis explains the greater distress caused by unpredictable shock by postulating that shock, itself, hurts more when it is not predicted. But there is an alternative view which is compatible with the evidence: shock, itself, does not hurt more when it is unpredictable; rather, the situation becomes more distressing because it lacks a predictor of *no* shock. When a stimulus reliably predicts the occurrence of electric shock, then safety, the absence of shock, is also usually predicted by the *absence* of the signal for shock. In Pavlovian language, the existence of a reliable CS^+ for shock (an excitor of fear) usually implies the existence of a reliable CS^- (a differential inhibitor of fear). The absence of the CS^+ is a reliable CS^-, because there is never a pairing of shock with absence of CS^+. The predictability of a shock-free period may be as important for S as the predictability of shock itself. It has been well established recently that animals can learn that a discrete stimulus predicts the absence of shock as well as that a stimulu predicts shock (Soltysik and Zielinski, 1962; Rescorla and LoLordo, 1965; Rescorla, 1967; LoLordo, 1967; Weisman, Denny, Platt and Zerbolio, 1966; Hammond, 1966; Moscovitch and LoLordo, 1968).

Assuming that what controls behavior in a shock situation is *the pres-*

ence of a reliable predictor of the absence of shock, as well as the presence of a reliable predictor of the occurrence of shock, then *if no safety
signal is present, the organism will remain in chronic fear.*

When applied to the data previously discussed, the safety signal hypothesis suggests that Ss prefer predictable to unpredictable shock, not
because predictable shock hurts less but because the situation in which
predictable shock occurs causes less total fear. For example, in Lockard's (1963) study, when the rat is in the predictable-shock side of the
apparatus, it is fearful only when the CS^+ is on. When the CS^+ is not
on, S is safe and can relax. On the unpredictable shock side, however,
the rat has no safety-signal, is constantly in the presence of CS^+ and is
fearful all of the time. The shocks themselves may not be differentially
painful; rather, the predictable shock situation elicits less fear, and thus
less distress because the rat can spend most of its time in the presence of
a safety signal.[9]

Similarly, the safety signal hypothesis argues that the *situation* in
which delayed shock occurs causes S to be in a fear state for a longer
period of time than does the immediate shock situation because organisms cannot "time" perfectly. If a brief shock is delivered immediately
on entering a chamber, and S is released 45 sec later (Knapp *et al.,*
1959), it receives a shock followed by 45 sec of a CS^- (safety). If the
shock is delayed for 45 sec, S receives 45 sec of CS^+, during the later
moments of which it is in a state of fear, followed by the shock. So the
rat chooses the chamber in which it is fearful less of the time.

The safety-signal hypothesis holds that a situation in which shock is
uncontrollable (response-independent) should arouse more fear than a
situation in which shock is response-contingent (see Section II,B). When
shock is response-contingent, witholding the response predicts that no
shock will occur and thus provides a CS^- (safety). Making the response
predicts shock and produces a CS^+ for fear. As long as the rat withholds
the response, it is in the presence of a fear-inhibiting stimulus. A yoked
rat (for which shock is response-independent) has no such safety signal,
and therefore remains in chronic fear.

We have seen that rats that receive light followed by shock 100% of
the time, and buzzer never followed by shock, form fewer ulcers than do
rats that receive half of the lights and half of the buzzers followed by
shocks (Sawrey, 1961). The safety signal hypothesis holds that for the
100% group, the buzzer is a CS^- because it is never followed by a shock.
For the 50% group, neither the buzzer nor the light is a safety signal.
The 50% group spends more total time in a state of fear and thus forms
more ulcers. Finally, Ss' subjective reports about the aversiveness of

---

[9]*Editor's note:* See also Denny's treatment (Chapter 4, this volume) of relaxation and relief for additional discussion relevant to this issue.

unpredictable shocks can also be understood using the safety signal hypothesis. Because Ss are in fear for a longer time with unpredictable than with predictable shocks, it follows that a higher level of background fear should occur in unpredictable shock situations. This deduction is supported by the two typical subjective reports about stress that characterize the experiments with humans: (a) the report that S can relax more of the time with predictable shocks, and (b) the report that unpredictable shocks hurt more. More relaxation follows directly from the safety signal hypothesis, and Melzack and Wall (1965), in their theory of pain-perception, suggest that pain should be enhanced when it occurs against a background of sympathetic activity. Unpredictable shocks, since they provide a background of fear, should cause felt shock to be more distressing. Predictable shocks, however, do not occur against such a background of fear and so should not be as distressing (cf. Hare and Petrusic, 1967).

Confirmation of the safety signal hypothesis requires E to show that S does actually remain in chronic fear when there is no reliable predictor of safety. The safety signal hypothesis holds that Ss receiving unpredictable shock should be in fear all the time in the shock situation because they have no safety signal. On the assumption that incidence of ulceration is a function of amount of time spent in a state of fear, these Ss should form more ulcers than do Ss which receive identical, but predictable, shocks. Seligman (1968) provided evidence for the hypothesis. He trained two groups of 8 rats each to bar-press for food on a VI schedule. In Phase I each group received sessions with CSs and shocks while they bar-pressed for food. One group (PR) received their CSs each followed by a shock. Another group (UN) received the same number of CSs and shocks, but in a random temporal relationship. The random presentation of shocks and CSs assured that no predictor either of shock or safety existed. In Phase II both groups received CS-free and shock-free bar-pressing sessions. Then in Phase III both groups received predictable shock paired with a new CS+. The groups differed only in Phase I, in that shock was unpredictable for the UN group but predictable for the PR group.

Figure 5 shows the total bar pressing over the shocked days of Phase I as a percentage of the bar pressing on the last shock free day (Day A). Every S in the PR Group showed reduced bar pressing when shock was first introduced. After several sessions, however, all Ss began to bar-press again. They pressed in the absence of the CS+ for shock (safety), but did not press during the CS+. In contrast, each S in the UN Group stopped bar pressing altogether and showed no sign of recovery.

In Phase II, all Ss were retrained so that the UN Group and PR

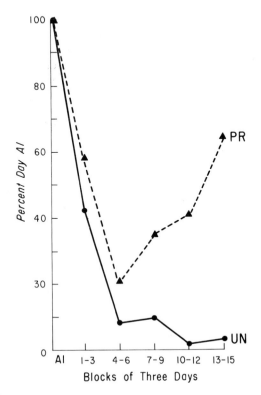

Fig. 5. The effects of unpredictable shocks on appetitive bar pressing in rats (from Seligman, 1968). The data is presented in the form of total bar pressing during block of days on which shock occurred as a percent of bar pressing on the last shock free day (Day A). Every S in the PR (predictable shocks) Group showed suppressed bar pressing initially, but after several sessions they bar-pressed again. In contrast, the rats in the UN (unpredictable shocks) Group stopped bar pressing and did not recover. This phenomenon is interpreted to be chronic fear in the UN Group.

Group exhibited the same bar-pressing rates. In Phase III, both groups received shocks predicted by a new signal. The PR Group recovered bar pressing more quickly than they had in Phase I, and again these Ss failed to press only during the signal. The UN Group, in contrast, stopped bar pressing completely and again did not recover. Finally, Ss in the UN Group, which had shown prolonged suppression of bar pressing, formed a median of 4.5 stomach ulcers. No S in the PR Group formed ulcers. Davis and McIntire (1969) independently performed essentially the same experiment as Phase I of Seligman (1968). The behavioral results were similar.

These results can be readily understood with the safety signal hypothesis and provide direct evidence that rats are in fear all the time in the absence of a predictor of safety. We know that fear suppresses bar pressing for food (Estes and Skinner, 1941). In Phase I, Ss in Seligman's (1968) UN group had no safety-signal and therefore should have remained in a chronic fear state. They should have *stopped bar pressing and shown no recovery*. They should not have pressed the bar either during the CS or in its absence. Ss in the group receiving predictable shock should have shown reduced bar pressing in the early sessions until they had learned to discriminate the safe periods: then they should have recovered bar pressing in the absence of the CS and should have failed to press the bar only during the CS^+. This should have been the case, because the absence of CS^+ should gradually have acquired the properties of a CS^-, a Pavlovian conditioned inhibitor of fear. This is what was found.

In Phase III, both groups received shocks *predicted* by a new signal. Group PR should then have shown less disruption of pressing in the absence of the new CS^+ than it had in Phase I, because, even though the CS^+ was new, the safety-signal (the chamber with CS^+ absent) was the same in both Phases. Group UN, however, should again have shown disruption of bar pressing and little or no recovery. This is because the new CS^- (the chamber in the absence of the CS^+) had not been a safety-signal in Phase I; so not only must a discrimination between CS^+ and CS^- now develop, but also extinction of fear to the new CS^- must also occur. This is what was found. Finally, the safety-signal hypothesis predicts that since Ss in the UN Group had been in chronic fear (as shown by the suppression of bar pressing), they should have shown more stomach ulcers than the PR Group. And this too was confirmed. Thus, Seligman's findings provide detailed support for the hypothesis.

The safety-signal hypothesis assumes that S remains in constant fear whenever it is not being exposed to a reliable predictor of safety. But how great is such chronic fear? Is it less intense than the peak of phasic fear caused by the onset of a reliable predictor of shock? Seligman (1968) found that rats which had received tones paired with shock showed discriminative conditioned suppression of bar pressing. Rats that had received tones and shocks randomly interspersed failed to bar press later in both the presence *and* the absence of the tone. We can reasonably assume that the *duration* of conditioned fear elicitation was longer for rats that received unpredictable shocks: but was the magnitude of fear different in the two groups? One could argue that it should have been because the probability of shock during any one minute of the unpredictable-shock sessions was considerably lower than the probability of shock during the one minute predictor of shock in the predictable shock sessions. However, the fact that the PR Group did not press at all during the tone, and the UN Group did not press at all throughout each session, suggests that the fear may have been the same in both groups. But this could have been due to a ceiling effect. Parametric studies of the effect of different intensities of predictable versus unpredictable shock should help to clarify this matter. With less intense shocks, a difference might emerge between the magnitudes of fear (indexed by suppression of bar pressing) in the predictable versus unpredictable shock situations. We would anticipate that the PR Group would be more afraid *during the* CS^+ than the UN Group would be throughout each session, because the probability of shock is greater during the CS^+ for the PR Group than it is during any equal period of time for the UN Group.[10]

3. Safety-Signal versus Preparatory Response Explanations

The safety-signal hypothesis does not exclude the possibility that some unknown preparatory response occurs when shock is signalled, and both theories may be useful. There is, however, no evidence yet that such a preparatory response occurs and serves the postulated instrumental function. The data of Seligman (1968) and of Davis and McIntire (1969) provide strong support for the safety-signal explanation of the effects of unpredictable shocks, and these data are not predicted easily by the preparatory response explanation. We must, however, be concerned with the existence of evidence that can be explained by the preparatory response theory but not by the safety-signal theory. One such line of evidence is that Ss choose predictable food over unpredictable food *e.g.*, Prokasy, 1956). The preparatory response theory can easily explain this: S prepares itself for food (*e.g.*, salivates) when food is signalled with the result that the food then tastes better when it is presented. Can the safety signal hypothesis also handle these data? Possibly. Assume that the motivation for food getting is a hunger (or starvation)-fear (*e.g.*, Mowrer, 1960). Assume further that in the absence of a reliable predictor of food, S remains in continual hunger-fear. Then less hunger-fear should occur in the signalled-food situation, and Ss should prefer it to the unsignalled food situation. Hunt, Scholosberg, Solomon, and Stellar (1941) have shown that food hoarding in the rat is greater if it has had past experience with starvation. The safety-signal hypothesis, when applied to appetitive situations, suggests that rats raised with unpredictable food should hoard more food than rats raised with predictable food because they will have experienced more hunger-fear. Mandler (1958) reared rats on different food-deprivation schedules. For one group, deprivation was variable (and food was unpredictable); it ranged between 6

[10]Seligman and Meyer (1970) recently confirmed this.

and 60 hr. For another group, deprivation was regular; 16 hr of *ad lib* food was alternated with 12 hr of deprivation. Mandler found that when both groups were later tested at the same deprivation level the variable group showed more rapid consummatory behavior and more rapid learning to bar press for food. The following observations were more directly to the point:

> The irregularly deprived animals were much more forceful in grabbing the pellets out of *E*'s hand, were more active, and showed one interesting pattern of behavior which was more pronounced than the control animals: Several pellets were put in the cage. When the rat had grabbed the first one, it wouldn't put it down in the rear of the cage and come get the next one (a fairly typical pattern for control rats). Rather it kept it in its mouth, grabbed at the next one with its paws, and appeared desperate as to how it could get the third one. The result was a lot of activity, circling around, accompanied by excited-looking behavior . . . . A second type of behavior, perhaps a little more like hoarding, was the reaction to removal of pellets at the end of a feeding period. The irregularly deprived animals would grab a pellet in their mouths at *E*'s approach to the cage and frequently considerable force was required to pull it out. They would also hold a pellet in their paws and huddle with it in the rear of the cage. This behavior also was consistent and recurrent and noticeable to all observers (Mandler, personal communication, 1967).

As the safety signal hypothesis suggests, irregularly-deprived animals may hoard more than do regularly deprived animals. If this is so, animals should prefer predictable to unpredictable food since they will experience less hunger-fear in the predictable food condition.

D.   The Effect of Prediction of Shock or Its Absence on Escape/Avoidance Behavior

Heretofore, we have discussed in detail the experiments which indicate that unpredictable shocks are more distressing than predictable shocks, and that *S*s prefer predictable shocks over unpredictable shocks. In addition, there are very striking properties acquired by specific stimuli that reliably predict either shocks or their absence, and which are revealed in their effect on escape/avoidance behavior. By varying the parameters of the Pavlovian conditioning space (See Figure 2) one can produce stimuli having markedly different effects on avoidance behavior.

Stimuli which predict shock will arouse fear and potentiate previously learned avoidance responses. Through the work carried out in our laboratory by Rescorla and LoLordo (1965), LoLordo and Rescorla (1966), LoLordo (1967), Rescorla (1967), and Moscovitch and LoLordo (1968), we now know that Pavlovian fear conditioning obeys the laws of Pavlovian salivary conditioning. These laws are strikingly revealed in the control of avoidance responding by Pavlovian CSs of many types. Some CSs are "danger signals," some are "safety signals," but all have one feature in common: they lie within the coordinates of the Pavlovian conditioning space (See Figure 2). Usually the CS^+ lies out at the 1.00 value on the abscissa, while the contrasting CS^- lies at the zero value on the ordinate and abscissa. We will review the techniques developed to create CSs^+ and CSs^- which later have the capacity to influence already established avoidance behavior.[11]

1. Excitation and Differential Inhibition

Rescorla and LoLordo (1965) trained dogs to jump a barrier in a shuttlebox to avoid shock on a Sidman, unsignallized shock schedule until a stable jumping rate was established. The dogs were then confined to one side of the shuttlebox and subjected to discriminative Pavlovian fear conditioning. A tone (CS^+) was paired with shock, and another tone (CS^-) was paired with absence of shock. Since the probability of shock given the (CS^+ was 1.0 and given the CS^- was 0, the predictability of shocks and safety was perfect. Later, in a test session, while the dog was jumping at a stable rate, a series of 5-sec test presentations of CS^+ and CS^- was superimposed on the existing schedule. The CS^+ produced an immediate tripling of the jumping rate whereas the CS^- reduced the jumping rate almost to zero. These results are illustrated in Figure 6. Thus, a stimulus which previously has been a perfect predictor of shock can, if presented, enhance or energize avoidance responding. A stimulus which has previously been a perfect predictor of absence of shock can, if presented, inhibit or de-energize avoidance responding.

2. Excitation and Conditioned Inhibition

Rescorla and LoLordo (1965) trained two other groups of dogs to avoid shock on a Sidman schedule in the shuttlebox. Then they subjected one group to a Pavlovian fear conditioning procedure in which CS^+ was followed by shock on half of the trials, but on the other half of the trials CS^+ was followed by CS^- and *no* shock. The second group, af-

[11]*Editor's note:* See also Chapter 4 by Denny and Chapter 2 by McAllister and McAllister.

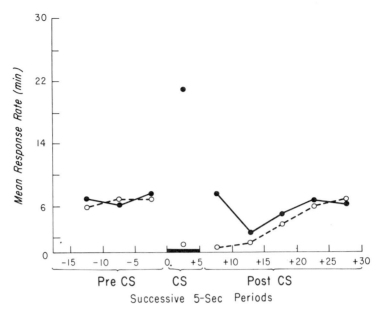

Fig. 6. Differential excitation and inhibition of fear in dogs (from Rescorla & Lo-Lordo, 1965). Prior to testing, *S*s had been trained with a Sidman contingency to avoid shocks reliably in the shuttlebox. Their typical response rate was 7 jumps/min. They were then given Pavlovian differential fear conditioning in the same shuttle box, while jumping was prevented. One tone served as CS^+, a contrasting tone was the CS^-. Later in a test session, while *S*s were jumping regularly in the shuttlebox, 5-sec test prods with each CS were given. The ordinate shows response rate in jumps per minute. The abscissa shows time before the test prod, during it, and after it. The response rates for CS^+ and CS^- are compared, the solid dots representing CS^+ and the open circles representing CS^-.

ter learning the Sidman avoidance response, was subjected to a different Pavlovian fear-conditioning procedure: CS^+ was followed by shock whenever it was presented without the CS^-, but on the other half of the trials CS^- was inserted 5 sec before the CS^+ and *no* shock followed. The CS^- in both procedures acquired fear-inhibiting properties in the sense that test presentations of CS^- reduced significantly the Sidman avoidance response rate. Presentations of CS^+ doubled the response rate. These findings are illustrated in Figure 7.

3.   *Inhibition by Temporal Delay*

Rescorla (1967b) trained dogs to avoid shock on a Sidman schedule in the shuttlebox. When the dogs had acquired a stable jumping rate, they were subjected to a Pavlovian fear-condition procedure in which a 30-sec tone (CS^+) was followed by shock. Later, while the dogs were perform-

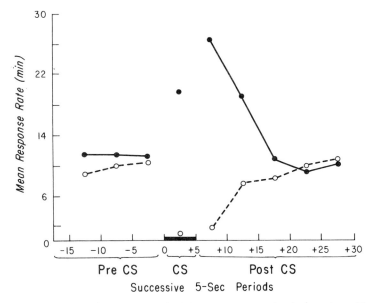

Fig. 7. Conditional excitatory and inhibitory control of instrumental avoidance responding by a Pavlovian CS$^+$ and CS$^-$. Prior to testing, Ss had been trained under a Sidman contingency to avoid shock in the shuttlebox. After their response rate was stable they were given Pavlovian conditioning, using the typical Pavlovian conditioned inhibition procedure: when CS$^+$ occurred alone it was always paired with shock, but when CS$^+$ and CS$^-$ occurred in close temporal sequence, no shock was given. Then, in a later session, while Ss were jumping in the shuttlebox, test prods with each CS were given. The ordinate shows jumps per minute. The abscissa shows time before the test prod, during it, and after it. Rates for CS$^+$ are represented by solid dots, for CS$^-$ by open circles.

ing their avoidance response in the shuttlebox, the 30-sec tone was presented from time to time. The effects of the tone are shown in Figure 8. The *onset* of the tone produced a *decrease* in jumping rate, and in the continued presence of the tone the rate gradually increased. At about 20-sec tone duration, the jumping rate went above the normal baseline rate, increasing steadily to the end of the interval, at which time the rate had approximately doubled. Cessation of the tone produced a decrease in jumping rate to a level below the normal baseline rate, followed by slow recovery to the baseline rate. Rescorla (1967b) has confirmed this finding in dogs trained to press a panel to avoid shock on a Sidman schedule. Here is another case in which *onset* of a predictor of shock *decreased* avoidance responding. Pavlov found similar inhibition of delay with salivary CSs and long-duration CSs, and he argued that the onset of the CS$^+$ is never closely paired with the US, and functions as a CS$^-$, inhibiting reflexes (Pavlov, 1927, p. 88). Rescorla's results show that the law

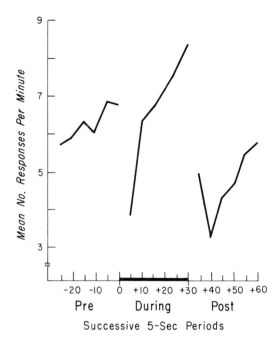

Fig. 8. Inhibition by temporal delay (adapted from Rescorla, 1967b). After avoidance training in the shuttlebox under a Sidman contingency, Ss were given simple Pavlovian conditioning with a 30-sec CS–UCS interval. There was no CS^-. In the test session, while Ss were jumping at a stable rate in the shuttlebox, the 30-sec CS^+ was presented from time to time. This figure shows that the onset of the CS^+ produced a *decrease* in jumping rate. Then, while CS^+ continued, the rate increased until it went above the pre-CS baseline rate.

of inhibition of delay holds for fear conditioning as well as for salivary conditioning. We can look at the onset of a long-delay CS as a predictor of temporary *absence* of shock, a special type of safety signal. Such an interpretation points up the need for a temporal dimension for the Pavlovian conditioning space of Figure 2. The conditional probability of a UCS, given the occurrence of a CS, is 1.00 for the whole CS–UCS interval. Yet it is zero for all time "slices" except that at the end of the interval.

4. Inhibition from Backward Conditioning

Backward conditioning might be considered a prime example of an inhibitory Pavlovian procedure. The CS should become inhibitory provided that the intertrial interval is long, because the CS is followed by a

UCS-free time interval. Moscovitch and LoLordo (1968) found this to be true for fear conditioning. Dogs were first trained to avoid shock on a Sidman schedule in the shuttlebox and were then penned in one side of the shuttlebox and given backward Pavlovian fear conditioning using a tone CS and shock US. The UCS–CS sequences were followed by a shock-free, variable intertrial interval with a mean of 2.5 min. Later, in a test session, short presentations of the tone resulted in a temporary *decrease* in jumping rate. We can infer that the backward CS functioned as a safety signal because it predicted a subsequent shock-free period.

5.   Inhibition from a Cessation Signal

Mowrer (1960) postulated that a cessation signal (a CS inserted shortly before shock terminates) should elicit a "relief" reaction. Moscovitch and LoLordo (1968) trained dogs to avoid shock with a Sidman contingency in a shuttlebox. Then the dogs had a Pavlovian conditioning session, during which 4-, 5-, and 6-sec shocks were presented in a random sequence. A CS was always presented 1 sec before each shock-termination, and it stayed on for 4 sec. The shock-free intertrial intervals following the CS were either 2.0, 2.5, or 3.0 min. Later, in a test session, while the dogs were jumping in the shuttlebox, test presentations of the CS produced a small, but significant *decrease* in jumping rate.

Did the cessation signal decrease Sidman avoidance responding because it predicted the termination of shock during conditioning or because it predicted at least 2.0 min of shock-free time? To answer these questions, Moscovitch and LoLordo (1968) compared the fear-inhibiting properties of these stimuli in dogs conditioned with backward CSs and cessation CSs. For all dogs the CSs predicted the same amount of shock-free time during fear conditioning. There were, however, three experimental groups which differed in the relation between the CS onset and shock-termination. In the cessation group, the CS came on 1 sec *before* the shock terminated. In two backward conditioning groups, the CS came on either 1 sec or 15 sec after termination of shock. It was found that the CS in both backward conditioning groups reduced the rate of Sidman avoidance responding *more* than did the CS in the cessation-signal group. This means that the backward CSs were *more* fear-inhibiting than was the cessation CS. This result is paradoxical because the cessation signal predicts both shock-termination and 2.0 min of shock-free time, whereas the backward CSs merely predict shock-free time. There is a theoretical resolution of this paradox if we assume that the cessation signal became a partial predictor of shock because of its temporal over-lap with shock. Assuming further that this property summated algebraically with the perfect prediction of shock-termination, we would expect the backward CSs to be more fear-inhibiting than the cessation CS. The Pavlovian conditioning space in Figure 2 does not take such possibilities into account but it does provide a simplified model from which such complex predictions could be derived.

The fact that variation in shock duration should determine the safety signal value of a cessation CS suggests an experiment in which, during a fear conditioning session, the duration of shocks are more variable than those used by Moscovitch and LoLordo. The CS, therefore, should reliably predict shock termination and might have powerful safety signal properties so that if imposed on Ss during Sidman avoidance, it would greatly reduce the response rate

6. *Inhibition from a CS Contingent upon the Occurrence of an Avoidance Response*

Rescorla (1968) trained dogs to jump in a shuttlebox on a Sidman schedule. After the dogs were performing stably, a 5-sec tone was introduced whenever a response occurred. After several sessions, during which the tone was produced by each jumping response, the tone was presented as a test stimulus while the dogs were performing the Sidman response. Such presentations of the tone reliably suppressed the Sidman jumping response rate, indicating that the tone had acquired the properties of a CS^-. This result suggests that avoidance responses themselves can acquire fear-inhibitory properties. Perhaps such a mechanism underlies the acquisition of both signalled and unsignalled (Sidman) avoidance responses (see Soltysik, 1963).

7. *Neutrality of CSs Randomly Related to Shocks*

Previously we have described the effects of CSs which lie along the axis of the Pavlovian conditioning space. We can, however, produce CSs which lie along the 45° independence line, for which it can be said that $p(UCS/CS) = p(UCS/\overline{CS})$. Rescorla (1966) trained dogs to shuttle on a Sidman schedule. The group of interest here was given a Pavlovian fear conditioning in which CSs and UCSs occurred randomly with respect to each other, *i.e.*, the occurrence of a CS predicted neither as UCS nor a $\overline{UCS}$, and the occurrence of a UCS predicted neither a CS nor a $\overline{CS}$. When the CS was later presented to the dogs while they were shuttling in the Sidman avoidance situation, the jumping rate was not affected. This outcome contrasts with those we have already described for CSs which reliably predict shocks and CSs which reliably predict absence of shocks, and with the findings of Seligman (1968) that unpredictable shocks produce chronic fear.

E. Summary

We have described the effects of some variations in the Pavlovian conditioning space. Situations in which shocks are unpredictable are more distressing than are situations in which shocks are predictable; this difference is reflected by both subjectively and by objectively-measured indices of preference and aversion. A "safety-signal" hypothesis or a "preparatory-response" hypothesis could account for such findings, but we prefer the "safety-signal" hypothesis because of its testability and comprehensiveness. This hypothesis asserts that stimuli which are located at different points in the Pavlovian conditioning space acquire different fear-arousing properties. Stimuli which reliably predict shocks (those on the abscissa of the conditioning space) will enhance or energize previously-learned avoidance responses, whereas, stimuli which reliably predict the absence of shocks (those on the ordinate of the conditioning space) will suppress or deenergize previously-learned avoidance responses.

IV. GENERAL SUMMARY

We have described a two-dimensional representation of the operations involved in instrumental training and in Pavlovian conditioning. This type of representation allows us to define the uncontrollability and unpredictability of aversive events, and it allows us to represent in a simple way the contingencies with which S may be faced in a wide variety of aversive treatments.

Uncontrollable shocks can have these effects on behavior:

(1) They interfere with the subsequent acquisition of active, two-way, shuttlebox escape/avoidance responses and of manipulandum, escape/avoidance responses.

(2) They either facilitate or have little effect on the acquisition of one-way, active, shuttlebox escape/avoidance responses.

(3) They facilitate the subsequent acquisition of passive escape/avoidance responses.

(4) They facilitate the performance of already-acquired, well-established escape/avoidance responses.

When one prior treatment with uncontrollable shock produces an interference effect in dogs, the effect fades so that it is undetectable after 48 hr. However, if S receives multiple exposures to uncontrollable shock, it then will be unable to learn to escape/avoid shocks even as long as one month later.

The interference effect is specifically the result of the uncontrollability of shocks rather than their severity or frequency of occurence, because only Ss which cannot control shock later fail to learn to escape/avoid shocks in the same situation or in a new training situation. Furthermore, if S is first given a short experience with controllable shocks in the escape/avoidance test situation, and is then given a series of uncontrollable shocks in a different situation, S then continues to escape/avoid shocks normally when it is returned to the test situation. Furthermore, Ss which, due to prior treatment with uncontrollable shocks are now incapable of acquiring an escape/avoidance response, can be "cured" by subjecting them to forcible exposure to the escape/avoidance contingencies.

Finally, uncontrollable shocks are more aversive, distressing, and physiologically stressful than are controllable shocks. Frequency of defecation, ulceration, and magnitude of weight loss, feeding inhibition, and the suppression of an operant baseline are all greater as a consequence of S's receiving uncontrollable shocks as compared with controllable shocks.

Unpredictable shocks also cause distress and physiological stress than do predictable shocks. The suppression of an operant baseline, the development of ulcers, the subjective reports of painfulness, unpleasantness, and anxiety level in human Ss, are all greater with unpredictable shocks than with predictable shocks. When given a choice between equated unpredictable and predictable shocks, both animal and human Ss choose the predictable shocks. In addition, Ss choose immediate shocks in preference to delayed shocks, and they choose response-contingent shocks over response-independent shocks.

Predictable shock and predictable absence-of-shock are conditions which affect both signallized and unsignalized (Sidman) avoidance learning. Predictors of shock (CS^+) and predictors of "safety" (CS^-) can control already-established avoidance responses; i.e., a variety of conditions producing excitation of fear by predictors of shock will energize already-established avoidance behavior, and a variety of conditions producing inhibition of fear by predictors of "safety" will suppress already-established avoidance behavior.

We have reviewed a number of theoretical interpretations of the effects of uncontrollable shocks on subsequent escape/avoidance learning, e.g., adaptation to shocks, sensitization to shocks, competing motor response, emotional exhaustion, and learned helplessness. None of them by itself adequately accounts for all of the known findings although the helplessness hypothesis seems to us to be the strongest and most comprehensive.

Two theoretical interpretations of the effects of unpredictable shocks on behavioral and physiological responses are discussed: the preparatory response hypothesis and the safety signal hypotheses. Of these, the safety signal hypothesis appears to us to be more useful.

ACKNOWLEDGMENT

This paper is based primarily on research supported by USPHS Grant MH-04202 and NSF Grant GB-2428 to Richard L. Solomon and by NIH Grant MH-16546 to Martin E.P. Seligman. The authors wish to thann Dorothy Brown, Steven Jones, and Bruce Halpern for a critical reading of this manuscript.

REFERENCES

Allison, J., Larson, D., & Jensen, D.D. Acquired fear, brightness preference, and one-way shuttlebox performance. *Psychonomic Science,* 1967, **8**, 269-270.

Anderson, D.C. Prior shock trauma and test-shock intensity as determinants of escape learning. *Psychological Reports,* 1966, **19**, 771-778.

Anderson, D.C., Cole, J., & McVaugh, W. Variations in unsignalled, inescapable preshock as determinants of responses to punishment. *Journal of Comparative and Physiological Psychology,* 1968, **65**, Monograph Supplement, 1-17.

Anderson, D.C., & Paden, P. Passive avoidance response learning as a function of prior tumbling trauma. *Psychonomic Science,* 1966, **4**, 129-130.

Anderson, D.C., Schwendiman, G., Packham, S., & Taylor, J. Does inescapable unsignaled preshock always produce conditioned apathy? Read at Western Psychological Association, 1967.

Anderson, N.H., & Nakamura, C.Y. Avoidance decrement in avoidance conditioning. *Journal of Comparative and Physiological Psychology,* 1964, **57**, 196-204.

Anderson, N.H., Rollins, H.A., & Riskin, S.R. Effects of punishment on avoidance decrement. *Journal of Comparative and Physiological Psychology,* 1966, **62**, 147-149.

Azrin, N.H. Some effects of two intermittent schedules of immediate and non-immediate punishment. *Journal of Psychology,* 1956, **42**, 3-21.

Badia, P., McBane, B., Suter, S., & Lewis, P. Preference behavior in an immediate versus variably delayed shock situation with and without a warning signal. *Journal of Experimental Psychology,* 1966, **72**, 847-852.

Badia, P., Suter, S., & Lewis, P. Preference for warned shock: information and/or preparation. *Psychological Reports,* 1967, **20**, 271-274.

Baum, M. The recovery-from-extinction of an avoidance response following an inescapable shock in the avoidance apparatus. *Psychonomic Science,* 1965, **2**, 7-8.

Baum, M. Dissociation of respondent and operant processes in avoidance learning. *Journal of Comparative and Physiological Psychology,* 1969, **67**, 83-88.

Beecroft, R.S. *Classical Conditioning,* Goleta, California: Psychonomic Press, 1966.

Behrend, E.R., & Bitterman, M.E. Sidman avoidance in the fish. *Journal of the Experimental Analysis of Behavior,* 1963, **13,** 229–242.

Brady, J.V., Porter, R.W., Conrad, D.G., & Mason, J.W. Avoidance behavior and the development of gastroduodenal ulcers. *Journal of the Experimental Analysis of Behavior,* 1958, **1,** 69–72.

Brady, J.P., Thornton, D., & deFisher, D. Deleterious effects of anxiety elicited by conditioned pre-aversive stimuli in the rat. *Psychosomatic Medicine,* 1962, **24,** 590–595.

Brimer, C.J., & Kamin, L.J. Disinhibition, habituation, sensitization and the conditioned emotional response. *Joucal of Comparative and Physiological Psychology,* 1963, **56,** 508–516.

Brookshire, K.H., Littman, R.A. & Stewart, C.N. Residua of shock trauma in the white rat: a three factor theory. *Psychological Monograph,* 1961, **75,** (10, Whole No. 514).

Brown, J.S., & Jacobs, A. The role of fear in the motivation and acquisition of responses. *Journal of Experimental Psychology,* 1949, **39,** 747–759.

Brush, F.R., & Levine, S. The relationship between avoidance learning and corticosterone levels. Paper read at Western Psychological Association Meeting, 1965.

Brush, F.R., Myer, J.S., & Palmer, M.E. Effects of kind of prior training and intersession interval upon subsequent avoidance learning. *Journal of Comparative and Physiological Psychology,* 1963, **56,** 539–545.

Carlson, N.J., & Black, A.H. Traumatic avoidance learning: the effects of preventing escape responses. *Canadian Journal of Psychology,* 1960, **14,** 21–28.

Church, R.M., LoLordo, V.M., Overmier, J.B., Solomon, R.L., & Turner, L.H. Cardiac responses to shock in curarized dogs. *Journal of Comparative and Physiological Psychology,* 1966, **62,** 1–7.

Cook, J., & Barnes, L.W. Choice of delay of inevitable shock. *Journal of Abnormal and Social Psychology,* 1964, **68,** 669–672.

D'Amato, M.R., & Gumenik, W.E. Some effects of immediate versus randomly delayed shock on an instrumental response and cognitive processes. *Journal of Abnormal and Social Psychology,* 1960, **60,** 64–67.

Davis, H., & McIntire, R.W. Conditioned suppression under positive, negative, and no CS–US contingency, *Journal of the Experimental Analysis of Behavior,* 1969, **12,** 633–640.

De Toledo, L., & Black, A.H. Effects of preshock on subsequence avoidance conditioning. *Journal of Comparative and Physiological Psychology,* 1967, **63,** 493–499.

Dinsmoor, J.A. Pulse duration and food deprivation in escape from shock training. *Psychological Reports,* 1958, **4,** 531–534.

Dinsmoor, J.A., & Campbell, S.L. Escape-from-shock training following exposure to inescapable shock. *Psychological Reports,* 1956a, **2,** 43–49.

Dinsmoor, J.A., & Campbell, S.L. Level of current and time between sessions as factors in adaptation to shock. *Psychological Reports,* 1956b, **2,** 441–444.

Estes, W.K., & Skinner, B.F. Some quantitative properties of anxiety. *Journal of Experimental Psychology,* 1941, **29,** 390–400.

Ferster, C.B., & Skinner, B.F. *Schedules of Reinforcement.* New York: Appleton, 1957.

Haggard, E. Some conditions determining adjustment during and readjustment following experimentally induced stress. In S. Tomkins (Ed.) *Contemporary psychopathology.* Cambridge, Massachusetts: Harvard University Press, 1943. Pp. 529–544.

Hammond, L.J. Increased responding to CS– in differential CER. *Psychonomic Science,* 1966, **5,** 337–338.

Hare, R.D. & Petrusic, W.M. Subjective intensity of electric shock as a function of delay in administration. Paper read at Western Psychological Association Meeting, San Francisco, May, 1967.

Hearst, E. Stress induced breakdown of an appetitive discrimination. *Journal of the Experimental Analysis of Behavior,* 1965, **8,** 135–146.

Hearst, E., & Whalen, R.E. Facilitating effects of D-Amphetamine on discriminated-avoidance performance. *Journal of Comparative and Physiological Psychology,* 1963, **36,** 124–128.

Hoffman, H.S., & Fleshler, M. Stimulus aspects of aversive controls: The effects of response contingent shock. *Journal of the Experimental Analysis of Behavior,* 1965, **8,** 89–96.

Honig, W.K. (Ed.) *Operant conditioning: Research and Application.* New York: Appleton, 1966.

Hunt, H.F. & Brady, J.V. Some quantitative and qualitative differences between "anxiety" and "punishment" conditioning. Paper read at American Psychological Association, 1951.

Hunt, H.F., & Brady, J.V. Some effects of punishment and intercurrent "anxiety" on a simple operant. *Journal of Comparative and Physiological Psychology,* 1955, **48,** 305–310.

Hunt, J. McV., Schlosberg, H., Solomon, R.L., & Stellar, E. Studies of the effects of infantile experience on adult behavior in rats: I. Effects of infantile feeding frustration on adult hoarding. *Journal of Comparative and Physiological Psychology,* 1947, **40,** 291–304.

Kalish, H.I. Strength of fear as a function of the number of acquisition and extinction trials. *Journal of Experimental Psychology,* 1954, **47,** 1–9.

Kelleher, R.T., Riddle, W.C., & Cook, L. Persistent behavior maintained by unavoidable shocks. *Journal of the Experimental Analysis of Behavior,* 1963, **6,** 507–517.

Kimmel, H.D. Instrumental factors in classical conditioning. In W. Prokasy, (Ed.), *Classical conditioning.* New York: Appleton, 1965.

Kimmel, H.D., & Pennypacker, H. Conditioned diminution of the unconditioned response as a function of the numbers of reinforcements. *Journal of Experimental Psychology,* 1962, **64,** 20–23.

Knapp, R.K., Kause, R.H., & Perkins, C.C., Jr. Immediate vs. delayed shock in T-maze performance. *Journal of Experimental Psychology,* 1959, **58,** 357–362.

Kurtz, K.H., & Walters, G. The effects of prior fear exposure on an approach-avoidance conflict. *Journal of Comparative and Physiological Psychology,* 1962, **55,** 102–108.

Leaf, R.C. Avoidance response evocation as a function of prior discriminative fear conditioning under curare. *Journal of Comparative and Physiological Psychology,* 1964, **58,** 446–449.

Lepanto, R., Moroney, W., & Zenhausern, R. The contribution of anxiety to the laboratory investigation of pain. *Psychonomic Science,* 1965, **3,** 475.

Levine, S., Chevalier, J., & Korchin, S. The effects of early shock and handling on later avoidance learning. *Journal of Personality,* 1956, **24,** 475–493.

Lindner, M. Hereditary and environmental influences upon resistance to stress. Unpublished doctoral dissertation, University of Pennsylvania, 1968.

Lockard, J.S. Choice of a warning signal or no warning signal in an unavoidable shock situation. *Journal of Comparative and Physiological Psychology,* 1963, **56,** 526–530.

LoLordo, V.M. Similarity of conditioned fear responses based upon different aversive events. *Journal of Comparative and Physiological Psychology,* 1967, **64,** 154–157.

LoLordo, V.M., & Rescorla, R.A. Protection of the fear-eliciting capacity of a stimulus from extinction. *Acta Biologica Experimentalis*, 1966, **26**, 251–258.

Lykken, D. Preception in the rat: Autonomic response to shock as a function of length of warning interval. *Science*, 1962, **137**, 665–666.

MacDonald, A. Effects of adaptation to the unconditioned stimulus upon the formation of conditioned avoidance responses. *Journal of Experimental Psychology*, 1946, **36**, 1–12.

Maier, S.F. Failure to escape traumatic shock: Incompatible skeletal motor responses or learned helplessness? *Learning and Motivation*, 1970, in press.

Maier, S.F., Seligman, M.E.P., & Solomon, R.L. Pavlovian fear conditioning and learned helplessness. In B.A. Campbell and R.M. Church (Eds), *Punishment and Aversive Behavior*. New York: Appleton, 1969, 299–343.

Mandler, J. Effect of early food deprivation on adult behavior in the rat. *Journal of Comparative and Physiological Psychology*, 1958, **51**, 513–517.

Mandler, J. Personal communicaton, 1967.

McCulloch, T.L., & Bruner, J.S. The effect of electric shock upon subsequent learning in the rat. *Journal of Psychology*, 1939, **7**, 333–336.

Melzack, R., & Wall, P.D. Pain Mechanisms: A new theory. *Science*, 1965, **150**, 971–979.

Morrow, M.C. Recovery of conditioned UCR diminution following extinction. *Journal of Experimental Psychology*, 1966, **71**, 884–888.

Moscovitch, A., & LoLordo, V.M. Role of safety in the Pavlovian Procedure. Backward fear conditioning. *Journal of Comparative and Physiological Psychology*, 1968, **66**, 473–479.

Mowrer, O.H. *Learning theory and behavior*. New York: Wiley, 1960.

Mowrer, O.H., & Viek, P. An experimental analogue of fear from a sense of helplessness. *Journal of Abnormal and Social Psychology*, 1948, **43**, 193–200.

Mullin, A.D., & Mogenson, G.J. Effects of fear conditioning on avoidance learning. *Psychological Reports*, 1963, **13**, 707–710.

Nakamura, C., & Anderson, N.H. Test of a CER interpretation of the avoidance decrement phenomenon. *Journal of Comparative and Physiological Psychology*, 1968, **66**, 759–763.

Overmier, J.B. Interference with avoidance behavior: Failure to avoid traumatic shock. *Journal of Experimental Psychology*, 1968, in press.

Overmier, J.B., & Leaf, R.C. Effects of discriminative Pavlovian fear conditioning upon previously or subsequently acquired avoidance responding. *Journal of Comparative and Physiological Psychology*, 1965, **60**, 213–217.

Overmier, J.B., & Seligman, M.E.P. Effects of inescapable shock upon subsequent escape and avoidance responding. *Journal of Comparative and Physiological Psychology*, 1967, **63**, 28–33.

Paré, W.P. The effect of chronic environmental stress on the stomach ulceration adrenal function and consumatory behavior in the rat. *Journal of Psychology*, 1964, **57**, 143.

Pavlov, I.P. *Conditioned reflexes*. New York: Dover, 1927.

Pearl, J., Walters, G., & Anderson, R.C. Suppressive effects of aversive stimulation on subsequently punished behavior. *Canadian Journal of Psychology*, 1964, **18**, 343–348.

Perkins, C.C., Jr., Levin, D., & Seymann, R. Preference for signal-shock vs. shock signal. *Psychological Reports*, 1963, **13**, 735–738.

Perkins, C.C., Jr., Seymann, R., Levis, D.J., & Spencer, R. Factors affecting preference for signal shock over shock-signal. *Journal of Experimental Psychology*, 1966, **72**, 190–196.

Pervin, L.A. The need to predict and control under conditions of threat. *Journal of Personality,* 1963, **31**, 570–585.

Pinckney, G. Avoidance learning in fish as a function of prior fear conditioning. *Psychological Reports,* 1967, **20**, 71–74.

Premack, D. Reinforcement theory. In M. Jones (Ed.) *Nebraska Symposium on Motivation,* 1965.

Prokasy, W.F. The acquisition of observing responses in the absence of differential external reinforcement. *Journal of Comparative and Physiological Psychology,* 1956, **49**, 131–134.

Prokasy, W.F. Classical eyelid conditioning: Experimenter operations, task demands, and response shaping. In Prokasy, W.F. (Ed.) *Classical conditioning,* New York: Appleton, 1965.

Rachlin, H., & Herrnstein, R. Hedonism revisited: On the negative law of effect. In B.A. Campbell and R.M. Church (Ed.) *Punishment and Aversive Behavior.* New York Appleton, 1969, 83–109.

Rescorla, R.A. Predictability and number of pairings in Pavlovian fear conditioning. *Psychonomic Science,* 1966, **4**, 383–384.

Rescorla, R.A. Pavlovian conditioning and its proper control procedures. *Psychological Review,* 1967, **74**, 71–79.

Rescorla, R.A. Inhibition of delay in Pavlovian fear conditioning. *Journal of Comparative and Physiological Psychology,* 1967b, **14**, 114–120.

Rescorla, R.A. Pavlovian conditioned fear in Sidman avoidance learning. *Journal of Comparative and Physiological Psychology,* 1968, **65**, 55–60.

Rescorla, R.A., & LoLordo, V.M. Inhibition of avoidance behavior. *Journal of Comparative and Physiological Psychology,* 1965, **59**, 406–410.

Sawrey, W. Conditioned responses of fear in the relationship to ulceration. *Journal of Comparative and Physiological Psychology,* 1961, **54**, 347–348.

Seligman, M.E.P. Chronic fear produced by unpredictable shock. *Journal of Comparative and Physiological Psychology,* 1968, **66**, 402–411.

Seligman, M.E.P., & Groves, D. Non-transient learned helplessness. *Psychonomic Science,* 1970, **19**, 191–192.

Seligman, M.E.P., & Maier, S.F. Failure to escape traumatic shock. *Journal of Experimental Psychology,* 1967, **74**, 1–9.

Seligman, M.E.P., & Meyer, B. Chronic fear and ulceration in rats as a function of unpredictability of safety. *Journal of Comparative and Physiological Psychology,* 1970, in press.

Seligman, M.E.P., Maier, S.F., & Geer, J. The alleviation of learned helplessness in the dog. *Journal of Abnormal Psychology,* 1968, **73**, 256–262.

Seward, J.P., & Humphrey, G.L. Avoidance learning as a function of pretraining in the cat. *Journal of Comparative and Physiological Psychology,* 1967, **63**, 338–341.

Sidman, M., Herrnstein, R.J., & Conrad, D.G. Maintenance of avoidance behavior by unavoidable shocks. *Journal of Comparative and Physiological Psychology,* 1957, **50**, 553–557.

Sines, J.O., Cleeland, C., & Adkins, J. The behavior of normal and stomach lesion susceptible rats in several learning situations. *Journal of Genetic Psychology,* 1963, **102**, 91–94.

Sokolov, Y.N. *Perception and the conditioned reflex.* Oxford: Pergamon Press, 1963.

Soltysik, S. Inhibitory feedback in avoidance conditioning. *Boletin del Instituto de Estudios Médicos y Biológicos*. Universidad Nacional de Mexico, 1963, **21**, 433.

Soltysik S., & Zielinski, K. Conditioned inhibition of the avoidance reflex. *Acta Biologica Experimentalis*, 1962, **22**, 157–167.

Waller, M.B., & Waller, P.F. The effects of unavoidable shocks on a multiple schedule having an avoidance component. *Journal of the Experimental Analysis of Behavior*, 1963, **6**, 29–37.

Weismann, R.C., Denny, M.R., Platt, S.A., & Zerbolio, D.J., Jr. Facilitation of extinction by a stimulus associated with long non-shock confinement periods. *Journal of Comparative and Physiological Psychology*, 1966, **62**, 26–30.

Weiss, J.M. Effects of coping response on stress. *Journal of Comparative and Physiological Psychology*, 1968, **65**, 251–260.

Weiss, J.M. Effects of predictable and unpredictable shock on development of gastrointestinal lesions in rats. *Proceedings, 76th Annual American Psychological Convention*, 1968b, 263–264.

Weiss, J.M., Krieckhaus, E.E., and Conte, R. Effects of fear conditioning on subsequent avoidance behavior. *Journal of Comparative and Physiological Psychology*, 1968, **65**, 413–421.

CHAPTER 7

Retention of Aversively Motivated Behavior

F. ROBERT BRUSH
University of Oregon Medical School
Portland, Oregon

It is generally assumed that retention by animals of instrumental and Pavlovian conditioned responses is exceptionally good, even after rather long intervals of time. This assumption, although widely endorsed, is based on relatively few experimental findings. The experiments of Liddell, James and Anderson (1934) and Hilgard and Marquis (1935) indicate that Pavlovian conditioned responses established by aversive unconditioned stimuli can be retained with only minor loss for periods of several years. More recently, Hoffman, Fleshler and Jensen (1963) reported relatively trivial loss of conditioned suppression by pigeons after a two-year retention interval. There appear to be no studies of retention of Pavlovian conditioned alimentary responses, although their retention is generally expected to be good (Youtz, 1938).

Retention of instrumentally rewarded responses is also rather good. For example, Skinner (1938, p. 93) reported very small differences in resistance to experimental extinction in rats tested 1 or 45 days after barpress training for food. Gagne (1941) found evidence of at least some retention 28 days after reacquisition of a previously extinguished running response in a straight alley, and Gleitman and Jung (1963) found essentially no loss of a spatial discrimination by rats over a 44-day retention interval unless proactive interference from prior learning of the reverse discrimination was provided. Furthermore, the now commonplace finding that animals can learn well with only one trial each day (*e.g.*, Weinstock, 1958) is ample evidence that the effects of a single reinforcer can persist for periods up to 24 hr. On the aversive side, there is evidence (*e.g.*, Azrin, 1960; Boe and Church, 1967) which suggests that the suppressive effects of punishment are relatively permanent. And similarly, instrumental avoidance responses have long been noted for their persistence over time. Using rats, Hunter (1935) found good retention of an avoidance response after 30 days; Kirby (1963) reported similar findings after 50 days. Wendt (1937) observed good retention of a leg flexion avoidance response by dogs after 2½ yr.

It has also been assumed that what little forgetting does occur, even over relatively long time intervals, is nonetheless a *monotonic* function of the duration of disuse. This inference is probably based on the classical work on retention of verbal material by humans. Certainly, the monotonic character of the retention function, first described by Ebbinghaus and replicated hundreds of times since then, needs no documentation.[1] Therefore, it was somewhat surprising when Kamin (1957) reported that relearning (retention) of an incompletely learned shuttlebox avoidance response by rats was a U-shaped function of time after original training. This finding was so unexpected that it set off a chain of research by a number of investigators. The U-shaped retention function has now been obtained under a wide variety of conditions so that its generality and reproducibility are beyond question. But the function has resisted analysis, and only a few of its determining variables have been identified. The purpose of this chapter is to review what is known about the phenomenon so that the range of conditions under which the function is obtained and the variables which control it can be specified as completely as current research permits. Finally, theoretical analyses of the phenomenon will be reviewed and their adequacy assessed.

Although we are concerned here with the problem of retention of a class of behaviors learned by animals, because of limited space, we will not be able to address the more general problem of memory, its experiential determinants, or its neurophysiological and biochemical mechanisms. Later in this chapter we will discuss some of the relationships between pituitary and adrenal activity and retention, but we will not be able to explore at this time the biochemical actions of these hormones at the cellular level which may mediate their apparent control of retention.

I. THE DEFINING EXPERIMENT

Kamin (1957) gave 25 trials of avoidance training to experimentally naive hooded rats (sex not specified) in a two-directional shuttlebox which measured 36 × 4 × 4¾ in. high. The unconditioned stimulus (US) was reported to be a 1.1-mA ac electric shock delivered through the grid

---

[1]In this context, we can safely exclude reminiscence as a significant exception to the monotonicity of the retention function inasmuch as the phenomenon is transitory and occurs only under the special conditions of massed practice, and is subject to the criticism that rehearsal is usually inadequately controlled.

floor of each compartment, and the conditiōned stimulus (CS) was a 74-dB buzzer located outside the shuttlebox. The CS–US interval was 5 sec (delayed-conditioning) and the intertrial interval was 1 min. Upon completion of the 25 trials of original training, the animals were divided into 6 randomly constituted groups which received 25 retraining trials after retention intervals of 0 (no interruption of training), 0.5, 1, 6, or 24 hr or 19 days. All animals but those in the 0-interval group were removed to their cages during the retention interval.

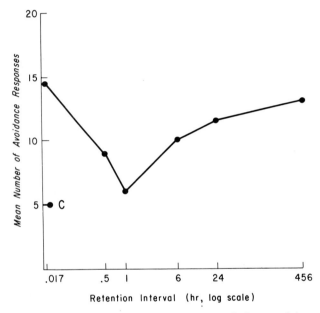

Fig. 1.   Adjusted mean number of avoidance responses during retraining as a function of retention interval. The overall mean number of avoidance responses that occurred during original training is indicated by the point labeled C on the ordinate. (From Kamin, 1957.)

Figure 1 illustrates the principal results of the experiment: mean total number of avoidance responses during retraining decreased from 0 to 1 hr and then increased from 1 hr to 19 days. The groups tested at 24 hr and 19 days were not significantly different from each other or from the 0-interval group (performance during retraining was adjusted by covariance for variation in number of avoidance responses made during original training). The 1-hr group, however, made significantly fewer avoidance responses than either the 0- or 24-hr group, and the 0.5- and 6-hr groups avoided significantly less frequently than the 0-hr group.

During the first 10 trials of retraining, the minimum of the function was at 6 hr; in contrast, the minimum was at 1 hr during the last 10 retraining trials.

A. Early Replications

Kamin's experiment was replicated by Denny (1958) using retention intervals of 0, 1, or 24 hr. Following Kamin's procedure, the rats in Denny's experiment received 25 trials of avoidance training and after the appropriate intervals received another 25 trials of training. Denny's animals learned considerably faster than Kamin's: 10.5 versus 5.0 mean number of avoidance responses during original training. Despite this notable difference in learning rate, the animals in Denny's experiment showed a significant U-shaped retention function, the mean number of avoidance responses during retraining being 17.8, 10.1, and 18.4 for the 0-, 1-, and 24-hr groups, respectively. Thus, the original experiment was replicated and the U-shaped retention function was shown to be invariant with changes in learning rate over a range of 2:1.

In a subsequent study (Denny and Ditchman, 1962), the time course of the U-shaped retention function was plotted in 15-min intervals around the 1-hr minimum. Denny and Ditchman used a shuttlebox having the dimensions (36 × 4 × 14 in. high) which had been determined to produce significant interference with retraining at a 1-hr retention interval (Denny and Thomas, 1960). The CS was a 70-dB buzzer mounted outside the box, and the US was a pulsing dc shock of approximately 1.7 mA. The CS–US interval was 5 sec, and both CS and US were terminated by the running response. Following 25 trials of original avoidance training, independent groups of hooded rats of both sexes spent retention intervals of 0.5, .75, 1.0, 1.25, and 1.5 hr in their home cages. Retraining consisted of 25 additional trials. Again, a significant U-shaped retention function was obtained with the minimum of the function at 1 hr. It is interesting to note that in Kamin's (1957) experiment the minimum of the function shifted from 6 to 1 hr as retraining progressed, whereas Denny and Ditchman (1962) found the minimum of the function at 1 hr regardless of whether retraining data were derived from early or late stages of the retention test.

At variance with these findings are those reported by Segal and Brush (1959) who found that the minimum of the retention function was either at 1 or 24 hr when intervals of 1 min, 1 hr, 1, 5, 10, or 20 days intervened between each of five successive avoidance training sessions of 20 trials each. In this experiment a 16 + 5½ + 7¾-in. high shuttlebox was used. The CS was a 10-sec clicking sound and flashing light presented in the compartment occupied by the rat, the US was scrambled ac electric shock of 0.15 mA, and a 5-sec CS–US interval was used in a delayed-conditioning procedure. In common with all of the preceding experiments, the intertrial interval was 1 min. Although the average percent frequency of avoidance responses in all groups during the second and subsequent sessions was around 75 to 80%, animals tested with 1- or 24-hr intervals between successive sessions showed a persistent warm-up decrement so that fewer avoidance responses occurred in these groups than in any of the others, even though their terminal performance each day was about the same as the others.

Thus, Kamin's basic finding that rate of relearning of a shuttlebox avoidance response by rats is a U-shaped function of the retention interval was replicated in three experiments despite the fact that rate of learning, shuttlebox dimensions, nature and locus of the CS, and kind and intensity of electric shock were varied. Not surprisingly, the results of these experiments differed in detail so that questions arose regarding (a) the determinants of the location of the minimum of the function, and (b) the reasons for the presence, and occasional absence, of a shift of the minimum of the function during the course of relearning (these questions will be discussed later in this chapter). But the remarkable thing about these experiments is their unanimity in finding the retention function to be U-shaped despite gross changes in procedure.

B. Early Theoretical Analyses

Although there was general agreement regarding the shape of these retention functions, the same cannot be said for interpretations of them. Kamin (1957) originally postulated two opposing processes to account for the U-shaped function, at that time regarding a unitary nonlinear process as unreasonable. He likened the descending portion of the retention function to forgetting, *i.e.*, to a progressive decrease of positive transfer from original to retraining, and he suggested that warm-up decrements, attributable to loss of postural adjustments or dissipation of emotional effects of electric shock, could increase for some period of time after original training and thus account for the progressive deterioration of performance as retention interval increased up to 1 hr or so. If the rising portion of the retention function is to be explained, these effects must be offset by some other process which serves to increase performance with time, and Kamin suggested that such a process might be an incubation effect, *i.e.*, a progressive increase of S's conditioned emotional response as a function of time after conditioning. By algebraic summation of two opposite effects, each of which reaches an asymptote within the time course of the experimental manipulation, the U-shaped retention function can be derived.

In a later analysis Kamin (1963) retained the monotonic increasing warm-up decrement but changed the opposite monotonic incubation effect to an inverted U-shaped function which describes interference with performance as a function of time, the peak of the function being at 1 hr after original learning. He declined to take a position on the question of whether the poor performance at the peak of the inverted U-shaped function occurred because of too much or too little fear of the CS.

Denny, on the other hand, took a clear position on this point. He asserted (1958) that a single nonlinear process could account for the U-shaped retention function and that that process is characterized by a short-term incubation of anxiety followed by a gradual dissipation of anxiety. The peak of the incubation phase is assumed to be reached about 1 hr after original learning, and complete dissipation of anxiety (to some basal or control level?) is assumed to occur within 24 hr. Poor performance during a retraining session 1 hr after original training would occur because rats typically freeze when intensely anxious and such freezing interferes with the instrumental avoidance response of running.

In a somewhat more "physiologizing" analysis, Brush, Myer, and Palmer (1963) suggested that the U-shaped retention function could be accounted for by a "parasympathetic overreaction" following aversive conditioning. These investigators assumed that the animal is in a state of sympathetic dominance (Gellhorn, 1957) during avoidance training, and that in the process of restoring homeostasis during the retention interval the autonomic nervous system overshoots to a state of parasympathetic dominance. It was argued that if retraining were attempted while the animal was in such a "parasympathetic overreaction" then performance would be relatively poor because that kind of autonomic imbalance is incompatible with avoidance learning and would have to be reversed during the course of the retraining session.

C. Memorial versus Motivational Interpretations of Retention

It is interesting to note that all of these early theoretical analyses of the U-shaped retention function utilized emotional and motivational constructs rather than terms derived from the study of memory, e.g., short-term and long-term storage, consolidation, retrieval, etc. One reason for this may be that poor retention at intermediate intervals fo lowed by improved retention at longer intervals requires that memories of originally learned responses not be lost but be temporarily "unavailable," and a model of such temporally controlled deficits in retrieval has not yet been developed. Furthermore, motivational analyses can make the traditional assumption that original learning (habit strength) is permanent and can account for the U-shaped retention function by invoking fluctuations in the motivation (drive and/or incentive) to perform the remembered response. One is tempted to comment that invocation of motivational constructs to "explain" the unexplainable is still looked on with favor in some sectors despite the scientific inadequacy of doing so, but one should also add that the explanatory value of a deficiency of retrieval is not much better than that of motivation or emotion. Furthermore, the use of motivational constructs is perhaps forgivable in view of the fact that until very recently the goal of identifying the neurophysiological bases of motivational constructs seemed much nearer realization than the corresponding goal of identifying the neural mechanisms of memory and retrieval.

Another reason for the use of motivational rather than memorial constructs may be that most investigators assumed that this peculiar retention function is unique to aversively motivated behaviors, if only because it had never been reported in the context of more thoroughly researched appetitive conditioning and learning situations. Certainly, one of the outstanding differences between aversive and appetitive learning situations is the high intensity emotional display in the former and its virtual absence in the latter. So focusing attention on emotional and motivational mechanisms to account for the U-shaped retention function seems not entirely unreasonable.

II.   REQUISITE ANTECEDENT CONDITIONS

All of the experiments described previously used a two-way shuttlebox and administered a fixed number of avoidance training trials to establish the original learning that preceded the retention interval so it is not clear which component(s) of that avoidance training, electric shock, escape training, fear conditioning, or the entire complex of avoidance training is(are) necessary to produce the U-shaped retention function. Similarly, neither the requisite amount of training nor the range of avoidance training procedures that are sufficient to produce the effect was determined by those experiments. However, additional research has settled some of these issues.

A. Pavlovian Conditioning of Fear Is Necessary and Sufficient

A series of experiments by Brush, Myer, and Palmer (1963) were conducted in an attempt to identify the necessary and sufficient antecedent conditions for obtaining the U-shaped retention function. In the first experiment avoidance training was carried out in automatic shuttleboxes in which the CS was a flashing light and clicking sound, both operated at 10 Hz, and the US was a scrambled ac electric shock of 0.26 mA. The CS–US interval was 5 sec in a delayed-conditioning procedure, and the intertrial interval was 1 min. Following a pretest, animals were trained to a criterion of 3 avoidance responses, not necessarily consecutive, and were then removed to their home cages. Groups of 10 rats were matched with respect to the mean number of trials required to reach the criterion of original learning and were tested after retention intervals of .08, 1, 4, 24, and 168 hr. Following the appropriate retention interval, each S received 40 trials of avoidance training using the same procedures as those of original training. Again, a U-shaped retention function was obtained. In terms of median trials to criterion, relearning scores of the 1- and 4-hr groups were not different from their values in *original* training, *i.e.*,they showed no evidence of positive transfer from original to relearning, whereas the .08-, 24-, and 168-hr groups showed marked improvement in relearning relative to original acquisition. Poor performance by the 1- and 4-hr groups persisted throughout the 40 trials of retraining. It should be noted that, as in Kamin's experiment (1957), the minimum of the function in this experiment also shifted from 4 to 1 hr as relearning progressed.

In an effort to fractionate the original avoidance training into its components, Ss in a second experiment were trained using an instrumental escape paradigm without a warning signal of any kind. The temporal pattern of shocks was the same as that generated by the average S in the previous experiment. Following appropriate intervals of time, Ss were given 40 trials of avoidance training, and although the retention function obtained was somewhat variable, there was no suggestion of a U-shaped retention function such as that seen following avoidance training. It was concluded that the electric shock stress of avoidance training is not sufficient to produce the U-shaped retention function. In a third experiment, fear conditioning was added to the training just described, by using instrumental escape training with a 0.5-sec CS–US interval. This interval permits pairing of CS and US under conditions nearly optimal for fear conditioning but precludes instrumental avoidance of the shock. The U-shaped retention function that follows avoidance training was duplicated in detail by various measures taken from the 40 trials of avoidance train-

ing that followed this training procedure. This suggests that fear conditioning plus escape training is sufficient to produce the phenomenon.
Psuedoconditioning control groups, which were trained in a fourth experiment, failed to show evidence of the U-shaped retention function
indicating that sensitization is not a sufficient condition for the effect.
These experiments lead to the conclusion that fear, conditioned to the
CS but not to apparatus cues, might be both necessary and sufficient to
initiate the processes underlying the U-shaped retention function.

The validity of this hypothesis was seriously questioned as a result of
an experiment by Kamin (1963, Experiment 3). He used three retention
intervals: 0, 1, or 24 hr, and original training consisted of 15 trials of
escape training, classical conditioning, or unsignaled shock. In the case
of escape training, unsignaled shocks were terminated by S's shuttling
response. In the classical conditioning procedure, Ss were confined first
to one side of the shuttlebox for 8 trials then to the other side for an
additional 7 trials. The CS–US interval was 5 sec, the US was 1 sec, and
CS and US terminated simultaneously. The unsignaled shock procedure
was identical to the classical conditioning procedure except that the CS
was omitted. Following the appropriate intersession intervals, 25 avoidance training trials were given. The mean number of avoidance responses that occurred during avoidance training showed no suggestion of the
U-shaped retention function following any of these training procedures.
Indeed, the only difference which approached significance occurred following classical conditioning and in that instance the 1-hr group tended
to avoid *more* frequently than the 0-hr group.

These results appeared to refute the conclusion of Brush *et al.* (1963)
that fear conditioned to the CS is probably the feature of original learning that is essential to produce the U-shaped retention function. Subsequently, however, Brush (1964) showed that fear conditioning is
sufficient to produce the effect. The U-shaped retention function was
seen again to follow escape training with a short CS–US interval, but in
this experiment the CS and US parameters were different from those
used earlier (Brush *et al.,* 1963): the CS was an increase in illumination
and presentation of 78 dB of white noise in the compartment occupied
by S and the US was a scrambled ac shock of 0.3 mA. A fear-conditioning procedure and an unsignaled shock procedure were also used.
During escape training the CS–US interval was 0.5 sec, and both CS and
US were terminated by the escape response. During fear conditioning,
Ss were confined to one side of the shuttlebox; the CS–US interval was
again 0.5 sec, but the shock was a fixed duration of 0.5 sec and was coterminous with the CS. The unsignaled shock procedure was the same as
fear conditioning except that no CS was presented. Twenty-five condi-

tioning or training trials were presented in each case, and retention was measured by performance during 40 trials of avoidance training. Intervals of .08, 1, 4, 24, and 168 hr were used following each pretraining procedure.

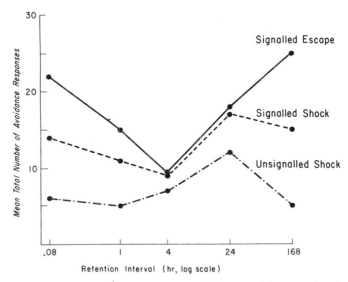

Fig. 2. Mean number of avoidance responses during retraining as a function of time after signaled escape training and after signaled and unsignaled fixed-duration shock. (From Brush, 1964.)

Figure 2 presents the results of this experiment. Both escape training with short CS–US interval and fear conditioning produce the U-shaped retention function. The absence of the U-shaped retention function in the case of *S*s pretrained with unsignaled shock is also apparent in Figure 2. Thus, the earlier inference by Kamin (1963) that classical conditioning of fear, in the absence of instrumental escape responding, cannot produce the U-shaped retention function is erroneous and probably attributable to inadequate sampling of retention intervals. The reader will note that the minima of these functions is at 4 hr, a retention interval not used by Kamin (1963).

Three other experiments have also reported finding the U-shaped retention function after fear conditioning. Brush and Levine (1966) obtained comparable results using the procedures outlined above, but two others have reported the effect using somewhat different procedures. Walrath (1968) gave rabbits 5 trials of fear conditioning in one side of a shuttlebox, and, after intervals of 2, 20, or 63 min, 3.3, 10.5, or 33.3 hr, they were given avoidance training to a criterion of 5 consecutive avoidance responses or for a maximum of 70 trials. For conditioning and avoidance training the CS was a 70-dB, 420-Hz tone, and the US was a 40-mA ac electric shock delivered through the grid floor of each compartment. The CS-US interval was 10 sec during both conditioning and training, and in each case the CS and US were terminated simultaneously. However, during avoidance training the stimuli were terminated by the shuttle response, whereas during fear conditioning the US duration was fixed at 0.6 sec. Intertrial interval averaged 3 min. The retention function was clearly U-shaped with poorest performance occurring in the 3.3- and 10.5-hr groups.

Using a somewhat different paradigm, Bintz, Braud and Brown (1970) trained rats to run down a straight alley for food reward in 20 trials spaced over 5 days. On the 6th day the S s were placed in the goal box and given two 60-V ac shocks of 0.25-sec duration. An additional nonrewarded trial was conducted 5 min, or 3 or 48 hr later, and the amount of approach to the goal box end of the straight alley was measured. The group tested 3 hr after conditioning showed significantly greater approach to the goal than did the other two groups. Control animals that received no fear conditioning approached the goal box to the same degree at all three retention intervals.

It seems safe to conclude from these results that Pavlovian conditioning of fear is both necessary and sufficient to set off whatever processes or mechanisms may be involved in producing the U-shaped retention function. However, questions regarding the requisite antecedent conditions remain unanswered by these experiments. For example, the minimum amount of fear conditioning that is required to produce the effect has not been determined, and the assumption that fear conditioning is sufficient to produce the effect implies that it be generated by all aversive training situations since they all necessarily include fear conditioning as a component of training.

B. Degree of Original Learning or Conditioning

The minimum amount of fear conditioning necessary to produce the U-shaped function has not been determined. However, a number of experiments in the literature have varied the degree of original learning rather widely so that something can be said about the effect of this variable despite the fact that the experiments do not attack this issue directly.

For example, among the experiments already reviewed extent of original training was varied over a considerable range. Kamin (1957) gave 25 trials of original avoidance training and his animals avoided about 5 times, whereas in Denny's (1958) replication, original avoidance training also continued for 25 trials but the animals avoided twice as often. Brush et al. (1963) gave original avoidance training to a criterion of 3 avoidance responses which required an average of 19 trials. All three experiments found significantly U-shaped retention functions which indicates that varying degree of original learning over a range of 3:1 does not determine the occurrence or nonoccurrence of the function although it may determine the location of its minimum, an issue that will be discussed later. Among the experiments using fear conditioning in original training, Brush (1964) used 25 trials, Walrath (1968) gave 5 trials and Bintz et al. (1970) used only two fear conditioning trials, but all three found evidence of the U-shaped retention function although other features of the experiments differed greatly. Again, there was suggestive evidence that this variable may control the locus of the minimum of the retention function. Two experiments by Pinel and Cooper (1966) using a one-trial passive avoidance procedure also obtained U-shaped retention functions (see Section C,4,a).

From these results one might be tempted to conclude that degree of original learning has little influence on the occurrence or nonoccurrence of the phenomenon. However, the picture was muddied by Anderson, Johnson, Schwendiman and Dunford (1966) who conducted a number of experiments in which rats were trained to avoid shock in a two-way shuttlebox. Original training was continued to various criteria and retention was measured during 40 trials of retraining. Retention intervals of .08, 1, 4, and 24 hr were used. A number of these experiments failed to produce significant variation in retention although many of them did, in fact, show U-shaped retention functions. In these experiments various features of the shuttlebox were manipulated and shock intensity was varied, but they had in common using criteria of either 2 or 3 avoidance responses during original training. When the criterion was reduced to 1 avoidance response, then highly significant U-shaped retention functions were obtained in two experiments. Taken together, the results of these experiments by Anderson et al. suggest that the U-shaped retention function is characteristic of poorly learned or poorly discriminated avoidance responses, not of more completely learned responses.

Following up this suggestion, Gabriel (1968) studied the effect of amount of original learning on the retention function using rabbits as Ss and an extinction test instead of relearning. His apparatus was the Brogden and Culler (1936) rotating wheel in which the CS was an 80-dB, 4000-Hz tone. Shock intensity was not specified except in behavioral terms. The CS–US interval was 4 sec, and both CS and US were terminated by the response, with the restriction that maximum duration of the US was 10 sec. The variable intertrial interval averaged 17.5 sec. A Sidman contingency was present in Gabriel's procedure because a response during the intertrial interval reset the interval.

Independent groups of Ss were given original avoidance training to criteria of 4 or 10 consecutive avoidance responses, or to 10 consecutive avoidance responses plus 150 additional trials (over training). Following retention intervals of 7 min or 1, 12, 24, 36, or 48 hr, groups of 10 Ss each received 150 extinction trials. Retention was measured by the number of conditioned responses elicited in extinction, and a U-shaped function was obtained only in animals trained to a criterion of 4 consecutive avoidance responses and then only during the first 30 trials of extinction. This function showed a significant decrease from 7 min to 1 hr and a significant increase from 1 hr to 12 hr with no further change at longer intervals. Retention functions following training to more stringent criteria or derived from later portions of the extinction session showed only monotonic increasing functions. Although inferences from Gabriel's experiment are limited by the noncomparability of subjects, apparatus, and training and testing procedures, nonetheless, his results tend to support Anderson's conclusion that the U-shaped retention function characterizes poorly learned avoidance behavior.

The results of an experiment by Klein and Spear (1969) are consistent with the above inference and show that age may also be an important variable that interacts with degree of original learning. Their apparatus was a one-way black-white box in which the CS was presentation of a flashing light in the white compartment and raising the door above the barrier separating the two compartments. The US was a 1.6-mA ac electric shock. The CS–US interval was 5 sec; the 30-sec intertrial interval was spent in a holding cage. After meeting an original learning criterion, the Ss were returned to their home cages for retention intervals of .17, 1, 4, or 24 hr, after which they received training to a criterion of five consecutive avoidance responses or for a maximum of 15 trials. .

Animals that were 25 or 95 days of age and trained to a criterion of one avoidance response in original training showed significant U-shaped functions which had their minima at 4 hr. In contrast, 16-day-old rats failed to show this form of retention unless they were trained to a more stringent criterion of five consecutive avoidance responses in original training. Thus, it is clear that the U-shaped retention function is consistently found following training to weak criteria of avoidance learning (as few as one avoidance response in post-weaning rats or as few as five avoidance responses in pre-weanlings), but in some experiments the function has not been found when original training continued to or surpassed a criterion of 10 consecutive avoidance responses.

However, a study by Brush and Sakellaris (1968) reported finding the U-shaped retention function in an extinction test given to adult rats at various times after they had met a criterion of 10 consecutive avoidance responses in original training. In their experiment Ss received a pretest, 25 trials of escape training with a 0.5-sec CS–US interval and avoidance training with a 5.0-sec CS–US interval which continued until the criterion of 10 consecutive avoidance responses was met or until a maximum of 100 avoidance training trials had been given. The CS was an increase in illumination and 78-dB of white noise in the compartment occupied by S and the US was a 0.3-mA ac electric shock delivered through the grid floor. A delayed-conditioning procedure was used, and the intertrial interval was constant at 1 min except in pretest where it was 2 min. Independent groups of 17 Ss each were matched for rate of original learning and were tested after intervals of .08, 1, 2, 4, 24, or 168 hr. The extinction test consisted of 100 trials on which the CS alone was presented; a shuttle response terminated the CS, but in the absence of a response the CS was terminated 5 sec after its onset.

Figure 3 presents the findings from this experiment. All three response classes: elicited (responses with latency $\leq$ 5.0 sec), intertrial, and total,

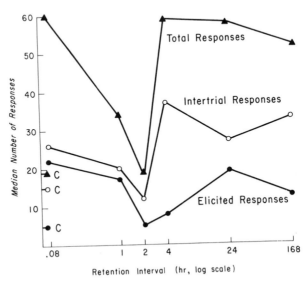

Fig. 3. Median number of elicited, intertrial and total responses in extinction as a function of time after avoidance training. Operant levels determined by untrained control animals are indicated for each response measure by the points labeled C on the ordinate. (From Brush & Sakellaris, 1968.)

show a significant effect of retention interval and the form of each of these functions is obviously nonlinear. All three measures show the minimum to be at 2 hr, although there was a tendency for the minimum to shift from 4 to 2 hr during the course of extinction.[2]

Despite the two exceptions provided by Anderson *et al.* (1964) and Gabriel (1968), we can conclude that degree of original learning or conditioning above the irreducible minimum of one fear conditioning trial is not an important variable in determining the presence or absence of the U-shaped retention function. The variant results obtained by Gabriel probably can be attributed to some combination of differences arising from species, apparatus, and training paradigms, while those of Anderson *et al.* might have arisen because samples as small as theirs frequently fail to generate statistically significant differences in training situations such as these that are notorious for their large within-group variances.

C. Kind of Original Training

The conclusion that the U-shaped retention function requires some degree of prior fear conditioning suggests that *all* forms of aversively motivated learning should be able to produce the effect inasmuch as all such training situations necessarily include the essential features of Pavlovian aversive conditioning, either explicitly or implicitly. Certainly, not all aversive training situations have been used in studies of retention, but a considerable number of them have been. So we can partially assess the validity of the fear conditioning hypothesis by reviewing the kinds of original training situations that have been used and noting any exceptions to our expectation.

1. Active Avoidance Training

 a. *Two-way shuttlebox training.* The original investigators of this problem used active avoidance training to establish original learning in their experiments, and they all used two-way shuttlebox training (Denny, 1958; Denny and Ditchman, 1962; Kamin, 1957; Segal and Brush, 1959). Their success in producing the U-shaped retention function need not be documented further.

It should also be noted that this form of the retention function can be obtained when the original active avoidance training is established in a two-way shuttlebox in which the unconditioned stimulus is not electric

---

[2]It should be noted that this experiment, in addition to demonstrating the U-shaped retention function after extensive avoidance training, also shows that changes in sensitivity or responsiveness to electric shock are not responsible for the shape and time course of the function.

shock. Greenberg and Kenyon (1965) used heat from infrared lamps as the US. The CS was a buzzer, the CS–US interval was 5 sec, and the intertrial interval was 1 min. Twenty-five avoidance training trials were given prior to and following retention intervals of 0, 1, 24, or 480 hr. Performance during retraining was a U-shaped function of the interval, the minimum being at 1 hr.

The retention function was also found in an interesting experiment by Bintz (1970), which used a somewhat more complex training procedure. In this instance, rats received 30 trials of active two-way shuttle-box avoidance training to each of two different conditioned stimuli—a light and a tone. The US was an ac electric shock. Following retention intervals of .08, 2, or 24 hr, retraining trials were given. When retraining consisted of 30 trials of continued active avoidance training to each of the stimuli, percent frequency of avoidance responding to each stimulus was a U-shaped function of the magnitude of the retention interval. This replicates the findings of the original experiments. However, if retraining consisted of 30 trials of active avoidance training to one of the stimuli (light for half the Ss, tone for the other half), and of 30 trials of *passive* avoidance training to the other stimulus (active-passive reversal learning for this stimulus), then the percent frequency of correct (avoidance) responding to each stimulus was an inverted U-shaped function of the magnitude of the retention interval.

These results are not easily interpreted in terms of any of the theoretical analyses outlined above. However, they do indicate that when a training situation is shifted from an active-active to an active-passive paradigm, *i.e.,* when a negative transfer situation is used with at least one conditioned stimulus, then the retention function for each stimulus is inverted relative to its usual form. It is an oversimplification to suggest that forgetting a prior active avoidance response at intermediate retention intervals will facilitate subsequent acquisition of a passive avoidance response because a concurrent continuation of active avoidance training to the other stimulus shows the same facilitation at intermediate retention intervals. Bintz's control animals (active-active tested on active-active) showed the usual U-shaped retention function so the inversion of form must be associated with changing the kind of training to one of the stimuli from active to passive, not with the use of concurrent training and testing of two conditioned stimuli. Although this analysis is hardly satisfactory, more adequate explanations must await additional experimentation on the problem. However, this experiment is an important one because it demands cautious interpretation of other experiments that use negative transfer paradigms to study the retention function. (See also Section IV.)

b.   One-way active avoidance training. The experiment by Klein and Spear (1969) which used one-way active avoidance training in a black-white two-compartment box has already been noted as successfully producing the U-shaped retention function in rats of widely different ages if degree of original training is appropriately varied. Baum (1968) also used this kind of original training and found the U-shaped retention function. However, Baum's experiment is noteworthy because he used reversal learning to measure retention and controlled for brightness preferences in original learning by training half of his *S*s to run from black to white, the other half to run from white to black. The CS in his experiment consisted of raising the guillotine door between the two compartments which produced a loud click as well as visual and other auditory stimuli. The US was a 115-V ac shock delivered to the grid floor through 100 kΩ resistance. The CS–US interval was 5 sec, and the intertrial interval was 30 sec, during which *S* remained in the safe compartment. Original training continued to a criterion of 10 consecutive avoidance responses whereupon the animals were returned to their home cages for retention intervals of 0, 1, 4, 22, or 44 hr. *S*s in the 0-hr group were held in *E*'s hand for 10 sec.

Following the retention period, the *S*s received reversal training to the same learning criterion that was used in original training. Here, *S*s originally trained to run from the black to the white compartment were placed in the white compartment and were required to run to the black one. The other *S*s trained in the opposite direction, were similarly reversed.

Baum's principal results are presented in Figure 4 in terms of median trial number of the 1st, 3rd, and 5th avoidance response as functions of the retention interval. It is clear that these functions are nonlinear; those produced by other measures of reversal training, *e.g.,* number of avoidance responses during the first 10 reversal training trials and number of errors before meeting the reversal criterion, were also significantly nonlinear. They show that reversal learning was relatively fast at short and at long retention intervals, whereas it was relatively slow at intermediate intervals. Inasmuch as nearly all *S*s showed positive transfer between original learning and reversal learning,[3] these functions indicate that re-

---

[3]Baum has kindly provided the overall median trial numbers of the 1st, 3rd, and 5th avoidance responses in original training, which were not reported in his published paper. They are 7.0, 10.0, and 13.0, respectively, and they indicate clearly that his training situation is one involving positive transfer even though a form of reversal learning is required of the animals. Very likely Baum's *S*s learned to "respond whenever possible" and were able to transfer that habit when the safe- and shock-cues were reversed.

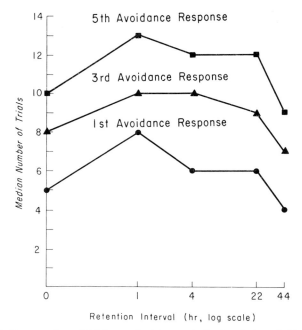

Fig. 4. Median number of trials required to reach the 1st, 3rd, and 5th avoidance response during reversal training as a function of time after original avoidance training. (From Baum, 1968.)

tention of original learning first decreases and then increases with time, *i.e.*, is a U-shaped function.

Another experiment by Klein and Spear (1970, Experiment 1) reports an interesting variant on Baum's reversal learning procedure. Klein and Spear gave their 26-day-old rats one-way active avoidance training (all *S*s ran from white to black) to a criterion of five consecutive avoidance responses. In their apparatus the CS consisted of a 2-Hz flashing light in the white compartment and lowering the door between the compartments. The US was a 1.6-mA ac electric shock in the white chamber, and the CS–US interval was 5 sec. The 30-sec intertrial interval was spent in a holding cage rather than in the safe black compartment. When the criterion of original learning had been met, *S*s were returned to their home cages for retention intervals of .08, 1, 4, or 24 hr, after which they received passive avoidance training to a performance criterion. In this phase of the experiment the animals were returned to the white compartment, and if they ran to the black, previously safe, compartment anytime within 60-sec of CS onset, they received a 0.2-mA

shock of 1-sec duration. Return to the white compartment was prevented by closing the door between the compartments. This training was
continued until S remained in the white compartment for 60 sec on three
consecutive trials.

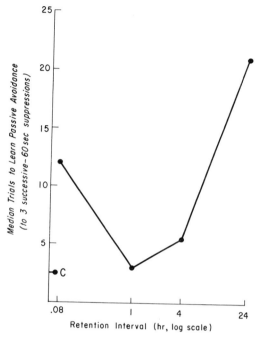

Fig. 5. Median number of trials required to reach a criterion of passive avoidance
learning as a function of time after original active avoidance training. The same measure
for experimentally naive animals is shown by the point labeled C on the ordinate. (From
Klein & Spear, 1970.)

Figure 5 represents the findings of their experiment and shows clearly
that median number of trials to reach the reversal learning criterion is a
U-shaped function of time. Quite obviously, prior active avoidance
learning interferes with subsequent passive avoidance learning at short
and at long intervals, whereas at intermediate intervals, especially at
1 hr, there is no transfer effect whatever. Because we know the learning
rate of experimentally naive Ss, we can be confident that the magnitude
of the negative transfer effect is reduced nearly to zero at intermediate
retention intervals. This suggests that at those intervals the original
learning is either nearly completely forgotten or rendered virtually ineffective.

Both the results of this experiment and those of Baum (1968) show that retention of original learning is a U-shaped function of time. Baum's experiment is a positive transfer situation which results in poor performance at intermediate intervals, whereas Klein and Spear's experiment (1970) is a negative transfer paradigm which results in good performance when the original learning is "forgotten" at intermediate intervals.

Although the findings of these experiments are consistent with the assumption that retention of original learning is a U-shaped function of time, caution should be exercised before adopting a purely memorial analysis of these retention functions. The same effects could be seen in both of these forms of reversal learning if the motivation to perform the previously learned response were a U-shaped function of time, so it is not necessary, in view of these data, to invoke a change of memory over time. To avoid taking a position on this issue we will use the term retention only in its operational sense and will not suggest whether the changes in retention are attributable to memory or to motivation.

   c. *Other forms of active avoidance training.* The only other form of active avoidance training that has been studied in retention is the running response by rabbits in the Brogden–Culler running wheel (Gabriel, 1968). We have already seen that this experiment did not generate the familiar U-shaped retention function except under very particular conditions: weak criterion of original learning and retention tested early in extinction. Whether or not rats in a similar training situation would produce results comparable to those of one- or two-way active avoidance training is not known at the present time, but even using rabbits, Gabriel did find the U-shaped function under some conditions.

2. Signaled Escape Training

We have already seen in the experiments by Brush *et al.* (1963) and Brush (1964) that if original training consists of signaled escape training in a two-way shuttlebox then performance during subsequent avoidance training is a U-shaped function of time after original training. This is true for the special training conditions used in those experiments, *i.e.*, 0.5-sec CS–US interval, response termination of CS and US, and moderate intensity electric shock (US). But it is not known whether such a function would occur following escape training with a longer CS–US interval. Use of a longer CS–US interval could provide short delays of punishment for anticipatory avoidance responses and might also eliminate the adventitious reinforcement of avoidance responses by subsequent short-latency termination of shock which characterizes escape training with a short CS–US interval. These may be training parameters that are critical for producing the U-shaped retention function, but research directly addressed to these questions is lacking. Punishment has been used in original learning and will be discussed later in the context of passive avoidance training.

Pinel (1968) used a one-trial escape training procedure to study retention. In his study experimentally naive male hooded rats received two pretraining trials in which they were placed daily in the white compartment of a two-compartment box and the latency with which they entered the opposite black compartment was recorded, whereupon they were removed to their home cages. On the third day the grid floor of the white compartment was electrified (2-mA ac) when Ss were placed in the white compartment, and they were allowed to escape to the black compartment from which they were removed 10 sec later. Independent groups of 10 or 11 Ss were returned to the white compartment (no shock present) after intervals of 5 sec, 1 min, or 24 hr. Control groups were comparably treated except that they received no shock. Latency of entry into the black compartment was measured on the test trial up to a limit of 5 min. Retention of the previous one-trial escape training decreased monotonically with time which was attributed by Pinel to the acquisition of a conditioned emotional response or a freezing response, but which may, in fact, be closely related to an effect of amount of training on the time course of the retention function (see Section III). Because Pinel did not assess retention at longer intervals, interpretations of the function he reports will have to remain speculative.

3. Pavlovian Conditioning of Fear

The experiments of Bintz et al. (1970), Brush (1964), Brush and Levine (1966) and Walrath (1968), already reviewed, showed that Pavlovian conditioning of fear can produce the U-shaped retention function, and they need no further discussion here. However, McMichael (1966, Experiment 2) also reported a U-shaped retention function following fear conditioning. Ten shocks were presented to rats in the black side of a black-white shuttlebox intermixed with shock-free periods in the white side of the apparatus. Amount of time spent in each side during a subsequent 10-min period of free choice was used to measure retention of conditioned fear after intervals of .03, .5, 1, 2, 4, 6, 24, 48, and 504 hr. Amount of time spent on the previous safe side gradually decreased as a function of retention interval, but this measure was reduced in the 4-hr group to a level equal to that of nonshocked control Ss. Thus, it could be argued that a U-shaped retention function having its minimum at 4 hr was observed in this experiment. However, as McAllister and Mc-Allister (1967) point out, these data, except for the 4-hr group, indicate that conditioned fear changes relatively little over time. Furthermore, it seems somewhat risky to conclude on the basis of only one data point that an otherwise fairly linear function is really U-shaped. But if some credence is given to the data of McMichael's 4-hr group, then these results together with those of experiments previously cited substantiate the conclusion that Pavlovian aversive conditioning can produce the U-shaped function under circumstances so varied that the conclusion need not be limited to a particular conditioning procedure or to a peculiar feature of the test situation.

Probably the first experiment to examine retention of Pavlovian aversive conditioning was one which appeared to obtain a different function. The experiment (Brady, 1952) was concerned with temporal parameters that affect the retrograde amnesia produced by electroconvulsive shock (ECS), but control Ss that received no ECS were also trained and tested; their data are relevant here. These Ss were first trained to press a lever for water reinforcement which was available on a variable interval (VI) schedule. Then a signal (clicking sound) was paired with shock on eight trials which were scattered throughout a 31-day training period. The CS–US interval was 3 min and CS and US were coterminous. After intervals of 30, 60, or 90 days pseudo-ECS treatments were begun and retention was measured in terms of resistance to extinction of the conditioned suppression of lever pressing. The data from control Ss indicate that strength of conditioned fear increased with time so that after 60 or 90 days the conditioned fear response was more resistant to extinction than it was immediately after conditioning. It should be noted, however, that this experiment only reported changes over long time intervals and did not measure retention at short and intermediate intervals where the U-shaped function appears to be located. Thus, the monotonic increasing retention function reported here cannot be taken as evidence against the fear conditioning hypothesis of Brush et al. (1963).

4. Passive Avoidance Training

Although there are some discrepancies in the details of the retention functions following various forms of active avoidance training, signaled escape training or Pavlovian fear conditioning, all of the experiments that use those paradigms and assess the appropriate intervals show that retention of original learning first decreases and then increases with time, i.e., that the retention functions for these forms of aversive conditioning or learning are U-shaped. This appears not to be the case with sóme forms of passive avoidance training although even here some of the retention functions are clearly U-shaped and similar in other respects to those which characterize conditioning and the active avoidance or escape paradigms. In this section we will examine first those experiments which produce the expected U-shaped retention function and then compare them with those which produce other forms of the function so that the variables which may control its form can be identified.

   a. U-shaped retention functions following passive avoidance training. Probably the first experiments to show the customary U-shaped retention function for a passive avoidance response were those by Pinel and Cooper (1966). In their first experiment male hooded rats were first trained to press a lever for water on a continuous reinforcement schedule (CRF). Then, one trial of avoidance training was given by presenting a 0.01-sec, 5-mA foot shock contingent upon the first bar press after S had been in the box for 20 sec on the training day. Immediately following the shock, each S was removed to his home cage for a retention interval of 1 min or 2 or 8 hr. In order to hold water deprivation constant during retention testing, different groups received their avoidance training under different deprivation conditions. Although the authors fail to specify this procedural point, retention was presumably tested with CRF water reinforcement and no shock. Retention was measured as the difference between the number of responses made during the last 10 min of the last CRF session and the number of presses that occurred during the 10-min retention test. Measured in this way retention was a U-shaped function which decreased from 1 min to 2 hr and then increased from 2 to 8 hr.
   In a second similar experiment, Ss were trained to drink from a water spout and duration of drinking was used as the dependent variable rather than frequency of bar pressing. During passive avoidance training, shock duration was apparently contingent on continued drinking, *i.e.,* the maximum duration of shock was 0.1 sec, but shock was terminated if the rat stopped drinking sooner than that. Again, the passive avoidance response was established by a single shock contingent upon drinking and again avoidance of the spout was a U-shaped function of the retention interval. The animals spent approximately 80 sec drinking from the spout following a 2-hr retention interval, whereas animals tested 1 min or 8 or 25 hr after avoidance training did not drink at all from the spout.
   It should be noted that in these experiments, degree of original learning is not well controlled, because only one shock is given and performance is not measured prior to the retention test. Furthermore, the

nonlinear shape of these functions is determined by only one group. However, the effects were statistically significant, were consistent in the two rather different experiments, and their implications are of some significance for analyses of the U-shaped retention function. It should be noted that in passive avoidance tests, poor retention is indexed by active responding which can result from forgetting (loss of memory) or from a decrease of fear which Pinel and Cooper noted can result in elevated response rates either because there is less motivation to avoid or because there is less freezing behavior. In any case, because retention of passive avoidance training showed a U-shaped retention function, one may infer that the deterioration of performance at intermediate intervals is associated with a decrease rather than an increase of fear which Denny's (1958) theory requires. Pinel and Cooper also noted that because their passive avoidance procedure used only one shock, it is difficult to invoke warm-up effects to account for their data which reduced the impact of Kamin's (1963) analysis, depending, as it does, on warm-up decrements.

A study designed similarly to Pinel and Cooper's first experiment was reported recently by Singh and Brush (1969). Male hooded rats were first trained to press a bar on a CRF schedule. However, in this experiment the animals were deprived of food on a daily feeding schedule that reduced their body weight by 25%. Thus, changes in skin resistance from variation in water deprivation could not result in different degrees of original learning which could alter the amount apparently retained at a later time. The animals were fed in their home cages 5 hr before the daily training sessions. After making approximately 800 reinforced lever presses over an 8- to 9-day period, the animals received passive avoidance training which consisted of superimposing a 2-min fixed interval (FI) schedule of response-contingent ac electric shock (0.55 sec, 0.3 mA) on the CRF base line schedule. The FI schedule was initiated by the beginning of the training session so that the first shock was not presented until after the animal had made a number of reinforced lever presses during the first 2 min. Passive avoidance training continued until a criterion of no responses for 10 min was achieved, after which the animals were returned to their home cages for retention intervals of .08, 1, 2, 4, 8, or 16 hr. Following the retention interval they received a 1-hr test session in which lever presses produced only the CRF food reward. In the absence of feeding during the interval, retention tests occurred at progressively greater levels of food deprivation.

Figure 6 presents the results of this experiment in terms of the median time required to emit the 1st, 3rd, and 5th lever presses as functions of the retention interval. Clearly, retention of this passive avoidance response (long latency to press the lever) is a U-shaped function of time

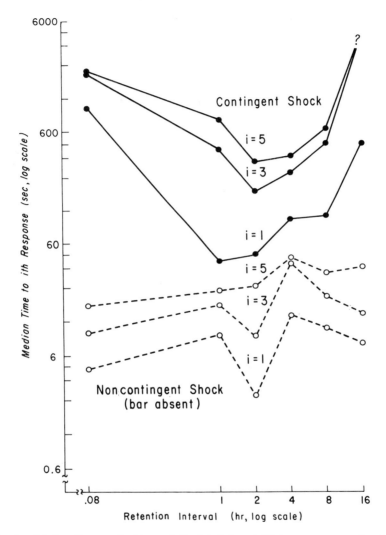

Fig. 6. Median time required to emit the 1st, 3rd, and 5th bar presses as a function of time after passive avoidance training (contingent shock) or free shock (noncontingent). See text for procedural details. (From Singh & Brush, 1969.)

and good retention returns at relatively long intervals despite the progressively stronger motivation to press the lever. Additional animals were trained to press the lever as described above, but instead of being given passive avoidance training these animals received an equal number of free shocks in the apparatus with the lever covered. Thus, the temporal pattern and duration of shock were matched to those generated by the median animal that received passive avoidance training, but in this case the shocks were not contingent on the animal's behavior. Their data are also presented in Figure 6 and show clearly that the U-shaped retention function is dependent on the contingency between response and shock and is not the result of fear conditioned to apparatus cues.

Both Pinel and Cooper (1966) and Singh and Brush (1969) used suppression of an appetitively rewarded response and tested for retention by maintaining appetitive reinforcement and by extinguishing the passive avoidance response. Contrasting with this approach is an experiment by Klein and Spear (1970, Experiment 2) in which acquisition of an active one-way avoidance response is used to measure retention of a previously learned passive avoidance response established in the same situation. In their experiment, rats were trained not to enter the black compartment of a black-white shuttlebox and to remain in the presence of the CS (a flashing light and raising the door between the two compartments) for 60 sec on three consecutive trials. If Ss entered the black compartment, which they did with some nonzero probability prior to training, the door was lowered and they received a 0.2-mA ac shock of 1-sec duration. Following retention intervals of .08, 1, 4, or 24 hr, the Ss received active avoidance training in which the same CS was used, but the shock was 0.5 mA and was terminated by S's escaping to the black compartment. The CS–US interval was 5 sec, and training continued until a criterion of five consecutive avoidance responses was met.

Figure 7 presents the results of their experiment in terms of median number of trials required to reach the active avoidance criterion. Because this is a negative transfer paradigm, retention of previous passive avoidance responses interferes with learning an active response and such interference (retention) occurs at short and at long retention intervals, whereas at 1-hr retention of the prior habit is so poor that the animals learn the active avoidance response as rapidly as naive rats. Thus, retention of passive avoidance learning has been shown to be a U-shaped function of time in four experiments which used widely different degrees of original training, three different responses, either reversal learning or extinction tests of the passive avoidance response, and three different approach motivations to support the base line behavior.

One additional experiment has reported a U-shaped retention function for passive avoidance learning, but the time course of the curve is quite different from those described above. In that experiment Irwin, Kalsner and Curtis (1964) placed 10-week-old male mice in a 2 × 7.25-in. box which was separated by a 1-in. barrier from a larger, 8.5 × 7.25-in.

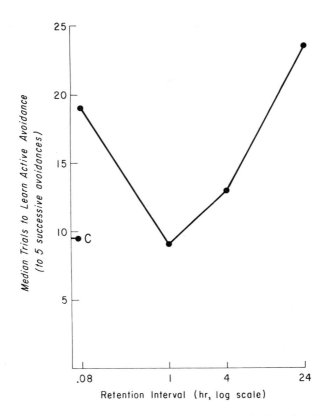

Fig. 7. Median number of trials required to reach a criterion of active avoidance learning as a function of time after original passive avoidance training. The same measure for experimentally naive animals is shown by the point labeled *C* on the ordinate. (From Klein & Spear, 1970.)

chamber. Both boxes were made of black acrylic plastic. Most of the animals tended to enter the larger compartment within 50 sec, and upon crossing the barrier, they received a single 0.2-mA electric shock of 2 sec duration. Independent groups of animals were tested after retention intervals of 0, 0.5, 2, 15, and 60 min by being placed once again in the small compartment of the apparatus. They crossed the hurdle with mean latencies of: 127, 88, 59, 74, and 122 sec, respectively. Thus, retention of passive avoidance learning was a U-shaped function of time, but the minimum of the function was at 2 min. This experiment is open to the criticisms that uncontrolled variation of the amount of original learning could have produced the obtained results and that no statistical analyses are provided in the published abstract of this experiment. Furthermore, the time course of this retention function is much reduced and may not even be comparable to that shown by rats in other training paradigms. There has been no research which establishes whether the different time course is due to the difference in species or to variations in the training paradigm, but, as we will see in the next section, this U-shaped function with the brief time course may be a part of a biphasic retention function that has been observed in other experiments. But it is clear that the U-shaped retention function having the usual time course can follow a wide variety of passive avoidance training procedures, especially those that involve suppression in rats of a reasonably well established appetitive or aversive instrumental or consummatory response.

   b. Biphasic retention functions following passive avoidance training. Irwin and Banuazizi (1966) found a retention function in mice that first declined then rose and then declined again. Their experiments were concerned with the effects of strychnine and pentylenetetrazol (metrazol) on retention of one-trial passive avoidance learning, but saline injected control animals were also tested and their data are relevant here. Using intervals of 0, 5, 15, 30, or 90 min or 24 hr, Irwin and Banuazizi found that retention, as indexed by response latency on Trial 2, decreased rapidly from 0 to 5 min and then increased from 5 to 90 min with a reversal of lesser magnitude from 90 min to 24 hr. This function replicated the one reported earlier by Irwin *et al.* (1964) in considerable detail. Additional control Ss were tested in a second experiment in this report, but the 0- and 15-min groups were omitted. As a result, only the rising portion of the function was presented, and in this experiment the 24-hr group gave different results from the comparable group of the preceding experiment. Here, the response latency on Trial 2 decreased markedly from the 90-min to 24-hr retention interval. Thus, a confusing and potentially misleading picture is presented by these two experiments, one showing a biphasic curve with the U-shaped dip being predominant and the other showing just an inverted U-shape.

   In an effort to unravel some of these inconsistencies, Irwin, Banuazizi, Kalsner and Curtis (1968) investigated a number of parameters of their training situation and found that the decline in retention after 24 hr resulted from transferring the animals from their wire home cages where food and water were normally available to plastic cages in the experimental room where access to food and water was not permitted. If the animals were kept in their home cages, which were moved to the experimental room, and had *ad lib.* access to food and water throughout the experiment, then the decline in retention at 24 hr did not occur, although the earlier dip at 5 to 8 min was maintained. The important factor in this complex manipulation appears not to be food or water deprivation since manipulation of that variable alone did not significantly alter the retention function.

Concerned with this same problem of 24-hr retention, Calhoun and Murphy (1966) showed that sensory stimulation for 30 min immediately after the passive avoidance training trial causes retention loss 24 hr later, whereas the same stimulation before training did not interfere with 24-hr retention.

But most disquieting is the observation of Irwin *et al.* (1968) that control animals that did not receive foot shock when they stepped over the hurdle on Trial 1 also showed increased response latency on Trial 2 and that the increase on Trial 2 was significantly greater after 90 min than after only 5 min. Furthermore, seasonal variations also appeared to influence Trial 2 latencies after a 24-hr retention period. One might be tempted to reject the one-trial passive avoidance paradigm as capable of producing behavior which is sufficiently significant and reliable to warrant study of its retention. However, a number of Irwin's experiments have reliably produced a short-term retention deficit (U-shaped function with minimum at 5–8 min) even though the long-term retention deficit at 24 hr appears not to be reliable except under poorly specified conditions of housing, season of the year, posttrial stimulation, etc.

  c. Inverted U-shaped functions following passive avoidance training. In a recent paper the functions of both of Irwin and Banuazizi's experiments were described as "inverted U-shaped function(s) of the conditioning-test interval with maximum latency at 90 min" (Zammit-Montebello, Black, Marquis, & Suboski, 1969, p. 579). Although their description hardly fits the Irwin and Benuazizi data, their own research on retention of one-trial passive-avoidance learning in rats does show a function that unambiguously has that shape.

The first experiment reported by these investigators examined the effects of shock intensity and amount of pretraining on the retention function. Their training apparatus consisted of a white compartment (17 × 14 × 16 in.) that was brightly illuminated by a 150-W flood lamp suspended 12 in. above the floor and a black compartment (14 × 14 × 16 in.) that was not directly illuminated. The floor of the black compartment was an electrifiable grid, whereas the floor of the white compartment was made of clear plexiglas. The two compartments were connected at floor level by a 3 × 3-in. opening with a guillotine door. Experimentally naive male hooded rats received either 1, 2, 4, or 8 daily training trials which consisted of placing the animals in the white compartment. When they entered the dark compartment, which they invariably did upon encountering the doorway, the door was lowered and they were confined to the dark compartment for 2 min after which they were returned to their home cages until the next day. On the last training trial for each animal a 2-sec electric shock of either 0.5, 1.0, or 2.0 mA was given 10 sec after entry into the black compartment.[4] Retention of the passive avoidance learning acquired on that one trial was measured in terms of the latency with which the animals entered the dark compartment on the next trial which occurred either 10 or 100 sec, 16 min, or 2.75 or 27.75 hr later.

Latency of entering the dark compartment increased at all retention intervals as shock intensity increased and, although there were a few reversals, latency decreased at all retention intervals as number of pretraining trials increased. Retention functions that appeared to be increasing monotonically, decreasing monotonically, or first increasing and then decreasing (inverted U-shaped) were described but no significance can be attached to the shapes of the various functions because the data were only analyzed statistically in the context of a complete factorial analysis of variance.

However, they reported a second experiment using basically the same procedures except in this one, four pretraining trials were used, the guillotine door was removed, and a 1-mA foot shock was employed. Retention was indexed by mean latency on trial 2 which occurred after 11 different intervals, ranging in half-log units from 3.2 sec ($10^{.5}$ sec) to 87.75 hr ($10^{5.5}$ sec); a randomly selected group of 15 Ss was tested at each retention interval. The latency function obtained in this rather massive experimental endeavor was clearly inverted U-shaped in form with maximum latency (retention) occurring in the 5.25- and 16-min groups. It is noteworthy that in addition to inverting the function relative to that of other experiments, this function has a time scale which is more similar to those of the Irwin experiments which used mice than to those previously reported which used rats.

Another inverted U-shaped retention function was reported by Adams and Calhoun (1969). In their experiment, an electric shock was administered when their mice stepped down from a small 7.6-cm diameter plat-

[4]It should be noted that this training procedure is probably, in fact, similar to the Klein and Spear (1970) active-passive paradigm because these Ss are probably being punished for making a well-established active response that allows them to escape from a brightly illuminated (aversive) environment. However, in this experiment passive avoidance training was continued for only one trial, degree of learning was not assessed prior to measuring its retention, and rate of passive avoidance learning in Ss not previously trained in active escape is not known.

form to a larger surrounding platform; following the technique outlined
by Essman and Alpern (1964), they slowly lowered the small platform
from 20.3 to 1.27 cm above the surrounding one, which usually induced
the animal to step down. After receiving the shock, Ss were removed to
a small wire cage to await Trial 2 which occurred after intervals of 0, 1,
2, 7, or 15 min. Retention, as measured by the percent increase of step-
down latency, increased from 0 to 2 min and decreased thereafter. Other
Ss were identically trained but tested for spontaneous activity level in a
separate photo-cell apparatus. Activity was a U-shaped function of the
retention interval, and the minimum of the function was at 2 min, the
interval at which retention of the passive avoidance response was greatest. Thus, Adams and Calhoun's results are directly opposite to those
obtained by Irwin *et al.* (1964) and Irwin and Benuazizi (1966) and suggest that spontaneous activity may be a variable to be considered when
interpreting retention curves, regardless of their form. Although the data
are sparce, it seems not unlikely that seasonal and environmental stimuli
could significantly affect activity level and thus might possibly contribute
to the variously shaped functions reported by Irwin *et al.* (1968).

   d.   Monotonic retention functions following passive avoidance training.
An unpublished experiment by McGaugh and Alpern, which was cited by
McGaugh (1966), studied retention of one-trial passive avoidance learning in mice. In their experiment, Ss were placed one at a time on a small
platform attached to the side of a box and were allowed to enter the
dark interior through a small hole, whereupon each S received a foot
shock as it entered. Retention was tested either 5 or 30 sec, 2 min, or 1,
or 24 hr later and was measured in terms of the percentage of Ss that
failed to step through the hole within 10 sec of being placed on the platform. Retention so measured increased significantly from 5 sec to 2 min,
increased slightly from 2 min to 1 hr, and then decreased slightly between 1 and 24 hr. In another experiment, Ss were given two trials
spaced 2 min apart. Retention at all intervals tested (2 min and 1 and 24
hr) was greater in these Ss than in those given only a single trial, but no
significant effect of retention interval was obtained. Similar effects were
obtained using 2 min of massed trials in original training. Thus, the
monotonic increasing retention function obtained in this experiment
appears to be limited to passive avoidance learning acquired in only one
trial.

   Clark (1967) conducted an experiment similar to McGaugh and Alpern's but he used different intervals and obtained different results.
Clark used essentially the same apparatus that McGaugh and Alpern
used, but he delivered a single 0.7-mA shock that was either 0.7, 1.4, or

2.8 sec in duration in different groups of mice, whereas McGaugh and Alpern used a 3.0-mA shock of unspecified duration. Clark tested retention at intervals of 0.5, 2, 7, 32, 166, or 512 hr, whereas McGaugh and Alpern used retention intervals of 5 and 30 sec, 2 min, and 1 and 24 hr. Furthermore, McGaugh and Alpern used a 10-sec cutoff in testing for retention, *i.e.*, they measured the percent frequency of animals remaining on the platform (avoidance response) for 10 sec. Clark, on the other hand, used 30 sec without entry into the dark compartment as the criterion for occurrence of the avoidance response. Whereas McGaugh and Alpern found an *increasing* monotonic function, Clark reported retention was a monotonic *decreasing* function of time.

It should be added, however, that the significant rise in retention in McGaugh and Alpern's data occurred only over the first 2 min with the slight additional improvement at 1 hr being insufficient to reach statistical significance. Similarly, the slight decrease at 24 hr was not statistically reliable. Clark, on the other hand, did not test retention in the range where McGaugh and Alpern found that it was improving, and instead found that retention decreased from .5 to 512 hr. If allowance is made for some variation in performance because of the differences in procedure, then it is possible that McGaugh and Alpern, on the one hand, and Clark, on the other, were simply measuring opposite sides of an inverted U-shape function that was comparable to the one described within a single experiment by Zammit-Montebello *et al.* (1969).

e. Recapitulation. It seems safe to infer from the literature on retention of passive avoidance learning: (1) that there are two basic forms of the retention function, U-shaped and inverted U-shaped, (2) that the time scale of the U-shaped function is such that the minimum is reached in 1 to 6 hr with nearly complete recovery in 16 to 24 hr, whereas the time scale of the inverted U-shaped function is such that the maximum is reached in a matter of minutes (range is 2–90) with significant loss occurring again in 24 hr or more, (3) that the inverted U-shaped function may be biphasic under some set of conditions that is not well specified, and (4) that the U-shaped function is usually associated with multitrial suppression of reasonably well-established instrumental or consummatory responses in rats, whereas the inverted U-shaped or biphasic function has never been observed except following one-trial training procedures which invariably involve suppression, in either rats or mice, of a relatively unlearned response that occurs with relatively high probability on the first trial.

Clearly, there are exceptions to these conclusions, but the weight of evidence seems to be in their favor. Thus, the extensive search of Irwin *et al.* (1968) for the determinants of the 24-hr retention loss seems fruit-less in view of the results of Zammit-Montebello *et al.* (1969), Clark (1967) and McGaugh and Alpern (McGaugh, 1966) which suggested that the relatively minor retention loss usually found at 24 hr is only one point on a progressively decreasing curve that extends for many more hours.' Rather, the striking feature of the Irwin data is the detection of good retention immediately after the training trial followed by a decline over 5 to 10 min. Inasmuch as the biphasic function is unique to Irwin's laboratories, and the inverted U-shaped function, albeit with somewhat varying time courses, has been found in a number of different laborato-ries, the weight of evidence would appear to indicate that the inverted U form characterizes the time course of retention of one-trial passive avoidance learning in rats and mice and that circumstances unique to Irwin's technique are responsible for his consistently finding the biphasic form with its initial decline of retention. Additional research which care-fully analyzes features of the experimental apparatus and training and testing procedures is needed before this issue can be settled.

Two additional experiments present conflicting data which remain unresolved. They are the U-shaped retention functions reported by Pinel and Cooper (1969), both of which follow one-trial passive avoidance training, and the inverted U-shaped functions which are reported by almost all of the other studies using one-trial passive avoidance training. Somehow, the one-trial suppression of an operant or consummatory base line (Pinel & Cooper, 1966) results in a U-shaped function, but one-trial suppression of relatively unlearned locomotor response (Adams & Calhoun, 1969; Irwin *et al.*, 1968; Zammit-Montebello *et al.*, 1969) produces the inverse function with a different time scale.

Spevack and Suboski (1967) are undoubtedly correct when they sug-gest that emotional conditioning and avoidance training are confounded in the one-trial passive avoidance paradigm, but noting that fact is of lit-tle assistance in accounting for the Pinel and Cooper data. One could assume that Pavlovian emotional conditioning can occur in one trial (a debatable point at best) and that instrumental avoidance training re-quires many more trials. Then the one-trial procedures would tend to emphasize emotional conditioning over avoidance learning, whereas mul-titrial procedures would reverse that emphasis. One could further assume that retention of one-trial emotional conditioning is an inverted U-shaped function of time. However, special additional assumptions are required regarding the relative ease of conditioning fear to cues pro-duced by different kinds of responses, and/or regarding the relative ease of learning the response-shock contingency for different kinds of respon-ses if the Pinel and Cooper data are to be reconciled with the data of the other one-trial passive avoidance training procedures. Such additional assumptions would be gratuitous at present, but even if made they would still leave us at the level of description rather than explanation.

In reconciling the multitrial procedures of Klein and Spear (1970) and of Singh and Brush (1969) with one-trial procedures of Adams and Calhoun (1969) and Zammit-Montebello *et al.* (1969), one could make the above assumption that the rate of Pavlovian conditioning is greater than the rate of instrumental learning and that the retention functions following multitrial procedures assess memory of instrumental learning, whereas those following one-trial procedures assess memory of Pavlovian conditioned emotional responses. This assumption is also gratuitous, however, because it has never been established empirically that emotional conditioning, as distinct from sensitization or the aftereffects of electric shock, is established in these one-trial experiments. Until the adequate control groups establish the nature of the learning or conditioning that occurs as a result of one response-contingent shock, it seems simpler to conclude that experiments using one-trial procedures are merely examining the aftereffects of electric shock or the dissipation of sensitization, whereas those using multitrial procedures are studying motivational or memorial changes associated with emotional conditioning and/or instrumental learning.

5. Assessment of Fear Conditioning Hypothesis

To date, it would appear that there is only one class of experiments which provides exceptions to the hypothesis that fear conditioning is necessary and sufficient to produce the U-shaped retention function when retention is measured in the same situation in which original conditioning or learning occurred. The sole exception is provided by the one-trial passive avoidance paradigms in which an unlearned locomotor response is suppressed by shock. In such cases, as we have seen, retention is either an inverted U-shaped or a biphasic function, with time scales measured in minutes rather than hours. Inasmuch as a unique base line behavior is used in those experiments, and because they all are open to the criticisms that probability of the base line response as well as the extent of original avoidance learning are not assessed prior to the retention interval, it seems reasonable to conclude that they are not measuring comparable phenomena, especially in view of the different time courses of the U-shaped and inverted U-shaped (or biphasic) functions. Thus, the fear conditioning hypothesis appears valid and need only be qualified to the extent of specifying the time course over which the retention function varies or of limiting it to exclude one-trial punishment of unlearned locomotor responses.

III. DETERMINANTS OF THE INTERVAL OF MINIMUM RETENTION

A number of experiments have reported variations in the locus of the minimum of the U-shaped retention function, some as a result of explicit experimental manipulations, others as a result of *post hoc* analyses of individual differences in training. These experiments will be reviewed in this section.

A. Rate of Original Learning

In a search for variables which might influence the shape of the U-shaped retention function, Brush, Myer, and Palmer (1964) selected intertrial interval on the grounds that it bears a close logical relation to retention interval since both intervals separate adjacent trials. They differ only in that the intertrial interval is usually relatively brief and the animal usually remains in the apparatus during it, whereas the retention interval is usually relatively long in duration and the animal usually is removed to his home cage for its duration. In Brush *et al.* (1964), animals were given original avoidance training to a criterion of three avoidance responses using a 10-Hz click and flash for the CS, a 0.26-mA scrambled ac electric shock for the US, and a 5-sec CS–US interval in a delayed-conditioning paradigm. A 3×5 factorial design was used in which there were three intertrial intervals, 0.5, 1, and 2 min and five retention intervals, .08, 1, 4, 24, and 168 hr. Following the retention interval, which the animal spent in his home cage, 40 trials of retraining were conducted under conditions identical to those of the *S*'s original training.

As Figure 8 shows, the median number of trials required to reach the learning criterion in original training is inversely related to intertrial interval. The same measure from the retraining session shows that poorest performance occurs after a retention interval of 24 hr when a 0.5-min intertrial interval is used, whereas with intertrial intervals of 1 and 2 min poorest performance occurs following a 4-hr retention interval.[5] This interaction between intertrial interval and retention interval was seen also in the frequency of avoidance responses during the first 10 trials of retraining, *i.e.*, the minimum of the function there is at 24 hr when the intertrial interval is 0.5 min and at 4 hr when the intertrial intervals are

---

[5]A similar interaction using fewer values of each variable was reported in an unpublished experiment by Denny and Fisher (1962).

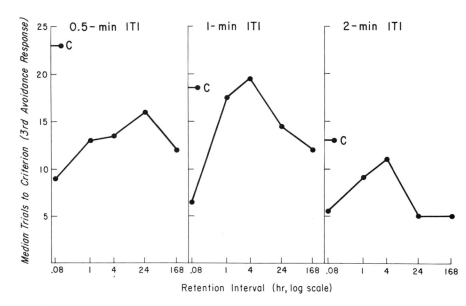

Fig. 8. Median number of trials required to reach a criterion of avoidance learning as a function of time after original training at each of three intertrial intervals (ITI). The median number of trials required to reach criterion in original acquisition is indicated by the point labeled C on the ordinate of each panel. (From Brush *et al.,* 1964.)

1 or 2 min. During subsequent blocks of 10 retraining trials the minima of the retention functions are at 1 hr for all intertrial-interval groups and, as a result, the functions generated by frequency of avoidance responding during the entire retraining session also have minima at 1 hr. Apparently, the effect of intertrial interval on the retention function is changed by the relearning process and is revealed only during the early stages of relearning. Somehow, the events associated with relearning override the effect of the intertrial interval and produce retention functions with minima uniformly at 1 hr.

Kamin (1963) presented data showing that learning rate, manipulated by *post hoc* analyses of individual differences, is also a determinant of the minimum of the function. In this experiment, degree of original learning was controlled by training hooded rats in a shuttlebox to a criterion of three consecutive avoidance responses. The CS–US interval was 5 sec, the CS was a 74-dB buzzer and the US a 1.1-mA ac electric shock. After retention intervals of 0 (1 min), 0.5, 1, 6, or 24 hr or 20 days, 25 trials of avoidance retraining were given. The usual U-shaped function was obtained, but Kamin plotted the data separately for the five *S*s that learned slowest and the five that learned fastest in each group during original training.

The function for the combined subgroups showed equally poor performance at the 1- and 6-hr intervals, whereas the function generated by the slow learners had a clear minimum at 6 hr, and the function for the fast learners showed poorest performance occurring in the 1-hr group. Speed of original learning was indexed by the number of shocks received so that the slow learners received a greater but unspecified number of Pavlovian conditioning trials than their fast learning counterparts. Thus, Kamin found an inverse relation between rate of original learning and the magnitude of the interval at the minimum of the retention function, which is in good agreement with the above results of Brush *et al.* (1963).

B. Extent of Original Conditioning or Training

In the experiments of Brush *et al.* (1963) and Kamin (1963) degree of original learning was held constant and the influence of *rate* of original learning on retention was examined. Under those conditions *direct* relations were obtained between number of CS–US pairings or number of training trials and the locus of the minimum of the U-shaped retention function. In other experiments, however, the number of conditioning or training trials has been manipulated directly while rate of conditioning or learning was held constant by randomly assigning subjects to retention groups which were trained under identical conditions. In these experiments opposite relationships were obtained. For example, Brush (1963) gave male hooded rats either 10 or 25 Pavlovian conditioning trials using a 0.5-sec CS–US interval and a 0.5-sec shock duration; CS and US were coterminous. After intersession intervals of .08, 1, 4, 24, or 168 hr, Ss were returned to the shuttlebox in which they had been conditioned and received 40 trials of avoidance training using a 5-sec CS–US interval in a delayed-conditioning paradigm. Shock intensity during avoidance training was 0.3 mA for all groups, but during Pavlovian conditioning shock intensity was 0.3 for half the Ss in each group and 0.6 mA for the other half. (The effects of this variable will be discussed in the next section.)

Ss receiving both 10 and 25 conditioning trials showed U-shaped retention functions in terms of various indices of rate of avoidance learning. However, the minimum of the function after 10 conditioning trials was at 4 hr, whereas the minimum after 25 trials was at 1 hr. The data showing this effect in terms of median total number of avoidance responses are shown in Figure 9.

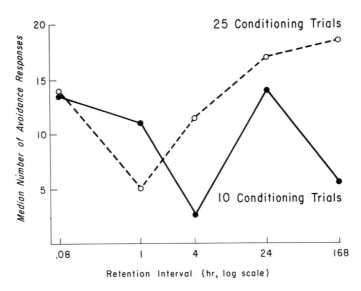

Fig. 9.   Median number of avoidance responses as a function of time after 10 and after 25 fear conditioning trials. (From Brush, 1963.)

This effect of number of original conditioning trials was confirmed in a more recent study in our laboratory (Brush, 1968, unpublished) which used either 5 or 25 trials of signaled escape training instead of Pavlovian conditioning. Retention was measured by performance during avoidance training, which was administered after intervals of .08, 1, 2, 4, 24, or 168 hr. Again, retention following both 5 and 25 trials of signaled escape training was a U-shaped function of the interval, but following 5 trials poorest avoidance performance occurred at 4 hr, whereas after 25 trials the 1-hr group showed the lowest frequency of avoiding shock.

C.   An Empirical Generalization Which Extends the Fear Conditioning Hypothesis

In experiments which hold degree of learning constant, the interval producing the poorest retention is *directly* related to number of original training trials (inversely to rate of original learning). That is, the U-shaped retention functions of animals that learn rapidly and who receive relatively few shocks reach their minima sooner than do the similarly shaped functions of animals that learn slowly and who receive relatively many shocks. On the other hand, in experiments which hold rate of original learning constant, the interval associated with poorest retention is *inversely* related to the number of original conditioning or training trials. Thus, it is not the number of trials or shocks, *per se,* that controls the interval at the minimum of the function. Rather, it appears that the interval of poorest retention is an inverse function both of *rate of learning* and of *extent of training or conditioning* when the opposite variable is held constant. This empirical generalization can be tied to the fear conditioning hypothesis by noting that in those experiments in which rate or degree of instrumental learning is manipulated, rate or degree of fear conditioning is probably varied also. It seems reasonable, therefore, to assert that it is the fear conditioning rather than the instrumental learning which controls the locus of the minimum of the U-shaped retention function.

This assertion, furthermore, has the merit of possibly explaining how rate and degree of conditioning come to exert the same effect on the U-shaped retention function. We know from experiments which used 10 or 25 trials of fear conditioning (Brush, 1963) that degree of conditioning *per se* inversely affects the locus of minimum retention. However, in the experiments of Brush *et al.* (1963) and Kamin (1963) rate of avoidance learning was altered or allowed to vary while the degree of instrumental learning was held constant. Degree of conditioning was free to vary within limits imposed by the training conditions and rate of conditioning.

In the Brush *et al.* (1963) experiment, the issue reduces to how much a given change of intertrial interval changes rate of Pavlovian conditioning relative to rate of instrumental learning. If the effect of intertrial interval is greater on conditioning than on learning, then an animal trained with fewer trials at a long intertrial interval could be better conditioned than one trained to the same criterion of instrumental learning with a greater number of trials at a short intertrial interval. Similarly, an animal in Kamin's (1963) experiment that learns to avoid relatively rapidly may also condition relatively rapidly and be more thoroughly conditioned than his slow learning (and slow conditioning) counterpart.

This extension of the fear conditioning hypothesis, then, states that fear conditioning is necessary and sufficient to produce the U-shaped retention function and that the magnitude of the interval at the minimum of the function is *inversely* related to degree of conditioning. We have seen confirmation of the latter portion of the hypothesis in the context of experimental manipulation and in a *post hoc* analysis of individual differences. Inasmuch as the hypothesis does not limit how this parameter may be varied, it can be tested in retention experiments that manipulate shock intensity and CS–US interval during a fixed number of original conditioning trials. Since both variables affect rate of conditioning, degree of conditioning will vary if all groups receive the same number of conditioning trials.

D. Tests of the Extension of the Fear Conditioning Hypothesis

1. Shock Intensity during Pavlovian Conditioning

It was noted in the preceding section that shock intensity (0.3 or 0.6 mA) during original conditioning was manipulated as part of the factorially designed experiment of Brush (1963). When the effect of number of Pavlovian conditioning trials was ignored, this variable altered the location of the minimum of the U-shaped retention function independently of the number of trials of Pavlovian conditioning. Figure 10 illustrates the effect in terms of the median total number of avoidance responses made during the 40 trials of avoidance training (shock intensity was 0.3 mA for all groups) that followed Pavlovian conditioning at the indicated shock intensity. An analysis of variance showed that shock intensity *per se* did not exert a significant effect on retention, *i.e.*, did not change the

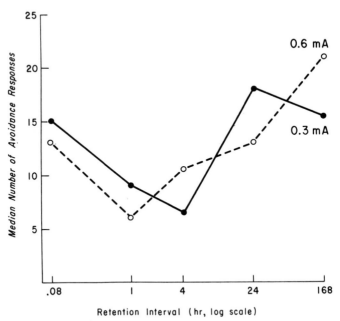

Fig. 10. Median number of avoidance responses as a function of time after fear conditioning using either 0.3- or 0.6-mA shock. (From Brush, 1963.)

overall level of the retention function. However, the minima are clearly different, being at 1 hr for the 0.6-mA group and at 4 hr for the 0.3-mA group. If one assumes that degree of original conditioning after n trials is directly related to shock intensity, perhaps because of an effect of shock intensity on *rate* of conditioning, then these results are consistent with the inverse relation between the interval of minimum retention and degree of conditioning. However, a note of caution is in order because in addition to the shock intensity being higher during conditioning in the 0.6- than in the 0.3-mA group, the 0.6-mA group also experienced a *change* of shock intensity when shifted from conditioning to avoidance training, whereas shock intensity was held constant in the 0.3-mA group. Inasmuch as avoidance learning in a two-way shuttlebox is exceptionally poor when shock intensity is as high as 0.6 mA, it is virtually impossible to unconfound the effects of intensity and change of intensity in this experimental paradigm. Nonetheless, it seems safe to conclude, at least tentatively, that the minimum of the U-shaped retention function is inversely related to degree of original conditioning, regardless of how manipulation of that parameter is accomplished.

2. Shock Intensity during Instrumental Training

Experiments which manipulate shock intensity during an original instrumental training session and test for retention at a later time have not yet been reported. However, effects similar to those reported for Pavlovian conditioning would be expected in instrumental situations so long as shock intensity and rate of instrumental learning were directly related, *e.g.*, in passive and in one-way active avoidance training. On the other hand, in two-way shuttlebox avoidance training, where learning rate and shock intensity are inversely related, the opposite effect of this variable on the interval of minimum retention might be expected, were it not possible that increasing shock intensity could facilitate fear conditioning and interfere with instrumental avoidance learning to nearly the same extent. Thus, the interval of minimum retention of shuttlebox avoidance learning might not be affected by shock intensity because these effects, being opposites, would tend to cancel each other. Obviously, this is a question that is answerable only by additional research which uses paradigms that unconfound retention of conditioning and retention of learning, but the hypothesis makes a clear prediction about the effects on the interval of minimum retention if the relation between a given variable and degree of original conditioning is specifiable and effects of the variable on instrumental learning can be controlled.

3. CS–US Interval during Pavlovian Conditioning

It is generally accepted that Pavlovian conditioning proceeds faster when the CS–US interval is short than when it is long. Thus, the hypothesis that the interval of minimum retention is inversely related to degree of original conditioning predicts that the retention function following a fixed number of conditioning trials with a short CS–US interval will reach its minimum sooner than the comparable function following conditioning for an equal number of trials with a long CS–US interval. Although addressed to another problem, another experiment in the report by Brush (1963) tests this prediction. Twenty-five trials of Pavlovian conditioning were given to male hooded rats confined to one side of a shuttlebox. The CS was a 78-dB white noise and a moderate increase in illumination, the US was a 0.3-mA ac shock of 1-sec duration, and the CS–US interval was either 0.5 or 5.0 sec; CS and US terminated simultaneously.

Retention was measured by performance during subsequent avoidance training in which the same CS and US were used except that the US was terminated by the shuttle response; the CS–US interval was 5.0 sec, and the intertrial interval was 1 min. Forty trials of avoidance training were given after retention intervals of .08, 1, 4, 24, and 168 hr.

In general, the retention functions after conditioning with a 5.0-sec CS–US interval were shallower than those that followed conditioning with the 0.5-sec CS–US interval; for most measures the effect of retention interval was not statistically significant after conditioning with the longer interval although all of the measures suggested that the retention function was U-shaped. Measures derived from early stages of avoidance learning showed poorest performance uniformly at 4 hr for groups conditioned with either CS–US interval. However, retention measured in terms of total frequency of avoidance responding showed functions which suggested that the minimum following conditioning with a 0.5-sec CS–US interval was at 4 hr, in agreement with the functions derived from early stages of training, whereas the minimum after conditioning with a 5.0-sec CS–US interval appeared to be at 1 hr. However, the difference between the 1- and 4-hr points in the 5.0-sec function was not great (certainly far short of statistical significance), so it is probably safe to conclude that in this instance manipulation of CS–US interval did not affect the interval of minimum retention.

4. Summary

Either the 10-fold difference in CS–US interval was not sufficient to shift the locus of the function or the hypothesis is incorrect, at least with respect to varying degree of conditioning by manipulating CS–US interval. At the risk of appearing unwilling to surrender a hypothesis in the face of an empirical test, we favor the former alternative since Kamin (1965) reported only very slight effects on CER suppression when CS–US interval was varied over a much wider range than was used in the present experiment. Probably, trace- rather than delayed-conditioning procedures should be used in experiments of this sort because the effects of CS–US interval are greater with the former than with the latter.

In summary, then, the data support the hypothesis that the interval of minimum retention is inversely related to degree of conditioning. Two experiments have tested the hypothesis, one confirming it, the other neither confirming nor disconfirming it so that additional quantitative research will be required to adequately assess its validity.

IV. THE PROBLEM OF STIMULUS GENERALIZATION

We have already seen in an experiment by Bintz (1970) that if retention of active avoidance responding to each of two stimuli is tested by continuing the active avoidance training to one stimulus and initiating passive avoidance training to the other, then *both* stimuli show an inversion of the usual U-shaped retention function. The change of stimulus conditions created by the initiation of passive avoidance training is responsible for the inversion, because if retention is tested by continuing the active avoidance training to each stimulus, then the usual U-shaped retention function is obtained for each stimulus. Two other experiments that also introduced stimulus changes between training ana test sessions were concerned with the retention of conditioned fear.

In the first, Tarpy (1966) studied retention of conditioned aversiveness in a conditioned suppression (CER) paradigm by measuring the effect of superimposing the CS used in active two-way shuttlebox avoidance training on a base line rate of lever pressing for food reward. He first deprived male albino rats of food until they stabilized at 80% of normal body weight. He then trained them to press a lever in a Skinner box on a 0.5-min variable interval (VI) schedule of food reward. After 6 days of training, Ss received two-way shuttlebox avoidance training using a 5.0-sec CS–US interval and a 1-min intertrial interval; the CS was a buzzer and the US was a 0.5-mA electric shock. Ss were trained for a maximum of 30 trials or to a criterion of three avoidance responses, not necessarily consecutive. After retention intervals of 0, 1, 4, 24, and 168 hr, they were returned to the Skinner box for 30 min of bar pressing reinforced on the 0.5-min VI schedule. During the first 10 min no CS was presented, but for the remainder of the test the buzzer was presented for 5 sec during each minute. Response suppression was measured in terms of rate of lever pressing during the second and third 10-min portions of the test session relative to response rate during the first 10 min when the CS was not present at all.

During the second 10-min period (CS present) suppression increased as retention interval increased from 0 to 4 hr and then decreased slightly, but not significantly, from 4 to 168 hr; this suggests that retention of conditioned fear increased monotonically with time. However, since the aversiveness of the CS was established in another situation and the acoustical properties of two chambers are rarely, if ever the same, one must assume that stimulus generalization is also involved in mediating this monotonic increasing function. No significant effect of retention interval was found in the third 10-min period.

McMichael (1966) used the same basic paradigm that Tarpy (1966) employed and compared the aversiveness of a Pavlovian CS to that of a CS for instrumental avoidance learning. In this experiment male albino rats were first trained to press a lever for food reward on a 6.5 variable ratio (VR) schedule. Half the Ss were then given two-way shuttlebox avoidance training using a 5-sec CS–US interval and a 1-min intertrial interval. The CS was a 73-dB white noise and the US was electric shock (170-V ac through 150kΩ resistance). Avoidance training continued to a criterion of three consecutive avoidance responses. The other Ss received 10 trials of Pavlovian conditioning of fear in which the CS–US interval was 5 sec and the US duration 1 sec; CS and US were coterminous. Two additional groups served as controls: one received pseudoconditioning in which a 1-sec US preceded the 6-sec CS by an interval of 1 sec; the other received 10 CS presentations without shock.

Following retention intervals of .03, .5, 1, 4, 6, 24, or 504 hr, Ss were returned to the Skinner box and, after the first 10 lever presses, responses during three successive 3-min periods were counted. The CS was presented during the second period, and suppression of response rate during the CS was measured relative to the average rate in the absence of the CS (periods 1 and 3 combined). Following Pavlovian conditioning, suppression increased from .03 to 6 hr, leveled off, and then declined slightly from 48 to 504 hr. A comparable function was observed following avoidance training, and even though the decrement at the longer retention intervals was greater than that following conditioning, in neither case was it statistically reliable. The two control groups were tested only at 4 hr, where the experimental groups showed maximal suppression, and neither showed detectable amounts of suppression. Since CS duration changed rather drastically between conditioning and test, stimulus generalization is very likely to be a determinant of these findings as well as Tarpy's.

In two experiments, then, a conditioned aversive stimulus was established either by shuttlebox avoidance training or by Pavlovian conditioning, and retention of its aversiveness was assessed in another situation by measuring the suppression of an operant response rate that resulted from superimposing the CS on the base line response. In all three instances, retention increased significantly as a function of time and all three cases showed nonsignificant reversals at the longer retention interval. This suggests that retention in these situations may, in fact, be an inverted U-shaped function of time, even though that relation was not seen as a statistically reliable effect. Failure to detect such a functional relationship could have occurred for a number of reasons, e.g., insufficient sample size for such highly variable data, insensitivity of the specific testing procedures, or shifts in the base line response rate. (See Chapter 2 by McAllister and McAllister, Section II,B for other data and comments relevant to these problems.)

In any event, three independent functions have shown a trend in this direction so we may not be too far wrong to regard the function as inverted U-shaped in form. If it is, then it is consistent with the data from the acquired-drive or escape-from-fear paradigms which are summarized in Figure 2 of Chapter 2 of this volume which shows the retention function of conditioned fear for animals conditioned in one situation and given hurdle-jumping tests in another. It should be noted that McAllister and McAllister (1968) have shown that the retention loss at long intervals is associated with the conditioned aversiveness of apparatus stimuli, not of the CS, and that the apparent increase in retention over shorter intervals cannot be attributed to changes of fear *per se*. Rather, the increase is most likely the result of an increase over time of the perceived similarity between the conditioning and test situations, the relevant stimuli being apparatus cues, extra-apparatus stimuli, or possibly even the CS. These inferences are based solely on research using the escape-from-fear paradigm, and their applicability to the experiments of Tarpy (1966) and McMichael (1966) has not been assessed. Nonetheless, the obvious similarity between the two paradigms warrants the tentative conclusion that these mechanisms may be at work in the latter experiments. Certainly, their results are similar to those summarized by McAllister and McAllister (Chapter 2, this volume).

It may also be reasonable to conclude, at least tentatively, that the same mechanisms are at work in the experiments reviewed in Section

II,C,4 which shows comparably shaped functions (albeit with varying time courses) for retention of the passive avoidance learning established by one trial. Those situations might well be particularly sensitive to temporal changes in stimulus detection inasmuch as the discrimination which results from that training can, at best, be poorly established since the animal receives only one exposure to the complex external and response-produced stimulus situation that must become associated with the punishing shock. Similarly, these processes may also be involved in the inversion of the U-shaped function that Bintz (1970) reported when active avoidance training to each of two stimuli is shifted in retention tests to active training to one stimulus and passive training to the other.

In spite of these considerations, however, the McAllister and McAllister analysis suggests that changes of conditioned fear are not involved in mediating the U-shaped retention functions that are generated by the training-interval-retraining paradigms since they do not involve stimulus changes between training and test. The McAllisters have found no evidence of change of conditioned fear in a situation that unconfounds retention of conditioned fear and retention of the index response. Thus, the U-shaped retention function, although it requires fear conditioning as an antecedent condition and is sensitive to the degree of fear conditioning, does not appear to involve contemporaneous changes of conditioned fear. Rather, it seems necessary to postulate that fear conditioning initiates a series of internal events, as yet unspecified, that change over time and that functionally alter the probability that previously established Pavlovian CRs will be elicited by the stimuli employed in the prior conditioning situation. It is clear that these internal events could alter performance either by directly blocking or facilitating retrieval of information from permanent memory or by modifying the internal motivational cues or states that mediate instrumental avoidance responding or suppression of other ongoing behavior. In the concluding sections of this chapter we will examine some of the properties of these internal events and explore some recent efforts that have been made to identify them.

V. NONASSOCIATIVE MANIPULATIONS OF THE U-SHAPED RETENTION FUNCTION

There are three experimental reports which indicate that the temporal sequence of the internal events that are postulated to mediate the U-shaped retention function can be abruptly altered. Two of them suggest that the sequence of events, once initiated by original conditioning, can recur if started again by a brief series of free shocks, regardless of when the shocks are given. The third study suggests that the temporal pattern of events can be suspended at any point in the sequence at which an electroconvulsive shock (ECS) is administered. We view these experiments as demonstrating opposite but closely related kinds of manipulations, because they suggest that the U-shaped retention function is mediated by events that are subject to experimental interventions which are not principally associative in nature, even though fear conditioning, clearly an associative process, is required to initiate them.

A. Recurrence of the Function

Denny (1958), as we have already seen, replicated the basic U-shaped retention function using intervals of 0, 1, or 24 hr and the original Kamin paradigm, *i.e.,* 25 trials of avoidance training—retention interval —25 trials of avoidance retraining. He also trained an additional experimental group of Ss on the avoidance task, and gave them a series of shocks which were not contingent on time or a particular response by S. The free shocks were given in a different apparatus 23 hr after original avoidance training, and retention was tested in a retraining session 1 hr later, *i.e.,* 24 hr after original training. Retention was quite poor whereas control Ss, not given the free shocks, showed good retention 24 hr after training. These Ss, then, behaved as if the free shocks had reset the retention function and when tested 1 hr later, retention was that of a normal 1-hr group.

Klein (1970) reported a similar experiment in which free shocks were given 145 min after original one-way avoidance training. Just 5 min later (2.5 hr after training) the retention test was given, which in this experiment consisted either of continued active avoidance training or acquisition of a passive avoidance response (Klein & Spear, 1970). In both cases, these Ss showed no retention loss and behaved just like the 10-min or 24-hr control Ss, whereas the untreated 2.5-hr control group showed the usual poor retention that characterizes tests at intermediate intervals after original avoidance training. Additional groups of Ss were given free shocks 5 min before retention tests which occurred 10 min or 24 hr after original training, and they showed clearly that at these retention intervals free shock did not affect performance relative to that of unshocked controls. Since the 10-min and 24-hr groups were not at the limit of performance, the facilitating effect of free shock given 5 min before a retention test could have occurred at any interval, but did so only at the intermediate retention intervals.

In Klein's experiment, then, Ss tested 2.5 hr after training and 5 min after free shock, behaved like 5- or 10-min Ss, whereas Denny's Ss tested 24 hr after training and 1 hr after free shock, behaved like 1-hr Ss. Making use of the fear conditioned to apparatus cues, Denny (1958) showed that if Ss remain in the experimental apparatus for a 1-hr retention period they behave like 5-min Ss, *i.e.,* they show good retention rather than the usual poor retention of 1-hr Ss that spent the interval in their home cages.[6] It can be argued that spending the 1-hr interval in the presence of aversively conditioned apparatus cues maintains the internal state associated with avoidance training so that these Ss behave just like Klein's Ss that have that state reinstated by the free shock immediately before testing. Similarly, a series of free shocks given 24 hr after training apparently can set off the temporal sequence of events that the original avoidance training initiates, because 1 hr later, poor retention rather than the good retention of 24-hr Ss prevails.

These experiments on recurrence of the U-shaped retention function favor a motivational rather than a purely memorial explanation because it is difficult to imagine a memory that is first present, then lost, and finally regained, that can be lost a second time if a few shocks are given after it is regained, and that can be rapidly restored if a similar series of free shocks is given at the time it is normally completely lost.

The most adequate analysis seems to be one which combines a kind of memory mechanism with motivational processes. We would suggest that Overton's (1964) notion of state-dependent learning is applicable here and that original conditioning establishes the presence of internal events which constitute a significant fraction of the set of motivational (emotional) cues that normally initiate instrumental avoidance responses. When returned to a nonaversive environment for the retention interval, the internal events subside and may even become relatively refractory so that the motivational cues necessary for performance of the avoidance response are absent or reestablished with some difficulty, with the result that avoidance performance is poor at intermediate retention intervals. Maintenance of the aversive environment or reinstatement of the motivational cues by a series of free shocks just prior to the test provides the necessary conditions for good avoidance behavior and the semblance of good retention of prior learning.

The data, however, require that this model also incorporate some mechanism whereby the requisite motivational cues return spontaneously after 16 to 24 hr or at least be more easily and quickly reinstated when

---

[6]This effect was also seen following 25 trials of fear conditioning (Brush and Levine, 1966).

retention testing is resumed. Furthermore, the recurrence data require that the dissipation of the internal events that follows original conditioning and mediates the retention loss at intermediate intervals be repeated if a series of free shocks are given after a 23- or 24-hr interval. One repetition of this process is plausible, but surely adaptation mechanisms would preclude an indefinitely long series of unchanging repetitions.

B.   Suspension of the Function

An experiment which suggests that the time course of the U-shaped retention function can be either temporarily or permanently suspended was recently reported by Suboski and Weinstein (1969). In their experiment, male albino rats were given 30 trials of avoidance training in a two-way shuttlebox in which the CS was a 5-Hz click, the US was intermittent ac shock of 0.8 mA, which was on for 0.5 sec and off for 4.0 sec. The CS–US interval was 10 sec, and the intertrial interval was 1 min. After intervals of 1 min, 1 or 16 hr, 20 trials of retraining of the avoidance response were given in order to measure retention of prior learning. A U-shaped function was obtained. Additional Ss were given a seizure induced by one electroconvulsive shock (ECS) treatment (50 mA at 1200 V for 0.5 sec through ear clips), either 1 min or 1 or 16 hr after original training, i.e., at the times the other groups of animals had been tested for retention. The ECS animals were tested for retention 24 , 23, or 8 hr later, i.e., 24 hr after original training. Although the group given ECS 1 min after training avoided significantly less often when tested 24 hr later than the comparable 1-min retention group, all other ECS groups were identical in performance to their non-ECS controls that were given retention tests without an intervening ECS treatment. Thus, the ECS seems, in this experiment, to prevent the temporal sequence of events from running their normal course and to hold those events fixed, for at least 23 to 24 hr, in whatever state they were in at the time ECS was given. There is also a suggestion in the data that the ECS, when given as soon as 1 min after original training, may in fact cause a partial retrograde amnesia for the prior learning.

Inasmuch as the modes of action of ECS with respect to memory are not understood, the finding that a single ECS treatment can apparently suspend the temporal sequence of events mediating the U-shaped retention function does little to aid our identification or understanding of those mediating events. Nevertheless, the Suboski and Weinstein experiment, together with those of Denny (1958) and of Klein (1970) suggest strongly that nonassociative interventions, in addition to associative variables of the conditioning situation, can be employed to manipulate the retention function experimentally. We are far from a clear understanding of how these nonassociative manipulations produce recurrence and suspension of the function, but the fact that they do is encouraging to investigators of a phenomenon which has successfully resisted analysis for a number of years.

VI.   THE SEARCH FOR THE EVENTS THAT MEDIATE THE U-SHAPED RETENTION FUNCTION

Our review of research on the U-shaped retention function has found that:

(1)   Pavlovian conditioning of fear is necessary and sufficient to produce the U-shaped retention function.

(2)   The interval of minimum retention is an inverse function of degree of conditioning.

(3)   Conditioned fear does not change with time, and, therefore, does not directly mediate the U-shaped retention function.

(4)   If stimulus generalization, especially of apparatus cues, is involved, then perceptual mechanisms produce what appears to be an inversion of the function.

(5)   Fear conditioning initiates a temporal sequence of internal events that mediate the behavioral U-shaped function, and that sequence can be made to recur at least once or to be suspended at least temporarily.

Relatively little research has been done to identify these mediating events, but temporally controlled changes in the activity of the pituitary-adrenal axis have been proposed as likely candidates for a number of reasons. The mediators of the U-shaped function must change relatively slowly with time, which tends to eliminate purely neural processes that typically proceed at high speed. Furthermore, the pituitary-adrenal system, which does respond relatively slowly and typically recovers homeostasis even more slowly, is activated by painful stimuli such as those used in aversive conditioning. Other hormonal systems (*e.g.,* gonadal) are accepted as having profound effects on reproductive behaviors, and recent research indicates that the pituitary-adrenal system may exert comparable control over aversively motivated behavior.

Thus, the pituitary-adrenal system has the fundamental properties that would be required if it were to mediate the U-shaped retention function. It now remains for us to review briefly the basic neuroendocrinology of this hormonal system, to examine the behavioral effects of the pituitary-

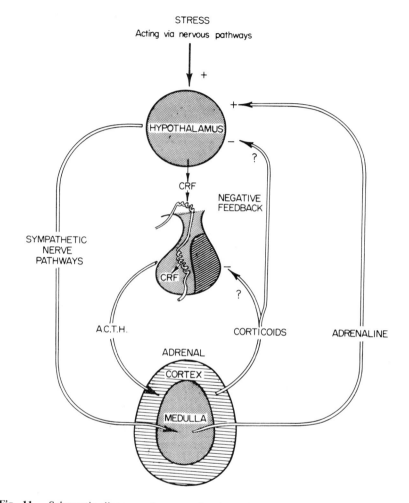

Fig. 11. Schematic diagram of neuroendocrinological integration of pituitary-adrenal system. (From Clegg & Clegg, 1969.)

adrenal hormones, and to determine whether the temporal fluctuations of hormonal secretion that occur following fear conditioning are appropriate and sufficient to mediate the U-shaped retention function.

A. Neural and Hormonal Integration of the Pituitary-Adrenal System

The basic interrelationships among the various components of this system are schematically illustrated in Figure 11. Primary aversive stimuli (those that elicit pain), as well as conditioned aversive stimuli that in S's past have been associated with pain, provide afferent input to the hypothalamus that can cause neurosecretory cells to release cortrophin releasing factor (CRF) in the region of the median eminence. The CRF is carried via the hypothalamic-hypophyseal portal veins to the anterior pituitary where it causes the adenohypophysis to release adrenocorticotrophic hormone (ACTH) into the general circulation. The blood-borne ACTH, in turn, causes the adrenal cortical cells to release glucocorticoids into the blood stream—corticosterone in the rat and hydrocortisone in man and monkey. Negative feedback loops have been postulated which would permit high concentrations of circulating glucocorticoids to suppress ACTH either by direct action on the pituitary or by indirect action via the hypothalamus and CRF, or both. However, as suggested by the question marks in the figure, the existence of these negative feedback loops is a subject of controversy. Smelik (1963a,b), for example, presented evidence that these negative feedback loops may operate only if supraphysiological concentrations of corticosterone are achieved by exogenous administration. At physiological concentrations, regulation of corticosterone may be achieved in part by the rate at which it is cleared from the blood, which in turn may be a direct function of its circulating concentration. See Smith (1965) for a critical evaluation of the issues in this controversy.

Also illustrated in Figure 11 is a pathway that has received relatively little attention but which may be of some importance here. Noxious afferent input can also activate sympathetic neural pathways and, when the chromaffine tissue of the adrenal medulla is stimulated, epinephrine is released into the general circulation. By some unspecified mechanism epinephrine causes a number of trophic hormones, including ACTH, to be released by the pituitary. Adrenal *medullary* activity, therefore, can indirectly stimulate adrenal *cortical* secretion.

This brief outline grossly oversimplifies the neural and hormonal integrations of an exceedingly complex system. However, the relatively slow response of the system to noxious stimuli is not surprising in view of the number of events that intervene between the application of the eliciting stimulus and the final adrenocortical response. In most cases, detectable changes in plasma concentration of corticosterone in the rat do not occur until 2 to 4 min after the application of an initial noxious stimulus and homeostasis after a maximal acute response may not be achieved for several hours.

The various metabolic effects of ACTH and the glucocorticoids need not concern us here since our interest is in behavioral changes that occur in normal animals that apparently are not debilitated in any way by the phasic changes induced by behaviorally relevant noxious events like aversive conditioning or avoidance training. However, when gross interventions such as adrenalectomy or hypophysectomy are involved, then the resultant metabolic derangements can have significant behavioral effects and need to be taken into account.

Before leaving this brief account of the control of the pituitary-adrenal system we should note some interactions in it that may have important implications for our analysis of the processes mediating the U-shaped retention function. Knigge, Penrod and Schindler (1959) reported evidence which suggests that for some time after the stress of immobilization or scalding the pituitary-adrenal system is temporarily unable to respond. The adrenal cortex is not depleted, because exogenous ACTH induces a normal response at that time. Rather, the relative refractoriness of the system appears to reside in the pituitary itself or in neural, presumably hypothalamic mechanisms associated with release of CRF into the portal veins.

In a related experiment, Kitay, Holub, and Jailer (1959) found that a single injection of .2 or .4 mg of epinephrine in rats produced significant ACTH release as measured by the 2-hr adrenal response (adrenal ascorbic acid concentration, which is depleted by the secretion of glucocorticoids, was reduced 2 hr after the epinephrine injection). That finding demonstrates experimentally the sympathetic-adrenal-medullary route of stimulating ACTH release. More importantly, however, these investigators noted that 24 hr after a single epinephrine injection, the ACTH release that is acutely induced by etherization was reduced significantly below the level of controls, even though adrenal ascorbic acid concentrations were normal at that time. The adrenal apparently was capable of responding normally to ACTH, and some ACTH was released by the pituitary, but the amount was less than normal. This effect was even more pronounced if epinephrine were injected daily for several days. Even though the magnitude of the pituitary response to this *chronic* epinephrine treatment was maintained, the *acute* response to etherization given at a later time was reduced despite significant recovery of pituitary stores of ACTH. As a result of these findings, the inhibition noted by Knigge *et al.* (1959) apparently resides in the hypothalamic release of CRF or in other neural events that precede CRF release.

These experiments show that a temporary inhibition of the pituitary response to acute stress can follow activation of the system by epinephrine, which may be important for two reasons. First, it might be an alternative regulatory mechanism to the postulated negative feedback control of ACTH by blood concentrations of glucocorticoids. A temporary inhibition of *acute* ACTH release following stimulation by epinephrine which leaves intact the pituitary's response to chronic, sustained stress, might be an important phasic regulatory mechanism that is quite separate structurally as well as functionally from the disputed negative feedback loop which may be involved in *tonic* control mechanisms.

Second, the period of pituitary inhibition following epinephrine injection is longer lasting than that following corticosterone injection (Yates, Leeman, Glenister, & Dallman, 1961), and it can be induced by concentrations of epinephrine that are more likely to be near physiological levels than is the case with corticosterone (Smelik, 1966a,b). It seems reasonable to suppose, therefore, that Pavlovian conditioning of fear could cause an endogenous release of epinephrine by the adrenal medulla as a result of sympathetic neural activity and that a period of inhibition of ACTH (and corticosteroid) release could follow the initial pituitary response when the noxious conditioned and unconditioned stimuli are removed. If either ACTH, or the glucocorticoids released by ACTH, or both, can be shown to have direct effects on aversively motivated behavior, then a good case will have been made for the possibility that temporal patterns of activity in the pituitary-adrenal system are the mediators of the U-shaped retention function. Confirmation of this, of course, would also depend on empirically demonstrating the requisite sequence of epinephrine-induced activation and inhibition of the pituitary-adrenal system following fear conditioning or other training procedures that include aversive conditioning.

B.   Behavioral Effects of Pituitary-Adrenal Hormones

The relatively small body of research on this topic has recently been reviewed by Levine (1968), and the reader is referred to that excellent treatment. Here, we will simply summarize those findings and add to Levine's coverage the few studies that have been reported since his review was completed. The effects on aversively motivated behavior of each of the relevant hormones will be taken up in turn.

1.   CRF

No behavioral effects of any kind have been reported for this hormone. It seems unlikely that CRF would have nonpituitary effects on the central nervous system, especially of a behaviorally relevant sort, but the possibility should not be overlooked.

2.   ACTH

Work by de Wied (1964) showed that adenohypophysectomized rats learned an active avoidance response more slowly than controls, the effect probably being attributable to sensory and motor debilitation. The effects could be counteracted by ACTH injection, but treatment with thyroxine, cortisone, and testosterone showed similar beneficial effects. In de Wied's hands ACTH did not facilitate avoidance learning in intact controls. However, an unpublished dissertation by Beatty (1969) showed clearly that exogenous ACTH administered to normal rats could facilitate avoidance learning when high (1.5 mA) but not low (0.5 mA) shock intensity was used. Adrenalectomy which reduced plasma concentration of glucocorticoids and presumably elevated endogenous ACTH concentration in the blood also facilitated avoidance learning at high shock intensity. Exogenous dexamethasone, a synthetic steroid with powerful ACTH suppressant effects, did not affect learning which suggests that the facilitation of avoidance learning by ACTH is not mediated by the adrenal but is a direct behavioral effect.

ACTH has been shown in a number of studies to inhibit extinction of an avoidance response. Miller and Ogawa (1962) showed the effect in adrenalectomized rats and de Wied (1967) found that the increased resistance to extinction of an avoidance response seen in adrenalectomized animals was reduced to normal by hypophysectomy. de Wied (1966) also showed that dexamethasone facilitated extinction. However, this effect can also be seen in hypophysectomized animals so the action of dexamethasone in facilitating extinction could be direct, could be mediated by its effect on ACTH, or both. Comparable effects on the maintenance of passive avoidance behavior have also been reported by Levine and Jones (1965) in intact animals and by Anderson, Winn, and Tam (1968) in hypophysectomized rats.

3. Glucocorticoids

We have already noted that dexamethasone facilitates extinction of avoidance learning in hypophysectomized rats (de Wied, 1966). Another effect on aversively motivated behavior that is clearly attributable to glucocorticoid action was reported by Wertheim, Conner, and Levine (1967). In that experiment rats were trained on a Sidman schedule and both ACTH and dexamethasone produced a decrease in response rate which resulted in increased efficiency of avoiding shock. These hormones also had the effect of reducing the duration of the warm-up that typically occurs at the beginning of each training session. In unpublished work, Levine (1968) found ACTH and dexamethasone facilitated the timing behavior required by a DRL (differential reinforcement of low response rates) schedule which is generally assumed to be an aversive schedule of reinforcement. It should be noted, however, that in both timing experiments, performance is improved by a reduction of response rate. No effects of the glucocorticoids on discrete-trial avoidance learning have been reported either in intact or hypophysectomized animals.

4. Epinephrine

This hormone has not been found to have consistent behavioral effects. Some investigations (Moyer & Bunnell, 1958) found no effect on acquisition of an avoidance response; Sines (1959) reported a decrement in acquisition; Kosman and Gerard (1955) found a decrement in performance. On the other hand, Latane and Schachter (1962) found that a low dose facilitated avoidance learning which raised the possibility that the behavioral effects may be an inverted U-shaped function of epinephrine concentration. It may be worth noting in this connection that the doses of epinephrine used by Kitay et al. (1959) to produce delayed pituitary inhibition were between the two doses (0.0125 and 0.500 mg/100 gm) used by Stewart and Brookshire (1967). These investigators found these doses had no effect on avoidance learning in female rats but produced a dose related interference with learning in males. Kitay et al. used male rats also. Thus, the interference with learning found by Stewart and Brookshire could be related to the delayed pituitary inhibition described by Kitay et al.

5. Summary

Obviously, not much is known about the effects on behavior of the hormones of the pituitary-adrenal system. ACTH appears to facilitate avoidance learning under special circumstances and more generally to facilitate performance of previously learned active and passive avoidance responses.

The glucocorticoids appear to facilitate timing behavior and extinction of avoidance responding, and it is tempting to speculate that these effects are accomplished by a general suppression of responding. However, Kendall (1969) has found that dexamethasone induces dramatic increases in spontaneous running by rats in activity wheels.

Epinephrine seems to facilitate or inhibit avoidance learning depending, at least in part, on the dosage. In all of this research the need for careful determination of dose-response and dose-time-response functions is apparent.

C. Temporal Changes of Pituitary-Adrenal Activity following Fear Conditioning

A large number of studies could be cited to document the elevation of plasma corticosterone concentration in rats following a wide variety of stressors, but few have plotted the time course over which basal concentrations are recovered. Even fewer have examined the effects of various behaviorally relevant stressors, such as fear conditioning or avoidance training, either on the magnitude of the elevation of corticosteroid concentration or on the recovery function following that elevation. Because of the technical difficulties encountered in measuring ACTH by *in vivo* or *in vitro* assay, virtually nothing is known about the magnitude of the pituitary response following fear conditioning or avoidance training. The many complex interactions in the system preclude estimating the pituitary response from information about plasma glucocorticoid concentration. A similar wealth of ignorance exists regarding the phasic changes in epinephrine concentration after aversive conditioning.

Because the measurements are technically relatively simple, a little more is known about the temporal changes of plasma corticosterone concentration after aversive conditioning. For example, Brush and Levine (1966) plotted the recovery function for corticosterone following 25 trials of fear conditioning in which the CS–US interval was 0.5 sec, the shock duration 0.5 sec, and the shock intensity 0.3 mA. These data are presented in Figure 12. Steroid concentration is elevated 5 min after the end of the fear conditioning session and declines to basal concentrations within 1 hr. Other Ss were used to generate the U-shaped retention function following fear conditioning, and immediately after the retention test, which consisted of 40 trials of avoidance training with a 5-sec CS–US interval, plasma corticosterone concentrations were also determined. Total duration of shock received during the retention test varied greatly among the various groups because of the U-shaped retention function, and so the corticosterone concentrations after the avoidance training session were adjusted for variation in shock duration by an analysis of covariance. The upper function in Figure 12 shows a tendency for avoidance training to elicit a greater steroid response as time after fear conditioning increases. These data suggest that the sensitivity or responsiveness of the pituitary-adrenal system may increase with time after fear conditioning, but this conclusion is admittedly speculative.

Recovery functions comparable to the one shown in Figure 12 were also found following avoidance training to a criterion of three avoidance responses (Levine and Brush, 1967) and following either 5 to 25 trials of signalled escape training (Brush, 1968). In all cases basal levels were reached within 1 hr after training. Even though the number of trials of signalled escape training altered the interval of minimum retention, basal concentrations of plasma corticosterone were reached at the same time, a result that is consistent with the absence of any clear-cut effect of glucocorticoids on acquisition of an avoidance response. These data force

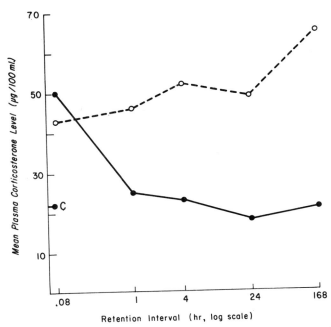

Fig. 12.   Mean plasma corticosterone concentration as a function of time after 25 trials of fear conditioning (solid line) and after completion of avoidance training (dashed line). See text for procedural details. (From Brush & Levine, 1966.)

the conclusion that either changes of ACTH secretion mediate the U-shaped retention function or the hormone hypothesis, as presently stated, is incorrect.

Inasmuch as there are no reports of direct measurements of plasma ACTH concentrations for the relevant time periods following aversive conditioning, the data which could provide a crucial test of the hypothesis are not available. However, there is indirect evidence to support the notion that extra-adrenal behavioral effects of ACTH can mediate the U-shaped function. Levine and Brush (1967) showed that if the post-training decline in plasma corticosterone concentration is prevented by administering ACTH immediately after completion of avoidance training, then the decline in avoidance relearning 1 hr later did not occur; glucocorticoid replacement did not prevent the 1-hr retention loss. Similar effects of ACTH were observed by Brush and Sakellaris (1968) who used an extinction test to measure retention of a well-learned avoidance response.

On the other side of the coin, a paper by Marquis and Suboski (1969) has been cited by Klein and Spear (1969) as showing the Kamin effect in adrenalectomized rats. However, Marquis and Suboski only examined two retention intervals, 15 min and 4 hr, so it is difficult to assert that the U-shaped function was obtained in that experiment. Their data do show that the effect of retention interval was not different in groups of rats that were adrenalectomized or adrenalectomized and treated with hydrocortisone injections and that those groups were not different from surgical controls. The authors suggested that ACTH may be involved. Certainly, the crucial data on this point have not been reported. We should note, however, that even in the adrenalectomized rat acute release of ACTH in response to noxious stimulation still occurs. It is also possible that the epinephrine-induced period of pituitary inhibition could survive adrenalectomy because extra-adrenal chromaffine tissue exists, and it may secrete a sufficient quantity of epinephrine to produce a nearly normal relative refractory period of pituitary secretion. It would be surprising, however, if the time course of the function were left undisturbed by adrenalectomy.

D. Summary

The picture that emerges from this welter of direct and indirect evidence is that if the pituitary-adrenal axis in anyway mediates the U-shaped retention function that follows fear conditioning then ACTH is most likely the predominant hormone involved. This hormone appears to facilitate performance of avoidance responses, and a mechanism is available whereby acute noxious stimulation may cause a phasic release of ACTH followed by a period of pituitary suppression. Thus, the poor retention at intermediate intervals may be related to a decreasing concentration of ACTH and to a period of pituitary inhibition. The recovery of retention at long intervals may be related to the decreasing refractoriness of the pituitary response to a second acute exposure to noxious stimulation, which the retention test certainly constitutes.

VII. CONCLUSION

We have now reviewed virtually all of the experimental work on retention of aversively motivated behavior. It is apparent that the U-shaped retention function is a reliable and reproducible effect that occurs under remarkably varied circumstances. The phenomenon was seen first in a savings paradigm where retention of original avoidance learning was measured, after the appropriate intervals, by performance during a continuation of that training. But the effect has also been seen using a variety of original training paradigms: fear conditioning, signaled escape training, and active and passive avoidance training; and a variety of testing procedures: initial or continued avoidance learning, extinction, learning the opposite response (active-passive and vice versa), and learning to avoid the previously safe stimulus. The function also appears not to be limited to any particular degree of learning or conditioning since it has been seen following as few as one training trial and as many as 100 or more. Rather, the time scale of the U-shaped retention function appears to be accelerated by more extensive conditioning since the interval of minimum retention has been shown to be inversely related to degree of original conditioning.

The crucial feature of original training seems to be Pavlovian conditioning of fear since the U-shaped function has never been seen following unsignalled shock, but has been obtained in virtually all experiments that include controlled or measured amounts of Pavlovian conditioning as part of original training. Apparent exceptions are those that use only one trial of passive avoidance training, the effects of which are largely unknown. These experiments are particularly difficult to evaluate, because there seems to be little evidence that significant amounts of conditioning or learning are produced in one trial, at least none is detectable immediately or shortly afterward. Controls are also lacking in most of the passive avoidance experiments so that effects of handling, electric shock, and exposure to apparatus cues cannot be eliminated.

Experiments that change stimuli, especially apparatus cues, between conditioning and retention report what appears to be the inverse of the U-shaped retention function. However, it appears likely that changes in detection of stimulus differences can account for these results and that stimulus generalization involves other processes that are unrelated to those that mediate the U-shaped retention function.

A nonassociative manipulation like a series of free foot shocks in another apparatus appears able to cause the sequence of events that mediate the function to recur, and a single ECS-induced seizure can apparently suspend that sequence of events. The ways in which these effects are achieved is unknown but both warrant replication and experimental analysis.

Finally, we have examined the current status of the hypothesis that temporal changes in pituitary-adrenal activity mediate the U-shaped retention function. This hormonal system seems to have the required properties for that mediation, and it appears that fear conditioning could result in an epinephrine-induced period of pituitary inhibition of ACTH release which may be associated with the poor retention at intermediate intervals. This hypothesis is admittedly speculative and very likely to be wrong. Crucial data are lacking and will be technically difficult to obtain, but the hypothesis is a testable one, and it represents our best guess at present.

ACKNOWLEDGMENT

Preparation of this chapter and the research conducted in my laboratory were supported by research grants MH-03337, MH-14350, and Research Scientist Development Award 5-K2-MH-38660 from the National Institute of Mental Health, United States Public Health Service.

REFERENCES

Adams, R.M., & Calhoun, W.H. Time-dependent memory storage: An alternative interpretation of some data. *Psychonomic Science,* 1969, **18**, 42–43.

Anderson, D.C., Johnson, L., Schwendiman, G., & Dunford, G. Retention of an imcompletely learned avoidance response: Some problems with replication. *Psychonomic Science,* 1966, **6**, 23–24.

Anderson, D.C., Winn, W., & Tam, T. Adrenocorticotropic hormone (ACTH) and acquisition of a passive avoidance response: A replication and extension. *Journal of Comparative and Physiological Psychology,* 1968, **66**, 497–499.

Azrin, N.H. Effects of punishment intensity during variable-interval reinforcement. *Journal of the Experimental Analysis of Behavior,* 1960, 3, 123–142.

Baum, M. Reversal learning of an avoidance response and the Kamin effect. *Journal of Comparative and Physiological Psychology,* 1968, **66**, 495–497.

Beatty, P.A. The effects of ACTH, adrenalectomy and dexamethasone on the acquisition of an avoidance response in rats. Unpublished Doctoral Dissertation, University of Wisconsin, 1969.

Bintz, J. Time-dependent memory deficits of aversively motivated behavior. *Learning and Motivation,* 1970, **1**, 382–390.

Bintz, J., Braud, W.G., & Brown, J.S. An analysis of the role of fear in the Kamin effect. *Learning and Motivation,* 1970, **1**, 170–176.

Boe, E.E., & Church, R.M. Permanent effects of punishment during extinction. *Journal of Comparative and Physiological Psychology,* 1967, **63**, 486–492.

Brady, J.V. The effect of electro-convulsive shock on a conditioned emotional response: The significance of the interval between the emotional conditioning and the electroconvulsive shock. *Journal of Comparative and Physiological Psychology,* 1952, **45**, 9–13.

Brogden, E.J., & Culler, E. A device for the motor conditioning of small animals. *Science,* 1936, **83**, 269–270.

Brush, F.R. Some variables influencing transfer from classical fear conditioning to instrumental avoidance training. Paper presented at the meeting of the Psychonomic Society, Bryn Mawr, Pennsylvania, August 1963.

Brush, F.R. Avoidance learning after fear conditioning and unsignalled shock. *Psychonomic Science,* 1964, **1,** 405–406.

Brush, F.R. Avoidance learning and plasma corticosterone concentration as a function of time after varying amounts of signalled escape training. 1968, unpublished.

Brush, F.R., & Levine, S. Adrenocortical activity and avoidance learning as a function of time after fear conditioning. *Physiology and Behavior,* 1966, **1,** 309–311.

Brush, F.R., Myer, J.S., & Palmer, M.E. Effects of kind of prior training and intersession interval upon subsequent avoidance learning. *Journal of Comparative and Physiological Psychology,* 1963, **56,** 539–545.

Brush, F.R., Myer, J.S., & Palmer, M.E. Joint effects of intertrial and intersession interval upon avoidance learning. *Psychological Reports,* 1964, **14,** 31–37.

Brush, F.R., & Sakellaris, P.C. Extinction as a function of time after avoidance training. Paper presented at the meeting of the Psychonomic Society, St. Louis, Missouri, October 1968.

Calhoun, W.H., & Murphy, R.J. Pre- and post-trial stimulation: Effects on retention. *Psychonomic Science,* 1966, **5,** 435–436.

Clark, R. Retention of a passive avoidance response in mice. *Psychonomic Science,* 1967, **7,** 29–30.

Clegg, P.C., & Clegg, A.G. *Hormones, cells and organisms.* Stanford, California: Stanford University Press, 1969.

Denny, M.R. The "Kamin-effect" in avoidance conditioning. Paper presented at the meeting of the American Psychological Association, Washington, D. C., September, 1958.

Denny, M.R., & Ditchman, R.E. The locus of maximal "Kamin effect" in rats. *Journal of Comparative and Physiological Psychology,* 1962, **55,** 1069–1070.

Denny, M.R., & Fisher, M.D. The interaction of intertrial interval and retention interval as to the locus of the "Kamin effect" in avoidance learning. Paper presented at the meeting of the Psychonomic Society, Washington University, August 1962.

Denny, M.R., & Thomas, J.O. Avoidance learning and relearning as a function of shuttlebox dimensions. *Science,* 1960, **132,** 620–621.

de Wied, D. Influence of anterior pituitary on avoidance learning and escape behavior. *American Journal of Physiology,* 1964, **207,** 255–259.

de Wied, D. Inhibitory effect of ACTH and related peptides on extinction of conditioned avoidance behavior in rats. *Proceeding of the Society for Experimental Biology and Medicine,* 1966, **122,** 28–32.

de Wied, D. Opposite effects of ACTH and glucocorticoids on extinction of conditioned avoidance behavior. In L. Martini, F. Faschini, and M. Motto (Eds.), *Hormonal steroids.* The Hague: Mouton, 1967.

Essman, W.B., & Alpern, H. Single trial conditioning: Methodology and results with mice. *Psychological Reports,* 1964, **14,** 731–740.

Gabriel, M. Effects of intersession delay and training level on avoidance extinction and intertrial behavior. *Journal of Comparative and Physiological Psychology,* 1968, **66,** 412–416.

Gagné, R.M. The retention of a conditioned operant response. *Journal of Experimental Psychology,* 1941, **29,** 296–305.

Gellhorn, E. *Autonomic Imbalance and the Hypothalamus.* Minneapolis, Minnesota: University of Minnesota Press, 1957.

Gleitman, H., & Jung, L. Retention in rats: The effect of proactive interference. *Science,* 1963, **142,** 1683–1684.

Greenberg, G., & Kenyon, G.Y. Anxiety in avoidance conditioning: The Kamin effect. Paper presented at the meeting of the Eastern Psychological Association, Atlantic City, April 1965.

Hilgard, E.R., & Marquis, D.G. Acquisition, extinction, and retention of conditioned lid responses to light in dogs. *Journal of Comparative Psychology,* 1935, **19,** 29–58.

Hoffman, H.S., Fleshler, M., & Jensen, P. Stimulus aspects of aversive controls: The retention of conditioned suppression. *Journal of the Experimental Analysis of Behavior,* 1963, **6,** 575–583.

Hunter, W.S. Conditioning and extinction in the rat. *British Journal of Psychology,* 1935, **6,** 135–148.

Irwin, S., & Banuazizi, A. Pentylenetetrazol enhances memory function. *Science,* 1966, **152,** 100–102.

Irwin, S., Banuazizi, A., Kalsner, S., & Curtis, A. One-trial learning in the mouse: I. Its characteristics and modification by experimental-seasonal variables. *Psychopharmacologia (Berl.), 1968,* **12,** 286–302.

Irwin, S., Kalsner, S., & Curtis, A. Direct demonstration of consolidation of one-trial learning. *Federation Proceedings,* 1964, **23,** 102. (Abstract)

Kamin, L.J. Retention of an incompletely learned avoidance response. *Journal of Comparative and Physiological Psychology,* 1957, **50,** 457–460.

Kamin, L.J. Retention of an incompletely learned avoidance response: Some further analyses. *Journal of Comparative and Physiological Psychology,* 1963, **56,** 713–718.

Kamin, L.J. Temporal and intensity characteristics of the conditioned stimulus. In W.F. Prokasy (Ed.), *Classical conditioning: A symposium.* New York: Appleton, 1965.

Kendall, J.W. Personal communication, 1969.

Kirby, R.H. Acquisition, extinction and retention of an avoidance response in rats as a function of age. *Journal of Comparative and Physiological Psychology,* 1963, **56,** 158–162.

Kitay, J.I., Holub, D.A., & Jailer, J.W. "Inhibition" of pituitary ACTH release after administration of reserpine or epinephrine. *Endocrinology,* 1959, **65,** 548–554.

Klein, S.B. Reinstatement of the memory of one-way active-avoidance learning after intermediate retention intervals. Paper presented at the meeting of the Eastern Psychological Association, Atlantic City, New Jersey, April 1970.

Klein, S.B., & Spear, N.E. Influence of age on short-term retention of active-avoidance learning in rats. *Journal of Comparative and Physiological Psychology,* 1969, **69,** 583–589.

Klein, S.B., & Spear, N.E. Forgetting by the rat after intermediate intervals ("Kamin Effect") as retrieval failure. *Journal of Comparative and Physiological Psychology,* 1970, **71,** 165–170.

Knigge, K.M., Penrod, C.H., & Schindler, W.J. *In vitro* and *in vivo* adrenal corticosteroid secretion following stress. *American Journal of Physiology,* 1959, **196,** 579–582.

Kosman, M.E., & Gerard, R.W. The effect of adrenaline on a conditioned avoidance response. *Journal of Comparative and Physiological Psychology,* 1955, **48,** 506–508.

Latane, B., & Schachter, S. Adrenalin and avoidance learning. *Journal of Comparative and Physiological Psychology,* 1962, **55,** 369–372.

Levine, S. Hormones and conditioning. In W.J. Arnold (Ed.), *Nebraska Symposium on Motivation.* Lincoln, Nebraska: University of Nebraska Press, 1968.

Levine, S., & Brush, F.R. Adrenocortical activity and avoidance learning as a function of time after avoidance training. *Physiology and Behavior,* 1967, **2**, 385–388.

Levine, S., & Jones, L.E. Adrenocorticotropic hormone (ACTH) and passive avoidance learning. *Journal of Comparative and Physiological Psychology,* 1965, **59**, 357–360.

Liddell, H.S., James, W.T., & Anderson, O.D. The comparative physiology of the conditioned motor reflex based on experiments with the pig, dog, sheep, goat and rabbit. *Comparative Psychology Monographs,* 1934, **11**(Whole No. 51).

Marquis, H.A., & Suboski, M.D. Adrenal function in the incubation of one-trial passive avoidance, CER, and two-way shuttlebox responses. Paper presented at the meeting of the Eastern Psychological Association, Philadelphia, Pennsylvania, April 1969.

McAllister, Dorothy E., & McAllister, W.R. Incubation of fear: An examination of the concept. *Journal of Experimental Research in Personality,* 1967, **2**, 180–190.

McAllister, Dorothy E., & McAllister, W.R. Forgetting of acquired fear. *Journal of Comparative and Physiological Psychology,* 1968, **65**, 352–355.

McGaugh, J.L. Time-dependent processes in memory storage. *Science,* 1966, **153**, 1351–1358.

McMichael, J.S. Incubation of anxiety and instrumental behavior. *Journal of Comparative and Physiological Psychology,* 1966, **61**, 208–211.

Miller, R.E., & Ogawa, N. The effect of adrenocorticotrophic hormone (ACTH) on avoidance conditioning in the adrenalectomized rat. *Journal of Comparative and Physiological Psychology,* 1962, **55**, 211–213.

Moyer, K.E., & Bunnell, B.N. Effect of injected adrenalin on an avoidance response in the rat. *Journal of Genetic Psychology,* 1958, **92**, 247–251.

Overton, D.A. State-dependent or "dissociated" learning produced with pentobarbital. *Journal of Comparative and Physiological Psychology,* 1964, **57**, 3–12.

Pinel, J.P.J., & Cooper, R.M. Demonstration of the Kamin effect after one-trial avoidance learning. *Psychonomic Science,* 1966, **4**, 17–18.

Segal, E.M., & Brush, F.R. Intersession interval in avoidance conditioning. Paper presented at the meeting of the Eastern Psychological Association, Atlantic City, New Jersey. April 1959

Sines, J.O. Reserpine, adrenaline and avoidance learning in the rat. *Psychological Reports,* 1959, **5**, 321–324.

Singh, P.J., & Brush, F.R. Retention of passive avoidance learning. Paper presented at the meeting of the Psychonomic Society, St. Louis, Missouri, November 1969.

Skinner, B.F. *The behavior of organisms.* New York: Appleton, 1938.

Smelik, P.G. Failure to inhibit corticotrophin secretion by experimentally induced increases in corticoid levels. *Acta Endocrinologica,* 1963, **44**, 36–46. (a)

Smelik, P.G. Relation between blood level of corticoids and their inhibiting effect on the hypophyseal stress response. *Proceedings of the Society for Experimental Biology and Medicine,* 1963, **113**, 616–619. (b)

Smith, G.P. Neural control of the pituitary-adrenocortical system. In W. Yamamoto and J. Brobeck (Eds.), *Physiological Controls and Regulations.* Philadelphia, Pennsylvania: Saunders, 1965.

Spevack, A.A., & Suboski, M.D. A confounding of conditioned suppression in passive avoidance: ECS effects. *Psychonomic Science,* 1967, **9**, 23–24.

Stewart, C.N., & Brookshire, K.H. Shuttlebox avoidance learning and epinephrine. *Psychonomic Science,* 1967, **9**, 419–420.

Suboski, M.D., & Weinstein, L. An ECS-maintained Kamin effect in rats. *Journal of Comparative and Physiological Psychology,* 1969, **69,** 510–513.

Tarpy, R. Incubation of anxiety as measured by response suppression. *Psychonomic Science,* 1966, **4,** 189–190.

Walrath, L.C. Interference of avoidance in rabbits. Unpublished manuscript, 1968.

Weinstock, S. Acquisition and extinction of a partially reinforced running response at a 24-hour intertrial interval. *Journal of Experimental Psychology,* 1958, **56,** 151–158.

Wendt, G.R. Two and one half year retention of a conditioned response. *Journal of General Psychology,* 1937, **17,** 178–180.

Wertheim, G.A., Conner, R.L., & Levine, S. Adrenocortical influences on free-operant avoidance behavior. *Journal of Experimental Analysis of Behavior,* 1967, **10,** 555–563.

Yates, F.E., Leeman, S.E., Glenister, D.W., & Dallman, M.F. Interaction between plasma corticosterone concentration and adrenocorticotropin-releasing stimuli in the rat: Evidence for the reset of an endocrine feedback control. *Endocrinology,* 1961, **69,** 67–80.

Youtz, R.E.P. The change with time of a Thorndikian response in the rat. *Journal of Experimental Psychology,* 1938, **23,** 128–140.

Zammit-Montebello, A., Black, M., Marquis, H.A., & Suboski, M.D. Incubation of passive avoidance in rats: Shock intensity and pretraining. *Journal of Comparative and Physiological Psychology,* 1969, **69,** 579–582.

PROBLEMS OF PUNISHMENT

CHAPTER 8

Some Effects of Noncontingent Aversive Stimulation

JAMES S. MYER

The Johns Hopkins University
Baltimore, Maryland

I. INTRODUCTION

Most contemporary accounts of the suppression of behavior by punishment place considerable emphasis upon the occurrence of responses which interfere with the punished act. As these competing responses are seldom directly manipulated or measured, the theorist must make some assumption about the general nature of the responses elicited by the punishing stimulus. Depending upon the mechanism presumed to underlie the suppressive effects of punishment, various theorists have emphasized a number of different and sometimes mutually exclusive behavioral effects of aversive stimulation. Aversive stimuli are said to produce a general suppression of behavior, to serve as drive which energizes behavior, to elicit unconditioned skeletal responses, to activate escape and avoidance behavior, to induce aggressive attack, and to arouse fear. Everyday observation and a considerable body of experimental evidence indicate that aversive stimuli do produce these varied effects, but it is clear that they cannot all occur simultaneously. The major purpose of this chapter is to survey a number of studies in which the behaviors elicited by aversive stimuli have been studied directly and to analyze the effects of noncontingent aversive stimulation on ongoing behavior in order to determine the conditions under which the various reactions to aversive stimulation occur.

If aversive stimuli have varied and sometimes contrasting effects on behavior, it is clear that there are certain problems inherent in specifying a simple behavioral indication that a stimulus is "aversive." Within a given experimental context, the problem of definition may be avoided by analyzing the phenomena under consideration in terms of the behavioral effect being studied, rather than in terms of the characteristics of the stimulus. For example, Azrin and Holz (1966) argue that one can study the variables influencing the suppressive effects of punishment without recourse to any particular specification of what constitutes a "punishing" stimulus other than the demonstrated fact that the stimulus reduces the probability of responses which it follows. Similarly, analyses of escape or avoidance conditioning need not independently verify the "aversiveness" of the stimuli in order to study the parametric control of the behavior. It is only when the focus of attention is on the stimuli that it becomes necessary to specify what is meant by "aversive stimulation."

The most common measure of the aversiveness of a stimulus is its capacity to evoke escape behavior; a stimulus is regarded as aversive if the organism will actively perform responses which terminate it. This definition has considerable intuitive appeal, but there are serious difficulties in using the motivation of escape behavior as the sole index of aversiveness. First, the escape procedure confounds the response-eliciting and motivating properties of the stimulus. There is considerable evidence that under some conditions the "natural" response to apparently aversive stimulation is not withdrawal, but an inhibition of behavior. In such cases escape behavior might be difficult to demonstrate, even though by other criteria the stimulus would be regarded as aversive. This is particularly a problem when one attempts to compare the aversiveness of different stimuli; some stimuli may be more effective than others in motivating escape behavior, whereas the opposite effect may be obtained if effectiveness as a punisher or as an unconditioned stimulus for conditioned suppression were considered. Furthermore, the escape procedure requires that the stimulus be of sufficient duration to mediate escape learning. A brief stimulus may never be escaped, even though it may produce other behavioral manifestations of aversion.

Difficulties are also encountered when aversiveness is defined solely in terms of the capacity of the stimulus to function as a "punisher," weakening responses upon which it is contingent. In free response situations, the unconditioned responses produced by the "punishing" stimulus may interfere with or facilitate the rate of the indicator response independently of any motivational properties of the stimulus, and the introduction of any stimulus, aversive or not, may disrupt behavior simply because the stimulus situation has changed. Furthermore, the weakening effects of the stimulus will depend in part upon the characteristics and strength of the baseline behavior, so that the apparent aversiveness of the stimulus will be influenced by such factors as deprivation conditions, previous history of positive reinforcement, and response requirements. This difficulty could be overcome if, as Irwin (1961) suggests, the aversiveness of different stimuli were compared by pitting them against one another as outcomes of choice behavior. Testing preferences among aversive events in a choice situation raises the problem of motivating the animal to choose at all, but this difficulty could be overcome by making either response effective in terminating some third stimulus which is more aversive than either of the "punishers." However, defining aversiveness in terms of the suppressive effects of the stimulus introduces the same basic problem as a definition in terms of the escape procedure; it is possible that different stimuli produce different effects, so that either definition would make it extremely difficult to demonstrate the aversiveness of some stimuli which would meet the criterion set by the other.

It is obvious that the difficulties inherent in defining "aversive" stem largely from the insistence that all stimuli which are called aversive have some common behavioral effect. Yet the experimental paradigms for studying aversive learning fall into two contrasting classes, one emphasizing active withdrawal from stimulation, and the other emphasizing the inhibition of behavior in the presence of aversive stimuli. Observers who have studied the behavior of animals in natural situations describe two types of defensive behavior, flight and immobility. There is also evidence that different neural systems may underlie active and passive defensive reactions (McCleary, 1961; Gerbrandt, 1965) and they are differentially affected by a variety of drugs (Kelleher & Morse, 1964). There are certainly no grounds for regarding either the escape-evoking or the suppressive effects of stimulation as the sole index of "aversiveness." Accordingly, it would seem to be more profitable at this stage of analysis to regard a stimulus as aversive if it either motivates the performance of learned escape responses or reduces the probability of responses upon which it is contingent, and to focus attention upon the behavioral effects of such stimuli in the hope of more clearly specifying how aversive stimuli influence behavior.

II. RESPONSES ELICITED BY AVERSIVE STIMULATION

A. Reactions to Electric Shock

Although considerable theoretical importance has been attached to the behavioral effects of electric shock, there have been surprisingly few systematic observational studies of the unconditioned responses which it elicits. The first direct study of behavior during shock (Muenzinger & Mize, 1933) was conducted to determine rats' threshold of reaction to shock, and, accordingly, employed very low shock intensities. It was reported that the first reliably detectable response to shock was an abrupt flinching reaction, and that the threshold for this reaction was at approximately .08 mA. An analysis of behavior in response to more intense shocks was subsequently reported by Kimble (1955), who confined rats in a small oblong box and presented brief shocks varying in intensity from 0.1 to 0.9 mA. Kimble found that at low shock intensities the predominant response to shock was "flinching," and that as shock intensity increased above 0.3 mA, flinching decreased in frequency and "jumping" emerged as the dominant response. These findings were confirmed by Trabasso and Thompson (1962), who employed a somewhat different experimental situation but used the same stimulus parameters as Kimble. The results of the two studies were strikingly similar; in both the occurrence of flinching was maximal at 0.3 mA, and in both studies "jumping" occurred with almost the same frequency at comparable intensities. Trabasso and Thompson further analyzed the behaviors categorized by Kimble as "jumping" into three sub-classes, "jump," "run," and "prance." All three behaviors were increasing functions of shock intensity, and prancing was the dominant response at the higher intensities.

More recently, Goodman, Dyal, Zinser, and Golub (1966) reported an observational study which extended the range of shock intensities to 3.0 mA. At lower shock intensities their observations corresponded closely to those of previous investigators. As shock intensity increased beyond 1.0 mA, jumping declined in frequency and prancing and running were the principle behaviors observed. In another experiment, Goodman et al. showed that the differential effects of shock intensity are independent of experience with variations in intensity; data obtained when three independent groups of rats were presented shocks of 0.6, 1.6, or 2.5 mA, respectively, did not differ from the results obtained at the same intensities when a repeated measurements design was employed. Campbell and Teghtsoonian (1958) provided further support for the conclusion that increasing shock intensity produces an increase in locomotor activity even in rats which have experienced only a single shock intensity. They presented shocks of different intensities and from different types of sources to independent groups of rats in pivoted tilting cages. A switch closed and produced an activity count when the rat moved across the center of the cage or jumped vigorously. With near-threshold shocks, the effect of increasing intensity depended upon the shock generator, but at clearly suprathreshold levels of shock, activity increased with increasing shock intensity.

Reports that the flinching reaction to shock onset is maximal at a fairly low intensity and declines with increasing shock intensity have been questioned by Hoffman, Fleshler and Abplanalp (1964), who studied rats in a spring-mounted cage which was arranged to permit quantitative recording of sudden flinching movements, but was relatively insensitive to the slower movements involved in locomotion. Brief shocks were administered through the grid floor of the cage. In a very thorough series of experiments they found that the flinching response occurs at very low shock intensities; probably below threshold for producing escape, conditioned suppression, or punishment effects. Increasing shock intensity increased the frequency, amplitude, and speed of flinching responses, and there were no inversions of the functions with shocks up to 2.7 mA. Hoffman *et al.* quite reasonably argue that the previously reported decrease in flinching responses with increasing shock intensity is due to an inability to observe the flinching response before running, jumping, and other gross behaviors begin to occur.

It seems clear that the rat's unconditioned reaction to electric shock is an immediate flinching response, followed by skeletal activity which is graded according to stimulus intensity. Although systematic observational data on other species are rare, many investigators have informally described the behavior of Ss subjected to electric shocks. These reports uniformly agree that moderately intense electric shock elicits vigorous skeletal responding in a wide variety of Ss. Furthermore, a systematic study of the reaction of cats to electric shock (Stewart, Abplanalp, & Warren, 1965) yielded results confirming those obtained with rats. The cats exhibited flinching at quite low shock intensities, and the threshold of the flinch response was similar to that reported by Muenzinger and Mize (1933) for rats. As shock intensity increased, locomotion became the dominant response, and although the Ss' threshold for locomotion was higher than that reported for rats, the same monotonic increasing relationship between shock intensity and frequency of running responses was obtained. Additional quantitative comparative data on unconditioned responses to shock would be most helpful in analyzing the characteristics of aversive learning in various species, but existing evidence permits us to conclude with considerable confidence that foot shock elicits skeletal activity, rather than an inhibition of behavior.

These experiments dealt with inescapable shock delivered through grid floors. One might suppose that a more localized shock would elicit precise, adaptive withdrawal responses, rather than the diffuse locomotor activity exhibited in studies with grid shock. However, this does not seem to be the case. In conditioning experiments using shock as the unconditioned stimulus for discrete flexion responses, it is a common observation that on early trials the shock elicits vigorous and diffuse activity, and this behavior is quite persistent (Culler & Mettler, 1934; Liddell, James, & Anderson, 1934). This is true not only when the S is closely restrained, but also when considerable freedom of movement is permitted (Gibson, 1952).

It is clear that the predominant unconditioned response to inescapable shock is vigorous skeletal activity. Analysis of the effects of shock on the behavior exhibited during the shock-free periods in the situation, however, reveals a quite different pattern of behavior. Brush, Mook and Davis (1960) confined rats to one compartment of a shuttlebox and presented ten inescapable 1-sec shocks at 1-min intervals. A flashing light and clicking sound came on 5 sec before shock onset and terminated with the shock. Five independent groups of rats received shocks of different intensities ranging from .10 to 1.58 mA. During shock the Ss exhibited behavior similar to that observed in other studies; active responding increased and crouching decreased with increasing shock intensity. The predominant response to the conditioned stimulus at all intensities was crouching, while exploration and forward locomotion during the conditioned stimulus declined over trials. The only other response exhibited with moderate frequency during the CS was standing upright on the hind legs. Collectively, these "freezing" responses almost completely dominated behavior during the CS. Similarly, there was a suppression of activity during the stimulus-free periods immediately preceding presentation of the conditioned stimulus, although the weak shock groups showed less suppression during this stimulus-free period than during the CS presentations.

The "freezing" response exhibited by rats in the presence of stimuli associated with shock is very readily conditioned and extremely persistent. Blanchard, Dielman, and Blanchard (1968) allowed rats to explore a grid box for ten minutes, then administered a single 2-sec duration, 1.3 mA shock. A time sampling method was used to record the behavior of the shocked animals and of unshocked controls during the subsequent 3 hr. During the first 30 min after shock, crouching by the Ss occurred on 74% of the observations, whereas the unshocked controls crouched only 30% of the time. Crouching decreased in both groups during the observation period, but the shocked Ss crouched more than the control Ss for the entire 3 hr. The suppression of behavior after shock is clearly elicited by stimuli in the shock situation, rather than a result of some residual effect of shock itself. Blanchard and Blanchard (1969) showed that rats shocked in one box and immediately moved to a different situation for observation did not crouch any more than unshocked controls, but when they were returned to the shock boxes an hour later they displayed more crouching than rats which spent the first postshock hour in the shock situation. The observation that a severe suppression of behavior occurs after a single shock casts considerable doubt on the notion that crouching is learned because it reduces the effects of shock. Blanchard and Blanchard also presented further evidence that crouching is not learned as an escape response during shock. Four independent groups of rats were observed in the shock boxes for a 10-min period during which one group was not shocked, and the other groups were administered continuous shock of .4, .8 or 3.0 mA, respectively. Almost no crouching was observed in the experimental groups during the 10-min shock period.

Contrasting effects of unconditioned and conditioned stimuli have also been observed in studies of the effects of shock on exploratory behavior. Montgomery and Monkman (1955) shocked rats which were exploring an enclosed checkerboard maze. During shock there was a marked increase in locomotor activity, but suppression of "exploratory" activity occurred after shock. Baron (1964) presented varying numbers of brief, intense shocks to mice in an open field, and observed exploratory behavior during the subsequent 30 min. Locomotor activity was markedly suppressed after shock, and the degree of suppression increased with the number of shocks administered. Mice which had previously explored the test environment displayed greater suppression than those which had no previous experience with the environment, leading Baron to suggest that activity in novel environments had previously been reinforced by escape from fear-arousing cues, whereas escape attempts were reduced or absent in the Ss which had previously explored the environment and failed to find a means of escape.

B. Pain, Fear, and Reactions to Aversive Stimulation

For the past thirty years interpretations of aversive learning phenomena have centered around the concept of "fear" or "anxiety." Electric shock is regarded as "painful," producing a complex of skeletal and autonomic responses, some of which are readily conditionable. The readily conditionable components of the "pain" response are considered to be a "fear" response. Thus shock produces a "pain-fear reaction," and the reaction produced by stimuli which have acquired aversiveness through association with shock is called "fear" or "anxiety" (Mowrer, 1939; Solomon & Brush, 1956). The data from the observational studies discussed above easily can be reconciled with this sort of analysis simply by assuming that the unconditioned response to pain is skeletal activity; when in pain the organism engages in behaviors which will remove him from the source of painful stimulation. Fear, on the other hand, produces an inhibition of activity; the fearful animal crouches, remaining alert but silent and immobile. This interpretation is compatible with discussions of defensive behavior based on observation of behavior in more "natural" situations; the threat of impending danger, such as the detection of a predator, is often observed to produce immobility, a reaction which is regarded as having survival value because it greatly reduces the likelihood that the fearful animal will be detected (Hediger, 1955; Konorski, 1967). Although this interpretation of the contrasting effects of shock and conditioned aversive stimuli has considerable intuitive appeal, it raises several vexing problems. If pain is defined as the reaction to shock, and fear as the reaction produced by conditioned stimuli associated with shock, the terms are no more than shorthand descriptions of the specific stimulus conditions. To generalize to other stimuli it is necessary to specify how pain and fear differ. Unfortunately, learning theorists have seldom grappled with the problem of defining pain, either relying on a phenomenological acceptance that certain stimuli are painful and others are not or simply using the terms "pain" and "shock" interchangeably.

The extreme emphasis in recent years on "fear" as a conditioned response based on electric shock has led to neglect of a considerable body of earlier literature in which fear was regarded as a reaction to sudden, intense, or "surprising" stimuli which have had no association with pain and which produce a pronounced inhibition of skeletal activity. In his discussion of the expression of fear in animals, Darwin provided a graphic description of the behavioral consequences of extreme fear:

> With all or almost all animals, even with birds, terror causes the body to tremble. The skin becomes pale, sweat breaks out, and the hair bristles. The secretions of the alimentary canal and of the kidneys are increased, and they are involuntarily voided, owing to the relaxation of the sphincter muscles ... . The breathing is hurried, The heart beats quickly, wildly, and violently; ... The mental faculties are much disturbed. Utter prostration soon follows, and even fainting. A terrified canary-bird has been seen not only to tremble and to turn white about the base of the bill, but to faint ... (Darwin, 1872, p. 77).

In contrasting the reactions to fear and pain, Darwin asserted:

> Pain, if severe, soon induces extreme depression or prostration; but it is at first a stimulant and excites to action, as we see when we whip a horse ... Fear again is the most depressing of all the emotions, and it soon induces utter, helpless prostration (Darwin, 1872, p. 81).

Turning to the expression of fear in man, Darwin discussed a continuum

of expression from "attention" through "surprise" to "terror," and emphasized the increasing inhibition of movement produced by sudden or
strange stimuli. He suggested that the "blind flight" sometimes exhibited
in extreme terror be interpreted in terms of his "principle of serviceable
associated habits;" that an extreme state of fear will evoke habits previously associated with the emotional state even though the action is not
adaptive in the particular situation.

In developing his behavioristic treatment of emotion, Watson also
emphasized the inhibitory effects of fear, concluding that in human in-
fants the only unconditioned stimuli for fear are loud sounds and loss of
support (Watson, 1930). It is interesting that his pioneering studies of
the conditioning of fear (Watson & Rayner, 1920) did not involve the
use of shock or other "painful" unconditioned stimuli, and Watson
(1930) expressed uncertainty concerning the relationship between the
"fear reactions" he described and the responses evoked by burning,
freezing, cutting, and the like. Although Watson's views of emotional
development met with considerable criticism, especially in terms of the
number of unconditioned stimuli eliciting fear, the universality of facial
expressiveness, and the precise course of the development of fear, subsequent investigators continued to view fear as an unconditioned response
to a variety of nonpainful stimuli, and to accept the inhibitory action of
fear as a matter of course. With the appearance of Mowrer's (1939) influential article on anxiety as a conditioned form of the pain reaction
and anxiety reduction as a reinforcer, the focus of attention of research
on fear shifted to an analysis of fear as a reaction to pain and as a
source of drive. Mowrer argued that fear is always a conditioned response, based on the association of some previously nonaversive stimulus with pain. He rejected Watson's apparent demonstration of
conditioning with "fear-arousing" unconditioned stimuli by asserting
that loud sounds are painful, and that loss of support is almost inevitably followed by pain, and thus was a conditioned fear stimulus at the
beginning of Watson's studies. Mowrer went on to propose that anxiety
activates behavior and that anxiety reduction is a powerful reinforcing
event. The growing popularity of Hull's (1943) stimulus-response drive-
reduction theory of learning and the willingness of Mowrer (1939),
Miller and Dollard (1941), and others to extend the conditioned anxiety
concept to a wide variety of problems in clinical, personality, and social
psychology led to ready acceptance of Mowrer's position. Although
Miller (1951), Tinbergen (1951), and others pointed out that some stimuli are apparently aversive even though there is no reason to believe that
they are "painful," for the subsequent two decades the study of aversive
learning was dominated by the analysis of active escape and avoidance

learning (Solomon & Brush, 1956). The view that active withdrawal is the basic response to all aversive stimuli was accompanied by the development of theories of punishment emphasizing the interfering role of escape (Gwinn, 1949) or avoidance (Mowrer, 1947) responses in accounting for the suppressive effects of punishment, relegating punishment, as Azrin and Holz (1966) have pointed out, to the role of a secondary process.

There are, however, good grounds for questioning the assumptions that all fears are conditioned responses based on the association of previously nonemotional stimuli with pain and that fear always serves as drive which energizes active skeletal responding. For example, the termination of noise has been shown to reinforce escape behavior in humans (Azrin, 1958), monkeys (Klugh & Patton, 1959), cats (Barry & Harrison, 1957), rats (Harrison and Abelson, 1959), and mice (Barnes & Kish, 1957). Response-contingent noise has been shown to suppress responding in humans (Azrin, 1958), rats (Bolles & Seelbach, 1964), mice (Barnes & Kish, 1957), and pigeons (Holz & Azrin, 1962). It is clear that intense noise is aversive, even though there is no compelling reason to believe that the noise levels used are "painful" or that the stimulus has acquired its aversiveness through conditioning. There have been few direct observational studies of the unconditioned responses elicited by noise. Existing evidence, however, is consistent in indicating that the initial reaction to the sudden onset of noise is a stereotyped "flinching" response, followed by an inhibition of behavior. For example, Montgomery and Monkman (1955) sounded a loud buzzer while rats were exploring a Y-maze, and found that the buzzer produced "freezing," thereby inhibiting exploratory behavior. Bolles and Seelbach (1964) report that rats in a small observation chamber displayed a momentary flinching reaction when sound level was increased from 55 to 98 dB, and that rats subjected to repeated brief increases in sound intensity displayed a general suppression of locomotor activity and grooming.

In the rat, intense light is also capable of motivating escape learning, and the vigor of performance of the learned escape responding increases with stimulus intensity (Keller, 1941; Jerome, Moody, Connor, & Fernandez, 1957). Intense light can also serve as an unconditioned stimulus for avoidance learning (Hefferline, 1950). As is the case with noise, the unconditioned response to intense light onset is a flinching reaction, followed by crouching and immobility rather than vigorous activity (Hefferline, 1950; Kaplan, 1957).

In addition to intense, diffuse sounds and lights, a number of more complex patterns of auditory and visual stimulation are apparently aversive in that they release various species-typical patterns of defensive behavior. Unfortunately, the effects of these stimuli are seldom studied independently of the observation of the behaviors they release, so their "aversiveness" is an inference from the unconditioned responses which they produce, and the responses are regarded as "defensive" largely because of the nature of the eliciting stimuli. In many naturalistic studies little is known of the past experience of the subjects, so reactions to presumably aversive stimuli may reflect a previous history of reinforcement for active or passive responding. There are, however, a number of studies of the ontogenetic development of defensive reactions to various patterns of visual stimulation by animals reared in controlled environments which indicate that the initial reaction to such stimuli is freezing and immobility, and that active withdrawal in the presence of such stimuli is a later development, dependent upon experience (Bronson, 1968).

There are other stimuli whose behavioral effects mimic those of shock. For example, Glaser (1910) dropped rats into a tank of water and measured the time it took them to find a small hole in the lid and escape. He reported very rapid acquisition of the escape response. In Glaser's experiment the water was at five degrees centigrade, and subsequent experimenters have often employed cold water, assuming that extremes of temperature are more aversive than simply being forced to swim. This assumption was confirmed experimentally by Wever (1932), who gave rats extensive training in escaping from water by swimming down a runway and climbing out, then measured swimming speeds in water ranging from 10 to 40°C. The rats swam faster as the water temperature deviated from body temperature in either direction. The finding that cooling the water produces more vigorous escape behavior has been confirmed in a number of subsequent experiments (Hack, 1933; Braun, Wedekind, & Smudski, 1957). Another means of increasing the aversiveness of immersion in water is to force the animal to swim under water. Mason and Stone (1953) found that asymptotic escape latencies are shorter when rats are forced to swim under water than when they can hold their heads above the surface, and Broadhurst (1957) showed that underwater swimming speed is a monotonic increasing function of air deprivation, manipulated by restraining the animals underwater in the start box for varying periods of time up to eight seconds. The behavioral effects of immersion in water are quite similar to the effects of shock; vigorous attempts to escape occur, and the vigor of the behavior is increased by making the water very hot or cold or by forcing the animal underwater. Indeed, Mason and Stone described the behavior of rats forced to swim under water as indicating "panic," and found, as did Broadhurst, that performance was sometimes disrupted by extreme air deprivation.

Most studies of learned responding for temperature change have been primarily concerned with long-term thermoregulation rather than aversive learning phenomena, and thus have employed conditions which lead to gradual alterations of body temperature, rather than abrupt application of aversive thermal stimuli. Such evidence as is available indicates that unconditioned responses to contact with an extremely hot or cold surface are similar to those elicited by electric shock. For example, rats placed on an extremely hot or cold metal plate display scrambling, jumping, and vigorous attempts to escape (Ulrich & Azrin, 1962). Similarly, strong blasts of air evoke active, rather than passive defensive reactions (Masserman, 1943).

It is clear from the preceding discussion that the initial response to an aversive stimulus is a flinching response, followed either by vigorous withdrawal, struggling, and locomotion, or by crouching, immobility, and an inhibition of activity. Among the stimuli eliciting "active" responding are electric shock, air blasts, immersion in hot or cold water, air deprivation, and contact with an extremely hot or cold surface. Stimuli with inhibitory action include intense lights and sounds, certain complex patterns of visual and auditory stimulation, and visual and auditory conditioned aversive stimuli. The contrasting effects of different aversive stimuli might be accounted for by assuming that they vary along an intensity dimension; that lights, sounds, and conditioned aversive stimuli are less painful than shock, extremes of temperature, and the like, and that the response to mildly aversive stimuli is freezing, replaced by increasingly vigorous withdrawal behavior as the aversiveness of the stimulus increases. It does seem that electric shock, even at quite low intensities, is extremely aversive as compared with more "natural" stimuli. Campbell and Bloom (1965) placed rats in a cage arranged so that the animals were free to cross from one side, where shock was continuously present, to the other, where they were subjected to one of eight levels of white noise, ranging from 45 to 115 dB in intensity. Although the animals exposed themselves to very weak shock when the noise was extremely intense, with slightly more intense. shock they remained in the presence of noise. A similar comparison of the relative "aversiveness" of noise and cold water is provided in a study by Woods and Campbell (1967). Rats were exposed to 90, 100, or 110 dB white noise in one chamber and could terminate the noise by entering a second chamber which contained ½ inch of water, varying in temperature from 32 to 12°C. At the beginning of the experiment the rats refused to enter the chamber containing water at body temperature, regardless of the intensity of the noise. After shaping the animals to escape from noise by running into the other compartment without water present, Woods and

Campbell again introduced water in the second chamber. An unreported number of rats still refused to enter the water, and were discarded from the experiment. For the remaining animals, the amount of time spent in the water decreased with reductions in water temperature and with decreases in the intensity of the noise presented in the other compartment. As in the comparison of noise and shock, it appears that noise is much less aversive than cold water, a finding consistent with the view that mildly painful stimuli suppress behavior, and more painful ones produce active withdrawal. However, the "spatial preference" situation employed by Campbell and his associates confounds the response-eliciting and motivational properties of the stimuli. If, as the evidence summarized above seems to indicate, shock and immersion in water elicit movement and noise inhibits activity, the marked "preference" for intense noise may be due at least in part to these factors, rather than the relative "aversiveness" of the stimuli.

If it were the case that stimuli which suppress behavior and those which activate behavior simply vary along an "aversiveness" dimension, the transition from suppression to activity should be observed with variations in intensity along a single stimulus dimension. The observational studies discussed previously consistently fail to reveal any such effect. After the flinching response, the first detectable reaction to electric shock is jumping, not an inhibition of activity. Increasing shock intensity or air deprivation or decreasing water temperature increases the vigor of the behaviors exhibited, but low levels of stimulation with shock, cold water and the like have not been reported to produce the characteristic inhibition of behavior exhibited in the presence of aversive visual and auditory stimuli. Similarly, increasing the intensity of lights and sounds increases, rather than decreases, the resulting freezing and inhibition of activity. There is little evidence that the different types of behavior elicited by these two groups of stimuli are due to simple quantitative differences in their aversiveness.

There is one clear difference between stimuli which induce vigorous withdrawal, struggling and locomotion and those which induce crouching, immobility and an inhibition of ongoing behavior. Those which evoke vigorous movement are all "proximal" stimuli, in the sense that they are effective only when the receptor surface is actually in contact with the source of stimulation. The inhibitory stimuli described are all "distal," in the sense that the source of stimulation is not in contact with the animal. While little experimental data is available, some observations suggest that these lists could be expanded to include chemical stimuli; many animals "freeze" when they encounter species-typical "alarm" pheromones or the odor of predators (Griffith, 1920; Marler &

Hamilton, 1966), whereas the animal which encounters an aversive taste actively rejects the stimulus (Pavlov, 1927). It is interesting that this distinction between distal and proximal aversive stimuli corresponds well with the phenomenological distinction between painful and nonpainful aversive stimulation, and with the view that "fear" is a response to "danger signals," rather than to painful stimulation itself. This analysis is not, however, intended to differentiate between pain and fear as psychological states. The generalization advanced here is that all aversive stimuli evoke an emotional "fear" reaction, but the pattern of skeletal responding elicited by aversive stimuli on the surface of the body is dominated by activity which may be effective in removing the organism from the source of stimulation, whereas aversive stimuli which are perceived through distance receptors produce a suppression of ongoing behavior. Whether or not a somesthetic stimulus is phenomenologically painful or not undoubtedly depends upon a myriad of factors other than its locus and intensity (Melzack & Wall, 1965). What is suggested is simply that if such a stimulus is demonstrably aversive either in escape or in punishment situations, the unconditioned response to its presentation will be activation rather than suppression of skeletal activity, whereas the natural reaction to aversive visual and auditory stimuli, whether conditioned or unconditioned, is an inhibition of ongoing behavior.

The view that aversive visual and auditory stimuli exercise inhibitory effects on behavior must be reconciled with the fact that animals do learn to escape intense lights and sounds. The available evidence, however, suggests that escape from intense light and sound occurs despite the unconditioned response to these stimuli, rather than because of them. Investigators studying escape learning motivated by light or sound have frequently mentioned problems in obtaining the desired behavior because of the suppressive effects of the stimuli. Furthermore, when the escape situation is arranged so that the subject must emit a number of responses to terminate the stimulus, increasing the intensity of the stimulus sometimes reduces rather than increases the vigor of escape responding. Kaplan (1952) found that rats pressing a bar to escape light displayed a monotonic increase in response rate with increasing light intensity when every response was reinforced by light termination, but when a fixed interval schedule was introduced, so that continued responding in the presence of the light was required, response rate was maximal at an intermediate intensity. Barry and Harrison (1957) obtained a similar result with cats responding to escape noise on a variable interval schedule; the suppressive effects of extremely intense noise resulted in a decrease in response rate. Recent work has shown that at extremely high light intensities escape responding is suppressed even when every response is reinforced with light termination (Kaplan, Jackson, & Sparer, 1965). It appears that in escape situations using light or sound as an aversive stimulus the response requirements are pitted against the unconditioned inhibitory effects of the stimuli.

A similar argument can be advanced with regard to shock-avoidance studies employing visual or auditory conditioned stimuli. Failures to learn are notoriously common when lever pressing is the avoidance response (Meyer, Cho, & Wesemann, 1960), and are not infrequently encountered in acquired drive and shuttlebox situations as well (Miller, 1948; Brush, 1966). There is considerable reason to believe that the acquisition of avoidance responding usually involves the transfer of a previously learned shock-escape response to the warning signal rather than the direct activation of flight reactions by the conditioned aversive stimulus. In discussing his classic "acquired drive" experiments, Miller suggested that acquisition of a response reinforced by escape from conditioned stimuli associated with shock would be facilitated if the required response were similar to the former shock-escape response. Brush examined data from a large number of rats trained in a typical shuttlebox avoidance situation, and found that the best single predictor of whether or not an animal would learn to avoid was escape latency; rats which failed to escape quickly from shock also failed to learn to avoid. A direct comparison of avoidance learning with or without escape responding is provided by a study by Church and Solomon (1956), who found that dogs trained to escape shock in a shuttlebox prior to avoidance training learned the avoidance response faster than dogs without prior escape training. Apparently active avoidance learning is possible without escape, but it is greatly facilitated by prior escape learning.

A recent series of experiments by Weiss, Krieckhaus and Conte (1968) provided a direct demonstration of the interfering effects of crouching in the presence of the conditioned stimulus in an avoidance situation. On each of two successive days rats were confined to one side of a shuttlebox and given four pairings of a 1000-Hz tone and a 1.0-mA shock. Control groups received presentations of the conditioned stimulus without shock in the shuttle box, the shock without a conditioned stimulus in a different box, or pairings of a blinking light and shock in the different box. All four groups then underwent conventional avoidance training in the shuttlebox, with the tone as the conditioned stimulus. Prior conditioning of fear to the auditory stimulus severely retarded acquisition of avoidance responding in the experimental group as compared with the three control groups, and the attenuation of avoidance responding persisted through a total of 150 avoidance training trials administered over an eight day period. Weiss *et al.* report that the poor avoidance performance of the prior fear conditioning group was correlated with freezing in the presence of the conditioned stimulus. The shock itself elicited the familiar jumping and running, so that the prior fear conditioning did not interfere with acquisition of shock-escape behavior. In another experiment Weiss et al. showed that the administration of inescapable CS–US pairings does not interfere with subsequent performance of a previously learned active avoidance response to the conditioned stimulus. Rats were trained to avoid shock by running in the presence of a visual or auditory stimulus. They then were confined to one side of the shuttlebox and given four CS–US pairings on each of two successive days. When an additional ten trials of avoidance training were administered the following day, avoidance latencies were shorter than on the last ten trials of avoidance training, indicating that the inescapable fear conditioning facilitated performance of a previously learned active withdrawal response to the conditioned stimulus.

Additional evidence that the unconditioned "freezing" responses to visual and auditory stimuli in avoidance situations interfere with the acquisition of the response comes from studies on the effect of shock intensity on avoidance learning. Blanchard and Blanchard (1969) have shown that the tendency to freeze in the presence of stimuli associated with shock increases with shock intensity. If the inhibitory effects of such stimuli increase with their aversiveness, increasing shock intensity should retard acquisition of active avoidance responding. That this is true has been shown both in the shuttlebox and the lever-pressing situations (Moyer & Korn, 1964; D'Amato & Fazzaro, 1966). The fact that animals can learn to actively respond to terminate aversive visual and auditory stimulation does not require a modification of the hypothesis that the basic reaction to such stimuli is an inhibition of activity. Instead, the inhibition hypothesis seems to aid in understanding some otherwise paradoxical results of avoidance conditioning experiments.

III. EFFECTS OF AVERSIVE STIMULATION ON ONGOING BEHAVIOR

Observational studies of behavior elicited by aversive stimulation are usually conducted simply by placing the S in a chamber, administering the stimulation, and recording S's reactions. In the typical punishment experiment, quite different conditions prevail. Motivating conditions, the stimulus situation, and reinforcement contingencies are arranged to assure that some particular behavior will occur with a high probability before the introduction of punishment. Thus observational studies of reactions to aversive stimulation in impoverished and often unfamiliar environments may yield results quite different from those which would be obtained if the aversive stimuli were presented to an S engaging in some well-established, positively motivated behavior. As with the general question of the unconditioned responses elicited by aversive stimulation, there is no unanimity among students of aversive learning concerning the effects of aversive stimulation on ongoing behavior. Some emphasize the suppressive effects of aversive stimulation (Estes & Skinner, 1941; Brady & Hunt, 1955), others the energizing or drive-inducing effects (Hull, 1943; Amsel & Maltzman, 1950), and still others stress the importance of the compatibility of the responses elicited by the aversive stimulus and the ongoing behavior, arguing that whether aversive stimulation facilitates or interferes with ongoing behavior depends upon the particular responses involved (Guthrie, 1935; Fowler, 1963). Thus we are in the familiar position of attributing contradictory effects to aversive stimulation without specifying the conditions under which these varied effects occur. The purpose of this section is to examine a number of studies of the effects of noncontingent aversive stimulation on ongoing behavior. These studies fall in three broad methodological groups. One is the "conditioned emotional response" paradigm, in which a conditioned aversive stimulus is presented to an organism which is engaging in some previously established behavior (Estes & Skinner, 1941). The effect of the stimulus is not assessed by directly observing behavior during stimulation, but rather by measuring the change in the baseline behavior which occurs during its presentation. A second group of investigations has attempted to study the effects of "emotionality" free of any associative effects conditioned to stimuli correlated with the aversive stimulus (Amsel & Maltzman, 1950). In these experiments the aversive stimulus is administered in a situation different from that in which the reference behavior is established, and the residual effects of aversive stimulation are subsequently assessed in the test situation. The third approach is to administer a noncontingent unconditioned aversive stimulus while the organism is engaging in some positively motivated behavior, and to determine the resulting change in the reference behavior. As the administration of the aversive stimulus is independent of S's behavior, this procedure is identical to the conditioned emotional response paradigm except that the effects of an unconditioned stimulus, rather than a warning signal, are assessed.

A. The Conditioned Emotional Response

The view that the predominant behavioral consequence of aversive visual and auditory stimulation is an inhibition of behavior receives its major support from the extensive literature on the "conditioned emotional response" (CER). Estes and Skinner (1941) showed that if a previously neutral stimulus regularly precedes shock during food-reinforced operant responding, the rate of responding is severely reduced in the presence of the stimulus. Since the original demonstration of conditioned suppression the basic finding that conditioned aversive stimuli interfere with ongoing positively motivated behavior has been repeatedly confirmed, and the conditioned suppression technique has been widely employed to assess the effects of a variety of physiological manipulations on the hypothesized underlying emotional state (Brady & Hunt, 1955). More recently, several investigators have utilized the conditioned suppression paradigm to analyze the basic phenomena of classical conditioning, and a series of studies by Kamin and his associates have led Kamin (1965) to conclude that the parametric control of the conditioned emotional response is quite similar to that found in Pavlovian salivary conditioning.

It is important to remember that the conditioned suppression technique is not a punishment procedure; presentations of the conditioned and unconditioned stimuli are not contingent upon any particular behavior by the animal. In some instances there may be a fortuitous correla-.ion of the presentation of the stimuli and the occurrence of the indicator response, but conditioned suppression can be produced by pairing the stimuli outside the experimental situation, so that the unconditioned stimulus is never presented during performance of the reference behavior (Libby, 1951). It is also important for our purpose to note that suppression can be conditioned to the general experimental situation without presenting an explicit warning signal. Such conditioning presumably was responsible for the suppression of activity during shock-free periods in the observational studies described in the preceding section.

The finding that conditioned stimuli associated with shock suppress ongoing behaviors does not in itself show that the basic response to such stimuli is an inhibition of behavior. If the stimuli elicit withdrawal or flight reactions, they will have interfering effects in many situations. However, investigators who have directly observed the "competing" behavior occurring during CER suppression have consistently reported an inhibition of movement, rather than the elicitation of vigorous overt competing behaviors by the CS. Hunt and Brady (1955), for example, observed that during conditioned suppression of lever pressing rats displayed freezing and crouching, not active movement. Davitz, Mason, Mowrer and Viek (1957) found that the presentation of a light which had previously been paired with shock suppressed locomotor exploratory activity by rats, and Bindra and Palfai (1967) showed that presentation of a clicking sound which was previously paired with shock suppressed locomotion and grooming by rats in a small observation box. In these studies it was clear that the "competing behavior" elicited by the conditioned stimulus was an inhibition of movement, rather than the elicitation by the stimulus of competing "active" responses.

The view that a previous history of escape and avoidance learning can modify the usual inhibitory effects of aversive visual and auditory stimuli also receives considerable support from studies of the conditioned emotional response. Sidman, Herrnstein, and Conrad (1957) found that monkeys previously trained to press a lever to postpone shock displayed an increase in rate of responding upon presentation of a clicking sound signalling an unavoidable and inescapable shock. Herrnstein and Sidman (1958) showed that food-motivated responding will also be enhanced in the presence of a warning signal for shock if the S has previously made the same response to avoid shock. They trained monkeys to lever-press for food, then presented a clicker which terminated with a brief, inescapable shock. The usual suppression of behavior during the signal was demonstrated. They then eliminated food reinforcement and trained the monkeys to prevent shock by pressing the lever. After this response was well established, shock was discontinued and the former food-reinforcement schedule was reinstated. When the shock signal was presented during food reinforced responding, the rate of responding increased rather than decreased.

The facilitation of previously acquired avoidance responses by "fear" does not require that the aversive stimulus associated with the warning signal be the same as that used to establish the avoidance behavior. LoLordo (1967) has shown that dogs will display an increase in rate of responding to prevent shock when presented a conditioned stimulus previously associated with loud noise. LoLordo pointed out that the increase in rate of avoidance responding during the signal for noise occurred despite the fact that the noise itself reduced response rate. Evidently the previous learning of active responding to avoid shock was sufficient to overcome the natural suppressive effects of the conditioned stimuli, but not the more powerful suppression induced by the intense noise.

To summarize, the extensive literature on the "conditioned emotional response" is consistent with the hypothesis that the "natural" response to visual and auditory stimuli which have acquired aversiveness through association with unconditioned aversive stimulation is an inhibition of ongoing behavior. Facilitation of ongoing behavior in the presence of such stimuli occurs if the behavior in question has previously been learned as an escape or avoidance response. It would be of considerable interest to know what effect a tactile conditioned stimulus would have in the conditioned emotional response paradigm, but apparently no such experiment has been conducted.

B. Residual Effects of Aversive Stimulation

The finding that conditioned "fear" stimuli suppress positively motivated behaviors is rather embarrassing for theories which propose that fear is a drive which evokes or facilitates learned responses based on other motivational states. This contradiction can be resolved by invoking the familiar "competing responses," arguing that responses conditioned to the fear stimulus will interfere with the indicator response, masking the energizing effects of fear. According to this view, if one could induce fear without conditioning it to any of the stimuli controlling the behavior studied, facilitation of the indicator response should occur. The first purported demonstration of facilitation of positively ·motivated behavior by "emotionality" was an experiment by Siegel and Siegel (1949), who were interested in the relationship between salivation and thirst. The Siegels assumed that emotionality inhibits salivation and thus should enhance drinking. They deprived rats of food and water for four hours each day, measuring water intake during the subsequent two hours. After several days of measurement, half of the Ss were subjected to "fairly intense" intermittent shocks immediately before receiving water at the end of the deprivation period. The remaining rats served as an unshocked control group. To measure urine output during shock, the shocks were administered in a metabolism cage, and the rats were immediately returned to their living cages for the drinking test. The mean water intake of the shocked group was higher than that of the control group, leading Siegel and Siegel to conclude that emotionality did increase water intake. Examination of their data, however, casts considerable doubt on this conclusion. Only 2 out of 20 Ss in the control group and 5 out of 20 in the experimental group drank more than 1 ml. of water. The elevation of the experimental group mean was due largely to the presence of a single S which drank 11.5 ml. No other S in either group drank more than 4 ml.

The hypothesis that in the absence of competing responses "emotionality" will facilitate positively motivated behavior was advanced the following year by Amsel and Maltzman (1950). They placed thirsty rats in drinking compartments and measured their water intake for 10 min each day for 14 days. On the next three days the Ss received shock immediately before the drinking tests in boxes intended to be quite different from the drinking cages. The next day half of the rats were preshocked and the others were not, and the following day these conditions were reversed for the two groups. As Figure 1 shows, mean water intake on

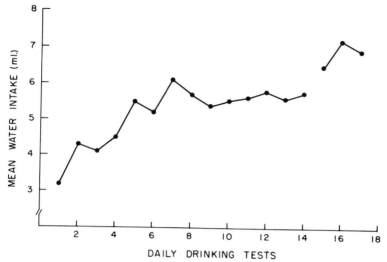

Fig. 1. Mean water intake on a 10-min drinking test on 14 control days followed by 3 days on which shock was administered immediately before the tests (Amsel & Maltzman, 1950).

the 3 preshock days was slightly higher than intake at the end of the control period. Although the mean water intake following preshock was significantly higher than on the last 3 control days, the effect was small, and the function suggests that water intake was not asymptotic at the end of the control period. A more appropriate comparison for determining the effects of preshock on subsequent drinking is provided by the data of the shocked and unshocked Ss on the last 2 days of the experiment. The differences between groups did not approach statistical significance. The conservative conclusion seems to be that preshock had no effect on drinking in this experiment.

Other experiments by Amsel and his collaborators showed that preshock suppresses drinking if it is administered in the presence of cues similar to those in the drinking situation (Amsel, 1950) and that the severity of the suppression depends upon the degree of similarity of the cues (Amsel & Cole, 1953). No evidence of facilitation of drinking was obtained in these experiments. Levine (1958) studied the effects of shock in a separate shock box on subsequent water consumption in the home cage and also found consistent evidence of suppression of drinking during the 10-min postshock tests. These results are, of course, further confirmation of the view that stimuli associated with shock suppress ongoing behavior, and that their suppressive effects generalize to similar stimuli.

The first fairly convincing demonstrations of a facilitation of drinking by "emotionality" were provided by some recent experiments by Moyer and his collaborators. Moyer and Baenninger (1963) found that simply placing rats which had received little previous handling in grill boxes for a few minutes severely depressed drinking on a subsequent test in another situation, but that drinking gradually recovered over a period of days. When preshock was then introduced, very weak shock had no effect, but intense preshock facilitated subsequent drinking. Moyer (1965) argued that if the animal had not previously experienced emotionality in the drinking situation, the novelty of the emotionality, like any novel stimulus, could interfere with drinking and thus overcome the facilitative effects of emotionality as a drive state. He partially corroborated this hypothesis in a very thorough experiment in which emotionality was evoked in different groups of rats by handling, shock, or placement in a shock box. Some of the Ss in each group underwent the prewatering treatment every day for five consecutive days, while others received the treatment only on the first and fifth days of this period. On the first day of the experiment, brief handling had no effect on subsequent drinking, but both shock and placement in the grill box without shock suppressed drinking. Drinking gradually recovered in the Ss which were placed or shocked in the grill boxes every day, and on the fifth day they displayed facilitation of drinking. The group which was shocked in the grill box only on the first and fifth days failed to show either facilitation or suppression on the fifth day, and the group placed in the grill box on the first and fifth days again displayed suppression. Although the facilitative effects reported by Moyer are not large, they are statistically significant and are consistent with his hypothesis that there must be habituation of the novelty of "emotionality" before facilitative effects can appear. Bolles (1967) has suggested that the animals drank more on the fifth day of the experiment simply because they had reduced intake previously, but examination of Moyer's data lends little support to this interpretation. It is unfortunate that the experiment was terminated on the first day facilitation occurred, as information about the persistence of the phenomenon would be most helpful in evaluating its importance.

More evidence of a small but reliable facilitation of drinking by prior aversive stimulation is provided by Levine (1965), who measured rats' water intake after .8-mA shock or after placement in the grill box without shock. The Ss in one shock group and one placement group received a single 20-sec exposure immediately before the 10-min drinking test, and another pair of groups received four 20-sec exposures separated by 10-min intervals, with the drinking test following the last exposure each day. Figure 2 shows the effects of the various treatments on subsequent drinking, expressed as deviations from mean intake during the 14-day

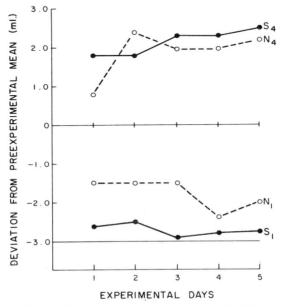

Fig. 2. Mean deviation of water consumption from control level by rats administered 1 or 4 shocks (S1, S4) or 1 or 4 exposures to a novel environment (N1, N4) prior to five daily drinking tests (Levine, 1965).

control period. Levine's results are of interest for several reasons. This is a clear demonstration in the same experimental situation of both facilitation and suppression of drinking by prior aversive stimulation. Although Levine does not specify the absolute amount of water consumed, the effects appear to be of sufficient magnitude to merit serious attention. The lack of difference between the shocked and "placed" groups corroborates Moyer's previous report that exposure to a novel environment, as well as shock, will affect subsequent drinking. The fact that the rats in Levine's experiment had a history of handling immediately before the drinking test prior to the introduction of the experimental treatment is consistent with Moyer's argument that habituation of responses to the novelty of emotionality is necessary to demonstrate facilitative effects.

The replication of the effects over a period of several days and the fact that Levine's Ss had free access to water in their living cages for 12 hr ·ach day seem to rule out an interpretation of the facilitation in terms of increased thirst due to previous suppression of drinking.

Although Levine has demonstrated both facilitation and suppression of drinking by prior aversive stimulation, it is not clear what are the critical determinants of these contrasting effects. Levine suggests that because of adaptation the level of "drive" induced by four trials is less than that induced by one. An alternative to this explanation may be that the critical difference between the one-trial and four-trial groups in this experiment lies in the temporal intervals between the stimulations and the test. Although both groups were tested for drinking immediately after their last stimulation, for the four-trial groups the drinking test occurred 30 min after the first stimulation. This finding is reminiscent of the well-known decrement in avoidance performance when a delay is imposed between successive avoidance conditioning sessions (Kamin, 1957), and is consistent with the view that the avoidance decrement is due to a parasympathetic over-reaction after fear conditioning (Brush, Myer, & Palmer, 1963; Brush & Levine, 1966). Systematic variation of the interval between aversive stimulation and subsequent drinking test should clarify this issue.

Demonstration of the facilitation of drinking by prior aversive stimulation raises the obvious question of the generality of the effect. Siegel and Siegel (1949) originally ascribed their supposed demonstration of a facilitation of drinking to an inhibition of salivation, but a subsequent study of the effects of preshock on feeding (Siegel, & Brantley, 1951) led Siegel to adopt a generalized drive position similar to that proposed by Amsel (1950). Siegel and Brantley measured food intake of rats on a 22-hr deprivation schedule. After adaptation to the feeding schedule, 8 Ss were taken to another room, shocked, then returned to their living cages and fed. The shocked rats ate a mean of 10.41 g during the subsequent hour, while a control group which had remained in the living cages averaged 9.24 g, a difference which Siegel and Brantley report is statistically significant. Strongman (1965) also reported a facilitation of feeding by preshock. Rats were adapted to a 23-hr feeding cycle in their home cages. On the test day they were administered a single 2.6 mA shock in a special shock compartment immediately before feeding, and food intake was measured in the home cage during the subsequent hour. Independent groups received shocks of either 3-, 30-, or 300-sec duration, and half of the ss in each shock group were fed their standard ration, whereas for the other half a small amount of quinine was added to the food. In addition to the six experimental groups, two control groups which were not taken from their cages prior to the eating test were employed; one tested with normal and the other with adulterated food. The results of this experiment are shown in Figure 3. It is clear that intake of

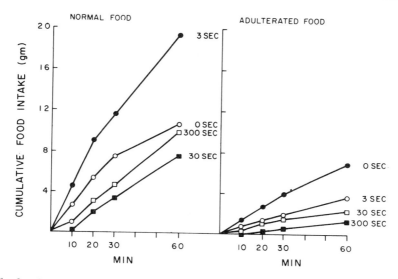

Fig. 3. Cumulative intake of normal or quinine-adulterated food during 1 hr beginning immediately after administration of a single shock of the indicated duration (Strongman, 1965).

the quinine adulterated food was suppressed by all three durations of preshock, and that these effects were maintained throughout the hour. The 30- and 300-sec duration preshocks were relatively less suppressive for the groups fed the standard ration, and the suppression was largely due to a failure to eat shorly after the shock. The 3-sec preshock markedly increased intake of the normal ration immediately after the shock, and the rats continued to eat throughout the hour, ultimately consuming almost twice as much food as the control group.

In interpreting these results, Strongman suggested that high levels of emotionality block the hunger drive, whereas lower levels increase sensitivity to the incentive properties of the food. According to his interpretation, at low levels anxiety will enhance eating a "positive incentive" and depress eating a "negative incentive." At high levels, anxiety will first block feeding entirely, and as anxiety dissipates the interaction of emotionality and the incentive value of the food will be revealed, reducing intake of negative foods and increasing intake of positive foods. This interpretation is adequate as a *post hoc* analysis of Strongman's findings, but without some clarification of what is meant by "positive" and "negative" incentive it has little predictive value. It is not at all clear why one would want to refer to a food that an animal will eat as "negative" except in comparison with some other food. A more likely explanation of the contrasting effects of the weak shock on eating the two different kinds of food is simply that the adulterated food not only was bitter, it was also a novel stimulus in the eating situation. According to this interpretation, any change in the test situation will magnify the suppressive effects of prior shock administered in another situation. This "generalization of novelty" view predicts that increasing the "incentive value" of the food by sweetening it would also reverse or attenuate the facilitative effect of preshock. Regardless of interpretation, Strongman's results clearly indicate that preshock facilitates feeding, assuring that the effect is not specific to drinking.

There have been a number of studies of the effects of prior aversive stimulation on behaviors other than feeding and drinking, but little evidence for generalized "energizing" effects has emerged. Baron (1963, 1964) shocked mice in a small compartment and observed subsequent exploratory behavior in an open field. Preshock consistently suppressed exploratory behavior. Similarly, Baron and Antonitis (1961) found that preshock reduced the level of unconditioned responding by mice in a lever box. These findings are consistent with the view that stimulus generalization from the shock situation to the test situation will result in suppression; there are obvious similarities between being placed in a shock compartment and being placed in a novel environment. Campbell and Candland (1961) avoided this problem by shocking rats in their living cages. The shocked Ss' subsequent exploratory behavior did not differ from that of unshocked controls, whereas another group shocked outside the living cages displayed a considerable inhibition of activity in the test environment.

There is also little evidence that aversive stimulation enhances subsequent performance of instrumental responses. Miller (1948) reported that rats previously trained to run a T-maze for food ran faster and chose more accurately if they were shocked immediately before a trial. This finding can readily be interpreted by assuming that at least part of the motivation of maze running is based upon reinforcement by escape from the maze. Furthermore, Ellis (1957) failed to find any effect of preshock on rats running to food in a straight alley, and Anderson, Cole and McVaugh (1968) report that preshock interferes with subsequent acquisition of running. Bevan, Bell, and Lankford (1967) trained rats to lever-press for water, then gave separate groups .25, .50, or .75 mA shocks before the daily sessions. All three preshock groups displayed suppression relative to unshocked controls. Strongman (1967) also found that preshock suppressed subsequent lever pressing for food. The only report of an apparent facilitation of free operant responding by preshock is an experiment by Ducharme and Belanger (1961). They trained rats to press a lever for water, then shocked the animals before each daily session, increasing the shock intensity each day. There was a very small tendency for responding to increase as shock intensity increased to .16 mA, then to decrease with further increases in intensity. The increase in responding at low shock intensities was very small, and there was no unshocked control group. No information is available as to the daily variation in response rate before the introduction of shock, so the possibility that the rise is due to some factor other than the introduction of preshock cannot be discounted. Certainly the bulk of the available evidence indicates that preshock suppresses operant responding, a finding which is not surprising considering the difficulty of preventing the generalization of fear conditioned to the shock situation to cues in the typical operant conditioning apparatus.

The suppressive effects of preshock on subsequent positively motivated behavior are readily accounted for in terms of generalization of conditioned fear, but a satisfactory account of facilitation of feeding and drinking is considerably more difficult. In view of the elusiveness of the phenomenon and the small magnitude of many of the reported effects, it is tempting to regard the positive results simply as illustrations of the statistical "Type 1 error." However, the magnitude and consistency of the effects reported in some of these experiments simply cannot be ignored. This is particularly true of Strongman's demonstration of an 80% increase in food intake after preshock under deprivation conditions which induced a very high rate of eating in the control condition. There seems to be little reason, however, to maintain the deception that after administration of aversive stimuli there exists some state of "pure emotionality" which is independent of the stimuli in the test situation and which can multiply with other existing drives to facilitate any arbitrarily chosen behavior. This view is apparently predicated on the assumption that the only readily conditionable emotion is fear. Considering the mounting evidence that stimuli associated with positive incentives acquire motivational or emotional properties (Bindra, 1968; Mowrer, 1960; Rescorla & Solomon, 1967), it is clear that whatever residual "emotionality" exists after aversive stimulation must interact with the "emotionality" evoked by the cues in the test situation. Thus deprivation and incentive conditions, prior experience in the test situation, and a host of other characteristics of the reference behavior may be as important as the parameters of aversive stimulation in determining the residual effects of painful stimulation.

C. Unconditioned Aversive Stimulation

Very little is known of the direct effects of unconditioned aversive stimuli on ongoing behavior. Investigators who are interested in "conditioned emotionality" are careful to choose conditioning stimuli which are not initially aversive, and when sounds, lights, and shocks are used as unconditioned aversive stimuli in CER or punishment situations they are usually so brief as to preclude any real analysis of their effects on ongoing behavior. Even if a brief unconditioned stimulus does momentarily disrupt behavior, the effect can be readily attributed to interference due to the startle response which characteristically occurs at the onset of any intense stimulus (Landis & Hunt, 1939), rather than to a general suppressive or facilitative effect of the stimulus. Similarly, suppression of behavior when a more enduring stimulus is occasionally presented during an experimental session may be due to "external inhibition," rather than to the aversiveness of the stimulus (Pavlov, 1927; Winnick & Hunt, 1951). There are scattered reports of suppression of ongoing behavior by visual and auditory stimuli which apparently are not attributable simply to startle reactions or to the "novelty" of the stimuli. For example, Green (1954) trained rats to press a lever for food on a 2-min variable interval schedule, then changed the illumination level in the chamber once each minute during the daily sessions. There was clear evidence of an inverse relationship between illumination level and rate of responding for food. A suppressive effect of intense light was also demonstrated by Henderson (1957), who trained six groups of rats to run a straight alley to food under different illumination conditions. The Ss received 10 trials on each of the first two days, and 20 trials on each of the subsequent 3 days. As Figure 4 shows, on the first day of training the rats run under low illumination were slightly faster than those run in darkness, whereas higher illumination levels reduced running speed. By the third day of the experiment, differences among the low illumination groups had disappeared, but the group run under the most intense illumination was slower than the others throughout the experiment. Indirect evidence of a suppressive effect can also be found in experiments employing lights or sounds as discriminative stimuli. When the presence of a light or sound signals that reinforcement is in effect and the absence of the stimulus signals nonreinforcement, response rate during reinforcement is some-

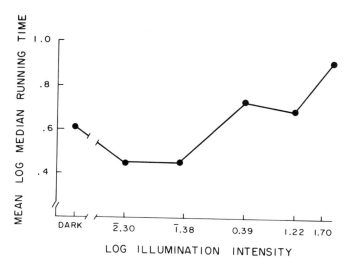

Fig. 4. Running times on first day of runway training under various illumination conditions (Henderson, 1957).

times reduced as compared with rates exhibited when the stimuli conditions are reversed (Skinner, 1938), and intense lights and sounds are sometimes so inhibitory as to preclude their use as discriminative stimuli (Keller & Schoenfeld, 1950). The scant data available are consistent with the hypothesis that the natural response to aversive visual and auditory stimuli is an inhibition of ongoing behavior, regardless of whether the aversiveness of the stimuli is due to conditioning. More extensive study of the effects of intense lights and sounds on ongoing behavior should reveal whether they mimic the effects of conditioned stimuli in the "conditioned emotional response" situation. It would be especially interesting to know if various physiological manipulations which influence the "emotional state" presumed to underlie conditioned suppression would have similar effects on "unconditioned suppression" in the presence of intense lights and sounds.

Laboratory studies of the effects of shock generally have concentrated on two broad classes of reaction, the inhibition of behavior and active withdrawal from the stimulus. Often in natural situations the source of aversive stimulation is another organism, and the reaction is to engage in various species-typical aggressive and defensive behaviors appropriate to the environmental context and the stimulus situation. The study of aggressive behavior in response to aversive stimulation first was brought under laboratory control by O'Kelly and Steckle (1939), who found that vigorous fighting resulted when shock was administered to a group of

rats confined in a grid cage. The basic observation that shock elicits aggressive behavior has been subsequently confirmed not only with the rat
and other mammals, but with birds and reptiles as well (Ulrich, Hutchinson, & Azrin, 1965). The behavior elicited by shock in social situations
is not simply a blind striking out at any object in the environment. The
form of the behavior is markedly dependent upon the stimulus situation
and the characteristics of the "spontaneous" aggressive behavior exhibited by the animal in natural situations. In domestic rats the reaction is
highly stereotyped, lacking much of the flexibility of behavior displayed
in spontaneous fighting. With the onset of shock, paired rats rear up,
stand stiffly facing one another, and strike with their forepaws. This posture, which Barnett (1963) calls "boxing" is generally regarded as a "defensive" or "ambivalent" posture when it occurs in "spontaneous"
fighting (Grant & Mackintosh, 1963). If the shocks occur at brief intervals the animals may maintain the upright position without striking during the intertrial interval, but they usually relax between shocks if the
shocks are relatively infrequent (Daniel, 1943). Because of the defensive
nature of shock-induced fighting in the rat, the behavior depends upon
the animals being in very close contact with one another. Ulrich and
Azrin (1962) found that pairs of rats in a 6 × 6-in. chamber fought in
response to almost every shock, whereas almost no fighting occurred in
an 18 × 18-in. chamber. Some other species exhibit more flexible and
complex behavior during shock. Hamsters (Ulrich & Azrin, 1962) and
squirrel monkeys (Azrin, Hutchinson, & Hake, 1963) persist in fighting
after shock termination. Vicious and continued shock-induced fighting
has also been reported in the wild rat (Richter, 1950) and by the strain
of domestic rats employed in the original study of O'Kelly and Steckle
(1939), suggesting that domestication has played a role in converting social responses during aversive stimulation from attack to defensive behaviors.

   The form of the behavior elicited by shock also depends upon the
stimulus characteristics of the protagonist. If a rat is paired with a ham-
ster, both animals exhibit the stereotyped "boxing" response (Ulrich &
Azrin, 1962), just as both species exhibit the behavior in intraspecies
"spontaneous" fighting (Grant & Mackintosh, 1963). Guinea pigs do
not exhibit the upright posture when fighting (Grant & Mackintosh,
1963), nor do they exhibit it when shocked (Ulrich & Azrin, 1962). If
shock is administered to a rat paired with a guinea pig, the rat modifies
the boxing posture, crouching so as to keep its head level with that of
the guinea pig (Ulrich & Azrin, 1962). In accord with the "defensive"
nature of the behavior, rats do not exhibit the boxing posture when
shocked in the presence of a nonmoving stimulus such as a toy doll or a

dead rat (Ulrich & Azrin, 1962). The dependency of the behavior induced by shock upon stimulus factors and the general experimental situation was demonstrated further in a recent experiment by Azrin, Rubin and Hutchinson (1968). Rats were closely restrained in a plastic tube with a metal, rubber, or wood target directly in front of their mouths. Under these conditions repeated shocks to the tail induced biting at the target, and different targets consistently elicited different frequencies of biting.

Squirrel monkeys exhibit biting attack when shocked in the presence of another animal, whether it is another monkey, a rat, or a mouse, and will bite at inanimate objects as well. Despite the wide variety of objects attacked by monkeys during shock, it is evident that the behavior is under stimulus control, for different stimuli differ in their effectiveness as elicitors of attack. For example, Azrin, Hutchinson, and Sallery (1964) have shown that squirrel monkeys shocked in the presence of a ball and a metal box almost invariably bite the ball. Further evidence that in monkeys shock induces a directed attack rather than simply eliciting biting comes from the demonstration that biting during shock is rewarding. Azrin, Hutchinson, and McLaughlin (1965) presented brief inescapable shocks to monkeys restrained in a chair. If the monkey pulled a nearby chain, it obtained a ball for a period of 2 sec. The monkeys learned to pull the chain to obtain and bite the ball, and persistently did so immediately after shocks. Two different chains were then introduced, and ball presentations were made contingent upon responses to one and not the other. The Ss quickly learned to pull the chain which produced the ball, and reversed the behavior when the response-reinforcement contingency was reversed. Biting the ball was reinforcing only when the animals were shocked, as almost no chain-pulling responses occurred during a shock-free session. This experiment clearly shows that in the squirrel monkey shock does not simply elicit biting attack, but rather it motivates the animal to bite. Differences in the form of aggressive behavior induced by shock are not only associated with species differences, but also with characterictic differences in the social behavior of individuals of a given species. Monkeys and chickens typically form dominance hierarchies in natural situations (Etkin, 1964). When pairs of monkeys or chickens are repeatedly shocked, similar relations emerge, with one animal attacking and the other engaging in defensive behavior (Ulrich, Hutchinson, & Azrin, 1965).

It is evident that the form of shock-induced aggressive behavior depends in part on the stimulus characteristics of the other animal and on the general experimental situation. Within a given experimental context, however, the most striking feature of the behavior is its consistency and persistence. In paired rats the characteristic "boxing" posture to shock occurs repeatedly with little sign of habituation even if several thousand responses are elicited in a single session (Ulrich & Azrin, 1962), and response frequency increases rather than decreases with successive elicitations (Ulrich & Craine, 1964). The latter finding suggests that the behavior is somehow adaptive as an escape response, but there is considerable evidence against this interpretation. For example, an extensive series of experiments by Azrin, Hutchinson and Hake (1967) has shown that in rats and monkeys the presence of another animal or an object to attack interferes with learning to press a lever to terminate shock and disrupts performance of a previously learned escape response. Roberts and Larson (1967) showed that rats shocked individually in the experimental chamber for a number of days before being tested in pairs show the same increased probability of fighting as do animals with an equally long history of shock-induced fighting. Simply placing rats in the chamber for the same number of days, either alone or in pairs, reduced the probability of shock-induced fighting on a subsequent test. Apparently in rats the increase in shock-induced fighting which occurs across repeated sessions is due to being shocked in the chamber, rather than to the repeated elicitation of fighting. These findings are consistent with the view that the response of paired rats to shock is a "defensive attack"; repeated shock in the situation might well be expected to sensitize such behavior, and adaptation to the presence of the other rat in the situation to reduce it.

In rats, some shock-induced fighting occurs with shocks as weak as .05 mA, and the probability of fighting increases as intensity is raised from 2.0 to 3.0 mA (Ulrich & Azrin, 1962; Dreyer & Church, 1968). At higher intensities the frequency of fighting in response to shock falls off somewhat, presumably because of the debilitating effects of the shock (Ulrich & Azrin, 1962). Increasing the duration of shock also increases the probability of fighting in paired rats (Azrin, Ulrich, Hutchinson, & Norman, 1964). This effect is evidently not simply due to reciprocity of shock intensity and duration, for Dreyer and Church (1968) found that although the probability of fighting was a linear function of the logarithm of both intensity and duration, the slope of the function for intensity was about twice the slope for duration. The probability of fighting by paired cats also depends upon shock intensity, but there is insufficient data available to specify the relationship precisely. Using three pairs of cats, Ulrich, Wolff, and Azrin (1964) found that fighting was occasionally exhibited in response to shocks of 1.6 mA, and shock of 2.0 mA elicited fighting on about half the presentations. Increasing the shock intensity to 3.0 mA produced a small increase in the frequency of fighting, and the authors reported that the fighting was more intense at the higher level. They also found that the probability that the cats would attack rats increased with increasing shock intensity, but they did not provide quantitative data. Squirrel monkeys will bite at an inanimate object immediately after shock. The effect of increasing shock intensity on this response is to increase the number of bites emitted immediately after each shock (Hutchinson, Azrin, & Renfrew, 1968). Figure 5 shows

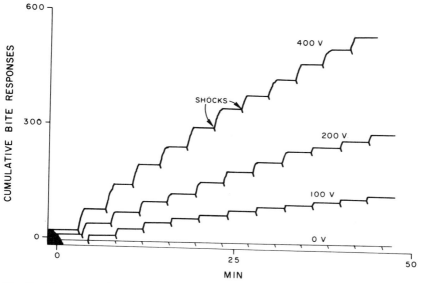

Fig. 5. Cumulative biting responses by a monkey during administration of shocks of different intensities administered at 6-min intervals (Hutchinson, Azrin, & Renfrew, 1968).

the effect of shock intensity upon the response of biting at a rubber tube by a monkey which was presented shocks once every four minutes. The data, which were recorded automatically through a pneumatic system attached to the tube, vividly illustrate the stereotypy of the behavior within a given set of stimulus conditions. The number of bites emitted increased with the duration as well as the intensity of the shock.

The close dependence of shock-induced aggression on the shock parameters raises the question of the effect of other aversive stimuli in social situations. Ulrich and Azrin (1962) administered a variety of presumably aversive stimuli to paired rats. Placing the rats in a chamber with a preheated floor induced fighting behavior similar to that exhibited during shock. Cooling the floor did not have a similar effect, but Ulrich and Azrin noted that no pain was perceived by a human upon touching the floor unless contact was sustained. More recently, Azrin, Hake and Hutchinson (1965) reported that squirrel monkeys will bite at a ball if their tails are pinched. Using a pneumatically operated piston that pinched the tail for one second, they found that the probability of biting increases with the intensity of the stimulus, controlled by varying air pressure on the piston. Attempts to induce fighting with auditory stimuli have consistently failed. Ulrich and Azrin (1962) presented intense noise (135 dB) to paired rats and guinea pigs, but did not observe fighting.

These findings suggest that aversive tactile stimuli activate species-typical aggressive behaviors, whereas aversive auditory stimuli suppress such behavior. If this is so, it should be difficult to classically condition shock-induced aggression using a sound as the conditioned stimulus. There have been two reports of purported classical conditioning of shock-induced fighting in rats. Creer, Hitzing, and Schaeffer (1966) paired rats in a small chamber and presented .05-sec duration sounds and shocks simultaneously at 3-sec intervals. After 1000 stimulations, the buzzer was presented alone on a series of 25 test trials. No fighting occurred on the test trials. After an additional 810 CS–US pairings, another series of test trials was conducted, this time by interposing the buzzer alone between successive blocks of 10 additional conditioning trials. Again no fighting occurred in response to the buzzer. The intensity of the conditioning stimulus was then increased to 80 dB and the animals were given an additional series of 130 conditioning trials, followed by sequences of 10 conditioning trials and a test trial, continuing until a total of 9 test trials had occurred. This procedure was repeated on 4 successive days. Creer *et al.* report that some fighting did occur in response to the buzzer alone under these conditions. A second experiment reported by these investigators employed delayed conditioning, rather than the simultaneous conditioning procedure of the first experiment. The 80-dB buzzer came on .5 sec before the shock. In the four daily sessions in which conditioning was claimed to be demonstrated the two pairs of rats received 100 conditioning trials, then 10 successive blocks of 10 conditioning trials and one test trial. Thus a total of 800 conditioning trials and 40 test trials were presented over a 4-day period. One pair of rats exhibited fighting on 10 test trials, and the other on 24 test trials.

Vernon and Ulrich (1966) also attempted to demonstrate classical conditioning of shock-induced fighting to an auditory CS. A 1-sec duration, 60-dB tone terminated simultaneously with a .5-sec shock of either 2.0, 2.5, or 3.0 mA intensity. Three pairs of rats were studied at each shock intensity. Trials were administered in blocks of ten with the shock omitted on every tenth trial. The frequency of fighting in response to the tone alone gradually increased, reaching a level of about 25 to 50% at the end of the 2000-trial session.

Neither of these studies provides a very firm basis for concluding that shock-induced fighting can be classically conditioned to an auditory stimulus. First, the level of "conditioning" reported is very low, with responses to the conditioned stimulus occurring on fewer than half of the test trials after hundreds of CS–US pairings. This level of performance is especially unimpressive when one considers that the probability of a fighting response is a joint function of the conditioning of either of the two paired Ss. Even if one accepts the significance of the occurrence of fighting in response to the CS at the end of these experiments, there are serious reasons to question the conclusion that "conditioning" was demonstrated. In both investigations pretests with the CS and US were conducted before beginning the conditioning sessions, but there were no further controls for sensitization. Both studies employed intense shock as an unconditioned stimulus, very short inter-trial intervals, long training sessions, and a testing procedure consisting of occasional trials with the CS alone interspersed in a series of conditioning trials. These conditions seem almost ideally suited to produce sensitization. In the absence of appropriate controls to determine the nonassociative effects of shock (Rescorla, 1967), and lacking any evidence on the retention or resistance to extinction of the response, there seems to be no reason to conclude that these experiments demonstrate the classical conditioning of shock-induced fighting. It seems much more likely that had more customary conditioning procedures been employed, the conditioned stimulus would have come to elicit fear, and, if anything, suppressed attack behavior during shock.

The fact that aggressive responses are induced or facilitated by painful stimulation raises an interesting question concerning the effects of punishment on aggressive behavior. Some theorists propose that punishment will suppress behavior if the punishing stimulus elicits responses incompatible with the punished act, but will facilitate performance if the punished response is similar to responses elicited by the punishing stimulus. Such reasoning suggests that the administration of painful stimulation contingent upon the occurrence of an aggressive behavior should produce little suppression, and might even potentiate the behavior. The opposite result was obtained in a study of the effects of punishment on the attack behavior of rats (Myer, 1966). Twelve rats which spontaneously and consistently attacked and killed mice in the absence of shock were presented one mouse each day and administered a single 3-sec duration shock when they first seized the mouse. If no attack occurred within 5 min, no shock was administered and the mouse was removed. Punishment continued until a suppression criterion of failure to attack on 3 successive days was attained, after which shock was discontinued, but daily mouse presentations were continued until the rats killed on 10 successive trials. The Ss almost always continued biting the mice during shock, and often continued biting for a short time after shock termination. Despite the failure of shock to disrupt attack behavior directly, punishment had a marked suppressive effect. Eleven rats reached the suppression criterion after 1–3 punishments, and the remaining S stopped attacking after 6 shocks. Three rats reached the recovery criterion within 15 days, including the ten criterion tests, but the other 9 Ss required 29–58 days to recover. The observation that attack behavior by mouse-killing rats is suppressed by attack-contingent shock has subsequently been confirmed under a variety of experimental conditions (Myer, 1967, 1968).

A study by Myer and Baenninger (1966) showed not only that punishment with response-contingent shock suppresses attack behavior, but also that noncontingent shock potentiates the behavior. Ten rats that consistently attacked and killed mice were presented mice at 30-min intervals and administered a single shock contingent upon each attack. After reaching a suppression criterion of failure to attack on 3 successive trials, the Ss were presented four additional mice at 30-min intervals. Beginning 2 min after presentation of the mouse on these 4 trials, 5 of the Ss were administered a series of ten 3-sec duration shocks, with 3-sec intervals between shocks. The remaining 5 Ss served as an unshocked control group. None of the 5 shocked Ss attacked mice during the 2-min preshock periods, but they invariably attacked and killed mice during shock administration. During shock the Ss repeatedly bit at the bodies of the mice, but they did not attack during the 2-min postshock period. The unshocked control Ss continued to exhibit the punishment-induced suppression of attack behavior. None of them killed mice on the first three trials, and only one killed on the fourth test. The noncontingent shock administered to the experimental group did not simply elicit random biting and "accidental" killing. The attacks were well-coordinated and indistinguishable from the "spontaneous" attacks exhibited prior to punishment. Furthermore, the attacks seemed to be under normal stimulus control. Myer and Baenninger tested rats that do not normally kill mice under the same noncontingent shock conditions, and the killing response was not exhibited during shock. Instead, the nonkillers assumed the upright boxing posture exhibited by paired rats, batting at the mice but not exhibiting the stereotyped biting response directed at the nape of the neck which is displayed by rats that kill mice. Similarly, rats that kill mice do not normally kill rat pups, due to an inhibition of killing controlled by the odor of the pups (Myer, 1964). When rats that killed mice but not rat pups were paired with rat pups in the noncontingent shock situation, they "boxed" with the rat pups instead of killing them.

The suppression of attack behavior by punishment with an aversive stimulus which itself potentiates the punished response obviously cannot be interpreted in terms of elicited or learned "competing responses." These findings are easily reconciled, however, with the proposition that in punishment situations there is classical conditioning of fear to distal stimuli associated with emission of the punished response, and that this fear inhibits behavior. If this general line of reasoning is correct, mouse-killing should also be suppressed by visual and auditory stimuli previously associated with noncontingent shock. This prediction was confirmed by Baenninger (1967). Rats that consistently killed mice were presented 5 mice each day at one hour intervals. A buzzer was turned on 30 sec before mouse presentation and remained on for 97 sec, terminating with a 7-sec shock. Within a few trials attack behavior was suppressed during the 60 sec between mouse presentation and the onset of shock. The shock itself always induced an immediate attack. Rats in another group were yoked to those in the first; each S received the same pattern of buzzer and shock presentations as his counterpart in the first group, but no mice were present on the conditioning trials. When subsequently tested for killing in the absence of either buzzer or shock, the Ss in the former group displayed severe suppression of attack behavior as compared with the Ss which had not received mice in association with shock, indicating that for the group which had received mice on the conditioning trials, the mouse, as well as the buzzer, had become a conditioned suppressor of killing. After attack behavior had recovered, both groups received buzzer-mouse-shock pairings on alternate days, with presentations of mice alone on the intervening days. Under these conditions both groups showed a clear differentiation between the mouse alone and the buzzer-mouse combination, suppressing attack in the presence of the buzzer but not when it was absent. The presentation of shock at the end of the buzzer continued to overcome the suppression and induce the Ss to attack and kill the mice.

Discussions of "shock-elicited aggression" usually emphasize the view that there is some fundamental and unique relationship between pain and aggression; that pain is a "primary stimulus" for aggression (Scott, 1958). The marked dependence of the shock-induced behavior upon the stimulus situation and the animal's characteristic mode of reaction, however, suggests an alternative interpretation. It seems possible that the effect of moderate pain is to potentiate any "active" behavior which has a high probability of occurrence in the situation. Being crowded together in a small, unfamiliar chamber might well "prime" two rats to be ready to engage in "aggressive-defensive" behavior, which then "goes off" upon the occurrence of shock. The extreme importance of arranging the situation to maximize the probability that the Ss will be near one another when shock is administered seems to support this view, as does the finding (Roberts and Larson, 1967) that shock does not elicit fighting in rats with an extensive history of adaptation to one another in the apparatus. The observation that the kind of behavior induced by shock depends upon the S's characteristic reaction to the stimulus adds support to a "prepotent response" interpretation.

More direct evidence for this interpretation is provided by a recent experiment by Barfield and Sachs (1968). Male rats were placed with receptive females in a small chamber, and 6 males which proved sexually active on pretests were selected for further study. Skin electrodes were attached to the male rats, and a shock intensity which elicited jumping and squealing was determined for each rat in isolation. The rats then underwent 4 tests of mating behavior, separated by weekly intervals. No shocks were administered on the first and third tests, but on the other two tests, .5-sec duration shocks were administered at 30-sec intervals beginning 15 sec after the receptive female was introduced into the chamber. Previous research would lead one to expect that under these conditions the shocked S would fight the other animal. Instead, the shock produced a pacing of the S's mating behavior. The female was approached and mounted immediately after each shock. As Figure 6 shows, under the control condition the intervals between mounts were quite variable, whereas during the experimental sessions the temporal distribution of mounting was closely tied to the shock. The potentiation of sexual behavior by shock was also apparent during the postejaculatory refractory period, which was significantly decreased by shock.

The only systematic studies of nonsocial behavior during shock have been concerned with eating. Ullman (1951) reduced rats to 80% of their normal body weight and observed them in an eating compartment for 20 min each day, recording the number of small food pellets taken during each 5-sec period. Beginning on the sixth day of the experiment, he administered a .245-mA shock during the first 5 sec of each minute. After 4 days the shock intensity was increased to .32 mA and the same procedure was followed for another 4 days. On the final 4 days of the experiment the Ss continued to receive .32-mA shock during the first 5 sec of each minute, but were fed to satiation immediately before the experimental sessions. The animals displayed a steady increase in total amount eaten during the experimental sessions from day to day, and a marked decrease in food intake when the satiation procedure was introduced.

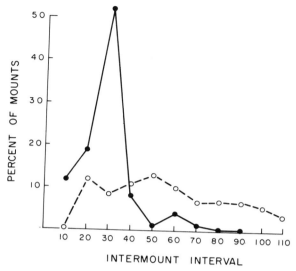

Fig. 6. Frequency distributions of intervals between successive mounts by male rats during administration of unavoidable shocks at 30-sec intervals (solid line) and during shock-free control sessions (dashed line) (Barfield & Sachs, 1968).

The increase in feeding was most likely due to an increase in hunger or to increasing familiarity with the experimental situation, and need not concern us here. The data that is pertinent in the present context is the relative amount eaten during shock and during the shock-free periods within the daily sessions. The lower intensity shock apparently had no effect on eating; food intake during shock did not differ significantly from intake during shock-free periods of corresponding duration. When shock intensity was increased to .32 mA, a significant increase in relative intake during shock occurred. On the fourth day of high shock, all 8 Ss took more food during shock than during any other 5-sec period, and the smallest amount of food was taken during the 5-sec periods immediately after the shocks. Under conditions of satiation, the facilitative effect of shock on feeding was even more dramatic. Almost half of the total amount of food eaten during the 20-min tests was taken during the 100 sec that shock was on.

Ullman (1952) reported a factorial experiment varying amount of training to eat in the apparatus before the introduction of shock (1 or 5 days), shock intensity (.245 or .30 mA), and hunger (10 or 20% reduction in body weight). After appropriate experience eating in the apparatus, the Ss were shocked for the first 5 sec of each minute during 20-min eating periods on four successive days. This procedure continued for another four days, during which the rats were fed before the tests. The only data reported is the number of pellets taken during the 5-sec shock period. An analysis of variance of the data from the first 4 days of the experiment revealed a significant effect of level of hunger, and the effect of shock intensity approached statistical significance, with more food eaten by the groups administered more intense shock. Feeding the animals before the experimental session on the next 4 days eliminated the effects of hunger, but the high shock groups ate significantly more than those subjected to low shock. Neither the effect of amount of training to eat in the apparatus nor any of the interaction terms approached statistical significance.

Ullman's experiments clearly show that when rats are periodically shocked in a feeding situation they eat a disproportionately large amount of food during administration of shock. These findings are reminiscent of Strongman's (1965) report of a facilitation of feeding by preshock. The absence of unshocked control groups, however, leaves open the question of whether eating was facilitated during shock or depressed during the shock-free periods. This deficiency in design was corrected by Sterritt (1962). A group of rats not subjected to shock was compared with groups presented .5- or 1.0-mA shocks during the first 5 sec of each minute of a 20-min eating test. The Ss were maintained at 80% of their free feeding body weight for the first 4 experimental days, and food satiated on the next 4 days. The results clearly confirmed Ullman's report that periodic shock produces an increase in food intake relative to that exhibited during shock-free periods in the situation, and further showed that this effect was due both to an increase in intake during shock and to a decrease after shock. The facilitative effect of shock was greater with the more intense shock and relatively greater under satiation conditions than under deprivation. Subsequent experiments showed that as shock intensity increased from 0 to .8 mA, the amount eaten during shock reached a maximum at .2 to .3 mA and then declined, eventually falling below the control level. The amount eaten during the shock-free periods was a decreasing function of shock intensity throughout this range (Sterritt, 1965; Sterritt and Shemberg, 1963).

The reduction of feeding after shock in these experiments can readily be interpreted as due to the suppressive effects of fear conditioned to apparatus cues, but the increases in eating during shock have been subject to a variety of interpretations. Ullman suggested that eating is normally a response to "hunger fear" which is sufficiently similar to "shock fear" to produce generalization of the eating response to shock. Sterritt suggested that eating during shock was the result of superstitious learning, based on adventitious reinforcement by shock termination following eating. This interpretation could account for the continuation of eating during shock throughout the experiment, but it is not clear how the superstition could have been acquired in the first place. Later Sterritt seems to have abandoned this notion, simply suggesting that eating reduces fear (Sterritt and Shemberg, 1963). The latter interpretation, however, is rather difficult to reconcile with the fact that feeding was suppressed during the shock-free intervals.

The observation of an increase in eating during shock again raises the question of the effect of response-contingent shock on a positively motivated behavior which is potentiated by noncontingent shock. Lichtenstein (1950) administered 2-sec duration shocks to dogs whenever they began eating. The Ss chewed the food vigorously during shock, so that the major behavior occurring both at the onset and the termination of shock was eating. Nevertheless, a rapid and remarkably enduring suppression of feeding occurred after the introduction of punishment. As was the case with attack behavior in rats, it is clear that punishment with response-contingent shock reduced the future probability of eating, even though the administration of the shock itself did not produce skeletal responses incompatible with the punished act.

Demonstrations of facilitation of behaviors such as fighting, copulation, feeding, and drinking during or immediately after shock suggest that at moderate intensities shock may potentiate whatever behavior is prepotent in the situation. An alternative possibility is that there is some unique relationship between shock and consummatory behavior. Unfortunately, very little is known of the effects of shock on instrumental behavior. The shocks employed in studies of conditioned suppression are usually so brief as to preclude analysis of the characteristics of the reference behavior during shock, and there have been no systematic studies of the effects of more prolonged noncontingent shock on instrumental behavior. Church, Raymond, and Beauchamp (1967) administered response-contingent, 3-sec duration shocks to rats lever-pressing for food on a variable interval schedule, and observed that the animals withdrew from the lever and ran around the chanber during shock. It is not clear, however, whether this behavior was exhibited on the early punishment trials or developed as a result of the response-shock contingency. Facilitation of bar-pressing by an aversive stimulus which might be expected to have effects similar to those of shock was reported by Webb and Goodman (1958). They trained rats to press one of two levers for food. After training, the S were satiated and tested in the lever box for 5 min, during which they emitted an average of 1.85 responses on the reinforced lever and 2.15 responses on the unreinforced lever. The box was then flooded with ½ in. of water. During the subsequent 5 min the Ss averaged 8.38 responses on the food lever, and only 4.77 on the other, leading Webb and Goodman to conclude that the emotionality produced when the box was flooded energized the previously learned behavior. This rather surprising finding was confirmed by Siegel and Sparks (1961), who replicated the Webb and Goodman experiment with almost identical results. Without additional experimental data, one can only speculate about the effects of shock on positively motivated instrumental responding. Very intense shock would surely interfere with ongoing behavior by directly producing competing skeletal responses, but it is not at all clear that similar effects would be produced by relatively mild shocks, sufficiently intense to suppress behavior in punishment or conditioned suppression situations, but not so strong as to extremely produce vigorous skeletal responding.

IV. NONCONTINGENT AVERSIVE STIMULATION AND THE SUPPRESSIVE EFFECTS OF PUNISHMENT

A. Comparisons of Contingent and Noncontingent Aversive Stimulation

There is overwhelming evidence that ongoing behavior is suppressed in the presence of visual and auditory stimuli associated with aversive stimulation. Accordingly, it seems reasonable to assume that the suppression of behavior by punishment is due at least partly to the generalized suppressive effects of aversive stimulation in the punishment situation (Church, 1963). Estes (1944) reported a series of experiments which suggested that the suppressive effects of punishment are largely due to such generalized emotional conditioning. In one of Estes' experiments, rats were trained to lever-press for food, then subjected to a series of extinction sessions. On the first day of extinction, shocks were administered at intervals of approximately 30 sec, but never immediately after a response. The shocked rats displayed suppression of responding relative to an unshocked control group, and the magnitude of the effect was similar to that observed with response-contingent shock in an earlier experiment. Another experiment tested the hypothesis that the recovery of responding after the termination of punishment is due to extinction of generalized conditioned suppression, rather than to the emission of unpunished responses. After appropriate training, three groups of rats underwent a 10 min extinction session, during which one group was not shocked, the second group received response-contingent shock, and for the third group the levers were removed and inescapable shocks were administered at 60-sec intervals. The following day, half of the Ss in each group were placed in the boxes with the levers removed for a period of 1 hr, while the others remained in their living cages. When extinction training was resumed the next day, the groups which had been shocked and had not been subsequently exposed to the apparatus displayed a marked suppression of lever pressing relative to the unshocked control group. There were no significant differences among the groups which received 1 hr of adaptation to the boxes, indicating that extinction of the suppression previously conditioned to the apparatus cues was equally effective in overcoming the suppression of responding produced by punishment and by noncontingent aversive stimulation.

Hunt and Brady (1955) provided a detailed comparison of the effects of response-contingent and noncontingent shock on lever-pressing. Four groups of rats were trained to respond for food on a 1-min variable interval schedule during 12-min daily sessions. After responding was established, some Ss received a series of aversive conditioning sessions, interspersed with adaptation sessions during which no aversive stimuli were presented. On conditioning days, a clicking sound was presented to all four groups during the fourth through sixth minute of the session. For one group, all responses made during the CS presentation were punished, and for another group the punishment contingency was in effect during the last 1.5 min of the CS. The other two groups did not receive shock for responding in the presence of the CS, but received two brief, inescapable shocks either at the middle or the end of the stimulus presentation. The experiment concluded with a 10-day series of sessions in which the CS alone was administered. As differences between the two punishment groups and between the two noncontingent shock groups were negligible, they were combined into a single punishment group and a single "CER" group. Lever pressing was almost completely suppressed in the presence of the CS in both groups, suggesting similar effects of contingent and noncontingent shock. Further analysis, however, revealed a number of interesting differences between the two groups. The CER group displayed a much greater suppression of responding in the absence of the CS than did the punishment group, and when the CS was presented without shock at the end of the experiment the punishment group recovered much more rapidly than the CER group. Furthermore, Hunt and Brady reported that the behavior exhibited during suppression of lever pressing was quite different in the two groups. The CER group displayed crouching and immobility, whereas the Ss in the punishment group were more active, and frequently made anticipatory responses to the lever. It appears that although both procedures suppressed lever-pressing, the effects of the punishment procedure were much more specific to the lever-pressing response.[1]

Hunt and Brady's report of more rapid recovery of responding after punishment than after conditioned suppression is somewhat difficult to interpret. It is possible that the punishment procedure had much more "response specific" effects; that the emission of a few unpunished responses was followed by much more rapid extinction of suppression than occurred following a more generalized suppression conditioned to many stimuli in the situation. However, the animals under the punishment condition received many fewer shocks than those in the CER group, for whom suppression did not prevent shock. It is possible that the persistence of the conditioned suppression after noncontingent shock was due simply to the fact that the noncontingent shock group received more shocks than the punished Ss.

Some investigators (Bolles & Seelbach, 1964; Hoffman & Fleshler, 1965) have attempted to meet the problem of equating the number and pattern of shock presentations under response-contingent and noncontingent conditions by employing a "yoked control" procedure. Each S in the punishment group is paired with an S in the noncontingent shock group, who then receives the pattern of aversive stimulation produced by his punished partner, regardless of his own behavior. Unfortunately, as Church (1964) has pointed out, this procedure also may lead to certain difficulties of interpretation. Beginning with the null hypothesis that the response-contingent and noncontingent procedures are equally effective in producing suppression, and assuming that there are no systematic differences between the pairs of Ss in the strength of the baseline behavior, one must assume that differences among Ss assigned to a given treatment are due to individual differences in reactivity to shock. If this is so, there may also be differences in reactivity to shock within each pair of Ss assigned to the two different experimental conditions. If within a given pair the S administered noncontingent shock is more sensitive to shock than the punished S, he will stop responding, but will continue receiving shock only until the punished S is also suppressed. If, on the other hand, the punished S is more sensitive to shock than the control S, he will stop responding and thus stop administering shocks to the yoked control, who can then continue responding indefinitely without further shock. Thus the "yoked control" procedure is biased in favor of demonstrating greater suppression in subjects receiving response-contingent punishment than in controls under the noncontingent procedure. It

[1]*Editor's note:* See Chapter 6 by Seligman, Maier, and Soloman for additional discussion of this point.

also seems to be biased toward demonstrating more rapid recovery in the punished Ss than the controls, for under the response-contingent procedure the Ss receive just enough shock to maintain suppression, whereas the yoked controls may continue to receive shock even though responding is completely suppressed. These considerations render interpretation of comparisons of the contingent and noncontingent procedures employing a yoked control procedure ambiguous.

Azrin (1956) trained pigeons to peck a key for food on a 3-min variable interval schedule. After responding was well established, the response key was alternately illuminated with an orange and a blue light every 2 min. The food reinforcement schedule remained in effect regardless of the color of the key, but a shock contingency was introduced in the presence of the orange light. Each S was subjected to four different shock procedures, with shock-free recovery periods interposed between the different procedures. Under the noncontingent shock conditions, an inescapable shock was administered either a fixed or a variable time after the orange light came on. Thus the orange light was a warning signal for an impending shock, regardless of the S's behavior. Under the punishment conditions, a shock was "due" some fixed or variable time after onset of the orange light, but was not administered unless the pigeon pecked the key. If no response occurred between the time the punishment contingency came into effect and the end of the 2-min stimulus period, the color of the key was changed and no shock was administered. There were variations in the pattern of responding in the presence of the orange light depending upon whether the shock occurred after a fixed or variable interval, but with either schedule of administration of shock there was much greater suppression of responding under the response-contingent procedure than when shock presentations were independent of behavior.

Marked differences in the suppressive effects of shock associated with the emission of a response and shock associated with the discriminative stimuli controlling the response also have been found in studies of instinctive or consummatory behaviors. Myer (1968) compared the effects of stimulus-contingent and response-contingent shock on rats which immediately and consistently attacked and killed mice. Four groups of 10 rats were presented 5 mice at 30-min intervals each day. The bodies of killed mice were immediately removed, and mice that were not killed were removed after 5 min. For the stimulus-contingent group a single 1.5-sec duration, 2-mA shock was presented ½ sec after each mouse presentation, regardless of the S's behavior. The Ss in an immediate-punishment group received a single shock when they first seized the mouse, and a delayed-punishment group was shocked 30 sec after the initiation of an attack. A noncontingent shock group was included to control for the general suppressive effects of shock in the experimental situation. This group was also presented mice at 30-min intervals, and a shock was administered at the middle of the intertrial interval, 15 min after the mouse was presented and at least 10 min after it was removed. For all 4 groups these procedures continued for 5 days. The Ss' behavior during this 5-day session was presumably jointly determined by any enduring associative effects of the various patterns of shock and also by the immediate energizing or inhibitory effects of shock within each daily set of trials. To determine the effects of the various treatments in the absence of the immediate effects of shock, the Ss were tested for attack and killing without shock on the day after the completion of this 5-day session. The following day a second 5-day "aversive stimulation" session began, during which all 4 groups received shock immediately contingent upon attack, using the procedure employed with the "immediate punishment" group during the first experimental session. At the conclusion of this immediate-punishment session another shock-free test was administered.

The effect of the various experimental treatments during the first session is shown on the left of Figure 7. As was expected in view of the po-

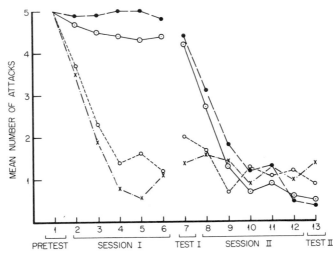

Fig. 7. Mean number of attacks by rats which in Session 1 received shock 15 min after mouse presentation (noncontingent shock), immediately after mouse presentation (stimulus-contingent shock), immediately contingent upon attacks (immediate punishment) or contingent upon and 30 sec after attacks (delayed punishment). All groups received immediate punishment in Session II (Myer, 1968). (●) Stimulus-contingent shock; (⊙) noncontingent shock; (×) immediate punishment; (○) delayed punishment.

tentiating effect of shock on attack behavior, the stimulus-contingent shock group continued to exhibit killing throughout the session, even though they were shocked immediately after every mouse presentation. Two Ss failed to kill 1 of the 25 mice presented to them during the session, another failed to kill on 2 trials, and the remaining 7 Ss killed all the mice presented. Shocks presented during the intertrial interval also had little suppressive effect. All the Ss in the noncontingent shock group killed some mice every day, and 6 of the 10 Ss killed all the mice presented during the session. By contrast, response-contingent shock rapidly suppressed attack behavior. The differential effects of the various treatments were maintained when the Ss were tested in the absence of shock. The stimulus-contingent and noncontingent shock groups displayed very little suppression, whereas marked suppression was exhibited by the punishment groups. When shock was made immediately contingent upon attack in the second experimental session, the former punishment groups remained suppressed, and, as is shown on the right of Figure 7, the former stimulus-contingent and noncontingent shock groups displayed a decline in attack behavior similar to that of the punishment groups in the first session. Thus shock contingent upon mouse presentation or presented during the intertrial interval exercised almost no suppressive effect as compared with response-contingent shock, and also did not increase sensitivity to subsequent punishment. These findings suggest that the suppression of attack behavior does not depend upon association of shock with the stimulus which arouses attack, but rather on the association of shock with the act of attacking. Similar results were obtained by Lichtenstein (1950) in his study of the effects of punishment on feeding by dogs; shock contingent upon the initiation of eating produced a marked and enduring suppression, whereas shock correlated with food presentation had little suppressive effect.

B. Gradients of Delay of Punishment

A somewhat different approach to analyzing the importance of the response contingency in determining the suppressive effects of punishment is to compare Ss presented immediate response-contingent punishment with Ss who are also punished for responding, but who receive the punishment some time after the response occurs. The assumption underlying this approach is that there are two factors involved in the suppression of behavior by punishment. One is a specific suppression of the punished response due to the association of punishment with the emission of the behavior. As associative learning depends upon the temporal relationship between the events to be associated, increasing delay of punishment would result in poorer learning, with a consequent reduction of the suppressive effects of punishment. The second factor is a nonspecific suppression of behavior in the experimental situation, which is relatively independent of the interval between the response and punishment. If the response-punishment interval is short, response suppression should occur because of the joint operation of these two factors. If punishment is delayed beyond the limits within which associative learning can occur, any suppression induced by punishment must be due solely to the non-specific effects of shock in the situation, and further increases in delay of punishment will have no further effect. If this analysis is correct, there should be a monotonic increasing gradient of delay of punishment, reaching asymptote when the limits of associative learning are reached.

The results of early experiments on the effects of delay of punishment on the suppression of positively motivated behaviors were rather contradictory. A complex study of punishment for erroneous choices by rats in a Y-maze (Warden and Diamond, 1931) seemed to provide evidence for a delay of punishment gradient, but a similar experiment by Bevan and Dukes (1955) failed to demonstrate any difference in the suppressive effects of shock delayed from two to seventeen seconds. The first study reporting a fairly systematic relationship between delay of punishment and the suppression of positively motivated behavior was provided by Baron (1965). Thirsty rats were trained to run a straight alley for water, then divided into 5 groups and administered a brief, intense shock 0, 5, 10, 20, or 30 sec after entering the goal compartment. Punishment severely reduced running speeds in all the punished groups as compared with unpunished controls, and running speed was inversely related to the delay of punishment. The delay of punishment gradient was rather irregular. The immediate-punishment group was virtually completely suppressed, and on the majority of the punishment trials the animals refused to run at all. The 5-sec and 10-sec delay groups were faster than the immediate punishment group, but apparently did not differ from one another in mean running speeds. They were somewhat slower than the 20-sec and 30-sec groups, between which there was also no difference in average speed. Baron noted that punishment in the goal box severely disrupted drinking, so the delay of punishment gradient may have been influenced by variations in the relationship between shock and consummatory behavior rather than by differences in the temporal relationship between punishment and the running response. It is possible that the "step-wise" function relating delay of punishment and running speed obtained in Baron's experiments reflects this confounding of delay of punishment and the nature of the last response before punishment. The immediate-punishment group received shock while running. The 5-sec and 10-sec delay groups were shocked during or soon after drinking, and shock presumably was not closely associated either with running or drinking in the longer delay groups.

The possible importance of analyzing the behavior intervening between the punished response and the administration of delayed punishment is further illustrated by an experiment by Banks and Vogel-Sprott (1965). The subjects were college students who were told that the experiment involved tests of perceptual motor skill and that they might expect to occasionally receive electric shocks through finger electrodes. The Ss were then instructed to press three buttons in front of them in any sequence they wished when signaled to do so by a tone. They were rewarded if they emitted one particular sequence of presses. After the correct sequence was learned, they were asked to perform a series of digit-symbol substitution tests. While the Ss were working on these tests, the tone was occasionally sounded, and they could press the buttons to receive reward. During this phase of the experiment, a .5-sec duration, 2.5-mA shock was contingent upon pressing the buttons. For 4 independent groups, the shock was delayed for 0, 30, 60, or 120 sec after the sequence of responses was completed. The immediate-punishment group made a mean of 3.9 responses, whereas the Ss in the delayed punishment groups responded on almost all of the 15 trials. The 3 delayed-punishment groups did not differ from each other. The failure to find differences among the delayed punishment groups might be regarded as showing that the delay-of-punishment gradient was asymptotic at 30 sec, and that the slight reduction in responding exhibited by the delay groups was due to a generalized suppressive effect of shock. It is possible, however, that college students can associate events separated by intervals somewhat longer than thirty sec, and that their failure to do so in this experiment was due to the interpolation of the digit-symbol task during the intervals. It is unfortunate that Banks and Vogel-Sprott did not report whether performance on the interpolated task was suppressed by the introduction of punishment.

A basic problem facing the investigator who wishes to compare immediate and delayed response-contingent punishment is the choice of the intensity of punishment to be employed. If the punishment is too weak, it will have little effect regardless of the delay interval. If it is quite intense, it may, as in Baron's experiment, markedly suppress the response regardless of the delay of punishment. A recent experiment by Camp, Raymond, and Church (1967) directly analyzed the role of punishment intensity in determining the relative suppression induced by immediate and delayed punishment. The experiment employed 11 groups of rats, including a control group which received no punishment. After training to press a lever for food reinforcement on a 1-min variable interval schedule, punishment on a fixed ratio schedule was introduced. The ratio schedule of punishment for each S was based on its response rate during the last training session, so that the S would receive an average of 1 punishment per minute if its response rate remained the same. For 5 groups, punishment was administered immediately after the ratio was completed, and for the other 5 groups, punishment occurred 30 sec after the last response in the ratio. Within these two sets of 5 groups, the shock intensity was .1, .2, .3, .5, or 2.0 mA. A number of features of this design should be noted. First, as a variable interval schedule of positive reinforcement was employed, the delayed punishment did not always follow the consummatory response. Second, the use of a free operant situation assured that there was no discrete discriminative stimulus, so that there was no confounding of the interval between presentation of the discriminative stimulus and shock presentation with the response-punishment interval. Finally, it must be emphasized that the Ss in the delayed-punishment groups were free to respond during the 30-sec delay interval, so that while there was a minimum interval of 30 sec between the "punished" response as defined by the experimenters and the presentation of shock, the last response before punishment might occur at any time during the interval.

To reduce variability due to individual differences in baseline response rate, the number of responses by each S during each punishment session was divided by the sum of the number of responses during that session and the number of responses on the last training day before the introduction of punishment. If response rate was unchanged during punishment, this ratio was .50, and decreases or increases in rate relative to the control session were reflected in corresponding decreases or increases in the suppression ratio. The unpunished control group displayed a slight increase in response rate during the 10 days of punishment training, producing a mean ratio of approximately .60. The mean suppression ratios over the 10 days for the 10 experimental groups are presented in Table 1. As is clear from the table, the overall effects of both shock intensity and delay were significant and in the predicted direction. The differences between delay groups at each intensity were generally small, however, and at the intermediate intensities the within-group variability was large. The only significant differences between immediate and delayed groups at a given shock intensity were at .2 mA and at 2.0 mA.

Camp *et al.* employed a similar design in another experiment, but presented punishment on an interval rather than a ratio schedule. Rats were trained to respond for food on a 1-min variable interval schedule, then were divided into 0-, 2-, and 30-sec delay-of-punishment groups. The "punished response" was the first response which occurred after a pun-

TABLE I

Mean Suppression Ratio for the Final 10 Sessions and the Standard Deviations of the Suppression Ratios for all Experimental Groups[a]

Intensity	Immediate		Long Delay	
	Suppression ratio	SD	Suppression ratio	SD
0.1	.52	.06	.56	.10
0.2	.46	.07	.57	.02
0.3	.44	.20	.47	.13
0.5	.18	.11	.30	.16
2.0	.03	.02	.06	.04

[a]From Camp *et al.* (1967).

ishment was "due" according to a 2-min variable interval program. The 0-sec delay group received a .25 mA shock immediately after this response, and, as in the preceding experiment, the delayed-punishment groups were free to respond during the delay intervals. All 3 groups displayed considerable suppression of lever pressing during the first few punishment sessions. As the experiment continued, there was a marked recovery of responding in the 30-sec delay group, and the 2-sec delay group recovered slightly, whereas responding was virtually completely suppressed in the immediate-punishment group throughout the 10 days of punishment. Further experimentation showed that the magnitude of suppression and the frequency distribution of response-shock intervals obtained with a delay of punishment of 30 sec were identical to those obtained with noncontingent shocks administered on the same 2-min variable interval schedule.

In a final experiment, Camp *et al.* attempted systematically to explore the delay of punishment gradient under conditions which minimized responding during the delay interval. Six groups of rats were trained to press a lever when a clicking sound was presented. The sound occurred on an average of once each minute. Responses in the absence of the sound were not reinforced, and if a response occurred during the 15 sec before the sound came on, its onset was delayed for 15 sec. When a response occurred in the presence of the sound, a pellet of food was presented and the sound was terminated. If no response occurred within ten sec, the stimulus automatically terminated. After this discrimination was established, partial reinforcement was introduced so that responses during the sound were reinforced only on 50% of the trials. On the unreinforced trials response-contingent punishment was administered to 4 groups, with delays of 0, 2.0, 7.5, or 30 sec. There were also a noncontingent shock group, which received a shock on the average of once every 2 min in the absence of the sound, and an unshocked control group. Figure 8 shows the mean percentage of "trials" (discriminative stimulus presentations) on which responses occurred for the 6 groups. As in the preceding experiment, the delayed-punishment groups and the noncontingent shock groups showed a considerable disruption of responding soon after the introduction of punishment, followed by recovery during subsequent punishment sessions. All of the shocked groups showed suppression relative to the unshocked control group, and the immediate-punishment group made significantly fewer responses than the other groups. The noncontingent shock and 30-sec delay groups did not differ significantly from one another, and showed less suppression than any of the other shocked groups. Again, it is clear that immediate punishment is more suppressive than delayed punishment, and that with long delays response-contingent punishment is no more suppressive than noncontingent shock. The delay of punishment gradient was rather irregular. As Figure 8 shows, there was little difference between the 2.0-sec and the 7.5-sec delay groups, a finding reminiscent of the "step-like" delay of punishment gradient obtained in the straight alley by Baron (1965).

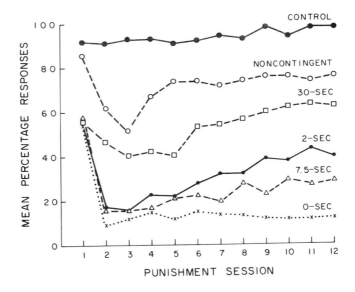

Fig. 8. Mean percentage of responses in 12 punishment sessions by rats administered no shock, noncontingent shocks, or response-contingent shock administered 0, 2, 7.5, or 30 sec after the response (Camp, Raymond, & Church, 1967).

Irregular delay of punishment gradients were also reported by Renner (1966), who compared the effects of delay of reward and of punishment in a choice situation. Rats were placed in a small start box from which they could enter either of 2 delay compartments, which in turn led to goal boxes and eventual removal from the situation. On each trial a door in the center of the start box was raised through the floor under the *S*, forcing choice of one of the delay boxes. The punished groups were administered a single shock either immediately after entering the "incorrect" delay chamber or after delays of 3, 7, 15, 30, or 60 sec. After the shock the *S*s were permitted to enter the goal box and the trial was terminated. If the "correct" delay compartment was entered, the *S*s were not shocked, but were simply held for the appropriate delay interval and then given access to the goal box. For 3 other groups, a similar delay procedure was employed, with delays of 0, 7, or 30 sec, but no shocks were presented. Instead, the *S*s were food-deprived and given food in the "correct" goal box. Under both conditions, 10 trials were administered each day, continuing to a criterion of 18 correct responses in a 2-day period. Examination of Renner's graphs indicates that varying delay of punishment from 0 to 15 sec had little or no effect on rate of learning, either in terms of days to criterion or error scores. Only the 30-sec and 60-sec delayed-punishment groups seem to have shown a retardation of learning as compared with the immediate-punishment condition. The positive reinforcement groups displayed the typical steep, monotonic increasing delay of reward gradient.

A failure to obtain differential effects of short delays of punishment during the course of suppression was also reported by Solomon, Turner, and Lessac (1968). Hungry dogs were presented two dishes of food, one containing dry laboratory chow, and the other containing canned meat, a highly preferred food. The dogs in one group were swatted with a newspaper if they touched the meat, and those in the other two groups were similarly punished 5 or 15 sec after they began eating. This punishment training continued until the dogs ate only the dry food on 20 consecutive days. The groups did not differ significantly in terms of number of punishments or number of days required to reach the suppression criterion. Eating is, of course, a "continuing" behavior, so that all 3 groups were punished while eating, although the punishment was administered at different times after the initiation of the behavior. Solomon *et al.* did obtain differential effects of delay of punishment when recovery from punishment-induced suppression was studied. When tested for eating the meat in the absence of the experimenter, who presumably was a discriminative stimulus for punishment, time to recovery was inversely related to the delay interval.

A similar failure to obtain an effect of delay of punishment on the suppression of a continuing behavior was reported by Myer (1968), who found that immediate attack-contingent shock and shock delayed for 30 sec after the initiation of an attack were equally effective in suppressing mouse-killing by rats. Although shock was temporally remote from the initiation of attack for the delayed punishment group, the rats were usually still biting at the body of the mouse at the time of shock onset. When administered a single 5-trial block of shock-free test trials on the day after the last day of immediate or delayed punishment, the groups did not differ. However, as both groups were virtually completely suppressed on the test day, the possibility that differences might have emerged during recovery was not adequately tested.

The effect of delay on the punishing effects of intense sound was investigated by Bolles and Warren (1966). Their study is also of interest because it experimentally tested a differential prediction of the "competing response" and "escape" hypotheses concerning the suppressive effects of punishment. Eight groups of rats were placed in a wooden box which had a 1-in. diameter hole in one wall. If the S broke a photocell beam across the hole, a response was recorded. Four groups were subjected to a punishment procedure; a 40-dB increase in noise level was contingent upon the response. A 2×2 factorial design was employed, such that the onset of punishment was either immediately contingent upon the response or delayed for 1.5 sec, and the termination of noise either occurred immediately after the S withdrew from the window or 1.5 sec after withdrawal. Four additional groups underwent analogous escape procedures. The intense noise was present except when the S broke the photobeam. When the photobeam was broken, the noise level was reduced either immediately or after a 1.5-sec delay; if the S moved away from the photobeam the noise came back on either immediately or after a delay. Figure 9 shows the percentage of time spent investigating the window by the various experimental groups during successive 3-min periods. It is clear that the escape procedure, in which the noise level was reduced if the animal investigated the window, resulted in much more window investigation than the punishment procedure. It is also clear that in the escape procedure the critical temporal interval was that between the initiation of the response and the termination of the aversive stimulus, and that in the punishment procedure the important interval is that between the initiation of the response and the onset of noise. The latter result is the opposite of that predicted by the "escape hypothesis," which regards the learning of a response which terminates the aversive stimulus as the critical determinant of the suppressive effects of punishment.

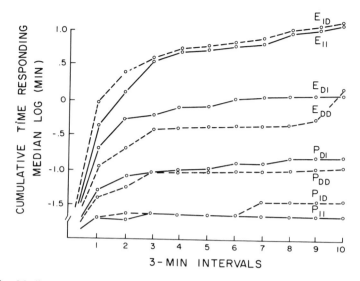

Fig. 9. Median occurrence of a window-investigation response over a 30-min session during which the criterion response produced (P) or terminated (E) intense noise. The changes in noise level were either immediate (I) or delayed (D) after the initiation or termination of the window investigation response. For example, group E_{ID} was run under escape conditions, with immediate noise reduction when the response was initiated, and noise onset delayed for 1.5 sec after the response was terminated. Group P_{DI} was punished with noise onset, which was delayed until 1.5 sec after initiation of the response, and received immediate termination of noise when the response was terminated (Bolles and Warren, 1966).

A regular, graded effect of delay of punishment on a positively motivated behavior was obtained in a recent study of punishment of the feeding reaction of goldfish. Myer and Ricci (1968) placed goldfish in glass bowls for daily feeding sessions in which 20 small clusters of Tubifex worms were presented at 150-sec intervals. After the feeding response was established, a shock was administered through electrodes immersed in the water on two sides of the bowls, either when the fish seized a cluster of worms or after delays of 2.5, 5, 10, or 20 sec. On the first "punishment" day the transformer controlling the shock was set at zero, and the voltage was increased by 5 V each day for each fish, continuing until the fish reached a suppression criterion of 15 or more failures to feed on 3 successive days. The effects of punishment were evaluated by determining a suppression threshold, which was the shock voltage employed on the day the animal reached the suppression criterion. All the fish reached the suppression criterion, showing that punishment was effective ın suppressıng feeding even with response-shock intervals as long as 20 sec. The amount of punishment required to suppress feeding was an increasing function of delay of punishment. The delay of punishment gradient, shown in Figure 10, increased sharply as the delay of punishment increased from 0 to 10 sec. Further increase in the response-shock interval had no effect on the suppression thresholds.

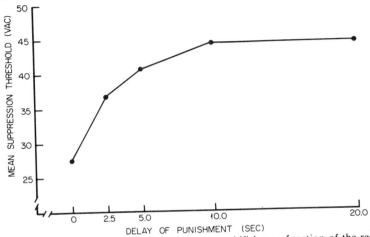

Fig. 10. Thresholds of suppression of feeding by goldfish as a function of the response-shock interval (Myer & Ricci, 1968).

This experiment showed that as the delay of punishment increased from 0 to 10 sec, an increasing amount of punishment was required to suppress the feeding reaction. In a second experiment, Myer and Ricci employed a more traditional experimental design to explore further the effects of punishment intensity and delay and to analyze the effect of delay of punishment upon the subsequent recovery of the feeding response. Six groups of fish were punished either with 10-V or 25-V shock and with delays of 0, 5, or 10 sec. Ten punishment trials were administered each day for 10 days, after which a 10-day recovery session was conducted. As Figure 11 shows, at every delay interval the high shock was more suppressive than the low shock, and within each shock intensity the magnitude of the suppression was inversely related to the delay of punishment. After termination of punishment, individual Ss generally exhibited rather abrupt all-or-none recovery functions, feeding consistently after a few unpunished responses. The recovery of the immediate-punishment groups was similar at both shock intensities, whereas the groups punished with 10-V shock after delays of 5 and 10 sec displayed

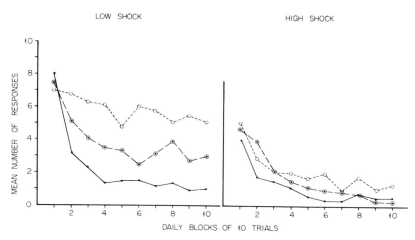

Fig. 11. Suppression of feeding by goldfish during immediate and delayed punishment with 10- and 25-V shock (Myer & Ricci, 1968). (●) 0-sec delay; (⊙) 5-sec delay; (o) 10-sec delay.

significantly less enduring suppression than the corresponding high shock groups. There were no differences among the three high shock groups in rate of recovery, and the two delayed low shock groups did not differ, but both recovered significantly faster than the corresponding immediate punishment group. The data suggested that the course of recovery was primarily due to the amount of suppression which occurred during punishment, rather than to a residual effect of delay. The high shock groups and the immediate-punishment low shock group were severely suppressed at the end of punishment, and recovered slowly. The other groups were only moderately suppressed, and thus resumed feeding much earlier in the unpunished recovery period.

The results of these experiments are quite consistent with the theory of punishment presented previously. According to this analysis, at very low intensities punishment was suppressive only if it was closely associated with the emission of the response. With increasing delays of punishment, an increasing punishment intensity was required to suppress the feeding response. Increasing the delay from 10 to 20 sec presumably had no additional effect because the suppression exhibited was due entirely to the generalized suppressive effects of shock in the experimental situation, rather than to more explicit associative learning. This interpretation is consistent with the results of a study of the role of the interstimulus interval in classical trace conditioning in goldfish (Bitterman, 1964), which indicated that little if any conditioning occurs with CS–US intervals longer than 10 sec. It must be emphasized, however, that delay of punish-

ment gradients derived from studies employing a discrete trials procedure do not necessarily demonstrate the importance of the response-
punishment contingency, as the interval between the presentation of the
discriminative stimulus for the response and the occurrence of punishment is also systematically varied. Thus it is clear from this sort of study
that the interval between the occasion of emission of the response and
the administration of punishment is important in determining the suppressive effects of punishment, but it is unclear whether the occurrence
of the response itself plays a major role.

The foregoing analysis of the effects of delay of punishment is based
upon the traditional assumption that learning depends upon a close
temporal association of the response and reinforcement; an assumption
which has been repeatedly verified in conventional learning experiments.
Some recent studies of the development of gustatory aversions suggest
that under certain conditions punishment may have highly specific suppressive effects even after very long delays. It has been known for some
time that if a rat eats a distinctively flavored poisoned food and sur-
vives, it may subsequently exhibit a specific aversion to that food. This
"bait shyness" may occur even though the poison is slow acting, so that
the illness it produces may not be experienced until some time after the
food is eaten (Barnett, 1963). A number of recent laboratory studies
seem to have shown that these "punishment" effects may occur even if
the nausea is induced several hours after the distinctively flavored solution is tasted. Revusky (1968) gave rats a single 5-min experience of
drinking from a tube containing a sucrose solution, followed by illness-
inducing X-irradiation seven hours later. On a subsequent test they
displayed a marked reduction in sucrose consumption relative to
irradiated controls which ate a familiar laboratory chow prior to the
irradiation treatment. Smith and Roll (1967) obtained similar results,
using saccharine and sucrose to flavor the water.

The aversions which result from illness after tasting a distinctively
flavored solution seem to be specific to the taste and odor of the food,
rather than associated with visual and auditory stimuli associated with
the feeding situation. A very nice demonstration of the stimulus
specificity of gustatory aversions is provided by a series of experiments
by Garcia and Koelling (1966), in which consumption of water with a
distinctive taste or accompanied by a distinctive complex of visual and
auditory stimulation was followed by sickness induced by radiation or
by poisoning, or by immediate or delayed shock. Water-deprived rats
were accustomed to licking at a tube connected to a drinkometer to
obtain water. The taste of the water could be varied by adding flavors,
and a distinctive pattern of visual and auditory stimulation could be

associated with the water by arranging a circuit so that every lick at the tube produced a momentary flash of light and a click from a relay. In the irradiation study, the rats received three conditioning trials, separated by 3-day intervals. On the conditioning trials the drinkometer contained a 1% saccharine solution, and the light and sound were correlated with licking. The X-rays were administered during the trial. On subsequent test trials the Ss were presented either the saccharine solution without the light-sound contingency, or unsweetened "bright-noisy" water. The results were quite striking; there was a marked suppression of drinking the sweetened water, whereas drinking "bright-noisy" water was unaffected. In the poisoning study, the Ss drank a solution of lithium chloride, which produces anorexia, nausea, and other toxic symptoms in man and gastroenteritis in animals, associated with the light-click stimulus. They were tested with a salt solution which rats do not readily distinguish from the lithium chloride solution used (Nachman, 1963) and also with "bright-noisy" water. As in the X-ray study, suppression was exhibited when the solution tasted like the one drunk before the animal became ill, but not when the visual and auditory stimulation which had accompanied drinking the solution was presented with water. The delayed shock study was conducted simultaneously with the lithium chloride study. The animals drank the nontoxic saline solution. While the animals were drinking, shock was introduced with a gradually increasing intensity, so as to produce a drinking pattern similar to that exhibited by the animals drinking the lithium chloride solution. On test trials the Ss did not show a suppression of drinking when the salt solution was presented without the light-noise contingency, but did display a suppression of drinking when water was presented and the light-noise contingency was in effect. Similar results were obtained in another study in which shock was immediately contingent upon the first lick at the tube during the punishment sessions. These results, combined with those of a number of other experiments (Garcia and Ervin, 1968) have clearly shown that punishment with electric shock produces suppression of the punished response in the presence of visual and auditory stimuli associated with punishment, but does not produce an aversion to tastes present during punishment. Nausea is associated with tastes and odors, but not with visual and auditory stimulation.

The results of studies in the development of gustatory aversions again point up the dangers inherent in drawing broad generalizations concerning the behavioral effects of "aversive stimulation" from the available experimental literature. Almost all of our current knowledge of the effects of punishment is based upon studies of the effect of electric shock contingent upon food-motivated instrumental responding by domestic rats. It is tempting to simply dismiss from consideration studies using "unusual" aversive stimuli, motivating conditions, reference behaviors, or organisms when they yield results at variance with findings derived from more conventional experimental situations. It is, however, hard to justify such selection of data. If any of the aversive stimuli employed in laboratory investigations is "unnatural," it is electric shock. It is difficult to understand why lever pressing or running down an alley should be regarded as more useful in gaining understanding of behavior than feeding, copulation, or attack behavior; why hunger should be considered the fundamental motive underlying behavior; or why the domesticated rat should be regarded as the prototypic organism. Until the scope of research is broadened to include a greater variety of stimuli, responses, and organismic conditions, any conclusions about the mechanisms underlying the suppressive effects of punishment must be highly tentative.

ACKNOWLEDGMENT

Preparation of this chapter was completed under the tenure of Grant GB - 8041 from the National Science Foundation. The author would like to thank Alan Baron, Russell M. Church, Paul Van Hemel, and Susan Van Hemel for their helpful and detailed criticisms of an earlier version of the manuscript.

REFERENCES

Amsel, A. The effect upon level of consummatory response of the addition of anxiety to a motivational complex. *Journal of Experimental Psychology,* 1950, **40,** 709–715.

Amsel, A., & Cole, K.F. Generalization of fear motivated interference with water intake. *Journal of Experimental Psychology,* 1953, **46,** 243–247.

Amsel, A., & Maltzman, I. The effect upon generalized drive strength of emotionality as inferred from the level of consummatory response. *Journal of Experimental Psychology,* 1950, **40,** 563–569.

Anderson, D.C., Cole, J., & McVaugh, W. Variations in unsignaled inescapable preshock as determinants of responses to punishment. *Journal of Comparative and Physiological Psychology,* 1968, **65,** (3), Part 2.

Azrin, N.H. Some effects of two intermittent schedules of immediate and non-immediate punishment. *Journal of Psychology,* 1956, **42,** 3–21.

Azrin, N.H. Some effects of noise on human behavior. *Journal of the Experimental Analysis of Behavior,* 1958, **1,** 183–200.

Azrin, N.H., Hake, D.F., & Hutchinson, R.R. Elicitation of aggression by a physical blow. *Journal of the Experimental Analysis of Behavior,* 1965, **8,** 55–57.

Azrin, N.H., & Holz, W.C. Punishment. In W.K. Honig (ed.), *Operant behavior: Areas of research and application.* New York: Appleton, 1966. Pp. 380–447.

Azrin, N.H., Hutchinson, R.R., & Hake, D.F. Pain-induced fighting in the squirrel monkey. *Journal of the Experimental Analysis of Behavior,* 1963, **6,** 620–621.

Azrin, N.H., Hutchinson, R.R., & Hake, D.F. Attack, avoidance, and escape reactions to aversive shock, *Journal of the Experimental Analysis of Behavior,* 1967, **10,** 131–148.

Azrin, N.H., Hutchinson, R.R., & McLaughlin, R. The opportunity for aggression as an operant reinforcer during aversive stimulation. *Journal of the Experimental Analysis of Behavior,*1965, **8,** 171–180.

Azrin, N.H., Hutchinson, R.R., & Sallery, R.D. Pain-aggression toward inanimate objects. *Journal of the Experimental Analysis of Behavior,* 1964, **7,** 223–228.

Azrin, N.H., Rubin, H.B., & Hutchinson, R.R. Biting attack by rats in response to aversive shock. *Journal of the Experimental Analysis of Behavior,* 1968, **11,** 633–639.

Azrin, N.H., Ulrich, R.E., Hutchinson, R.R., & Norman, D.G. Effect of shock duration on shock-induced fighting. *Journal of the Experimental Analysis of Behavior,* 1964, **7,** 9–11.

Baenninger, R. Contrasting effects of fear and pain on mouse killing by rats. *Journal of Comparative and Physiological Psychology,* 1967, **63,** 298–303.

Banks, R.K., & Vogel-Sprott, M. Effect of delayed punishment on an immediately rewarded response in humans. *Journal of Experimental Psychology,* 1965, **70,** 357–359.

Barfield, R.J. & Sachs, B.D. Sexual behavior: stimulation by painful electric shock to the skin in male rats. *Science,* 1968, **161,** 393–395.

Barnes, G.W. & Kish, G.B. Reinforcing properties of the termination of intense auditory stimulation. *Journal of Comparative and Physiological Psychology,* 1957, **50,** 40–43.

Barnett, S.A. *The rat: A study in behavior.* Chicago, Illinois: Aldine, 1963.

Baron, A. Differential effects of fear on activity in novel and familiar environments. *Psychological Reports,* 1963, **13,** 251–257.

Baron, A. Suppression of exploratory behavior by aversive stimulation. *Journal of Comparative and Physiological Psychology,* 1964, **57,** 299–301.

Baron, A. Delayed punishment of a runway response. *Journal of Comparative and Physiological Psychology,* 1965, **60,** 131–134.

Baron, A., & Antonitis, J.J. Punishment and preshock as determinants of bar-pressing behavior. *Journal of Comparative and Physiological Psychology,* 1961, **54,** 716–720.

Barry, J.J., Jr., & Harrison, J.M. Relation between stimulus intensity and strength of escape responding. *Psychological Reports,* 1957, **3,** 3–8.

Bevan, W., Bell, R., & Lankford, H.G. The residual effect of shock upon bar-pressing for water. *Psychological Record,* 1967, **17,** 23–28.

Bevan, W., & Dukes, W.F. Effectiveness of delayed punishment on learning performance when preceded by premonitory cues. *Psychological Reports,* 1955, **1,** 441–448.

Bindra, D. Neuropsychological interpretation of the effects of drive and incentive-motivation on general activity and instrumental behavior. *Psychological Review,* 1968, **75,** 1–22.

Bindra, D. & Palfai, T. Nature of positive and negative incentive-motivational effects on general activity. *Journal of Comparative and Physiological Psychology,* 1967, **63,** 288–297.

Bitterman, M.E. Classical conditioning in the goldfish as a function of the CS–US interval. *Journal of Comparative and Physiological Psychology,* 1964, **58,** 359–366.

Blanchard, R.J. & Blanchard, D.C. Crouching as an index of fear. *Journal of Comparative and Physiological Psychology,* 1969, **67,** 370–375.

Blanchard, R.J., Dielman, T.E., & Blanchard, D.C. Prolonged after-effects of a single foot shock. *Psychonomic Science,* 1968, **10,** 327–328.

Bolles, R.C. *Theory of motivation.* New York: Harper, 1967.

Bolles, R.C., & Seelbach, S.E. Punishing and reinforcing effects of noise onset and termination for different responses. *Journal of Comparative and Physiological Psychology,* 1964, **58,** 127–131.

Bolles, R.C., & Warren, J.A., Jr. Effects of delay on the punishing and reinforcing effects of noise onset and termination. *Journal of Comparative and Physiological Psychology,* 1966, **61,** 475–477.

Brady, J.V., & Hunt, H.F. An experimental approach to the analysis of emotional behavior. *Journal of Psychology,* 1955, **40,** 313–324.

Braun, H.W., Wedekind, C.E., & Smudski, J.F. The effect of an irrelevant drive on maze learning in the rat. *Journal of Experimental Psychology,* 1957, **54,** 148–152.

Broadhurst, P.L. Emotionality and the Yerkes-Dodson law. *Journal of Experimental Psychology,* 1957, **54,** 345–352.

Bronson, G. W. The fear of novelty. *Psychological Bulletin,* 1968, **69,** 350–358

Brush, F.R. On the differences between animals that learn and do not learn to avoid electric shock. *Psychonomic Science,* 1966, **5,** 23–24.

Brush, F.R., & Levine, S. Adrenocortical activity and avoidance learning as a function of time after fear conditioning. *Physiology and Behavior,* 1966, **1,** 309–311.

Brush, F.R., Mook, D.G., & Davis, C.G. Conditioned and unconditioned responses as a function of shock intensity. Paper presented at Eastern Psychological Association Meeting, New York, 1960.

Brush, F.R., Myer, J.S., & Palmer, M.E. Effects of kind of prior training and intersession interval upon subsequent avoidance learning. *Journal of Comparative and Physiological Psychology,* 1963, **56,** 539–545.

Camp, D.S., Raymond, G.A., & Church, R.M. Temporal relationship between response and punishment. *Journal of Experimental Psychology,* 1967, **74,** 114–123.

Campbell, B.A., & Bloom, J.M. Relative aversiveness of noise and shock. *Journal of Comparative and Physiological Psychology,* 1965, **60,** 440–442.

Campbell, B.A., & Candland, D.K. Effects of prior shock on the emotionality of young rats in an open field. *Canadian Journal of Psychology,* 1961, **15,** 1–5.

Campbell, B.A., & Teghtsoonian, R. Electrical and behavioral effects of different types of shock stimuli on the rat. *Journal of Comparative and Physiological Psychology,* 1958, **51,** 185–192.

Church, R.M. The varied effects of punishment on behavior. *Psychological Review,* 1963, **70,** 369–402.

Church R.M. Systematic effect of random error in the yoked control design. *Psychological Bulletin,* 1964, **62,** 122–131.

Church, R.M., Raymond, G.A., & Beauchamp, R.D. Response suppression as a function of intensity and duration of a punishment. *Journal of Comparative and Physiological Psychology,* 1967, **63,** 39–44.

Church, R.M., & Solomon, R.L. Traumatic avoidance learning: The effects of delay of shock termination. *Psychological Reports,* 1956, **2,** 357–368.

Creer, T.L., Hitzing, E.W., & Schaeffer, R.W. Classical conditioning of reflexive fighting. *Psychonomic Science,* 1966, **4,** 89–90.

Culler, E., & Mettler, F.A. Conditioned behavior in a decorticate dog. *Journal of Comparative Psychology,* 1934, **18**, 291–303.

D'Amato, M.R., & Fazzaro, J. Discriminated lever-press avoidance learning as a function of type and intensity of shock. *Journal of Comparative and Physiological Psychology,* 1966, **61**, 313–315.

Daniel, W.J. An experimental note on the O'Kelly-Steckle reaction. *Journal of Comparative Psychology,* 1943, **35**, 267–268.

Darwin, C. *The expression of the emotions in man and animals.* New York: Appleton, 1872.

Davitz, J.R., Mason, D.J., Mowrer, O.H., & Viek, P. Conditioning of fear: A function of the delay of reinforcement. *American Journal of Psychology,* 1957, **70**, 69–74.

Dreyer, P.I., & Church, R.M. Shock-induced fighting as a function of the intensity and duration of the aversive stimulus. *Psychonomic Science,* 1968, **10**, 271–272.

Ducharme, R., & Belanger, D. Influence d'une stimulation electrique sur le niveau d'activation et la performance. *Canadian Journal of Psychology,* 1961, **15**, 61–68.

Ellis, N.R. The immediate effect of emotionality upon behavior strength. *Journal of Experimental Psychology,* 1957, **54**, 339–344.

Estes, W.K. An experimental study of punishment. *Psychological Monographs,* 1944, **57** (whole # 263).

Estes, W.K., & Skinner, B.F. Some quantitative properties of anxiety. *Journal of Experimental Psychology,* 1941, **29**, 390–400.

Etkin, W. (ed.) *Social behavior and organization among vertebrates.* Chicago, Illinois: University of Chicago Press, 1964.

Fowler, H. Facilitation and inhibition of performance by punishment: The effects of shock intensity and distribution of trials. *Journal of Comparative and Physiological Psychology,* 1963, **56**, 531–538.

Garcia, J., & Ervin, F.R. Gustatory-visceral and telereceptor-cutaneous conditioning-adaptation in internal and external milieus. *Communications in Behavioral Biology,* 1968, **2**, 389–415.

Garcia, J., & Koelling, R.A. Relation of cue to consequence in avoidance learning. *Psychonomic Science,* 1966, **4,** 123–124.

Gerbrandt, Lauren K. Neural systems of response release and control. *Psychological Bulletin,* 1965, **64**, 113–123.

Gibson, Eleanor J. The role of shock in reinforcement. *Journal of Comparative and Physiological Psychology,* 1952, **45**, 18–30.

Glaser, O.C. The formation of habits at high speed. *Journal of Comparative Neurology,* 1910, **20**, 165–184.

Goodman, E.D., Dyal, J.A., Zinser, O., & Golub, A. UCR morphology and shock intensity. *Psychonomic Science,* 1966, **5**, 431–432.

Grant, E.C., & Mackintosh, J.H. A comparison of the social postures of some common laboratory rodents. *Behaviour,* 1963, **21**, 246–259.

Green, E.J. An anchoring effect in the operant responding of rats. *American Journal of Psychology,* 1954, **67**, 141–142.

Griffith, C.R. The behavior of white rats in the presence of cats. *Psychobiology,* 1920, **2**, 19–28.

Guthrie, E.R. *The psychology of learning.* New York: Harper, 1935.

Gwinn, G.T. Effect of punishment on acts motivated by fear. *Journal of Experimental Psychology,* 1949, **39**, 260–269.

Hack, E.R. Learning as a function of water temperature. *Journal of Experimental Psychology*, 1933, **16**, 442–445.

Harrison, J.M., & Abelson, R.M. The maintenance of behavior by the termination and onset of intense noise. *Journal of the Experimental Analysis of Behavior*, 1959, **2**, 23–42.

Hediger, H. *Studies of the psychology and behavior of captive animals in zoos and circuses.* London and Washington, D.C.: Butterworth, 1955.

Hefferline, R.F. An experimental study of avoidance. *Genetic Psychology Monographs*, 1950, **42**, 231–334.

Henderson, R.L. Stimulus-intensity dynamism and secondary reinforcement. *Journal of Comparative and Physiological Psychology*, 1957, **50**, 339–344.

Herrnstein, R.J., & Sidman, M. Avoidance conditioning as a factor in the effects of unavoidable shocks on food-reinforced behavior. *Journal of Comparative and Physiological Psychology*, 1958, **51**, 380–385.

Hoffman, H.S., & Fleshler, M. Stimulus aspects of aversive controls: The effects of response contingent shock. *Journal of the Experimental Analysis of Behavior*, 1965, **8**, 89–96.

Hoffman, H.S., Fleshler, M., & Abplanalp, P.L. Startle reaction to electrical shock in the rat. *Journal of Comparative and Physiological Psychology*, 1964, **58**, 132–139.

Holz, W.C., & Azrin, N.H. Recovery during punishment by intense noise. *Psychological Reports*, 1962, **11**, 655–657.

Hull, C.L. *Principles of behavior.* New York: Appleton, 1943.

Hunt, H.F., & Brady, J.V. Some effects of punishment and intercurrent "anxiety" on a simple operant. *Journal of Comparative and Physiological Psychology*, 1955, **48**, 305–310.

Hutchinson, R.R., Azrin, N.H., & Renfrew, J.W. Effects of shock intensity and duration on the frequency of biting attack by squirrel monkeys. *Journal of the Experimental Analysis of Behavior*, 1968, **11**, 83–88.

Irwin, F.W. On desire, aversion, and the affective zero. *Psychological Review*, 1961, **68**, 293–300.

Jerome, E.A., Moody, J.A., Connor, T.J., & Fernandez, M.B. Learning in a multiple-door situation under various drive states. *Journal of Comparative and Physiological Psychology*, 1957, **50**, 588–591.

Kamin, L.J. The retention of an incompletely learned avoidance response. *Journal of Comparative and Physiological Psychology*, 1957, **50**, 457–460.

Kamin, L.J. Temporal and intensity characteristics of the conditioned stimulus. In W.F. Prokasy (Ed.). *Classical conditioning: A symposium.* New York: Appleton, 1965.

Kaplan, M. The effects of noxious stimulus intensity during intermittent reinforcement of escape behavior, *Journal of Comparative and Physiological Psychology*, 1952, **45**, 538–549.

Kaplan, M. Amplitude of respiratory movements as a function of noxious stimulus intensity. *Psychological Reports*, 1957, **3**, 429–438.

Kaplan, M., Jackson, B., & Sparer, R. Escape behavior under continuous reinforcement as a function of aversive light intensity. *Journal of the Experimental Analysis of Behavior*, 1965, **8**, 321–323.

Kelleher, R.T., & Morse, W.H. Escape behavior and punished behavior. *Federation Proceedings*, 1964, **23**, 808–817.

Keller, F.S. Light-aversion in the white rat. *Psychological Record*, 1941, **4**, 235–250.

Keller, F.S., & Schoenfeld, W.N. *Principles of psychology.* New York: Appleton, 1950.

Kimble, G.A. Shock intensity and avoidance learning. *Journal of Comparative and Physiological Psychology*, 1955, **48**, 281–284.

Klugh, H.E., & Patton, R.A. Escape behavior of monkeys from low intensity tone. *Psychological Reports*, 1959, **5**, 573–578.

Konorski, J. *Integrative activity of the brain: An interdisciplinary approach*. Chicago, Illinois: University of Chicago Press, 1967.

Landis, C., & Hunt, W.A. *The startle pattern*. New York: Farrar and Rinehart, 1939.

Levine, S. Noxious stimulation in infant and adult rats and consummatory behavior. *Journal of Comparative and Physiological Psychology*, 1958, **51**, 230–233.

Levine, S. Water consumption: Emotionally produced facilitation or suppression? *Psychonomic Science*, 1965, **3**, 105–106.

Lichtenstein, P.E. Studies of anxiety: 1. The production of a feeding inhibition in dogs. *Journal of Comparative Physiology*, 1950, **43**, 16–29.

Libby, A. Two variables in the acquisition of depressant properties of a stimulus. *Journal of Experimental Psychology*, 1951, **42**, 100–108.

Liddell, H.S., James, W.T., & Anderson, O.D. The comparative physiology of the conditioned motor reflex. *Comparative Psychology Monographs*, 1934, **11**, (1 Whole number 51).

LoLordo, V.M. Similarity of conditioned fear responses based upon different aversive events. *Journal of Comparative and Physiological Psychology*, 1967, **64**, 154–158.

Marler, P.R., & Hamilton, W.J. *Mechanisms of animal behavior*. New York: Wiley, 1966.

Mason, W.A., & Stone, C.P. Maze performance of rats under conditions of surface and underwater swimming. *Journal of Comparative and Physiological Psychology*, 1953, **46**, 159–165.

Masserman, J.H. *Behavior and neurosis*. Chicago, Illinois: University of Chicago Press, 1943.

McCleary, R.A. Response specificity in the behavioral effects of limbic system lesions in the cat. *Journal of Comparative and Physiological Psychology*, 1961, **54**, 605–613.

Melzack, R., & Wall, P. D. Pain mechanisms: A new theory. *Science*, 1965, **150**, 971–979.

Meyer, D.R., Cho, C., & Wesemann, A.F. On problems of conditioning discriminated lever-press avoidance responses. *Psychological Review*, 1960, **67**, 224–228.

Miller, N.E. Studies of fear as an acquirable drive: 1. Fear as motivation and fear-reduction as reinforcement in the learning of new responses. *Journal of Experimental Psychology*, 1948, **38**, 89–101.

Miller, N.E. Theory and experiment relating psychoanalytic displacement to stimulus-response generalization. *Journal of Abnormal and Social Psychology*, 1948, **43**, 155–178.

Miller, N.E. Learnable drives and rewards. Chapter 13, In S.S. Stevens, (Ed.) *Handbook of experimental psychology*. New York: Wiley, 1951.

Miller, N.E., & Dollard, J. *Social learning and imitation*. New Haven, Connecticut: Yale University Press, 1941.

Montgomery, K.C., & Monkman, J.A. The relation between fear and exploratory behavior. *Journal of Comparative and Physiological Psychology*, 1955, **48**, 132–136.

Mowrer, O.H. A stimulus-response analysis of anxiety and its role as a reinforcing agent. *Psychological Review*, 1939, **46**, 553–565.

Mowrer, O.H. On the dual nature of learning—A reinterpretation of conditioning and problem solving. *Harvard Educational Review*, 1947, **17**, 102–148.

Mowrer, O.H. *Learning theory and behavior.* New York: Wiley, 1960.

Moyer, K.E. Effect of experience with emotion provoking stimuli on water consumption in the rat. *Psychonomic Science,* 1965, **2,** 251–252.

Moyer, K.E., & Baenninger, R. Effect of environmental change and electric shock on water consumption in the rat. *Psychological Reports,* 1963, **13,** 179–185.

Moyer, K.E., & Korn, J.H. Effect of UCS intensity on the acquisition and extinction of an avoidance response. *Journal of Experimental Psychology,* 1964, **67,** 352–359.

Muenzinger, K.F., & Mize, R.H. The sensitivity of the white rat to electric shock: Threshold and skin resistance. *Journal of Comparative Psychology,* 1933, **15,** 139–148.

Myer, J.S. Stimulus control of mouse-killing rats. *Journal of Comparative and Physiological Psychology,* 1964, **58,** 112–117.

Myer, J.S. Punishment of instinctive behavior: Suppression of mouse-killing by rats. *Psychonomic Science,* 1966, **4,** 385–386.

Myer, J.S. Prior killing experience and the suppressive effects of punishment on the killing of mice by rats. *Animal Behavior,* 1967, **15,** 59–61.

Myer, J.S. Associative and temporal determinants of facilitation and inhibition of attack by pain. *Journal of Comparative and Physiological Psychology,* 1968, **66,** 17–21.

Myer, J.S., & Baenninger, R. Some effects of punishment and stress on mouse killing by rats. *Journal of Comparative and Physiological Psychology,* 1966, **62,** 292–297.

Myer, J.S., & Ricci, D. Delay of punishment gradients for the goldfish. *Journal of Comparative and Physiological Psychology,* 1968, **66,** 417–421.

Nachman, M. Learned aversion to the taste of lithium chloride and generalization to other salts. *Journal of Comparative and Physiological Psychology,* 1963, **56,** 343–349.

O'Kelly, L.I., & Steckle, L.C. A note on long enduring emotional responses in the rat. *Journal of Psychology,* 1939, **8,** 125–131.

Pavlov, I.P. *Conditioned reflexes.* Translated by G.P. Anrep. London and New York: Oxford University Press, 1927.

Renner, K.E. Temporal integration: Relative value of rewards and punishments as a function of their temporal distance from the response. *Journal of Experimental Psychology,* 1966, **71,** 902–907.

Rescorla, R.A. Pavlovian conditioning and its proper control procedures. *Psychological Review,* 1967, **74,** 71–80.

Rescorla, R.A., & Solomon, R.L. Two-process learning theory: Relationships between Pavlovian conditioning and instrumental learning. *Psychological Review,* 1967, **74,** 151–182.

Revusky, S.H. Aversion to sucrose produced by contingent x-irradiation: Temporal and dosage parameters. *Journal of Comparative and Physiological Psychology,* 1968, **65,** 17–22.

Richter, C.P. Domestication of the Norway rat and its implications for the problem of stress. In H.G. Wolff *et al.* (Eds.), *Life stress and bodily disease.* Baltimore, Maryland: Williams and Wilkins, 1950.

Roberts, C.L., & Larson, C. Shock history and adaptation as parameters of elicited aggression in rats. *Psychological Record,* 1967, **17,** 425–428.

Scott, J.P. *Aggression.* Chicago, Illinois: University of Chicago Press, 1958.

Sidman, M., Herrnstein, R.J., & Conrad, D.G. Maintenance of avoidance behavior by unavoidable shocks. *Journal of Comparative and Physiological Psychology,* 1957, **50,** 553–557.

Siegel, P.S., & Brantley, J.J. The relationship of emotionality to the consummatory response of eating. *Journal of Experimental Psychology*, 1951, **42**, 304–306.

Siegel, P.S., & Siegel, H.S. The effect of emotionality on water intake in the rat. *Journal of Comparative and Physiological Psychology*, 1949, **42**, 12–16.

Siegel, P.S., & Sparks, D.L. Irrelevant aversive stimulation as an activator of an appetitional response: A replication. *Psychological Reports*, 1961, **9**, 700.

Skinner, B.F. *The behavior of organisms: An experimental analysis.* New York: Appleton, 1938.

Smith, J.C., & Roll, D.L. Trace conditioning with x-rays as the aversive stimulus. *Psychonomic Science*, 1967, **9**, 11–12.

Solomon, R.L., & Brush, E.S. Experimentally derived conceptions of anxiety and aversion. In M.R. Jones (Ed.), *Nebraska Symposium on Motivation.* Lincoln, Nebraska: University of Nebraska Press, 1956.

Solomon, R.L., Turner, L.H., & Lessac, M.S. Some effects of delay of punishment on resistance to temptation in dogs. *Journal of Personality and Social Psychology*, 1968, **8**, 233–238.

Sterritt, G.M. Inhibition and facilitation of eating by electric shock. *Journal of Comparative and Physiological Psychology*, 1962, **55**, 226–229.

Sterritt, G.M. Inhibition and facilitation of eating by electric shock: III. A further study of the role of strain and of shock level. *Psychonomic Science*, 1965, **2**, 319–320.

Sterritt, G.M., & Shemberg, K. Inhibition and facilitation of eating by electric shock: II. Shock level, shock schedule and strain of rats. *Journal of Psychosomatic Research*, 1963, **7**, 215–223.

Stewart, C.N., Abplanalp, P.H., & Warren, J.M. Unconditioned responses to electrical shock by cats. *Journal of Comparative and Physiological Psychology*, 1965, **60**, 449–451.

Strongman, K.T. The effect of anxiety on food intake in the rat. *Quarterly Journal of Experimental Psychology*, 1965, **17**, 255–260.

Strongman, K.T. The effect of prior exposure to shock on a visual discrimination by rats. *Canadian Journal of Psychology*, 1967, **21**, 57–58.

Tinbergen, N. *The study of instinct.* London and New York: Oxford University Press, 1951.

Trabasso, T.R., & Thompson, R.W. Supplementary report: Shock intensity and unconditioned responding in a shuttle box. *Journal of Experimental Psychology*, 1962, **63**, 215–216.

Ullman, A.D. The experimental production and analysis of a "compulsive eating symptom" in rats. *Journal of Comparative and Physiological Psychology*, 1951, **44**, 575–581.

Ullman, A.D. Three factors involved in producing "compulsive eating" in rats. *Journal of Comparative and Physiological Psychology*, 1952, **45**, 490–496.

Ulrich, R.E., & Azrin, N.H. Reflexive fighting in response to aversive stimulation. *Journal of the Experimental Analysis of Behavior*, 1962, **5**, 511–520.

Ulrich, R.E., & Craine, W.H. Behavior: Persistence of shock-induced aggression. *Science*, 1964, **143**, 968–970.

Ulrich, R.E., Hutchinson, R.R., & Azrin, N.H. Pain-elicited aggression. *Psychological Record*, 1965, **15**, 111–126.

Ulrich, R.E., Wolff, P.C., & Azrin, N.H. Shock as an elicitor of intra- and inter-species fighting behavior. *Animal Behavior*, 1964, **12**, 14–15.

Vernon, W., & Ulrich, R. Classical conditioning of pain-elicited aggression. *Science,* 1966, **152,** 668–669.

Warden, C.J., & Diamond, S.A. A preliminary study of the effect of delayed punishment on learning in the white rat. *Journal of Genetic Psychology,* 1931, **39,** 455–461.

Watson, J.B. *Behaviorism.* (Rev. ed.) Chicago, Illinois: University of Chicago Press, 1930.

Watson, J.B., & Rayner, R. Conditioned emotional reactions. *Journal of Experimental Psychology,* 1920, 3, 1–14.

Webb, W.B., & Goodman, I.J. Activating role of an irrelevant drive in absence of the relevant drive. *Psychological Reports,* 1958, **4,** 235–238.

Weiss, J.M., Krieckhaus, E.E., & Conte, R. Effects of fear conditioning on subsequent avoidance behavior and movement. *Journal of Comparative and Physiological Psychology,* 1968, **65,** 413–421.

Wever, E.G. Water temperature as an incentive to swimming activity in the rat. *Journal of Comparative Psychology,* 1932, **14,** 219–224.

Winnick, W.A., & Hunt, J. McV. The effect of an extra stimulus upon strength of responses during acquisition and extinction. *Journal of Experimental Psychology,* 1951, **41,** 205–215.

Woods, P.J., & Campbell, B.A. Relative aversiveness of white noise and cold water. *Journal of Comparative and Physiological Psychology,* 1967, **64,** 493–495.

CHAPTER 9

Suppression and Facilitation by Response Contingent Shock

HARRY FOWLER

University of Pittsburgh
Pittsburgh, Pennsylvania

I. INTRODUCTION TO THE STUDY OF PUNISHMENT

Current theoretical opinion on the subject of punishment seems to prevail much as a negative reaction to the viewpoint that was popularized during the thirties and forties. Following Thorndike's (1932) restatement of the law of effect, in which the consequences of verbal "annoyers" were relegated to an ineffective status, the now classic bar-slap study by Skinner (1938) and the related more extensive experimental work by Estes (1944) involving electric shock highlighted an effect of punishment that was, at best, only temporarily suppressing: Applied during the extinction of a bar-press response, punishment suppressed response rate in accord with the severity of the punishing stimulus but responding recovered with the removal of the punisher, even to the point of suggesting an increase in rate compensatory for the suppression that had initially been produced. These observations, coupled with those relating to the clinical interpretation of punishment as something inevitably disruptive, leading possibly to neurotic outcome (*e.g.,* Maier, 1949; Masserman, 1943), soon fostered the widespread belief—or "legend" as Solomon (1964) has characterized it—that punishment was ineffective in eliminating behavior, and therefore a procedure to be avoided whenever possible.

Contrasting with this earlier attitude, present-day accounts of punishment (*e.g.,* Azrin & Holz, 1966; Church, 1963; Solomon, 1964) have stressed that, as a behavioral control, punishment is at least as effective if not better than other procedures used to eliminate responding. It can work, and when it works, it invariably suppresses the behavior that it follows. Clearly, the accumulation of present findings on punishment supports such a contention, and thus at a descriptive level, one must agree that punishment can have the effect of suppressing behavior, temporarily or even permanently (*e.g.,* Boe & Church, 1967; Appel, 1963;

Storms, Boroczi, & Broen, 1962). Nonetheless, it should be considered that such an emphasis on the effectiveness of punishment in reducing or eliminating behavior, like the opposite argument of prior years, may seriously hinder our understanding of the nature of the phenomenon, causing us possibly to confuse the *functions* and *mechanisms of operation* of the punishment contingency with its currently renowned and pronounced *effect* of producing suppression. In part, this confusion finds its basis in our failure to provide a clear distinction between a punishing stimulus and the punishment procedure, and similarly to treat clearly the several varieties of definition that have been applied to the latter.

A. Approaches to a Definition of Punishment

Definitions of punishment range from the generally employed procedural statement of presenting some noxious stimulus contingent upon an active response[1] to the more specialized designation of punishment as an "annoying after-effect," as "discomfort" following a response (Thorndike, 1911, 1913), or in a more theoretical vein as the occurrence of a response-produced drive state (*cf.* Dollard & Miller, 1950). These latter definitions have been looked upon disparagingly by current researchers (*e.g.,* Azrin & Holz, 1966) primarily because of their reference to "subjective" states and theoretical inferences about behavior, and the difficulty attendant on measuring any such inferred states of the organism. Contrary to this opinion, however, the "subjective" definitions have had a firm empirical base. Thus, Thorndike (1913) was careful to define the "discomfort" of punishment as a condition which the organism would independently avoid or abandon: "one which the organism does nothing to preserve, often doing things which put an end to it." (Thorndike, 1913, p. 2.) Comparably, with reference to the designation of punishment as a drive state, recognition of the usual defining operation of drive as intense stimulation implicates punishment as a "relatively sudden and painful increase of stimulation following the performance of some act." (Mowrer, 1947, p. 136.) Placed in their proper perspective, then, these specialized definitions of punishment reflect exactly that, special cases of the generally accepted procedural definition of presenting a noxious stimulus contingent upon some response.

---

[1]Although not generally acknowledged, investigations of punishment implicate an active response (*i.e.,* a specific *motor* reaction) as opposed to the passive behavior that is "punished" in escape and avoidance tasks where, contrariwise, termination or postponement of the noxious timulus is made contingent upon a specific motor reaction. Considering that a class of "not doing" or "stopping" behaviors could be specified as the punished reaction, however, a procedural definition of punishment would seem to require the designation of only a *specific* response, that is, apart from its active or passive nature.

In this light, the problem of defining punishment may be reduced to one of determining whether a stimulus is aversive or not, and then of determining whether the aversive stimulus occurs in a contingent relationship to the specified response. (Hereafter, the terms *noxious* and *aversive* will be used interchangeably in designating the punishing stimulus.)

Either of two approaches may be adopted to determine whether a stimulus is aversive: the *operational* or transituational approach where, independent of the punishment procedure, the stimulus is shown to be aversion-producing, as for example in generating escape or avoidance behaviors; and the *functional* or intrasituational approach where the aversion-producing properties of the stimulus are reflected within the punishment situation itself, *i.e.,* by an effected suppression of the punished act. With both of these approaches, punishment is thus viewed as the counterpart of reinforcement: in the functional sense of producing the specific *effect* of suppressing rather than reinforcing a certain behavior; and, in the operational sense of providing an independent basis by which it can be demonstrated that the animal will escape or avoid the stimulus, as opposed to selecting and approaching it, as in a preference task. Over the years, most investigators have subscribed to the operational definition of punishment (*e.g.,* Dinsmoor, 1954; Keller & Schoenfeld, 1950; Skinner, 1953; Solomon, 1964; Thorndike, 1911, 1913). presumably because of the independence of operations for noxious and punishing stimuli, and hence, the absence with this approach of any confounding of aversion and punishment effects. Nonetheless, this general subscription to the operational approach has not precluded an outcropping of objections to it.

While there is no particular difficulty in demonstrating aversion to a noxious stimulus, as in escape or avoidance tasks, there does prevail the foremost problem of insuring that the parameters of the noxious-stimulus condition used to generate escape and avoidance are in fact the same as those employed in the punishment procedure. It does no good, for example, to demonstrate that an animal will avoid the shock side of a tilt-box preference arrangement where shock has been presented continuously or discontinuously over an extended period or session of training and then to employ the same intensity of shock in a punishing situation where the shock is administered but for a brief duration. Strictly considered, the parameters (*i.e.,* the duration and frequency of occurrence) of the punishing stimulus are not those of the aversive stimulus defined in the tilt-box experiment. Similarly, one must insure that the treatment history of the animals subjected to aversion testing, as well as the particular animal population itself, is duplicated in punishment testing.

Another problem prevails regarding a possible dual effect of a single stimulus, as for example both an aversion and an approach-producing effect. Logan and Wagner (1965) have suggested that attempts to treat

punishment as the reciprocal operation of reward may run afoul of findings like Bower and Miller's (1958) which show that a rat will learn to
press a bar to turn on an electrical stimulus to its brain and then press
another bar to turn the same stimulus off. It would seem, however, that
this problem may be reduced to a matter of parameter specification also,
since the time course of the rewarding and punishing effects of brain
stimulation is disparate. Consequently, it can be argued that the aversion
produced by the brain stimulus, once it is on for a period, is sufficient to warrant its use as a noxious stimulus in the punishment procedure, *i.e.*, under the
same temporal conditions.

Other, less formidable objections to the operational approach have
stressed that the prerequisite demonstration of escape or avoidance
places punishment in the perspective of a secondary process, and similarly that the effects of punishment are then to be viewed as resulting
indirectly from an escape or avoidance reaction (Azrin & Holz, 1966).
These objections cannot be taken seriously, however, if one considers
that in reverse fashion the punishment procedure could just as well be
employed to provide an independent demonstration of the noxiousness
of a stimulus that is then to be used in an escape or avoidance task, that
is, with the point of focus now being on the latter.

It would appear then, in this process of distilling objections to the
operational approach, that the only major consideration is one of an
identity of parameters across independent situations, *i.e.*, across punishment and aversion conditions. In this respect, the problem may be
viewed simply as a matter of additional work and/or experimental re-
finement. But, herein prevails the crux of the problem—indeed, the
singular objection. Serious effort simply has not been given to
demonstrating independently the noxiousness of the stimulus to be employed in the punishment procedure. Virtually all studies on punishment are without such effort and consequently in practice, if not in
principle, investigators have favored the functional approach.

B. Implications of a Functional Definition

Commitment to a functional definition of punishment has not been by
default alone, for several investigators (*e.g.*, Azrin & Holz, 1966; Church,
1963; Deese, 1958) have presented positive arguments for it. For example, Azrin and Holz (1966) maintain that beyond the practical consideration of not having to be concerned with independent demonstrations of
the noxiousness of the punishing stimulus, it is similarly not necessary to
record "hypothesized—but thus far unrecorded—escape responses that
are presumed to produce the response reduction." (Azrin & Holz, 1966,
p. 382.) Furthermore, the functional approach "focuses the investigator's

attention on the independent variables [presumably relating to the punishing stimulus] rather than on a set of 'competing' behaviors that are often given 'explanatory' status." (*ibid.*) Whether these considerations represent a distinct advantage of the functional approach is a matter open to dispute; indeed, even the empirical basis for these statements may be questioned. Nonetheless, it is not to be denied that, along with its practical advantage, the functional approach has been highly productive in enabling a determination of those parameters of the punishing stimulus that are effective in suppressing behavior. In particular, the work by Azrin and Holz (1966; see also Church, 1969) has shown that amount of suppression is positively related to (a) the severity of the punishing stimulus, in terms of both its intensity and duration, (b) the immediacy of presentation of the punishing stimulus following the punished act, (c) the abruptness of its introduction or increment, (d) its scheduled frequency of occurrence, as in continuous versus intermittent schedules, and (e) its variability of presentation as in VI versus FI schedules. Collectively, these findings support the contention that punichment is a process similar to reinforcement in terms of its determinants, but opposite in terms of its effects; as such, the data speak well of a functional approach to the definition of punishment.

Unfortunately, the matter of response suppression is not so simple, for there are variables other than the parameters of punishment that are influential with respect to a determination of the degree of suppression that is attained, as well as the fact of suppression itself. Recent work by several investigators suggests that the degree of suppression of a punished act may well relate to the degree of control that the animal exerts over the punishment contingency. Thus, Leitenberg (1965) has shown that a nonreinforced operant is more effectively suppressed when the punishment (intense light) is of a fixed duration than when its duration is controlled by the rat's latency of escape from the punishing stimulus. This finding seems not to be explained simply on the basis of longer and possibly more severe punishment with the fixed duration condition since essentially the same outcome prevails when the average duration of punishment in the escape condition is matched through the use of a yoked control (Leitenberg, 1967; but see Church, 1964).

In a similar vein, it has been shown for pigeons that suppression by shock of a food-reinforced pecking response is far more effective when there exists an alternative unpunished response that also leads to food reinforcement (see Azrin & Holz, 1966), or when an additional response is available which is not food reinforced but permits the animal to escape (*i.e.*, gain a period of safety) from the punishment schedule (Azrin, Hake, Holz & Hutchinson, 1965). Particularly impressive are the correlative findings reported by Azrin *et al.* (1965) showing that this alternative "escape" response can be maintained by FR and FI schedules of escape reinforcement, will continue to prevail even though the frequency of food reinforcement is reduced as a consequence of escape responding, and most important, that the escape response will initially develop at intensities of punishment that have little or no effect on a response where escape is not possible. Here are circumstances where, from the standpoint of a functional approach, a particular stimulus is to be classified as a punisher, but this same stimulus when of comparable severity and yet even greater frequency (as a consequence of a procedure that does not permit escape) does not so qualify.

The same considerations prevail with respect to the role that reinforcement can have in determining whether a particular stimulus is to be classified as a punisher. In contrast to the operational approach, where the aversiveness of a stimulus can be assayed via escape from that stimulus alone, the functional approach is typically committed to an outcome based on the interaction of both aversive and reinforcing stimuli. This occurs for the reason that, in order to demonstrate a suppression effect, the punished response must initially be developed and maintained at some strength, as is generally effected through the administration of reinforcement. In this light, it is not surprising that the degree of suppression which obtains from the same punishing stimulus varies considerably with the magnitude of reinforcement (*e.g.*, Bower & Miller, 1960; but see Ferraro, 1966) or with the frequency and schedule of reinforcement (*e.g.*, Azrin, 1959; Azrin & Holz, 1966). Differences in outcome associated with the use of different schedules of reinforcement are especially significant. Whereas punishment of each response under FI reinforcement typically results in a reduced rate of responding, the same schedule of punishment with FR reinforcement does not, despite the fact that there can be a considerably greater frequency of punishment with reinforcement administered on an FR schedule. (The main effect of punishment with FR reinforcement is to increase the postreinforcement pause, with the "run" of responses being relatively unaltered; see Azrin & Holz, 1966.)

These considerations point up the fact that, by adopting a functional approach to the definition of punishment, we are committed to saying that a particular stimulus is a punisher under one condition of reinforcement and not under another. Yet, whether we adopt a functional or an operational approach to the definition of punishment, we are committed to a procedural operation for punishment which is based on an aversive-stimulus contingency, and not on the specification of reinforcement, its amount, frequency, or schedule of occurrence. The foregoing findings indicate, however, that our acceptance of the functional definition requires a comparable acceptance of the parameters of reinforcement as determinants of the punishment effect—and thus of the punishing stimulus itself.

Although there are other considerations bearing on the implications of a functional approach, as for example whether the effects of punishment do in fact mirror those of reward—a circumstance which also seems not to prevail (see Logan & Wagner, 1965), the foregoing should suffice to point up a significant fact: The functional approach requires a *circularity* in the definition of punishment which simply cannot be dismissed. What is determined by a fuctional definition to be a punisher in one context is not always the same punisher in another, and is sometimes not a punisher at all. Indeed, as the remainder of this chapter shows, there are those situations in which punishment does not have a weakening or suppressing effect, but comparable to the strengthening effect of reward, it actually facilitates the behavior that is being punished. Selectively considered, these facilitating effects of punishment would suggest that the function of punishment is to strengthen the punished response; of course, such an approach would be equally restrictive. For this reason, it is imperative that consideration be given not simply to the suppressing effects of punishment but rather to the varied effects of punishment, not simply for the reason of challenging a suppression interpretation of the function of punishment, but rather for the broader purpose of pointing up possibily different and yet equally important functions of the punishment procedure.

C. Plan and Scope of the Chapter

In order to illuminate different functions of the punishment procedure, the remainder of this chapter reflects a "reverse" strategy in which it is asked, not under what conditions does punishment suppress behavior, but rather under what conditions does punishment operate so as to facilitate the behavior that is being punished. By selectively focusing on these facilitating effects of punishment, we are committed to a determination of those functions of punishment which are apart from any suppressing function. This is not to say that we shall dismiss completely the suppressing effects of punishment, for to the extent that varied effects reflect varied functions, it is likely similarly that the singular effect of suppression can be mediated by different functions. Thus, a secondary aim of this chapter will be to evaluate the extent to which the suppression produced by punishment is actually indicative of a suppression function. Furthermore, by assaying the varied functions of punishment, we shall be in a position to compare these functions with those of a nonaversive stimulus contingency, *i.e.*, where the procedural operation for punishment is met through the use of a "neutral" rather than a noxious stimulus. In turn, these comparisons should enable us to determine which of those functions of punishment are in fact peculiar to the aversive-stimulus contingency.

It should be made clear that our concern will not be simply with facilitation in general, but specifically with those instances of so-called "paradoxical" facilitation. There are many circumstances under which punishment can facilitate performance, as for example when punishment is selectively administered in a choice context for incorrect responses, and as a result acquisition of the correct, food-reinforced response is facilitated (*e.g.*, Yerkes & Dodson, 1908; Hoge & Stocking, 1912; Warden & Aylesworth, 1927). Or to cite a more recent phenomenon, when punishment is administered for responses in a temporal sequence that is generated by differential reinforcement of low rates (DRL), and as a consequence of the increased frequency of long inter-response times effected by punishment, performance is similarly facilitated (*e.g.*, Bruner, 1967; Holz, Azrin & Ulrich, 1963). These findings of facilitated performance are consistent with a suppression interpretation of the function of punishment in that wrong responses or short interresponse times leading to punishment, or more frequent punishment, are reduced and eliminated. However, there are those paradoxical effects of punishment which show facilitated performance where a suppression effect is clearly expected. A classic example is Muenzinger's (1934) finding that punishment of a correct, food-reinforced response in a visual discrimination task does not retard the learning of this response, but instead facilitates it, and almost as well as when the same punishment is administered for the incorrect response.

Along with a selective emphasis on paradoxical facilitation, our attention will be restricted to those circumstances where such facilitation is produced by response-contingent electric shock. Our purpose in focusing on shock as a punishing stimulus is actually twofold: First, studies on punishment have generally used electric shock to satisfy the aversive-stimulus contingency required by the punishment operation. More importantly, however, our plan to assay those functions of punishment that may be reflected by paradoxical facilitation commits us essentially to an operational approach in which the noxiousness of the punishing stimulus must be independently substantiated. Fortunately, recent psychophysical research by Campbell and Masterson (1969) indicates that the difference in detection and aversion thresholds to electric shock is at best a small one, if indeed there is any difference at all. Thus, when electric shock of any intensity is used as a punishing stimulus, it is a *relatively* safe assumption that the aversive-stimulus contingency has been met. This, of course, is not to dismiss the above-noted limitations of the operational approach or even the observation that under some conditions, particularly those simulating sensory deprivation, extremely weak shock may serve in itself as a positive reinforcer (*e.g.*, Harrington & Linder, 1962; Harrington & Kohler, 1966). For these reasons, we shall endeavor where possible to point up both facilitating and suppressing effects of the same shock stimulus applied as a punisher under comparable conditions of experimentation.

Following the above plan, the remaining sections of this chapter are structured about two broad (and arbitrary) classes of study of paradoxical effects: the first bearing on the possible stimulus or "cue" functions of punishment, and the second relating to the response-eliciting functions of punishment. This classification is essentially representative of a treatment in which punishment is viewed primarily with respect to its effects as a stimulus, first as conditioned stimulus (CS) and secondly as an unconditioned stimulus (US) or response elicitor.

II. STIMULUS (CUE) PROPERTIES OF PUNISHMENT

Note has already been made of the fact that punishment is usually administered along with reinforcement, for the reason that some fairly high level of responding must initially prevail so as to permit a suppressing effect of punishment to be evident. Considered further, however, it is apparent that this general procedure implicates a specific temporal patterning of events in which the response in question is followed by punishment and *then* by reinforcement. That is to say, when both punishment and reinforcement are immediately contingent upon a response, the operations involved are such as to promote a continguous presentation of the punishing and reinforcing stimuli, but the nature and topography of the responses to these stimuli generally permit the punishment to antedate the reinforcement. In the case of a rat that is bar-pressing for both food and shock, for example, the shock is circuited such that it is delivered immediately upon execution of the response, *and similarly the food,* but following the response and delivery of both food and shock, the animal must still approach the food cup in order to gain the reinforcer; indeed, even if the shock were contingent upon the *S*'s contact with food, and barring whatever withdrawal reactions might be elicited by the shock, the punishment would still antedate the reinforcement occasioned with the *S*'s consummation of the food object.

So considered, the punishment procedure is one in which an aversive stimulus, like shock, can actually signal and thereby mediate the influence of reinforcement. In effect, the aversive stimulus becomes a CS for food, an observation which Pavlov (1927) accorded specific note:

The organism responds by a violent motor reaction directed towards removal of the nucuous stimulus or to its own removal from it. But we may, nevertheless, make use even of these stimuli for the establishment of a new conditioned reflex. Thus in one particular experiment a strong nocuous stimulus—an electric current of great strength—was converted into an alimentary conditioned stimulus, so that its application to the skin did not evoke the slightest defence reaction. Instead, the animal exhibited a well-marked alimentary conditioned reflex, turning its head to where it usually received the food and smacking its lips, at the same time producing a profuse secretion of saliva. (Pavlov, 1927, p. 29 f.)

Taken together with the noted patterning of punishing and reinforcing events, Pavlov's observations (see also Masserman, 1943) lead us to consider the manner in which *response-contingent* shock might similarly serve as a "cue" for continued responding, as in an operant context, or as a CS mediating reinforcement of the punished response itself. Accordingly, in the following subsections, attention is directed to shock's potential function within the punishment procedure both as a discriminative stimulus and as a secondary reinforcer, and then apart from these two functions, simply as a highly discernible or distinctive cue.

A   Discriminative Stimulus Function

Formal investigation of the role of response-contingent shock as a signal (*i.e.,* as a discriminative stimulus) for responding in an operant context, and thus as a basis by which punishment could facilitate performance, was first accomplished by Holz and Azrin (1961, 1962). Previously, however, in a study focusing on schedules that involved multiple aversive control, Appel (1960b) inadvertently uncovered a discriminative control by shock-punishment.

In Appel's (1960b) experiment, monkeys were initially trained on a Sidman avoidance schedule to postpone shock for 20 sec by making a lever press; then, the Ss were confronted with a multiple schedule in which the avoidance contingency was signalled by a white light and a punishment component (*i.e.,* response-contingent shock presented on a VI 1-min schedule) signalled by a green light. Under this multiple schedule, the Ss quickly learned to discriminate between the signal lights, showing a continued high rate of responding during the white light (avoidance period) and a low, suppressed rate of responding during the green light (punishment period). In a subsequent phase of the experiment, however, the stimulus lights were removed with the avoidance and punishment components being presented alternately in a mixed schedule. Herein, the Ss continued to show just as proficient discrimination performance as they had previously, even though all external stimulus controls were now absent. The nature of the discriminative control was indicated, however, when the punishment programmer accidentally broke down and, as a consequence, the S was confronted with a mixed avoidance-extinction schedule, *i.e.,* shock presented every 20 sec in the absence of a response or no shock at all. During the inadvertent extinction periods (no punishment) responding abruptly increased to the level observed during the avoidance period; however, when the punishment programmer was fixed and response-contingent shock reintroduced, responding again dropped to a low level. Apparently, in the absence of external stimulus controls, the presence of punishment was conducive to the formation of a discrimination, because without the punishment contingency there was no discrimination at all.

Because the discriminative control apparently effected by shock punishment in Appel's (1960b) experiment was associated with a period when the S should not respond (since responding produced shock rather than postponing it), it is difficult to attribute the S's performance to a discriminative function of the shock, rather than to its possible suppressing function. A clearer separation of the two functions could be achieved if shock-punishment signalled a period when the S should respond (as for food reinforcement) and this is precisely what the Holz and Azrin (1961) experiment demonstrated. Pigeons were first trained to make a pecking response for food reinforcement on a 2-min VI schedule and then shock-punishment was introduced for each response, with the intensity of the punishment regulated so as to produce a moderate suppression. After a period of training in which responding in the combined punishment-reinforcement sessions stabilized, additional sessions were introduced in which neither punishment nor reinforcement was administered. These extinction sessions were irregularly alternated with the punishment-reinforcement sessions until responding virtually disappeared in the extinction session and yet continued at a fairly high rate in the punishment-reinforcement session. As in the Appel (1960b) experiment, this difference in response rate between the two sessions indicated a discriminative control by punishment, particularly in view of the fact that, during the punishment-reinforcement session, shock-punishment occurred with each response whereas reinforcement occurred only on an irregular basis, thereby simulating the absence of reinforcement as in the extinction session. The possibility prevailed, nevertheless, that reinforcement and not punishment produced the observed difference in response rate.

To preclude an influence of reinforcement, Holz and Azrin (1961)

continued training the pigeons but now with the reinforcement temporarily omitted from the punishment-reinforcement session; *i.e.*, the *S* was
confronted with sessions in which it received either punishment (and no
reinforcement) for responding or nothing at all. Under these conditions,
a discriminative control by punishment was clearly illustrated for the pigeon continued to respond at a fairly high rate when punished, but virtually not at all when not punished. As an additional and even more
demanding test of the shock's discriminative-stimulus function, punishment was introduced in the middle of an extinction session when responding was at an extremely low rate. Here, shock-punishment led to a
rapid increase in response rate; conversely, when the punishment was removed responding fell back to the low rate that was characteristic of the
extinction session. The same findings prevailed when, in place of
response-contingent shocks, response-independent and thus unavoidable
shocks were introduced into the extinction session. The occasional presentation of these response-independent shocks produced a slight "flurry"
of responding shortly after their delivery, thereby indicating the discriminative control exerted by the shock. Indeed, as these unavoidable
shocks became more frequent, responding also became more frequent.

Although the foregoing results indicate that punishment can serve as a
cue for responding, a question prevails as to whether punishment can
also serve as a cue for not responding. To treat this question, a final
part of the Holz and Azrin (1961) experiment entailed training a pigeon
under conditions that were comparable to those for prior *S*s except that
shock was now associated with the extinction session rather than the
reinforcement session. So as to permit an evaluation of the discriminative rather than aversive property of the shock, the intensity of the
shock-punishment employed was extremely mild, being set at an intensity which did not suppress responding when applied during reinforcement. As with prior conditions, training under the present set of
reinforcement and punishment-extinction conditions eventually led to a
discrimination in which responding occurred at a very low rate in the
punishment-extinction session, but remained at a high rate in the reinforcement session. In itself, this finding is suggestive of a discriminative
control by shock-punishment; but more important is the result that prevailed when punishment was temporarily omitted during the sessions
that normally paired punishment and extinction: Responding abruptly
increased and occurred at a rate characteristic of the reinforcement session. Evidently, punishment had come to serve as a cue for not responding since its absence set the occasion for responding even when food
reinforcement was unavailable.

In a subsequent study assaying the interaction of aversive and discriminative properties of punishment, Holz and Azrin (1962) trained pigeons on a FI schedule of food reinforcement wherein shock-punishment was selectively applied to different portions of the reinforcement interval. With an FI schedule of reinforcement, the S is essentially confronted with a temporal discrimination in which responding during the initial portion of the interval is not associated with reinforcement but responding at the end of the interval is. Consequently, a stimulus that is selectively applied to the initial or end portion of the interval may serve to enhance the temporal discrimination by designating more clearly (as a discriminative stimulus) when the S should or should not respond. Precisely this effect was obtained when shock-punishment was selectively applied to the S's responses: Relative to performance in the absence of any external signal, the application of a mild (50-V) shock to responses in the first three-quarters of the interval suppressed responding; on the other hand, the application of the same shock-punishment to responses during the last quarter of the interval facilitated responding. An interaction of the discriminative and aversive properties of shock was then tested by increasing the intensity of the punishment. When applied as above to responding during the first three-quarters of the interval, a more severe (100-V) punishment suppressed responding even further, but when applied to responses during the last quarter of the interval, this stronger shock attenuated the heightened level of responding that was present with the milder, 50-V shock. These findings indicate that the discriminative and aversive properties of punishment may, depending upon the manner in which punishment is applied, operate so as to complement, offset, or even override one another.

A similar interaction between the discriminative and aversive properties of punishment may be illustrated with reference to escape and avoidance behaviors. In a study by Migler (1963), rats were trained under conditions in which a bar press permitted them either to escape a 1.0-mA shock for 10 sec (R_E–S interval) or, if the response occurred between scheduled shocks, to postpone the shock for 10 sec (R_A–S interval). Because the Ss developed a bar-holding tendency—a fairly typical occurrence within this context—Migler scheduled punishment-shocks of the same intensity but of very short duration (.05 sec) to occur whenever the rat held the bar for 2.5 sec. Contrary to Migler's expectations, these punishment shocks "not only failed to eliminate the bar holding but in some cases even seemed to strengthen it." From an extended series of related experiments, Migler (1963) found that the development of this "self-punishment" effect was primarily dependent upon the concurrent operation of the escape contingency: after initial escape training, punishment-shocks were introduced with the escape shocks eliminated and bar holding tended to drop out almost immediately; however, when the escape contingency was gradually eliminated by progressively increasing over sessions the R_f–S interval from the original 10 sec to 3 min or more, self-punished bar holding tended to be maintained.

As an interpretation of these findings, Migler (1963) suggests that the rats continued to bar hold in the face of punishment because the punishment-shock was of very brief duration and therefore may have reinforced, by its quick termination, the "superstition" that bar holding was effective in terminating whatever shock (presumably escape shock from the S's viewpoint) that was present. In this respect, then, the onset of punishment would have served as a signal correlated with adventitious reinforcement to continue making the bar-holding response. Such an interpretation accords well with the fact that when the duration of the punishment-shock was increased from .05 to .5 sec, thereby increasing punishment severity as well as altering its cue characteristics, bar holding was for the most part eliminated. Hurwitz (1965) has reported a related effect in the context of discriminated avoidance training: when the discrimination performance conditions are made increasingly stringent, i.e., the interval between the warning signal and shock becomes so short that avoidance responding is highly correlated with shock onset, the avoidance response drops out for rats that have been trained to bar-press on an avoidance-only procedure; however, for Ss originally trained on a combined escape-avoidance procedure, stringent discrimination conditions can lead to an increase in bar-press rate, and correspondingly a better maintenance of the avoidance response. Thus, animals trained on a procedure where the onset of shock has originally provided a cue for bar-press escape responding, resort to this behavior rather than suppress bar-press responding.

These findings highlighting the cue properties of punishment would also seem to relate to the facilitation of performance that obtains with punishment of a conditioned avoidance response, an effect that may be illustrated by reference to the Appel (1960b) experiment noted above. As will be recalled, monkeys were initially trained to bar-press so as to postpone shock for 20 sec (Sidman avoidance) in the context of both white and green signal lights that were alternately presented during an experimental session. In a subsequent phase of the experiment, a multiple avoidance-punishment schedule was put into effect with the avoidance contingency being withdrawn during the green light and replaced by a VI 1-min punishment schedule. Upon confrontation with this multiple schedule, the Ss showed not only an increase in bar-press rate during both signal lights, but also their rate in the green (punishment) period exceeded that in the white (avoidance) period. The

Ss. eventually learned to stop responding in the presence of the punishment contingency, but before this suppression took place, additional punishment-shocks occurred with the result that the level of avoidance responding also increased. Similar findings on the effect of shock-punishment have been reported in a study by Black and Morse (1961; see also Solomon, Kamin & Wynne, 1953): Dogs trained to postpone shock by jumping a barrier in a shuttlebox showed an initial increase in response rate and then eventual suppression when given shock during an extinction phase. The effect has also been observed in studies using unavoidable, *i.e.,* response-independent as opposed to response-contingent, shocks, (Appel, 1960a; Sidman, 1958; Sidman, Herrnstein & Conrad, 1957).

More recently, Sandler and his associates (Sandler, Davidson, Greene & Holzschuh, 1966a; Sandler, Davidson & Holzschuh, 1966b; Sandler, Davidson & Malagodi, 1966c; Sandler & Davidson, 1967) have reported findings showing that punishment of bar-press avoidance generally results in response facilitation irrespective of whether the punishment is introduced during training or extinction, or the avoidance contingency is of the Sidman or signalled variety. Furthermore, while the effect is sometimes short-lived, it can be enhanced if the punishment is introduced gradually during training so as to reduce the discriminability of punishment and avoidance contingencies (Sandler *et al.,* 1966c); and it will be maintained for considerable lengths of time despite the presence of an unpunished alternative (Sandler & Davidson, 1967). As Sandler and his associates suggest, there seems little doubt from these results and the nature of the avoidance task that the initial escape component of avoidance learning exerts a continuing influence throughout the punished avoidance sessions. That is to say, punishment superimposed on the avoidance contingency serves the function of a discriminative stimulus by reinstating conditions which originally caused the *S* to make an escape response. Consequently, when punished, the *S* attempts to escape with the result that another shock is received, leading in a "vicious circle" fashion (Mowrer, 1950) to a burst of punished responses.

One other study to be noted with reference to the function of shock as a discriminative stimulus is the recent investigation by McMillan and Morse (1967). To assay the discriminative properties of shock under conditions comparable to those employed to study the discriminative control exerted by other stimuli, McMillan and Morse used repeated pulses of weak shock as an S_D or S_Δ for food reward on an FR schedule. That shock so employed could serve as a discriminative stimulus was well indicated in the performance of their *Ss*: Monkeys learned to discriminate the shock conditions (as shown by shorter latencies of responding during reinforcement periods and fewer responses during non-reinforcement periods), were able to maintain this performance when the length of the nonreinforcement period was varied, and even showed a reversal of performance when the shock conditions correlated with S_D and S_Δ periods were reversed.

In view of McMillan and Morse's (1967) procedure of administering brief pulses of shock repeatedly throughout periods of reinforcement or nonreinforcement, their findings indicate that shock need not be present as a punishing stimulus (*i.e.*, made response contingent) in order to gain a discriminative control over performance. Essentially, this same finding prevailed with the avoidance studies that used response-independent shocks (*e.g.*, Sidman *et al.*, 1957) and with the Holz and Azrin (1961) study wherein response-contingent shocks that were initially associated with reinforcement were then introduced on an unavoidable basis during extinction—all with the result of facilitating responding. These observations of the effects of response-independent shock make clear then the discriminative control by shock *punishment*, for they illustrate that the action of such shock, when associated with reinforcement, is not in the backward direction of strengthening the preceding response (as when the shock is response independent), but rather in the forward direction of signalling the occasion for additional responding.

B. Secondary Reinforcing Function

The fact that punishment can operate as a discriminative stimulus signaling additional responding in no way vitiates the possibility that response-contingent shock can also exert a facilitating action in a "backward" direction, *i.e.*, as a secondary reinforcer for the punished response. Indeed, reviews of the literature on secondary reinforcement relating both to positive and negative primary reinforcers (*e.g.*, Beck, 1961; Myers, 1958) indicate that the operation of a stimulus as a secondary reinforcer may well be dependent upon its initial establishment as a discriminative stimulus. However, to demonstrate that shock-punishment can secondarily reinforce the punished response (*i.e.*, mediate the effect of the primary reinforcer), it is necessary to employ a procedure which precludes the use of shock-punishment, not as a signal for reinforcement, but as a signal for continued responding which may lead to the reinforcement. In effect, such procedure is accomplished in either of two ways: through the use of a heterogeneous response chain where the initial component-response, which is punished, is topographically different from a subsequent component-response which leads to the reinforcer; or, perhaps more directly, through the use of a discrete-trial arrangement where within "separate" trials or units of time, as in a T-maze arrangement, the S is enabled a single response that is both punished and reinforced.

Of several studies that have used a discrete-trial procedure to assess a potential secondary reinforcing function of shock-punishment, most have originated from Muenzinger's early finding of a "shock-right" facilitation effect, *i.e.*, the facilitated choice performance of rats receiving shock for the correct, food-reinforced response in a T-maze visual discrimination task (*e.g.*, Muenzinger, 1934; Muenzinger, Bernstone & Richards, 1938). These findings, together with an associated increment in choice-point pausing and VTE activity on the part of Ss receiving either shock-right (SR) or shock-wrong (SW) training, led Muenzinger to argue that in the context of discrimination learning punishment serves the general function of alerting the animal to relevant discriminanda. The fact, however, that punishment was selectively administered for either the correct or incorrect response allowed the possibility that shock could serve as a differential cue, and in the case of the SR condition, as a conditioned positive reinforcer. Acknowledging this interpretation, Freeburne and Taylor (1952) trained rats on a visual discrimination task wherein the operation of shock-punishment as a cue selectively associated with reinforcement was precluded by the administration of shock for *both* correct and incorrect responses. Comparable to the effects reported by Muenzinger for SR and SW training, however, Freeburne and Taylor (1952) found that this shock-both (SB) condition led to improved performance over a no-shock (NS) control, and thus they were led to interpret their findings as being consonant with Muenzinger's general alerting hypothesis.

The conclusion drawn by Freeburne and Taylor (1952) was subsequently questioned by Prince (1956) on the basis that their reported difference was only marginally reliable and derived from a restricted sample. Apparently, as a result of the imposition following choice of a 5-sec delay in a neutral gray chamber, and similarly the occasioning of reinforcement in another gray chamber away from the discriminative stimuli, Freeburne and Taylor's simple black-white discrimination problem was made so difficult that nearly one-third of the Ss failed to reach a moderate learning criterion within 500 trials. Under these conditions any improvement in performance from SB training might well have derived from its potential effect in suppressing position habits. More importantly, when Prince (1956, Experiment 1) repeated Freeburne and Taylor's study, but without the complicating delay aspects, he found no evidence that SB training facilitated performance relative to that of an NS control. Prince's results, therefore, could be viewed as indirect support for a secondary reinforcing function of shock for the correct response because, without a differential cue function (as in SB training), facilitated performance did not occur. However, the issue was far from settled for neither Prince (1956) nor Freeburne and Taylor (1952) employed an SR control against which the presence or absence of SB facilitation could be assessed.

Pursuing the matter further, Lohr (1959) attempted to assess a secondary reinforcing function of shock-punishment in the context of a "spatial" problem, as opposed to the simultaneous visual discrimination task employed by prior investigators. In the first of two experiments which utilized a symmetrical choice apparatus having parallel arms that converged to a common goal at either end, rats were trained for 0, 250, or 500 trials to shuttle back and forth for food reinforcement at each goal. Then, moderate or strong shock-punishment was introduced into one of the arms: in the 0-trial condition, shock was presented to half of the Ss either on the left or the right; in the 250- and 500-trial conditions, where every S had developed a pronounced position preference, shock was administered on the S's preferred side. The results of Lohr's first experiment showed that shock, even though associated with food reinforcement at the goal, had the general effect of suppressing the punished response, especially so under the condition of strong shock and less preshock training. An interesting aspect of Lohr's data, however, related to the performance of Ss that received moderate shock after 500 preshock trials. Rather than showing any tendency to select the unpunished, alternative route to food, these Ss continued to exhibit their position preferences despite the fact that they were continually punished. Thus, it appeared to Lohr as if they had acquired "a compulsion for taking unnecessary punishment."

Lohr (1959) acknowledged that the results of his first experiment did not provide any evidence for a secondary reinforcing function of shock since the pronounced position preferences of the "compulsive" Ss had been acquired well prior to the introduction of punishment. For these Ss, with their extensive training, moderate shock punishment was simply not effective in disrupting the position response. As a consequence, Lohr (1959) attempted in his second experiment to demonstrate that animals would actually *learn* to go to that position which led through shock-punishment to food. To that end, extremely mild shock was introduced at the beginning of training (either in the right or left arm) and then progressively increased over the course of 500 trials until it finally reached the "strong" shock intensity employed in the first experiment. Quite amazingly, the results of Lohr's second experiment showed that 12 out of 16 Ss developed a position response leading through shock-punishment. Furthermore, in marked contrast to those Ss that had not acquired a preference for the shocked arm, the "compulsive" Ss failed to show a single digression to the other (unpunished) arm during the last 100 trials, even though shock-punishment had reached the "strong" intensity. It seemed evident therefore that shock had made "some positive contribution to the strength of the habit."

Lohr's (1959) results are most impressive, but a question prevails as to the manner in which shock did in fact make a "positive contribution." Inspection of Lohr's data and methodology points up at least two important considerations. First, the effective shock intensity for the rat at the beginning of training (.014 mA) was "well below the avoidance threshold," and not until after some 150 training trials did the shock reach a value (.037 mA) which would appear representative of an aversion threshold (cf. Campbell and Teghtsoonian, 1958). Second, within this period of training, viz., 150 trials, all but one of the Ss showed clear evidence of having developed a position habit and, of these, 12 were already responding to the "punished" alternative. In contrast to these Ss who continued on subsequent trials to display the compulsion of running through shock (now supra-threshold), those Ss who had not early acquired a position response to the "punished" side never developed this behavior. Thus, it would appear that the function of shock in Lohr's second experiment was not to set the occasion for the learning of a position response but, like its effect in the first experiment, to "fixate" an already acquired response. On this point, the results of an earlier study by Farber (1948) are instructive.

Farber (1948) similarly trained rats on a spatial discrimination problem, but apart from the complicating procedural aspects of Lohr's second experiment, Farber's Ss were permitted 40 food-reinforced trials on their perferred side of a T-maze without any shock being administered. Then, for half of the Ss, shock in either arm was added to the food-reinforcement contingency present in the preferred arm with the result that the shocked Ss continued to display their initial position habits and, like Lohr's Ss, with fewer digressions to the nonpreferred side than the control, no-shock Ss. Most important is the fact that when shock was removed after 60 such trials and all animals were then confronted with a reversal wherein food was shifted to their nonpreferred side, the previously shocked Ss showed the fixated behavior of running significantly more often to the originally food-reinforced side.

Farber's interpretation of these data also implicated a secondary reinforcing effect, but not that relating to the shock. Indeed, the compulsive behavior of the experimental Ss could not have been maintained by any acquired reinforcing effect of the shock because during the reversal problem shock was not present at all. Rather, Farber suggested that, as a result of their initially reinforced preferences, the experimental Ss were able to run through shock and thereby terminate any fear conditioned to the situational cues. Thus, it was this form of secondary reinforcement, *viz.,* "anxiety" reduction, which was responsible for the added strengthening of the position habit, as well as its maintenance during the reversal problem. Acknowledging the applicability to Lohr's data of this interpretation, or even one relating to the possible *negative* reinforcement deriving from S's escape from the punishing shock itself[2], we are confronted with the conclusion that there is no discrete-trial study deriving from Muenzinger's early work on SR facilitation which clearly implicates the role of shock as a conditioned positive reinforcer.

Another line of research relating to the potential function of shock as a secondary reinforcer derives from Pavlov's (1927) observation of a counter-conditioning effect, *i.e.,* the attenuation of the aversiveness of a painful electric shock when presented as a CS for the US of food. In an effort to demonstrate this phenomenon in an operant conflict arrangement, Williams and Barry (1966) trained rats to press a lever for food reinforcement on a 1-min VI schedule. Then, a punishing shock of .5-sec duration was introduced at intensities increasing to .5 mA. For all Ss, both shock and food were programmed on comparable 1-min VI schedules; however, to assess the relationship of shock and food, the two schedules were either arranged so that food and shock occurred "simultaneously" for the same response (counter-conditioning procedure) or started at different times so that only one event, food or shock, occurred immediately following a response (control procedure). Furthermore, with both punishment conditions, timing on the food and shock schedules was halted as soon as either event (or both) was programmed for delivery. In this way, it was possible to structure events in the control condition such that the probability of occurrence of shock was equal to that for food, and yet neither event signalled the other.

Williams and Barry's (1966) results showed that, relative to terminal performance on a training schedule entailing food reinforcement alone, the initial effect of shock was to suppress responding under both punishment conditions. Over the course of ten daily sessions, however, re-

---

[2]Church (1963) has pointed out that an interpretation of Farber's results is complicated by the fact that an occasional shock had to be administered in the stem of the T maze in order to have the experimental Ss continue making a choice. Thus, the fixation shown by the experimental Ss may have related to a greater resistance to extinction of their "escape" response as opposed to the "approach" response acquired by the control Ss. This consideration not withstanding, Church's interpretation would seem equally if not more applicable to the negative reinforcement deriving from the S's escape from punishment-shock administered in the T arm.

For a review which highlights the role of escape reinforcement in studies on fixation, see Seward (1969).

sponse rate under the paired shock-food arrangement (counter-conditioning) quickly rose to and surpassed the terminal acquisition level, whereas response rate under the control condition stabilized at the level of initial suppression. Besides demonstrating this counter-conditioning effect, Williams and Barry (1966) showed that the effect could be offset by increasing the strength of shock-punishment. Thus, the imposition of shocks progressively increasing in intensity from 0.5 to 1.0 mA led to a rapid suppression of behavior, to the point where the difference in response rate between the two punishment conditions was negated.

Comparable findings in support of a counter-conditioning effect have also been reported in a study by Akhtar (1967). Using an operant, bar-press arrangement, Akhtar showed that rats' resistance to continuous shock-punishment (without food reinforcement) depended directly on the extent of S's prior training with shock interspersed in a continuous food-reinforcement schedule, and particularly the manner in which the shock functioned as a cue. When shock was interspersed with continuous food reinforcement such that the shock signalled the subsequent event of food, resistance to continuous punishment without food reinforcement increased; on the other hand, when shock signalled the advent of additional shocks, resistance to continuous punishment decreased. Akhtar's (1967) results showed therefore, like those of Williams and Barry (1966), that the suppressive effect of shock-punishment could be attenuated by associating the shock with food reinforcement. Nevertheless, both of these studies are insufficient insofar as they bear on the potential function of shock as a conditioned positive reinforcer. In the Akhtar (1967) experiment, the cue function of shock-punishment was specifically structured so as to control subsequent responding; hence, it cannot be ascertained that shock as a *positive* cue operated in the "backward" direction of strengthening (or maintaining) those responses which led to the shock. This discriminative-stimulus function of the shock is ruled out in the Williams and Barry (1966) experiment, since the VI programs for shock and food both terminated with the same response, but the recovery of rate observed with the counter-conditioning procedure, even though higher than terminal acquisition performance when food alone was administered, cannot be adequately assessed. As Williams and Barry themselves acknowledge, terminal acquisition performance "may not indicate the extent to which responding would have risen had shock not been introduced."

A comparable but more expanded approach to the study of shock as a secondary reinforcer has been to administer both food and shock events on an intermittent, 50% schedule with shock punishment in an antedating position relative to food reinforcement and, most importantly, its occurrence scheduled in either a positive, negative, or uncorrelated fashion with the occurrence of food reinforcement. Employing this scheduling in a discrete-trial procedure, Logan (1960) trained rats to run down an alley through a brief 100-V shock at the end of the runway to food reinforcement at the goal. During early training, all Ss showed comparable acquisition performance, but in later stages, when shock was progressively increased to 200 V, Ss of the positively correlated condition ran consistently, albeit not reliably, faster than those of the negatively correlated condition suggesting therefore a counter-conditioning effect. The surprising result, however, was that both the positively and negatively correlated groups were consistently inferior to the uncorrelated group, a result which certainly could not be taken in support of a secondary reinforcing function of the shock. Logan's interpretation of these findings is that the uncorrelated group had the most widely varied number of goal events and, with moderate shock-punishment, such stimulus variation at the goal may have a beneficial effect. Furthermore, within the context of a discrete-trial procedure, shock may function as a cue for continued running into the goal. That is to say, if Ss of the positively and negatively correlated conditions learned to run into the goal depending on whether shock at the entrance to the goal was present or absent, then these Ss might slow down as they approached the locus of the "informational" stimulus, viz., shock or its absence, as opposed to Ss of the uncorrelated condition who, without such a cue, would continue to run to the food cup in the goal.

A more recent study which also manipulated the correlation of shock and food events, but in the context of a two-component operant chain, is that by Murray and Nevin (1967). These investigators trained rats in a two-bar chamber wherein responding on the left bar (A), on a FI 30-sec schedule starting from darkness, produced light above the bars and shock (0.4 mA) with a probability of 0.5. In the positively correlated condition employed by the investigators, the occurrence of light plus shock indicated the availability of water reinforcement for a response on the right bar (B), whereas light without shock indicated no reinforcement. In the negatively correlated condition, the discriminative stimuli (i.e., light with or without shock) were reversed in significance; and for the uncorrelated condition, both shock on bar A and reinforcement on bar B were presented with a probability of 0.5, but in a manner such that neither the presence nor the absence of shock with light served as a discriminative stimulus for water reinforcement. To reinstitute the FI 30-sec schedule on bar A, the light associated with reinforcement for all three conditions was terminated following a bar B response or, in the absence of that response, after 2 sec.

Murray and Nevin's (1967) results showed that, relative to initial baseline performance in the absence of shock, response rate on bar A was at first suppressed to a small extent under the positively correlated condition, but then recovered over sessions to the point where performance was actually facilitated relative to the previous unpunished baseline and to a subsequent baseline that was determined by removing the shock. In contrast, bar A response rate under the negatively correlated condition was initially suppressed to a greater extent and did not recover appreciably over further sessions until shock-punishment was finally removed; with the uncorrelated condition, performance on bar A was intermediate to that of the two correlated conditions. Thus, Murray and Nevin's (1967) findings showed that across the three correlational conditions, from positive to negative, terminal performance on bar A (for which the effect of shock-punishment could only operate in a "backward" direction) ranged significantly from facilitation to suppression. These effects were also found to be regulated by the intensity of shock-punishment: when shock was increased from 0.4 to 0.8 mA in a second phase of the experiment, comparable and substantial suppression resulted under all three correlations of shock-punishment and food reinforcement.

A final point to be noted in reference to Murray and Nevin's (1967) findings bears on the relationship between shock's backward-acting effect on bar A performance and its forward-acting, discriminative-stimulus function for bar B performance. Although discriminative control over the second component, for which reinforcement was available 50% of the time, depended to some extent on the correlation of shock and food events, for the most part change in rate and terminal performance on the first component were unrelated to performance on the second component. Hence, it would appear that the backward-acting effect of shock on bar A performance functioned independently of its operation as a discriminative stimulus for bar B performance, although, as the investigators point out, their experimental arrangement was not structured so as to be sensitive to a discriminative control by shock-punishment, and therefore the relationship may have been obscured. These observations notwithstanding, Murray and Nevin's (1967) findings provide the best evidence that shock-punishment can function as a conditioned positive reinforcer. Their results show that the suppressive effect of the punishing stimulus is not merely attenuated but actually altered to the point where it facilitates a response for which punishment could not have functioned as a discriminative stimulus.

C. Distinctive Cue Function

In the preceding section, note was made of Muenzinger's (1934) shock-right (SR) facilitation effect, and the unsuccessful attempts by other investigators to relate this finding to a secondary reinforcing function of the shock. Actually, an interpretation of SR facilitation was far from simple because the phenomenon was beset by two major complications.[3] First, not all investigators were able to show that moderate shock-punishment for the correct response would, in fact, facilitate discrimination learning. Thus, Wischner (1947) found that in the context of noncorrection training, as opposed to the correction training procedure used by Muenzinger and other investigators, shock-wrong (SW) training led to facilitated performance but SR training did not. Indeed, even with correction training, the effect was not always reliably present (see Fairlie, 1937). Second, underlying these empirical discrepancies were procedural and methodological variations in the designs that were employed, as is evident in the Muenzinger-Wischner differences, as well as a failure to treat the parameters of shock-punishment in any systematic fashion. As early as his original experiment, Muenzinger (1934) had stated that only "moderate" shock-punishment would be facilitating, but systematic manipulation of the intensity of the shock or of any of its other parameters had not been accomplished.

In view of the need for a systematic program of research on the SR phenomenon, the author in collaboration with Professor Wischner undertook a series of investigations designed to assay the functional relationships between the parameters of shock-punishment and such nonshock methodological variables as training-procedure, performance-factor and discriminative-stimulus manipulations. In two, initial experiments (Wischner, Fowler & Kushnick, 1963; Wischner & Fowler, 1964) which focused on shock parameters, rats received noncorrection training on a simple, light-dark T-maze discrimination problem wherein shock of varying intensities and durations (45, 60, and 75 V, .3 MΩ; 0.1, 0.2, and 0.4 sec) was factorially administered for either the correct or incorrect response. For the most part, the findings of this initial research were significant in pointing up only an avoidance-producing effect of the shock. Thus, in the intensity study (Wischner et al., 1963) errors were found to decrease over increasing SW intensities and to increase over increasing SR intensities. Likewise, in the duration study (Wischner & Fowler, 1964), which utilized a moderate shock intensity of 60 V, an inverse relationship prevailed between error frequency and SW duration; however, with respect to the SR condition, comparable durations of shock of the same intensity were found to have no systematic effect ei-

---

[3]For a comprehensive account critically reviewing early work on SR facilitation, see Fowler and Wischner (1969).

ther in augmenting or reducing errors. While these results showed no SR facilitation, they indicated in view of the significant SW effects that some other factor or factors were operating to offset an avoidance-producing effect of shock for the correct response. Because of the discrete-trial procedure imposed by the T-maze arrangement, any such additional factor could not have related to the function of shock as a discriminative stimulus.[4] There prevailed the possibility, however, that the avoidance-producing effect of shock was being offset by a counter-conditioning effect or even that the shock had acquired positive reinforcing properties.

In view of this latter possibility, as well as the limitations of prior research assessing the potential function of shock as a secondary reinforcer, a subsequent study (Fowler & Wischner, 1965b) was addressed to this problem in the context of an extinction paradigm. Initially, rats received either no-shock (NS) or SR acquisition training on a light-dark discrimination where, through the use of a semiforced-choice procedure, occasions of reinforcement were equated across training conditions and balanced (similarly for shock) over left and right maze arms. Then, after 200 such trials, the Ss received free-choice extinction training in which the NS control group (hereafter designated NS–C) was continued as before without shock, and the experimental Ss in subgroups were subjected to the following conditions: SR, shock for the previously correct response; SW, shock for the previously incorrect response; and NS, a no-shock experimental group serving as a control for the shock-right experiences of acquisition training. In this experiment, as well as in all subsequent research, shock was set and maintained at the intermediate values of 60 V, 0.2 sec.

The results of our extinction study (Fowler & Wischner, 1965b) showed that, on the free-trial components of the forcing procedure employed during acquisition training, performances for the control and experimental Ss were virtually identical. Hence, this finding matched well those results of our prior duration study (Wischner & Fowler, 1964). Even so, the extinction data of the present study provided no evidence that shock had acquired a secondary reinforcing property via its associa-

---

[4]Azrin and Holz (1966) have argued that SR facilitation can be explained by a discriminative-stimulus function of shock, but their position is simply untenable. In the discrete-trial procedure, there is no basis by which shock per se can serve as a cue for the correct choice since the administration of shock is always subsequent to that response. The argument may be extended to include the potential role of fear as a discriminative stimulus, but one must acknowledge that *selective* conditioning of fear to the positive discriminative stimulus is dependent upon the S having already formed the discrimination or, at least, having differentially "detected" the discriminanda; consequently, even the role of fear as a discriminative stimulus would seem superceded by that of the actual visual discriminative stimulus.

tion with food reinforcement, or even that its aversiveness had been attenuated. Indeed, relative to performances under both control conditions (NS and NS-C), the SR extinction condition had the pronounced effect of rapidly increasing responses to the non-shocked "incorrect" arm, rather than as a secondary reinforcer protracting responses to the "correct" arm. Similarly, as the SW Ss extinguished their "correct" response tendency, making additional "errors" and thereby increasing their receipt of shock, their responses to the nonshocked "correct" arm were abruptly augmented. Thus, for both SR and SW Ss, the only apparent effect of shock administered during extinction was to suppress those responses with which the shock was associated.

Along with the above study, we considered an alternative interpretation of our prior results which focused on the likelihood that not simply shock but all of the stimuli associated with food reinforcement in the correct arm (e.g., physical features and discriminative stimulus) should acquire reinforcing properties. So considered, the operation of secondary reinforcement would not be limited to correct-arm cues alone, but would be mediated by any such similar stimuli (e.g., physical features) in the incorrect arm; that is, there would be a *generalization* of secondary reinforcement from correct to similar incorrect-arm cues. From this standpoint, the introduction of shock into one maze arm should serve to alter the complex of stimuli comprising that arm, such that this arm is now more readily perceived by S as being different from a similar, alternative arm which is without the shock. Operating in this fashion as a "distinctive" cue which increases the discriminability of the stimulus alternatives, the function of shock should be to *limit* the generalization of secondary reinforcement from the food-associated correct-arm cues to those in the incorrect arm; and in comparison with no-shock Ss, this limitation to the secondary reinforcing properties of the incorrect-arm cues should lead for the shocked Ss to a reduction in errors. Moreover, because this distinctive-cue function of shock is independent of an association with food reinforcement, it should operate so as to facilitate performances for both SR and SW Ss; however, in the case of SR Ss, any such facilitation could easily be countered by the shock's aversive property with the resultant that no obvious or apparent effect of the shock is manifested.

With its emphasis on the discriminability (or, perhaps more specifically, the dissimilarity) of the stimulus alternatives, the foregoing interpretation suggests that a distinctive-cue effect of the shock should be less predominant in the typically utilized light-dark discrimination where the alternatives, as served by the visual discriminative stimuli, are already highly discriminable and thus generalization of secondary reinforcement relatively small. For this reason we conducted an experiment (Fowler & Wischner, 1965a) in which rats received either SR or SW training on a set of more difficult, bright-dim discriminations, *i.e.*, where problem difficulty was systematically increased by reducing the difference in relative brightness of the visual discriminanda. The results of this study were clear in showing that performance was progressively retarded across increasing levels of problem difficulty. But, most important was the finding that, in comparison with respective NS groups, SR groups were reliably facilitated at all problem levels and SW groups even more so. Here then were findings which pointed up both a distinctive-cue and an avoidance-producing effect of the shock, the former as reflected in SR facilitation and the latter in the superior performance of SW over SR *S*s.

Tangential note should be given to the results of a study by Curlin and Donahoe (1965) which appeared almost coincidentally with those of our problem-difficulty study (Fowler & Wischner, 1965a). In Curlin and Donahoe's study, rats also received "SR" or "SW" training but in the context of an operant arrangement where mild or strong shock-punishment (.13 or .30 mA, 0.5 sec) was administered for each bar-press response during either the positive (light on) or negative (light off) period of a successive visual discrimination. The results of this study generally showed facilitated discrimination performance for the shocked groups, but in the case of SR trained *S*s, such facilitation was limited to the mild punishment condition. As a consequence, Curlin and Donahoe suggested that prior discrepant findings on the effect of SR training might relate to the particular levels of shock employed. The fact, however, that we were able in our problem difficulty study (Fowler & Wischner, 1965a) to obtain SR facilitation with the same intensity and duration of shock that had previously been ineffective in our parametric research (*e.g.*, Wischner & Fowler, 1964) indicated that the particular effect of SR training depended not on shock parameters alone, but on the interaction of these parameters with the specific conditions of training. In this respect, it is noteworthy that Curlin and Donahoe's discrimination problem, although apparently "easy" as effected by the presence or absence of a stimulus light above the manipulanda, may well have been made relatively difficult by the continuous operation of a house light. This consideration notwithstanding, an interpretation of their results regarding a distinctive-cue function of the shock is complicated by the fact that their operant procedure enabled the shock to function as a discriminative stimulus.

Other studies in our program of research, for the most part unpublished, have been reported in a recent article by Fowler and Wischner (1969). Two of these unpublished studies are particularly important for our purpose since they bear on the question of whether our problem difficulty findings might be attributed to some general alerting function of the shock, as Muenzinger (1934) had earlier suggested. In one of the unpublished studies, both light-dark and bright-dim discriminations were employed to evaluate the effects of NS and SR training, as well as those of two other conditions, shock-both (SB) and shock-paired (SP). As in earlier research (*e.g.,* Freeburne & Taylor, 1952), *S*s of the SB condition received shock for both correct and incorrect responses; similarly, in the SP condition *S*s received shock for both responses but only when a paired running mate of the SR condition made a correct response and received shock. Thus, both the SB and SP conditions permitted a potential sensitizing function of the shock to be operative, but both precluded any distinctive-cue effect since the shock was not selectively associated with one or the other of the stimulus alternatives; in addition, the SP condition controlled for the number and order of shock experiences received by SR *S*s. Comparable to the results of our problem difficulty study, the findings of the present study showed facilitated performance for SR *S*s but only on the more difficult, bright-dim discrimination. In contrast, the performances of the SB and SP groups did not differ reliably from that of the NS group on either of the two problem conditions, indicating therefore that the obtained SR facilitation effect could not be attributed to the operation of some general alerting function of shock-punishment.[5]

In the other unpublished study reported by Fowler and Wischner (1969), an effort was made to manipulate task difficulty within the context of an easy, light-dark discrimination problem, *i.e.,* in a way independent of the similarity of the discriminative stimuli and thus independent of a distinctive-cue effect of the shock. This was accomplished by varying for rats the number of nondifferentially reinforced *pretraining* trials with the light and dark alternatives prior to the *S*s' receipt of either NS or SR discrimination training on the same alternatives. Consistent with the results of earlier studies on the effect of nondifferential pretraining (*e.g.,* Bitterman & Elam, 1954; Crawford, Mayes & Bitterman, 1954), the results of the present study showed that discrimination performance was progressively retarded with increasing amounts of such pretraining, ranging from 0 to 64 trials. However, the

[5]In relation to those earlier studies (Freeburne & Taylor, 1952; Prince, 1956) which utilized the SB condition to assess a secondary reinforcing function of shock, the present results might be construed as supporting such an interpretation. However, the fact that SR facilitation occurred only at the more difficult bright-dim discrimination level argues strongly against this interpretation, for there is no basis by which the operation required to establish shock as a conditioned positive reinforcer can be differentially related to the variable of problem difficulty. The same holds true regarding a discriminative-stimulus interpretation of the effect of shock or of its associated fear component (see footnote 4).

extent of the retardation resulting at any level of pretraining was comparable for both NS and SR groups. These results indicated therefore, in accord with the distinctive-cue interpretation, that the SR facilitation obtaining with bright-dim discriminations was not due merely to the increased amount of training required for task mastery at these more difficult problem levels. Furthermore, insofar as the retarding effects of nondifferential pretraining have been attributed to the diminution of observing responses directed toward the discriminative stimuli (Wyckoff, 1952), or to the loss of functional significance of the discriminative stimuli (Bitterman & Elam, 1954), the present results are consistent with those of our shock-both study in arguing against a general sensitizing effect of the shock.

Other studies in the series have focused on performance-factor manipulations relating to the role of "approach" and "avoidance" variables such as drive, incentive, shock intensity and the like. In one such study, a Ph.D. thesis by R.P. Hawkins (1965), the effects of drive (10 or 15 gm daily ration) and incentive (1 or 4 pellets food reinforcement) were investigated in conjunction with NS or SR training on light-dark and bright-dim discriminations. As anticipated, the results of Hawkin's study showed that higher amounts of drive and incentive facilitated performance on both easy and difficult discrimination problems, and consistent with the results of our earlier research, SR training had the effect of facilitating performance, but only at the difficult problem level. A particularly interesting aspect of Hawkin's data related to the interaction of the drive and incentive variables with SR training: although incentive did not have an appreciable influence on SR facilitation, high drive had the effect of augmenting SR facilitation, but again only within the difficult problem condition. These results are amenable to the interpretation that the effect of shock, acting as a distinctive cue which limits the generalization of secondary reinforcement from correct to incorrect-arm cues, operates essentially through the development of differential associative strengths for correct and incorrect response tendencies (i.e., a habit difference) which may be amplified by increased drive.

Because the results of our prior research indicated the operation of distinctive-cue and avoidance-producing effects of shock-punishment, we attempted in a recent study (Fowler, Goldman, & Wischner, 1968) to separate these two functions, as well as to assess their relationship to the intensity of the shock experience. This was accomplished by training rats under the influence of sodium amytal and different intensities of shock for the correct response (0-120 V, 0.2 sec) in a moderately difficult, bright-dim discrimination. Sodium amytal has elsewhere been shown (e.g., Miller, 1961) to reduce the fear or anxiety which motivates avoidance in conflict situations, and thus its utilization in the present study was for the purpose of evaluating a distinctive-cue effect of the shock apart from its avoidance-producing effect. The results of this study showed that the performance of both placebo and no-injection control Ss was initially facilitated and then retarded as the intensity of shock for the correct response increased. Similarly, the performance of the drugged Ss was increasingly facilitated over low intensities, but in contrast, did not give way to retardation at the stronger intensities. Indeed, consistent with the discriminable properties of stimuli in general, the data for the drugged Ss indicated that the cue effect of the shock was an S-shaped function of the intensity of the shock stimulus.

Although the foregoing findings are sufficient to illustrate a distinctive-cue function of shock-punishment, some comment should be offered on the relationship of our findings to those of Muenzinger (1934), in particular, the fact that Meunzinger consistently obtained SR facilitation in the context of correction training on an *easy* black-white discrimination. Considering that our results showed SR facilitation in the context of noncorrection training, but only at a more difficult bright-dim problem level, we endeavored in another study (Fowler, Spelt & Wischner, 1967) to assess the relationship of problem difficulty and training procedure by comparing the effects of SR training on light-dark and bright-dim discrimination problems entailing both correction and noncorrection procedures. The results of this study were consistent with our prior research in showing SR facilitation with noncorrection training, but only at a difficult problem level; and, equally consistent with Muenzinger's findings, the present results showed SR facilitation with correction training on both easy and difficult problems, although more so with the latter. Most important in this respect were the performances of the NS controls for the two training conditions within each problem level: for these groups, errors increased progressively from easy to difficult-problem noncorrection training, through easy to difficult-problem correction training. Hence, the results of this study showed a *unitary* dimension of task difficulty based on the interaction of training procedure and problem level. This dimension of task difficulty was found to bear a direct relationship to the magnitude of SR facilitation obtaining across the different training conditions, illustrating therefore that correction training is productive of a more difficult problem and that associated with this increased difficulty is greater SR facilitation.

These findings now make possible an interpretation of the results of experiments using both correction and noncorrection procedures. Along with any generalized secondary reinforcement for incorrect responses, there is, in correction training, a related secondary reinforcing effect which derives from a delay of primary reinforcement for each incorrect response, specifically, as a consequence of the S retracing towards the positive discriminative stimulus following an error and finally obtaining food reinforcement. Thus, correction training should lead to poorer performance in comparison with noncorrection training, wherein an "infinite" delay of reinforcement (*i.e.*, no reinforcement) prevails for each incorrect response, and as a consequence of the additional or more potent secondary reinforcement available for incorrect responses in the correction procedure, shock for the correct response should additionally facilitate performance. This should occur because, as a distinctive cue, shock can increase the discriminability of the sequential stimulus-response components involved in correcting, and thereby limit any generalization of secondary reinforcement from late to early components (as well as that deriving from the physical similarity of the stimulus alternatives). Furthermore, as an aversive or fear-producing stimulus, shock can cause the S to slow down upon correcting (and even to enter the stem of the T-maze, as indeed was observed), thereby increasing the time required to correct and thus *increasing* the delay of primary reinforcement contingent upon an incorrect response. Collectively, then, the findings indicate that, as a distinctive cue, shock-punishment can facilitate discrimination performance to the extent that secondary reinforcement for the incorrect response is augmented, either by increasing the similarity of the stimulus alternatives or by using correction instead of noncorrection training.

III.   RESPONSE ELICITING PROPERTIES
OF PUNISHMENT

The present section also focuses on a stimulus property of punishment, but whereas prior treatment was directed to the role of shock-punishment as a cue or a CS which is associated with reinforcement, current emphasis is directed to its role as a US, that is, as a stimulus which can elicit specific motor and/or general emotional (fear) reactions. The relevance of such a consideration for an understanding of the punishment process lies in the fact that the reactions elicited by punishment can become conditioned to those neutral stimuli in the situation which are contiguous with the aversive US (punishment) and, via the process of trace or delayed conditioning, as well as stimulus generalization, to those stimuli which antedate the punishment. In this manner fractional components (r_p) of the punishment-produced reactions can occur during the response sequence leading to punishment, thereby influencing if not preventing the occurrence of the punished response.

Theoretically, the basis for operation of anticipatory responses to punishment is quite varied, and is dependent upon the following types of cues: general stimuli as represented, for example, by the physical features of the situation; specific discriminative stimuli that are associated with shock-punishment (as well as with the positive reinforcer maintaining the punished response); and within this latter classification, the proprioceptive or "feedback" stimuli of the punished response itself. All of these stimuli, via their association with shock-punishment, may serve as CS's for the reactions directly elicited by punishment. However, with the conditioning of anticipatory punishment reactions to any such cues controlling the punished response, the whole process is compounded for the responses leading to punishment (or some segment thereof) can themselves be associated with and thus conditioned to the stimulus or feedback components of the anticipatory punishment reactions. The import of this association is made apparent when one considers that the feedback components (s_p) of anticipatory punishment reactions may then mediate any and all of the cue effects treated previously with reference to the function of punishment itself. Accordingly, *anticipatory* fear may well function as a discriminative stimulus, as a distinctive cue, and quite possibly as a result of its association with the reinforcer maintaining the punished response, as a conditioned positive reinforcer. In this fashion, shock-punishment can actually postdate the occurrence of a reinforcer and yet provide the basis (through the r_p-s_p mechanism) by which performance of the punished act is altered, maintained or even facilitated.

To point up these response-eliciting functions of punishment apart from a general suppressing function, our concern for the most part will again be with "paradoxical" facilitation. In the following subsections, focus is placed first on specific motor reactions elicited by shock-punishment, and then on general emotional or fear responses, and relatedly the manner in which such fear can function as a cue. Finally, consideration is given to the basis for *escape* from both punishment and fear that prevails with the motor reactions elicited by punishment (and possibly also by fear) and hence the basis for negative reinforcement that is occasioned with the administration of punishment itself.

A. Motor Eliciting Function

Several investigations have been directed to an assessment of the reactions produced by shock of different intensities (*e.g.,* Goodman, Dyal, Zinser & Golub, 1966; Kimble, 1955; Trabasso & Thompson, 1962). The results of these studies are consistent in showing for rats a predominance of "flinch" reactions over low intensities, followed by an increasing frequency of "jump" reactions from about 0.3 to 0.9 mA (Kimble, 1955), where "prancing" and "running" become dominant over jumping (Trabasso & Thompson, 1962), and are then maintained without diminution to an intensity of 3.0 mA (Goodman *et al.* 1966). These "active" kinds of motor reactions are to be expected for the reason that they derive from experimental arrangements in which shock is administered to a passive animal; but, what of the case where the animal is already engaged in an active response, as is customarily the case when punishment is administered? In this context, shock may well elicit a general class of "stopping" behaviors, such as cringing or "freezing," as well as the more active modes of behavior noted above. Indeed, depending upon the type of reaction elicited by shock-punishment and conditioned to the cues in the situation, anticipatory punishment effects may either complement or interfere with the responses leading to punishment, so that measured performance may be either facilitated or disrupted.[6]

The relationship between behaviors leading to shock and the type of reaction directly elicited by the shock was initially treated in a study by Sheffield (1948). Attempting to relate the differences earlier reported by Brogden, Lipman and Culler (1938) between the effect of avoidable as opposed to unavoidable shock as a US for a conditioned running response, Sheffield (1948) trained guinea pigs to run to a tone CS in an activity wheel (as did Brogden, Lipman, and Culler, 1938), but took special note of the behaviors elicited by unavoidable shock during the course of a conditioned run. These observations showed that the shock US produced a range of responses such that the S either continued running or engaged in "incompatible" behaviors, like sprawling, turning around, or stopping, when shocked in response to the tone. When these different types of shock-produced reactions were related to performance on the next trial, Sheffield found that the strength of the conditioned running response reliably increased or decreased depending, respectively, on whether the S had continued running or stopped in response to the shock. In a subsequent paper, Sheffield (1949) noted a similar relationship between performance and whether rats initially escaped shock in an obstruction box by running forward or backing away. Ss that had initially responded to the shock by running forward often showed the behavior of "dashing out of the experimentor's hand, taking the shock and

---

[6]*Editor's note:* See also Chapter 3 by Bolles and Chapter 8 by Myer, this volume, for other treatments extending the significance of the variation in reactions produced by shock.

ignoring the lure on the far side of the grill." (Sheffield, 1949, p. 286.) In such cases, increasing the intensity of the shock only led to more vigorous running into the shock.

Similar findings on the relationship between punishment facilitation and punishment intensity were reported by Gwinn (1949). In Gwinn's study, which was actually designed to show that punishment would facilitate rather than inhibit performance when the response to the punishing stimulus was compatible with the punished act, rats were trained to escape a moderate 60-V shock in a circular alley by running forward and jumping out of the end compartment. Then, with the escape shock omitted and the running response now motivated presumably by fear, experimental Ss received either the same 60-V or a stronger 120-V shock-punishment in a distinctive segment of the alley just prior to the goal compartment. In comparison with control Ss that did not receive shock during this "extinction" phase of the experiment, the experimental Ss ran faster into the punishing shock and for a greater number of trials, with these effects being reliably augmented by the more severe punishment condition.

The fact that the punished Ss of Gwinn's (1949) study did finally extinguish their running was attributed by Gwinn to a conditioned intensification of fear in the distinctive punishment segment of the alley, and relatedly, the increased incidence of competing reactions (*i.e.*, startle and pausing) that occurred for the punished Ss as they approached this section. This subsequently developing inhibitory effect of punishment was also apparent in the performance of animals of both shock intensity conditions that had received extinction training under a condition where shock-punishment was administered on an intermittent, 30% schedule. During the latter stages of extinction, speed of running for these partially punished Ss was reliably slower following shock trials than following nonshock trials, indicating therefore that punishment had a specific inhibiting effect despite its general effect of facilitating performance relative to that of the unpunished controls. Taken together, Gwinn's (1949) results provided evidence both for an inhibiting and a facilitating effect of punishment, with these opposed effects apparently relating in the former case to the startle-pausing reactions elicited by fear of the punishment sections of the alley and in the latter case to the responses of running forward that were elicited and maintained by the shock-punishment itself.

Combined facilitating and inhibiting effects of punishment were also observed in a study by Fowler (1963), but with both of these effects apparently stemming from the reactions directly elicited by shock-punishment. In Fowler's study an effort was made to assess the potential dynamogenic effect of punishment that might occur as a consequence of an increased or residual emotionality resulting from the shock experience. Accordingly, rats received massed or distributed training running down a straight alley to food and different intensities of shock-punishment (0–110 V, .25 MΩ) at the goal. The findings showed that early in training stronger shocks had the uniform effect across training conditions of producing slower speeds; however, by the end of training, the distribution of speed scores for every group of shocked Ss was bimodal, with the fast and slow Ss within each distribution running reliably faster and slower, respectively, than appropriate counterparts of the unpunished control group. These effects were generally amplified by the intensity of shock-punishment so that stronger shocks produced greater facilitation and greater inhibition, respectively, for the "fast" and "slow" performers within each group of Ss.

To assay those factors underlying the bimodality of speeds, as well as the differential effect of punishment intensity on the "fast" and "slow" performers, Fowler (1963) made observations of the rat's behavior at the moment that shock was delivered. These observations showed quite consistently that the slow performers tended upon receipt of food at the goal to stand with all four feet on the grid through which shock was delivered and to lurch *back* when shocked. In contrast, the fast performers tended to stand with their front paws off the grid upon receipt of food and to lurch *forward* when shocked. Thus, the goal behavior of the shocked Ss indicated that shock-punishment had the effect of eliciting different reactions, which were stronger as a function of punishment intensity and, being either compatible or incompatible with the act of running to the goal, presumably served via their anticipatory occurrence to facilitate or retard performance of the punished response.

Because of the correlational nature of Fowler's (1963) findings, alternative interpretations are possible. For example, if shock-punishment is facilitating as a consequence of a dynamogenic effect at intensities just above threshold, and only aversive at stronger intensities, the obtained performance differences might well have resulted from the slow performers receipt of shock on their less calloused, smaller, and therefore more sensitive front paws, so that the effective intensities for these Ss were greater than those for the fast performers that received shock primarily on their hind paws. To assess this alternative interpretation, as well as demonstrate experimentally the facilitation and inhibition of performance produced by punishment, Fowler and Miller (1963) conducted a follow-up study in which rats were trained to run in the same apparatus to food and to different intensities of shock-punishment (0–75 V) at the goal, but now with shock specifically administered either to S's hind or front paws. The results of this study were consistent with those of the former investigation: Ss receiving hind-paw shock were facilitated relative to unpunished controls, whereas Ss that received front-paw shock were generally retarded. Furthermore, these effects were again amplified by the intensity of the punishment experience, and in no case did the milder punishment conditions facilitate the performance of Ss receiving shock on the front paws. Consequently, the results could not be attributed to any facilitating influence of shock-punishment *per se.*

In view of the interpretation offered by Fowler and Miller (1963), that the responses elicited by punishment could become anticipatory and thereby weaken or augment the punished running response, an effort was made to determine whether hind-paw punishment produced a "gradient" of facilitation within the instrumental response chain. This was accomplished by measuring the speeds of the hind-paw Ss within successive 2-ft sections along the runway and comparing these scores with respective section-speeds of the unpunished control Ss. As anticipated, the section-speed ratios showed facilitated performance on the part of the hind-paw shocked Ss, and indicative of an "approach" gradient, the ratios became larger with nearness to the goal. Furthermore, the effect of stronger hind-paw punishment was to raise the height of the entire approach gradient. It is especially noteworthy that these gradients matched as inverted images the *avoidance* gradients reported by Karsh (1962) for rats run in the same apparatus to food and shock intensities that were considerably stronger (75–300 V), although not specific to S's hind or front paws.

The importance of the response-eliciting function of punishment is not limited to the kind or type of reaction produced, but may relate as well to the point of development of the reaction within the training sequence. Such an effect is indicated in the results of a study by Karsh (1963) addressed to the effects of changes in the strength of punishment. Rats were briefly trained to run down an alley to food reinforcement, following which they received extended training wherein either a moderate (120-V) or a more severe (200-V) shock-punishment was consistently administered along with food reinforcement at the goal. When speeds under the two punishment intensities stabilized at different levels, the Ss were divided into subgroups with some of the Ss then being continued on the same shock intensity as before, and others being switched to the other of the two intensities. The results of Karsh's experiment showed that speeds for the switched groups changed only gradually and approached a level of performance intermediate to that of the unswitched groups. Thus, her data indicated that performance subsequent to a change in punishment intensity was still subject to the influence of the prior shock experience. In relation to these incomplete shifts in performance, Karsh noted a stereotypy in the responses elicited by shock-punishment at the goal: whereas moderate shock-punishment initially produced a reaction of shuddering or lurching back and severe shock-punishment the more vigorous reaction of actually jumping away and withdrawing from the food cup where shock was delivered, an upward or downward change in the intensity of punishment tended to elicit the reaction that had previously been established under the original punishment intensity. These findings, along with those considered above, indicate that how the animal learns to respond to shock, both in manner and magnitude, constitutes a major determinant of the punishment effect.

In our earlier discussion of the function of shock as a discriminative stimulus (Section II,A), note was made of the manner in which shock-punishment could so serve in the context of escape-avoidance training, that is, as a cue which would reinstate previously conditioned escape responses after the avoidance response was established. A recent study by Kurtz and Shafer (1966) has shown that comparable to the response-eliciting effects of punishment in the case of appetitive reinforcement (Fowler & Miller, 1963; Karsh, 1963), performance in the case of avoidance training is also influenced by the type of reaction directly elicited by punishment. Specifically, rats were trained to make a shuttle response to a light CS in order to avoid the US of shock which followed CS onset by 6 sec. A control group received a standard conditioning procedure whereby, depending upon elapsed time from CS onset, shock was either omitted (by a successful avoidance) or administered while S was engaged in shuttling or not responding at all. The Ss of two experimental groups also received shock if they made no response within the CS–US interval, but with the added contingency that shock was withheld for one group and added for the other group if the S began to shuttle at any point within the CS–US interval. Hence, the "shock-added" group was always punished for responding to the CS (as well as the control group occasionally) whereas the "shock-withheld" group was never punished for shuttling. Kurtz and Shafer observed that, for the shock-added and control groups, response-contingent shock had the effect of increasing the incidence of "freezing" behaviors and that these behaviors became conditioned to the light CS. Consequently, during subsequent trials, when a standard training procedure was in effect for all three groups, both the control and shock-added groups showed more "freezing" and therefore inferior avoidance performance in comparison with the shock-withheld group.

A final study to be noted in the context of the eliciting function of shock is the recent investigation by Morse, Mead and Kelleher (1967). In this experiment, brief shock administered every 60 sec to the tails of monkeys was found to elicit a stereotyped pulling and biting of the monkeys' neck collars. Following a number of such training sessions, shock was scheduled so that the first collar-response 30 sec after a shock produced the next shock (FI-30) or, if no response occurred, shock was again presented after 60 sec. Under these conditions, the collar response soon came to antedate the occurrence of shock to the point where every shock was then produced by a response. These findings are especially significant for they illustrate that shock-punishment can maintain responding when the only programmed consequence of responding is the scheduled presentation of the shock (see also Migler, 1963). Collectively, the findings of this section illustrate that the type and magnitude of the reaction elicited by shock and conditioned to the cues which antedate the shock constitute characteristics of the punishment situation which may distinguish it from learning with reward alone.

B. Emotion (Fear) Producing Function

As suggested earlier, the responses elicited by an aversive stimulus like shock may include not only specific motor reactions, but emotional or fear reactions as well. Furthermore, being subject to the same principle of anticipatory responding as noted with reference to the motor reactions produced by punishment, fear responses should be capable of being conditioned to the cues which antedate the shock, and therefore should be capable of influencing any and all performance occurring in the context of the shock-antedating cues. Much evidence exists on the phenomenon of fear conditioning, especially with regard to the role of fear as a secondary motivational system by which other behaviors can be acquired, maintained and even intensified (*e.g.,* Brown & Jacobs, 1949; Brown, Kalish & Farber, 1951; May, 1948; Miller, 1948; Mowrer, 1940). In the context of punishment training, however, the role of fear has often been summarily dismissed because of its conceptual status as an unobservable entity (*e.g.,* Azrin & Holz, 1966; Dinsmoor, 1954, 1955). It is further argued (*e.g.,* Dinsmoor, 1954) that, apart from a potential disruptive influence of anticipatory fear—as, for example, in producing cringing or "freezing"—the suppressing effects of punishment are derivable simply on the basis of the conditioned aversive properties of those cues which antedate the punishment and which the animal can thus "passively" avoid by engaging in behaviors that offset or compete with the active response sequence leading to punishment.[7] In view of these opinions, it becomes especially important that we examine the potential role of fear within a punishment paradigm by treating those cases where punishment has the paradoxical effect of facilitating performance or, at least, of maintaining a response which could reasonably be expected to be suppressed or eliminated.[8]

Anecdotal evidence has been reported on the ability of animals, both human and infrahuman, to learn to approach rather than withdraw from the cues of conditioned fear and thereby to resist and even overcome the decremental effects of punishment (see Miller, 1954). However, systematic experimental investigation of this phenomenon was initiated only recently. In the first of three experiments reported by Miller (1960), rats were trained to run down an alley for food reward and then, after reaching asymptotic performance, they received additional trials during which increasingly intense shock-punishments (125–335 V) were administered along with food reinforcement at the goal. Miller found that Ss of this "gradual" shock condition were progressively slowed down as a consequence of stronger shocks, but relatively little at the maximum intensity in comparison with "sudden" shock Ss that received the maximum intensity (335 V) on the first and remaining of their punishment trials. Because the gradual shock Ss had an extensive number of training contacts with shock at the goal, the possibility existed that their resistance to punishment was due to a physiological adaptation to the shock. In Miller's second experiment, however, control Ss that received the same gradual series of shocks in a distinctively different box outside of the alley (30 min after their daily trials) were shown to be comparable in performance to the sudden group, i.e., when finally tested in the alley with the maximum shock intensity. These results indicated that mere exposure to shock was not the factor responsible for the heightened resistance to punishment. Similarly, the effect could not be attributed to the point of introduction of shock-punishment within the training sequence because in Miller's third experiment sudden shock-punishment administered early in training i.e., coincidental with the first punishment trial for a gradual

---

[7] In reference to this position, Mowrer (1960) has astutely argued that *conditioned* aversiveness is not a property gained by a neutral stimulus in its own right, but rather a property acquired by the S; that is to say, the physical features of a neutral stimulus are not altered by its association with a primary aversive event like shock, but only the responses of the animal that are elicited by the stimulus.

[8] *Editor's note:* See especially Chapter 2 by McAllister and McAllister for additional discussion of conditioned punishment as an index of fear.

group, produced a performance decrement comparable to that of sudden shock-punishment administered late in training, *i.e.,* coincidental with the first *test* trial for the gradual group.

Despite the control features of Miller's (1960) study, his findings cannot be taken in support of the operation of fear nor of the cues of conditioned fear serving as discriminative stimuli for the response of continued running. As Miller himself notes, the gradual shock *S*s showed considerably less of a reaction to punishment at the goal in comparison with the violent lurching back and running away from the goal exhibited by the sudden shock *S*s. Consequently, the resistence to punishment exhibited by the gradual *S*s (and relatedly their less vigorous reactions to shock) could well have been due to a counter-conditioning effect in which the aversiveness of the shock experience was attenuated by the extensive association of shock and food reward. Furthermore, in view of Karsh's (1963) results showing that the magnitude of the motor reaction elicited by moderate shock-punishment tends to persist with an increase in punishment intensity, we may question whether the results are directly attributable to this factor rather than to the production of fear.

Miller's (1960) findings were subsequently extended in an investigation by Feirstein and Miller (1963), and with essentially the same outcome: Rats that received gradually increasing shock-punishments (10–430 V), but now on an intermittent basis in the *center* of the runway, showed far greater resistance to the maximum shock intensity of 430 V than did a sudden shock group that also received its shock in the center of the alley but at a considerably lower intensity of at first 100 V and then 250 V.[9] These results are impressive in view of the discrepancy in shock intensity for the gradual and sudden groups, but again the findings cannot be selectively attributed to the operation of conditioned fear nor to its role as a discriminative stimulus for continued responding. Appropriately, Feirstein and Miller note that with initially weak intensities, the gradual center-shock procedure enables the response of continuing to run forward to be elicited by the shock itself, as well as reinforced both by escape from shock and food reward at the goal. The complicating response-eliciting features of shock, as well as a potential counter-conditioning effect produced by the shock's antedating position relative to food reinforcement, would not apply however to the training procedure that was employed by Feirstein and Miller (1963) for other *S*s whereby

---

[9]Uhl (1967) has reported similar results using an operant analog of the runway procedure, *viz.,* discrete FR "trials" with gradually increasing shocks programmed in the middle of the FR schedule.

shock-punishment was administered 5 sec *after* S received food reinforcement at the goal. With this end-shock procedure, the investigators
again found considerably greater resistence to punishment on the part of
a gradual than sudden shock group. Hence, these findings, which would
seem independent of all of the previously considered functions of punishment, may suggest that fear became anticipatory and served both as a
cue and as an additional motivational impetus for the response of running to the goal.

Feirstein and Miller's (1963) findings are also supported by the results
of a series of studies by Banks (1966a, 1966b, 1967). In place of gradual
increments in the intensity of shock-punishment, however, Banks employed a procedure for rats whereby, following initial training to run
down an alley for food reward alone, the Ss received food along with a
constant goal-shock intensity (.32 mA, 0.1 sec) that was administered on
an intermittent, 30% schedule. Experimental Ss receiving this intermittent punishment (IP), as well as control Ss that did not receive any punishment during training, were then subjected to a test phase of
continuous punishment (CP) of the same intensity that was administered
along with food reward at the goal. The results of Bank's (1966a) experiment showed, comparable to Feirstein and Miller's (1963) results, that
the experimental Ss were far more resistant to CP than the control Ss,
and indicated therefore that persistence in the face of response-contingent aversive stimulation could be learned. But like Miller's (1960) results and those obtained by Feirstein and Miller (1963) with the gradual
center-shock procedure, Bank's (1966a) findings are subject to the criticism that his procedure of pairing shock-punishment with food reinforcement at the goal allowed the possibility of a counter-conditioning
effect. In Bank's (1966b) second experiment, however, IP was administered together with intermittent food reinforcement but the punishment
occurred only on nonreinforced trials. Again, experimental Ss subjected
to CP (now also without food reinforcement) showed significantly
greater resistance to the effects of punishment than did control Ss that
received either no punishment during preliminary training or the same
schedule of IP administered outside of the apparatus (specifically, 1 min
after the nonreinforced trials). Because all of the punishments administered during both training and testing were paired with nonreward,
Bank's (1966b) results cannot be attributed to an attenuation of the
aversiveness of the shock either by counter-conditioning or, in view of
the shock control, by mere exposure to the shock. Thus, the findings
argue strongly that resistance to punishment can be learned and mediated by the cues of anticipatory fear.

A complete analysis of the above results requires that one consider the extent to which a learned resistance to response-contingent shock is conditioned in part, if not wholly, to cues other than those of anticipatory fear, as for example apparatus cues. Logically, such an interpretation is ruled out by the fact that control Ss receive comparable training in making an approach response to the same set of apparatus cues and yet do not show comparable resistance to CP when administered in the context of these same cues. Confirmation of this argument is afforded by the results of Bank's (1967) third experiment: Hungry rats received IP and food reward in one runway apparatus and then, under the influence of water deprivation alone, they received water-reward training *without* punishment in a second grossly different runway, followed by a CP test phase. Under these conditions, where apparatus cues, as well as drive and reinforcement cues (*i.e.*, $S^D$and sg) were altered .from one training situation to the other, IP Ss again showed reliably greater resistance to CP than did control Ss that received the same schedule of IP during the first training phase but outside the apparatus. In view of these results, it seems especially clear that the observed resistance to punishment develops from an association between the cues of anticipatory punishment, *i.e.,* the stimulus feedback of an anticipatory fear reaction, and the instrumental response, for only the cues of fear would be common to both situations. In this context note should also be made of the results of a study by Terris and Wechkin (1967) pointing up the generality of the phenomenon. Subjecting rats initially to punishment training which entailed for experimental groups either a mild shock or a mild air blast together with food reinforcement at the goal of a runway, Terris and Wechkin found that, in comparison with control Ss that had not received punishment training, experimental Ss were more resistent to a subsequent, more intense punishment whether this punishment was the same as or different from that received in original training.

On the basis of these findings, which highlight a discriminative-stimulus function of fear, one may consider further whether fear, as a "motivational" stimulus, will serve not only to elicit but also to intensify the responses instrumental to punishment, and thereby lead to a facilitation of the punished response. It is interesting in this respect that Bank's (1966a, 1967) research shows an initial suppression followed by a subsequent recovery in the performance of Ss receiving IP training. These findings are analogous to those reported for intermittent nonreward (see Amsel, 1962) which, together with demonstrating an increment in resistance to extinction, also illustrate an intensification of the instrumental response during *acquisition* training (*e.g.,* Goodrich, 1959.) In the context of punishment training, comparable facilitating effects relating to the "energizing" aspects of anticipatory fear have been reported in a study by Martin and Ross (1964). Training rats to run down an alley to continuous water reinforcement and gradually increasing consummatory-response punishments (electric shocks) administered on an intermittent, 50% schedule, Martin and Ross found that starting speeds at the end of acquisition training, as well as combined starting and running speeds, were reliably faster for punished Ss than for control Ss that had not received punishment. That this facilitation derived from an *aversive* stimulus contingency (*i.e.,* that the shock-punishment had not been attenuated by its association with water reinforcement) was shown by a reliable suppression of the consummatory response on the punishment trials. At the onset of extinction, however, when both water reinforcement and shock-punishment were removed, consummatory responding as well as goal speeds for the experimental Ss were reliably facilitated, suggesting an intensification of these behaviors as well by the fear conditioned to the cues at the goal. Similar extinction results have been reported by Brown and Wagner (1964) and by Logan (1960).

On the basis of their findings, Martin and Ross (1964; also Martin, 1963) have suggested that whenever an approach response is sufficiently dominant to offset any cringing or "freezing" produced by anticipatory fear, such fear may "feed into" and thereby augment the approach response. This dependency between the facilitation produced by anticipatory punishment and the strength of the response leading to punishment seems indicated in the results of the previously cited Ph.D. thesis by Hawkins (1965). It will be recalled that rats in Hawkins' study received shock-right (SR) or no-shock (NS) training in a T-maze visual discrimination task wherein both drive (food deprivation) and incentive (food reinforcement) were factorially manipulated in conjunction with problem difficulty, specifically, light-dark and bright-dim problem conditions. With regard to speed of choice as measured from the start to S's occlusion of a photobeam just beyond the choice point in either arm, Hawkins' (1965) results showed that high drive and high incentive had the additive effect of increasing speed of choice within both problem conditions. However, when the discriminative stimuli were highly dissimilar (as in the easy light-dark problem) so that any fear conditioned as a consequence of SR training was selectively associated with the correct-response alternative, such SR training had the reliable effect of suppressing choice speeds to a comparable extent under all conditions of drive and incentive. On the other hand, when the discriminative stimuli were highly similar (as in the more difficult, bright-dim problem) so that fear was conditioned not only to the correct arm but also by generalization, to the similar incorrect arm, SR training had the effect of facilitating choice speeds under the high incentive condition; under conditions of low incentive, the effect of SR training was to suppress choice speeds comparably in both the easy and difficult problems. Considered together, these findings suggest that when fear is not selectively operating in one response alternative and therefore is less likely to elicit reactions removing S from this alternative in particular, it may facilitate the response of approaching the punished alternative providing that this approach response is made especially dominant, *e.g.,* by a high incentive condition.

Hawkins' (1965) results are particularly interesting because, in addition to pointing up an energizing function of fear, they provided evidence of a distinctive-cue function of shock-punishment itself. In our prior discussion of these data (Section II,C), it was noted that SR training had the effect of facilitating correct *choices* as well, but only within the difficult problem-condition and only under the condition of high drive. These results were suggested as being amenable to the interpretation that a distinctive-cue function of shock-punishment operates through the development of differential habit strengths which can be amplified by high drive. Their significance in the present context, however, is in pointing up the likelihood that not only shock-punishment but also the stimuli provided by conditioned fear can function as distinctive cues; and so operating, they may comparably facilitate performance by increasing the discriminability of the stimulus alternatives. That is to say, as with shock punishment itself, stimuli produced by conditioned fear can serve to limit the generalization of secondary reinforcement from a correct, food-reinforced alternative to a similar incorrect alternative and thereby reduce errors. This interpretation of the role of fear, which in effect argues that fear can mediate an *acquired* distinctiveness of cues (*cf.* Dollard & Miller, 1950) may be illustrated by reference to the findings of a study by Muenzinger and Baxter (1957).

In Muenzinger and Baxter's (1957) experiment, rats received food reward training in either a black or white runway where different groups in both situations had either to approach and cross an electrified grid "on their own initiative" or, being dropped onto the grid, to escape shock by running into the food compartment. Then, for T-maze discrimination training on a black-white problem, the brightness of the runway (black or white) was employed as a shock-substitute cue so as to stimulate either SR or SW training. As would be expected on the basis of the different reactions conditioned during runway training, the "approach" group was found to be superior to the "escape" group when the shock-substitute cue designated the correct alternative and simulated the SR condition; conversely, the escape group was superior to the approach group when the shock-substitute cue designated the incorrect alternative and simulated the SW condition. The perplexing result, however, was that with either the simulated SR or SW condition, both escape and approach trained Ss were superior to controls that had received runway training without the shock. These data indicated that, apart from the specific motor reactions elicited by shock and conditioned to the cues in the runway, these cues could facilitate performance when selectively designating *either* a correct or an incorrect response alternative. Muenzinger and Baxter (1957) interpreted this finding in terms of general sensitization, but now of course on the basis of the fear conditioned to the shock-substitute cues. An interpretation more in keeping with current findings on the effect of SR training (see Section II,C; also Fowler & Wischner, 1969) suggests instead that fear mediated an acquired distinctiveness of the shock-substitute cues; and, when selectively designating either the correct or incorrect response alternative, these fear-producing cues served to limit the generalization of secondary reinforcement from the correct to the incorrect alternative, thereby facilitating the performance of the prior shocked Ss.

Other equally important applications of the cue function of anticipatory fear may be noted as, for example, with regard to the effect of punishment in spatial discrimination learning. From those findings highlighting the association that can develop between anticipatory fear and the approach response leading to punishment (*e.g.*, Banks, 1966b; Hawkins, 1965; Martin & Ross, 1964), it follows that such a response should continue to be elicited and be maintained by fear of the punished alternative even when the S is confronted with an extinction or a reversal problem wherein the punishment is omitted. Consequently, in comparison with unpunished controls, punished Ss should show the persistent, maladaptive behavior of "fixating" on the previously punished alternative (*cf.* Farber, 1948). Koski and Ross (1965) have reported results which seem to illustrate this effect rather nicely. Rats that received consummatory-response punishment from the onset of spatial discrimination training (thereby allowing fear to become anticipatory and be associated with the response leading to punishment) showed retarded performance on a reversal for water reinforcement alone in comparison with either control Ss that had not received punishment or other experimental Ss that had received punishment on the original problem but only after learning had been accomplished. These findings and the others noted above indicate that whether shock-punishment will facilitate performance depends not only on the specific cue function of shock and the motor reactions elicited by it, but also on the function of shock in producing fear and the manner in which stimuli produced by this fear, on becoming anticipatory as the fear response does so, may themselves function as cues in eliciting, maintaining, and additionally intensifying behaviors that lead to punishment.

C.   Escape-Permitting Function

An analysis of the response-eliciting properties of punishment would not be complete without reference to the associated escape-permitting aspects of the punishment situation, in particular, the negative reinforcement that can derive from *termination* of the punishing stimulus and can serve to strengthen those reactions that are elicited by the punishment. A question may be posed regarding the relevance of escape responding for situations in which the duration of the punishing stimulus is so short as to prevent the S from emitting, within the temporal extent of the aversive stimulus, any reaction which would "remove" it from that stimulus. However, the temporal extent of the punishing stimulus does not vitiate the operation of negative reinforcement through pain termination, nor of that deriving potentially from a reduction of fear via the S's "withdrawal" from the cues associated with punishment—or even from the punishment contingency itself (*cf.* Azrin *et al.* 1965). So considered, the responses that follow punishment and lead to escape from both fear and pain, or are *adventitiously* associated with such escape, represent potentially important determinants of the particular effect that punishment will have on performance. Indeed, in situations where the response leading to punishment is not altered but is maintained by the punishing stimulus, the behavior that is punished should also be reinforced, and as a consequence, performance can be paradoxically facilitated.

Throughout prior discussion, frequent reference has been made to the role of escape responding in different contexts relating both to the cue and to the response-eliciting properties of punishment: specifically, with regard to the function of punishment as a discriminative stimulus (*e.g.*, Migler, 1963), as a potential secondary reinforcer (*e.g.*, Lohr, 1959), as an elicitor of specific motor reactions (*e.g.*, Gwinn, 1949), and as a US for conditioning fear (*e.g.*, Feirstein & Miller, 1963). Even in the context of "shock-right" training, where current findings are illustrative of a distinctive-cue function of punishment the results of early research (*e.g.*, Muenzinger, 1934; Muenzinger, *et al.*, 1938) seem largely attributable to the reinforcement of escape responses (see Fowler & Wischner, 1969). Despite these varied contexts pointing up the role of escape, isolation of this process is made extremely difficult by reason of the fact that it is virtually always confounded with other functions of the punishment procedure. Recently, however, a phenomenon has appeared which perhaps best illustrates the involvement of escape training in the context of punishment-produced facilitation. Initially termed "vicious circle" behavior, but more recently coming under the label "self-punitive," the phenomenon was first uncovered via a serendipitous observation by Judson Brown, as reported in Mowrer (1947): Rats trained to escape shock by running from an electrified start box and alley to an uncharged goal continued to run through shock in the alley when shock in the starting region was omitted; *i.e.*, the Ss ran into shock even though it was no longer necessary for them to run from shock.

The self-punitive effect observed by Brown received only perfunctory experimental treatment until recently, when the phenomenon was subjected to systematic investigation by Brown, Martin and Morrow (1964). In the first of two experiments utilizing a trap-door starting mechanism, rats were dropped onto a charged grid (60–75 V through 10 kΩ) and were permitted to escape shock in the start and alley regions by running to an uncharged goal that was distinctively different in several respects from the rest of the apparatus. Following 40 such trials, when "extinction" was introduced for all Ss by removing shock from the start region, different subgroups received shock-punishment throughout the entire alley (but not the goal), in the last two feet of the alley, or no punishment at all. The results of this first study provided some evidence that both the "short" and "long" punishment conditions would prolong extinction, but for the most part differences among the groups were unreliable. In the second experiment, however, when the same escape procedure and apparatus were employed but with fewer acquisition trials, slightly reduced shock intensities (45–50 V), a gradual reduction in start-box shock intensity from acquisition to extinction, and a buzzer in place of a flashing light that had been associated with the drop delivery, the extinction results unequivocally favored the punishment Ss. Whereas unpunished Ss showed a decrement in running speed over the course of extinction, the long-punishment Ss showed relatively constant speeds, and were faster than the short-punishment Ss which in turn were faster than the unpublished controls. These results could not be attributed simply to the eliciting properties of punishing shock, for the short-shock Ss were also faster than the control Ss in the initial 4-ft section of the alley that was not electrified. Furthermore, in comparison with the slowing down on the part of the unpunished Ss, the short-punishment Ss actually speeded up as they approached the locus of punishment in the final 2-ft alley segment, suggesting therefore an anticipatory shock-escape reaction analogous to the operation of incentive motivation (*i.e.*, anticipatory goal responding) in the context of appetitive conditioning (see Spence, 1956).

The findings reported by Brown *et al.* (1964) soon led to an intensification of research on self-punitive behavior with the result, however, that not all investigators were able to demonstrate a reliable effect as had been the case in the first experiment reported by Brown *et al.* (1964) as well as in some earlier research (*e.g.,* Moyer, 1957; Seward & Raskin, 1960). The issue was additionally complicated by the fact that more recent studies, tending to use avoidance training followed by punished extinction (*e.g.,* Campbell, Smith & Misanin, 1966; Seligman & Campbell, 1965; Smith, Misanin & Campbell, 1966), even obtained negative results showing a suppression rather than a facilitation of the punished response. Despite these failures at duplicating self-punitive behavior, the number of recent studies that have reported positive findings (about 20 or so using *either* an escape or an avoidance procedure) has been sufficient to establish the validity of the phenomenon beyond any doubt.[10] The differences in outcome are instructive, however, for they lead us to consider the manner in which the prior-noted functions of punishment may relate to the obtainment of self-punitive behavior. In particular, three aspects of the methodology seem of paramount importance:

1. Cue and Eliciting Properties of Punishment.

A seemingly major, if not primary, requirement for the obtainment of self-punitive behavior is that the response leading to punishment be sufficiently strong so that, upon receipt of punishment, the *S* does not withdraw or lurch back but instead continues to run forward to the unelectrified goal." In this fashion, punishment can serve to elicit continued running and, as a consequence, it can function as a discriminative stimulus for the response, as well as a motivator of it. So considered, the relationship between the strength of the "approach" response and the strength of the punishment will also be important, for to the extent that forward progress (*i.e.,* continued running) is not disrupted, stronger punishments may additionally intensify and thereby further sustain the behavior.

2. Cue and Eliciting Properties of Punishment-Produced Fear

Because the response leading to punishment must be maintained during "extinction" training, *i.e.,* when shock is removed from the start re-

---

[10]For an excellent review of the history of this problem, both current and past, as well as for a critical accounting of procedural factors and related theoretical principles underlying differences outcome in studies on self-punitive behavior, see Brown (1969).

[11]*Editor's note:* See Chapter 3 by Bolles for a discussion of this point relative to avoidance learning.

gion, it is equally important that this response and the fear produced by shock during acquisition training be well established to the cues of the start region. Consequently, with the start-area cues producing fear and the S having learned to run in the context of these cues, anticipatory fear deriving from punishing shock in extinction can then serve as a cue to elicit running, as opposed to competing reactions of cringing or "freezing." Important methodological features in this respect bear on the development of a strong conditioned fear reaction to the start-area cues, as effected through the use of salient and intense CSs (cf. Whittleton, Kostanek & Sawrey, 1965)—like the drop delivery and associated buzzer stimulus used in the Brown, et al. (1964) study[12]—and a sufficiently intense US or escape shock (cf. Anderson & Johnson, 1966). Furthermore, in order that punishing shock, as a US, may reinstate or maintain the fear conditioned to the start area, it may well be advantageous to have the punishing shock in a proximal position relative to the start region, so as to insure an optimal CS–US interval (cf. Martin & Melvin, 1964; Melvin, Athey & Heasley, 1965), and to have the punishment area of the alley similar in physical features to the start area, so as to promote a generalization of fear of punishment to the start region.

3. Reinforcement via Escape from Both Fear and Pain of Punishment

So that both fear and pain of punishment can serve as cues which will elicit, as well as intensify, the response of running forward, it is critical that they be maintained as effective signals for the response via their association with the reinforcement deriving from escape from punishment. Indeed, if escape were precluded or even diminished, as would be effected by extending punishing shock into the goal region, then these cues would lose their functional significance as signals for safety, since they would now be associated with, and thus signal, nonreinforcement or extinction. (Note here that the customary operation for "extinction" in studies on self-punitive behavior is not that of removing the reinforcement, i.e., preventing escape from shock, but rather the pseudo operation of removing the shock that elicits running from the start.) Additionally, it is important that the punishment area of the alley be separate and distinct from the uncharged goal region, so that the same response of running forward through shock can be immediately reinforced by escape

---

[12]Consistent with this interpretation, the findings of an unpublished study by the author, in collaboration with M.J. Moskowitz and P.F. Spelt, indicate that the saliency of start-area cues, as manipulated by the presence or absence of drop delivery or of buzzer CS, is a major determinant of the eliciting properties of the start cues and relatedly of the presence or absence of self-punitive behavior.

not only from pain, but also from the fear conditioned to the punishment and start areas. That the goal area be distinctively different from
the rest of the apparatus, as in the Brown *et al.* (1964) study, is also
required from the standpoint of precluding any generalization of fear to
this region. Finally, the intensity of punishing shock will be important
for to the extent that both fear and pain of punishment are effectively
reduced via escape, more intense punishment may set the occasion for
greater reinforcement of the escape response and consequently a stronger
self-punitive effect.

Factors other than those listed above should be important in determining self-punitive behavior, as for example the time between the S's
start and the delivery of the motivating shock (*i.e.*, CS–US interval, as in
avoidance training) and the number of acquisition trials (*i.e.*, CS–US
pairings). Nevertheless, the foregoing analysis should suffice in pointing
up those functions of punishment and the related procedural manipulations by which self-punitive behavior may be obtained. Because our concern is primarily with the escape-permitting aspects of the punishment
situation, we shall limit further discussion of self-punitive behavior to
those studies which not only report the phenomenon, but in addition
show an actual strengthening of the response leading to punishment—an
outcome seemingly related to the operation of escape reinforcement.

Some evidence for a reinforcement effect is provided in a study by
Melvin and Martin (1966) which extended the original self-punitive paradigm by using two, qualitatively different aversive stimuli. Rats were
trained via a drop delivery onto a runway to escape either a buzzer stimulus (101 dB, *re* .0002 dynes/cm^2) or a shock (50 V, 10 kΩ), and then, when
the escape stimulus was omitted for "extinction" training, different
subgroups from each of the two training conditions received either no
punishment or a 0.3-sec buzzer or shock-punishment administered immediately upon S's entry into the alley. Both the buzzer and shock-trained
Ss learned effective escape responses during acquisition training, but the
performance of the shock-escape group was far superior to that of the
buzzer group, indicating that shock was much more of an aversive stimulus than the buzzer in motivating escape. Consistent with these results,
shock-punishment had the pronounced effect of protracting extinction
for both buzzer and shock-trained Ss, whereas this self-punitive effect
was considerably reduced with buzzer-punishment, and in fact, was present reliably only for the shock-trained subgroups. The more interesting
aspect of the data for our purposes related to the difference in extinction
performance between buzzer and shock-trained Ss that received shock-
punishment: whereas shock-trained Ss showed a gradual decrement in
running speed with the onset of extinction training, buzzer-trained Ss

actually showed an abrupt increment in running speed, illustrating therefore that shock-punishment could not only maintain the behavior but
also lead to the kind of imporvement in performance characteristic of
learning. Caution must be exercised in attributing this result to the reinforcement of escape responses, however, for the effect could also relate
to the greater aversiveness of shock as a punisher (for buzzer-trained Ss),
and hence to the greater production of fear and pain as *elicitors* of self-
punitive running.

The reinforcement of escape responses in the "acquisition" of self-punitive behavior during extinction training seems more clearly indicated in
the results of a series of studies by Beecroft and his associates (Beecroft,
1967; Beecroft & Bouska, 1967; Beecroft, Bouska & Fisher, 1967; Beecroft & Brown, 1967). In an initial study actually concerned with the
learning of self-punitive running, Beecroft and Bouska (1967) used the
original apparatus including the drop delivery and associated buzzer CS
of Brown et al. (1964, Experiment 2) but limited the amount of shock-
escape training for rats to 10 trials, so that running at the outset of extinction would be slow enough to permit an improvement in performance. Relative to unpunished controls which showed a progressive
decrement in speed over the course of 10 extinction trials, punished Ss
showed a gradual rise in running speed, measured either in the initial
4-ft segment of the alley that was not electrified or in the last 2-ft segment
where shock-punishment (55 V, 10kΩ) was administered. The same effect
was also observed in a study by Beecroft (1967) where, in place of initial
shock-escape training, an avoidance procedure was employed by delay-
ing the onset of shock for 3 sec following the S's drop delivery onto the
alley grid. In this study, the rise in self-punitive running was more con-
strained, however, presumably as a result of faster, and hence more
nearly asympototic, running speeds which prevailed at the outset of extinction training.

That avoidance training can lead to an improvement in running during punished extinction is also reported by Beecroft and Brown (1967).
Attempting to capitalize on the fact that shock-punishment administered
near the goal of a runway, for example, the short-punishment condition
in Brown et al. (1964), would more closely duplicate training with an
avoidance procedure whereby S eventually learns to run in the absence
of shock in the start and initial alley sections, Beecroft and Brown utilized an escape-avoidance procedure in which the CS–US interval between drop delivery and the onset of shock (55 V, 10 kΩ) was set for
different groups at 0, 1, 2 or 4 sec. Over the course of 50 training trials,
running speed in a 6-ft alley correlated directly with the "demands" of
the avoidance schedule: *i.e.*, speeds were progressively faster with shorter

CS–US intervals except in the case of the 0-sec (escape) condition where performance was comparable to that of the 2-sec avoidance condition. During extinction training, however, when punishing shock of the same intensity was administered, but only in the last 2-ft alley segment, the 2- and 4-sec avoidance groups showed a marked rise in running speed from their original low levels of performance, in comparison with the 1-sec avoidance group which maintained its previously high performance level. Thus, these results showed that, depending on the requirements imposed by shock scheduling, the avoidance *S*s either learned to run fast during acquisition training, as in the 1-sec condition, or they *learned* to run fast during extinction, as in the 2- and 4-sec conditions. However, when the conditions of prior training were considerably altered by the administration of punishing shock near the goal, as for the 0-sec (escape) group, speeds did not increase but tended to be maintained or even to decrease over the course of extinction.

The final study in the series, that by Beecroft, *et al.* (1967), highlights the role of both training procedure and punishment intensity as determinants of self-punitive running. Using the general methodology of prior studies and a 3-sec interval between drop delivery and the onset of shock (55 V, 10 kΩ), Beecroft *et al.* (1967) trained rats to a criterion of one successful avoidance, following which extinction was introduced with shock-punishment administered in the final 1-ft segment of the alley and set for different groups at 0, 40, 55 or 70 V. Self-punitive behavior occurred for all of the punished groups, with the 55-V group showing the greatest resistance to extinction as measured both by the number of *S*s continuing to run during extinction and by mean trials to an extinction criterion. These findings, as well as similar results from a subsidiary experiment using a different training voltage (*viz.,* 70 V) indicated that the cues provided by shock during avoidance training became associated with continued running and that an alteration of these cues, as when shock intensity was increased or decreased, degraded their eliciting function. This eliciting effect, however, did not contravert the intensifying and potential reinforcing aspects of punishment, as related to shock intensity, for during the early part of extinction, running speeds varied directly with punishment intensity. In fact, relative to terminal acquisition speeds, which were maintained at a constant level by the 55-V punishment group, speeds for the 40-V group tended to decrease whereas those for the 70-V group increased.

Other studies pointing up instances of "learned" self-punitive behavior have been reported by Melvin and Smith (1967) and Melvin and Stenmark (1968). These two studies are especially noteworthy because, in contrast to the above investigations, they illustrate that such learning may occur prior to the acquisition of an escape or an avoidance response, or subsequent to its extinction. This latter effect is shown in the Melvin and Smith (1967) study wherein rats received avoidance training in a 4-ft alley followed by regular (no-shock) extinction for 30 trials and then punishment training with shock administered in the second foot of the runway. Running speeds decreased progressively during regular extinction but with the onset of punishment training, speeds abruptly increased. (The effect was also obtained but in reverse order for a comparison group that received punishment training followed by regular extinction.) Even more dramatic findings for our purposes are those reported by Melvin and Stenmark (1968). To assess the role of fear conditioning, these investigators gave rats 18 paired presentations of a buzzer and a shock (65V, 10kΩ) in the start box of an alley but prevented the Ss from running; then, following 3 additional trials in which shock was omitted and the S now permitted to leave the start and run to the goal, 40 more trials were administered with experimental Ss being punished for running. Despite the fact that running had never been associated with shock, punished Ss showed a consistent improvement in running speed in comparison with the gradual decrement in running speed shown by unpunished controls. It is particularly noteworthy that the learning exhibited by the punished Ss was facilitated by middle-alley as opposed to far (near-goal) punishment and, consistent with the results of Beecroft *et al.* (1967), by stronger as opposed to weaker (75 versus 55 V) shocks—although this latter effect was not statistically reliable.

The foregoing studies, especially those by Melvin and his associates, would seem highly indicative of the reinforcement deriving from escape from punishment; but, the findings cannot be taken to vitiate the cue and eliciting functions of fear and pain of punishment, nor their role in the learning of self-punitive behavior. For example, in the Melvin and Smith (1967) study wherein rats received regular extinction training prior to punishment training, a question prevails as to the role of punishment as a US in reinstating the fear conditioned to the start-area cues and hence in reinstating the cues for running (*cf.* Baum, 1965). Similarly, in the Melvin and Stenmark (1968) study in which running had not previously been associated with shock, one cannot dismiss the possibility that such running was partially conditioned to fear of the start area during the three preshock (prior to punishment) trials, and that punishment training then served to maintain this association as well as to promote its further development. These confounding effects relating to the cue and eliciting properties of punishment would seem completely obviated, however, in the unpublished research most recently reported by Brown (1969). Attempting to transmute running based on food-reward training to self-punitive running, Brown initially trained rats when hungry to run in an alley to food reinforcement at the goal; then, increasingly intense and progressively more frequent shock punishments (0-40 V, 10 kΩ) administered in the middle of the alley were interspersed in training when the Ss were *not* hungry and *not* rewarded by food at the goal, so that finally the Ss received nothing but punishment for running. Not all of Brown's Ss continued to run when punishment was completely substituted for food reinforcement, but more ran than when shock punishment was not so substituted, as for unpunished controls. Furthermore, in comparison with a steady decline in running speed shown by the unreinforced and unpunished Ss, the punished Ss learned to run faster and faster.

On the basis of Brown's (1969) reported findings, particularly the fact that his punished Ss had never experienced shock nor the fear produced by shock in the start of the alley, and thus had never previously run in the context of shock and fear cues, one is confronted with the fact that punishment, like food, operated essentially as a reinforcer. But, by virtue of the fact that shock-punishment entails an aversive-stimulus contingency (and relatedly the fact that not all of Brown's punished Ss continued to run), one cannot reasonably attribute the reinforcement effect to the *presentation* of the aversive stimulus, as analogous to the positive reinforcement provided by presentation of food. Consequently, it seems clear that the learning produced by punishment related to the *negative* reinforcement of escape from both fear and pain of the aversive stimulus, as would prevail in the context of simple escape conditioning where, in place of the appetitive motivation used in Brown's (1969) research, performance is continuously motivated by the presentation of shock and reinforced by its reduction or elimination. In view of this comparison, it is indeed unfortunate that no study on self-punitive behavior has, to the writer's knowledge, investigated the effect of administering punishment with and without the escape contingency: for when the reduction of shock in instrumental escape conditioning is of a small magnitude (*cf.* Bower, Fowler & Trapold, 1959) or its termination considerably delayed (*cf.* Fowler & Trapold, 1962), acquisition of the running response simply does not prevail.

IV.   THE NATURE OF PUNISHMENT:
SUMMARY AND INTERPRETATION

At the beginning of this chapter, reference was made to the varied effects of punishment as indicators of comparably varied functions of punishment. Following this orientation, selective consideration of the facilitating effects of punishment demonstrated both cue and eliciting properties of punishment apart from a presummed suppressing function. With reference to the role of punishment as a signal or as a CS for food reinforcement, note was made of its specific function as a discriminative stimulus, as a secondary reinforcer, and even as a highly discernible or distinctive cue. It is now to be emphasized that these cue functions of punishment are not necessarily dependent upon the association of punishment with food reinforcement, as was argued previously regarding the function of punishment as a distinctive cue in the context of "shock-wrong" training, *i.e.,* when punishment is applied to the incorrect (nonreinforced) response. Similarly, with reference to the discriminative properties of punishment, it will be recalled that punishment can function equally well as a signal for nonreinforcement and, although not previously detailed, punishment should also be effective as a secondary "frustrative" stimulus; *i.e.,* like its role as a secondary reinforcer in mediating the effect of food reinforcement, punishment should also operate as a mediator of the effect of nonreinforcement when selectively designating a condition of nonreward. In this light, it would seem that much of what has been attributed to a suppressing function of punishment is equally ascribable to its function as a cue, when associated with nonreward.

The same holds true regarding the function of punishment in eliciting specific motor and/or fear reactions, and in providing a basis for reinforcement via escape from both fear and pain of punishment. Although these functions derive from an analysis based on the facilitating effects of punishment, it should be apparent that the eliciting properties of punishment are equally applicable to suppression effects, for example, the case of punishment producing motor reactions that cause the S to withdraw or lurch back from the aversive stimulus and which, on becoming anticipatory, interfere or compete with the response leading to punishment. Similarly, the response leading to punishment may be disrupted (*i.e.,* "suppressed") through cringing and "flinching" movements that are produced by anticipatory fear.[13] Finally, one may expect that anticipatory reactions, which interfere with the response leading to punishment and which therefore are effective in removing the animal from further punishment, will be negatively reinforced via the S's escape from or reduction of both fear and pain of punishment. Consequently, not

[13]It is noteworthy that recent work by Spevack and Suboski (1967) has successfully demonstrated a confounding of "conditioned suppression" (*i.e.,* the conditioning of a "freezing" response to situational cues) in a one-trial "passive avoidance" situation where shock is administered contingent upon a bar-press response.

only facilitating effects but suppressing effects as well are derivable on the basis of both the CS and US properties of punishment.

It should not be gained from the foregoing, however, that the specified cue and eliciting properties of punishment necessarily obviate a suppressing function or for that matter other functions of the punishment procedure. Prior discussion also had reference to the potential function of punishment in "sensitizing" or alerting the S to the discriminanda (*e.g.*, Muenzinger, 1934; see also Strain, 1953), and in producing stimulus variation, as when punishment is administered on an intermittent basis (*e.g.*, Logan, 1960). Other possible functions, not considered, would have reference to the action of punishment in producing a "compensatory increase" in response rate, as when punishment is eliminated from a free response context (*e.g.*, Azrin, 1960; Estes, 1944) or, like reinforcement, in producing a "contrast" effect, as when punished Ss exhibit higher rates on an alternative or subsequently unpunished response in comparison with the rate shown on this response by unpunished controls (*e.g.*, Brethower & Reynolds, 1962; Holz, Azrin & Ulrich, 1963).

These additional "facilitating" effects of punishment must eventually be considered with regard to the possible additional functions of punishment that they illuminate, as well as the extent to which they can be subsummed by the cue and eliciting properties of punishment already noted. Thus, one may consider punishment as a distinctive cue in obviating any sensitizing function (see Section II,C), or as a discriminative stimulus in accounting for a "compensatory increase" via the signalling of reinforcement that may be occasioned with the removal of punishment from an extinction phase (see Estes, 1944), or even as a primary elicitor of fear in accounting for a "contrast" effect via the reduction of *generalized* fear and hence the additional reinforcement that prevails for an alternative unpunished response. To the extent, however, that we have been able to isolate different functions of the punishment procedure, as well as to relate these functions to the varied effects of punishment, it behooves us to consider which of the noted functions are in fact peculiar to punishment as a process distinct from others.

A. Functions Specific to Punishment

In those studies we have considered that point up the facilitating effects of punishment, as well as in virtually all studies on punishment, the experimental paradigms have involved a comparison of response-contingent shock (punishment) with the absence of shock (no punishment), and/or with the absence of the contingency, as in noncontingent or response-independent shock. These comparisons are most important in extracting the particular effects of punishment, and indeed, as illustrated, in highlighting different functions of the punishment procedure. But insofar as these comparisons isolate functions and effects peculiar to punishment, they are grossly inadequate, for although they control for the presence of an aversive stimulus, like shock, and the contingency involved, they do not control for the combination of these two factors as would be provided by a contingency entailing nonaversive stimuli. Consequently, an analysis of the nature of punishment as a process distinct from others must have reference to those functions of punishment which are peculiar to an aversive-stimulus contingency and not to one based on nonaversive or "neutral" stimuli.

When this type of comparison is considered, it becomes eminently clear that the noted cue or CS functions of punishment are, for the most part, not peculiar to the punishment process. That is to say, nonaversive or neutral stimuli, when contingent upon a response and associated with reinforcement, may also function as discriminative stimuli for continued responding or as secondary reinforcers which mediate the effect of food reinforcement. The same holds true, of course, regarding the discriminative properties of punishment (and correspondingly of nonaversive stimuli) as signals for nonreward and relatedly as cues which may produce anticipatory frustration. Generally considered, the function of punishment as a distinctive cue would also be subsummed by nonaversive stimuli, but in this respect a qualification may be in order. Because a distinctive-cue function of punishment bears on the extent to which the aversive stimulus is distinctive and, as such, may increase discriminability of the stimulus alternatives (thereby limiting the generalization of secondary reinforcement from food-associated, correct cues to incorrect cues), the aversive stimulus may be inherently more distinctive as a result of its subjective intensity. That is to say, nonaversive stimuli may function as distinctive cues, but the extent to which distinctiveness or increased discriminability of the alternatives is gained should be governed by the intensity of these stimuli. Consequently, a neutral stimulus made more intense will be more distinctive, but such an increase in its intensity may effectively promote it to the threshold of aversiveness, as in the case of bright lights, loud noises, etc. So considered, then, a distinctive-cue function may be viewed as peculiar to punishment in so far as aversiveness is represented by an intensive dimension.

It is the intensive dimension of aversive stimulation that also sets the punishment process apart regarding its US or eliciting properties. Nonaversive or neutral stimuli can serve as USs (cf. Fowler, 1965, 1967), but the innate reactions elicited by these stimuli will be comprised of responses of orienting, attending to or detecting the stimuli. Thus, the nature of the reaction elicited by a nonaversive stimulus will differ drastically from that produced by an aversive stimulus, like shock, unless of course the response to the nonaversive or neutral stimulus is established through prior conditioning (as in the case of conditioned aversiveness) or the nonaversive stimulus itself is of such an intensity as to promote flinching, "freezing", and concomitant emotional reactions. Such reactions to an intense US may, on becoming anticipatory, interfere with the response that leads to the US and thereby promote the US to the position of an effective suppressor or "punisher" of behavior. In this respect, then, it is not the eliciting function of the aversive stimulus that is peculiar to the punishment process, but rather the type and magnitude of the reaction that is elicited by punishment by virtue of its intensity.

The significance of the intensiveness of aversive stimulation is brought out even more clearly with reference to the role of punishment in reinforcement. As noted previously, the escape-permitting aspects of the punishment situation may effect either a facilitation of performance, as in learned self-punitive behavior, or a disruption of performance via the negative reinforcement prevailing for anticipatory reactions that remove the S from both fear and pain of punishment. Nonaversive or neutral stimuli that are contingent on a response may also provide reinforcement, *i.e.*, via sensory change and stimulus variation (*cf.* Kish, 1966), but herein the reinforcement is comparable to that afforded by food reinforcement, as effected by the presentation of the stimulus rather than by its removal or termination. Indeed, only when the neutral stimulus is made sufficiently intense so as to produce aversion will its alleviation be comparable to that of punishment in permitting reinforcement via escape. From this vantage point, we are confronted with the conclusion that it is the response-eliciting functions of punishment, namely, its motor-eliciting, emotional and escape aspects, which characterize and represent the mechanics or principles of operation of punishment as a process distinct from others.

B.   Theoretical Mechanisms of Punishment

By our continual reference to the functions, as well as to the effects of punishment, we have attempted to evaluate the principles of operation of the punishment process, *i.e.*, the theoretical mechanisms by which punishment may exert its effect either in facilitating or suppressing behavior. And, on the basis of the noted functions of punishment, in particular, those deriving from the foregoing comparisons involving aversive and nonaversive stimuli, we have argued that specific to this process are the response-eliciting and escape-permitting properties of the aversive-stimulus contingency. Consequently, with reference now to the theoretical mechanisms of punishment, these functions may be translated to hypotheses involving (1) a *competing-response* mechanism, (2) a *fear* mechanism and (3) an *escape* mechanism. That is to say, in elaboration (1) that punishment-produced motor reactions will, via the principles of classical conditioning and stimulus generalization, occur in the context of the cues that antedate punishment and, depending upon the type and strength of the reactions elicited, either compete with or complement the response leading to punishment; (2) that fear, on similarly becoming anticipatory, will suppress the punished response via the flinching and cringing reactions that it can produce, or if associated with a dominant approach response, provide the discriminative and motivational basis for the continuation of this response; or (3) that escape from both fear and pain of punishment will, via the principle of reinforcement, strengthen anticipatory reactions of withdrawing from punishment or perseverative reactions of "running through" punishment.

Apart from these hypotheses involving competing-response, fear and escape mechanisms, there are those in which the operation of punishment is related to a *suppression* or an *avoidance* mechanism (see Church, 1963). Herein, the action of punishment in reducing or eliminating (but not facilitating) behavior is thought to be via a suppression or a direct inhibition of the punished response—as opposed to its interference via, for example, competing-response or fear mechanisms—or, from the standpoint of an avoidance mechanism which does not entail inhibition of the punished response, that punishment-associated cues, either situational or response-produced, become conditioned aversive stimuli which the S then learns to avoid by engaging in responses that are instrumental to their removal or termination; with the termination of these discriminative stimuli controlling the punished response, the behavior is thus disrupted. Although this latter hypothesis is quite similar to those based on the response-eliciting mechanisms of punishment, it can be distinguished from them by way of its emphasis, not on the anticipatory occurrence of punishment-produced reactions, but rather on the instrumental learning of responses that occur in the context of punishment-associated cues.[14] This similarity notwithstanding, interpretations involving suppression or avoidance mechanisms, as described, are severely restricted by virtue of the fact that they cannot be employed to

---

[14]The distinction is, of course, further removed when the possibility is noted that startle and withdrawal reactions to anticipatory fear can be reinforced, *i.e.*, instrumentally learned, on the basis of the S's escape from fear.

account for punishment effects inclusive of paradoxical facilitation. Indeed, our purpose in selectively focusing on facilitating effects was to point up functions (and correlative mechanisms) of punishment which were apart from a suppression or an avoidance mechanism. It behooves us, however, to consider one final basis for differentiating the various mechanisms of punishment, one that relates specifically to the effect of punishment in suppressing behavior.

In an overview of the theoretical mechanisms of punishment, Church (1963) has pointed out an important distinction regarding the correlation of aversive stimuli and the response to which such stimulation is applied. Regarding the elimination of a response, both suppression and avoidance interpretations of the function of punishment necessarily involve a correlation of this response with the punishing stimulus, so that this response in particular, rather than some other response, will be inhibited (*i.e.*, suppressed) and/or its associated "feedback" stimuli established as conditioned aversive stimuli. In contrast, hypotheses based on competing-response, fear and escape mechanisms do not necessarily require that the aversive stimulus be correlated with the response, for their action is indirectly established through the responses that are produced by the aversive stimulus and are conditioned to the cues antedating the punishment. Thus, an important basis for differentiating hypotheses involving "correlated" and "uncorrelated" mechanisms relates to the effect produced by administering aversive stimulation either on a response-contingent or a response-independent basis; *i.e.*, where the interval between the response and the aversive stimulus is of a short duration, so as to promote a contingency between the response and the aversive stimulus, or of a relatively long and/or varied duration, so as to effect an independence of the response and the aversive stimulus.

Hypotheses involving either correlated or uncorrelated mechanisms have no difficulty in accounting for the suppressing effect of response-contingent aversive stimulation (*viz.*, punishment) since the temporal proximity of the response to punishment will enable the response to be influenced directly by a suppression mechanism, for example, or indirectly by the competing reactions that are produced by punishment and conditioned to the cues controlling the punished response. Furthermore, a direct suppressing action or an indirect interfering action of punishment should be comparably regulated by the intensity of the punishment since with greater punishment intensity, suppression will be greater and the interfering responses produced by punishment stronger. The effect of correlated and uncorrelated mechanisms would not be expected to be the same, however, regarding aversive stimulation that is administered independently of the response, *i.e.*, on a noncontingent basis. Herein, the aversive stimulus, be it weak or strong, should be ineffective in disrupting behavior via a direct suppressing mechanism since the response in question is temporally removed from the aversive stimulus and its possible inhibiting action. Similarly, by virtue of this temporal disparity, response-produced stimuli will be degraded as conditioned aversive stimuli and thus less capable of producing avoidance. The same holds true for uncorrelated mechanisms when the aversive stimulus is of weak intensity and hence the reactions (URs) elicited by the stimulus too weak to be effectively conditioned to situational cues or any other stimuli that may be associated with the response. But if, in the presence of general situational cues or traces of specific external stimuli associated with the response, the reactions elicited by the aversive stimulus are sufficiently strong as a result of the intensity of the aversive stimulus as a US, then effective conditioning should be accomplished. And, to the extent that the cues present in the context of the reactions produced by the aversive stimulus are the same as or similar to those prevailing at the time of the response antedating the aversive stimulus, then performance should be disrupted.

Totally, the foregoing analysis suggests that, with respect to the suppressing effects of punishment in particular, the function of punishment in eliciting specific motor and/or general emotional reactions, as well as in permitting escape, will be highly influential depending upon the temporal relation of the aversive stimulus to the response, the similarity of the cues associated with both the aversive stimulus and the response, and especially important, the intensity of the aversive stimulus itself. Taking into account the role of these factors, an analysis of the effects of contingent and noncontingent procedures should, as Church (1963) suggested, prove particularly illuminating with respect to the manner and mechanisms by which punishment can disrupt performance. Nonetheless, to the extent that punishment can facilitate performance, and indeed it can, the operation of mechanisms relating to the response-eliciting properties of punishment seems clearly well established.

ACKNOWLEDGMENT

This paper was prepared while the author was on sabbatical leave to the Department of Psychology, University of New Mexico. Grateful acknowledgement is made to Dr. Frank A. Logan, Chairman, for the facilities generously provided.

Preparation of the paper was supported in part by Grant MH-08482 from the National Institutes of Health, United States Public Health Service.

REFERENCES

Akhtar, M. Increased resistance to punishment as a function of counterconditioning. *Journal of Comparative and Physiological Psychology,* 1967, **64,** 268–272.

Amsel, A. Frustrative nonreward in partial reinforcement and discrimination learning: Some recent history and a theoretical extension. *Psychological Review,* 1962, **69,** 306–328.

Anderson, D.C., & Johnson, L. Conditioned fear as a function of US intensity under conditions of drive constancy. *Psychonomic Science,* 1966, **5,** 443–444.

Appel, J.B. The aversive control of an operant discrimination. *Journal of the Experimental Analysis of Behavior,* 1960, **3,** 35–47. (a)

Appel, J.B. Some schedules involving aversive control. *Journal of the Experimental Analysis of Behavior,* 1960, **3,** 349–359. (b)

Appel, J.B. Punishment and shock intensity. *Science,* 1963, **141,** 528–529.

Azrin, N.H. Punishment and recovery during fixed-ratio performance. *Journal of the Experimental Analysis of Behavior,* 1959, **2,** 301–305.

Azrin, N.H. Sequential effects of punishment. *Science,* 1960, **131,** 605–606.

Azrin, N.H., Hake, D.F., Holz, W.C., & Hutchinson, R.R. Motivational aspects of escape from punishment. *Journal of the Experimental Analysis of Behavior,* 1965, **8,** 31–44.

Azrin, N.H., & Holz, W.C. Punishment. In W.K. Honig (Ed.), *Operant behavior: Areas of research and application.* New York: Appleton, 1966. Pp. 380–447.

Banks, R.K. Persistence to continuous punishment following intermittent punishment training. *Journal of Experimental Psychology,* 1966, **71,** 373–377. (a)

Banks, R.K. Persistence to continuous punishment and nonreward following training with intermittent punishment and nonreward. *Psychonomic Science,* 1966, **5,** 105–106. (b)

Banks, R.K. Intermittent punishment effect (IPE) sustained through changed stimulus conditions and through blocks of nonpunished trials. *Journal of Experimental Psychology,* 1967, **73,** 456–460.

Baum, M. The recovery-from-extinction of an avoidance response following an inescapable shock in the avoidance apparatus. *Psychonomic Science,* 1965, **2,** 7–8.

Beck, R.C. On secondary reinforcement and shock termination. *Psychological Bulletin,* 1961, **58,** 28–45.

Beecroft, R.S. Near-goal punishment of avoidance running. *Psychonomic Science,* 1967, **8,** 109–110.

Beecroft, R.S. & Bouska, S.A. Learning self-punitive running. *Psychonomic Science,* 1967, **8,** 107–108.

Beecroft, R.S., Bouska, S.A., & Fisher, B.G. Punishment intensity and self-punitive behavior. *Psychonomic Science,* 1967, **8,** 351–352.

Beecroft, R.S., & Brown, J.S. Punishment following escape and avoidance training. *Psychonomic Science,* 1967, **8,** 349–350.

Bitterman, M.E., & Elam, C.B. Discrimination following varying amounts of nondifferential reinforcement. *American Journal of Psychology,* 1954, **67,** 133–137.

Black, A.H., & Morse, Patricia. Avoidance learning in dogs without a warning signal. *Journal of the Experimental Analysis of Behavior,* 1961, **4,** 17–23.

Boe, E.E., & Church, R.M. Permanent effects of punishment during extinction. *Journal of Comparative and Physiological Psychology,* 1967, **63,** 486–492.

Bower, G.H., Fowler, H., & Trapold, M.A. Escape learning as a function of amount of shock reduction. *Journal of Experimental Psychology*, 1959, **58**, 482–484.

Bower, G.H., & Miller, N.E. Rewarding and punishing effects from stimulating the same place in the rat's brain. *Journal of Comparative and Physiological Psychology*, 1958, **51**, 669–674.

Bower, G.H., & Miller, N.E. Effects of amount of reward on strength of approach in an approach-avoidance conflict. *Journal of Comparative and Physiological Psychology*, 1960, **53**, 59–62.

Brethower, D.M., & Reynolds, G.S. A facilitative effect of punishment on unpunished behavior. *Journal of the Experimental Analysis of Behavior*, 1962, **5**, 191–199.

Brogden, W.J., Lipman, E.A., & Culler, E. The role of incentive in conditioning and extinction. *American Journal of Psychology*, 1938, **51**, 109–117.

Brown, J.S. Factors affecting self-punitive locomotor behavior. In B.A. Campbell & R.M. Church (Eds.), *Punishment and Aversive Behavior*. New York: Appleton, 1969. Pp. 467–514.

Brown, J.S., & Jacobs, A. The role of fear in the motivation and acquisition of responses. *Journal of Experimental Psychology*, 1949, **39**, 747–759.

Brown, J.S., Kalish, H.I., & Farber, I.E. Conditioned fear as revealed by magnitude of startle response to an auditory stimulus. *Journal of Experimental Psychology*, 1951, **41**, 317–328.

Brown, J.S., Martin, R.C., & Morrow, M.W. Self-punitive behavior in the rat: Facilitative effects of punishment on resistance to extinction. *Journal of Comparative and Physiological Psychology*, 1964, **57**, 127–133.

Brown, R.T., & Wagner, A.R. Resistance to punishment and extinction following training with shock or nonreinforcement. *Journal of Experimental Psychology*, 1964, **68**, 503–507.

Bruner, A. Food-based timing behavior sharpened by the selective punishment of short interresponse times. *Psychonomic Science*, 1967, **8**, 187–188.

Campbell, B.A., & Masterson, F.A. Psychophysics of punishment. In B.A. Campbell & R.M. Church (Eds.), *Punishment and Aversive Behavior*. New York: Appleton, 1969. Pp. 3–42.

Campbell, B.A., Smith, N.F., & Misanin, J.R. Effects of punishment on extinction of avoidance behavior: Avoidance-avoidance conflict or vicious-circle behavior? *Journal of Comparative and Physiological Psychology*, 1966, **62**, 495–498.

Campbell, B.A., & Teghtsoonian, R. Electrical and behavioral effects of different types of shock stimuli on the rat. *Journal of Comparative and Physiological Psychology*, 1958, **51**, 185–192.

Church, R.M. The varied effects of punishment on behavior. *Psychological Review*, 1963, **70**, 369–402.

Church, R.M. Systematic effect of random error in the yoked control design. *Psychological Bulletin*, 1964, **62**, 122–131.

Church, R.M. Response suppression. In B.A. Campbell & R.M. Church (Eds.), *Punishment and Aversive Behavior*. New York: Appleton, 1969. Pp. 111–156.

Crawford, F.T., Mayes, G.L., & Bitterman, M.E. A further study of differential afferent consequences in non-differential reinforcement. *American Journal of Psychology*, 1954, **67**, 717–719.

Curlin, Elizabeth R., & Donahoe, J.W. Effects of shock intensity and placement on the learning of a food-reinforced brightness discrimination. *Journal of Experimental Psychology*, 1965, **69**, 349–356.

Deese, J. *The psychology of learning.* (2nd ed.) New York: McGraw-Hill, 1958.

Dinsmoor, J.A. Punishment: I. The avoidance hypothesis. *Psychological Review,* 1954, **61,** 34–46.

Dinsmoor, J.A. Punishment: II. An interpretation of empirical findings. *Psychological Review,* 1955, **62,** 96–105.

Dollard, J., & Miller, N.E. *Personality and psychotherapy: An analysis in terms of learning, thinking, and culture.* New York: McGraw-Hill, 1950.

Estes, W.K. An experimental study of punishment. *Psychological Monographs,* 1944, **57,** (3, Whole No. 263).

Fairlie, C.W. The effect of shock at the 'moment of choice' on the formation of a visual discrimination habit. *Journal of Experimental Psychology,* 1937, **21,** 662–669.

Farber, I.E. Response fixation under anxiety and non-anxiety conditions. *Journal of Experimental Psychology,* 1948, **38,** 111–131.

Feirstein, A.R., & Miller, N.E. Learning to resist pain and fear: Effects of electric shock before versus after reaching goal. *Journal of Comparative and Physiological Psychology,* 1963, **56,** 797–800.

Ferraro, D.P. Persistence to continuous punishment as a function of amount of reinforcement. *Psychonomic Science,* 1966, **6,** 109–110.

Fowler, H. Facilitation and inhibition of performance by punishment: The effects of shock intensity and distribution of trials. *Journal of Comparative and Physiological Psychology,* 1963, **56,** 531–538.

Fowler, H. *Curiosity and exploratory behavior.* New York: Macmillan, 1965.

Fowler, H. Satiation and curiosity: Constructs for a drive and incentive-motivational theory of exploration. In K.W. Spence & J.T. Spence (Eds.), *The psychology of learning and motivation.* Vol. I. New York: Academic Press, 1967. Pp. 157–227.

Fowler, H., Goldman, L., & Wischner, G.J. Sodium amytal and the shock-right intensity function for visual discrimination learning. *Journal of Comparative and Physiological Psychology,* 1968, **65,** 515–519.

Fowler, H., & Miller, N.E. Facilitation and inhibition of runway performance by hind- and fore-paw shock of various intensities. *Journal of Comparative and Physiological Psychology,* 1963, **56,** 801–805.

Fowler, H., Spelt, P.F., & Wischner, G.J. Discrimination performance as affected by training procedure, problem difficulty and shock for the correct response. *Journal of Experimental Psychology,* 1967, **75,** 432–436.

Fowler, H. & Trapold, M.A. Escape performance as a function of delay of reinforcement. *Journal of Experimental Psychology,* 1962, **63,** 464–467.

Fowler, H. & Wischner, G.J. Discrimination performance as affected by problem difficulty and shock for either the correct or incorrect response. *Journal of Experimental Psychology,* 1965, **69,** 413–418. (a)

Fowler, H., & Wischner, G.J. On the "secondary reinforcing" effect of shock for the correct response in visual discrimination learning. *Psychonomic Science,* 1965, **3,** 209–210. (b)

Fowler, H., & Wischner, G.J. The varied functions of punishment in discrimination learning. In B.A. Campbell & R.M. Church (Eds.), *Punishment and aversive behavior.* New York: Appleton, 1969. Pp. 375–420.

Freeburne, C.M., & Taylor, J.E. Discrimination learning with shock for right and wrong responses in the same subjects. *Journal of Comparative and Physiological Psychology,* 1952, **45,** 264–268.

Goodman, E.D., Dyal, J.A., Zinser, O., & Golub, A. UCR morphology and shock intensity. *Psychonomic Science,* 1966, **5,** 431–432.

Goodrich, K.P. Performance in different segments of an instrumental response chain as a function of reinforcement schedule. *Journal of Experimental Psychology,* 1959, **57,** 57–63.

Gwinn, G.T. The effects of punishment on acts motivated by fear. *Journal of Experimental Psychology,* 1949, **39,** 260–269.

Harrington, G.M., & Kohler, G.R. Sensory deprivation and sensory reinforcement with shock. *Psychological Reports,* 1966, **18,** 803–808.

Harrington, G.M., & Linder, W.K. A positive reinforcing effect of electrical stimulation. *Journal of Comparative and Physiological Psychology,* 1962, **55,** 1014–1015.

Hawkins, R.P. Effects of drive, incentive and problem difficulty on the facilitation of discrimination performance by punishment of correct responses. Unpublished doctoral dissertation. University of Pittsburgh, 1965.

Hoge, Mildred A., & Stocking, Ruth J. A note on the relative value of punishment and reward as motives. *Journal of Animal Behavior,* 1912, **2,** 43–50.

Holz, W.C., & Azrin, N.H. Discriminative properties of punishment. *Journal of the Experimental Analysis of Behavior,* 1961, **4,** 225–232.

Holz, W.C., & Azrin, N.H. Interactions between the discriminative and aversive properties of punishment. *Journal of the Experimental Analysis of Behavior,* 1962, **5,** 229–234.

Holz, W.C., Azrin, N.H., & Ulrich, R.E. Punishment of temporally spaced responding. *Journal of the Experimental Analysis of Behavior,* 1963, **6,** 115–122.

Hurwitz, H.M.B. Effect of preliminary training and signal duration on the maintenance of an avoidance response. *Psychonomic Science,* 1965, **3,** 529–530.

Karsh, Eileen B. Effects of number of rewarded trials and intensity of punishment on running speed. *Journal of Comparative and Physiological Psychology,* 1962, **55,** 44–51.

Karsh, Eileen B. Changes in intensity of punishment: Effect on running behavior of rats. *Science,* 1963, **140,** 1084–1085.

Keller, F.S., & Schoenfeld, W.N. *Principles of psychology.* New York: Appleton, 1950.

Kimble, G.A. Shock intensity and avoidance learning. *Journal of Comparative and Physiological Psychology,* 1955, **48,** 281–284.

Kish, G.B. Studies of sensory reinforcement. In W.K. Honig (Ed.), *Operant behavior: Areas of research and application.* New York: Appleton, 1966. Pp. 109–159.

Koski, C.H., & Ross, L.E. Effects of consummatory response punishment in spatial-discrimination learning and response fixation. *Journal of Experimental Psychology,* 1965, **70,** 360–364.

Kurtz, P.S., & Shafer, J.N. Response contingent shock and avoidance conditioning. *Psychonomic Science,* 1966, **6,** 223–224.

Leitenberg, H. Response initiation and response termination: Analysis of effects of punishment and escape contingencies. *Psychological Reports,* 1965, **16,** 569–575.

Leitenberg, H. Punishment training with and without an escape contingency. *Journal of Experimental Psychology,* 1967, **74,** 393–399.

Logan, F.A. *Incentive: How the conditions of reinforcement affect the performance of rats.* New Haven: Yale University Press, 1960.

Logan, F.A., & Wagner, A.R. *Reward and punishment.* Boston, Massachusetts: Allyn & Bacon, 1965.

Lohr, T.F. The effect of shock on the rat's choice of a path to food. *Journal of Expimental Psychology,* 1959, **58,** 312–318.

Maier, N.R.F. *Frustration: The study of behavior without a goal.* New York: McGraw-Hill, 1949.

Martin, B. Reward and punishment associated with the same goal response: A factor in the learning of motives. *Psychological Bulletin,* 1963, **60,** 441–451.

Martin, B., & Ross, L.E. Effects of consummatory response punishment on consummatory and runway behavior. *Journal of Comparative and Physiological Psychology,* 1964, **58,** 243–247.

Martin, R.C. & Melvin, K.B. Viscious circle behavior as a function of delay of punishment. *Psychonomic Science,* 1964, **1,** 415–416.

Masserman, J.H. *Behavior and neurosis.* Chicago: University of Chicago Press, 1943.

May, M.A. Experimentally acquired drives. *Journal of Experimental Psychology,* 1948, **38,** 66–77.

McMillan, D.E., & Morse, W.H. Schedules using noxious stimuli. II: Low intensity electric shock as a discriminative stimulus. *Journal of the Experimental Analysis of Behavior,* 1967, **10,** 109–118.

Melvin, K.B., Athey, G.I., Jr., & Heasley, F.H. Effects of duration and delay of shock on self-punitive behavior in the rat. *Psychological Reports,* 1965, **17,** 107–112.

Melvin, K.B., & Martin, R.C. Facilitative effects of two modes of punishment on resistance to extinction. *Journal of Comparative and Physiological Psychology,* 1966, **62,** 491–494.

Melvin, K.B., & Smith, F.H. Self-punitive avoidance behavior in the rat. *Journal of Comparative and Physiological Psychology,* 1967, **63,** 533–535.

Melvin, K.B., & Stenmark, D.E. Facilitative effects of punishment on the establishment of a fear motivated response. *Journal of Comparative and Physiological Psychology,* 1968, **65,** 517–519.

Migler, B. Experimental self-punishment and superstitious escape behavior. *Journal of the Experimental Analysis of Behavior,* 1963, **6,** 371–385.

Miller, N.E. Studies of fear as an acquirable drive: I. Fear as motivation and fear-reduction as reinforcement in the learning of new responses. *Journal of Expimental Psychology,* 1948, **38,** 89–101.

Miller, N.E. Fear. In R.H. Williams (Ed.), *Human factors in military operations.* Chevy Chase, Maryland: John Hopkins University, Operations Research Office, 1954. Pp. 269–281.

Miller, N.E. Learning resistance to pain and fear: Effects of overlearning, exposure, and rewarded exposure in context. *Journal of Experimental Psychology,* 1960, **60,** 137–145.

Miller, N.E. Some recent studies of conflict behavior and drugs. *American Psychologist,* 1961, **16,** 12–24.

Morse, W.H., Mead, Regina N., & Kelleher, R.T. Modulation of elicited behavior by a fixed-external schedule of electric shock presentation. *Science,* 1967, **157,** 215–217.

Mowrer, O.H. Anxiety-reduction and learning. *Journal of Experimental Psychology,* 1940, **27,** 497–516.

Mowrer, O.H. On the dual nature of learning—a reinterpretation of "conditioning" and "problem-solving." *Harvard Educational Review,* 1947, **17,** 102–148.

Mowrer, O.H. *Learning theory and personality dynamics.* New York: Ronald Press, 1950.

Mowrer, O.H. *Learning theory and behavior.* New York: Wiley, 1960.

Moyer, K.E. The effects of shock on anxiety-motivated behavior in the rat. *Journal of Genetic Psychology,* 1957, **91,** 197–203.

Muenzinger, K.F. Motivation in learning: I. Electric shock for correct responses in the visual discrimination habit. *Journal of Comparative Psychology*, 1934, **17**, 267–278.

Muenzinger, K.F., & Baxter, L.F. The effects of training to approach vs. to escape from electric shock upon subsequent discrimination learning. *Journal of Comparative and Physiological Psychology*, 1957, **50**, 252–257.

Muenzinger, K.F., Bernstone, A.H., & Richards, L. Motivation in learning: VIII. Equivalent amounts of electric shock for right and wrong responses in a visual discrimination habit. *Journal of Comparative Psychology*, 1938, **26**, 177–186.

Murray, Marcia, & Nevin, J.A. Some effects of correlation between response-contingent shock and reinforcement. *Journal of the Experimental Analysis of Behavior*, 1967, **10**, 301–309.

Myers, J.L. Secondary reinforcement: A review of recent experimentation. *Psychological Bulletin*, 1958, **55**, 284–301.

Pavlov, I.P. *Conditioned Reflexes.* (Translated by G.V. Anrep) London and New York: Oxford University Press, 1927.

Prince, A.I., Jr. Effect of punishment on visual discrimination learning. *Journal of Expimental Psychology*, 1956, **52**, 381–385.

Sandler, J., & Davidson, R.S. Punished avoidance behavior in the presence of a non-punished alternative. *Psychonomic Science*, 1967, **8**, 297–298.

Sandler, J., Davidson, R.S., Greene, W.E., & Holzschuh, R.D. Effects of punishment intensity on instrumental avoidance behavior. *Journal of Comparative and Physiological Psychology*, 1966, **61**, 212–216. (a)

Sandler, J., Davidson, R.S., & Holzschuh, R.D. Effects of increasing punishment frequency on Sidman avoidance behavior. *Psychonomic Science*, 1966, **5**, 103–104. (b)

Sandler, J., Davidson, R.S., & Malagodi, E.F. Durable maintenance of behavior during concurrent avoidance and punished-extinction conditions. *Psychonomic Science*, 1966, **6**, 105–106. (c)

Seligman, M.E.P. & Campbell, B.A. Effect of intensity and duration of punishment on extinction of an avoidance response. *Journal of Comparative and Physiological Psychology*, 1965, **59**, 295–297.

Seward, J.P. The role of conflict in experimental neurosis. In B.A. Campbell & R.M. Church (Eds.), *Punishment and aversive behavior.* New York: Appleton, 1969. Pp. 421–447.

Seward, J.P., & Raskin, D.C. The role of fear in aversive behavior. *Journal of Comparative and Physiological Psychology*, 1960, **53**, 328–335.

Sheffield, F.D. Avoidance training and the contiguity principle. *Journal of Comparative and Physiological Psychology*, 1948, **41**, 165–177.

Sheffield, F.D. Hilgard's critique of Guthrie. *Psychological Review*, 1949, **56**, 284–291.

Sidman, M. Some notes on "bursts" in free-operant avoidance experiments. *Journal of the Experimental Analysis of Behavior*, 1958, **1**, 167–172.

Sidman, M., Herrnstein, R.J., & Conrad, D.G. Maintenance of avoidance behavior by unavoidable shock. *Journal of Comparative and Physiological Psychology*, 1957, **50**, 553–557.

Skinner, B.F. *The behavior of organisms.* New York: Appleton, 1938.

Skinner, B.F. *Science and human behavior.* New York: Macmillan, 1953.

Smith, N.F., Misanin, J.R., & Campbell, B.A. Effect of punishment on extinction of an avoidance response: Facilitation or inhibition? *Psychonomic Science*, 1966, **4**, 271–272.

Solomon, R.L. Punishment. *American Psychologist,* 1964, **19**, 239–253.

Solomon, R.L., Kamin, L.J., & Wynne, L.C. Traumatic avoidance learning: The outcomes of several extinction procedures with dogs. *Journal of Abnormal and Social Psychology,* 1953, **48**, 291–302.

Spence, K.W. *Behavior theory and conditioning.* New Haven, Connecticut: Yale University Press, 1956.

Spevack, A.A., & Suboski, M.D. A confounding of conditioned suppression in passive avoidance: ECS effects. *Psychonomic Science,* 1967, **9**, 23–24.

Storms, L.H., Boroczi, G., & Broen, W.E. Punishment inhibits an instrumental response in hooded rats. *Science,* 1962, **135**, 1133–1134.

Strain, E.R. Establishment of an avoidance gradient under latent-learning conditions. *Journal of Experimental Psychology,* 1953, **46**, 391–399.

Terris, W., & Wechkin, S. Learning to resist the effects of punishment. *Psychonomic Science,* 1967, **7**, 169–170.

Thorndike, E.L. *Animal intelligence: Experimental studies.* New York: Macmillan, 1911.

Thorndike, E.L. *Educational psychology.* Vol. II. *The psychology of learning.* New York: Teachers College, Columbia University, 1913.

Thorndike, E.L. *The fundamentals of learning.* New York: Teachers College, Columbia University, 1932.

Trabasso, T.R., & Thompson, R.W. Supplementary report: Shock intensity and unconditioned responding in a shuttle box. *Journal of Experimental Psychology,* 1962, **63**, 215–216.

Uhl, C.N. Persistence in punishment and extinction testing as a function of percentages of punishment and reward in training. *Psychonomic Science,* 1967, **8**, 193–194.

Warden, C.J., & Aylesworth, M. The relative value of reward and punishment in the formation of a visual discrimination habit in the white rat. *Journal of Comparative Psychology,* 1927, **7**, 117–127.

Whittleton, J.C., Kostansek, D.J., & Sawrey, J.M. CS directionality and intensity in avoidance learning and extinction. *Psychonomic Science,* 1965, **3**, 415–416.

Williams, D.R., & Barry, H., III. Counter conditioning in an operant conflict situation. *Journal of Comparative and Physiological Psychology,* 1966, **61**, 154–156.

Wischner, G.J. The effect of punishment on discrimination learning in a noncorrection situation. *Journal of Experimental Psychology,* 1947, **37**, 271–284.

Wischner, G.J., & Fowler, H. Discrimination performance as affected by duration of shock for either the correct or incorrect response. *Psychonomic Science,* 1964, **1**, 239–240.

Wischner, G.J., Fowler, H., & Kushnick, S.A. Effect of strength of punishment for "correct" or "incorrect" responses on visual discrimination performance. *Journal of Experimental Psychology,* 1963, **65**, 131–138.

Wyckoff, L.B., Jr. The role of observing responses in discrimination learning. Part I. *Psychological Review,* 1952, **59**, 431–442.

Yerkes, R.M., & Dodson, J.D. The relation of strength of stimulus to rapidity of habit formation. *Journal of Comparative Neurology & Psychology,* 1908, **18**, 459–482.

Author Index

Numbers in parentheses refer to the pages on which the complete references are listed.

A

Abelson, R. M., 478, (532)

Abplanalp, P. L., 472, 473, (532, 535)

Ackerman, P. T., 61, 69, 75, 78, (98)

Adams, R. M., 430, 433, 434, (461)

Adelman, H. M., 235, 244, 246, 247, 248, (290, 291)

Ader, R., 221, (226)

Adkins, J., 361, (399)

Aiken, E. G., 50, (101), 110, 125, 141, (176)

Akhtar, M., 557, (598)

Allison, J., 206, (226), 370, (395)

Alpern, H., 431, (462)

Amsel, A., 112, 128, 132, 167, (170), 206, 210, 214, (226, 228), 245, 247, (290), 485, 488, 489, 492, (528), 578, (598)

Anchel, H., 222, (226)

Anderson, D. C., 110, 121, 142, (170, 173), 355, 357, 359, 366, (395), 412, 415, 455, (461), 494, (528), 585, (598)

Anderson, N. H., 186, 189, 203, (226, 227), 356, 373, (395, 398)

Anderson, O. D., 401, (464), 473, (533)

Anderson, R. C., 277, (291), 359, (398)

Anger, D., 126, 128, (170), 199, (226)

Annau, Z., 133, 137, 138, 142, 157, 161, (170)

Antonitis, J. J., 494, (529)

Appel, J. B., 537, 546, 547, 550, 551, (598)

Arbit, J., 87, (96)

Athey, G. I., Jr., 585, (602)

Atkinson, R. C., 193, (227), 304, 307, 325, (345)

Auld, F., 87, (96)

Aylesworth, M., 544, (604)

Ayres, J. J. B., 116, 144, 158, 161, (170)

Azrin, N. H., 130, (170), 189, (226), 377, (395), 401, (461), 469, 478, 480, 498, 499, 500, 501, 502, 513, (528, 529, 532, 535), 537, 538, 540, 541, 542, 544, 546, 547, 548, 552, 561, 574, 582, 592, (598, 601)

B

Bacon, W. E., 246, (290)

Badia, P., 218, (226), 376, 378, (395)

Baenninger, R., 490, 504, 505, (529, 534)

Bagne, C., 256, (290)

Banks, J. H., 87, (101)

Banks, R. K., 517, (529), 577, 578, 581, (598)

Banuazizi, A., 25, 28, 30, 33, 34, 42, 61, (96, 101)

Barfield, R. J., 506, 507, (529)

Barker, E., 193, 203, (226)

Barlow, J. A., 271, (290)

Barnes, G. W., 218, (227), 478, (529)

Barnes, L. W., 376, (396)

Barnett, S. A., 498, 526, (529)

Baron, A., 209, 213, 214, (226), 475, 494, 516, 520, (529)

Barrett, G. V., 246, (290)

Barry, H., 556, 557, (604)

Barry, J. J., Jr., 478, 482, (529)

Baum, M., 133, (170), 357, 373, (395), 417, 418, 420, (461), 589, (598)

Baxter, L. F., 580, 581, (603)

Beatty, P. A., 455, (461)

Beauchamp, R. D., 509, (530)

Beck, R. C., 271, (290), 552, (598)

Beecroft, R. S., 107, 132, 137, (171), 351, (395), 327, 328, 329, (345), 587, 588, 589, (598)

Behrend, E. R., 355, (396)

Belanger, D., 495, (531)

Bell, R., 494, (529)

Benuazizi, A., 428, 429, 431, 433, (463)

Bergmann, G., 106, (171)

Berman, A. J., 7, (103)

Bernstone, A. H., 553, 582, (603)

Bertsch, G. J., 167, (174)

Bevan, W., 494, 516, (529)

Bindra, D., 81, (96), 222, (226), 487, 495, (529)

Bintz, J., 411, 412, 416, 421, 443, 446, (461)

Bitterman, M. E., 83, (96), 106, 108, 140, (171), 222, (228), 355, (396), 525, (529), 564, 565, (598, 599)

Bixenstine, V. E., 193, 203, (226)

Black, A. H., 25, 26, 28, 30, 31, 33, 34, 36,

605

Subject Index

A

Acquired distinctiveness of cues, 580

Acquired drive, *see also* Conditioned fear
  avoidance response difference from escape response, 206ff
  avoidance response same as escape response, 205ff
  defining procedures, 204f
  no escape response, 209ff
  similarity of avoidance and escape responses, 213ff

ACTH, 451f
  behavioral effects, 454f

Adaptation, 362

Adrenalectomy, 459

Adventitious punishment, 364

Adventitious reinforcement, 363f, 550, 582

Anticipatory responses
  conditioned fear, 577
  escape from shock, 583
  to punishment, 568

Anxiety, 347

Attention in avoidance learning, 201

Autonomic conditioning
  cardiovascular responses, 4
  emotion and, 11
  failure of, 24
  operant vs. voluntary control, 12
  psychosomatic medicine and, 12

Autonomic response
  as index of classical conditioning, 92f
  as preparatory CR, 378ff

Aversive stimulation, 347
  definition, 470
  effects on behavior, 469, 484ff
  reactions to noise, 478

Aversive stimuli
  cooling, 501
  heating, 501
  tactile, 502

Aversiveness, 360

Avoidance extinction as counterconditioning, 325

Avoidance learning
  avoidance operator, a_o, 303
  avoidance same as escape, 202
  choice of response, 190ff
  choice reversal, 340ff
  commutativity of operators, 304ff
  conditioned fear, 220
  CS-termination contingency, 215ff
  effective reinforcement, 184, 199ff
  effective responses, 183ff
  escape contingency, 190ff
  failure to learn, 186ff
  intermittent shock, 197
  long nonshock confinement, 267
  mathematical models of, 298
  mathematical notation for, 299f
  Markov models of, 298, 307ff
  no CS, 198ff
  no escape response, 195ff
  punishment for errors in extinction of, 285f
  response chains, 223f
  Sidman procedure, 198ff
  shock frequency, 199f
  shock operator, 303
  similarity of avoidance and escape responses, 202ff
  temporal discrimination in, 200
  sources of reinforcement, 190f
  species-specific defense reaction as avoidance response, 185ff
  two-choice discrimination, 262ff
  two-factory theory of, 91f
  two-operator linear model of, 302ff
  weakening of ineffectual species-specific defense reactions, 219ff

Avoidance response
  escape response different from, 192ff
  escape response same as, 192ff
  Latency distributions of Markov states, 332f
  lever pressing, 187f, 197

S